Professional
Java®
JDK® 6 Editi〔

W. Clay Richardson, Donald Avondolio, Scot Schrager,
Mark W. Mitchell, and Jeff Scanlon

BICENTENNIAL
1807
WILEY
2007
BICENTENNIAL

Wiley Publishing, Inc.

Professional Java, JDK 6 Edition

Published by
Wiley Publishing, Inc.
10475 Crosspoint Boulevard
Indianapolis, IN 46256
www.wiley.com

ISBN-13: 978-0-471-77710-6
ISBN-10: 0-471-77710-2

Manufactured in the United States of America

10 9 8 7 6 5 4 3 2 1

1O/RU/RS/QW/IN

For general information on our other products and services or to obtain technical support, please contact our Customer Care Department within the U.S. at (800) 762-2974, outside the U.S. at (317) 572-3993 or fax (317) 572-4002.

Library of Congress Cataloging-in-Publication Data

Professional Java JDK, 6 Edition / W. Clay Richardson ... [et al.].
    p. cm.
 Includes index.
 ISBN-13: 978-0-471-77710-6 (paper/website)
 ISBN-10: 0-471-77710-2 (paper/website)
 1. Java (Computer program language) I. Richardson, W. Clay, 1976-
 QA76.73.J38P7623 2007
 005.13'3—dc22

                              2006032740

Wiley also publishes its books in a variety of electronic formats. Some content that appears in print may not be available in electronic books.

*This book is dedicated to all those who make the daily sacrifices,
especially those who have made the ultimate sacrifice, to ensure our
freedom and security.*

About the Authors

W. Clay Richardson is a software consultant concentrating on agile Java solutions for highly specialized business processes. He has fielded many Java solutions, serving in roles including senior architect, development lead, and program manager. He is a co-author of *More Java Pitfalls* and *Professional Portal Development with Open Source Tools* (Wiley), and *Professional Java, JDK 5 Edition*. As an adjunct professor of computer science for Virginia Tech, Richardson teaches graduate-level coursework in object-oriented development with Java. He holds degrees from Virginia Tech and the Virginia Military Institute.

Donald Avondolio currently serves in a lead position as an architect/developer on an enterprise development project. In his spare time, Donald loves fly-fishing, watching baseball and lacrosse, running triathlons (not very well), and sitting around his house complaining about things.

Scot Schrager has consulted extensively in the domains of pharmaceuticals, supply chain management, and the national security market. He has led and participated in various project teams using Java and Object Oriented Analysis & Design techniques. Most recently, Schrager has been focused on distributed application architecture using J2EE technology.

Mark W. Mitchell has extensive experience in enterprise application integration, particularly Web Services integration between Java and the Microsoft platform. He has developed and deployed several mission-critical web applications. Mitchell holds a degree in computer science from the University of Virginia.

Jeff Scanlon is a software development consultant from Virginia. He holds both the Sun Certified Java Developer and Microsoft Certified Solutions Developer certifications, and has been published in *Software Development* magazine.

Credits

Acquisitions Editor
Robert Elliott

Development Editor
Brian Herrmann

Technical Editor
David Parks

Production Editor
Kathryn Duggan

Copy Editor
Kim Cofer

Editorial Manager
Mary Beth Wakefield

Production Manager
Tim Tate

Vice President and Executive Group Publisher
Richard Swadley

Vice President and Executive Publisher
Joseph B. Wikert

Project Coordinator
Kristie Rees

Graphics and Production Specialists
Carrie A. Foster
Brooke Gracyzk
Denny Hager
Joyce Haughey
Barbara Moore
Barry Offringa
Alicia B. South
Ronald Terry

Quality Control Technicians
John Greenough
Charles Spencer
Brian H. Walls

Proofreading and Indexing
Techbooks and Stephen Ingle

Anniversary Logo Design
Richard Pacifico

Contents

Acknowledgments	**xv**
Introduction	**xvii**

Part I: Thinking Like a Java Developer   1

Chapter 1: Key Java Language Features and Libraries   3

Introducing Derby	**3**
Using Derby	**4**
Language Features Added in Java 5	**7**
Generics	7
Enhanced for Loop	16
Additions to the Java Class Library	17
Variable Arguments	18
Boxing and Unboxing Conversions	19
Static Imports	21
Enumerations	24
Metadata	26
Important Java Utility Libraries	**34**
Java Logging	35
Java Preferences	70
Summary	**77**

Chapter 2: Tools and Techniques for Developing Java Solutions   79

Principles of Quality Software Development	**80**
Habits of Effective Software Development	**81**
Communicate	81
Model	81
Be Agile	81
Be Disciplined	82
Trace Your Actions to Need	82
Don't Be Afraid to Write Code	83
Think of Code as a Design, not a Product	83

Contents

Read a Lot   84
Build Your Process from the Ground Up   84
Manage Your Configuration   84
Unit Test Your Code   85
Continuously Integrate   85
Maintaining Short Iterations   86
Measure What You Accomplished — Indirectly   87
Track Your Issues   87
Development Methodology   **88**
Waterfall Methodology   88
Unified Process   90
Extreme Programming   91
Observations on Methodology   92
Practical Development Scenarios   **93**
Ant   93
Maven 2   101
TestNG   106
XDoclet   110
JMeter   117
Summary   **120**

Chapter 3: Exploiting Patterns in Java   **123**

Why Patterns Are Important   **124**
Keys to Understanding the Java Programming Language   124
Keys to Understanding Tools Used in Java Development   125
Keys to Developing Effective Java Solutions   126
Building Patterns with Design Principles   **127**
Designing a Single Class   127
Creating an Association between Classes   128
Creating an Interface   129
Creating an Inheritance Loop   129
Important Java Patterns   **131**
Adapter   131
Model-View-Controller   134
Command   142
Strategy   146
Composite   150
Summary   **154**

Part II: A Broad Understanding of Java APIs, Tools, and Techniques   155

Chapter 4: Developing Effective User Interfaces with JFC   157

Layout Managers   **158**
BorderLayout   158
BoxLayout   164
FlowLayout   173
GridLayout   177
GridBagLayout   189
SpringLayout   194
CardLayout   202
GroupLayout   208
Mustang Release Desktop Enhancements   **214**
Managing Navigation Flows in Swing Applications   **225**
Summary   **235**

Chapter 5: Persisting Your Application Using Files   237

Application Data   **237**
Saving Application Data   239
Sample Configuration Data Model for an Application   239
Java Serialization: Persisting Object Graphs   **241**
Key Classes   242
Serializing Your Objects   243
Extending and Customizing Serialization   257
When to Use Java Serialization   261
JavaBeans Long-Term Serialization: XMLEncoder/Decoder   **262**
Design Differences   262
Serializing Your JavaBeans   265
When to Use XMLEncoder/Decoder   269
Flexible XML Serialization: Java API for XML Binding (JAXB)   **270**
Sample XML Document for the Configuration Object   271
Defining Your XML Format with an XML Schema   273
JAXB API Key Classes   280
Marshalling and Unmarshalling XML Data   281
Creating New XML Content with JAXB-Generated Classes   283
Using JAXB-Generated Classes in Your Application   283

Contents

Annotating Existing Java Classes for Use with JAXB   290

When to Use JAXB   307

Where JAXB Fits in the JDK   308

Summary   **308**

Chapter 6: Persisting Your Application Using Databases   311

JDBC API Overview   **312**

Setting Up Your Environment   **313**

JDBC API Usage in the Real World   **313**

Understanding the Two-Tier Model   313

Understanding the Three-Tier Model   314

Effectively Using JDBC 4.0   **315**

Overview   315

Managing Connections   316

Understanding Statements   318

Utilizing Result Sets   328

Advanced Concepts   333

Hibernate   **335**

Hibernate Components   336

Hibernate Example   341

Summary   **354**

Chapter 7: Developing Web Applications Using the Model 1 Architecture   355

What Is Model 1? Why Use It?   **356**

JSP 2.0 Overview   357

Integrated Expression Language (EL)   365

JSTL 1.1 Overview   366

Developing Your Web Application Visualizations with JSTL 1.1   370

Developing Your Web Application Visualizations with JSP 2.0   376

AJAX   381

Summary   **391**

Chapter 8: Developing Web Applications Using the Model 2 Architecture   393

The Problem   **393**

What Is Model 2?   **393**

Why Use Model 2?   **395**

Developing an Application with WebWork   **396**

What Is Inversion of Control and Why Is it Useful?   397

Architecture   399

Extending the Framework to Support Hibernate   402
Preventing the Hanging Session   403
Defining Your Domain Model   405
Implementing Your Use Cases with Actions   412
Developing Your Views   415
Configuring Your Application   422
Adapting to Changes   424
Summary   **426**

Chapter 9: Interacting with C/C++ Using Java Native Interface   **427**

A First Look at Java Native Interface   **427**
Creating the Java Code   428
Creating the Native Code and Library   429
Executing the Code   431
Java Native Interface   **432**
Data Types   432
Strings in JNI   432
Arrays in JNI   436
Working with Java Objects in C/C++   442
Handling Java Exceptions in Native Code   449
Working with Object References in Native Code   451
Advanced Programming Using JNI   455
Developing an Email Client   **460**
System Design   460
User Interface   461
Summary   **471**

Chapter 10: EJB 3 and the Java Persistence API   **473**

New Features   **474**
Java Persistence API (JPA)   **475**
Entities   475
Query Language   475
EntityManager   476
What Are Session Beans? The Demise of Entity Beans?   480
Interceptors   481
EJB 3 and Java Persistence API Web Component Examples   485
Summary   **517**

Contents

Chapter 11: Communicating between Java Components and Components of Other Platforms **519**

Component Communication Scenarios	**520**
News Reader: Automated Web Browsing	520
A Bank Application: An EJB/Java EE Client	520
A Portal: Integrating Heterogeneous Data Sources and Services	521
Overview of Interprocess Communication and Basic Network Architecture	**521**
Sockets	**522**
The Java Socket API	523
Implementing a Protocol	530
Remote Method Invocation	**542**
Core RPC/RMI Principles	542
Common Object Request Broker Architecture	**547**
CORBA Basics	547
RMI-IIOP: Making RMI Compatible with CORBA	551
How to Turn an RMI Object into an RMI-IIOP Object	551
When to Use CORBA	553
Distributed File System Notifications: An Example CORBA System	554
Web Services	**563**
Random-Weather.org	564
Platform-Independent RPC	566
Summary	**597**

Chapter 12: Service Oriented Integration **599**

Service Oriented Architecture	**599**
Enabling Technology	**600**
Java Management Extensions	**600**
Why Is JMX Important?	601
The JMX Architecture	601
Creating and Managing a Standard MBean	602
JMX Management	606
Java Messaging Service	**610**
Why Is JMS Important?	610
Endpoints: Queues and Topics	610
Sending and Receiving Messages	611
System Integration Patterns	**619**
Processing Chain	619
Request-Reply	619
Split-Aggregate	621
Summary	**623**

Chapter 13: Java Security   625

Java Cryptography Architecture and Java Cryptography Extension (JCA/JCE)   **625**
JCA Design and Architecture   626
Java Cryptography Extension   656
Program Security Using JAAS   **666**
User Identification   667
Executing Code with Security Checks   668
Authorization   672
Summary   **673**

Chapter 14: Packaging and Deploying Your Java Applications   675

Examining Java Classpaths   **675**
Investigating the Endorsed Directory   **680**
Exploring Java Archives   **681**
Manipulating JAR Files   **681**
Examining the Basic Manifest File   684
Examining Applets and JARs   685
Signing JAR Files   686
Examining the JAR Index Option   690
Creating an Executable JAR   691
Analyzing Applets   **691**
Basic Anatomy of an Applet   692
Packaging an Applet for Execution   693
Examining Applet Security   694
Exploring Web Applications   **694**
Examining the WAR Directory Structure   695
Understanding the WAR Deployment Descriptor   696
Packaging Enterprise JavaBeans   **698**
Inspecting Enterprise Archives   **699**
The EAR Descriptor File   700
Deployment Scenario   700
Jumping into Java Web Start   **702**
Examining the TicTacToe Example   702
Summarizing Java Web Start   709
Using Ant with Web Archives   **709**
Installing Ant   709
Building Projects with Ant   710
Summary   **713**

Index   **715**

Acknowledgments

First, I could not have had any chance of actually getting this book done without the support of my wonderful wife, Alicia. She and my daughter Jennifer, who has far less sophisticated expectations of my literary skills, are the joy in my life and I look forward to spending more time with them. I love both of you more than words can describe. Stephanie, we love you and will never forget you. I would like to thank our technical editor, David Parks for the outstanding job he did on this project—you had NO IDEA what you were agreeing to do when I recruited you into this job! My fellow authors—Donnie, Mark, Scot, and Jeff—have been terrific with their hard work on a demanding project. I appreciate each of your contributions to this book. I would like to thank Bob Elliott and Brian Herrmann for all of their hard work and perseverance while working with us on this project. I would like to acknowledge my leadership, Joe Duffy, Bruce Feldman, Jim Moorhead, Don Heginbotham, Jon Grasmeder, and Augie Dunheimer, for their dedication to the simple concept of doing the right thing for the right people. It is very refreshing to work at a company that exercises the inverse of the cynical "zero sum game." I would like to thank my parents, Bill and Kay, my in-laws, Stephen and Elaine Mellman, my sister Kari, my brother-in-law Grayson, my brother Morgan, and my stepfather Dave for always being there. I would like to acknowledge my grandmothers, Vivian and Sophie, for being what grandmothers should be.

I would also like to acknowledge my team members for the great things they do every day to make the world a better place: Jon Simasek, Rob Brown, Keith Berman, Mauro Marcellino, Terry Trepel (welcome back from Iraq!), Marshall Sayen, Joe Sayen, Hanchol Do, Scot Schrager, Don Avondolio, Brian Stearns, Cliff Toma, Mike Clarke, Brad Phillips, Jeff Lane, Nhon Pham, Julia Lee, Vic Fraenckel (welcome back from the dead!), Morgan Ruther, Lonnie Haaland, George Burgin, and Mark (Mojo) Mitchell. Matt Tyrrell, I was going to write something witty or amusing, but I think Jennifer put it best, "What time is Uncle Matt coming over?"—WCR

First, I'd like to thank these people for inspiring me in the workplace: Swati Gupta, Chi Louong, Bill Hickey, and Chiming Huang. Thanks to all of the great professors at the Virginia Tech Computer Science/Information Technology Departments: Shawn Bohner, Tarun Sen, Stephen Edwards, and John Viega. I am indebted to all of my students who taught me so much through their dedication, hard work, and insight, which has allowed me to incorporate their development wisdom for instruction in this book. Appreciation goes out to the sponsors, volunteers, and organizers of The Great Cow Harbor Run (Northport, NY) and The Columbia Triathlon (Columbia, MD) for organizing world-class events I like to participate in, but more importantly for inspiring me to be a more disciplined and focused person. Special thanks to my friends, the Wieczoreks, Devaneys, Keanes, O'Donohoes, Howards, and Pujols.

Lastly, I wish to thank all of the co-authors, who are fun guys to work with and be around: Jeff, Mark, Scot, and Clay and my co-workers: Mauro Marcellino, Joe and Marshall Sayen, Jon Simasek, Terry Trepel and his wonder-dog Ontio, Hanchol Do, Keith Berman, Rob Brown, Dave Parks, Brian Stearns, Mike Clarke, Morgan Ruther, Cliff Toma, Matt Tyrrell, the Thoman family (Brettie-boy, Cindy, and baby Zoe),Vic Fraenckel, Nhon Pham, Julia Lee, and to my fishing buddy George Burgin. To all of my family: Mom, Dad, Michael, John, Patricia, Keil, Jim, Sue, Reenie, Donna, Kelly, Stephen, Emily, Jack, and Gillian, Matt and Danielle, you guys are great. To my wife Van, whom I love more than anything for her continual support during the writing of this book.—DJA

Acknowledgments

The first person I would like to thank is Heather. Seven years together and a wonderful eleven-month-old son, you have made me the luckiest guy on earth. Thanks for saying, "I do." I also need to thank my parents. First I'd like to thank my mom, because she has always been on my side, in support of me and my decisions. And my dad, because he's the kind of dad I'd like to one day become. I would also like to thank my family who supported me; my sister and her family; Fern, Gary, and Isabel. In addition, I would thank my extended family, Joe, Sabina, Robin, Peter, Brandon, Abby, Christiana, Joe Jr., Chris, Ann, Paige, and Liam. I also need to thank my co-workers who make every day an experience. Clay, thanks for providing the vision and drive to keep this work interesting. We are not in the one's and zero's business, we solve problems. Don, thanks for putting up with me. Dave, thanks for putting up with Don and me. Cliff, thanks for doing all the hard work, and please tell Gerry thanks too. I'd also like to thank Marty, Melinda, Brett, Mike, Mark, Terry, Mauro, Marshall, and Keith.—SRS

I would like to first thank my wife, Elisa, for supporting me through this book. Projects like this always seem like they will take less time than they actually do, and I thank her for supporting me through my optimistic time estimates. I'd like to thank Clay for giving me the opportunity to write with him, and Don for guiding me through it. I'd also like to thank our technical and development editors, Dave and Brian, for helping me with my chapters. I would like to thank the people I have worked closely with recently: Keith, Jeff, Jon, Terry, Nhon, Matt, Marshall, Joe, Brad, Carlton, Todd, Bryan, Hanchol, Vic, and everyone I have worked with in the past. I have learned a lot simply through watching and listening. There is no greater work atmosphere than the one where you are the least experienced—there is something to be learned from everyone every day. I'd like to thank my parents; my dad for sparking my interest in computer science, and my mom for helping me learn to write. Most of all I would like to thank God, as writing this book has been an exercise in faith and trust. Last but not least I would like to thank all of my family and friends for supporting me around book deadlines and understanding where all my time was going.—MWM

The following deserve acknowledgment: Dave Nelson for introducing me to programming and for being the main reason I am where I am; my parents and family; our editors at Wiley, Brian Herrmann and Robert Elliott; and Dave Parks, our technical reviewer. To my most important teachers: Alfred Martin and Paul D'Andrea. And finally, to Phil Bickel, Eric Anderton, John Tarcza, Keith Obenschain, Robert Burtt, Joseph Kapp, Randy Nguyen, Leo Pak, Mark Orletsky, Randy Shine, David Hu, Min Soo Yi, and Corey Chang for their support.—JS

Introduction

Professional Java Programming provides a bridge from the "how to" language books that dominate the Java space (*Teach Yourself Hello World in Java in 24 Hours*) and the more detailed, but technologically stove-piped books on topics such as EJB, J2EE, JMX, JMS, and so on. Most development solutions involve using a mix of technologies, and the books for all of these technologies would stand several feet tall. Furthermore, the reader needs but a fraction of the overall content in these books to solve their specific problems. *Professional Java Programming* provides background information on the technology, practical examples of using the technology, and an explanation of where the reader could find more detailed information. It strives to be a professional reference for the Java developer.

Who This Book Is For

This book serves three types of readers:

❑ The newly introduced reader who has graduated from *Beginning Java*, by covering more advanced Java solutions and language features.

❑ The Java developer who needs a good all-purpose reference and a first source when tackling new Java problems that may be outside their technological experience.

❑ The developer who has already had experience with certain solutions, but may not, for example, think it worthwhile to read 500 pages on JMS alone to see if JMS could fit into their solution space. This book can provide reduced barriers to technological entry for these developers.

What This Book Covers

Professional Java JDK 6 Edition builds upon *Ivor Horton's Beginning Java 2*, to provide the reader with an understanding of how professionals use Java to develop software solutions. It starts with a discussion of the tools and techniques of the Java developer, continues with a discussion of the more sophisticated and nuanced parts of the Java SDK, and concludes with several examples of building real Java solutions using Java APIs and open source tools. *Professional Java JDK 6 Edition* leaves the reader with a well-rounded survey of the professional Java development landscape, without losing focus in exhaustive coverage of individual APIs. This book is the bridge between Java language texts, methodology books, and specialized Java API books. For example, once you have mastered the basics of the Java language, you will invariably encounter a problem, like building a database-driven web site, which requires you to use a collection of technologies like JSP, and tools like Hibernate; this book provides a concrete solution that integrates both of them. The following figure provides a context to this book's coverage in relation to other Java books. As you start with the beginning Java books, you would use this book as a solution primer to introduce you to more in-depth books on a particular subject, such as patterns, Web Services, or JDBC.

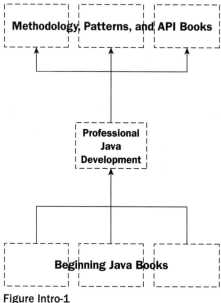

Figure Intro-1

How This Book Is Structured

Working as an effective professional Java developer requires two major skills: thinking like a Java developer and having a broad understanding of Java APIs, tools, and techniques to solve a wide variety of Java problems. Reviewing the structure of the book, you can see how the chapters help you realize the goal of improving these skills.

Part I: Thinking Like a Java Developer

Experienced Java developers recognize that there is a particular mindset among effective Java developers. The first three chapters provide you with strong coverage of topics that will help you achieve that mindset.

Chapter 1: Key Java Language Features and Libraries

Any introductory Java book will cover the features of the Java programming language. This chapter picks up where those books leave off by focusing on a number of the key sophisticated Java language features such as regular expressions, preferences, and Java logging. Most importantly, this chapter introduces Derby, a lightweight database new to Java 6, and reviews language features that were introduced in Java 2 Standard Edition 5.0. These features include generics, metadata, autoboxing, and more.

Chapter 2: Tools and Techniques for Developing Java Solutions

Making the jump from someone who knows the Java language to a Java developer is an interesting transition. Typically, developers find books that teach the language and books that teach the methodologies.

Furthermore, methodology books are often written defensively, as if they are defending a dissertation or prescribing a diet. These books often prescribe ritualistic adherence to their methodology, lest you risk failure. New developers can find this approach quite exhausting, because rarely do you start in a position where you can dictate a team's process. In this book, you will find a developer's focused view on methodology and tools with practical insights into how to allow tools to make your work easier and more productive.

Chapter 3: Exploiting Patterns in Java

Patterns provide an invaluable resource to developers in trying to communicate solutions to common problems. However, as software problems are generally very abstract, understanding common solutions to them—or even the value of the approach—can be a very overwhelming experience.

However, as you might imagine, there are some key problems that recur throughout the Java solution space, and therefore, frameworks and APIs are built upon patterns. As such, having a utilitarian understanding of patterns is invaluable, and arguably unavoidable in becoming an effective Java developer. This chapter explains the critical importance of patterns, provides a practical understanding of patterns, and demonstrates examples of common patterns found in the Java world.

Part II: A Broad Understanding of Java APIs, Tools, and Techniques

The Java platform has extended beyond being a simple applet development language at its inception to three distinct editions targeted at three different platforms. Not only has the platform evolved into a huge undertaking, but the open source movement and the Java community have also added features and tools that provide even more options to the Java developer.

Therefore, you can find yourself easily overwhelmed. This part of the book provides a series of common problems across the Java development space. In each area, you will be introduced to a problem, and a focused solution to that problem. These solutions do not attempt to provide comprehensive coverage of all of the involved APIs, but rather a primer needed to solve that problem. From there, you could bridge into a book with more specialized coverage. The primary intent is to not require a three-foot tall stack of books to address a simple end-to-end solution to a common development problem.

Chapter 4: Developing Effective User Interfaces with JFC

Commonly referred to simply as Swing, the Java Foundation Classes provide the functionality to build user interfaces and desktop applications. As these classes frequently make up most of the logical examples within introductory Java books, it makes logical sense to start with a Swing example. However, this chapter covers the intricacies of Swing in more detail, including some advanced topics like Layout Managers and Java 2D.

Chapter 5: Persisting Your Application Using Files

One of the more important things for any application to be able to do is persist (that is, save) its state. In this chapter, you will discover techniques to implement save and restore functionality, using two different methods, Java object serialization and the Java API for XML Binding (JAXB).

Chapter 6: Persisting Your Application Using Databases

Files are traditionally used to share data in a single-threaded mode—one user at a time. When data must be shared throughout the enterprise, you use a database. In this chapter, you learn the more advanced features of the Java Database Connectivity API (JDBC) 4.0. Furthermore, this chapter addresses one of the more popular object persistence frameworks (and the foundation for the development of the new EJB 3.0 specification)—Hibernate.

Chapter 7: Developing Web Applications Using the Model 1 Architecture

Those who have been developing web applications for a long time recognize that the page-centric paradigm, also known as the Model 1 Architecture, has been used across many technology platforms (ASP, Cold Fusion, Perl, and so on) to develop web applications. Java supports this paradigm through its Java Server Pages and Java Standard Tag Library specifications. In this chapter, you learn about these frameworks as well as other best practices in developing web applications within the Model 1 Architecture.

Chapter 8: Developing Web Applications Using the Model 2 Architecture

As web applications have evolved, there has been recognition of some weaknesses in the page-centric approach of the Model 1 Architecture. In this chapter, you learn about these weaknesses and how they gave rise to the Model 2 Architecture, which is component-centric. You will see how using a component framework like WebWork allows for easy integration of other components like Hibernate.

Chapter 9: Interacting with C/C++ Using Java Native Interface

Frequently, you have application components that are regrettably not written in the Java programming language, often not alleviating the need for those components to be accessible by your application. The solution to this problem is the Java Native Interface. This chapter explains the intricacies of JNI, as well as a number of the potential pitfalls.

Chapter 10: EJB 3 and the Java Persistence API

Enterprise JavaBeans (EJB) is Java's distributed component technology and the cornerstone of the Java 2 Enterprise Edition platform. EJB 3.0 represents a significant improvement in the Java language by leveraging the Plain Old Java Object (POJO) paradigm with the Java Persistence API to provide reliable, robust, and transparent object persistence. This chapter explains the EJB 3 specification and the Java Persistence API and demonstrates their utility to developing enterprise Java solutions.

Chapter 11: Communicating between Java Components and Components of Other Platforms

While RMI has proven to be a good solution for Java-to-Java communication, there are still a tremendous number of needs to access (or provide access to) components of other platforms. This is particularly true of the Microsoft .NET platform. This chapter explains the basics of interprocess communication, discusses several techniques for interprocess communication, and culminates in an example using Web Services.

Chapter 12: Service Oriented Integration

When performing enterprise application integration of components distributed across many machines and platforms, it is often necessary for you to be able to spread the workload across many different steps. There are two APIs that are particularly useful in this regard, the Java Message Service (JMS) and the Java Management Extensions (JMX). In this chapter, you see the core of these two APIs tied together to provide a highly useful architecture.

Chapter 13: Java Security

Information security is tremendously important to Java development. In this chapter, you see how your application can be secured using the Java Authorization and Authentication Service (JAAS) and your data can be secured using the Java Cryptography Extensions (JCE). Also detailed in this chapter is the new XML digital signature support introduced in Java 6, useful in building security for Web Services.

Chapter 14: Packaging and Deploying Your Java Applications

One of the trickiest and most painful things about developing Java applications, whether they are enterprise or desktop applications, is packaging and deploying your application. There are a multitude of deployment descriptors and packaging rules that exist in many of the Java APIs. There are JARs, WARs, EARs, and more on the way. Often you get cursory understanding of these formats and specifications within each of the stovepipe books. In this chapter, you learn about a number of the packaging mechanisms that exist in Java, as well as descriptions of the deployment descriptors for each of those mechanisms.

What You Need to Use This Book

This book is based upon Java 2 Standard Edition version 6.0. You might find it helpful to have an Integrated Development Environment (IDE) of your choice—Eclipse is a very good and popular one (www.eclipse.org). Furthermore, depending on the chapter, you may need to use an application server like JBoss (www.jboss.org) or Tomcat (http://jakarta.apache.org/tomcat). The need to download an application server, as well as any other downloads (of APIs and so on), is addressed in each chapter.

Conventions

To help you get the most from the text and keep track of what's happening, a number of conventions are used throughout the book.

> **Boxes like this one hold important, not-to-be forgotten information that is directly relevant to the surrounding text.**

Tips, hints, tricks, and asides to the current discussion are offset and placed in italics like this.

As for styles in the text, the following are standard for the book:

❑ Important words are *highlighted* when they are introduced.

❑ Keyboard strokes are shown like this: Ctrl+A.

❑ File names, URLs, and code within the text are like so: `persistence.properties`.

❑ Code is presented in two different ways:

```
In code examples, new and important code is highlighted with a gray background.
```

```
The gray highlighting is not used for code that's less important in the present
context, or has been shown before.
```

Source Code

As you work through the examples in this book, you may choose either to type in all the code manually or to use the source code files that accompany the book. All of the source code used in this book is available for download at `www.wrox.com`. Once at the site, simply locate the book's title (either by using the Search box or by using one of the title lists) and click the Download Code link on the book's detail page to obtain all the source code for the book.

Because many books have similar titles, you may find it easiest to search by ISBN; for this book the ISBN is 978-0-471-77710-6.

Once you download the code, just decompress it with your favorite compression tool. Alternatively, you can go to the main Wrox code download page at `www.wrox.com/dynamic/books/download.aspx` to see the code available for this book and all other Wrox books.

Errata

We make every effort to ensure that there are no errors in the text or in the code. However, no one is perfect, and mistakes do occur. If you find an error in one of our books, like a spelling mistake or faulty piece of code, we would be very grateful for your feedback. By sending in errata you may save another reader hours of frustration and at the same time you will be helping us provide even higher quality information.

To find the errata page for this book, go to `www.wrox.com` and locate the title using the Search box or one of the title lists. Then, on the book details page, click the Book Errata link. On this page you can view all errata that has been submitted for this book and posted by Wrox editors. A complete book list including links to each book's errata is also available at `www.wrox.com/misc-pages/booklist.shtml`.

If you don't spot the error you are experiencing on the Book Errata page, go to `www.wrox.com/contact/techsupport.shtml` and complete the form there to send us the error you have found. We'll check the information and, if appropriate, post a message to the book's errata page and fix the problem in subsequent editions of the book.

p2p.wrox.com

For author and peer discussion, join the P2P forums at `http://p2p.wrox.com`. The forums are a web-based system for you to post messages relating to Wrox books and related technologies and interact with other readers and technology users. The forums offer a subscription feature to e-mail you topics of interest of your choosing when new posts are made to the forums. Wrox authors, editors, other industry experts, and your fellow readers are present on these forums.

At `http://p2p.wrox.com` you will find a number of different forums that will help you not only as you read this book, but also as you develop your own applications. To join the forums, just follow these steps:

1. Go to p2p.wrox.com and click the Register link.

2. Read the terms of use and click Agree.

3. Complete the required information to join as well as any optional information you wish to provide and click Submit.

4. You will receive an e-mail with information describing how to verify your account and complete the registration process.

You can read messages in the forums without joining P2P, but to post your own messages, you must join.

Once you join, you can post new messages and respond to messages other users post. You can read messages at any time on the Web. If you would like to have new messages from a particular forum e-mailed to you, click the Subscribe to this Forum icon by the forum name in the forum listing.

For more information about how to use the Wrox P2P, be sure to read the P2P FAQs for answers to questions about how the forum software works as well as many common questions specific to P2P and Wrox books. To read the FAQs, click the FAQ link on any P2P page.

Part I: Thinking Like a Java Developer

Chapter 1: Key Java Language Features and Libraries

Chapter 2: Tools and Techniques for Developing Java Solutions

Chapter 3: Exploiting Patterns in Java

Key Java Language Features and Libraries

The past two major releases of the JDK have seen some significant changes. JDK 5 introduced new features at the language level, something that has not happened since Java was first released. Some of the most significant features added to the language are generics (parameterized types), enumerations, and metadata. With JDK 6, one of the biggest changes is the inclusion of a lightweight database known as Derby, which is from the Apache Database project.

The first half of this chapter introduces Derby and reviews the new language features from JDK 5. The second half of this chapter details certain key utility packages in the `java.util` branch of the class library that are useful for professional programming in Java.

Introducing Derby

New to Java 6 is a lightweight database called Derby, a product of the Apache Database project. Derby is a transactional, relational database and provides a small footprint on disk. As of the July 13, 2006 release of the Java 6 JDK, Derby is installed (by default) in `C:\Program Files\Java\jdk1.6.0\db` and includes the core libraries, demonstration programs, and an example database. Derby started its life as CloudScape, a product IBM acquired with Informix. In 2004, IBM decided to open source CloudScape and it became an incubator project under the Apache Software Foundation with the name Derby. The real benefits to using Derby are that it has minimal administration needs and a small footprint. The databases are small on disk, roughly 2MB for a basic database. The fact that administration is minimal allows you, as a developer, to easily create and use databases in code. This speeds up development. Deployment is made that much easier because Derby supports storage of a database archived in a JAR file, allowing you to simply distribute the JAR file.

Because Derby is an involved topic, this section serves only to introduce Derby and its features, using the included command-line tool and a brief exploration of using the JDBC driver. Derby is revisited later in this book.

Using Derby

As mentioned, Derby is automatically installed as part of the JDK. Derby provides a command-line tool called `ij`, which is an abbreviation for interactive JDBC scripting tool. This tool provides a way to connect to and manipulate Derby databases. You must have the following JAR files in your classpath before using this tool. The `derby.jar` file contains the JDBC drivers, and `derbytools.jar` contains the `ij` tool itself:

```
c:\Program Files\Java\jdk1.6.0\db\lib\derby.jar
c:\Program Files\Java\jdk1.6.0\db\lib\derbytools.jar
```

After your classpath is configured, start the tool and connect to the example database (toursdb) included with Derby:

```
c:\>java org.apache.derby.tools.ij
ij version 10.2
ij> connect 'jdbc:derby:c:\Program Files\Java\jdk1.6.0\db\demo\databases\toursdb';
ij>
```

Don't forget the semicolon at the end of a command. If you leave this off, `ij` may seem like it's processing a command, but it isn't. This provides for ease of entering multiline commands such as creating tables or complicated select statements. These semicolons are confined to `ij` and are not passed to the database.

The tool works much as you would expect it to, such as issuing a select statement to retrieve a partial listing of data from the countries table (a table that is part of the example toursdb):

```
ij> select * from countries where country like 'A%';
COUNTRY                        |C&|REGION
-----------------------------------------------------------------
Afghanistan                    |AF|Asia
Albania                        |AL|Europe
Algeria                        |DZ|North Africa
American Samoa                 |AS|Pacific Islands
Angola                         |AO|Africa
Argentina                      |AR|South America
Armenia                        |AM|Europe
Australia                      |AU|Australia and New Zealand
Austria                        |AT|Europe
Azerbaijan                     |AZ|Central Asia
```

To create a new database from `ij`, include the parameter `create=true` to the connection string. Because you're already connected to the toursdb, first disconnect. The `select` statement proves you're disconnected. Then issue the new `connect` statement:

```
ij> disconnect;
ij> select * from countries;
IJ ERROR: Unable to establish connection
ij> connect 'jdbc:derby:DerbyTestDB;create=true';
ij>
```

The database name (in this case, DerbyTestDB) is created as a subdirectory of the directory where you started the `ij` tool. The database appears on disk in the directory `C:\DerbyTestDB`. Exploring this directory is strictly for curiosity's sake — you should never have to modify any file in this directory, including the `service.properties` file that may seem tempting to play with. The creation of a database also creates a `derby.log` file at the same level as the DerbyTestDB, so the file in this case is `C:\derby.log`. This log file is an error log and is useful to check to get more information about the inevitable problems that arise during real development. If you create multiple databases they will share this log file.

Now that you have a new database, create a table, insert some data, and query it:

```
ij> create table zipcodes(zipcode varchar(5), city varchar(20), state varchar(2));
0 rows inserted/updated/deleted
ij> insert into zipcodes values ('22030', 'Fairfax', 'VA');
1 row inserted/updated/deleted
ij> insert into zipcodes values ('22003', 'Annandale', 'VA');
1 row inserted/updated/deleted
ij> insert into zipcodes values ('90210', 'Beverly Hills', 'CA');
1 row inserted/updated/deleted
ij> select * from zipcodes;
ZIPC&|CITY                |STA&
------------------------------
22030|Fairfax             |VA
22003|Annandale           |VA
90210|Beverly Hills       |CA

3 rows selected
ij>
```

By default, auto-commit is on from the `ij` tool, so you don't have to issue the `commit;` command to save changes to the database. You can control auto-commit by issuing the command "autocommit on;" or "autocommit off;" Type "exit;" to exit from the `ij` tool.

Now that you have seen the basics of using the `ij` tool, look at an example of querying your newly created database from a Java program using the JDBC driver. Because the standard JDBC mechanism is used, there are no surprises with the import statements:

```java
import java.sql.Connection;
import java.sql.DriverManager;
import java.sql.ResultSet;
import java.sql.SQLException;
import java.sql.Statement;

import java.util.Properties;

public class DerbyTestDBClient {
    public static void main(String[] args)
    {
        DerbyTestDBClient testClient = new DerbyTestDBClient();

        testClient.showZipCodes();
    }
```

The showZipCodes method actually opens the connection and performs the query. The driver used is org.apache.derby.jdbc.EmbeddedDriver. Derby also includes a ClientDriver for connecting to Derby in network mode, where Derby runs a network server providing for a client/server approach to using Derby:

```java
public void showZipCodes()
{
    try {
        String driver = "org.apache.derby.jdbc.EmbeddedDriver";

        Class.forName(driver).newInstance();
        Connection conn = null;
        conn = DriverManager.getConnection("jdbc:derby:DerbyTestDB");
        Statement s = conn.createStatement();
        ResultSet rs = s.executeQuery("SELECT city, state, zipcode
                                    FROM zipcodes");

        while(rs.next()) {
            System.out.println("City   : " + rs.getString(1));
            System.out.println("State  : " + rs.getString(2));
            System.out.println("Zipcode: " + rs.getString(3));
            System.out.println();
        }

        rs.close();
        s.close();
        conn.close();
    } catch(Exception e) {
        System.out.println("Exception: " + e);
        e.printStackTrace();
    }
}
```

Here's the output from the previous code:

```
c:\>java DerbyTestDBClient
City   : Fairfax
State  : VA
Zipcode: 22030

City   : Annandale
State  : VA
Zipcode: 22003

City   : Beverly Hills
State  : CA
Zipcode: 90210
```

Derby is a thriving project and continues to implement more features. You can keep an eye on its development at http://db.apache.org/derby.

Language Features Added in Java 5

Several useful syntactic elements were introduced in Java 5. All these features are supported by an updated compiler, and all translate to already defined Java bytecode, meaning that virtual machines can execute these features with no need for an update:

- ❑ **Generics:** A way to make classes type-safe that are written to work on any arbitrary object type, such as narrowing an instance of a collection to hold a specific object type and eliminating the need to cast objects when taking an object out of the collection.

- ❑ **Enhanced `for` loop:** A cleaner and less error-prone version of the `for` loop for use with iterators.

- ❑ **Variable arguments:** Support for passing an arbitrary number of parameters to a method.

- ❑ **Boxing/unboxing:** Direct language support for automatic conversion between primitive types and their reference types (such as `int` and `Integer`).

- ❑ **Type-safe enumerations:** Clean syntax for defining and using enumerations, supported at the language level.

- ❑ **Static import:** Ability to access static members from a class without need to qualify them with a class name.

- ❑ **Metadata:** Coupled with new tools developed by third-party companies, saves developers the effort of writing boilerplate code by automatically generating the code.

These features update the Java language to include many constructs developers are used to in other languages. They make writing Java code easier, cleaner, and faster. Even if you choose not to take advantage of these features, familiarity with them is vital to read and maintain code written by other developers.

Generics

Java 5 introduced generics, also known as parameterized types. Generics allow you to write a class that can operate on any type but that specific type is not specified until declaration of an instance of the class. Because this type is not specified as part of the class definition, the class becomes generic, gaining the ability to work on any type specified. The most obvious example, and a great use of generics, is the collection classes. The `ArrayList` class, for example, was written to hold, simply, `Object`. This means objects lose their type when added to the `ArrayList` and a cast is needed when accessing an element of the `ArrayList`. However, code that uses a generic version of the `ArrayList` can say "I want this `ArrayList` to hold only `String`s." This adds additional type-safety to Java because, if anything other than a `String` is added to the collection, the compiler will catch it. This also means that a cast is no longer needed when accessing elements — the compiler knows it only holds `String`s and will produce an error if the elements are treated as anything other than a `String`. Specifying `String` as the parameterized type is as easy as placing the type in angle brackets:

```
ArrayList<String> listOfStrings; // <TYPE_NAME> is new to the syntax
String stringObject;

listOfStrings = new ArrayList<String>(); // <TYPE_NAME> is new to the syntax
listOfStrings.add(new String("Test string")); // Can only pass in String objects
stringObject = listOfStrings.get(0); // no cast required
```

Generics are also known as *parameterized types* where a type is the parameter. As can be seen in the previous example, `String` is the *formal* type parameter. This same parameterized type must be used when instantiating the parameterized type.

Because one of the goals of the new language features in Java 5 was to not change the Java instruction set, generics are, basically, syntactic sugar. When accessing elements of the `ArrayList`, the compiler automatically inserts the casts that you now don't have to write. It's also possible to use the primitive data types as a parameterized type, but realize that these incur boxing/unboxing costs because they are implicitly converted to and from `Object`. Nonetheless, there are benefits in increased type-safety and increased program readability.

Type Erasure

A generic type in Java is compiled to a single class file. There aren't separate versions of the generic type for each formal parameterized type. The implementation of generics utilizes type erasure, which means the actual parameterized type is reduced to `Object`. Strangely, the decision to use erasure, although requiring no bytecode changes, hobbles the generics mechanism in its determination to maintain strong typing, as you'll soon see.

By way of example, the following code will not compile:

```
interface Shape {
    void draw();
}

class Square implements Shape {
    public String name;

    public Square()
    {
        name = "Square";
    }

    public void draw()
    {
        System.out.println("Drawing square");
    }
}

public class ErasureExample {
    public static <T> void drawShape(T shape)
    {
        shape.draw();
    }

    public static void main(String args[])
    {
        Square square = new Square();
    }
}
```

The compiler issues the following error:

```
ErasureExample.java:23: cannot find symbol
symbol  : method draw()
location: class java.lang.Object
      shape.draw();
             ^
1 error
```

If you replace the drawShape method with the following, the compiler is now happy to compile the program:

```
public static <T> void drawShape(T shape)
{
   System.out.println("Hashcode: " + shape.hashCode());
}
```

Why this discrepancy? It's the result of type erasure. The hashCode method belongs to Object, however the draw method belongs only to objects of type Shape. This little experiment demonstrates that the parameterized type is actually reduced to an Object. The next example shows how this relates to use of a generic class with different parameterized types.

Start with a new generic class to hold a data item of arbitrary type:

```
public class CustomHolder<E>
{
   E storedItem;

   public E getItem()
   {
      return(storedItem);
   }

   public void putItem(E item)
   {
      System.out.println("Adding data of type " + item.getClass().getName());
      storedItem = item;
   }
}
```

By convention, single letters are used for formal type parameters, usually E for element and T for type. Add a main method to this class:

```
public static void main(String args[])
{
   CustomHolder<String> stringHolder = new CustomHolder<String>();
   CustomHolder<Object> objectHolder = new CustomHolder<Object>();
   String str = new String("test string");
   String str2;

   stringHolder.putItem(str);
```

```
            objectHolder.putItem(str);

            str2 = stringHolder.getItem();
            //str2 = objectHolder.getItem();
        }
```

Look at the last two lines. Retrieving an element from `stringHolder` and assigning it to a string is fine. However, if you uncomment the second line, which tries to access the same string in the `objectHolder`, you get the following compiler error.

```
c:\>javac CustomHolder.java
CustomHolder.java:28: incompatible types
found    : java.lang.Object
required: java.lang.String
        str2 = objectHolder.getItem();
                                    ^
1 error
```

This makes sense because the actual type parameter (in this case, `String` or `Object`) dictates the type. When you add a `String` to the `objectHolder`, it is simply stored as an `Object`. When you attempt to assign the `Object` to the `String` (in the call to `objectHolder.getItem`), you now need an explicit cast to the `String` type.

Because of type erasure, it is possible to assign a generic class reference to a reference of its nongeneric (legacy) version. Therefore, the following code compiles without error:

```
Vector oldVector;
Vector<Integer> intVector;

oldVector = intVector; // valid
```

However, though not an error, assigning a reference to a nongeneric class to a reference to a generic class will cause an unchecked compiler warning. This happens when an erasure changes the argument types of a method or a field assignment to a raw type if the erasure changes the method/field type. As an example, the following program causes the warnings shown after it. You must pass `-Xlint:unchecked` on the command line to `javac` to see the specific warnings:

```
import java.util.*;

public class UncheckedExample {
    public void processIntVector(Vector<Integer> v)
    {
        // perform some processing on the vector
    }

    public static void main(String args[])
    {
        Vector<Integer> intVector = new Vector<Integer>();
        Vector oldVector = new Vector();
        UncheckedExample ue = new UncheckedExample();

        // This is permitted
```

```
            oldVector = intVector;
            // This causes an unchecked warning
            intVector = oldVector;
            // This is permitted
            ue.processIntVector(intVector);
            // This causes an unchecked warning
            ue.processIntVector(oldVector);
        }
    }
```

Attempting to compile the previous code leads to the following compiler warnings:

```
UncheckedExample.java:16: warning: unchecked assignment: java.util.Vector to
java.util.Vector<java.lang.Integer>
        intVector = oldVector; // This causes an unchecked warning

UncheckedExample.java:18: warning: unchecked method invocation:
processIntVector(java.util.Vector<java.lang.Integer>) in UncheckedExample is
applied to (java.util.Vector)
        ue.processIntVector(oldVector); // This causes an unchecked warning

2 warnings
```

Wildcards and Bounded Type Variables

Because you can't use CustomHolder<Object> as if it were a super-type of CustomHolder<String>, you can't write a method that would process both CustomHolder<Object> and CustomHolder<String>. There is, however, a special way to accomplish this. As part of the generics syntax, a wildcard is introduced, which, when used, basically means "any type parameter." Revisit the previous example and show how the wildcard, a single question mark, is used.

Take the CustomHolder class and add a few new methods and a new main as follows:

```
    public static void processHolderObject(CustomHolder2<Object> holder)
    {
        Object obj = holder.getItem();

        System.out.println("Item is: " + obj);
    }

    public static void processHolderString(CustomHolder2<String> holder)
    {
        Object obj = holder.getItem();

        System.out.println("Item is: " + obj);
    }

    public static void processHolderWildcard (CustomHolder2<?> holder)
    {
        Object obj = holder.getItem();

        System.out.println("Item is: " + obj);
```

```
    }

    public static void main(String args[])
    {
        CustomHolder2<String> stringHolder = new CustomHolder2<String>();
        CustomHolder2<Object> objectHolder = new CustomHolder2<Object>();
        String str = new String("test string");
        String str2;

        stringHolder.putItem(str);
        objectHolder.putItem(str);

        //processHolderObject(stringHolder);
        processHolderObject(objectHolder);

        processHolderString(stringHolder);
        //processHolderString(objectHolder);

        processHolderWildcard(stringHolder);
        processHolderWildcard(objectHolder);
    }
```

The two lines that are commented will prevent the program from compiling. If both these lines are uncommented, the compiler issues the following errors:

```
c:\>javac CustomHolder2.java
CustomHolder2.java:48: processHolderObject(CustomHolder2<java.lang.Object>) in C
ustomHolder2<E> cannot be applied to (CustomHolder2<java.lang.String>)
        processHolderObject(stringHolder);
        ^
CustomHolder2.java:52: processHolderString(CustomHolder2<java.lang.String>) in C
ustomHolder2<E> cannot be applied to (CustomHolder2<java.lang.Object>)
        processHolderString(objectHolder);
        ^
2 errors
```

This reminds you that the type parameter used must match the formal type parameter. However, notice that neither line that invokes processHolderWildcard is commented. This is because using the wildcard allows you to pass in either stringHolder or objectHolder. You can read the method parameter type CustomerHolder2<?> as "a CustomHolder2 of any type" as opposed to "of Object type" or "of String type."

A type parameter can be restricted to certain types by what is called a bound. A bound can be applied to a regular type parameter or a wildcard. Revisit the Shape example from earlier in the chapter, which defines a Shape interface:

```
import java.util.ArrayList;
import java.util.Iterator;

interface Shape {
    void draw();
```

```
    }

class Square implements Shape {
    public void draw()
    {
        System.out.println("Drawing square");
    }
}

class Circle implements Shape {
    public void draw()
    {
        System.out.println("Drawing circle");
    }
}
```

Now define a `PaintProgram` class to demonstrate bounds. If you add a `drawShape` method that defines a type parameter, this won't work:

```
public static <S> void drawShape(S shape)
{
    shape.draw();
}
```

So you must add a bound to the type parameter so Java treats the `shape` formal type parameter as a `Shape` and not an `Object`. By bounding the type parameter to `Shape`, you dictate that the object passed in must derive directly or indirectly from `Shape`. Because of this, Java knows that the object is a `Shape` and thus can invoke methods that belong to `Shape` instead of only `Object` methods:

```
public static <S extends Shape> void drawShapeBounded(S shape)
{
    shape.draw();
}
```

As alluded to earlier, this may make you wonder if generics really are that useful. If you have to explicitly state the bounds on a type parameter, you may as well just use the `Shape` interface to constrain a normal method parameter. One of the places generics really do shine is easing the use of collections, and this is probably the main justification for adding generics to Java.

Look at implementing a `drawAllShapes` method that takes a parameterized `ArrayList`. As expected, you need a bound here so Java does not treat the contents of the `ArrayList` as `Objects`:

```
public static <T extends Shape> void drawAllShapes(ArrayList<T> shapeList)
{
    T shape;
    Iterator<T> shapeIterator;

    shapeIterator = shapeList.iterator();
    while(shapeIterator.hasNext()) {
        shape = shapeIterator.next();
        shape.draw();
    }
}
```

By constraining the T type parameter, invoking draw is acceptable because Java knows it's a Shape.

If you want to specify multiple interfaces/classes to use as a bound, separate them with the ampersand (&). Also note that extends is used to specify bounds regardless of whether the type parameter is bounded by an interface or a class.

Using Generics

It is straightforward to create objects of a generic type. Any parameters must match the bounds specified. Although you might expect to create an array of a generic type, this is only possible with the wildcard type parameter. It is also possible to create a method that works on generic types. This section describes these usage scenarios.

Class Instances

Creating an object of a generic class consists of specifying types for each parameter and supplying any necessary arguments to the constructor. The conditions for any bounds on type variables must be met. Note that only reference types are valid as parameters when creating an instance of a generic class. Trying to use a primitive data type causes the compiler to issue an unexpected type error.

This is a simple creation of a HashMap that assigns Floats to Strings:

```
HashMap<String,Float> hm = new HashMap<String,Float>();
```

Arrays

Arrays of generic types and arrays of type variables are not allowed. Attempting to create an array of parameterized Vectors, for example, causes a compiler error:

```
import java.util.*;

public class GenericArrayExample {
    public static void main(String args[])
    {
        Vector<Integer> vectorList[] = new Vector<Integer>[10];
    }
}
```

If you try to compile that code, the compiler issues the following two errors. This code is the simplest approach to creating an array of a generic type and the compiler tells you explicitly that creating a generic type array is forbidden:

```
GenericArrayExample.java:6: arrays of generic types are not allowed
        Vector<Integer> vectorList[] = new Vector<Integer>[10];
                                       ^
GenericArrayExample.java:6: arrays of generic types are not allowed
        Vector<Integer> vectorList[] = new Vector<Integer>[10];
                                       ^
2 errors
```

You can, however, create an array of any type by using the wildcard as the type parameter.

Generic Methods

In addition to the generic mechanism for classes, generic methods are introduced. The angle brackets for the parameters appear after all method modifiers but before the return type of the method. Following is an example of a declaration of a generic method:

```
static <Elem> void swap(Elem[] a, int i, int j)
{
    Elem temp = a[i];
    a[i] = a[j];
    a[j] = temp;
}
```

The syntax for the parameters in a generic method is the same as that for generic classes. Type variables can have bounds just like they do in class declarations. Two methods cannot have the same name and argument types. If two methods have the same name and argument types, and have the same number of type variables with the same bounds, then these methods are the same and the compiler will generate an error.

Generics and Exceptions

Type variables are not permitted in `catch` clauses, but can be used in `throws` lists of methods. An example of using a type variable in the `throws` clause follows. The `Executor` interface is designed to execute a section of code that may throw an exception specified as a parameter. In this example, the code that fills in the `execute` method might throw an `IOException`. The specific exception, `IOException`, is specified as a parameter when creating a concrete instance of the `Executor` interface:

```
import java.io.*;

interface Executor<E extends Exception> {
    void execute() throws E;
}

public class GenericExceptionTest {
    public static void main(String args[]) {
        try {
            Executor<IOException> e =
                new Executor<IOException>() {
                public void execute() throws IOException
                {
                    // code here that may throw an
                    // IOException or a subtype of
                    // IOException
                }
            };

            e.execute();
        } catch(IOException ioe) {
            System.out.println("IOException: " + ioe);
            ioe.printStackTrace();
        }
    }
}
```

The specific type of exception is specified when an instance of the `Executor` class is created inside main. The `execute` method throws an arbitrary exception that it is unaware of until a concrete instance of the `Executor` interface is created.

Enhanced for Loop

The `for` loop has been modified to provide a cleaner way to process an iterator. Using a `for` loop with an iterator is error prone because of the slight mangling of the usual form of the `for` loop since the `update` clause is placed in the body of the loop. Some languages have a `foreach` keyword that cleans up the syntax for processing iterators. Java opted not to introduce a new keyword, instead deciding to keep it simple and introduce a new use of the colon. Traditionally, a developer will write the following code to use an iterator:

```
for(Iterator iter = intArray.iterator(); iter.hasNext(); ) {
    Integer intObject = (Integer)iter.next();
    // ... more statements to use intObject ...
}
```

The problem inherent in this code lies in the missing `update` clause of the `for` loop. The code that advances the iterator is moved into the body of the `for` loop out of necessity, because it also returns the next object. The new and improved syntax that does the same thing as the previous code snippet is as follows:

```
for(Integer intObject : intArray) {
    // ... same statements as above go here ...
}
```

This code is much cleaner and easier to read. It eliminates all the potential from the previous construct to introduce errors into the program. If this is coupled with a generic collection, the type of the object is checked versus the type inside the collection at compile time.

Support for this new `for` loop requires a change only to the compiler. The code generated is no different from the same code written in the traditional way. The compiler might translate the previous code into the following, for example:

```
for(Iterator<Integer> $iter = intArray.iterator(); $iter.hasNext(); ) {
    Integer intObject = $iter.next();
    // ... statements ...
}
```

The use of the dollar sign in the identifier in this example merely means the compiler generates a unique identifier for the expansion of the new `for` loop syntax into the more traditional form before compiling.

The same syntax for using an iterator on a collection works for an array. Using the new `for` loop syntax on an array is the same as using it on a collection:

```
for(String strObject : stringArray) {
    // ... statements here using strObject ...
}
```

However, the compiler expands the array version to code slightly longer than the collection version:

```
String[] $strArray = stringArray;

for(int $i = 0; $i < $strArray.length; $i++) {
    String strObject = $strArray[$i];
    // ... statements here ...
}
```

The compiler this time uses two temporary and unique variables during the expansion. The first is an alias to the array, and the second is the loop counter.

Additions to the Java Class Library

To fully support the new `for` loop syntax, the object iterated over must be an array or inherit from a new interface, `java.lang.Iterable`, directly or indirectly. The existing collection classes were retrofitted for the release of JDK 5. The new `Iterable` interface looks like this:

```
public interface Iterable {
    /**
     * Returns an iterator over the elements in this collection.  There are no
     * guarantees concerning the order in which the elements are returned
     * (unless this collection is an instance of some class that provides a
     * guarantee).
     *
     * @return an Iterator over the elements in this collection.
     */
    SimpleIterator iterator();
}
```

Additionally, `java.util.Iterator` will be retrofitted to implement `java.lang.ReadOnlyIterator`, as shown here:

```
public interface ReadOnlyIterator {
    /**
     * Returns true if the iteration has more elements. (In other
     * words, returns true if next would return an element
     * rather than throwing an exception.)
     *
     * @return true if the iterator has more elements.
     */
    boolean hasNext();

    /**
     * Returns the next element in the iteration.
     *
     * @return the next element in the iteration.
     * @exception NoSuchElementException iteration has no more elements.
     */
    Object next();
}
```

The introduction of this interface prevents dependency on the `java.util` interfaces. The change in the `for` loop syntax is at the language level and it makes sense to ensure that any support needed in the class library is located in the `java.lang` branch.

Variable Arguments

C and C++ are a couple of the languages that support variable length argument lists for functions. Java decided to introduce this aspect into the language. Only use variable argument parameter lists in cases that make sense. If you abuse them, it's easy to create source code that is confusing. The C language uses the ellipsis (three periods) in the function declaration to stand for "an arbitrary number of parameters, zero or more." Java also uses the ellipsis but combines it with a type and identifier. The type can be anything—any class, any primitive type, even array types. When using it in an array, however, the ellipsis must come last in the type description, after the square brackets. Because of the nature of variable arguments, each method can only have a single type as a variable argument and it must come last in the parameter list.

Following is an example of a method that takes an arbitrary number of primitive integers and returns their sum:

```
public int sum(int... intList)
{
    int i, sum;

    sum=0;
    for(i=0; i<intList.length; i++) {
        sum += intList[i];
    }

    return(sum);
}
```

All arguments passed in from the position of the argument marked as variable and beyond are combined into an array. This makes it simple to test how many arguments were passed in. All that is needed is to reference the `length` property on the array, and the array also provides easy access to each argument.

Here's a full sample program that adds up all the values in an arbitrary number of arrays:

```
public class VarArgsExample {
    int sumArrays(int[]... intArrays)
    {
        int sum, i, j;

        sum=0;
        for(i=0; i<intArrays.length; i++) {
            for(j=0; j<intArrays[i].length; j++) {
                sum += intArrays[i][j];
            }
        }

        return(sum);
```

```
    }

    public static void main(String args[])
    {
        VarArgsExample va = new VarArgsExample();
        int sum=0;

        sum = va.sumArrays(new int[]{1,2,3},
                           new int[]{4,5,6},
                           new int[]{10,16});
        System.out.println("The sum of the numbers is: " + sum);
    }
}
```

This code follows the established approach to defining and using a variable argument. The ellipsis comes after the square brackets (that is, after the variable argument's type). Inside the method the argument intArrays is simply an array of arrays.

Boxing and Unboxing Conversions

One tedious aspect of the Java language in the past is the manual operation of converting primitive types (such as int and char) to their corresponding reference type (for example, Integer for int and Character for char). The solution to getting rid of this constant wrapping and unwrapping is boxing and unboxing conversions.

Boxing Conversions

A boxing conversion is an implicit operation that takes a primitive type, such as int, and automatically places it inside an instance of its corresponding reference type (in this case, Integer). Unboxing is the reverse operation, taking a reference type, such as Integer, and converting it to its primitive type, int. Without boxing, you might add an int primitive to a collection (which holds Object types) by doing the following:

```
Integer intObject;
int intPrimitive;
ArrayList arrayList = new ArrayList();

intPrimitive = 11;
intObject = new Integer(intPrimitive);
arrayList.put(intObject); // cannot add intPrimitive directly
```

Although this code is straightforward, it is more verbose than necessary. With the introduction of boxing conversions, the preceding code can be rewritten as follows:

```
int intPrimitive;
ArrayList arrayList = new ArrayList();

intPrimitive = 11;
// here intPrimitive is automatically wrapped in an Integer
arrayList.put(intPrimitive);
```

The need to create an `Integer` object to place an `int` into the collection is no longer needed. The boxing conversion happens such that the resulting reference type's `value()` method (such as `intValue()` for `Integer`) equals the original primitive type's value. Consult the following table for all valid boxing conversions. If there is any other type, the boxing conversion becomes an identity conversion (converting the type to its own type). Note that due to the introduction of boxing conversions, several forbidden conversions referring to primitive types are no longer forbidden because they now can be converted to certain reference types.

Primitive Type	Reference Type
boolean	Boolean
byte	Byte
char	Character
short	Short
int	Integer
long	Long
float	Float
double	Double

Unboxing Conversions

Java also introduces unboxing conversions, which convert a reference type (such as `Integer` or `Float`) to its primitive type (such as `int` or `float`). Consult the following table for a list of all valid unboxing conversions. The conversion happens such that the `value` method of the reference type equals the resulting primitive value.

Reference Type	Primitive Type
Boolean	boolean
Byte	byte
Character	char
Short	short
Integer	int
Long	long
Float	float
Double	double

Valid Contexts for Boxing and Unboxing Conversions

Because the boxing and unboxing operations are conversions, they happen automatically with no specific instruction by the programmer (unlike casting, which is an explicit operation). There are several contexts in which boxing and unboxing conversions can happen.

Assignments

An assignment conversion happens when the value of an expression is assigned to a variable. When the type of the expression does not match the type of the variable, and there is no risk of data loss, the conversion happens automatically. The precedence of conversions that happen is the identity conversion, a widening primitive conversion, a widening reference conversion, and then the new boxing (or unboxing) conversion. If none of these conversions are valid, the compiler issues an error.

Method Invocations

When a method call is made, and the argument types don't match precisely with those passed in, several conversions are possible. Collectively, these conversions are known as method invocation conversions. Each parameter that does not match precisely in type to the corresponding parameter in the method signature might be subject to a conversion. The possible conversions are the identity conversion, a widening primitive conversion, a widening reference conversion, and then the new boxing (or unboxing) conversion.

The most specific method must be chosen anytime more than one method matches a particular method call. The rules to match the most specific method change slightly with the addition of boxing conversions. If all the standard checks for resolving method ambiguity fail, the boxing/unboxing conversion won't be used to resolve ambiguity. Therefore, by the time checks are performed for boxing conversions, the method invocation is deemed ambiguous and fails.

Combining boxing with generics allows you to write the following code:

```
import java.util.*;

public class BoxingGenericsExample {
    public static void main(String args[])
    {
        HashMap<String,Integer> hm = new HashMap<String,Integer>();

        hm.put("speed", 20);
    }
}
```

The primitive integer `20` is automatically converted to an `Integer` and then placed into the `HashMap` under the specified key.

Static Imports

Importing static data is introduced into the language to simplify using static attributes and methods. After importing static information, the methods/attributes can then be used without the need to qualify the method or attribute with its class name. For example, by importing the static members of the `Math` class, you can write `abs` or `sqrt` instead of `Math.abs` and `Math.sqrt`.

This mechanism also prevents the dangerous coding practice of placing a set of static attributes into an interface, and then in each class that needs to use the attributes, implementing that interface. The following interface should not be implemented in order to use the attributes without qualification:

```
interface ShapeNumbers {
    public static int CIRCLE = 0;
    public static int SQUARE = 1;
    public static int TRIANGLE = 2;
}
```

Implementing this interface creates an unnecessary dependence on the `ShapeNumbers` interface. Even worse, it becomes awkward to maintain as the class evolves, especially if other classes need access to these constants also and implement this interface. It is easy for compiled classes to get out of synchronization with each other if the interface containing these attributes changes and only some classes are recompiled.

To make this cleaner, the static members are placed into a class (instead of an interface) and then imported via a modified syntax of the import directive. `ShapeNumbers` is revised to the following:

```
package MyConstants;

class ShapeNumbers {
    public static int CIRCLE = 0;
    public static int SQUARE = 1;
    public static int TRIANGLE = 2;
}
```

A client class then imports the static information from the `ShapeNumbers` class and can then use the attributes `CIRCLE`, `SQUARE`, and `TRIANGLE` without the need to prefix them with `ShapeNumbers` and the member operator.

To import the static members in your class, specify the following in the import section of your Java source file (at the top):

```
import static MyConstants.ShapeNumbers.*; // imports all static data
```

This syntax is only slightly modified from the standard format of the import statement. The keyword `static` is added after the `import` keyword, and instead of importing packages, you now always add on the class name because the static information is being imported from a specific class. The chief reason the keyword `static` is added to the import statement is to make it clear to those reading the source code that the import is for the static information.

You can also import constants individually by using the following syntax:

```
import static MyConstants.ShapeNumbers.CIRCLE;
import static MyConstants.ShapeNumbers.SQUARE;
```

This syntax is also what you would expect. The keyword `static` is included because this is a static import, and the pieces of static information to import are each specified explicitly.

You cannot statically import data from a class that is inside the default package. The class must be located inside a named package. Also, static attributes and methods can conflict. For example, following are two classes (located in `Colors.java` and `Fruits.java`) containing static constants:

```
package MyConstants;

public class Colors {
    public static int white = 0;
    public static int black = 1;
    public static int red = 2;
    public static int blue = 3;
    public static int green = 4;
    public static int orange = 5;
    public static int grey = 6;
}
```

```
package MyConstants;

public class Fruits {
    public static int apple = 500;
    public static int pear = 501;
    public static int orange = 502;
    public static int banana = 503;
    public static int strawberry = 504;
}
```

If you write a class that tries to statically import data on both these classes, everything is fine until you try to use a static variable that is defined in both of them:

```
import static MyConstants.Colors.*;
import static MyConstants.Fruits.*;

public class StaticTest {
    public static void main(String args[])
    {
        System.out.println("orange = " + orange);
        System.out.println("color orange = " + Colors.orange);
        System.out.println("Fruity orange = " + Fruits.orange);
    }
}
```

The seventh line of the program causes the following compiler error. The identifier `orange` is defined in both `Colors` and `Fruits`, so the compiler cannot resolve this ambiguity:

```
StaticTest.java:7: reference to orange is ambiguous, both variable orange in
MyConstants.Colors and variable orange in MyConstants.Fruits match
        System.out.println("orange = " + orange);
```

In this case, you should explicitly qualify the conflicting name with the class where it is defined. Instead of writing `orange`, write `Colors.orange` or `Fruits.orange`.

Enumerations

Java introduces enumeration support at the language level in the JDK 5 release. An enumeration is an ordered list of items wrapped into a single entity. An instance of an enumeration can take on the value of any single item in the enumeration's list of items. The simplest possible enumeration is the `Colors` enum shown here:

```
public enum Colors { red, green, blue }
```

They present the ability to compare one arbitrary item to another, and to iterate over the list of defined items. An enumeration (abbreviated enum in Java) is a special type of class. All enumerations implicitly subclass a new class in Java, `java.lang.Enum`. This class cannot be subclassed manually.

There are many benefits to built-in support for enumerations in Java. Enumerations are type-safe and the performance is competitive with constants. The constant names inside the enumeration don't need to be qualified with the enumeration's name. Clients aren't built with knowledge of the constants inside the enumeration, so changing the enumeration is easy without having to change the client. If constants are removed from the enumeration, the clients will fail and you'll receive an error message. The names of the constants in the enumeration can be printed, so you get more information than simply the ordinal number of the item in the list. This also means that the constants can be used as names for collections such as `HashMap`.

Because an enumeration is a class in Java, it can also have fields and methods, and implement interfaces. Enumerations can be used inside `switch` statements in a straightforward manner, and are relatively simple for programmers to understand and use.

Here's a basic `enum` declaration and its usage inside a `switch` statement. If you want to track what operating system a certain user is using, you can use an enumeration of operating systems, which are defined in the `OperatingSystems` enum. Note that because an enumeration is effectively a class, it cannot be public if it is in the same file as another class that is public. Also note that in the `switch` statement, the constant names cannot be qualified with the name of the enumeration they are in. The details are automatically handled by the compiler based on the type of the `enum` used in the `switch` clause:

```java
import java.util.*;

enum OperatingSystems {
    windows, unix, linux, macintosh
}

public class EnumExample1 {
    public static void main(String args[])
    {
        OperatingSystems os;

        os = OperatingSystems.windows;
        switch(os) {
            case windows:
                System.out.println("You chose Windows!");
                break;
            case unix:
                System.out.println("You chose Unix!");
                break;
```

```
            case linux:
                System.out.println("You chose Linux!");
                break;
            case macintosh:
                System.out.println("You chose Macintosh!");
                break;
            default:
                System.out.println("I don't know your OS.");
                break;
        }
    }
}
```

The `java.lang.Enum` class implements the `Comparable` and `Serializable` interfaces. The details of comparing enumerations and serializing them to a data source are already handled inside the class. You cannot mark an `enum` as `abstract` unless every constant has a class body, and these class bodies override the abstract methods in the `enum`. Also note that enumerations cannot be instantiated using `new`. The compiler will let you know that `enum types may not be instantiated`.

Java introduces two new collections, `EnumSet` and `EnumMap`, which are only meant to optimize the performance of sets and maps when using `enums`. Enumerations can be used with the existing collection classes, or with the new collections when optimization tailored to enumerations is desired.

Methods can be declared inside an `enum`. There are restrictions placed on defining constructors, however. Constructors can't chain to superclass constructors, unless the superclass is another `enum`. Each constant inside the `enum` can have a class body, but because this is effectively an anonymous class, you cannot define a constructor.

You can also add attributes to the enumeration and to the individual `enum` constants. An `enum` constant can also be followed by arguments, which are passed to the constructor defined in the `enum`.

Here's an example enumeration with fields and methods:

```
enum ProgramFlags {
    showErrors(0x01),
    includeFileOutput(0x02),
    useAlternateProcessor(0x04);

    private int bit;

    ProgramFlags(int bitNumber)
    {
        bit = bitNumber;
    }

    public int getBitNumber()
    {
        return(bit);
    }
}

public class EnumBitmapExample {
    public static void main(String args[])
```

```
    {
        ProgramFlags flag = ProgramFlags.showErrors;

        System.out.println("Flag selected is: " +
                            flag.ordinal() +
                    " which is " +
                            flag.name());
    }
}
```

The `ordinal()` method returns the position of the constant in the list. The value of `showErrors` is 0 because it comes first in the list, and the ordinal values are 0-based. The `name()` method can be used to get the name of the constant, which provides for getting more information about enumerations.

Metadata

Another feature that Sun has decided to include in the JDK 5 release of Java is a metadata facility. This enables tagging classes with extra information that tools can analyze, and also applying certain blocks of code to classes automatically. The metadata facility is introduced in the `java.lang.annotation` package. An annotation is the association of a `tag` to a construct in Java such as a class, known as a *target* in annotation terminology. The types of constructs that can be annotated are listed in the `java.lang` `.annotation.ElementType` enumeration, and are listed in the following table. Even annotations can be annotated. `TYPE` covers classes, interfaces, and `enum` declarations.

ElementType Constant
ANNOTATION_TYPE
CONSTRUCTOR
FIELD
LOCAL_VARIABLE
METHOD
PACKAGE
PARAMETER
TYPE

Another concept introduced is the life of an annotation, known as the *retention*. Certain annotations may only be useful at the Java source code level, such as an annotation for the `javadoc` tool. Others might be needed while the program is executing. The `RetentionPolicy` enumeration lists three `type` lifetimes for an annotation. The `SOURCE` policy indicates the annotations should be discarded by the compiler, that is, should only available at the source code level. The `CLASS` policy indicates that the annotation should appear in the class file, but is possibly discarded at runtime. The `RUNTIME` policy indicates the annotations should make it through to the executing program, and these can then be viewed using reflection.

Several types of annotations are defined in this package. These are listed in the following table. Each of these annotations inherits from the `Annotation` interface, which defines an `equals` method and a `toString` method.

Annotation Class Name	Description
Target	Specifies to which program elements an annotation type is applicable. Each program element can appear only once.
Documented	Specifies annotations should be documented by `javadoc` or other documentation tools. This can only be applied to annotations.
Inherited	Inherits annotations from superclasses, but not interfaces. The policy on this annotation is `RUNTIME`, and it can be applied only to annotations.
Retention	Indicates how long annotations on this program element should be available. See `RetentionPolicy` discussed previously. The policy on this annotation is `RUNTIME`, and it can be applied only to annotations.
Deprecated	Marks a program element as deprecated, telling developers they should no longer use it. Retention policy is `SOURCE`.
Overrides	Indicates that a method is meant to override the method in a parent class. If the override does not actually exist, the compiler will generate an error message. This can be applied only to methods.

Two useful source level annotations come with JDK 5, `@deprecated` and `@overrides`. The `@deprecated` annotation is used to mark a method as deprecated — that is, it shouldn't be used by client programmers. The compiler will issue a warning when encountering this annotation on a class method that a programmer uses. The other annotation, `@overrides`, is used to mark a method as overriding a method in the parent class. The compiler will ensure that a method marked as `@overrides` does indeed override a method in the parent class. If the method in the child class doesn't override the one in the parent class, the compiler will issue an error alerting the programmer to the fact that the method signature does not match the method in the parent class.

Developing a custom annotation isn't difficult. Create a `CodeTag` annotation that stores basic author and modification date information, and also stores any bug fixes applied to that piece of code. The annotation will be limited to classes and methods:

```
import java.lang.annotation.*;

@Retention(RetentionPolicy.SOURCE)
@Target({ElementType.TYPE, ElementType.METHOD})
public @interface CodeTag {
    String authorName();
    String lastModificationDate();
    String bugFixes() default "";
}
```

The `Retention` is set to `SOURCE`, which means this annotation is not available during compile time and runtime. The doclet API is used to access source level annotations. The `Target` is set to `TYPE` (for classes/interfaces/enums) and `METHOD` for methods. A compiler error is generated if the `CodeTag` annotation is applied to any other source code element. The first two annotation elements are `authorName` and `lastModificationDate`, both of which are mandatory. The `bugFixes` element defaults to the empty string if not specified. Following is an example class that utilizes the `CodeTag` annotation:

```
import java.lang.annotation.*;

@CodeTag(authorName="Dilbert",
         lastModificationDate="May 7, 2006")
public class ServerCommandProcessor {
    @CodeTag(authorName="Dilbert",
             lastModificationDate="May 10, 2006",
             bugFixes="BUG0170")
    public void setParams(String serverName)
    {
        // ...
    }

    public void executeCommand(String command, Object... params)
    {
        // ...
    }
}
```

Note how annotation is used to mark who modified the source and when. The method was last modified a day after the class because of the bug fix. This custom annotation can be used to track this information as part of keeping up with source code modifications. To view or process these source code annotations, the doclet API must be used.

The doclet API (aka Javadoc API) has been extended to support the processing of annotations in the source code. To use the doclet API, include the `tools.jar` file (located in lib directory of a default JDK install, version 5 or higher) in your classpath. You use the doclet API by writing a Java class that extends `com.sun.javadoc.Doclet`. The `start` method must be implemented because this is the method that Javadoc invokes on a doclet to perform custom processing. A simple doclet to print out all classes and methods in a Java source file follows:

```
import com.sun.javadoc.*;

public class ListClasses extends Doclet {
    public static boolean start(RootDoc root) {
        ClassDoc[] classes = root.classes();
        for (ClassDoc cd : classes) {
            System.out.println("Class [" + cd + "] has the following methods");
            for(MemberDoc md : cd.methods()) {
                System.out.println("   " + md);
            }
        }
        return true;
    }
}
```

The `start` method takes a `RootDoc` as a parameter, which is automatically passed in by the `javadoc` tool. The `RootDoc` provides the starting point to obtain access to all elements inside the source code, and also information on the command line such as additional packages and classes.

The interfaces added to the doclet API for annotations are `AnnotationDesc`, `AnnotationDesc` `.ElementValuePair`, `AnnotationTypeDoc`, `AnnotationTypeElementDoc`, and `AnnotationValue`.

Any element of Java source that can have annotations has an `annotations()` method associated with the doclet API's counterpart to the source code element. These are `AnnotationTypeDoc`, `AnnotationTypeElementDoc`, `ClassDoc`, `ConstructorDoc`, `ExecutableMemberDoc`, `FieldDoc`, `MethodDoc`, and `MemberDoc`. The `annotations()` method returns an array of `AnnotationDesc`.

AnnotationDesc

This class represents an annotation, which is an annotation type (`AnnotationTypeDoc`), and an array of annotation type elements paired with their values. `AnnotationDesc` defines the following methods.

Method	Description
`AnnotationTypeDoc annotationType()`	Returns this annotation's type.
`AnnotationDesc .ElementValuePair[] elementValues()`	Returns an array of an annotation's elements and their values. Only elements explicitly listed are returned. The elements that aren't listed explicitly, which assume their default value, are not returned because this method processes just what is listed. If there are no elements, an empty array is returned.

AnnotationDesc.ElementValuePair

This represents an association between an annotation type's element and its value. The following methods are defined.

Method	Description
`AnnotationTypeElementDoc element()`	Returns the annotation type element.
`AnnotationValue value()`	Returns the annotation type element's value.

AnnotationTypeDoc

This interface represents an annotation in the source code, just like `ClassDoc` represents a `Class`. Only one method is defined.

Method	Description
`AnnotationTypeElementDoc[] elements()`	Returns an array of the elements of this annotation type.

AnnotationTypeElementDoc

This interface represents an element of an annotation type.

Method	Description
`AnnotationValue` `defaultValue()`	Returns the default value associated with this annotation type, or null if there is no default value.

AnnotationValue

This interface represents the value of an annotation type element.

Method	Description
`String toString()`	Returns a string representation of the value.
`Object value()`	Returns the value. The object behind this value could be any of the following.
	❑ A wrapper class for a primitive type (such as `Integer` or `Float`)
	❑ A `String`
	❑ A `Type` (representing a class, a generic class, a type variable, a wildcard type, or a primitive data type)
	❑ A `FieldDoc` (representing an `enum` constant)
	❑ An `AnnotationDesc`
	❑ An array of `AnnotationValue`

Here's an example using the annotation support provided by the doclet API. This doclet echoes all annotations and their values that it finds in a source file:

```
import com.sun.javadoc.*;
import java.lang.annotation.*;

public class AnnotationViewer {
    public static boolean start(RootDoc root)
    {
        ClassDoc[] classes = root.classes();

        for (ClassDoc cls : classes) {
            showAnnotations(cls);
        }

        return(true);
    }

    static void showAnnotations(ClassDoc cls)
    {
        System.out.println("Annotations for class [" + cls + "]");
```

```
        process(cls.annotations());

        System.out.println();
        for(MethodDoc m : cls.methods()) {
            System.out.println("Annotations for method [" + m + "]");
            process(m.annotations());
            System.out.println();
        }
    }

    static void process(AnnotationDesc[] anns)
    {
        for (AnnotationDesc ad : anns) {
            AnnotationDesc.ElementValuePair evp[] = ad.elementValues();

            for(AnnotationDesc.ElementValuePair e : evp) {
                System.out.println("  NAME: " + e.element() +
                                    ", VALUE=" + e.value());
            }

        }
    }
}
```

The `start` method iterates across all classes (and interfaces) found in the source file. Because all annotations on source code elements are associated with the `AnnotationDesc` interface, a single method can be written to process annotations regardless of with which source code element the annotation is associated. The `showAnnotations` method prints out annotations associated with the current class and then processes all methods inside that class. The doclet API makes processing these source code elements easy. To execute the doclet, pass the name of the doclet and name of the class to process on the command line as follows:

```
javadoc -doclet AnnotationViewer ServerCommandProcessor.java
```

The doclet echoes the following to the screen:

```
Loading source file ServerCommandProcessor.java...
Constructing Javadoc information...
Annotations for class [ServerCommandProcessor]
  NAME: CodeTag.authorName(), VALUE="Dilbert"
  NAME: CodeTag.lastModificationDate(), VALUE="May 7, 2006"

Annotations for method [ServerCommandProcessor.setParams(java.lang.String)]
  NAME: CodeTag.authorName(), VALUE="Dilbert"
  NAME: CodeTag.lastModificationDate(), VALUE="May 10, 2006"
  NAME: CodeTag.bugFixes(), VALUE="BUG0170"

Annotations for method [ServerCommandProcessor.executeCommand(java.lang.String,
java.lang.Object[])]
```

To access annotations at runtime, the reflection API must be used. This support is built in through the interface `AnnotatedElement`, which is implemented by the reflection classes `AccessibleObject`, `Class`, `Constructor`, `Field`, `Method`, and `Package`. All these elements may have annotations. The `AnnotatedElement` interface defines the following methods.

Method	Description
`<T extends Annotation> T getAnnotation(Class<T> annotationType)`	Returns the annotation associated with the specified type, or null if none exists.
`Annotation[] getAnnotations()`	Returns an array of all annotations on the current element, or a zero-length array if no annotations are present.
`Annotation[] getDeclaredAnnotations()`	Similar to `getAnnotations` but does not return inherited annotations—only annotations explicitly declared on this element are returned. Returns a zero-length array if no annotations are present.
`boolean isAnnotationPresent(Class<? extends Annotation> annotationType)`	Returns `true` if the `annotationType` is present on the current element, `false` otherwise.

Develop an annotation that might be useful in developing a testing framework. The framework invokes test methods specified in the annotation and expects a Boolean return value from these testing methods. The reflection API is used to both process the annotation and execute the test methods.

The annotation is listed as follows:

```
import java.lang.annotation.*;

@Retention(RetentionPolicy.RUNTIME)
@Target({ElementType.TYPE})
public @interface TestParameters {
    String testStage();
    String testMethods();
    String testOutputType(); // "db" or "file"
    String testOutput(); // filename or data source/table name
}
```

An example application of this annotation is to a class of utility methods for strings. You might develop your own utility class and develop testing methods to ensure the utility methods work:

```
@TestParameters(testStage="Unit",
                testMethods="testConcat,testSubstring",
                testOutputType="screen",
                testOutput="")
public class StringUtility {
    public String concat(String s1, String s2)
    {
        return(s1 + s2);
    }

    public String substring(String str, int startIndex, int endIndex)
    {
        return(str.substring(startIndex, endIndex));
```

```
        }

    public boolean testConcat()
    {
        String s1 = "test";
        String s2 = " 123";

        return(concat(s1,s2).equals("test 123"));
    }

    public boolean testSubstring()
    {
        String str = "The cat landed on its feet";

        return(substring(str, 4, 7).equals("cat"));
    }
}
```

Following is an example implementation of the testing framework. It uses reflection to process the annotation and then invoke the testing methods, writing the results to the screen (though other output destinations can be built into the framework).

```
import java.lang.reflect.*;
import java.lang.annotation.*;
import java.util.*;

public class TestFramework {
    static void executeTests(String className) {
        try {
            Object obj = Class.forName(className).newInstance();

            TestParameters tp = obj.getClass().getAnnotation(TestParameters.class);
            if(tp != null) {
                String methodList = tp.testMethods();
                StringTokenizer st = new StringTokenizer(methodList, ",");
                while(st.hasMoreTokens()) {
                    String methodName = st.nextToken().trim();

                    Method m = obj.getClass().getDeclaredMethod(methodName);
                    System.out.println("");
                    System.out.println(methodName);
                    System.out.println("----------------");
                    String result = invoke(m, obj);
                    System.out.println("Result: " + result);
                }
            } else {
                System.out.println("No annotation found for " + obj.getClass());
            }
        } catch(Exception ex) {
            System.out.println("Exception: " + ex);
            ex.printStackTrace();
        }
    }

    static String invoke(Method m, Object o) {
```

```
        String result = "PASSED";

        try {
            m.invoke(o);
        } catch(Exception ex) {
            System.out.println("Exception: " + ex + "\n" + ex.getCause());
            result = "FAILED";
        }

        return(result);
    }

    public static void main(String [] args) {
        if(args.length == 0) {
            System.out.println("Must specify class name (without an extension)");
        } else {
            executeTests(args[0]);
        }
    }
}
```

Executing the preceding class on the `StringUtility` class provides the following output:

```
C:\>java TestFramework StringUtility

testConcat
----------------
Result: PASSED

testSubstring
----------------
Result: PASSED
```

The `executeTests` method obtains a handle to the `TestParameters` annotation from the class and then invokes each method from the `testMethods()` element of the annotation. This is a simple implementation of the testing framework and can be extended to support the other elements of the `TestParameters` annotation, such as writing results to a database instead of the screen. This is a practical example of using metadata — adding declarative information to Java source that can then be utilized by external programs and/or doclets for generating documentation.

Important Java Utility Libraries

This section describes several key utility libraries in Java. These libraries are as follows:

- ❑ **Java logging:** A powerful logging system that is vital for providing meaningful error messages to end users, developers, and people working in the field.

- ❑ **Regular expressions:** A powerful "miniature language" used to process strings in a variety of ways, such as searching for substrings that match a particular pattern.

- ❑ **Java preferences:** A way to store and retrieve both system- and user-defined configuration options.

Each library is designed for flexibility of usage. Familiarity with these libraries is vital when developing solutions in Java. The more tools on your belt as a developer, the better equipped you are.

Java Logging

Java has a well-designed set of classes to control, format, and publish messages through the logging system. It is important for a program to log error and status messages. There are many people who can benefit from logging messages, including developers, testers, end users, and people working in the field that have to troubleshoot programs without source code. It is vital to include a high number of quality log messages in a program, from status updates to error conditions (such as when certain exceptions are caught). By using the logging system, it is possible to see what the program is doing without consulting the source code, and most importantly, track down error conditions to a specific part of the program. The value of a logging system is obvious, especially in large systems where a casual error with minimal or no log messages might take days or longer to track down.

The logging system in `java.util.logging` is sophisticated, including a way to prioritize log messages such that only messages a particular logger is interested in get logged, and the messages can be output to any source that a `Handler` object can handle. Examples of logging destinations are files, databases, and output streams. Take a close look at Figure 1-1 to see an overview of the entire logging system.

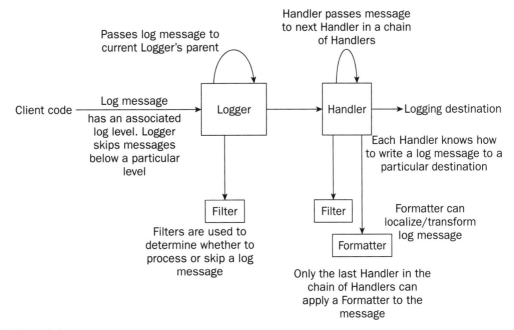

Figure 1-1

The specific `Logger` objects are actually hierarchical, and though not mandatory, can mirror the class hierarchy. When a `Logger` receives a log message, the message is also passed automatically to the parent of `Logger`. The root logger is named `" "` (the empty string) and has no parent. Each other `Logger` is usually named something such as `java.util` or `java.util.ArrayList` to mirror the package/class hierarchy. The names of the `Logger` objects, going down the tree, are dot-separated. Therefore, `java.util` is the parent `Logger` of `java.util.ArrayList`. You can name the loggers any arbitrary string, but keeping with the dot-separated convention helps with clarity.

The simplest use of the logging system creates a `Logger` and uses all system defaults (defined in a properties file) for the logging system. The following example outputs the log message using a formatting class called the `SimpleFormatter` that adds time/date/source information to the log message:

```java
import java.util.logging.*;

public class BasicLoggingExample {
    public static void main(String args[])
    {
        Logger logger = Logger.getLogger("BasicLoggingExample");

        logger.log(Level.INFO, "Test of logging system");
    }
}
```

The following is output from the `BasicLoggingExample`:

```
Feb 22, 2004 4:07:06 PM BasicLoggingExample main
INFO: Test of logging system
```

The Log Manager

The entire logging system for a particular application is controlled by a single instance of the `LogManager` class. This instance is created during the initialization of the `LogManager`. The `LogManager` contains the hierarchical namespace that has all the named `Logger` objects. The `LogManager` also contains logging control properties that are used by `Handlers` and other objects in the logging system for configuration. These configuration properties are stored in the file `lib/logging.properties` that is located in the JRE installation path.

There are two system properties that can be used to initialize the logging system with different properties. The first way is to override the property `java.util.logging.config.file` and specify the full path to your own version of `logging.properties`. The other property, `java.util.logging.config.class`, is used to point to your own `LogManager`. This custom `LogManager` is responsible for reading in its configuration. If neither of these properties is set, Java will default to the `logging.properties` file in the JRE directory. Consult the following table for properties that can be set on the `LogManager` in this file. You can also specify properties for `Loggers` and `Handlers` in this file. These properties are described later in this section.

Property Key	Property Value
`Handlers`	Comma-separated list of `Handler` classes. Each handler must be located somewhere in the system classpath.
`.level`	Sets the minimum level for a specific `Logger`.
	The `level` must be prefixed with the full path to a specific `Logger`. A period by itself sets the level for the root logger.

The LogManager Class

The `LogManager` class contains methods to configure the current instance of the logging system through a number of configuration methods, tracks loggers and provides access to these loggers, and handles certain logging events. These methods are listed in the following tables.

Configuration

The methods listed in the following table relate to storage and retrieval of configuration information in the `LogManager`.

Method	Description
`String getProperty(String name)`	Returns the value corresponding to a specified logging property.
`void readConfiguration()`	Reloads the configuration using the same process as startup. If the system properties controlling initialization have not changed, the same file that was read at startup will be read here.
`void readConfiguration(InputStream ins)`	Reads configuration information from an `InputStream` that is in the `java.util` `.Properties` format.
`void reset()`	Resets the logging system. All `Handlers` are closed and removed and all logger levels except on the root are set to null. The root logger's level is set to `Level.INFO`.

Logger Control

The methods listed in the following table relate to the storage, retrieval, and management of individual `Logger` references. These are the most commonly used methods on the `LogManager` class.

Method	Description
`static LogManager getLogManager()`	Returns the one and only instance of the `LogManager` object.
`boolean addLogger(Logger logger)`	Returns true if the `Logger` passed in is not already registered (its name isn't already in the list). The logger is registered.
	Returns false if the name of the `Logger` object already exists in the list of registered loggers.
`Logger getLogger(String name)`	Returns a reference to the `Logger` object that is named "name," or null if no logger is found.
`Enumeration getLoggerNames()`	Returns an `Enumeration` containing a list of the names of all currently registered loggers.

Events

The methods listed in the following table provide a way to add and remove references to listeners that should be notified when properties are changed on the LogManager.

Method	Description
void addPropertyChangeListener (PropertyChangeListener l)	Adds a property change listener to the list of listeners that want notification of when a property has changed. The same listener can be added multiple times.
void removePropertyChangeListener (PropertyChangeListener l)	Removes a single occurrence of a property change listener in the list of listeners.

The Logger Class

An instance of the Logger class is used by client code to log a message. Both the log message and each logger have an associated level. If the level of the log message is equal to or greater than the level of the logger, the message is then processed. Otherwise, the logger drops the log message. It is an inexpensive operation to test whether or not to drop the log message, and this operation is done at the entry point to the logging system — the Logger class. These levels are defined inside the Level class. Consult the following table for a full list of levels.

Logger Level	Description
SEVERE	Highest logging level. This has top priority.
WARNING	One level below severe. Intended for warning messages that need attention, but aren't serious.
INFO	Two levels below severe. Intended for informational messages.
CONFIG	Three levels below severe. Intended for configuration-related output.
FINE	Four levels below severe. Intended for program tracing information.
FINER	Five levels below severe. Intended for program tracing information.
FINEST	Lowest logging level. This has lowest priority.
ALL	Special level that makes the system log ALL messages.
OFF	Special level that makes the system log NO messages (turns logging off completely).

Logger Methods

The `Logger` is the main class used in code that utilizes the logging system. Methods are provided to obtain a named or anonymous logger, configure and get information about the logger, and log messages.

Obtaining a Logger

The following methods allow you to retrieve a handle to a `Logger`. These are static methods and provide an easy way to obtain a `Logger` without going through a `LogManager`.

Method	Description
`static Logger getAnonymousLogger()` `static Logger getAnonymousLogger(String resourceBundleName)`	Creates an anonymous logger that is exempt from standard security checks, for use in applets. The anonymous logger is not registered in the `LogManager` namespace, but has the root logger ("") as a parent, inheriting level and handlers from the root logger. A resource bundle can also be specified for localization of log messages.
`static Logger getLogger(String name)` `static Logger getLogger(String name, String resourceBundleName)`	Returns a named logger from the `LogManager` namespace, or if one is not found, creates and returns a new named logger. A resource bundle can also be specified for localization of log messages.

Configuring a Logger Object

The following methods allow you to configure a `Logger` object. You can add and remove handlers, set the logging level on this `Logger` object, set its parent, and choose whether or not log messages should be passed up the logger hierarchy.

Method	Description
`void addHandler(Handler handler)`	Adds a `Handler` to the logger. Multiple handlers can be added. Also note that the root logger is configured with a set of default `Handlers`.
`void removeHandler(Handler handler)`	Removes a specified handler from the list of handlers on this logger. If the handler is not found, this method returns silently.
`void setLevel(Level newLevel)`	Sets the log level that this logger will use. Message levels lower than the logger's value will be automatically discarded. If null is passed in, the level will be inherited from this logger's parent.

Table continued on following page

Method	Description
`void setParent(Logger parent)`	Sets the parent for this logger. This should not be called by application code, because it is intended for use only by the logging system.
`void setUseParentHandlers(boolean useParentHandlers)`	Specifies true if log messages should be passed to their parent loggers, or false to prevent the log messages from passing to their parent.
`Filter getFilter()`	Returns the filter for this logger, which might be null if no filter is associated.
`Handler[] getHandlers()`	Returns an array of all handlers associated with this logger.
`Level getLevel()`	Returns the log level assigned to this logger. If null is returned, it indicates the logging level of the parent logger that will be used.
`String getName()`	Returns the name of this logger, or null if this is an anonymous logger.
`Logger getParent()`	The nearest parent to the current logger is returned, or null if the current logger is the root logger.
`ResourceBundle getResourceBundle()`	Returns the `ResourceBundle` associated with this logger. Resource bundles are used for localization of log messages. If null is returned, the resource bundle from the logger's parent will be used.
`String getResourceBundleName()`	Returns the name of the resource bundle this logger uses for localization, or null if the resource bundle is inherited from the logger's parent.
`boolean getUseParentHandlers()`	Returns true if log messages are passed to the logger's parent, or false if log messages are not passed up the hierarchy.

Logging Messages

The following methods are all used to actually log a message using a `Logger`. Convenience methods are provided for logging messages at each logging level, and also for entering and exiting methods and throwing exceptions. Additional methods are provided to localize log messages using a resource bundle.

Method	Description
`void config(String msg)` `void fine(String msg)` `void finer(String msg)` `void finest(String msg)` `void info(String msg)` `void severe(String msg)` `void warning(String msg)`	The `Logger` class contains a number of convenience methods for logging messages. For quickly logging a message of a specified level, one method for each logging level is defined.
`void entering(String sourceClass, String sourceMethod)` `void entering(String sourceClass, String sourceMethod, Object param1)` `void entering(String sourceClass, String sourceMethod, Object params[])`	Log a message when a method is first entered. The variant forms take a parameter to the method, or an array of parameters, to provide for more detailed tracking of the method invocation. The message of the log is ENTRY in addition to the other information about the method call. The log level is `Level.FINER`.
`void exiting(String sourceClass, String sourceMethod)` `void exiting(String sourceClass, String sourceMethod, Object result)`	Log a message when a method is about to return. The log message contains RETURN and the log level is `Level.FINER`. The source class and source method are also logged.
`boolean isLoggable(Level level)`	Checks if a certain level will be logged. Returns true if it will be logged, or false otherwise.
`void log(Level level, String msg)` `void log(Level level, String msg, Object param1)` `void log(Level level, String msg, Object[] params)` `void log(Level level, String msg, Throwable thrown)` `void log(LogRecord record)`	Standard general logging convenience methods. Variants include the ability to specify a parameter or array of parameters to log, or `Throwable` information. The information is placed into a `LogRecord` object and sent into the logging system. The last variant takes a `LogRecord` object.

Table continued on following page

Method	Description
void logp(Level level, String sourceClass, String sourceMethod, String msg)	Take source class and source method names in addition to the other information. All this is put into a LogRecord object and sent into the system.
void logp(Level level, String sourceClass, String sourceMethod, String msg, Object param1)	
void logp(Level level, String sourceClass, String sourceMethod, String msg, Object[] params)	
void logp(Level level, String sourceClass, String sourceMethod, String msg, Throwable thrown)	
void logrb(Level level, String sourceClass, String sourceMethod, String bundleName, String msg)	Allow you to specify a resource bundle in addition to the other information. The resource bundle will be used to localize the log message.
void logrb(Level level, String sourceClass, String sourceMethod, String bundleName, String msg, Object param1)	
void logrb(Level level, String sourceClass, String sourceMethod, String bundleName, String msg, Object[] params)	
void logrb(Level level, String sourceClass, String sourceMethod, String bundleName, String msg, Throwable thrown)	
void throwing(String sourceClass, String sourceMethod, Throwable thrown)	Logs a throwing message. The log level is Level.FINER. The log record's message is set to THROW and the contents of thrown are put into the log record's thrown property instead of inside the log record's message.

The LogRecord Class

The LogRecord class encapsulates a log message, carrying the message through the logging system. Handlers and Formatters use LogRecords to have more information about the message (such as the time it was sent and the logging level) for processing. If a client to the logging system has a reference to a LogRecord object, the object should no longer be used after it is passed into the logging system.

LogRecord Methods

The LogRecord contains a number of methods to examine and manipulate properties on a log record, such as message origination, the log record's level, when it was sent into the system, and any related resource bundles.

Method	Description
Level getLevel()	Returns the log record's level.
String getMessage()	Returns the unformatted version of the log message, before formatting/localization.
long getMillis()	Returns the time the log record was created in milliseconds.
Object[] getParameters()	Returns an array of parameters of the log record, or null if no parameters are set.
long getSequenceNumber()	Returns the sequence number of the log record. The sequence number is assigned in the log record's constructor to create a unique number for each log record.
Throwable getThrown()	Returns the Throwable associated with this log record, such as the Exception if an exception is being logged. Returns null if no Throwable is set.
String getLoggerName()	Returns the name of the logger, which might be null if it is the anonymous logger.
String getSourceClassName()	Gets the name of the class that might have logged the message. This information may be specified explicitly, or inferred from the stack trace and therefore might be inaccurate.
String getSourceMethodName()	Gets the name of the method that might have logged the message. This information may be specified explicitly, or inferred from the stack trace and therefore might be inaccurate.
int getThreadID	Returns the identifier for the thread that originated the log message. This is an ID inside the Java VM.

Setting Information about Message Origination

The following methods allow you to set origination information on the log message such as an associated exception, class and method that logged the message, and the ID of the originating thread.

Method	Description
void setSourceClassName (String sourceClassName)	Sets the name of the class where the log message is originating.
void setSourceMethodName (String sourceMethodName)	Sets the name of the method where the log message is originating.

Table continued on following page

Method	Description
`void setThreadID (int threadID)`	Sets the identifier of the thread where the log message is originating.
`void setThrown (Throwable thrown)`	Sets a `Throwable` to associate with the log message. Can be null.

Resource Bundle Methods

The following methods allow you to retrieve and configure a resource bundle for use with the log message. Resource bundles are used for localizing log messages.

Method	Description
`ResourceBundle getResourceBundle()`	Returns the `ResourceBundle` associated with the logger that is used to localize log messages. Might be null if there is no associated `ResourceBundle`.
`String getResourceBundleName()`	Returns the name of the resource bundle used to localize log messages. Returns null if log messages are not localizable (no resource bundle defined).
`void setResourceBundle (ResourceBundle bundle)`	Sets a resource bundle to use to localize log messages.
`void setResourceBundleName(String name)`	Sets the name of a resource bundle to use to localize log messages.

Setting Information about the Message

The following methods configure the log message itself. Some of the information you can configure related to the log message are its level, the contents of the message, and the time the message was sent.

Method	Description
`void setLevel(Level level)`	Sets the level of the logging message.
`void setLoggerName(String name)`	Sets the name of the logger issuing this message. Can be null.
`void setMessage(String message)`	Sets the contents of the message before formatting/ localization.
`void setMillis(long millis)`	Sets the time of the log message, in milliseconds, since 1970.
`void setParameters(Object[] parameters)`	Sets parameters for the log message.

Method	Description
`void setSequenceNumber(long seq)`	Sets the sequence number of the log message. This method shouldn't usually be called, because the constructor assigns a unique number to each log message.

The Level Class

The `Level` class defines the entire set of logging levels, and also objects of this class represent a specific logging level that is then used by loggers, handlers, and so on. If you desire, you can subclass this class and define your own custom levels, as long as they do not conflict with the existing logging levels.

Logging Levels

The following logging levels are defined in the `Level` class.

Log Level	Description
OFF	Special value that is initialized to `Integer.MAX_VALUE`. This turns logging off.
SEVERE	Meant for serious failures. Initialized to 1,000.
WARNING	Meant to indicate potential problems. Initialized to 900.
INFO	General information. Initialized to 800.
CONFIG	Meant for messages useful for debugging. Initialized to 700.
FINE	Meant for least verbose tracing information. Initialized to 500.
FINER	More detailed tracing information. Initialized to 400.
FINEST	Most detailed level of tracing information. Initialized to 300.
ALL	Special value. Logs ALL messages. Initialized to `Integer.MIN_VALUE`.

Level Methods

The `Level` class defines methods to set and retrieve a specific logging level. Both numeric and textual versions of levels can be used.

Method	Description
static Level parse(String name)	Returns a Level object representing the name of the level that is passed in. The string name can be one of the logging levels, such as SEVERE or CONFIG. An arbitrary number, between Integer.MIN_VALUE and Integer.MAX_VALUE can also be passed in (as a string). If the number represents one of the existing level values, that level is returned. Otherwise, a new Level is returned corresponding to the passed in value. Any invalid name or number causes an IllegalArgumentException to get thrown. If the name is null, a NullPointerException is thrown.
boolean equals(Object ox)	Returns true if the object passed in has the same level as the current class.
String getLocalizedName()	Returns the localized version of the current level's name, or the non-localized version if no localization is available.
String getName()	Returns the non-localized version of the current level's name.
String getResourceBundleName()	Returns the name of the level's localization resource bundle, or null if no localization resource bundle is defined.
int hashCode()	Returns a hash code based on the level value.
int intValue()	Returns the integer value for the current level.
String toString()	Returns the non-localized name of the current level.

The Handler Class

The Handler class is used to receive log messages and then publish them to an external destination. This might be memory, a file, a database, a TCP/IP stream, or any number of places that can store log messages. Just like loggers, a handler has an associated level. Log messages that are less than the level on the handler are discarded. Each specific instance of a Handler has its own properties and is usually configured in the logging.properties file. The next section discusses the various handlers that are found in the java.util.logging package. Creating a custom handler is straightforward, because implementations of only close(), flush(), and publish(LogRecord record) are needed.

Handler Methods

The Handler class defines three abstract methods that need specific behavior in inheriting classes. The other methods available on the Handler class are for dealing with message encoding, filters, formatters, and error handlers.

Key Abstract Methods

When developing a custom handler, there are three abstract methods that must be overridden. These are listed in the following table.

Method	Description
`abstract void close()`	Should perform a `flush()` and then free any resources used by the handler. After `close()` is called, the `Handler` should no longer be used.
`abstract void flush()`	Flushes any buffered output to ensure it is saved to the associated resource.
`abstract void publish(LogRecord record)`	Takes a log message forwarded by a logger and then writes it to the associated resource. The message should be formatted (using the `Formatter`) and localized.

Set and Retrieve Information about the Handler

The methods listed in the following table allow you to retrieve information about the handler, such as its encoding, associated error manager, filter, formatter, and level, and also set this configuration information.

Method	Description
`String getEncoding()`	Returns the name of the character encoding. If the name is null, the default encoding should be used.
`ErrorManager getErrorManager()`	Returns the `ErrorManager` associated with this `Handler`.
`Filter getFilter()`	Returns the `Filter` associated with this `Handler`, which might be null.
`Formatter getFormatter()`	Returns the `Formatter` associated with this `Handler`, which might be null.
`Level getLevel()`	Returns the level of this handler. Log messages lower than this level are discarded.
`boolean isLoggable(LogRecord record)`	Returns true if the `LogRecord` passed in will be logged by this handler. The checks include comparing the record's level to the handler's, testing against the filter (if one is defined), and any other checks defined in the handler.
`void setEncoding(String encoding)`	Sets the encoding to a specified character encoding. If null is passed in, the default platform encoding is used.
`void setErrorManager (ErrorManager em)`	Sets an `ErrorManager` for the handler. If any errors occur while processing, the `Error Manager's error` method is invoked.
`void setFilter (Filter newFilter)`	Sets a custom filter that decides whether to discard or keep a log message when the `publish` method is invoked.
`void setFormatter (Formatter newFormatter)`	Sets a `Formatter` that performs custom formatting on log messages passed to the handler before the log message is written to the destination.
`void setLevel(Level newLevel)`	Sets the level threshold for the handler. Log messages below this level are automatically discarded.

Stock Handlers

The `java.util.logging` package includes a number of predefined handlers to write log messages to common destinations. These classes include the `ConsoleHandler`, `FileHandler`, `MemoryHandler`, `SocketHandler`, and `StreamHandler`. These classes provide a specific implementation of the abstract methods in the `Handler` class. All the property key names in the tables are prefixed with `java.util` `.logging` in the actual properties file.

The `StreamHandler` serves chiefly as a base class for all handlers that write log messages to some `OutputStream`. The subclasses of `StreamHandler` are `ConsoleHandler`, `FileHandler`, and `SocketHandler`. A lot of the stream handling code is built into this class. See the following table for a list of properties for the `StreamHandler`.

Property Name	Description	Default Value
StreamHandler.level	Log level for the handler	Level.INFO
StreamHandler.filter	Filter to use	undefined
StreamHandler.formatter	Formatter to use	java.util.logging .SimpleFormatter
StreamHandler.encoding	Character set encoding to use	Default platform encoding

The following methods are defined/implemented on the `StreamHandler` class.

Method	Description
void close()	The head string from the Formatter will be written if it hasn't been already, and the tail string is written before the stream is closed.
void flush()	Writes any buffered output to the stream (flushes the stream).
boolean isLoggable (LogRecord record)	Performs standard checks against level and filter, but also returns false if no output stream is open or the record passed in is null.
void publish(LogRecord record)	If the record passed in is loggable, the Formatter is then invoked to format the log message and then the message is written to the output stream.
void setEncoding(String encoding)	Sets the character encoding to use for log messages. Pass in null to use the current platform's default character encoding.
protected void setOutputStream (OutputStream out)	Sets an OutputStream to use. If an OutputStream is already open, it is flushed and then closed. The new OutputStream is then opened.

The `ConsoleHandler` writes log messages to `System.err`. It subclasses `StreamHandler` but overrides `close()` to only perform a flush, so the `System.err` stream does not get closed. The default formatter used is `SimpleFormatter`. The following table describes the properties that can be defined in the `logging.properties` file for the `ConsoleHandler`.

Property Name	Description	Default Value
ConsoleHandler.level	Log level for the handler	Level.INFO
ConsoleHandler.filter	Filter to use	Undefined
ConsoleHandler.formatter	Formatter to use	java.util.logging.SimpleFormatter
ConsoleHandler.encoding	Character set encoding to use	Default platform encoding

The SocketHandler writes log messages to the network over a specified TCP port. The properties listed in the following table are used by the SocketHandler. The default constructor uses the properties defined, and a second constructor allows the specification of the host and port SocketHandler(String host, int port). The close() method flushes and closes the output stream, and the publish() method flushes the stream after each record is written.

Property Name	Description	Default Value
SocketHandler.level	Log level for the handler	Level.INFO
SocketHandler.filter	Filter to use	undefined
SocketHandler.formatter	Formatter to use	java.util.logging.XMLFormatter
SocketHandler.encoding	Character set encoding to use	Default platform encoding
SocketHandler.host	Target host name to connect to	undefined
SocketHandler.port	Target TCP port to use	undefined

The FileHandler is able to write to a single file, or write to a rotating set of files as each file reaches a specified maximum size. The next number in a sequence is added to the end of the name of each rotating file, unless a *generation* (sequence) pattern is specified elsewhere. The properties for the FileHandler are listed in the following table.

Property Name	Description	Default Value
FileHandler.level	Log level for the handler.	Level.INFO
FileHandler.filter	Filter to use.	undefined
FileHandler.formatter	Formatter to use.	java.util.logging.XMLFormatter
FileHandler.encoding	Character set encoding to use.	Default platform encoding
FileHandler.limit	Specifies approximate maximum number of bytes to write to a file. 0 means no limit.	0

Table continued on following page

Property Name	Description	Default Value
FileHandler.count	Specifies how many output files to cycle through.	1
FileHandler.pattern	Pattern used to generate output filenames.	%h/java%u.log
FileHandler.append	Boolean value specifying whether to append to an existing file or overwrite it.	false

The FileHandler class supports filename patterns, allowing the substitution of paths such as the user's home directory or the system's temporary directory. The forward slash (/) is used as a directory separator, and this works for both Unix and Windows machines. Also supported is the ability to specify where the generation number goes in the filename when log files are rotated. These patterns are each prefixed with a percent sign (%). To include the percent sign in the filename, specify two percent signs (%%). The following table contains all the valid percent-sign substitutions.

Pattern	Description
%t	Full path of the system temporary directory
%h	Value of the user.home system property
%g	Generation number used to distinguish rotated logs
%u	Unique number used to resolve process conflicts

For example, if you're executing this on Windows 95 and specify the filename pattern %t/app_log.txt, the FileHandler class expands this to C:\TEMP\app_log.txt. Note that the %t and %h commands do not include the trailing forward slash.

The %u is used to account for when multiple threads/processes will access the same log file. Only one process can have the file open for writing, so to prevent the loss of logging information, the %u can be used to output to a log file that has a similar name to the others. For example, the filename pattern %t/logfile%u.txt can be specified, and if two processes open this same log file for output, the first will open C:\TEMP\logfile0.txt and the second will open C:\TEMP\logfile1.txt.

The MemoryHandler is a circular buffer in memory. It is intended for use as a quick way to store messages, so the messages have to be sent to another handler to write them to an external source. Because the buffer is circular, older log records eventually are overwritten by newer records. Formatting can be delayed to another Handler, which makes logging to a MemoryHandler quick. Conditions that will cause the MemoryHandler to send data (push data) to another Handler are as follows:

❑ A log record passed in has a level greater than a specified pushLevel.

❑ Another class calls the push method on the MemoryHandler.

❑ A subclass implements specialized behavior to push data depending on custom criteria.

The properties on the `MemoryHandler` are listed in the following table.

Property Name	Description	Default Value
`MemoryHandler.level`	Log level for the handler	`Level.INFO`
`MemoryHandler.filter`	Filter to use	undefined
`MemoryHandler.size`	Size of the circular buffer (in bytes)	1,000
`MemoryHandler.push`	Defines the push level — the minimum level that will cause messages to be sent to the target handler	`Level.SEVERE`
`MemoryHandler.target`	Specifies the name of the target `Handler` class	(undefined)

The constructors create a `MemoryHandler` with a default or specific configuration.

Constructor	Description
`MemoryHandler()`	Creates a `MemoryHandler` based on the configuration properties.
`MemoryHandler(Handler target, int size, Level pushLevel)`	Creates a `MemoryHandler` with a specified target handler, size of the buffer, and push level.

The methods provided by the `MemoryHandler` create and configure the behavior of the memory handler.

Method	Description
`void publish(LogRecord record)`	Stores the record in the internal buffer, if it is loggable (see `isLoggable`). If the level of the log record is greater than or equal to the `pushLevel`, all buffered records, including the current one, are written to the target `Handler`.
`void close()`	Closes the handler and frees the associated resources. Also invokes `close` on the target handler.
`void flush()`	Causes a `flush`, which is different from a `push`. To actually write the log records to a destination other than memory, a `push` must be performed.
`Level getPushLevel()`	Returns the current push level.
`boolean isLoggable (LogRecord record)`	Compares the log levels, and then runs the record through the filter if one is defined. Whether or not the record will cause a `push` is ignored by this method.
`void push()`	Sends all records in the current buffer to the target handler, and clears the buffer.
`void setPushLevel(Level newLevel)`	Sets a new `push` level.

The Formatter Class

The `Formatter` class is used to perform some custom processing on a log record. This formatting might be localization, adding additional program information (such as adding the time and date to log records), or any other processing needed. The `Formatter` returns a string that is the processed log record. The `Formatter` class also has support for `head` and `tail` strings that come before and after all log records. An example that will be implemented later in this section is a custom `Formatter` that writes log records to an HTML table. For this formatter, the head string would be the `<table>` tag, and the tail string is the `</table>` tag. The methods defined in the `Formatter` class are listed in the following table.

Method	Description
`abstract String format(LogRecord record)`	Performs specific formatting of the log record and returns the formatted string.
`String formatMessage(LogRecord record)`	The message string in the `LogRecord` is localized using the record's `ResourceBundle`, and formatted according to `java.text` style formatting (replacing strings such as `{0}`).
`String getHead(Handler h)`	Returns the header string for a specified handler, which can be null.
`String getTail(Handler h)`	Returns the tail string for a specified handler, which can be null.

Stock Formatters

The logging package comes already equipped with a couple of useful formatters. The `SimpleFormatter` provides a basic implementation of a formatter. The `XMLFormatter` outputs log records in a predefined XML format. These two stock formatters will cover a variety of basic logging scenarios, but if you need behavior not supplied by either of these formatters, you can write your own.

SimpleFormatter

The `SimpleFormatter` does a minimal level of work to format log messages. The format method of the `SimpleFormatter` returns a one- or two-line summary of the log record that is passed in. Logging a simple log message, such as `test 1`, using the `SimpleFormatter` will issue the following output:

```
Apr 18, 2004 12:18:25 PM LoggingTest main
INFO: test 1
```

The `SimpleFormatter` formats the message with the date, time, originating class name, originating method name, and on the second line, the level of the log message and the log message itself.

XMLFormatter

The `XMLFormatter` formats the log records according to an XML DTD. You can use the `XMLFormatter` with any character encoding, but it is suggested that it be used only with `"UTF-8"`. The `getHead()` and `getTail()` methods are used to output the start and end of the XML file, the parts that aren't repeated for each log record but are necessary to create a valid XML file.

Example output from the `XMLFormatter` follows:

```
<?xml version="1.0" encoding="windows-1252" standalone="no"?>
<!DOCTYPE log SYSTEM "logger.dtd">
<log>
<record>
  <date>2004-04-18T12:22:36</date>
  <millis>1082305356235</millis>
  <sequence>0</sequence>
  <logger>LoggingTest</logger>
  <level>INFO</level>
  <class>LoggingTest</class>
  <method>main</method>
  <thread>10</thread>
  <message>test 1</message>
</record>
<record>
  <date>2004-04-18T12:22:36</date>
  <millis>1082305356265</millis>
  <sequence>1</sequence>
  <logger>LoggingTest</logger>
  <level>INFO</level>
  <class>LoggingTest</class>
  <method>main</method>
  <thread>10</thread>
  <message>test 2</message>
</record>
</log>
```

The XML DTD that the logging system uses is shown here:

```
<!-- DTD used by the java.util.logging.XMLFormatter -->
<!-- This provides an XML formatted log message. -->

<!-- The document type is "log" which consists of a sequence
of record elements -->
<!ELEMENT log (record*)>

<!-- Each logging call is described by a record element. -->
<!ELEMENT record (date, millis, sequence, logger?, level,
class?, method?, thread?, message, key?, catalog?, param*, exception?)>

<!-- Date and time when LogRecord was created in ISO 8601 format -->
<!ELEMENT date (#PCDATA)>

<!-- Time when LogRecord was created in milliseconds since
midnight January 1st, 1970, UTC. -->
<!ELEMENT millis (#PCDATA)>

<!-- Unique sequence number within source VM. -->
```

```
<!ELEMENT sequence (#PCDATA)>

<!-- Name of source Logger object. -->
<!ELEMENT logger (#PCDATA)>

<!-- Logging level, may be either one of the constant
names from java.util.logging.Constants (such as "SEVERE"
or "WARNING") or an integer value such as "20". -->
<!ELEMENT level (#PCDATA)>

<!-- Fully qualified name of class that issued
logging call, e.g. "javax.marsupial.Wombat". -->
<!ELEMENT class (#PCDATA)>

<!-- Name of method that issued logging call.
It may be either an unqualified method name such as
"fred" or it may include argument type information
in parenthesis, for example "fred(int,String)". -->
<!ELEMENT method (#PCDATA)>

<!-- Integer thread ID. -->
<!ELEMENT thread (#PCDATA)>

<!-- The message element contains the text string of a log message. -->
<!ELEMENT message (#PCDATA)>

<!-- If the message string was localized, the key element provides
the original localization message key. -->
<!ELEMENT key (#PCDATA)>

<!-- If the message string was localized, the catalog element provides
the logger's localization resource bundle name. -->
<!ELEMENT catalog (#PCDATA)>

<!-- If the message string was localized, each of the param elements
provides the String value (obtained using Object.toString())
of the corresponding LogRecord parameter. -->
<!ELEMENT param (#PCDATA)>

<!-- An exception consists of an optional message string followed
by a series of StackFrames. Exception elements are used
for Java exceptions and other java Throwables. -->
<!ELEMENT exception (message?, frame+)>

<!-- A frame describes one line in a Throwable backtrace. -->
<!ELEMENT frame (class, method, line?)>

<!-- an integer line number within a class's source file. -->
<!ELEMENT line (#PCDATA)>
```

Creating Your Own Formatter

It isn't too difficult to develop a custom `Formatter`. As an example, here's an implementation of the `HTMLTableFormatter` that was mentioned previously. The HTML code that is output looks like this:

```
<table border>
    <tr><th>Time</th><th>Log Message</th></tr>
    <tr><td>...</td><td>...</td></tr>
    <tr><td>...</td><td>...</td></tr>
</table>
```

Each log record starts with `<tr>` and ends with `</tr>` because there is only one log record per table row. The `<table>` tag and the first row of the table make up the head string. The `</table>` tag makes up the tail of the collection of log records. The custom formatter only needs an implementation of the `getHead()`, `getTail()`, and `format(LogRecord record)` methods:

```java
import java.util.logging.*;

class HTMLTableFormatter extends java.util.logging.Formatter {
    public String format(LogRecord record)
    {
        return("   <tr><td>" +
                record.getMillis() +
                "</td><td>" +
                record.getMessage() +
                "</td></tr>\n");
    }

    public String getHead(Handler h)
    {
        return("<table border>\n   " +
                "<tr><th>Time</th><th>Log Message</th></tr>\n");
    }

    public String getTail(Handler h)
    {
        return("</table>\n");
    }
}
```

The Filter Interface

A filter is used to provide additional criteria to decide whether to discard or keep a log record. Each logger and each handler can have a filter defined. The `Filter` interface defines a single method:

```java
boolean isLoggable(LogRecord record)
```

The `isLoggable` method returns true if the log message should be published and false if it should be discarded.

Creating Your Own Filter

An example of a custom filter is a filter that discards any log message that does not start with `"client"`. This is useful if log messages are coming from a number of sources, and each log message from a particular client (or clients) is prefixed with the string `"client"`:

```java
import java.util.logging.*;

public class ClientFilter implements java.util.logging.Filter {
    public boolean isLoggable(LogRecord record)
    {
        if(record.getMessage().startsWith("client"))
            return(true);
        else
            return(false);
    }
}
```

The ErrorManager

The `ErrorManager` is associated with a handler and is used to handle any errors that occur, such as exceptions that are thrown. The client of the logger most likely does not care or cannot handle errors, so using an `ErrorManager` is a flexible and straightforward way for a `Handler` to report error conditions. The error manager defines a single method:

```java
void error(String msg, Exception ex, int code)
```

This method takes the error message (a string), the `Exception` thrown, and a code representing what error occurred. The codes are defined as static integers in the `ErrorManager` class and are listed in the following table.

Error Code	Description
CLOSE_FAILURE	Used when `close()` fails
FLUSH_FAILURE	Used when `flush()` fails
FORMAT_FAILURE	Used when formatting fails for any reason
GENERIC_FAILURE	Used for any other error that other error codes don't match
OPEN_FAILURE	Used when open of an output source fails
WRITE_FAILURE	Used when writing to the output source fails

Logging Examples

By default, log messages are passed up the hierarchy to each parent. Following is a small program that uses a named logger to log a message using the `XMLFormatter`:

```java
import java.util.logging.*;

public class LoggingExample1 {
    public static void main(String args[])
```

```
      {
          try{
              LogManager lm = LogManager.getLogManager();
              Logger logger;
              FileHandler fh = new FileHandler("log_test.txt");

              logger = Logger.getLogger("LoggingExample1");

              lm.addLogger(logger);
              logger.setLevel(Level.INFO);
              fh.setFormatter(new XMLFormatter());

              logger.addHandler(fh);
              // root logger defaults to SimpleFormatter.
              // We don't want messages logged twice.
              //logger.setUseParentHandlers(false);
              logger.log(Level.INFO, "test 1");
              logger.log(Level.INFO, "test 2");
              logger.log(Level.INFO, "test 3");
              fh.close();
          } catch(Exception e) {
              System.out.println("Exception thrown: " + e);
              e.printStackTrace();
          }
      }
}
```

What happens here is the XML output is sent to `log_test.txt`. This file is as follows:

```xml
<?xml version="1.0" encoding="windows-1252" standalone="no"?>
<!DOCTYPE log SYSTEM "logger.dtd">
<log>
<record>
  <date>2004-04-20T2:09:55</date>
  <millis>1082472395876</millis>
  <sequence>0</sequence>
  <logger>LoggingExample1</logger>
  <level>INFO</level>
  <class>LoggingExample1</class>
  <method>main</method>
  <thread>10</thread>
  <message>test 1</message>
</record>
<record>
  <date>2004-04-20T2:09:56</date>
  <millis>1082472396096</millis>
  <sequence>1</sequence>
  <logger>LoggingExample1</logger>
  <level>INFO</level>
  <class>LoggingExample1</class>
  <method>main</method>
  <thread>10</thread>
  <message>test 2</message>
</record>
</log>
```

Because the log messages are then sent to the parent logger, the messages are also output to `System.err` using the `SimpleFormatter`. The following is output:

```
Feb 11, 2004 2:09:55 PM LoggingExample1 main
INFO: test 1
Feb 11, 2004 2:09:56 PM LoggingExample1 main
INFO: test 2
```

Here's a more detailed example that uses the already developed `HTMLTableFormatter`. Two loggers are defined in a parent-child relationship, `ParentLogger` and `ChildLogger`. The parent logger will use the `XMLFormatter` to output to a text file, and the child logger will output using the `HTMLTableFormatter` to a different file. By default, the root logger will execute and the log messages will go to the console using the `SimpleFormatter`. The `HTMLTableFormatter` is extended to an `HTMLFormatter` to generate a full HTML file (instead of just the table tags):

```java
import java.util.logging.*;
import java.util.*;

class HTMLFormatter extends java.util.logging.Formatter {
    public String format(LogRecord record)
    {
        return("      <tr><td>" +
               (new Date(record.getMillis())).toString() +
               "</td>" +
               "<td>" +
               record.getMessage() +
               "</td></tr>\n");
    }

    public String getHead(Handler h)
    {
        return("<html>\n  <body>\n" +
               "    <table border>\n        " +
               "<tr><th>Time</th><th>Log Message</th></tr>\n");
    }

    public String getTail(Handler h)
    {
        return("    </table>\n  </body>\n</html>");
    }
}

public class LoggingExample2 {
    public static void main(String args[])
    {
        try {
            LogManager lm = LogManager.getLogManager();
            Logger parentLogger, childLogger;
            FileHandler xml_handler = new FileHandler("log_output.xml");
            FileHandler html_handler = new FileHandler("log_output.html");
            parentLogger = Logger.getLogger("ParentLogger");
            childLogger = Logger.getLogger("ParentLogger.ChildLogger");

            lm.addLogger(parentLogger);
```

```
                    lm.addLogger(childLogger);

                    // log all messages, WARNING and above
                    parentLogger.setLevel(Level.WARNING);
                    // log ALL messages
                    childLogger.setLevel(Level.ALL);
                    xml_handler.setFormatter(new XMLFormatter());
                    html_handler.setFormatter(new HTMLFormatter());

                    parentLogger.addHandler(xml_handler);
                    childLogger.addHandler(html_handler);

                    childLogger.log(Level.FINE, "This is a fine log message");
                    childLogger.log(Level.SEVERE, "This is a severe log message");
                    xml_handler.close();
                    html_handler.close();
                } catch(Exception e) {
                    System.out.println("Exception thrown: " + e);
                    e.printStackTrace();
                }
            }
        }
```

Here's what gets output to the screen:

```
Apr 20, 2004 12:43:09 PM LoggingExample2 main
SEVERE: This is a severe log message
```

Here's what gets output to the `log_output.xml` file:

```
<?xml version="1.0" encoding="windows-1252" standalone="no"?>
<!DOCTYPE log SYSTEM "logger.dtd">
<log>
<record>
  <date>2004-04-20T12:43:09</date>
  <millis>1082479389122</millis>
  <sequence>0</sequence>
  <logger>ParentLogger.ChildLogger</logger>
  <level>FINE</level>
  <class>LoggingExample2</class>
  <method>main</method>
  <thread>10</thread>
  <message>This is a fine log message</message>
</record>
<record>
  <date>2004-04-20T12:43:09</date>
  <millis>1082479389242</millis>
  <sequence>1</sequence>
  <logger>ParentLogger.ChildLogger</logger>
  <level>SEVERE</level>
  <class>LoggingExample2</class>
  <method>main</method>
  <thread>10</thread>
  <message>This is a severe log message</message>
</record>
</log>
```

The contents of the `log_output.html` file are as follows:

```
<html>
  <body>
    <table border>
      <tr><th>Time</th><th>Log Message</th></tr>
      <tr><td>Tue Apr 20 12:43:09 EDT 2004</td><td>This is a fine log
message</td></tr>
      <tr><td>Tue Apr 20 12:43:09 EDT 2004</td><td>This is a severe log
message</td></tr>
    </table>
  </body>
</html>
```

Note that the root logger, by default, logs messages at level INFO and above. However, because the ParentLogger is only interested in levels at WARNING and above, log messages with lower levels are immediately discarded. The HTML file contains all log messages because the ChildLogger is set to process all log messages. The XML file contains only the one SEVERE log message, because log messages below the WARNING level are discarded.

Regular Expressions

Regular expressions are a powerful facility available to solve problems relating to the searching, isolating, and/or replacing of chunks of text inside strings. The subject of regular expressions (sometimes abbreviated regexp or regexps) is large enough that it deserves its own book — and indeed, books have been devoted to regular expressions. This section provides an overview of regular expressions and discusses the support Sun has built in to the `java.util.regex` package.

Regular expressions alleviate a lot of the tedium of working with a simple parser, providing complex pattern matching capabilities. Regular expressions can be used to process text of any sort. For more sophisticated examples of regular expressions, consult another book that is dedicated to regular expressions.

If you've never seen regular expressions before in a language, you've most likely seen a small subset of regular expressions with file masks on Unix/DOS/Windows. For example, you might see the following files in a directory:

```
Test.java
Test.class
StringProcessor.java
StringProcessor.class
Token.java
Token.class
```

You can type `dir *.*` at the command line (on DOS/Windows) and every file will be matched and listed. The asterisks are replaced with any string, and the period is taken literally. If the file mask `T*.class` is used, only two files will be matched — `Test.class` and `Token.class`. The asterisks are considered meta-characters, and the period and letters are considered normal characters. The meta-characters are part of the regular expression "language," and Java has a rich set of these that go well beyond the simple support in file masks. The normal characters match literally against the string being tested. There is also a facility to interpret meta-characters literally in the regular expression language.

Several examples of using regular expressions are examined throughout this section. As an initial example, assume you want to generate a list of all classes inside Java files that have no modifier before the keyword `class`. Assuming you only need to examine a single line of source code, all you have to do is ignore any white space before the string `class`, and you can generate the list.

A traditional approach would need to find the first occurrence of `class` in a string and then ensure there's nothing but white space before it. Using regular expressions, this task becomes much easier. The entire Java regular expression language is examined shortly, but the regular expression needed for this case is `\s*class`. The backslash is used to specify a meta-character, and in this case, `\s` matches any white space. The asterisk is another meta-character, standing for "0 or more occurrences of the previous term." The word `class` is then taken literally, so the pattern stands for matching white space (if any exists) and then matching `class`. The Java code to use this pattern is shown next:

```
Pattern pattern = Pattern.compile("\\s*class");
// Need two backslashes to preserve the backslash

Matcher matcher = pattern.matcher("\t\t    class");
if(matcher.matches()) {
    System.out.println("The pattern matches the string");
} else {
    System.out.println("The pattern does not match the string");
}
```

This example takes a regular expression (stored in a `Pattern` object) and uses a matcher to see if the regular expression matches a specific string. This is the simplest use of the regular expression routines in Java. Consult Figure 1-2 for an overview of how the regular expression classes work with each other.

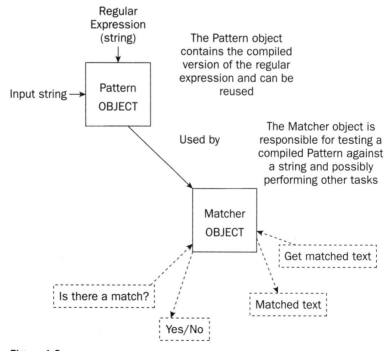

Figure 1-2

The designers of the regular expression library decided to use a *Pattern-Matcher* model, which separates the regular expression from the matcher itself. The regular expression is compiled into a more optimized form by the `Pattern` class. This compiled pattern can then be used with multiple matchers, or reused by the same matcher matching on different strings.

In a regular expression, any single character matches literally, except for just a few exceptions. One such exception is the period (.), which matches any single character in the string that is being analyzed. There are sets of meta-characters predefined to match specific characters. These are listed in the following table.

Meta-Character	Matches
\\	A single backslash
\0n	An octal value describing a character, where n is a number such that $0 <= n <= 7$
\0nn	
\0mnn	An octal value describing a character, where m is $0 <= m <= 3$ and n is $0 <= n <= 7$
\0xhh	The character with hexadecimal value hh (where $0 <= h <= F$)
\uhhhh	The character with hexadecimal value hhhh (where $0 <= h <= F$)
\t	A tab (character '\u0009')
\n	A newline (linefeed) ('\u000A')
\r	A carriage-return ('\u000D')
\f	A form-feed ('\u000C')
\a	A bell/beep character ('\u0007')
\e	An escape character ('\u001B')
\cx	The control character corresponding to x, such as \cc is control-c
.	Any single character

The regular expression language also has meta-characters to match against certain string boundaries. Some of these boundaries are the beginning and end of a line, and the beginning and end of words. The full list of boundary meta-characters can be seen in the following table.

Meta-Character	Matches
^	Beginning of the line
$	End of the line
\b	A word boundary
\B	A non-word boundary

Meta-Character	Matches
\A	The beginning of the input
\G	The end of the previous match
\Z	The end of the input before any line terminators (such as carriage-return or linefeed)
\z	The end of the input

Regular expression languages also have character classes, which are a way of specifying a list of possible characters that can match any single character in the string you want to match. If you want to specify a character class explicitly, the characters go between square brackets. Therefore, the character class [0123456789] matches any single digit. It is also possible to specify "any character except one of these" by using the caret after the first square bracket. Using the expression [^012], any single digit *except* for 0, 1, and 2 is matched. You can specify character ranges using the dash. The character class [a-z] matches any single lowercase letter, and [^a-z] matches any character except a lowercase letter. Any character range can be used, such as [0-9] to match a single digit, or [0-3] to match a 0, 1, 2, or 3. Multiple ranges can be specified, such as [a-zA-Z] to match any single letter. The regular expression package contains a set of predefined character classes, and these are listed in the following table.

Character Class Meta-Character	Matches
.	Any single character
\d	A digit [0-9]
\D	A nondigit [^0-9]
\s	A whitespace character [\t\n\x0B\f\r]
\S	A nonwhitespace character [^\s]
\w	A word character [a-zA-Z_0-9]
\W	A nonword character [^\w]

Additionally, there are POSIX character classes and Java character classes. These are listed in the following tables, respectively.

Character Class Meta-Character	Matches
\p{Lower}	Lowercase letter [a-z]
\p{Upper}	Uppercase letter [A-Z]
\p{ASCII}	All ASCII [\x00-\x7F]

Table continued on following page

Character Class Meta-Character	Matches
\p{Alpha}	Any lowercase or uppercase letter
\p{Digit}	A digit [0-9]
\p{Alnum}	Any letter or digit
\p{Punct}	Punctuation [!"#$%&'()*+,-./:;<=>?@[\]^_`{|}~]
\p{Graph}	A visible character: any letter, digit, or punctuation
\p{Print}	A printable character; same as \p{Graph}
\p{Blank}	A space or tab [\t]
\p{Cntrl}	A control character [\x00-\x1F\x7F]
\p{XDigit}	Hexadecimal digit [0-9a-fA-F]
\p{Space}	A whitespace character [\t\n\x0B\f\r]

Character Class	Matches
\p{javaLowerCase}	Everything that Character.isLowerCase() matches
\p{javaUpperCase}	Everything that Character.isUpperCase() matches
\p{javaWhitespace}	Everything that Character.isWhitespace() matches
\p{javaMirrored}	Everything that Character.isMirrored() matches

Another feature of the regular expression language is the ability to match a particular character a specified number of times. In the previous example, the asterisk was used to match zero or more characters of white space. There are two general ways the repetition operators work. One class of operators is greedy, that is, they match as much as they can, until the end. The other class is reluctant (or lazy), and matches only to the first chance they can terminate. For example, the regular expression .*; matches any number of characters up to the *last* semicolon it finds. To only match up to the first semicolon, the reluctant version .*?; must be used. All greedy operators and the reluctant versions are listed in the following two tables, respectively.

Greedy Operator	Description
X?	Matches X zero or one time
X*	Matches X zero or more times
X+	Matches X one or more times
X{n}	Matches X exactly n times, where n is any number
X{n,}	Matches X at least n times
X{n,m}	Matches X at least n, but no more than m times

Reluctant (Lazy) Operator	Description
X??	Matches X zero or one time
X*?	Matches X zero or more times
X+?	Matches X one or more times
X{n}?	Matches X exactly n times, where n is any number
X{n,}?	Matches X at least n times
X{n,m}?	Matches X at least n, but no more than m times

The language also supports capturing groups of matching characters by using parentheses inside the regular expression. A back reference can be used to reference one of these matching subgroups. A back reference is denoted by a backslash followed by a number corresponding to the number of a subgroup. In the string (A(B)), the zero group is the entire expression, then subgroups start numbering after each left parenthesis. Therefore, A(B) is the first subgroup, and B is the second subgroup. The back references then allow a string to be matched. For example, if you want to match the same word appearing twice in a row, you might use [([a-zA-Z])\b\1]. Remember that the \b stands for a word boundary. Because the character class for letters is inside parentheses, the text that matched can then be referenced using the back reference meta-character \1.

The Pattern Class

The Pattern class is responsible for compiling and storing a specified regular expression. There are flags that control how the regular expression is treated. The regex is compiled to provide for efficiency. The textual representation of a regular expression is meant for ease of use and understanding by programmers.

Method	Description
static Pattern compile(String regex) static Pattern compile(String regex, int flags)	The compile method accepts a regular expression in a string and compiles it for internal use. The variant form allows you to specify flags that modify how the regular expression is treated.
static boolean matches(String regex, CharSequence input)	Compiles a specified regular expression and matches it against the input. Returns true if the regular expression describes the input data, and false otherwise. Use this only for quick matches. To match a regular expression repeatedly against different input, the regular expression should be compiled only once.
static String quote(String s)	Returns a literal regular expression that will match the string passed in. The returned string starts with \Q followed by the string passed in, and ends with \E. These are used to quote a string, so what would be meta-characters in the regular expression language are treated literally.

Table continued on following page

65

Method	Description
`int flags()`	Returns an integer containing the flags set when the regular expression was compiled.
`Matcher matcher(CharSequence input)`	Returns a `Matcher` to use for matching the pattern against the specified input.
`String pattern()`	Returns the regular expression that was used to create the pattern.

`String[] split(CharSequence input)`
 	
`String[] split(CharSequence input, int limit)`
	Returns an array of strings after splitting the input into chunks using the regular expression as a separator. The `limit` can be used to limit how many times the regular expression is matched. The matching text does not get placed into the array. If `limit` is positive, the pattern will be applied at least "limit minus 1" times. If `limit` is 0, the pattern will be applied as many times as it can, and trailing empty strings are removed. If `limit` is negative, the pattern will be applied as many times as it can, and trailing empty strings will be left in the array.

The Matcher Class

The `Matcher` class is used to use a pattern to compare to an input string, and perform a wide variety of useful tasks. The `Matcher` class provides the ability to get a variety of information such as where in the string a pattern matched, replace a matching subset of the string with another string, and other useful operations.

Method	Description
`static String quoteReplacement(String s)`	Returns a string that is quoted with \Q and \E and can be used to match literally with other input.
`Matcher appendReplacement (StringBuffer sb, String replacement)`	First appends all characters up to a match to the string buffer, then replaces the matching text with `replacement`, then sets the index to one position after the text matched to prepare for the next call to this method. Use `appendTail` to append the rest of the input after the last match.
`StringBuffer appendTail (StringBuffer sb)`	Appends the rest of the input sequence to the string buffer that is passed in.
`MatchResult asResult()`	Returns a reference to a `MatchResult` describing the matcher's state.
`int end()`	Returns the index that is one past the ending position of the last match.

Method	Description
`int end(int group)`	Returns the index that is one past the ending position of a specified capturing group.
`boolean find()`	Returns true if a match is found starting at one index immediately after the previous match, or at the beginning of the line if the matcher has been reset.
`boolean find(int start)`	Resets the matcher and attempts to match the pattern against the input text starting at position `start`. Returns true if a match is found.
`boolean hitEnd()`	Returns true if the end of input was reached by the last match.
`boolean requireEnd()`	Returns true if more input could turn a positive match into a negative match.
`boolean lookingAt()`	Returns true if the pattern matches, but does not require that the pattern has to match the input text completely.
`boolean matches()`	Returns true if the pattern matches the string. The pattern must describe the entire string for this method to return true. For partial matching, use `find()` or `lookingAt()`.
`Pattern pattern()`	Returns a reference to the pattern currently being used on the matcher.
`Matcher reset()`	Resets the matcher's state completely.
`Matcher reset (CharSequence input)`	Resets the matcher's state completely and sets new input to `input`.
`int start()`	Returns the starting position of the previous match.
`int start(int group)`	Returns the starting position of a specified capturing group.
`Matcher usePattern (Pattern newPattern)`	Sets a new pattern to use for matching. The current position in the input is not changed.
`String group()`	Returns a string containing the contents of the previous match.
`String group(int group)`	Returns a string containing the contents of a specific matched group. The 0-th group is always the entire expression.
`int groupCount()`	Returns the number of capturing groups in the matcher's pattern.
`Matcher region(int start, int end)`	Returns a `Matcher` that is confined to a substring of the string to search. The caret and dollar sign meta-characters will match at the beginning and end of the defined region.
`int regionEnd()`	Returns the end index (one past the last position actually checked) of the currently defined region.
`int regionStart()`	Returns the start index of the currently defined region.

Table continued on following page

Method	Description
`String replaceAll(String replacement)`	Replaces all occurrences of the string that match the pattern with the string `replacement`. The `Matcher` should be reset if it will still be used after this method is called.
`String replaceFirst(String replacement)`	Replaces only the first string that matches the pattern with the string `replacement`. The `Matcher` should be reset if it will still be used after this method is called.

The MatchResult Interface

The `MatchResult` interface contains the group methods, and `start` and `end` methods, to provide a complete set of methods allowing for describing the current state of the `Matcher`. The `Matcher` class implements this interface and defines all these methods. The `toMatchResult` method returns a handle to a `MatchResult`, which provides for saving and handling the current state of the `Matcher` class.

Regular Expression Example

Use the `Pattern`/`Matcher` classes to process a Java source code file. All classes that aren't public will be listed (all classes that have no modifiers, actually), and also all doubled words (such as two identifiers in a row) are listed utilizing back references.

The input source code file (which does not compile) is shown as follows:

```
import java.util.*;

class EmptyClass {
}

class MyArrayList extends extends ArrayList {
}

public class RETestSource {
    public static void main(String args[]) {
        System.out.println("Sample RE test test source code code");
    }
}
```

The program utilizing regular expressions to process this source code follows:

```
import java.util.*;
import java.util.regex.*;
import java.io.*;

public class RegExpExample {

    public static void main(String args[])
    {
        String fileName = "RETestSource.java";

        String unadornedClassRE = "^\\s*class (\\w+)";
```

```
        String doubleIdentifierRE = "\\b(\\w+)\\s+\\1\\b";

        Pattern classPattern = Pattern.compile(unadornedClassRE);
        Pattern doublePattern = Pattern.compile(doubleIdentifierRE);
        Matcher classMatcher, doubleMatcher;

        int lineNumber=0;

        try {
            BufferedReader br = new BufferedReader(new FileReader(fileName));
            String line;

            while( (line=br.readLine()) != null) {
                lineNumber++;

                classMatcher = classPattern.matcher(line);
                doubleMatcher = doublePattern.matcher(line);

                if(classMatcher.find()) {
                    System.out.println("The class [" +
                                        classMatcher.group(1) +
                                "] is not public");
                }

                while(doubleMatcher.find()) {
                    System.out.println("The word \"" + doubleMatcher.group(1) +
                                    "\" occurs twice at position " +
                                    doubleMatcher.start() + " on line " +
                                    lineNumber);
                }
            }
        } catch(IOException ioe) {
            System.out.println("IOException: " + ioe);
            ioe.printStackTrace();
        }
    }
}
```

The first regular expression, ^\\s*class (\\w+), searches for unadorned class keywords starting at the beginning of the line, followed by zero or more white space characters, then the literal class. The group operator is used with one or more word characters (A–Z, a–z, 0–9, and the underscore), so the class name gets matched.

The second regular expression, \\b(\\w+)\\s+\\1\\b, uses the word boundary meta-character (\b) to ensure that words are isolated. Without this, the string public class would match on the letter c. A back reference is used to match a string already matched, in this case, one or more word characters. One or more characters of white space must appear between the words. Executing the previous program on the preceding test Java source file gives you the following output:

```
The class [EmptyClass] is not public
The class [MyArrayList] is not public
The word "extends" occurs twice at position 18 on line 6
The word "test" occurs twice at position 32 on line 11
The word "code" occurs twice at position 49 on line 11
```

Java Preferences

Programs commonly must store configuration information in some manner that is easy to change and external to the program itself. Java offers utility classes for storing and retrieving system-defined and user-defined configuration information. There are separate hierarchies for the user and system information. All users share the preference information defined in the system tree; each user has his or her own tree for configuration data isolated from other users. This allows for custom configuration, including overriding system values.

The core of the preferences class library is the abstract class `java.util.prefs.Preferences`. This class defines a set of methods that provides for all the features of the preferences library.

Each node in a preference hierarchy has a name, which does not have to be unique. The root node of a preference tree has the empty string ("") as its name. The forward slash is used as a separator for the names of preference nodes, much like it is used as a separator for directory names on Unix. The only two strings that are not valid node names are the empty string (because it is reserved for the root node) and a forward slash by itself (because it is a node separator). The root node's path is the forward slash by itself. Much like with directories, absolute and relative paths are possible. An absolute path always starts with a forward slash, because the absolute path always starts at the root node and follows the tree down to a specific node. A relative path never starts with a forward slash. A path is valid as long as there aren't two consecutive forward slashes in the pathname, and no path except the path to root ends in the forward slash.

Because preferences are implemented by a third-party implementer, changes to the preferences aren't always immediately written to the backing store.

The maximum length of a single node's name and any of its keys is 80 characters. The maximum length of a string value in a node is 8,192 characters.

The Preferences Class

The `Preferences` class is the main class used for dealing with preferences. It represents a node in the preference's tree and contains a large number of methods to manipulate this tree and also nodes in the tree. It is basically a one-stop shop for using preferences. The following sections outline the `Preferences` methods.

Operations on the Preferences Tree

The `Preferences` class defines a number of methods that allow for the creation/deletion of nodes and the retrieval of certain nodes in the tree.

Method	Description
`Preferences node(String pathName)`	Returns a specified node. If the node does not exist, it is created (and any ancestors that do not exist are created) and returned.
`boolean nodeExists(String pathName)`	Returns true if the path to a node exists in the current tree. The path can be an absolute or relative path.

Method	Description
`void removeNode()`	Removes this preference node and all of its children. The only methods that can be invoked after a node has been removed are `name()`, `absolutePath()`, `isUserNode()`, `flush()`, and `nodeExists("")`, and those inherited from `Object`. All other methods will throw an `IllegalStateException`. The removal may not be permanent until `flush()` is called to persist the changes to the tree.
`static Preferences systemNodeForPackage(Class c)`	This method returns a preference node for the package that the specified class is in. All periods in the package name are replaced with forward slashes.
	For a class that has no package, the name of the node that is returned is literally <unnamed>. This node should not be used long term, because it is shared by all programs that use it.
	If the node does not already exist, the node and all ancestors that do not exist will automatically be created.
`static Preferences systemRoot()`	This method returns the root node for the system preferences tree.
`static Preferences userNodeForPackage(Class c)`	This method returns a preference node for the package that the specified class is in. All periods in the package name are replaced with forward slashes.
	For a class that has no package, the name of the node that is returned is literally <unnamed>. This node should not be used long term, because it is shared by all programs that use it, so configuration settings are not isolated.
	If the node does not already exist, the node and all ancestors that do not exist will automatically get created.
`static Preferences userRoot()`	This method returns the root node for the user preferences tree.

Retrieving Information about the Node

Each node has information associated with it, such as its path, parent and children nodes, and the node's name. The methods to manipulate this information are shown here.

Method	Description
`String absolutePath()`	This method returns the absolute path to the current node. The absolute path starts at the root node, /, and continues to the current node.
`String[] childrenNames()`	Returns an array of the names of all child nodes of the current node.
`boolean isUserNode()`	Returns true if this node is part of the user configuration tree, or false if this node is part of the system configuration tree.
`String name()`	Returns the name of the current node.
`Preferences parent()`	Returns a `Preferences` reference to the parent of the current node, or null if trying to get the parent of the root node.

Retrieving Preference Values from the Node

The following methods act much like those from the `Hashtable` class. The key difference is that there are versions of the `get` for most primitive types. Each type is associated with a specific key, a string standing for the name of the configuration parameter.

Method	Description
`String[] keys()`	Returns an array of strings that contains the names of all keys in the current preferences node.
`String get(String key, String def)`	Returns the string associated with a specified key. If the key does not exist, it is created with the default value def and this default value is then returned.
`boolean getBoolean (String key, boolean def)`	Returns the `boolean` associated with a specified key. If the key does not exist, it is created with the default value def and this default value is then returned.
`byte[] getByteArray (String key, byte[] def)`	Returns the `byte` array associated with a specified key. If the key does not exist, it is created with the default value def and this default value is then returned.
`double getDouble(String key, double def)`	Returns the `double` associated with a specified key. If the key does not exist, it is created with the default value def and this default value is then returned.
`float getFloat(String key, float def)`	Returns the `float` associated with a specified key. If the key does not exist, it is created with the default value def and this default value is then returned.

Method	Description
`int getInt(String key, int def)`	Returns the `integer` associated with a specified key. If the key does not exist, it is created with the default value `def` and this default value is then returned.
`long getLong(String key, long def)`	Returns the `long` associated with a specified key. If the key does not exist, it is created with the default value `def` and this default value is then returned.

Setting Preference Values on the Node

Along with each `get` method is a `put` version intended for setting the information associated with a given configuration parameter's key name.

Method	Description
`void put(String key, String value)` `void putBoolean(String key, boolean value)` `void putByteArray(String key, byte[] value)` `void putDouble(String key, double value)` `void putInt(String key, int value)` `void putFloat(String key, float value)` `void putLong(String key, long value)`	These methods set a configuration parameter (the name of which is passed in as `key`) to a specific type. If `key` or `value` is null, an exception is thrown. The key can be at most 80 characters long (defined in `MAX_KEY_LENGTH`) and the value can be at most 8,192 characters (defined in `MAX_VALUE_LENGTH`).

Events

Two events are defined for the `Preference` class — one fires when a node is changed in the preference tree, and the second fires when a preference is changed. The methods for these events are listed in the next table.

Method	Description
`void addNodeChangeListener (NodeChangeListener ncl)`	Adds a listener for notification of when a child node is added or removed from the current preference node.
`void addPreferenceChangeListener (PreferenceChangeListener pcl)`	Adds a listener for preference change events — anytime a preference is added to, removed from, or the value is changed, listeners will be notified.
`void removeNodeChangeListener (NodeChangeListener ncl)`	Removes a specified node change listener.
`void removePreferenceChangeListener (PreferenceChangeListener pcl)`	Removes a specified preference change listener.

Other Operations

The following table lists the other methods in the `Preference` class, such as writing any pending changes to the backing store, resetting the preference hierarchy to empty, saving the hierarchy to disk, and other operations.

Method	Description
`void clear()`	Removes all preferences on this node.
`void exportNode (OutputStream os)`	Writes the entire contents of the node (and only the current node) to the output stream as an XML file (following the `preferences .dtd` listed in the following section).
`void exportSubtree (OutputStream os)`	Writes the entire contents of this node and all nodes located below this node in the preferences tree to the output stream as an XML file (following the `preferences.dtd` listed in the following section).
`void flush()`	Writes any changes to the preference node to the backing store, including data on all children nodes.
`void remove(String key)`	Removes the value associated with the specified key.
`void sync()`	Ensures that the current version of the preference node in memory matches that of the stored version. If data in the preference node needs to be written to the backing store, it will be.
`String toString()`	Returns a string containing `User` or `System`, depending on which hierarchy the node is in, and the absolute path to the current node.

Exporting to XML

The `Preferences` system defines a standard operation to export the entire tree of keys/values to an XML file. This XML file's DTD is available at `http://java.sun.com/dtd/preferences.dtd`. This DTD is also included here:

```
<?xml version="1.0" encoding="UTF-8"?>

<!-- DTD for a Preferences tree. -->

<!-- The preferences element is at the root of an XML document
     representing a Preferences tree. -->
<!ELEMENT preferences (root)>

<!-- The preferences element contains an optional version
     attribute, which specifies version of DTD. -->
<!ATTLIST preferences EXTERNAL_XML_VERSION CDATA "0.0" >

<!-- The root element has a map representing the root's preferences
     (if any), and one node for each child of the root (if any). -->
<!ELEMENT root (map, node*) >

<!-- Additionally, the root contains a type attribute, which
     specifies whether it's the system or user root. -->
```

```
    <!ATTLIST root
            type (system|user) #REQUIRED >

    <!-- Each node has a map representing its preferences (if any),
         and one node for each child (if any). -->
    <!ELEMENT node (map, node*) >

    <!-- Additionally, each node has a name attribute -->
    <!ATTLIST node
            name CDATA #REQUIRED >

    <!-- A map represents the preferences stored at a node (if any). -->
    <!ELEMENT map (entry*) >

    <!-- An entry represents a single preference, which is simply
         a key-value pair. -->
    <!ELEMENT entry EMPTY >
    <!ATTLIST entry
            key   CDATA #REQUIRED
            value CDATA #REQUIRED >
```

Using Preferences

The following example sets a few properties in a node in the user tree, prints out information about the node, and then exports the information to an XML file:

```java
import java.util.*;
import java.util.prefs.*;
import java.io.*;

public class PreferenceExample {
    public void printInformation(Preferences p)
        throws BackingStoreException
    {
        System.out.println("Node's absolute path: " + p.absolutePath());

        System.out.print("Node's children: ");
        for(String s : p.childrenNames()) {
            System.out.print(s + " ");
        }
        System.out.println("");

        System.out.print("Node's keys: ");
        for(String s : p.keys()) {
            System.out.print(s + " ");
        }
        System.out.println("");

        System.out.println("Node's name: " + p.name());
        System.out.println("Node's parent: " + p.parent());
        System.out.println("NODE: " + p);
        System.out.println("userNodeForPackage: " +
                Preferences.userNodeForPackage(PreferenceExample.class));
        System.out.println("All information in node");
```

```
            for(String s : p.keys()) {
                System.out.println("  " + s + " = " + p.get(s, ""));
            }
        }

    public void setSomeProperties(Preferences p)
        throws BackingStoreException
    {
        p.put("fruit", "apple");
        p.put("cost", "1.01");
        p.put("store", "safeway");
    }

    public void exportToFile(Preferences p, String fileName)
        throws BackingStoreException
    {
        try {
            FileOutputStream fos = new FileOutputStream(fileName);

            p.exportSubtree(fos);
            fos.close();
        } catch(IOException ioe) {
            System.out.println("IOException in exportToFile\n" + ioe);
            ioe.printStackTrace();
        }
    }

    public static void main(String args[])
    {
        PreferenceExample pe = new PreferenceExample();
        Preferences prefsRoot = Preferences.userRoot();
        Preferences myPrefs = prefsRoot.node("PreferenceExample");

        try {
            pe.setSomeProperties(myPrefs);
            pe.printInformation(myPrefs);
            pe.exportToFile(myPrefs, "prefs.xml");
        } catch(BackingStoreException bse) {
            System.out.println("Problem with accessing the backing store\n" + bse);
            bse.printStackTrace();
        }
    }
}
```

The output to the screen is shown here:

```
Node's absolute path: /PreferenceExample
Node's children:
Node's keys: fruit cost store
Node's name: PreferenceExample
Node's parent: User Preference Node: /
NODE: User Preference Node: /PreferenceExample
```

```
userNodeForPackage: User Preference Node: /<unnamed>
All information in node
  fruit = apple
  cost = 1.01
  store = safeway
```

The exported information in the XML file is listed here:

```
<?xml version="1.0" encoding="UTF-8"?>
<!DOCTYPE preferences SYSTEM "http://java.sun.com/dtd/preferences.dtd">
<preferences EXTERNAL_XML_VERSION="1.0">
  <root type="user">
    <map/>
    <node name="PreferenceExample">
      <map>
        <entry key="fruit" value="apple"/>
        <entry key="cost" value="1.01"/>
        <entry key="store" value="safeway"/>
      </map>
    </node>
  </root>
</preferences>
```

Summary

This chapter introduced Derby, a lightweight database from the Apache Database project, which is new in JDK 6. Also reviewed were the new language features that Sun built into the JDK 5 release of the Java programming language. You should have all you need to know to understand and utilize these new features. You may find that a number of programming tasks you've accomplished in the past are now made simpler and clearer, and perhaps even some problems that never had a good solution now do.

Also covered in this chapter are several of the most important utility libraries in Java. The preferences library allows you to store and retrieve configuration information for your application. The logging library provides a sophisticated package of routines to track what your program is doing and offer output in a variety of ways. The regular expression library provides routines for advanced processing of textual data.

Now that you have learned about the advanced language features in Java, the next two chapters take you inside a modern Java development shop. In Chapter 2, the habits, tools, and methodologies that make an effective Java developer are discussed.

2

Tools and Techniques for Developing Java Solutions

Many beginning Java developers master the concepts of the Java programming language fairly well and still have a difficult time reaching the next level as a professional Java developer.

This is because most Java books simply focus on teaching only the Java language, a Java tool (like Ant or TestNG), or a language-neutral software methodology. This leaves you to learn techniques and practices from other software developers or at the proverbial "school of hard knocks."

Chapter 1 discussed the advanced features of the Java language—a continuation on the theme of most beginning Java books. But now, you are starting the transition to a new kind of Java book, one more experience-centric, starting with this chapter. In this chapter, you will get a feel for the tools and techniques of modern Java development. It introduces you to "thinking like a professional Java developer," which continues in the next chapter—a discussion of Java design patterns.

By the end of this chapter, you should have acquired the following skills:

- ❑   Familiarity with the principles of quality software development
- ❑   Familiarity with the habits of an effective software developer
- ❑   Awareness of a number of the prominent software development methodologies
- ❑   Acquaintance with many of the tools commonly found in Java development environments

Principles of Quality Software Development

So, you have figured out how to build your Java applications, and they work just like the ones from which you learned. You are getting paid to write these applications, so you are now a professional Java developer. But how do you know if you are doing a good job?

There are literally thousands upon thousands of articles debating the measures of quality software with each of them offering you their own solution for how you should answer this question. Realizing that this discussion is well beyond the scope of this book (thankfully), this body of work can be boiled down to a few questions:

❑ **Does the software do what it is supposed to do?**

    ❑ Of course, this is a loaded question. It is entirely possible to say that a piece of software does what it is supposed to do (as defined by a requirements specification), but this is absolutely worthless. In essence, you are talking about a failure of your requirements gathering process, which leads you to build the wrong thing. Your software is being built to serve a particular need, and if it does not satisfy that need (for whatever reason), the software is a failure.

❑ **Does the software do things it shouldn't do?**

    ❑ Developers like to refer to this phenomenon as undocumented features, but your users will refer to them as bugs. Everyone prefers to build bug-free software, but in the real world, this just doesn't happen. All men may be created equal, but all bugs are not. Bugs that do not impact the functioning of the system — or the business process they support — are obviously far less important than those that do.

❑ **Did you deliver the software in a timely manner?**

    ❑ Timing is everything, and this is true nowhere more than in software in which the pace of change is incredible. If your software takes so long to deliver that it is no longer appropriate to the business process it supports, then it is worthless. The great untold secret behind the high percentage of software projects that end in failure is that many of them simply could not keep up with the pace of technological innovation — and died trying.

❑ **Could you do it again if you had to?**

    ❑ Of course, you will have to! This is *the job* — writing and delivering software that complies with the preceding questions. The key here is that you should not have to learn all of your hard knocks lessons every time you build software. You will invariably be asked to deliver your software again with fixes and enhancements, and you hopefully do not have to fix the same bugs over and over again nor have the same integration challenges repeatedly. "At least we don't have to deal with this next time" should be a truth that comforts you in your integration and bug fixing, and not a punch line to a development team joke.

These questions may seem like common sense — because they are! But there is an old saying that "common sense is neither," so it is important not to assume that everyone is on the same sheet of music. Furthermore, the U.S. Army Rangers have a saying, "Never violate any principles, and do not get wrapped up in technique." You will find this a helpful maxim in dealing with the maze of processes, products, and techniques involved in software development. These are the core principles of software development, and how you get there is technique. Do not lose sight of the distinction between these two things.

Habits of Effective Software Development

Motivational sayings and commonsense questions do not create a strategy for making you into an effective Java developer. You need to consider *the how* in delivering quality software. Along those lines, a set of habits is shared among effective software developers. They are outlined in the following sections.

Communicate

The picture of the egg-headed recluse software engineer sitting in the dark part of some basement while banging away on a keyboard like an eccentric secretary is an outmoded stereotype (well mostly, the dark is good). As you learned before, software is built to satisfy a need in some particular business process. To be successful, you need to tap in and really appreciate that need. This is very difficult to do by reading a specification. You want to talk to the users, and, if you cannot talk to the users, you want to talk to someone who was a user or speaks with users. You want to learn what it is they do, how they are successful, and how your software will help them be more successful. If the use of your software is simply by management fiat, then your software purpose is already on critical life support.

You also want to communicate with your fellow developers — explaining to them what you learned, learning from their mistakes, and coordinating how your software will work together. Make it a point to try to establish some social interaction among your teammates, even if it is an occasional lunch or brief chat. Software can be a hard and stressful job; it helps if you have a basic familiarity with your teammates.

Model

Before you go running out to buy the latest in fashion apparel, check the cover of this book. It is pretty clear that this book will not have you doing any posing! Modeling builds upon communication by allowing a more tangible way to visualize a given concept or idea.

Don't assume that everyone on your team needs to attend Unified Modeling Language (UML) training or buy thousands of dollars of UML modeling software. UML is a great package for expressing a lot of things in a common format that should be understandable by a wide variety of people — from users to developers. Indeed, you know this is not the case. The key to any notation is that it must be well understood by those who read it. If your team is UML-savvy or will commit to being that way, then it is a fantastic notation — planned out by a large committee of very smart people.

Of course, the old joke is, "A camel is a horse designed by a committee." This means that you should recognize that UML contains a toolset that extends well beyond what you may need for your project's modeling needs. The key is to find a notation that everyone (including users) understands and stick with it.

Also, if your tools provide more of a hindrance than an aid in your modeling, don't use them. Scott Ambler suggests in his book *Agile Modeling: Effective Practices for Extreme Programming and the Unified Process* that you can draw your models on a whiteboard, take a digital camera snapshot of the whiteboard, and have exactly what you need — without the burden or cost of a tool.

Be Agile

Change is an inevitable part of software development. Not only is technology consistently changing, but so is your customer's business process, if for no other reason than the fact that you have actually provided some automation support.

Teaching a course in Object Oriented Software Development, I often point out to my students that, despite being a sophisticated software engineering professional who has developed many software solutions to improve the way people do business, I could not easily come up with a set of requirements for a system that would improve my business process. The fact is — like most people in the working world — I don't spend a lot of time thinking about how I do what I do. If asked to do so, I would probably relate my ideal system as an approximation of what I already experience. This would immediately change when you, the software team, introduced a new system to me because my entire frame of reference is now relative to what you have placed before me. Things that I once thought were important would no longer be so — improvements that I assumed would be better turn out not to be, and so on. Ultimately, it is a very natural and appropriate thing for my requirements to change!

You frequently hear software engineers bemoan the fact that the requirements keep changing. This is quite puzzling because software engineers presumably chose their profession based on the desire to develop software, and changing requirements facilitate that goal. Changing requirements is not really the problem. The problem is that the software team is not in the habit of accommodating change; that is, they are not very agile.

Lou Holtz once said, "Life is 10 percent what happens to you and 90 percent how you respond to it." This saying goes a long way toward distilling the attitude that a software engineer should possess to be effective in modern Java development.

Be Disciplined

Before you go running out and hacking and slashing your way to programming heaven, ensure that you maintain your discipline. Discipline is about maintaining your focus in the presence of a tremendous amount of distraction. This is not about holding your hand over a hot candle or walking across burning coals. You do what you should do, not what you can do.

Recall the principles of quality software development and ensure that you are not violating any of them. Often, rushing to do something will actually cause you to take longer. Be mindful of things slipping, like little bugs that should have been caught before or lapses in judgment for the sake of expediency.

However, in the same regard, do not slow things down simply for the sake of caution. Simply slowing down to avoid making a mistake will not definitely allow you to avoid the mistake, but it will certainly reduce the amount of time you have to spend correcting it.

This is a very typical concern when trying to fix a bug or develop an innovative way to handle something that was unanticipated. By desiring to do something new and cool, you can lose sight of how important it really is in accomplishing the goal of the system.

Trace Your Actions to Need

Discipline goes hand in hand with tracing your actions to the need that your software is meant to address. It is very important that you are able to understand why each of you built each of the components of your system.

Traceability refers to the ability for you to follow your need all the way through the system. For example, you may have a need to provide a printed report. You would then see that traced into a set of use cases, or software requirements, which would then be realized in certain design elements, which would then be implemented in certain pieces of code, which would then be compiled into certain executables or libraries, which would then be deployed to a certain machine and so forth.

So, you are thinking, "Well, that is really neat, but what does all of that really buy me?" The answer is simple. Say you received a request to change the code to support another type of printer. The ability to trace your code through lets you understand where your potential adaptations could be made.

Traceability is not meant to be some huge undertaking requiring mountains of paperwork and a large database, spreadsheet, or document, nor does it require some dumbed-down version of the code to explain it to those who are not able to read or write code. Traceability only requires that someone who can do something about it should be able to find his or her way through the code.

Don't Be Afraid to Write Code

It seems self-evident, but you would be surprised how often coding is relegated to such a minor part of software development — particularly on complex systems, where it is most needed. Often, there is a desire to figure it out on paper first, find the right design pattern, or model it just right.

However, certain logical constructs are simply unable to be elegantly expressed anywhere but in the code. Also, a compiler verifies a number of assumptions in your design, and your runtime environment will do the same.

It is also easier to estimate how long it will take to do something if you actually do something very similar. A scaled-back prototype that covers the bounds of your system can go a long way to understanding exactly how complex or time-consuming a particular task may actually be.

Furthermore, in Java development, you simply do not have the luxury of assuming that you understand everything about your system. With the high degree of reuse that exists in Java development, your system is invariably dependent on code developed outside of your design space. So, it is foolish to assume that a given API works like you assume it does. There are too many variables involved in the equation.

Part of the fearlessness toward writing code involves changing code. *Refactoring* — changing the design of existing code — is an important part of software development. [FOWLER]

Think of Code as a Design, not a Product

Refactoring demonstrates a key habit in effective software development. Code should not be considered the product that you deliver. After all, you rarely actually deliver the source code to the user. Instead, you deliver them compiled byte code that operates in accordance with your source code.

This is because your source code is part of the design. As mentioned previously, there are some logical constructs that cannot be expressed anywhere but inside code. Furthermore, source code provides a human-understandable expression of logic that is then compiled into byte codes (and further gets converted into machine instructions).

You may be saying, "Well, of course, source code is not the product, who said it was?" You may never run into a problem with an organization that fails to realize this premise, but it is unlikely. Simply pay careful attention to the disproportionate focus paid to the design phase and the relative number of designers who cannot write code. This will demonstrate that the focus of the project is misplaced.

Read a Lot

This may seem like a shameless plug by a self-serving author, but the simple fact is that software is always changing and improving. There are new technologies, implementations, APIs, standards, and so forth. Software development is a knowledge occupation, and part of the job (as well as developing any system) is learning. Learning new technologies, learning better approaches, and even learning more about the tools and APIs currently used in your solutions are critical to success.

A large part of this has to do with the rise of the Internet and open source software. Java has extended beyond just being a programming language and more toward a software development community.

If you have a software problem, you should first check online to see if someone has already solved that problem. Furthermore, you could check to see how others in your situation have overcome problems you have yet to encounter.

Build Your Process from the Ground Up

Your process is the way you, as a team, do business. No matter what your management tries to do in terms of instituting a process, your team will have to buy into how you will do business. The key to building an effective process is to start from the ground up. Management will set expectations for the outcomes they want and how they will measure your performance. If they place a high value on documentation and paperwork, you need to ensure those expectations are met.

The key part is that your team will need to work together and that will decide how you meet the expectations of management. If you do not agree as a team to a process, then process can become a political football. You do not want to get into a situation where process is used to try to differentiate between co-workers. Once that starts happening, you will find that the techniques become more important than good software principles, and you start to lose the ability to trace your actions to your software's need.

An important consideration in building your process from the ground up is recognizing where your process really begins and ends. Development team wars have been waged simply on the basis of the question of integrated development environment (IDE) standardization, like Eclipse. You should ask yourselves whether you really want to standardize on an IDE. Even though you certainly need something to be able to interoperate among team members with effective configuration management (discussed subsequently), you still don't want to make someone have to fight their development tools. Software is hard enough without having to fight against your tools.

This is the key consideration in building your process. Decide what your team can agree on to make everyone the most effective. If you cannot agree, then management may have to get involved, but this should be avoided.

Manage Your Configuration

Configuration management is important because stuff happens. A hard drive goes bad, your latest improvement goes very badly, and so forth. These are all examples of things that happen in the normal course of software development.

You should recognize that there is a distinct difference between configuration management and source code control. Configuration management is a process in which you control how your system is put together. The key goal in configuration management is that you can replicate your configuration in another place. You do not just maintain configuration control of your source code but also your runtime environment (including dependent libraries, application server configuration, Java Runtime Environment, or database schema), that is, anything you would need in order to re-create your system.

Source code control using a tool like the Concurrent Versioning System (CVS) is used to allow multiple developers to work on files and integrate their changes while saving the history of previous revisions. CVS is the dominant tool in the open source environment and is cleanly integrated into most of the major IDEs. Of course, source control is useless if you do not *commit your changes*!

Unit Test Your Code

When you design and write code, you are writing test cases. You are writing test cases to handle the intended case, that is, how the system should behave as you go through the system. As you do that, you are making certain assumptions about how your system will react given a certain set of circumstances. For example, if I check to see that an object is not null here, I am assuming that it will not be null up to a certain point.

As you write code, you tend to develop your complex logic to support the intended case, checking for needed preconditions required for your code to work. However, there is often a set of scenarios for which your code was designed to work. Unit testing allows you to test those scenarios.

I will discuss how to use an open source tool called TestNG, which is a similar regression testing framework as JUnit, to perform unit testing, but unit testing becomes an important part of the habit known as *continuous integration*.

Continuously Integrate

Having a strong set of unit tests that ensure the functionality of the individual components of your system, you could now combine these together into one cohesive product and run all of the unit tests on all the components to see how well the system as a whole functions, as illustrated in Figure 2-1.

You should note that, even if you are not very good about unit testing, continuous integration can still apply and provide great value to your development team. As you combine the efforts of your entire development team, you will see how things actually play together and ensure valid assumptions toward each other's code.

The more you integrate your system together, the more confident you will become in the success of the product as a whole. This helps mitigate risk by discovering problems early when they can be fixed. Continuous integration ties directly into maintaining short development iterations.

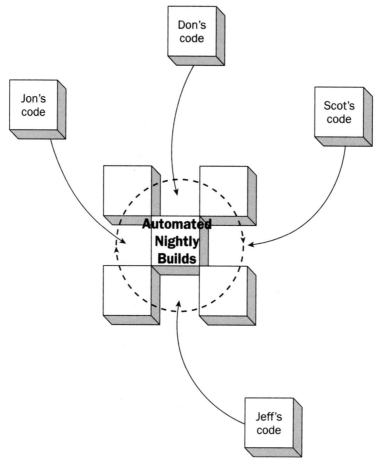

Figure 2-1

Maintaining Short Iterations

As previously noted, the sooner you discover problems, the less likely they are to affect your overall development success. The trick to doing this is to maintain short development iterations. This means that you should be able to go through the development life cycle (requirements, code, design, and test) in a short period of time.

You should try to involve your customer in each iteration if possible because, as mentioned previously, your software will change their context. This means they will start describing what they want within the context of what you built, not in some abstract concept.

How short depends on your team, but for the purposes of this discussion, you should measure it in weeks, not months. You want to put enough in an iteration to be meaningful in the shortest period of time. Two weeks to a month is a good rough estimate for your first iteration. After that, you can use your own success or failure to determine your next iteration.

Measure What You Accomplished — Indirectly

There is an old joke in software estimation, "What is the difference between a fairy tale and a software estimate? One doesn't start with once upon a time." This joke takes to task the idea that software estimation is really hard, and most techniques are frequently described as black magic.

However, successful software estimates are based on experience. Experience is based on trying to quantify what you have done before (and how long it took) as a predictor of how long the next thing will take. Because the typical workplace doesn't punish overestimation as much as underestimation — early is good, late is bad — you start to have these highly defensive estimates of software effort. These estimates start to build on one another and, because you cannot come in too low or your next estimate will not be as believable, you start to have down time. You start to gold plate (that is, add unnecessary and untraceable features) your system and gain a sense of inactivity.

The opposite phenomenon also occurs. Because software developers cannot be trusted to make estimates (because they are gold plating and sitting around), management steps in and promises software based on their guesses on how long something should take. Usually, they are setting aggressive schedules simply for some marketing purpose and frame it as a technical challenge to the developers. Developers are optimists and fighters, so they accept the ridiculous schedules until they get burned out and leave for a new job.

So, how do you avoid these dysfunctional circumstances? You measure what you have done by using an indirect measure to keep you honest. Extreme Programming (XP) has a concept known as *velocity*. XP is discussed subsequently, but the concept of velocity can be paraphrased as follows:

1. You have a set of tasks, each of which you assign a certain number of points related to how much effort it will take to accomplish it.

2. You then estimate how many points each of the developers on your team will be able to accomplish for a given iteration — taking into account leave and so forth. Your iteration is timeboxed to a specific amount of time (for example, two weeks is common).

3. You perform the work and keep track of how many points you were actually able to accomplish.

4. You start the process over for new tasks, adjusting them based on the actual results. As you get better or your system becomes better understood, your velocity will increase.

Of course, nothing scares developers more than metrics. As Mark Twain once said, "There are three types of lies: lies, damned lies, and statistics." Developers understand that metrics can be oversimplified or distorted beyond their actual meaning. This is why teamwork and communication is so important. You should only allow these metrics to be visible to those who actually are involved in using them. You can make it a secret handshake; that is, if you don't have a velocity, you don't get to know the velocity.

Of course, on the subject of sensitive but necessary measures of your development performance, you should also look into tracking your issues.

Track Your Issues

Another volatile subject on a development team is bug reporting and tracking. As previously mentioned, it is hard for you to understand what your customers want, and it is hard for them to understand what they want. Furthermore, your users will use your software in ways that you did not anticipate and they will discover undocumented features of your system.

However, if you get past the concept of blame and simply focus on the inevitability of bugs and changes, you can make your issue tracking system a good way of keeping track of things that need to be done.

Whether you use a sophisticated online system or a simple spreadsheet, it is important that you keep track of the loose ends. You will find that it is a great practice to allow your users to directly input feedback on your product. How you choose to triage your responses is up to you, but it is very helpful to always have an open ear to listen to the user. Of course, if you let them constantly enter things in the system, you will need to make it appear that you are actually listening on the other end.

Development Methodology

Now that you have reviewed the principles of quality software development and many of the habits that help to facilitate achieving those principles, it is time to learn some actual full up methodologies used in many Java development shops.

There is a joke, "What is the difference between a methodologist and a terrorist? You can negotiate with a terrorist!" This joke pokes fun at a very real problem. Often, methodologies are evaluated as if they must account for every possible circumstance in the development life cycle and must be ritualistically adhered to — or the methodology magic will not work. Of course, all methodologies have to be tailored to your own development scenario, but you need to know the particulars of a methodology before you can tailor it.

A full examination and comparison of development methodologies is beyond the scope of this book, but you will learn some of the most popular ones in use today.

Waterfall Methodology

The grandfather of all software methodologies is the Waterfall methodology. It is known as the Waterfall methodology because the sequences flow through each other sequentially, as demonstrated in Figure 2-2.

The Waterfall methodology consists of a series of activities separated by control gates. These control gates determine whether a given activity has been completed and would move across to the next activity. The requirements phase handles determining all of the software requirements. The design phase, as the name implies, determines the design of the entire system. Next, the code is written in the code phase. The code is then tested. Finally, the product is delivered.

The primary criticism of the Waterfall methodology is that it takes too long to gain feedback on how things are going. As you read previously, some parts of your software are well understood and others are not. Therefore, trying to do all of the requirements first (which is to say, quantify the need into tangible specifications) is very hard when your user may not have a good understanding of the problem at hand. Furthermore, if you make a mistake in the requirements, it will propagate to the design, the code, and so on. Also, there is no real capability to go back in the process. So, if you get into testing and discover that a part of the design simply doesn't work, you end up making changes to fix that issue, but you lose all context of your design activity — you are literally band-aiding the system on purpose!

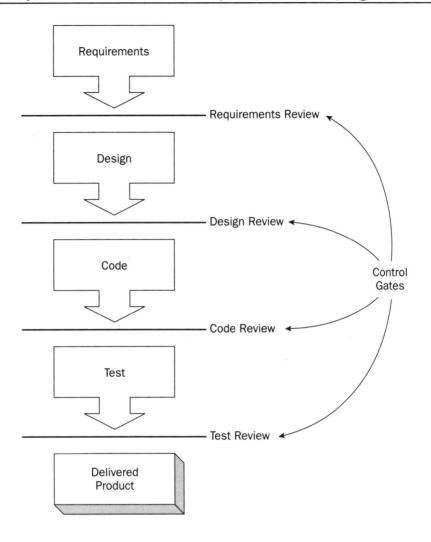

Figure 2-2

Recognizing this problem, the Waterfall methodology has been adapted in several other forms, like the spiral methodology, which entails simply having multiple waterfalls. The idea is to shorten the time of the life cycle; that is, create an iterative solution to the problem.

Ultimately, you cannot escape the waterfall, because it really is the commonsense approach. First, you decide what it is you are going to build. Then, you decide how you are going to build it. Next, you actually build it. Finally, you ensure that you actually built what you wanted (and it that works). The major distinction with the next two methodologies discussed has to do with how much of the overall effort you try to build at a time.

Unified Process

In Craig Larman's *Applying UML and Patterns,* he discusses an agile version of the Unified Process (UP), a process originally developed from the merger of several object-oriented development methodologies. The Unified Process entails short iterations of development based on tackling the most important aspects of your system first, which is illustrated in Figure 2-3. [LARMAN]

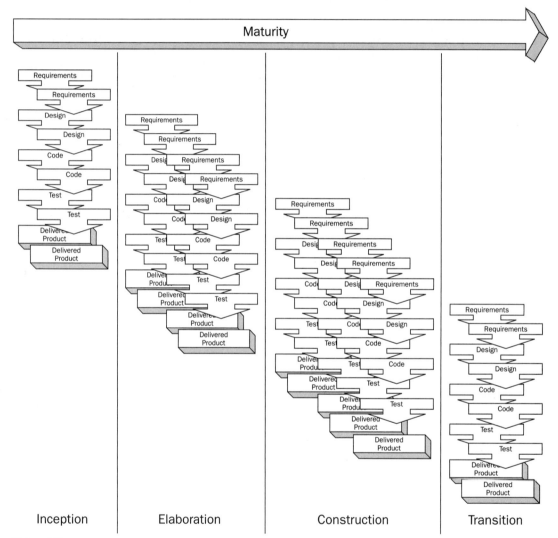

Figure 2-3

You develop a survey of use cases (that is, brief descriptions of user interactions with the system) and start working them off in the order in which they pose a risk to the overall success of the system. You can add or remove use cases from your survey, as appropriate, through your development. The phases illustrated in Figure 2-3 define and measure the relative maturity of the system.

The phases of the Unified Process are as follows:

- **Inception:** The system is still being felt out to determine the scope of the system — what will the system do and what are its boundaries. This phase can be very short if the system is well understood.

- **Elaboration:** You are mitigating the architectural risks to the system. This is a fancy way of saying, "Have you solved all of your hard problems?" or "Do you know how to do all the things you are going to need to do?"

- **Construction:** You are finishing all of the relevant use cases to make the system production ready, that is, to go into beta.

- **Transition:** You move the system through its final release stages and beta releases. It could include the operations and maintenance of the software.

This is an agile process that focuses on maintaining momentum, but it still sticks to a lot of the traditional practices of use case development, modeling, and so forth. The next methodology is also an agile process, but it has a different focus in terms of how to accomplish it.

Extreme Programming

Kent Beck's *eXtreme Programming eXplained* introduced a radically new methodology into the software development community. Based on his experiences on a project at Chrysler, he proposed making coding the central part of your development effort.

You have your user come up with stories describing how the system should work, and order them based on their relative importance. You then take on a set of stories for your team to accomplish in a given iteration, about two weeks in length — working 40-hour weeks. You split your team into pairs to work on each of the stories, allowing a certain amount of built-in peer review of the code as it is being written. You and your partner start by writing unit tests to go along with your source code. After you are done with your particular piece of code, you take it over to the integration machine where you add to the code baseline and run all of the unit tests accumulated from everyone's code. After each iteration, you should have a working system that your user can review to ensure that you are meeting their needs. This whole process is shown in Figure 2-4.

Note that XP doesn't place a high emphasis on designing the software; instead, it holds that most upfront design is not very helpful to the overall effort and ends up being changed with actual development.

XP is rather good at continuously having a working system. It can be tough when you lack an involved user or have a project of a large size (50 or more developers), when coordination and design activities actually could provide more value.

XP's system of velocity, described previously, provides a good sense of understanding the capability of your team so you can effectively plan, thus avoiding burning out your engineers or sandbagging your customer.

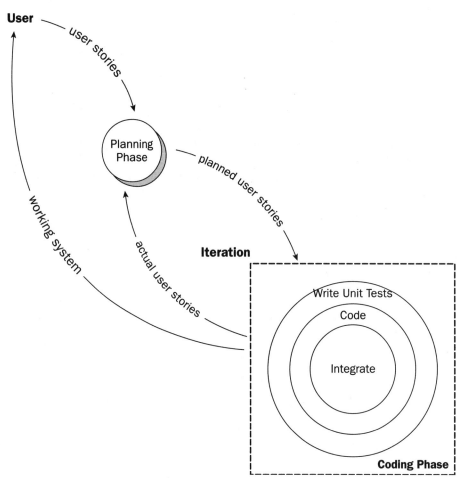

Figure 2-4

Observations on Methodology

You can take away several critical points from reviewing these three divergent methodologies:

❑ Ultimately, you are doing the same task in each methodology. How much scope you attempt to address in each activity defines the real difference.

❑ The agile methodologies, like UP and XP, seek to be reactive rather than proscriptive. That is, they attempt to assess the success and adjust direction of the effort continuously rather than relying on the pass/fail nature of waterfall control gates.

❑ The methodologies vary in how much importance they grant to the design phase and the accoutrements that surround them (UML modeling tools and so forth). The Waterfall process finds this phase incredibly important, and UP recognizes that for the part of the system you are addressing in your iteration. XP believes that coding is design, and all of the additional work is built around considering scenarios that are not actually addressed in the functionality of the system. After all, you are coding the actual user stories.

❑ All of the methodologies recognize the importance of use cases, but they address them in different forms. The Waterfall methodology sees use cases as a tool for generating the explicit requirements of the system, providing background information. UP finds them important as an inventory of scope. The survey report contains a simplified explanation of each use case and then relies upon them to build its design models in each of its iterations. XP is based directly on developing to satisfy what it calls user stories, which are more informal in format but still essentially the same as survey reports.

There is no one-size-fits-all methodology. As mentioned in *Habits of Effective Software Development*, it is important that you and your team determine the process by which you will accomplish addressing the need for which your software is being built. This section was meant to provide you with a background on some of the most common methodologies in software today, and the next section discusses some of the common tools used in software development in the context of practical development scenarios.

Practical Development Scenarios

Distributing J2EE applications across tiers is a challenging task to tackle because of all of the underlying implications of mixing and matching components with connectors across a system. The J2EE architecture consists of four tiers: the client, Web, business, and Enterprise Information System (EIS). The client tier is comprised of applets, HTML, and Java components. The Web tier is made up of servlets and Java Server Pages that operate in a web container. The business tier manages all of the data transactions and persistence mechanisms of a system as well as resource allocations. The EIS tier is accountable for all of the back-end database systems with which application components must integrate.

With all of these components and connectors, consideration must be given to the construction of processes that manage and test these entities to ensure that consistencies are attained during development and deployment. Many open source tools have been developed to facilitate technological timing issues so that business challenges can be met. The remaining sections of this chapter discuss some of these tools so you can apply them in your operations to realize those consistencies, which should facilitate your development activities and help you become more successful with your integrations and deployments.

This chapter investigates some scenarios on how to apply scripting tools like Ant, Maven 2, and XDoclet to manage your component builds and packaging, along with TestNG and JMeter to test your applications in an automated fashion to ensure that your development operations can behave in a harmonious manner.

Ant

All software projects need consistent builds from a common repository to ensure applications are deployed properly. For many software projects (both commercial and open source), Ant has been used to compile, test, and package components for distribution (see Figure 2-5).

With Ant, a series of targets are implemented to construct processes to build your system components. This section takes you through three different scenarios that you might encounter in your development activities that can be tackled with Ant.

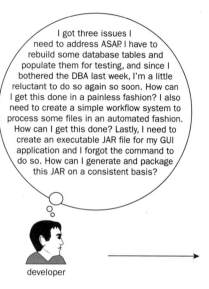

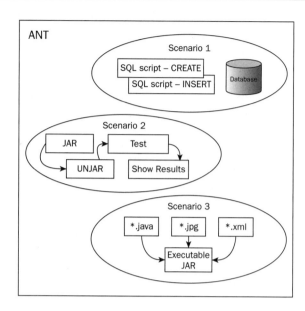

developer

Figure 2-5

Scenario 1

In general, most Ant scripts start with property settings that are used to establish proper directory structures for file creation and transfer during your build activities. Similarly, parameters that are needed for processing can be defined like they are for database operations used in all three target entries in the following Ant script. Users can also send these parameters to the Ant script from the command line using the -D operation:

```
<project name="Database creation" default="createTables_MySQL" basedir=".">
<!-- could use a property file, we opted for property settings in script
<property file="${basedir}/build.properties"/> -->

<property name="sql.driver" value="org.gjt.mm.mysql.Driver"/>
<property name="sql.url" value="jdbc:mysql://localhost/sample_project"/>

<property name="sql.user" value=""/>
<property name="sql.pass" value=""/>
```

The createTables_MySQL target executes three SQL scripts for employees, project, and timetable table creation. The idea here is to be able to generate your tables on the fly just in case you need to deploy your database tables on a new platform for testing and/or deployment:

```
<target name="createTables_MySQL">
    <sql driver="${sql.driver}" url="${sql.url}" userid="${sql.user}"
password="${sql.pass}" >
        <classpath>
        <pathelement location="mysql-connector-java-3.0.9-stable-bin.jar"/>
```

```
        </classpath>
            use sample_project;
            <transaction src="employees.sql"/>
            <transaction src="project.sql"/>
            <transaction src="timetable.sql"/>
        </sql>
    </target>
```

The `createDB_MySQL` script works in conjunction with the `sample_project.sql` file to create a database in MySQL so tables can be added to it. The following code snippet outlines how this is done, first by dropping any preexisting tables for `employees`, `project`, and `timetable`. After that has been performed, the database will be created for table aggregations:

```
BEGIN;
DROP TABLE IF EXISTS employees;
DROP TABLE IF EXISTS project;
DROP TABLE IF EXISTS timetable;
DROP DATABASE IF EXISTS sample_project;
COMMIT;

CREATE DATABASE sample_project;
    <target name="createDB_MySQL">
        <sql driver="${sql.driver}"
            url="${sql.url}"
            userid="${sql.user}"
            password="${sql.pass}"
            classpath="mysql-connector-java-3.0.9-stable-bin.jar"
            src="sample_project.sql"/>
    </target>
```

The last target, `dropDB_MySQL`, is used to drop the database, `sample_project`, just in case something has gone wrong and a user wants to start over from scratch. Prior to performing this operation, a user should probably provide a query asking the user if this operation is really desired, as shown in the following code:

```
    <target name="dropDB_MySQL">
        <input message="Do you really want to delete this table (y/n)?"
validargs="y,n" addproperty="do.delete" />
        <condition property="do.abort">
            <equals arg1="n" arg2="${do.delete}"/>
        </condition>
        <fail if="do.abort">Build aborted by user.</fail>
        <sql driver="${sql.driver}" url="${sql.url}" userid="${sql.user}"
password="${sql.pass}" >
            <classpath>
            <pathelement location="mysql-connector-java-3.0.9-stable-bin.jar"/>
        </classpath>
            drop database sample_project;
        </sql>
    </target>
</project>
```

Sequence	Target	Action
2	createTables_MySQL	Creates tables for operations/testing
1	createDB_MySQL	Creates database for table adds
3	dropDB_MySQL	Drops database

Scenario 2

For Scenario 2, a simple, linear workflow application that grades student homework submissions demonstrates how to use both Java and Ant to perform document collection and processing. The following `build.xml` script employs a custom Ant task to migrate archive files to a designated collection directory so that a small set of rules can be applied to individual source code files inside the archived artifact to ensure that proper requirements have been implemented in them.

The Ant script that follows implements the `taskdef` task so a custom-made task application named `CollectTask` can be run. The `path id` tags—labeled `compile.cp` and `run.cp`, respectively—reference dependencies that are needed to run both the `CollectTask` and `Test` applications. When the Ant build file is invoked, the default tag `main` is called, which in turn executes the `CollectTask` application that reads an archived file for processing by the subsequent `Test` program:

```xml
<?xml version="1.0"?>
<project name="Test" default="main" basedir=".">

    <property name="test.dir" value="." />
    <property name="ant.jar" value="ant.jar" />

    <taskdef name="testTask" classpathref="compile.cp" classname="CollectTask"/>

    <path id="compile.cp">
        <pathelement location="${test.dir}"/>
    </path>

    <path id="run.cp">
        <pathelement location="${ant.jar}" />
        <pathelement location="${test.dir}"/>
    </path>

    <target name="main">
        <testTask fileDirectory="C:\\Java_6_book\\ANT\\test\\jars"/>
        <java classpathref="run.cp" classname="com.javaSE6.Test"/>
    </target>

</project>
```

`CollectTask` extends the abstract `Task` class that serves as the base class for all Ant tasks. As you can see in the script, the `execute` method implements the task itself and receives the `directoryName` reference from the build file by means of inheritance so the application can retrieve archive files from that directory. Essentially, the application attempts to aggregate all archive files from the designated directory so they can be processed, or graded, by the workflow algorithms:

```java
import java.io.*;
import java.util.*;

import org.apache.tools.ant.BuildException;
import org.apache.tools.ant.Task;

public class CollectTask extends Task
{
    private String directoryName;

    // The method executing the task
    public void execute() throws BuildException {
        File dir = new File(directoryName);

        String[] children = dir.list();
        if (children == null) {
            System.out.println("Either directory " + directoryName + " does not exist
or is not a directory");
        } else {
            try {
                String outList[] = null;
                for (int i=0; i < children.length; i++) {
                    // Get filename of file or directory
                    String filename = children[i];
                    outList = runExecutable("jar xvf " + directoryName +
File.separatorChar + filename);
                }
            } catch(Exception e) {
                System.out.println("EXCEPTION: " + e.toString());
            }
        }
    }

}
```

The runExecutable method runs the external Java archive tool named jar to extract the files that reside in the archive. A List class is implemented to capture the sequence of events that are rendered to the Java console during execution so they can be returned to the execute method that invokes it:

```java
static public String[] runExecutable(String cmd) throws IOException
{
    List<String> list = new ArrayList<String>();
    Process proc = Runtime.getRuntime().exec(cmd);

    InputStream istream = proc.getInputStream();
    BufferedReader br = new BufferedReader(new InputStreamReader(istream));

    // read output lines from command
    String str;
    while ((str = br.readLine()) != null)
        list.add(str);

    try {
        proc.waitFor();
    } catch (InterruptedException e) {
```

```
            System.out.printf("%s\n",e.toString());
    }

    if (proc.exitValue() != 0)
        System.out.printf("%s\n","exit process status is non-zero");

    br.close();

    return (String[]) list.toArray(new String[0]);
}

    // The setter for the "fileDirectory" attribute
    public void setFileDirectory(String directoryName)
    {
        this.directoryName = directoryName;
    }
```

Once the archived contents are placed on the file system, the Test application parses comments from the individual files by means of regular expressions to ensure that the homework requirements have been properly incorporated into the submission:

```
package com.javaSE6;

import java.lang.reflect.*;
import java.util.logging.Logger;
import java.util.regex.*;
import java.io.*;

public class Test {
    private static Logger logger = Logger.getLogger("Test");

    public Test() {}

    public static int getComments(String filename) {
        int points = 0;
        String comment = "";
        try {
            System.out.printf("%s\n", filename);
            BufferedReader br = new BufferedReader(new FileReader(new
File(filename)));
            String line = "";
            StringBuffer buff = new StringBuffer();
            while ((line = br.readLine()) != null) {
                buff.append(line + "Z!Z");
            }
            br.close(); br = null;

            Pattern p1 = Pattern.compile ("/\\*\\*?([^\\*][^/]*)\\*/");
            Matcher m1 = p1.matcher(buff.toString());
```

The `while` loop in this code snippet processes comment notations detected from regular expression patterns so that individual lines can be marked and grading points can be established:

```
int ctr = 1;
while (m1.find()) {
    comment = m1.group(1);
    comment = comment.trim();

    // Remove the leading newline.
    comment = comment.replaceAll("^Z!Z", "");
    comment = comment.trim();

    // Remove the trailing newline.
    comment = comment.replaceAll("Z!Z$", "");
    comment = comment.trim();

    // Add in all the middle newlines.
    comment = comment.replaceAll("Z!Z", "\n");

    System.out.printf("%s\n", comment);
}
} catch (Exception e) {
    System.out.printf("%s\n", e.toString());
}
if ( comment.equals("") )
    points -= 5;
return points;
}
```

After the `Test` application is invoked by the Ant script, the `main` method will be run to test individual method implementations for proper return values and naming conventions by using the Java Reflection API, which serves as a mechanism to retrieve information about a class:

```
static public void main(String argv[]) {
    // starting grade
    int grade = 100;

    try {
        ActorImpSingleton ais1 = new ActorImpSingleton(new Actor1Imp());
        Actor1 actor1 = new Actor1();
        String s = actor1.displayReview();
        if (s == null) grade -= 5;

        Class c = Class.forName("com.javaSE6.Actor1");
        Method methodNames[] = c.getDeclaredMethods();
        for (int i = 0; i < methodNames.length; i++) {
            logger.info("method= " + methodNames[i].toString());
        }
        int points = getComments(".\\com\\javaSE6\\Actor1.java");
    }
    catch(Exception e)
    {
```

```
            logger.info("Exception: " + e.toString());
        }
        logger.info("FINAL grade is " + grade);
    }
}
```

Hopefully, the concepts implemented in the process flow application for Scenario 2 demonstrate the powerful scripting capabilities of Ant when combined with the error handling and string processing strengths of the Java programming language.

Scenario 3

Scenario 3 addresses the creation of executable JAR files for a sample GUI application called Book AuthorSearch. Notice the following <manifest> tag that specifies the application's main class name. This is provided so the create JAR file can be clicked and the application will be run automatically:

```
<project name="test" default="all" >

    <target name="init" description="initialize the properties.">
     <tstamp/>
     <property name="build" value="./build" />
    </target>

    <target name="clean" depends="init" description="clean up the output
directories.">
        <delete dir="${build}" />
    </target>

    <target name="prepare" depends="init" description="prepare the output
directory.">
        <mkdir dir="${build}" />
    </target>

    <target name="compile" depends="prepare" description="compile the Java
source.">
        <javac srcdir="./src/book" destdir="${build}">
        </javac>
    </target>

    <target name="package" depends="compile" description="package the Java classes
into a jar.">
        <jar destfile="${build}/BookAuthorSearch.jar" basedir="${build}">
          <manifest>
            <attribute name="Main-Class" value="book.BookAuthorSearch" />
          </manifest>
        </jar>
    </target>
```

The last target, run, is used to invoke the BookAuthorSearch JAR file for execution. The JAR file is an important feature that allows Java applications to be easily packaged for deployment:

```
    <target name="run" description="Run the application.">
        <classpath>
            <pathelement location=" BookAuthorSearch.jar "/>
        </classpath>
    </java>
</target>

<target name="all" depends="clean,package" description="Compile and package."/>

</project>
```

With tightened schedules, smaller development teams, and remote development operations, it is paramount for projects to employ Ant so important processes can be captured and implemented in an easy manner by anyone. Consistent process operations ensure that builds are not corrupted and development and deployment activities can go forward in a less painful way than those programs that operate in an ad hoc fashion.

Maven 2

Maven 2 is an alternative open source configuration management distribution that is similar to Ant, which can be used to build, test, and deploy components during the life cycle of a program. Maven 2 differs from its predecessor distribution, Maven 1, in that its directory structure consists of two subdirectories where source code and target output files should reside. Figure 2-6 shows a sample file system tree that outlines this structure for the following sample Maven 2 script to demonstrate its usage. File systems that do not adhere to this structure can be overridden by the project descriptor.

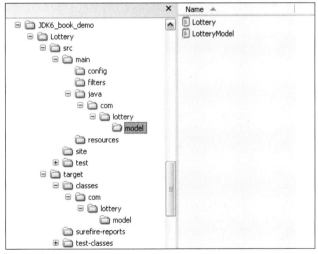

Figure 2-6

The Maven 2 demonstration script implements some Java classes for a lottery number generation application that performs simple generation and lookup operations of lottery numbers from a statically defined table. Notice that the `src` directory contains all of the source material needed to build the project, along with test code and other resources that might be needed to assist in the build. The `target` directory is utilized to collect all outputs that are derived from the build components in the `src` directory.

Here is a table that also visualizes how a Maven 2 tree structure might look. This outline reflects a more generic view of a Maven 2 project than Figure 2-6, which applies to the sample Lottery application. Typically, the `src` directory contains all of the source material for building the project, including the subdirectories for configuration and test applications. Naturally, license and readme file artifact inclusion would improve deployment and maintenance operations.

File System	Purpose
`src/main/java`	Application/Library sources
`src/main/resources`	Application/Library resources
`src/main/config`	Configuration files
`src/test/java`	Test sources
`LICENSE.txt`	Project's license
`README.txt`	Project's readme

Additional files like license information and readme files are shown to help users better understand how the Maven 2 is used, what dependencies are needed to operate the script, and what license constraints users need to know prior to deployment. Two important concepts—archetypes and transitive dependencies—are discussed subsequently to help users better understand and implement the Maven 2 build tool.

Archetypes

Archetypes serve as a templating toolkit in Maven 2, and are meant to be used to build generic templates for deployment. Maintenance stability occurs when programs manage and deploy applications with a consistent theme. Archetypes allow for this to happen.

By running the `mvn -e archetype:create -DgroupId=com.lottery -DartifactId=Lottery -Dpackagename=com.lottery` Maven 2 command from the user prompt, a simple directory structure will be established where users can add their code while adhering to a common, standardized template.

Transitive Dependencies

Transitive dependencies are a new feature in Maven 2, allowing for the automatic discovery of library dependencies. These library discoveries are managed through dependency mediation and dependency scope.

Dependency mediation is used to determine what version of a library is needed for an application to run properly. Maven 2 currently employs the "nearest definition" feature to ensure that a suitable library version is applied in your build. This means that you can specify that proper library version in the project's POM configuration file.

Dependency scope allows users to heap dependencies upon a Maven 2 script that are appropriate for a designated build stage. These dependencies consist of five different scopes: `compile`, `provided`, `runtime`, `test`, and `system`. The `compile` scope serves as the default scope that is applied across all classpaths. The `provided` scope is a non-transitive property that dictates that a particular Java Development Kit (JDK) or container will provide the scope needed to build an application. The `runtime` scope indicates to the build process that any dependencies that are required are not supplied during compilation operations. The `test` scope establishes a constraint on the build process that says dependencies are required only for the test and execution stages of a build. Lastly, the `system` scope is similar to the provided scope except that you have to provide the proper JAR files explicitly in your build. For the sake of brevity, this example does not include many of the project elements described previously. As shown in the Ant example previously, consistency across your builds is an important goal for development operations. Maven will allow you to satisfy your build and deployment goals, like Ant, but with a different technique. This scenario gives you a small taste of how to implement Maven to automate your build activities (see Figure 2-7).

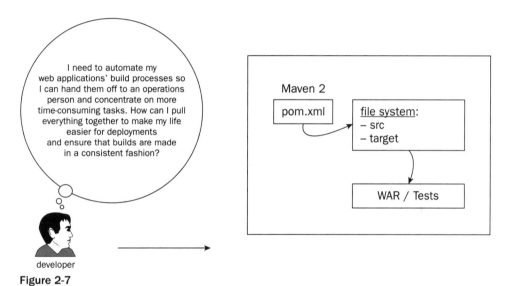

Figure 2-7

Maven implements a program descriptor file called the project object model, or POM for short, to describe all of the relevant components of a project that will be utilized for operation. This program description file is structured as a hierarchical XML file to outline a build process:

```
<project xmlns="http://maven.apache.org/POM/4.0.0"
xmlns:xsi="http://www.w3.org/2001/XMLSchema-instance"
  xsi:schemaLocation="http://maven.apache.org/POM/4.0.0
http://maven.apache.org/maven-v4_0_0.xsd">
  <modelVersion>4.0.0</modelVersion>
  <groupId>com.lottery</groupId>
  <artifactId>Lottery</artifactId>
  <packaging>jar</packaging>
  <version>1.0-SNAPSHOT</version>
  <name>Lottery number generator: Good Luck</name>
  <url>http://maven.apache.org</url>
  <dependencies>
```

```
        <dependency>
          <groupId>junit</groupId>
          <artifactId>junit</artifactId>
          <version>3.8.1</version>
          <scope>test</scope>
        </dependency>
      </dependencies>
      <build>
        <finalName>Lottery</finalName>
        <plugins>
            <plugin>
                <groupId>org.apache.maven.plugins</groupId>
                <artifactId>maven-compiler-plugin</artifactId>
                <configuration>
                    <source>1.5</source>
                    <target>1.5</target>
                </configuration>
            </plugin>
        </plugins>
      </build>
    </project>
```

A JavaBean implementation class named `Lottery` allows the Maven operation to create lottery objects for member and lottery number processing. Once an object has been created, it can easily be referenced by using the `accessor` methods to collect data affiliated with that object:

```
package com.lottery.model;

public class Lottery
{
    private String lotteryGroupMember;
    private String lotteryNumbers;

    public Lottery() {
        super();
    }

    public Lottery(String lotteryGroupMember, String lotteryNumbers) {
        super();
        this.lotteryGroupMember = lotteryGroupMember;
        this.lotteryNumbers = lotteryNumbers;
    }

    public String getLotteryGroupMember() {
        return lotteryGroupMember;
    }

    public void setLotteryGroupMember(String lotteryGroupMember) {
        this.lotteryGroupMember = lotteryGroupMember;
    }

    public String getLotteryNumbers() {
        return lotteryNumbers;
```

```
        }

        public void setLotteryNumbers(String lotteryNumbers) {
            this.lotteryNumbers = lotteryNumbers;
        }

    }
```

Data model and retrieval operations are performed by the `LotteryModel` class. The `lotteryObject` array houses individual `Lottery` objects for reference by the `findLotteryNumberByMember` method. The `getRandomNumbers` method generates a string value comprised of six random numbers. These numbers are retrieved by the `getLotteryNumbers` method in the `Lottery` class:

```java
package com.lottery.model;

import java.util.*;

public class LotteryModel
{
    private static Lottery[] lotteryObjects =
    {
        new Lottery("Louie", getRandomNumbers()),
        new Lottery("Joey", getRandomNumbers()),
        new Lottery("Timmy", getRandomNumbers())
    };

    public List<Lottery> findLotteryNumberByMember(String member)
    {
        List<Lottery> membersFound = new ArrayList<Lottery>();
        for(Lottery person : lotteryObjects)
        {
            if (person.getLotteryGroupMember().equals(member))
            {
                System.out.println("# generated = " + person.getLotteryNumbers() +
" for " + member);
                membersFound.add(person);
            }
        }
        return membersFound;
    }

    public static String getRandomNumbers()
    {
        StringBuffer sb = new StringBuffer();

        Random rand = new Random();
        for (int i=0; i < 6; i++)
        {
            sb.append(String.valueOf(rand.nextInt(60)));
            if (i + 1 != 6) sb.append(", ");
        }
        return sb.toString();
    }
}
```

Testing operations are performed by the `LotteryModelTest` class that instantiates a `LotteryModel` object that performs a lottery number lookup on the member name `Timmy` and invokes the `assertNotNull` method in the JUnit library to see if the member object is null and report if it is. Additionally, a member lookup is performed for user `Timmy` by the `getLotteryGroupMember` method in the `LotteryModel` class:

```
package com.lottery.model;

import java.util.List;
import junit.framework.TestCase;

public class LotteryModelTest extends TestCase
{
    public void testLotteryGroupMember()
    {
        LotteryModel model = new LotteryModel();
        List<Lottery> member = model.findLotteryNumberByMember("Timmy");
        assertNotNull(member);
        for(Lottery m : member)
        {
            assertEquals(m.getLotteryGroupMember(),"Timmy");
        }
    }
}
```

The implementation for the lottery member and number lookup application demonstrates how Maven POM files are declared and projects are structured on the file system to perform scripting operations. Project life cycles are managed with Maven so repetitive build tasks can be captured and run in an automated fashion without having to worry about "fat-fingering" scripts that can slow down and introduce problems to projects' maintenance activities.

Some might consider Maven to be an unnecessary complication to Ant, but both tools can be utilized in tandem or separately to build and manage Java-based projects during the life cycle of a program. Although Ant and its rich set of task libraries are more mature than Maven 2 at this point in time, Maven 2 eliminates a lot of dependencies that Ant creates and manages Java ARchive (JAR) files a lot better. Ultimately, these tools were developed to provide uniform software builds, facilitate project management operations, unify library implementations, and to propagate best practices across a project, which they both manage to deliver in their own distinct fashion.

TestNG

The TestNG test framework, developed by Cedric Buest and Alexandru Popescu, is based on the Annotations implementation distributed in the Java 5 Tiger release. TestNG's inherent strength lies in an XML configuration file, named `testng.xml`, that allows testers to support parallel testing, as well as support for method and group dependencies. Moreover, test plan designations are easily constructed and deconstructed by modifying the class names in the configuration file.

TestNG allows testers to perform test grouping operations by applying the `group` element to test methods so individual methods can be affiliated with a `group` tag. Each test suite outlined can specify whether or not a group will be included or excluded during functional testing invocations.

Figure 2-8 depicts a common scenario that all software developers encounter after code has been put into production. Inquiries are often made after new deployments by maintenance personnel and users concerning operations, application functionalities, and perceived irregularities. Developers, who often have moved on to new requirements, must refresh their memories about code artifacts that were crafted prior to new development activities. The TestNG application helps developers better understand the state of their code so determinations can be made about corrective actions that might be needed if source code has been corrupted by other developers or the code that was deployed did not accommodate user actions, which resulted in improper client-tier presentations. The source code in the TestExample application addresses this issue and could be beneficial in addressing this problem.

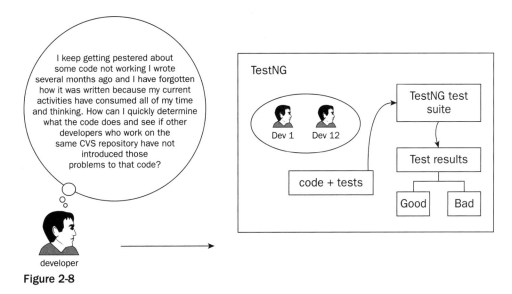

Figure 2-8

In the test example, the `testng.xml` file serves as the controller for all of the test plans scheduled to run within the TestNG application. A myriad of tags are available to testers within the framework to control the flow of test operations and the components marked for execution. Here is a sample `testng.xml` file that creates a generic test that has arranged to run only methods affiliated with the `testgroup2` community while excluding those written for the group named `testgroup1`. Notice that the `TestExample` program has been slated to run inside the test suite where its methods' annotations will dictate whether or not they will be invoked:

```
<!DOCTYPE suite SYSTEM "http://beust.com/testng/testng-1.0.dtd" >
<suite name="Example" >
    <parameter name="tester-name" value="HancholDo"/>
    <test name="Demo">
        <groups>
            <run>
                <exclude name="testgroup1"/>
                <include name="testgroup2"/>
                <include name="assert" />
            </run>
        </groups>
        <classes>
```

```
                <class name="com.javaSE6.TestExample" />
            </classes>
        </test>
    </suite>
```

Here is the Ant `build.xml` artifact that compiles and invokes the TestNG test application so that the test classes in the `testng.xml` file can be run. Proper configuration paths are established by property name inputs and `path id` references:

```
<project name="testng" default="all" basedir=".">

    <property file="build.properties"/>
    <property name="build.compiler" value="javac1.5" />
    <property name="test.output" value="${example.dir}/build/test-output"/>

    <target name="all" depends="prepare,compile,run"/>

    <path id="compile.cp">
       <pathelement location="${build.jdk15.dir}"/>
    </path>

    <path id="run.cp">
        <pathelement location="${jdk15.testng.jar}" />
        <path refid="compile.cp"/>
        <pathelement location="${example.dir}/build/classes"/>
    </path>

    <taskdef classpathref="compile.cp" name="testng"
classname="com.beust.testng.TestNGAntTask"/>

    <target name="compile" depends="prepare">
        <echo message="compiling code in ${src.dir}"/>
        <javac debug="true"
               source="1.5"
               classpathref="compile.cp"
               srcdir="${example.dir}/src"
               destdir="${example.dir}/build/classes"/>
    </target>

    <target name="prepare">
       <mkdir dir="${example.dir}/build/classes"/>
       <mkdir dir="${test.output}"/>
    </target>
```

Once the Ant application prepares the application to run, the `run` target invokes the `java` binary to run the `com.buest.testng.TestNG` application. The `-ea` argument is passed so that assertions are enabled in the program execution:

```
    <target name="run" depends="compile">
        <java fork="yes"
              classpathref="run.cp"
              classname="com.beust.testng.TestNG">
          <arg value="-d"/>
```

```
            <arg value="${test.output}"/>
            <arg value="${example.dir}/testng.xml"/>
            <jvmarg value="-ea"/>
        </java>
        <echo>Check out --> ${test.output}\index.html for a TestNG HTML report</echo>
    </target>

    <target name="clean">
        <delete dir="${example.dir}/build/classes"/>
        <delete dir="${test.output}"/>
        <antcall target="prepare"/>
    </target>

</project>
```

Now that the Ant `build.xml` file has invoked the `run` target on the `TestExample` application, all of the annotation and configuration constraints will be placed on it by `testng.xml` file. Methods that annotated with the `beforeSuite = true` reference are called before any tests in a test suite have been run. Moreover, methods annotated with the `afterTestClass = true` reference will be invoked after test classes have been run. Annotated methods implementing `before/afterTestMethod = true` tags have their methods run before and after the enabled methods dictated by the `testng.xml` are run:

```
package com.javaSE6;

import org.testng.annotations.Configuration;
import org.testng.annotations.ExpectedExceptions;
import org.testng.annotations.Test;

@Test(groups = { "testgroup2" }, enabled = true )
public class TestExample
{
  @Configuration(beforeSuite = true)
  public static void setupClass() {
   System.out.printf("%s\n","run Before Suite implementation");
  }

  @Configuration(afterTestClass = true)
  public static void tearDownClass() {
   System.out.printf("%s\n","Tearing down classes");
  }

  @Configuration(beforeTestMethod = true)
  public void beforeTestMethod() {
   System.out.printf("%s\n","run Before Method Invocation");
  }

  @Configuration(afterTestMethod = true)
  public void afterTestMethod() {
   System.out.printf("%s\n","run After Method Invocation");
  }
```

Group annotations are run when they are included in the `testng.xml` configuration file. Because the `testgroup2` groups have been enabled, they will be run and output their text accordingly:

```java
@Test(groups = { "testgroup1" })
public void testMethod1() {
  System.out.printf("%s\n",".....  TESTGROUP1");
}

@Test(groups = { "testgroup1" } )
public void testMethod2() {
  System.out.printf("%s\n",".....  TESTGROUP1");
}

@Test(groups = { "testgroup2" })
public void testMethod3() {
  System.out.printf("%s\n",".....  TESTGROUP2");
}

}
```

This sample TestNG script demonstrates a simple test execution on a fairly benign test application, but imagine how easy it can be applied to more difficult test activities by applying annotation tags to test methods and applications to dictate program flows and controlling them through the implementation of a flexible XML configuration file.

XDoclet

XDoclet is a wonderful tool that can be downloaded from the SourceForge web site at `http://xdoclet.sourceforge.net/` to ensure that consistencies are realized with your development operations. XDoclet can be especially helpful on projects that involve disparate sets of developers who are working from a common source code repository. Consider all the times you have halted your development activities because someone forgot to add entries in the deployment descriptor and included the code that refers to that entry or when the entry itself was delivered but the code was not checked in. That can be particularly frustrating during final deployment migrations. XDoclet can alleviate those occurrences because developers can embed their mappings in their code, and build files can parse through that code to generate the appropriate mappings needed for deployment. Additionally, extraneous mappings can be appended to the deployment descriptor (`web.xml`) by making entries in `servlets.xml` and `servlet-mappings.xml`. This scenario appends JavaServer Page (JSP) mappings to the deployment descriptor through the `servlets.xml` file for browser visualization (see Figure 2.9).

You can implement the following script to properly map your servlet and JSP entries in your deployment descriptor using the `XDoclet` libraries. Naturally, the first part of your script outlines the properties needed for file transfer, manipulation, and packaging:

```xml
<?xml version="1.0" encoding="UTF-8"?>
<project name="XDoclet servlet/jsp" default="build-war" basedir=".">
<description>XDoclet script generation for Servlets/JSPs</description>
<property name="app.name" value="resubmit"/>
<property name="src.dir" location="src"/>
  <property name="build.dir" location="build"/>
  <property name="dist.dir" location="dist"/>
  <property name="lib.dir" location="lib"/>
```

```
<property name="merge.dir" location="mergeDir"/>
<property name="generated.dir" location="generated"/>
<property name="web.deployment.dir" location="${generated.dir}/webdeployment"/>
<property name="xdoclet.lib.dir" location="xdocletlib"/>
<path id="compile.path">
  <fileset dir="${lib.dir}" includes="*.jar"/>
</path>
<path id="xdoclet.lib.path">
  <fileset dir="${lib.dir}" includes="*.jar"/>
  <fileset dir="${xdoclet.lib.dir}" includes="*.jar"/>
</path>
```

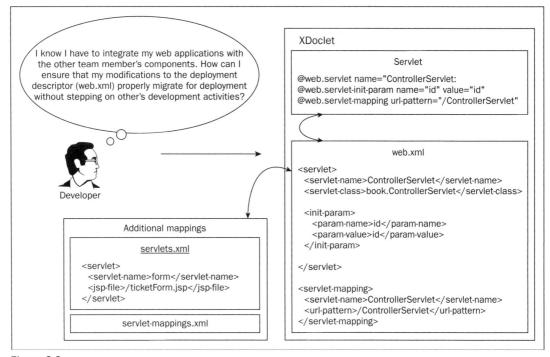

Figure 2-9

The `clean` target is typically used to clean up the environment prior to build operations so a clean slate can be worked on without having to worry about residual files corrupting processing activities. The target block also creates new directories for file transfer and deployment once the previous directories have been purged from the file system:

```
<target name="clean">
  <delete dir="${gen.src.dir}/org"/>
  <delete dir="${web.deployment.dir}"/>
  <delete dir="${build.dir}"/>
  <delete dir="${dist.dir}"/>
  <delete dir="${generated.dir}"/>
  <mkdir dir="${build.dir}" />
```

```
    <mkdir dir="${build.dir}/WEB-INF" />
    <mkdir dir="${build.dir}/WEB-INF/classes" />
    <mkdir dir="${build.dir}/WEB-INF/lib" />
</target>
```

The `generate-web` target implements the `WebDocletTask` libraries to parse the servlet source file to strip the servlet's mapping attributes. Once that has been performed, the Ant script copies the deployment descriptor to the `/WEB-INF` directory of the web application and the JavaServer Pages to the `Web` directory:

```
<target name="generate-web">
  <taskdef name="webdoclet" classname="xdoclet.modules.web.WebDocletTask"
classpathref="xdoclet.lib.path"/>
  <webdoclet destdir="${build.dir}/WEB-INF/classes" mergeDir="${merge.dir}">
    <fileset dir="${src.dir}">
      <include name="**/*.java" />
    </fileset>
    <deploymentdescriptor destdir="${web.deployment.dir}" distributable="false" />
  </webdoclet>
  <!-- copy files to appropriate directories -->
  <copy todir="${build.dir}/WEB-INF">
    <fileset dir="${web.deployment.dir}">
      <include name="**/*.xml" />
    </fileset>
  </copy>
  <copy todir="${build.dir}">
    <fileset dir="${basedir}/web/jsp">
      <include name="**/*.jsp" />
    </fileset>
  </copy>
</target>
```

The `compile` target is invoked from the `build-clean` target. This compiles the source code so it can be properly packaged for deployment:

```
<target name="compile" depends="generate-web">
  <javac destdir="${build.dir}/WEB-INF/classes" classpathref="xdoclet.lib.path">
    <src path="${src.dir}"/>
  </javac>
</target>
```

The `package` target creates a Web ARchive file (WAR) for distribution. Ideally, you could build a target to deploy the WAR file to your application server's `Web` container for execution:

```
<target name="package" depends="generate-web">
  <jar destfile="${build.dir}/${app.name}.war" basedir="${build.dir}"/>
</target>
<target name="build-clean" depends="clean,compile"/>
<target name="build-war" depends="build-clean,package"/>
</project>
```

The next scenario is common for many distributed system applications that use Hibernate as their Object/Relational (O/R) tool to gain access to back-end data with domain objects (see Figure 2-10).

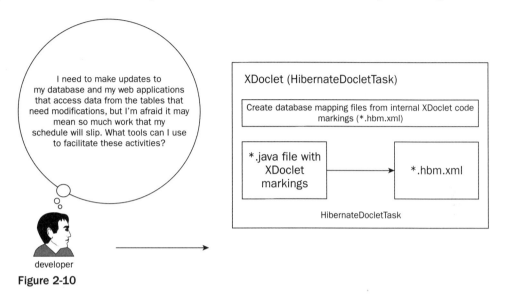

Figure 2-10

Here domain object modeling is shown for the Storefront application so object member data can easily be accessed through get/set accessor methods. Essentially, individual state items are matched to database attributes in the STOREFRONT database that is referenced by the @hibernate.class tag. Note, though, that this application only outlines the get/set methods for the productid attribute; methods also need to be created for the category, name, description, and stockdate attributes that were omitted for the sake of brevity. This program reveals how XDoclet operates as a code generation engine by creating external resource files from JavaDoc-like markings inside the class file. When the XDocletHibernateTask class is invoked from the Ant file, it reads this file and strips out the tags associated with the @ sign to create mappings used to access back-end data:

```
package com.domainobjects;

import java.math.BigDecimal;
import java.util.Date;

/**
    @hibernate.class table="STOREFRONT" mutable="false" schema="${db.schema}"
*/

public class Storefront
{
    private BigDecimal productid;
    private String category;
    private String name;
    private String description;
```

```
        private Date stockdate;

        /**
         *    @hibernate.id column="productid"  generator-class="assigned"
         *    @return Returns the productid
         */
        public BigDecimal getProductid() {
            return this.productid;
        }

        /**
         *    @param productid - The productid to set.
         */
        public void setProductid(BigDecimal productid) {
            this.productid = productid;
        }

        /* perform same operations for these attributes too
        column="CATEGORY"
        column="NAME"
        column="DESCRIPTION"
        column="STOCKDATE"
        */
}
```

Normally, good programming practices dictate that business logic should be placed in a JavaBean component to separate it from scripting logic in a Java Server Page (JSP), but in order to demonstrate the concepts of this rather simple example, it is included in this JSP to demonstrate how to invoke the Hibernate domain objects to collect and render database information from the Storefront database:

```
<%@ page language="java" import="net.sf.hibernate.*" %>
<%@ page language="java" import="java.util.*, java.sql.*, java.io.*" %>
<%@ page language="java" import="com.domainobjects.*" %>
<%@ page language="java" import="com.store.*" %>

<%
Session sess = null;
Transaction tx = null;

try {
    sess = HibernateSessionFactory.currentSession();
    tx = sess.beginTransaction();

    if (sess == null)
        System.out.println("[index.jsp] session is NULL.");
    else {
        String cat = "kitchen"; // retrieve kitchen items only
        List items = sess.find("from Storefront as s");
        %>
        <table>
          <tr>
            <td bgcolor="#cccccc">ProductID</td>
            <td bgcolor="#cccccc">Category</td>
```

```
                    <td bgcolor="#cccccc">Name</td>
            </tr>
            <%
            for (Iterator iter = items.iterator(); iter.hasNext();) {
                Storefront store = (Storefront) iter.next();
                %>
                <tr>
                    <td><%=store.getProductid()%></td>
                    <td><%=store.getCategory()%></td>
                    <td><%=store.getName()%></td>
                </tr>
                <%
            }
            tx.commit();
            sess.close();
            %>
        </table>
        <%
    }
} catch (HibernateException e) {
    // perform rollback and session closure here
}
%>
```

Hibernate domain object compilations and distributions are implemented in the build.xml file here by stepping through a sequence of Ant tasks. Java compilation operations rely on the classpath items set within the path_id reference.

```xml
<?xml version="1.0"?>
<project name="project" default="dist">

    <property file="build.properties" />
    <property name="app.name" value="hibernate" />
    <property name="app.version" value="1" />
    <property name="db.schema" value="<place database schema here>" />

    <path id="classpath.build">
        <fileset dir="lib\runtime" />
        <fileset dir="lib\build" />
        <fileset dir="lib" />
    </path>

    <target name="deploy" depends="compile">
        <copy todir="build">
            <fileset dir="web" />
        </copy>
        <copy todir="build\WEB-INF\lib">
            <fileset dir="lib\runtime" />
        </copy>
    </target>

    <target name="dist" depends="deploy">
        <copy todir="${deploy.home}\webapps\${app.name}">
```

```
            <fileset dir="build" />
        </copy>
    </target>

    <target name="compile" depends="config">
        <javac srcdir="src" destdir="build\WEB-INF\classes"
classpathref="classpath.build" debug="true" />
        <copy todir="build\WEB-INF\classes">
            <fileset dir="src">
                <exclude name="**/*.java" />
            </fileset>
        </copy>
    </target>
```

The config target depends on the init target to ensure that all of the directories are made where the build file classes and libraries will be placed. A task definition is crafted to link the HibernateDocletTask class with the hibernate tag so mappings will be generated from the Storefront XDoclet markings when it is invoked:

```
    <target name="config" depends="init">
        <taskdef name="hibernate" classpathref="classpath.build"
classname="xdoclet.modules.hibernate.HibernateDocletTask" />
        <hibernate destDir="build/WEB-INF/classes" mergeDir="merge" >
            <fileset dir="src">
                <include name="**/*.java" />
            </fileset>
            <hibernate version="2.0" />
        </hibernate>
        <copy todir="build/WEB-INF/classes">
            <fileset dir="src" includes="**/*.xml" />
        </copy>
    </target>

    <target name="init">
        <mkdir dir="build\WEB-INF\classes" />
        <mkdir dir="build\WEB-INF\lib" />
    </target>

    <target name="clean">
        <delete dir="build" />
    </target>

</project>
```

The hibernate.cfg.xml file outlines database configuration attributes so that the SessionFactory application can easily connect to the project's back-end database system. Here a reference is made to the Storefront mapping file, Storefront.hbm.xml, so it will be available to the client code that accesses data from the Storefront database:

```
<?xml version='1.0' encoding='utf-8'?>
<!DOCTYPE hibernate-configuration PUBLIC "-//Hibernate/Hibernate Configuration
DTD//EN" "http://hibernate.sourceforge.net/hibernate-configuration-2.0.dtd">
<hibernate-configuration>
  <session-factory name="SessionFactory">
    <!-- example connection pool. -->
    <property name="hibernate.connection.driver_class"
>oracle.jdbc.driver.OracleDriver</property>
    <property name="hibernate.connection.url"
>jdbc:oracle:thin:@<hostname>:1521:<SID></property>
        <property name="hibernate.connection.username" >user</property>
        <property name="hibernate.connection.password" >password</property>
        <property
name="hibernate.dialect">net.sf.hibernate.dialect.Oracle9Dialect</property>
        <property name="hibernate.show_sql">true</property>
        <property name="hibernate.statement_cache.size">0</property>
        <property name="hibernate.jdbc.use_scrollable_resultset">true</property>
        <property
name="net.sf.hibernate.connection.ConnectionProvider">net.sf.hibernate.connection.U
serSuppliedConnectionProvider</property>
        <property name="hibernate.outer_join">true</property>
        <!-- Mapping files -->
        <mapping resource="com/domainobjects/Storefront.hbm.xml" />
  </session-factory>
</hibernate-configuration>
```

As a software developer, you will consistently be asked to deliver your software with new features and code corrections throughout the life cycle of a program. The trick is to familiarize yourself with tools like XDoclet to generate code for you so that integration challenges can be mitigated.

JMeter

Software development typically is performed as a solitary endeavor until it is time to integrate with new and existing components on your deployment system. Understanding how your applications will perform under real-life conditions is a legitimate concern for all software developers.

With the JMeter application, available at `http://jakarta.apache.org/jmeter/`, you can generate and manage user simulations for your applications using a robust GUI application console to collect performance measurements. This is performed by adding ThreadGroups to your test plans to simulate users and configuration elements that simulate and stimulate your applications (see Figure 2-11).

With enterprise development efforts, performance discovery cannot be performed early enough in your development activities to determine what kind of loads your applications can handle alone and when packaged with other applications targeted for deployment.

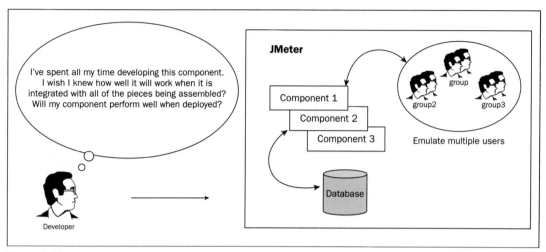

Figure 2-11

A simple Ant script is shown here to demonstrate how JMeter scripts can be run externally from the JMeter application where the tests were generated and recorded. To run these scripts, a Java archive file named `ant-jmeter.jar` needs to be added to the Ant execution path. This file can be procured from `www.programmerplanet.org/ant-jmeter/`. The `main` target invokes the `jmeter` task definition, which in turn runs the test plans specified within the task:

```xml
<?xml version="1.0"?>
<project name="Test" default="main" basedir=".">

  <property name="jmeter.dir" value="c:\Java_6_book\JMeter" />
  <property name="jmeter.save.saveservice.output_format" value="xml" />

  <taskdef name="jmeter"
classname="org.programmerplanet.ant.taskdefs.jmeter.JMeterTask"/>

  <target name="main">
    <jmeter jmeterhome="${jmeter.dir}"
resultlog="${jmeter.dir}/tests/JMeterResults.jtl">
      <testplans dir="${jmeter.dir}" includes="*.jmx"/>
    </jmeter>
    <xslt in="${jmeter.dir}/tests/JMeterResults.jtl"
          out="${jmeter.dir}/tests/JMeterResults.html"
          style="${jmeter.dir}/tests/jmeter-results-detail-report.xsl"/>
  </target>

</project>
```

This test example is fairly simplistic and easy to generate and run, but JMeter possesses many more sophisticated techniques and tools that can be utilized for optimizing applications for a program that complement its testing capabilities. But, rather than delving into a broad range of scenarios to demonstrate some of the other load testing capabilities of JMeter and the wide range of testing protocols that can be applied, it would probably be more beneficial to describe from a high-level view all of the different capabilities the tool possesses that can facilitate your development operations.

JMeter has eight different components that measure your application's performance in your development space. These components are as follows:

❑ **Logic Controllers** allow testers to customize logic flows in a test plan so requests are transmitted according to controller determinations. This means that applications can be run in preset loop intervals or in random algorithms to satisfy test objectives.

❑ **Listeners** are conduits to data that are collected by the JMeter application during testing operations. Data collections can either be saved off to files or shown in graphical representations like graphs and tables. Visual representations of test data enhance analysis operations so speculations about source code robustness can be gauged, which can lead to better software deployments.

❑ **Sampler plans** establish user requests that need to be passed to a user test plan. Some sampler requests are FTP, HTTP, JDBC, LDAP, and SOAP processes.

❑ **Config Elements** are used by the JMeter application to perform disparate protocol requests to back-end components like Web, database, and Lightweight Directory Access Protocol (LDAP) servers. TCP and FTP requests can also be performed to test your system's components.

❑ **Assertions** can be implemented to discover problems with HTML tags and error strings that are introduced by testing activities. These assertions enable users to test assumptions about a program, which fundamentally increases confidence that an application will be deployed properly and satisfy the customer requirements established at the onset of a project.

❑ **Pre- and Post-Processor** tests act like servlet filters that can manipulate code prior to and after tests have been run. When web components are pre-processed, requests can be modified prior to being passed along to a service end point. This would occur when a user attempts to translate an XML response to HTML prior to rendering content to a browser. Alternatively, postprocessing could be used to process response objects during web testing activities.

❑ **ThreadGroups** typically allow users to manually craft simulations through GUI controls in the JMeter console. Moreover, they are used to generate, capture, and replay tests automatically by recording navigation flows using the applications' Recording Controller.

❑ **Timers** allow the JMeter application to perform user-specified delay requests for threaded operations

The latest JMeter 2.1 release has introduced many new features, as shown in Figure 2-12, to load test the functional behavior of your system and gather performance metrics so your applications can be deployed with some assurance that they can handle difficult user loads.

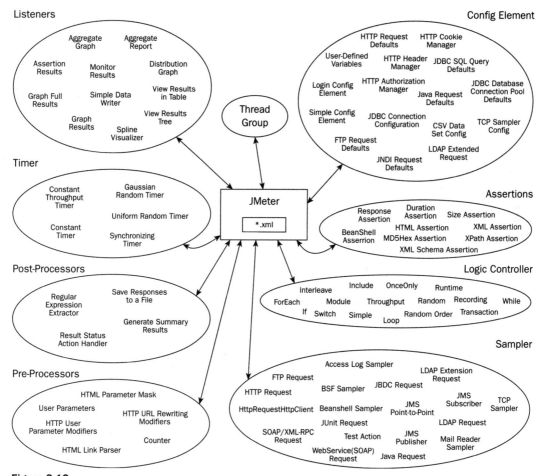

Figure 2-12

Summary

This chapter carried you from the abstract concepts of what it means to write quality software to the concrete details of how software tools are used in Java development environments. Along the way, you were provided information to give you a feel for what it is like to be a Java developer, including the following points:

- ❏ The principles of software quality by which developers live
- ❏ The habits that an effective software developer exhibits
- ❏ A few of the methodologies that software developers use
- ❏ How and why to use many of the tools found in Java development environments

Chapter 3 continues the brief aside into thinking like a professional Java developer by discussing design patterns, which provide an intellectual repository from which you can learn to avoid common problems that face many Java developers, as well as how the developers of the Java programming language solved many of their issues.

3

Exploiting Patterns in Java

In Chapter 2, you learned about half of "thinking like a Java developer" when software development methodologies were discussed. This chapter handles the other half—the use of patterns to make you an effective Java developer.

This is not a patterns book. This chapter is included because patterns are critical to understanding and communicating the designs of application programming interfaces, tools, and other applications. This is because the vast majority of these technologies are built on top of design patterns.

If I had to pick one aspect of software engineering that I absolutely love, hands down, it would be software design. Designing software well is challenging and it requires a combination of creativity and problem-solving skills. The experience of creating a solution in software can be very rewarding. If you are just becoming familiar with the Java programming language, software design can be a little overwhelming. It's like a blank canvas with a lot of colors from which to choose. Design decisions are difficult to make because—without experience—it is difficult to understand how the choices you make will affect the application later.

Learning design patterns is the single best way to increase your abilities as a software engineer. Technology changes very quickly. To give things a little perspective, learning a new technology is like reading a good book; learning patterns is like learning to read.

The focus of this chapter is to communicate why design patterns are important and highlight commonly occurring patterns. Hopefully, if you haven't been turned on to patterns already, this chapter will give you some reasons to pursue them.

> There are plenty of patterns books. I feel these three represent some of the best work written on the subject: Refactoring: Improving the Design of Existing Code *by Martin Fowler;* Design Patterns: Elements of Reusable Object-Oriented Software *by Erich Gamma, Richard Helm, Ralph Johnson, and John Vlissides; and* Applying UML and Patterns: An Introduction to Object-Oriented Analysis and Design and the Unified Process *by Craig Larman.*

This chapter provides you with a strong definition of a pattern, an understanding of why patterns are important, tricks to understanding a pattern, and an explanation of important Java patterns. This chapter is divided into three main sections. The first section discusses the rationale behind learning patterns and some examples of where they are used in software design. The second section, building patterns from design principles, walks you through a series of exercises that show how to form patterns from basic design principles. Finally, the important patterns section walks you through code examples of a subset of well-known design patterns.

Why Patterns Are Important

One of my father's favorite quotes was, "Experience is a good teacher, but a fool will learn from no other." In software, experience is a good teacher, but lessons learned from experienced designers can help accelerate your design skills. A pattern is a documented lesson learned.

A pattern is a proven solution to a software problem enabling reuse of software at the design level. The purpose of a pattern is to conceptually pair a problem with its design solution and then apply the solution to similar problems. Code-level reuse of software is desirable, but design-level reuse is far more flexible.

With each application you work on, none of them will be the same. There will be similarities. Being able to recognize these similarities, combined with your knowledge of design patterns, will help bring confidence to the design decisions you make.

Patterns are one of the greatest resources you will have in the design of object-oriented software. They will definitely help you to master the Java programming language, be more productive, and develop effective Java solutions.

Keys to Understanding the Java Programming Language

Patterns help you understand the Java programming language. Compared to other programming languages, Java has a steep learning curve. It's not that Java is harder to learn than other languages. Just the opposite, it has a very clean syntax and its structure is similar to other OO languages.

The language becomes difficult once you confront the vast number of APIs available to the Java programmer. The number of APIs available is a very good thing. Each API should be viewed as a tool in the toolbox for solving problems.

Leveraging existing software is a core practice in thinking like a professional Java developer. This allows you to save time and be more productive. The collection of APIs provided in the 1.6 JDK, as well as countless open source projects, represent what you don't have to build from scratch.

This book examines several APIs such as Collections, Java2D, JMX, XML, EJB, JMS, JDBC, RMI, and Web Service. The list is pretty long, but it only scratches the surface on the number of APIs available. The truth is you cannot sit down and learn them all. Thankfully, there is no reason to learn them all. This is why design patterns are so important to learning Java.

Design patterns allow you to learn a new API quickly. If you understand the patterns used in an API, you will be able to quickly understand, evaluate, and potentially integrate that code into your solution. It is much easier to learn and build on top of existing APIs than it is to reinvent the wheel and start from nothing.

This is especially true when working with the J2EE framework. If you are working on a project and hear that a decision has been made to ignore the distributed transaction processing capabilities of a J2EE application server in favor of a homegrown solution, run and don't look back. As a Java developer, you learn as much as you can and only build what you need.

J2EE is a standards-based solution. One misconception about the J2EE framework is that it is considered a product. J2EE is not a product, it is a specification. Sun publishes a set of requirements that describe a J2EE container. Software vendors then implement these specs and sell their container as part of a standards-based solution. This is important because the folks at Sun are pattern savvy. The APIs are all based on patterns. This is very good news for you and an excellent reason to gain a strong understanding of design patterns. If you do, you will be able to understand and leverage anything Sun throws your way.

Keys to Understanding Tools Used in Java Development

In addition to the wealth of APIs available to Java developers, there is also a large number of development tools for improving the software development process. A few tools are Ant, TestNG, and XDoclet. These tools offer extension points for integration as well as good working examples of the power of design patterns.

Ant

Ant is an XML-based build tool with several uses. One of the uses is to automate the building of a software project. It can also do the work of most scripting languages without being OS dependent. It's built using a combination of several design patterns.

TestNG

TestNG is a unit-testing framework. Establishing automated unit tests is an excellent way to prove code changes to prevent introducing new bugs into your software. To use TestNG, you must extend the framework. By understanding the patterns TestNG is built on, you will be able to take advantage of automated unit testing.

XDoclet

XDoclet is a code-generating framework. It allows you to embed metadata in the comments of your code. The metadata is used to generate supporting code as well as XML descriptor files. XDoclet makes it easy to sync derived software artifacts common when developing EJBs, servlets, and persistent data objects such as Hibernate and JDO.

Numerous other tools are available to the Java developer. Understanding the patterns these tools are built on takes some of the magic out of how they work. By understanding design patterns you will be able to use and extend these tools to build better software.

Keys to Developing Effective Java Solutions

Patterns help you build effective solutions using Java, helping you communicate design concepts as well as gain an appreciative knowledge of underlying design principles.

Develop Common Design Vocabulary

There is a lot of value in the pattern name. The name provides a common vocabulary for software engineers to use to communicate. The patterns in this book are taken from the widely accepted GoF.

For example, say you need two to parts of a system to communicate even though they expect different interfaces. Use the Adapter pattern. If you have a situation where several algorithms will solve the same problem, use the Strategy pattern. This chapter goes into those two patterns, as well as several others, in detail. The point of mentioning them now is to show that the name can easily convey the design.

Understand the Fundamentals of Design

This reason for learning patterns is near and dear to me. Initially, after being introduced to the concepts of object-oriented programming, I failed to see the relevance of the object-oriented concepts. It seems like more work with limited benefits. It wasn't until I was exposed to design patterns that I started to gain a real appreciation for the power of the OO concepts.

Patterns will help you fully understand fundamental design principles. Understanding the fundamentals of software design is critical to becoming a confident software designer. Patterns provide a concrete example of how to apply various design principles. Essentially, design is about making decisions. Knowing which decisions lead to good software design, and which lead to problems in the future, makes all the difference in building effective solutions.

Design decisions center on identifying the pieces of your software system and how they will work together to accomplish your objective. Good design is the result of the lessons often learned from living through a bad design nightmare.

Abstraction, *polymorphism*, and *inheritance* are the three principal concepts of object-oriented design. Abstraction is the practice of modeling the relevant aspects of real-world concepts. Polymorphism is type substitution allowing one class to take the place of another. Inheritance is the practice of creating specialization and generalization relationships between classes. These are the tools in object-oriented software that enable good design. The following is a list of design principles that are used to apply these tools.

Some design criteria to consider when building a Java solution include:

- ❑ **Protected variations.** This means that you need to isolate volatility in your application. If you feel an application component could change, then take steps to segregate that component using interfaces. Interfaces will allow you to change the implementing class without affecting existing application dependencies.

- ❑ **Low coupling.** The purpose of this design concept is to ensure that changes made in one section of code don't adversely affect another unrelated section. For example, does a user interface change require a change to the database? If so, the application could be brittle where any small change propagates throughout the software system.

- ❑ **High cohesion.** The practice of tying closely related things together tightly.

These tools and criteria are important to understanding design patterns because each pattern is the application of one or more design principles. Once you understand abstraction, polymorphism, and inheritance, it is easier to understand how patterns can reduce the complexity of software design.

Software design goals are important, but there is a large gap between goals and real implementations. Patterns bridge this gap and realize these goals; nothing teaches like a good example. The next section discusses some foundation on how to get started with patterns.

Building Patterns with Design Principles

At the core of any pattern is a collection of design principles. This section looks at a simple and unconventional approach to building patterns from the ground up. The approach is to start with a simple design and gradually make changes so the design is more flexible. Each step uses the object-oriented tools available to you in Java, as well as one or more of the design principles discussed in the previous section. Each design change becomes a step in building more complex design patterns. By following the exercises in this section, it will be clear how applying design principles makes software more flexible. This allows you to understand the mechanics behind patterns a small piece at a time.

This section starts off with the design of a single class. From this single class design, an association is added, followed by an interface. These two steps add flexibility to the single class design. Understanding this flexibility has important ramifications for understanding design patterns. The final section shows an example of merging the concepts of association and inheritance, which is common in a number of design patterns.

Designing a Single Class

A single class doesn't constitute a design pattern, but it is a design. And there is nothing wrong with simplicity. Part of the design process is assigning responsibility to an object, as in Figure 3-1.

It is very common for a class to become bloated with several methods not related to the abstraction the class represents. This can cause dependency problems down the line and does not fit with the high cohesion design principle. In this example, the `Teacher` class contains several methods related to teacher responsibilities. The solution is to *push to the right* or delegate the methods that do not belong with the abstraction. The phrase "do not belong" is subjective. Any design decision could be wrong. As long as you justify it with sound OO principles, don't worry — you can always change it later when the problem is clearer.

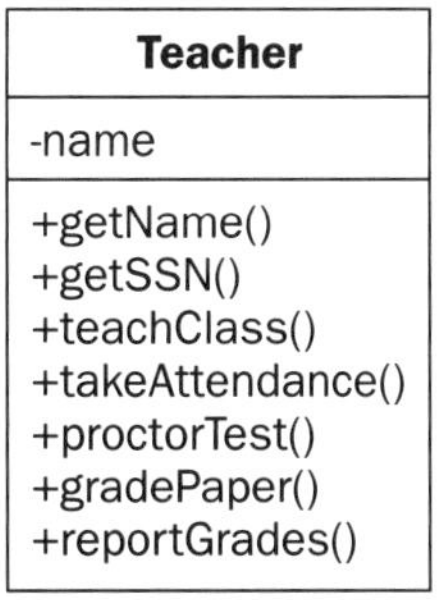

Teacher
-name
+getName() +getSSN() +teachClass() +takeAttendance() +proctorTest() +gradePaper() +reportGrades()

Figure 3-1

Creating an Association between Classes

All the teacher responsibilities have been delegated to a class called `TeacherResponsibilities`. Again visualize the methods being pushed to the right or delegated to another class. Figure 3-2 shows how responsibility has been delegated through an association.

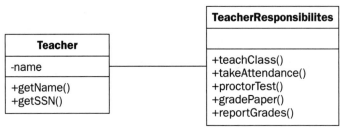

Figure 3-2

For the `TeacherResponsibilities` class to do work on behalf of the `Teacher` class, an association has to be created. The `Teacher` object holds a reference to the `TeacherResponsibilities`.

There are basically three ways this can happen:

1. The `TeacherResponsibilities` object is passed to the `Teacher` object as a parameter:

```
Teacher teacher = new Teacher("Heather");
TeacherResponsibilities responsibilities= new TeacherResponsibilities ();
teacher.setResponsibilities ( responsibilities);
```

2. The `Teacher` object creates the `TeacherResponsibilities` object:

```
public class Teacher {

private TeacherResponsibilities responsibilities = new TeacherResponsibilites();

}
```

3. The `TeacherResponsibilites` object is passed back from a method call:

```
public class Teacher {

private TeacherResponsibilities responsibilities;

    public Teacher() {
Administration admin = new Administration();
 responsibilities = admin.getResponsibilites();
    }
 }
```

These three methods determine the visibility an object shares with another in making up an association. The design might be done, but there is another design principle to address: *loose-coupling*. In specifying an association, a tight dependency between the `Teacher` and the `TeacherResponsibilites` classes has been created. The relationship is restricted to the `Teacher` and the `TeacherResponsibilites` types. That would be fine, except that it may be felt that the responsibilities will change over time. *How do you loosen the relationship and address this volatility?* The answer is to *push up* an interface.

Creating an Interface

An interface is a software contract between classes. By using the interface, the `Current` class is allowed to provide the implementation. If in the future the implementation changes, you can replace the current class with a new class. Because the `Teacher` class only depends on the `Responsibilities` interface, the `Teacher` class will not need to be modified. The UML for this design is shown in Figure 3-3.

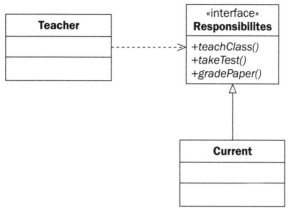

Figure 3-3

> Just a word of warning: each artifact you add to the design is one more thing to manage. Interfaces are great when establishing dependencies across components to isolate volatility, but they are not needed everywhere.

The next section combines delegation and inheritance, the concepts of the previous two sections, to create powerful object structures. An inheritance loop combines the pluggable functionality of inheritance with the separation of concerns gained with an association.

Creating an Inheritance Loop

By relating two classes with both an association and an inheritance, it is possible to create trees and graphs. Think of this as *reaching up* the class hierarchy. The inheritance relationship causes the nodes in the object structure to be polymorphic. In the example shown in Figure 3-4, a `WorkFriends` group can be manipulated using the same interface declared by the `Person` class. Another common example would be how files and folders on a file system have similar behavior. They both use common functionality such as copy, delete, and more. Composition, in the "Important Java Patterns" section of this chapter, is a good example of using an inheritance loop to allow type independent functionality.

Figure 3-4 shows the resulting class and object view of an *inheritance loop*. This is a common structure used in many design patterns including composition.

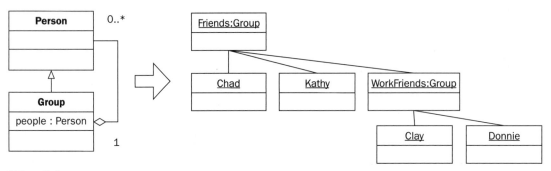

Figure 3-4

An inheritance loop is referred to as reaching up the hierarchy, as depicted in Figure 3-4. By reaching up the hierarchy, you create a relationship known as *reverse containment*. By holding a collection of a super-class from one of its subclasses it is possible to manipulate different subtypes as well as collections with the same interface.

Figure 3-5 shows one subtle change to the example in Figure 3-4. By changing the cardinality of the association between the super- and subtypes to many-to-many, it is possible to represent graphs as well as trees.

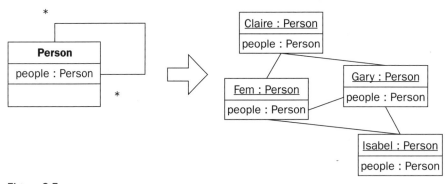

Figure 3-5

Finally, Figure 3-6 adds subtype relationships to the inheritance loop, allowing the representation of a complex data structure with methods that can be invoked with a polymorphic interface.

You have also created a common interface for each responsibility, allowing you to add new responsibilities with limited impact to the application.

The purpose of this section was to learn tricks to understanding patterns. By creating associations and using inheritance, you have been able to build some complex designs from these principles. You learned to apply these principles by remembering simple actions: push to the right, push up, and reach up. Learning these tricks will help you understand the well-known patterns in the next section.

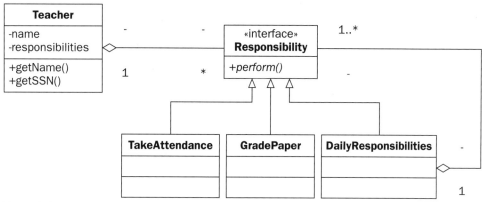

Figure 3-6

Important Java Patterns

This section shows examples of very important and well-known patterns. By learning each of these patterns, you will develop your pattern vocabulary and add to your software design toolbox. Each pattern discussed subsequently includes a description of the problem the pattern solves, the underlying principles of design at work in the pattern, and the classes that make up the pattern and how they work together.

The focus of this section is not to describe patterns in a traditional sense, but instead to provide code and concrete examples to demonstrate the types of problems that each pattern can solve. All the patterns discussed in this section are oft-adapted GoF patterns.

The patterns in this section include Adapter, Model-View-Controller, Command, Strategy, and Composite. Each pattern is discussed with a text description and a diagram showing the pattern as well as the example classes fulfilling their corresponding pattern role. The key takeaway in each case is to recognize how these classes collaborate to a solve specific problem.

Adapter

An Adapter allows components with incompatible interfaces to communicate. The Adapter pattern is a great example of how to use object-oriented design concepts. For one reason, it's very straightforward. At the same time, it's an excellent example of three important design principles: delegation, inheritance, and abstraction. Figure 3-7 shows the class structure of the Adapter pattern as well as the example classes used in this example.

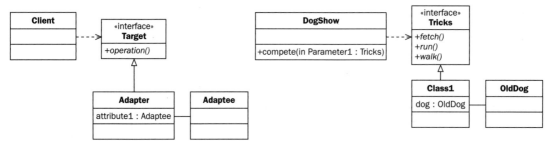

Figure 3-7

The four classes that make up the Adapter pattern are the `Target`, `Client`, `Adaptee`, and `Adapter`. Again, the problem the Adapter pattern is good at solving is incompatible interfaces. In this example, the `Adaptee` class does not implement the target interface. The solution will be to implement an intermediary class, an `Adapter`, that will implement the target interface on behalf of the `Adaptee`. Using polymorphism, the client can use either the `Target` interface or the `Adapter` class with little concern over which is which.

Target

Start off with the Target interface. The `Target` interface describes the behavior that your object needs to exhibit. It is possible in some cases to just implement the `Target` interface on the object. In some cases it is not. For example, the interface could have several methods, but you need custom behavior for only one. The `java.awt` package provides a Window adapter for just this purpose. Another example might be that the object you want to adapt, called the `Adaptee`, is vendor or legacy code that you cannot modify:

```
package wrox.pattern.adapter;

public interface Tricks {

    public void walk();
    public void run();
    public void fetch();
}
```

Client

Next, look at the client code using this interface. This is a simple exercise of the methods in the interface. The `compete()` method is dependent on the `Tricks` interface. You could modify it to support the `Adaptee` interface, but that would increase the complexity of the client code. You would rather leave the client code unmodified and make the `Adaptee` class work with the `Tricks` interface:

```
public class DogShow {

    public void compete( Tricks target){
        target.run( );
        target.walk( );
        target.fetch( );
    }
}
```

Adaptee

Now the `Adaptee` is the code that you need to use, but it must exhibit the `Tricks` interface without implementing it directly:

```java
package wrox.pattern.adapter;

public class OldDog {
  String name;

  public OldDog(String name) {
    this.name= name;
  }
  public void walk() {
    System.out.println("walking..");
  }
  public void sleep() {
    System.out.println("sleeping..");
  }
}
```

Adapter

As you can see from the `OldDog` class, it does not implement any of the methods in the `Tricks` interface. The next code passes the `OldDog` class to the `Adapter`, which does implement the `Tricks` interface:

```java
package wrox.pattern.adapter;

public class OldDogTricksAdapter implements Tricks {
  private OldDog adaptee;

  public OldDogTricksAdapter(OldDog adaptee) {
    this.adaptee= adaptee;
  }
  public void walk() {
    System.out.println("this dog can walk.");
    adaptee.walk();
  }
  public void run() {
    System.out.println("this dog doesn't run.");
    adaptee.sleep();
  }
  public void fetch() {
    System.out.println("this dog doesn't fetch.");
    adaptee.sleep();
  }
}
```

The `Adapter` can be used anywhere that the `Tricks` interface can be used. By passing the `OldDogTricksAdapter` to the `DogShow` class, you are able to take advantage of all the code written for the `Tricks` interface as well as use the `OldDog` class unmodified.

The next section of code looks at how to establish the associations and run the example:

```
package wrox.pattern.adapter;

public class DogShow {
  //methods omitted.

  public static void main(String[] args) {

    OldDog adaptee = new OldDog("cogswell");
    OldDogTricksAdapter adapter = new OldDogTricksAdapter( adaptee );
    DogShow client = new DogShow( );
    client.compete( adapter );

  }
}
```

Model-View-Controller

The purpose of the Model-View-Controller (MVC) pattern is to separate your user interface logic from your business logic. By doing this it is possible to reuse the business logic and prevent changes in the interface from affecting the business logic. MVC, also known as Model-2, is used extensively in web development. For that reason, Chapter 8 is focused completely on this subject. You can also learn more about developing Swing clients in Chapter 4. Figure 3-8 shows the class structure of the Model-View-Controller pattern along with the classes implementing the pattern in this example.

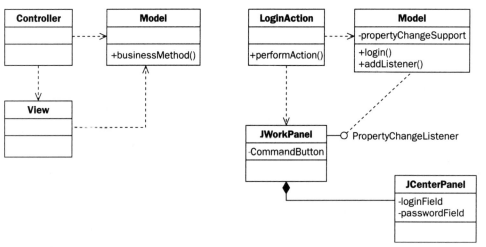

Figure 3-8

This pattern example will be a simple Swing application. The application will implement the basic login functionality. More important than the functionality is the separation of design principles that allow the model (data), controller (action), and the view (swing form) to be loosely coupled together.

Model-View-Controller is actually more than a simple pattern. It is a separation of responsibilities common in application design. An application that supports the Model-View-Controller design principle needs to be able to answer three questions. How does the application change the model? How are changes to the model reflected in the view? How are the associations between the model, view, and controller classes established? The next sections show how these scenarios are implemented in this example using a Swing application.

Scenario 1: Changing the Model

Changes to the model are pushed from the outside in. The example uses Java Swing to represent the interface. The user presses a button. The button fires an event, which is received by the controlling action. The action then changes the model (see Figure 3-9).

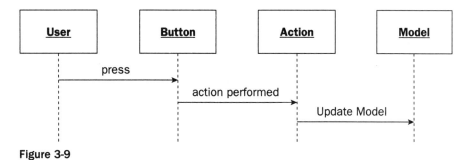

Figure 3-9

Scenario 2: Refreshing When the Model Changes

The second scenario assumes that the model has been updated by an action. The views might need to know this information, but having the model call the view directly would break the MVC separation principle requiring the model to have knowledge of the view. To overcome this, Java provides the Observer Design pattern, allowing changes from the model to "bubble out" to the view components. All views that depend on the model must register as a ChangeListener. Once registered, the views are notified of changes to the model. The notification tells the view to pull the information it needs directly from the model (see Figure 3-10).

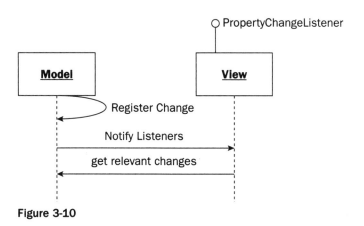

Figure 3-10

Scenario 3: Initializing the Application

The third scenario shows how to initialize the action, model, and view objects and then establish dependencies between the components (see Figure 3-11).

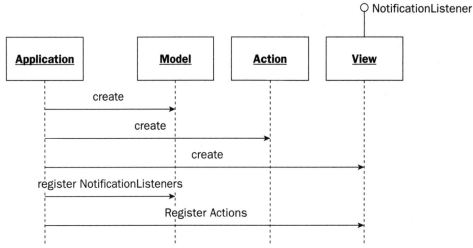

Figure 3-11

The views are registered with the model and the actions are registered with the views. The application class coordinates this.

Having discussed the collaboration scenarios between the model, view, and controller components, the next sections delve into the internals of each component, starting with the model.

Model

The Model can be any Java object or objects that represent the underlying data of the application, often referred to as the domain model. This example uses a single Java object called Model.

The functionality of the Model in this example is to support a login function. In a real application, the Model would encapsulate data resources such as a relational database or directory service:

```
package wrox.pattern.mvc;
import java.beans.PropertyChangeListener;
import java.beans.PropertyChangeSupport;

public class Model {
```

The first thing of interest in the Model is the PropertyChangeSupport member variable. This is part of the Event Delegation Model (EDM) available since JDK 1.1. The EDM is an event publisher-subscriber mechanism. It allows views to register with the Model and receive notification of changes to the Model's state:

```
    private PropertyChangeSupport changeSupport= new PropertyChangeSupport(this);
    private boolean loginStatus;
    private String login;
    private String password;
    public Model() {
      loginStatus= false;
    }
    public void setLogin(String login) {
      this.login= login;
    }
    public void getPassword(String password) {
      this.password= password;
    }
    public boolean getLoginStatus() {
      return loginStatus;
    }
```

Notice that the setLoginStatus() method fires a property change:

```
    public void setLoginStatus(boolean status) {
      boolean old= this.loginStatus;
      this.loginStatus= status;
      changeSupport.firePropertyChange("model.loginStatus", old, status);
    }

    public void login(String login, String password) {
      if ( getLoginStatus() ) {
        setLoginStatus(false);
      } else {
        setLoginStatus(true);
      }
    }
```

This addPropertyChangeListener() is the method that allows each of the views interested in the model to register and receive events:

```
    public void addPropertyChangeListener(PropertyChangeListener listener) {
      changeSupport.addPropertyChangeListener(listener);
    }
  }
```

Notice that there are no references to any user interface components from within the Model. This ensures that the views can be changed without affecting the operations of the model. It's also possible to build a second interface. For example, you could create an API using Web Services to allow automated remote login capability.

View

The View component of the application will consist of a Swing interface. Figure 3-12 shows what the user will see when the application is run.

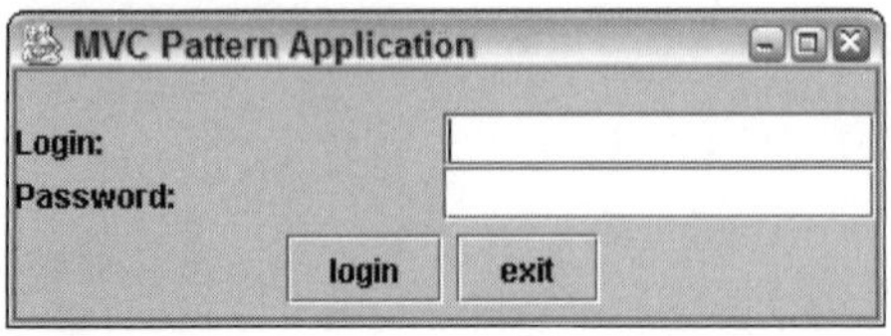

Figure 3-12

There are two `JPanel` components that make up the user interface. The first is the `CenterPanel` class that contains the login and password text boxes. The second is the `WorkPanel` that contains the login and exit command buttons as well as the `CenterPanel`.

The `CenterPanel` is a typical user data entry form. It's important to notice that there is no code to process the login in this class. Its responsibility is strictly user interface:

```
package wrox.pattern.mvc;
import java.awt.GridLayout;
import javax.swing.JLabel;
import javax.swing.JPanel;
import javax.swing.JTextField;

public class CenterPanel extends JPanel {

  private JTextField login= new JTextField(15);
  private JTextField password= new JTextField(15);

  public CenterPanel() {
    setLayout(new GridLayout(2, 2));
    add(new JLabel("Login:"));
    add(login);
    add(new JLabel("Password:"));
    add(password);
  }
  public String getLogin() {
    return login.getText();
  }
  public String getPassword() {
    return password.getText();
  }
}
```

The next user interface component, `WorkPanel`, contains `CenterPanel`. Notice that there are no references to the `WorkPanel` from the `CenterPanel`. This is an example of composition, allowing the `CenterPanel` to be switched out for another form or viewed in a different frame:

```
package wrox.pattern.mvc;
import java.awt.BorderLayout;
import java.beans.PropertyChangeEvent;
import java.beans.PropertyChangeListener;
import javax.swing.Action;
import javax.swing.JButton;
import javax.swing.JLabel;
import javax.swing.JPanel;
```

As you can see from the class declaration, the `WorkPanel` is a Swing component. In addition, it also implements the `PropertyChangeListener` interface. This allows the `WorkPanel` to register with the application model and have change notifications published to it when the Model changes. The `WorkPanel` is registered with the Model as a `PropertyChangeListener`. This allows the interface to change without affecting the domain Model, an example of low-coupled design:

```
public class WorkPanel extends JPanel implements PropertyChangeListener {
  private Model model;

  private JPanel center;
  private JPanel buttonPanel= new JPanel();
  private JLabel loginStatusLabel= new JLabel(" ");

  public WorkPanel(JPanel center, Model model) {
    this.center= center;
    this.model= model;
    init();
  }
  private void init() {
    setLayout(new BorderLayout());
    add(center, BorderLayout.CENTER);
    add(buttonPanel, BorderLayout.SOUTH);
    add(loginStatusLabel, BorderLayout.NORTH);
  }
```

When the Model changes, the `propertyChange()` method is called for all classes that registered with the Model:

```
public void propertyChange(PropertyChangeEvent evt) {
  if (evt.getPropertyName().equals("model.loginStatus")) {
    Boolean status= (Boolean)evt.getNewValue();
    if (status.booleanValue()) {
      loginStatusLabel.setText("Login was successful");
    } else {
      loginStatusLabel.setText("Login Failed");
    }
  }
}
```

The `addButton()` method allows you to do two things. First, you can configure any number of buttons. Second, it provides the action classes. They specify the work each performs when the button is pressed. The action represents the final part of the MVC pattern: the Controller. The Controller is discussed in the next section:

```
public void addButton(String name, Action action) {
  JButton button= new JButton(name);
  button.addActionListener(action);
  buttonPanel.add(button);
}

}
```

Controller

The purpose of the Controller is to serve as the gateway for making changes to the Model. In this example, the Controller consists of two `java.swing.Action` classes. These `Action` classes are registered with one or more graphical components via the components' `addActionListener()` method. There are two `Action` classes in this application. The first attempts to login with the Model. The second exits the application:

```
package wrox.pattern.mvc;

import java.awt.event.ActionEvent;
import javax.swing.AbstractAction;
```

The `LoginAction` extends the `AbstractionAction` and overrides the `actionPerformed()` method. The `actionPerformed()` method is called by the component, in this case the command button, when it is pressed. The action is not limited to registration with a single user interface component. The benefit of separating out the Controller logic to a separate class is so that the action can be registered with menus, hotkeys, and toolbars. This prevents the action logic from being duplicated for each UI component:

```
public class LoginAction extends AbstractAction {

    private Model model;
    private CenterPanel panel;
```

It is common for the Controller to have visibility of both the Model and the relevant views; however, the model cannot invoke the actions directly. Ensuring the separation of business and interface logic remains intact:

```
    public LoginAction(Model model, CenterPanel panel ) {
      this.model= model;
      this.panel = panel;
    }
     public void actionPerformed(ActionEvent e) {
       System.out.println("Login Action: "+ panel.getLogin() +" "+ panel.getPassword()
);
       model.login( panel.getLogin(), panel.getPassword()  );
    }
}
```

The `ExitAction` strictly controls the behavior of the user interface. It displays a message when the Exit button is pressed confirming that the application should close:

```
package wrox.pattern.mvc;
import java.awt.event.ActionEvent;
import javax.swing.AbstractAction;
import javax.swing.JFrame;
import javax.swing.JOptionPane;
public class ExitAction extends AbstractAction {

  public void actionPerformed(ActionEvent e) {

    JFrame frame= new JFrame();
    int response= JOptionPane.showConfirmDialog(frame,
                                   "Exit Application?",
```

```
"Exit",JOptionPane.OK_CANCEL_OPTION);
    if (JOptionPane.YES_OPTION == response) {
      System.exit(0);
    }
  }
}
```

Finally, you can view the `Application` class. The `Application` class is responsible for initialization, and it creates the associations that establish the MVC separation of logic design principles:

```
package wrox.pattern.mvc;
import java.awt.event.WindowAdapter;
import java.awt.event.WindowEvent;
import javax.swing.JFrame;

public class Application extends JFrame {
  private Model model;
```

The Swing application creates an association to the `Model` class, shown in the following code in the application constructor:

```
public Application(Model model) {
    this.model= model;
```

Then, create the Views to display the Swing interface:

```
CenterPanel center= new CenterPanel();
WorkPanel work= new WorkPanel(center, model);
```

Create the `Action` classes that represent the controller and register them with the command buttons:

```
work.addButton("login", new LoginAction(model, center));
work.addButton("exit", new ExitAction() );
model.addPropertyChangeListener(work);
setTitle("MVC Pattern Application");
```

Use Swing housekeeping to display the application:

```
getContentPane().add(work);
pack();
show();
addWindowListener(new WindowAdapter() {
  public void windowClosing(WindowEvent e) {
    System.exit(0);
  }
});
}
public static void main(String[] args) {
  Model model= new Model();
  Application application= new Application(model);
}
}
```

The Model-View-Controller pattern is a combination of best practices in software design. It prompts a separation of concern between the user interface and business layers of an application. This example covered a number of design patterns: composition, action, and event publish-subscribe. The next pattern is the Command pattern, which provides a consistent means of handling user requests.

Command

The Command pattern provides a standard interface for handling user requests. Each request is encapsulated in an object called a command. Figure 3-13 shows the classes involved in the Command pattern.

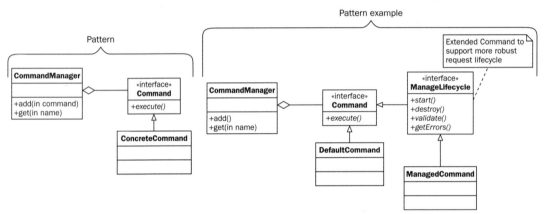

Figure 3-13

The three classes of the command pattern are the `Command`, `CommandManager`, and `Invoker`. The `Command` class represents an encapsulation of a single behavior. Each behavior in an application, such as save or delete, would be modeled as a command. In that way the behavior of an application is a collection of command objects. To add behavior to an application, all a developer needs to do is implement additional command objects. The next component in the Command pattern is the `CommandManager`. This class is responsible for providing access to the commands available to the application. The final component is the `Invoker`. The `Invoker` is responsible for executing the command classes in a consistent manner. The next section looks at the anatomy of the `Command` class.

Command

The first part of the Command pattern is the `Command` interface identified by a single method:

```
package wrox.pattern.command;

public interface Command {

    public void execute();
}
```

The life cycle is different from calling a typical method. For example, if you need to pass in an object parameter like the following method:

```
 public void getTotal(Sale) {
//calculate the sale.
}
```

As a command you would write the following:

```
public CalculateSale implements Command {
private Sale sale;

public void setSale( Sale sale ) {
this.sale = sale;
}
public void execute( ) {
// calculate the sale.
}
```

For the purpose of the example, use an empty command to demonstrate the interaction between the classes in this pattern:

```
package wrox.pattern.command;

public class DefaultCommand implements Command {

  public void execute() {
    System.out.println("executing the default command");
  }
}
```

The next section looks at the class that manages the command for an application.

CommandManager

The CommandManager class will process all requests. Using a HashMap, all of the commands will be initialized before requests are processed, then retrieved by name. They are stored using the add() method, and retrieved through the getCommand() method:

```
package wrox.pattern.command;
import java.util.HashMap;
import java.util.Map;
public class CommandManager {
  private Map commands= new HashMap();

  public void add(String name, Command command) {
    commands.put(name, command);
  }
  public Command getCommand(String name) {
    return (Command)commands.get(name);
  }
}
```

Invoker

A standalone client will demonstrate the execution of the Command pattern. When the `Client` constructor is called it adds the `DefaultCommand` to the manager:

```
package wrox.pattern.command;
import java.util.Collection;
import java.util.HashMap;
import java.util.Map;

public class Client {
  private CommandManager manager= new CommandManager();

  public Client() {
    manager.add("default", new DefaultCommand());
  }
```

Here, the command mapping has been hard coded. A more robust implementation would initialize the command map from a resource file:

```
<commands>
  <command name="default" class="wrox.Pattern.command.DefaultCommand" />
</commands>
```

Then, as requests are received by the `invoke(String name)` method, the command name is looked up in the `CommandManager` and the `Command` object is returned:

```
public void invoke(String name) {
  Command command= manager.getCommand(name);
    command.execute();
}

public static void main(String[] args) {
  Client client= new Client();
  client.invoke("default");
  }
}
```

This is an important part of most web frameworks like Struts or WebWork. In WebWork there is a specific Command pattern component called xWork, which is described in detail in Chapter 8. By handling each request as a `Command` object, it is possible to apply common services to each command. Some common services could be things such as security, validation, and auditing. The next section of code extends the current Command pattern and implements a `ManagedLifecycle` interface. This interface will define a set of methods that are called during each request:

```
package wrox.Pattern.command;

import java.util.Collection;
import java.util.Map;

public interface ManagedLifecycle extends Command {

  public void initialize();
  public void setApplicationContext(Map context);
```

```
    public boolean isValidated();
    public Collection getErrors( );
    public void destroy();

}
```

The `ManagedLifecycle` interface is a contract between the `Command` object and the client code.

The following is an example command that implements the `ManagedLifecycle` interface:

```
package wrox.pattern.command;
import java.util.Collection;
import java.util.Map;
import java.util.HashMap;

public class ManagedCommand implements ManagedLifecycle {
  private Map context;
  private Map errors= new HashMap( );
  public void initialize() {
    System.out.println("initializing..");
  }
  public void destroy() {
    System.out.println("destroying");
  }
  public void execute() {
    System.out.println("executing managed command");
  }
  public boolean isValidated() {
    System.out.println("validating");
    return true;
  }
  public void setApplicationContext(Map context) {
    System.out.println("setting context");
    this.context= context;
  }
  public Collection getErrors() {
    return errors.getValues();
  }
}
```

The following code shows initialization and invocation of two types of commands, the standard and managed:

```
package wrox.pattern.command;
import java.util.Collection;
import java.util.HashMap;
import java.util.Map;

public class Client {
  private Map context= new HashMap();
  private CommandManager manager= new CommandManager();

  public Client() {
    manager.add("default", new DefaultCommand());
```

A new `ManagedCommand` has been added to the `CommandManager`:

```
    manager.add("managed", new ManagedCommand());
  }
  public void invoke(String name) {
    Command command= manager.getCommand(name);
```

Next, a check is put in place to determine whether the command being executed implements the `ManagedLifecycle` interface:

```
    if (command instanceof ManagedLifecycle) {
      ManagedLifecycle managed= (ManagedLifecycle)command;
      managed.setApplicationContext(context);
      managed.initialize();
      if (managed.isValidated()) {
        managed.execute();
      } else {
        Collection errors = managed.getErrors();
      }
      managed.destroy();
    } else {
      command.execute();
    }
  }
```

The calling sequence of the `ManagedLifecycle` is richer with functionality compared with its single method version. First it passes required application data, calls the initialize method, performs validation, and then calls the `execute()` method.

> Allowing the client Invoker to pass resources to the command is a very powerful concept referred to as inversion of control (IOC), or dependency injection. This eliminates the need for the `Command` class to look up services and resources that are available to the invoker. (A good example of this is shown Chapter 8.)

Strategy

The Strategy pattern allows you to replace algorithms on the fly. To implement the solution, you represent each algorithm as a `Strategy` class. The application then delegates to the current `Strategy` class to execute the strategy-specific algorithm. Figure 3-14 shows the UML for the Strategy pattern alongside the example for this section.

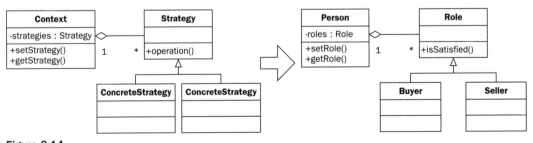

Figure 3-14

A common mistake in domain modeling is the overuse of *subtyping*. A subtype should be created only when a specific "is-a" type relationship can be described between a subtype and its super-type. For example, when modeling a person within a domain model, it is tempting to create a subtype for each type of person. There is no wrong way of modeling a problem, but in this case each person can take on several roles. This example looks at buyer and seller roles any person might participate in at a given time. This doesn't pass the "is-a" relationship test for subtyping. It is fitting that a person's behavior varies by his role; this concept can be expressed using the Strategy pattern.

The example application in this section looks at the roles of buyers and sellers, showing how their differing behavior can be abstracted out into a strategy.

Locking each person into one role or the other is a mistake. The ability to switch between the behaviors of classes in a class hierarchy is the motivation for using the Strategy pattern. Figure 3-15 shows the wrong way to model the "plays a role" relationship.

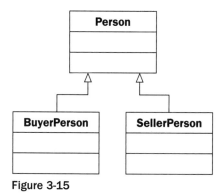

Figure 3-15

The Strategy pattern is made up of an interface that defines the pluggable behavior, implementing subclasses to define the behavior and then an object to make use of the strategy.

Strategy

The solution is to model each role as a class and delegate role-specific behavior from the `Person` class to the `Role` current state. First, look at the behavior that will differ by the current state object. The example uses the interface `Role` to declare the strategy behavior, and the two concrete classes, `Buyer` and `Seller`, to implement the differing behavior.

To provide a little context to the example, the `Buyer` and `Seller` are trying to agree on a product price. The `isSatisified()` method is passed a `Product` and a `Price` and both parties must determine if the deal is acceptable:

```java
package wrox.pattern.strategy;

public interface Role {

    public boolean isSatisfied( Product product, double price );
}
```

Of course, the `Seller` and `Buyer` have differing objectives. The `Seller` is looking to make a profit, setting a 20 percent profit margin on any products sold. The following code makes that assumption:

```
package wrox.pattern.strategy;
public class Seller implements Role {

  /*
   * Seller will be happy if they make 20% profit on whatever they sell.
   * (non-Javadoc)
   * @see wrox.Pattern.strategy.Role#isSatisfied(wrox.Pattern.strategy.Product,
  double)
   */
  public boolean isSatisfied(Product product, double price) {
    if (price - product.getCost() > product.getCost() * .2) {
      return true;
    } else {
      return false;
    }
  }
}
```

The `Buyer`, on the other hand, is looking for a product that is within a spending limit. It is important to note that the `Buyer` class is not limited to the methods described by the `Role` interface, making it possible to establish the `limit` member variable in the `Buyer` class that is not present in the `Seller` class.

The algorithm for what is acceptable is an arbitrary part of this example, but it is set so the `Buyer` cannot spend above the chosen limit and will not pay more that 200 percent of the initial product cost. The role of `Buyer` is expressed in the `isSatisfied()` method:

```
package wrox.Pattern.strategy;
public class Buyer implements Role {

  private double limit;

  public Buyer(double limit) {
    this.limit= limit;
  }
  /*
   * The buyer is happy if he can afford the product,
   *   and the price is less then 200% over cost.
   * @see wrox.Pattern.strategy.Role#isSatisfied(wrox.Pattern.strategy.Product,
  double)
   */
  public boolean isSatisfied(Product product, double price) {
    if ( price < limit && price < product.getCost() * 2 ) {
      return true;
    } else {
      return false;
    }

  }
}
```

The code example that follows uses a class for the abstraction of a product. It's a data object that is part of the scenario. The code is as follows:

```
package wrox.pattern.strategy;
public class Product {
  private String name;
  private String description;
  private double cost;

  public Product(String name, String description, double cost) {
      this.name = name;
      this.description = description;
      this.cost = cost;
  }
  // Setters and Getter Omitted.
```

The next section looks at the class that uses the pluggable strategy.

Context

Next, examine the `Person` class that manages the `Role` objects. First, the `Person` class has an association with the `Role` interface. In addition, it is important to note that there is a setter and getter for the `Role`. This allows the person's roles to change as the program executes. It's also much cleaner code. This example uses two roles: `Buyer` and `Seller`. In the future, other `Role` implementing objects such as `Wholesaler`, `Broker`, and others can be added because there is no dependency to the specific subclasses:

```
package wrox.pattern.strategy;

public class Person {
  private String name;
  private Role role;
  public Person(String name) {
    this.name= name;
  }
  public Role getRole() {
    return role;
  }
  public void setRole(Role role) {
    this.role= role;
  }
```

Another key point is that the satisfied method of the `Person` class delegates the `Role`-specific behavior to its `Role` interface. *Polymorphism* allows the correct underlying object to be chosen:

```
public boolean satisfied(Product product, double offer) {
    return role.isSatisfied(product, offer);
  }
}
```

Now, the code of the pattern has been implemented. Next, view what behavior an application can exhibit by implementing this pattern. To start, you can establish `Products`, `People`, and `Roles`:

```
package wrox.pattern.strategy;

public class Person {
// previous methods omitted.

  public static void main(String[] args) {
     Product house= new Product("house", "4 Bedroom North Arlington", 200000);
     Product condo= new Product("condo", "2 Bedroom McLean", 100000);
     Person tim= new Person("Tim");
     Person allison= new Person("Allison");
```

You are buying and selling houses. The next step is to establish initial roles and assign the roles to the people. The people will then exhibit the behavior of the role they have been assigned:

```
     tim.setRole(new Buyer(500000));
     allison.setRole(new Seller());

     if (!allison.satisfied(house, 200000)) {
       System.out.println("offer of 200,000 is no good for the seller");
     }
     if (!tim.satisfied(house, 600000)) {
       System.out.println("offer of 600,000 is no good for the buyer");
     }
     if (tim.satisfied(house, 390000) && allison.satisfied(house, 390000)) {
       System.out.println("They Both agree with 390,000 ");
```

To further demonstrate the capabilities of the Strategy pattern, switch the initial `Seller` to the `Buyer` by calling `setRole()` on the `Person` object. It is possible to switch to a `Buyer` without modifying the `Person` object:

```
     allison.setRole(new Buyer(190000));
     if (allison.satisfied(condo, 110000)) {
       System.out.println("As a buyer she can afford the condo ");
     }
   }
 }
}
```

By implementing the Strategy pattern, it is possible to change an object's behavior on the fly with no effect on its implementation. This is a very powerful tool in software design. In the next section, the composite patterns build on the same principle of abstracting behavior to treat a class hierarchy with a single common interface.

Composite

The Composite design pattern allows you to treat a collection of objects as if they were one thing. In this way you can reduce the complexity of the code required if you were going to handle collections as special cases. Figure 3-16 shows the structure of the Composite pattern in conjunction with the classes implementing the pattern in this example.

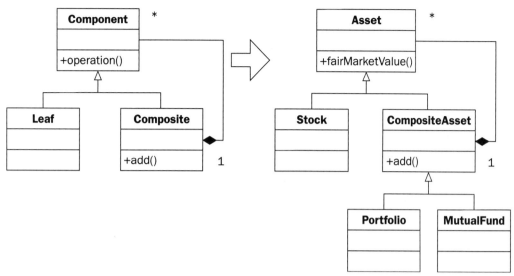

Figure 3-16

The example used here to demonstrate this behavior is a portfolio management system that consists of stocks and mutual funds. A mutual fund is a collection of stocks, but you would like to apply a common interface to both stocks and mutual funds to simplify the handling of both. This allows you to perform operations such as calculate Fair Market Value, buy, sell, and assess percent contribution with a common interface. The Composite pattern would clearly reduce the complexity of building these operations. The pattern consists of the Component, Leaf, and Composite classes. Figure 3-16 should look similar to Figure 3-6, where you were first introduced to the inheritance loop concept.

Component

First is the component interface; it declares the common interface that both the single and composite nodes will implement. The example is using fairMarketValue, an operation that can be calculated over stocks, mutual funds, and portfolios:

```
package wrox.pattern.composite;

public interface Asset {

  public double fairMarketValue();
}
```

Leaf

The Leaf class represents the singular atomic data type implementing the component interface. In this example, a Stock class will represent the leaf node of the pattern. The Stock class is a leaf node in that it does not hold a reference to any other Asset objects:

```
package wrox.pattern.composite;

public class Stock implements Asset {

  private String name;
```

```
    private double price;
    private double quantity;

    public Stock(String name, double price, double quantity) {
       this.name= name;
       this.price= price;
       this.quantity= quantity;
    }
```

Stock price is calculated by multiplying share price and quantity:

```
    public double fairMarketValue() {

       return price * quantity;
    }
 }
```

Composite

The following section declares the Composite object called `CompositeAsset`. Notice that `Composite Asset` is declared abstract. A valid composite asset, such as a mutual fund or portfolio, extends this abstract class:

```
    package wrox.pattern.composite;
    import java.util.ArrayList;
    import java.util.Iterator;
    import java.util.List;

    public abstract class CompositeAsset implements Asset {
       private List assets= new ArrayList();

       public void add(Asset asset) {
          assets.add(asset);
       }
```

Iterate through the child investments. If one of the child investments also happens to be a composite asset, it will be handled recursively without requiring a special case. So, for example, it would be possible to have a mutual fund comprising mutual funds:

```
    public double fairMarketValue() {
       double total = 0;
       for (Iterator i= assets.iterator(); i.hasNext();  ) {
          Asset asset= (Asset)i.next();
          total = total + asset.fairMarketValue();
       }
       return total;
    }
 }
```

Once that is complete, what follows is to build the concrete composite objects: `MutualFund` and `Portfolio`. Nothing significant is required for the `MutualFund` class; its behavior is inherited from the `CompositeAsset`:

```
package wrox.pattern.composite;

public class MutualFund extends CompositeAsset{

  private String name;

  public MutualFund(String name) {
    this.name = name;
  }

}
```

The `Portfolio` class extends `CompositeAsset` as well; the difference is that it calls the superclass directly and modifies the resulting calculation for fair market. It subtracts a two-percent management fee:

```
package wrox.pattern.composite;

public class Portfolio extends CompositeAsset {
  private String name;
  public Portfolio(String name) {
    this.name= name;
  }
  /* Market value - Management Fee
   * @see wrox.Pattern.composite.CompositeAsset#fairMarketValue()
   */
  public double fairMarketValue() {
    return super.fairMarketValue() - super.fairMarketValue() * .02;
  }

}
```

The only thing left to do is exercise the code. The next class is of an `Investor`. The `Investor` is the client code taking advantage of the Composite design pattern:

```
package wrox.pattern.composite;

public class Investor {
  private String name;
  private Portfolio porfolio;
  public Investor(String name, Portfolio portfolio) {
    this.name= name;
    this.porfolio= portfolio;
  }
```

By calling the fair market value on the investor's portfolio, the Composite pattern will be able to traverse the collection of stocks and mutual funds to determine the value of the whole thing without worrying about the object structure:

```
public double calcNetworth( ){

  return porfolio.fairMarketValue();
```

```
    }

    public static void main(String[] args) {
        Portfolio portfolio= new Portfolio("Frequently Used Money");
        Investor investor= new Investor("IAS", portfolio);

        portfolio.add(new Stock("wrox", 450, 100));

        MutualFund fund= new MutualFund("Don Scheafer's Intellectual Capital");
        fund.add(new Stock("ME", 35, 100) );
        fund.add(new Stock("CV", 22, 100) );
        fund.add(new Stock("BA", 10, 100) );
        portfolio.add(fund);

        double total =investor.calcNetworth();

        System.out.println("total =" + total);
    }
}
```

With the Composite pattern, it is very easy to simplify operations over complex data structures.

Summary

This chapter gave you a strong appreciation of the value of patterns in developing Java solutions. They are critical in learning from the experience of others, but also in understanding APIs used by the Java platform.

In this chapter, you learned about patterns, why they're important, tricks to understanding them, and several important patterns in Java programming.

Now that you have learned how to think like a Java developer, the rest of the book focuses on practical examples of developing Java solutions. These chapters are not comprehensive examinations of the technologies in each chapter, but rather a real-life example of a development problem, which is solved using various technologies.

The first chapter in this new phase of the book is Chapter 4. In that chapter, you learn how to use Swing to build Java desktop applications.

Part II: A Broad Understanding of Java APIs, Tools, and Techniques

Chapter 4: Developing Effective User Interfaces with JFC

Chapter 5: Persisting Your Application Using Files

Chapter 6: Persisting Your Application Using Databases

Chapter 7: Developing Web Applications Using the Model 1
Architecture

Chapter 8: Developing Web Applications Using the Model 2
Architecture

Chapter 9: Interacting with C/C++ Using Java Native Interface

Chapter 10: EJB 3 and the Java Persistence API

Chapter 11: Communicating between Java Components and
Components of Other Platforms

Chapter 12: Service Oriented Integration

Chapter 13: Java Security

Chapter 14: Packaging and Deploying Your Java Applications

Developing Effective User Interfaces with JFC

Java Foundation Classes (JFC) is a package of libraries for developing robust graphical user displays for client-side applications that can be implemented on enterprise systems. The JFC API libraries comprise five different components:

- ❑ **AWT.** The Abstract Windowing Toolkit (AWT) classes are comprised of legacy graphics code from Java 1.x that were developed to create simple user interfaces for applications and applets.

- ❑ **Accessibility.** The Accessibility classes accommodate assistive technologies that provide access to information in user interface components.

- ❑ **Java 2D.** The Java 2D classes contain a broad set of advanced graphics APIs that allow users to create and manipulate image, shape, and text components.

- ❑ **Drag and Drop.** The Drag and Drop classes allow users to initiate drag operations so components can be dropped on designated target areas. This is accomplished by setting up a drop target listener to handle drop events and a management object to handle drag-and-drop operations.

- ❑ **Swing.** The Swing classes are built atop of the AWT classes to provide high-quality GUI components for enterprise applications.

Large tomes have been written about JFC, specifically Swing libraries and their advanced presentation features, with numerous pages of APIs affiliated with those libraries that could easily be acquired by your Integrated Development Environment (IDE) or the Internet during your development activities. Along with those library presentations were some simple applications that provided little instructional value other than to demonstrate how things work in a basic fashion. Rather than getting bogged down with a recital of those voluminous APIs, this chapter concentrates the discussion on many of the Swing features that you will need to incorporate into your professional development activities to be successful. You'll learn advanced GUI applications that combine multiple layout managers to achieve relevant presentation applications that manage data and navigation flow in an efficient manner. All of the sample applications incorporate listeners and their interfaces to manage events generated by users in their navigation activities along with Gang of Four (GoF) design patterns to promote best practices in your modeling and implementation operations.

This chapter starts by demonstrating some foundation knowledge about layout managers so that you can conceptualize Swing layout designs from a high-level perspective and then implement them using JFC libraries in an efficient manner. With a solid handle on what these libraries can do for you, you will be able to approach your development tasks with greater confidence, which will result in more germane product development. The next two sections of this chapter cover some practical applications concerning the new Mustang desktop features and how navigation flows in your GUI application can be managed with the assistance GoF design patterns.

Layout Managers

Layout managers are used in Java Swing applications to arrange objects when they are added to a `Container` object. The `setLayout()` method is used to override default layout managers appropriated to `JPanel` (`FlowLayout`) and `JFrame` (`BorderLayout`) containers.

This section of the chapter discusses eight important layout managers:

- ❑ `BorderLayout`
- ❑ `BoxLayout`
- ❑ `CardLayout`
- ❑ `FlowLayout`
- ❑ `GridbagLayout`
- ❑ `GridLayout`
- ❑ `SpringLayout`
- ❑ `GroupLayout`

All of these layout managers are covered at length within interesting Swing applications that implement listeners to react to user selections on various visualization components. Most important, these applications demonstrate how the different layout managers can be amalgamated to craft relevant GUI presentations.

BorderLayout

The `BorderLayout` manager is the default layout for a frame. A `BorderLayout` uses five regions in its display space. Those regions are generally referred to as NORTH, SOUTH, WEST, EAST, and CENTER. Those regions generally refer to the same attributes that a map would use. The NORTH and SOUTH regions extend to the top and bottom areas of the Container, while the EAST and WEST regions extend from the bottom of the NORTH and top of the SOUTH regions and to the left and right sides of the Container, respectively. The CENTER region occupies all of the residual space that remains in the center of the Container.

The `BorderLayout` manager is typically generated by instantiating a new `BorderLayout` class with a constructor that has no parameters or with a constructor that specifies two integer values that specify the horizontal and vertical pixels between components in this fashion: `new BorderLayout(int hGap, int vGap)`.

The following `BorderLayout` example emulates a test application that quizzes the user with five fairly simple arithmetic queries. As a user sequentially steps through the test questions, a progress bar will track where the test taker is with respect to the end of the test and what the running score is. Figure 4-1 provides a model of the application and shows how the different GUI components will occupy the `BorderLayout` panel.

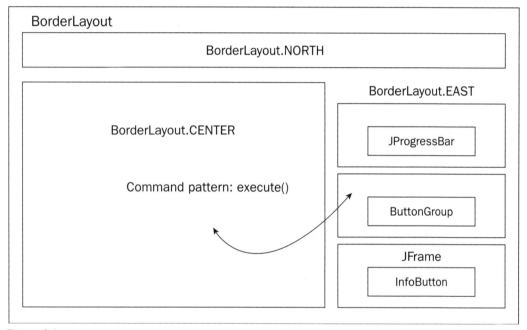

Figure 4-1

The `BorderLayoutPanel` application will incorporate the Command pattern to handle button requests for quiz questions and the answers to those questions by the user. Some of the benefits and drawbacks of the Command pattern are outlined in the table that follows.

Pattern	Benefits	Consequences
Command	Acts as a delivery mechanism that carries behavior rather than data in an application.	Creation of a lot of little classes to accommodate component actions.
	Delivers encapsulated actions to a method or object for easier program control.	

The following code segment outlines a `BorderLayoutPanel` implementation that is realized in the Arithmetic Test visualization shown in Figure 4-1. Many of these actions are omitted from this example, as well as many of the layout manager programs, to provide better reading clarity. Note that the `ButtonText` variable uses HTML scripting text to allow for the spanning of text in the `JButton` Swing component to which it will be applied. The Command pattern interface is implemented so the application can polymorphically derive proper event actions during runtime based on the user's navigation operations:

```
[BorderLayoutPanel.java]
// package name and import statements omitted

public class BorderLayoutPanel extends JPanel implements ActionListener {
  // some declarations omitted for the sake of brevity [Please check download code]
  private final static String[] ButtonText =
    { "<html><center><font size='+2'>Basic Arithmetic</font><br><br>( click for
question )</center></html>" };
  private static String[] questions =
                    { "1, 2, What is 1 + 1 ?, 0, 1, 2, 3",
                      "2, 0, What is 1 - 1 ?, 0, 1, 2, 3",
                      "3, 2, What is 5 - 3 ?, 0, 1, 2, 3",
                      "4, 3, What is 4 - 1 ?, 0, 1, 2, 3" };

  private Hashtable hashtableQuestions = new Hashtable();

  public interface Command {
     public void execute();
  }

  public BorderLayoutPanel(String FrameTitle) {
     initComponents();
  }
```

The `initComponents()` method is created to separate relevant initialization tasks so it can be invoked by the constructor during inception and when the user has finished the test and wants to reset the application. Here, all of the panels are derived that will be deployed by the `BorderLayout` manager:

```
public void initComponents() {
   try {
      removeAll();

      northPanel = new JPanel();
      answerPanel = new JPanel();
      centerPanel = new JPanel();
      eastPanel = new JPanel();
      msgText = new JLabel("Click button to start!");
      InfoScreenButton = new RulesButton("Rules");
      optGroup = new ButtonGroup();
      progressBar = new JProgressBar();

      questionCount = 1;
      correctAnswerCount = 0;
      numberQuestionsAnswered = 0;

      String[] strLine;
```

```
for (int x = 0; x < questions.length; x++) {
   strLine = questions[x].split(",");
   hashtableQuestions.put(strLine[0], strLine);
}

buttons = new JQuestionButton[numberButtons];
for (int i = 0; i < numberButtons; i++) {
   buttons[i] = new JQuestionButton("Question");
   buttons[i].setText(ButtonText[i]);
   centerPanel.add(buttons[i]);
   buttons[i].addActionListener(this);
}

InfoScreenButton.addActionListener(this);
```

At this point in the application, the layout of the Swing components are established and the answers for the quiz are saved to the `ButtonGroup` component for visual rendering. It is important to note how layout managers are intermingled to get the desired visual effect. The `answerPanel` uses the `GridLayout` class to enforce 0 rows and 1 column so the answers available to the user are lined up in a single column prior to being added to the `eastPanel` component below the progress bar and above the rules button:

```
centerPanel.setLayout(new GridLayout(0, 1));
answerPanel.setLayout(new GridLayout(0, 1));

Answer = new JRadioButtonAnswer[numberAnswers];
for (int i = 0; i < numberAnswers; i++) {
   Answer[i] = new JRadioButtonAnswer(A[i]);
   answerPanel.add(Answer[i]);
   Answer[i].addActionListener(this);
   optGroup.add(Answer[i]);
}

BlankRadioButton = new JRadioButton();
optGroup.add(BlankRadioButton);

northPanel.setBackground(new Color(255, 255, 220));
northPanel.add(msgText);

eastPanel.setLayout(new GridLayout(0, 1));
eastPanel.add(progressBar);
eastPanel.add(answerPanel);
eastPanel.add(InfoScreenButton);

setLayout(new BorderLayout());
add(eastPanel, "East");
add(northPanel, "North");
add(centerPanel, "Center");

setSize(600, 600);
questionAnswered = true;
answerPanel.setVisible(false);

progressBar.setMaximum(numberQuestions);
progressBar.setValue(0);
```

```
            progressBar.setIndeterminate(false);

            resetButton = new JResetButton("Reset Game");
            resetButton.addActionListener(this);

        } catch (Exception e) {
            logger.info("Exception: " + e.toString());
        }
    }
```

The `JQuestionButton` implements the `Command` interface so user invocations on that button will dynamically determine — through the `ActionListener` implementation — that the `execute()` method associated with this button should be invoked. Once invoked, the application will use a key based on the question count to search the `hashtableQuestions` collection class for the proper question to render on the display:

```
    private class JQuestionButton extends JButton implements Command {

        public JQuestionButton(String caption) { super(caption); }
        public void execute() {
            try {
                if (numberQuestionsAnswered < numberQuestions) {
                    answerPanel.setVisible(true);
                    northPanel.setBackground(new Color(255, 255, 220));
                    if (questionAnswered) {
                        optGroup.setSelected(BlankRadioButton.getModel(), true);
                        questionAnswered = false;
                        try {
                            String key = Integer.toString(questionCount);
                            if (hashtableQuestions.containsKey(key)) {
                                Question = (String[]) hashtableQuestions.get(key);
                                questionCount++;
                            } else {
                                logger.info("key NOT found" + key);
                            }
                        } catch (Exception e) { throw e; }

                        msgText.setText(Question[2]);
                        for (int i = 0, x = 3; i < numberAnswers; i++) {
                            Answer[i].setText(Question[x + i]);
                        }
                    }
                }
            } catch (Exception e) {
                logger.info("Exception: " + e.toString());
            }
        }
    }
```

The `JRadioButtonAnswer` class also implements the `Command` interface to polymorphically determine behavior needed when a user clicks the radio button answer to the question posed by the test application. If the user response is correct, the background color of the `northPanel` will be turned green, indicating a positive response to the question, and if another question is available, the `JButton setText()` method will be used to display the user's score, and the `progressBar` component will exhibit the percentage of the test that the user has covered:

```
private class JRadioButtonAnswer extends JRadioButton implements Command {
    public JRadioButtonAnswer(String caption) {}
    public void execute() {
        try {
            if (!questionAnswered) {
                if (Question[1].trim().equals(getText().trim())) {
                    msgText.setText("Correct!!!");
                    northPanel.setBackground(Color.green);
                    correctAnswerCount++;
                } else {
                    msgText.setText(
                        "Wrong!!! The correct answer is: " + Question[1]);
                    northPanel.setBackground(Color.red);
                }

                questionAnswered = true;
                numberQuestionsAnswered++;

                buttons[0].setText(
                    ("<html><center><font size='+2'>( click for question )</font>"
                    + "<br><br>"
                    + " Score= "
                    + correctAnswerCount
                    + "/"
                    + numberQuestionsAnswered).toString()
                    + "</center></html>");

                progressBar.setValue(numberQuestionsAnswered);
                progressBar.setStringPainted(true);
                progressBar.setString(
                Double.toString(Math.round(progressBar.getPercentComplete() * 100))+
"%");
                if (numberQuestionsAnswered >= numberQuestions) {
                    buttons[0].setBackground(new Color(255, 255, 220));
                    buttons[0].setText("Finished. Score= " + String.valueOf(
(float) correctAnswerCount / (float) numberQuestionsAnswered * 100) + "%");
                    // setup reset button
                    answerPanel.removeAll();
                    answerPanel.add(resetButton);
                }
            } else {
                msgText.setText(
                "You have answered this question, please select a new Question");
            }

        } catch (Exception e) {
            logger.info("Exception occured: " + e.toString());
        }
    }
}
```

The `actionPerformed` method is an implementation of the `ActionListener` interface, which is invoked when an event is created by user operations. The `Command` pattern implementation determines which button was selected by the user and the proper `execute()` method to invoke based on that event:

```
public void actionPerformed(ActionEvent e) {
    Command obj = (Command) e.getSource();
    obj.execute();
}
```

The `RulesButton` class also implements the `Command` interface so a new frame will be kicked off when a user selects the Rules button in the test application. The `JResetButton` button is used to supplant the answers in the `answerPanel` when all five questions have been answered by the test taker. This allows the user to retake the test by resetting the answers in the test. Ideally, you would want to randomize those answers to make the test more difficult, but this application was developed to demonstrate, in a simple fashion, how the `Border Layout` class can be used with other layout managers to develop relevant GUI applications:

```
class RulesButton extends JButton implements Command {

    public RulesButton(String Title) { super(Title); }
    public void execute() {
        JLabel InfoLabel = new JLabel(
            "<html> How To Play:<br> Click on button to generate questions "
            + "on the right side of the user display. A progress bar will "
            + "indicate where the tester is with respect to the entire test.");
        JFrame InfoFrame = new JFrame("How To Play");
        InfoFrame.getContentPane().add(InfoLabel);
        InfoFrame.setSize(400, 150);
        InfoFrame.show();
    }
}

private class JResetButton extends JButton implements Command {
    public JResetButton(String caption) {
        super(caption);
    }
    public void execute() {
        initComponents();
    }
}
}
```

Figure 4-2 represents the finished product of the `BorderLayoutPanel` application. Test questions are rendered in the NORTH section of the `BorderLayout`, and test progress statistics, answers, and a Rules component reside on the EAST. Users navigate through the test by clicking on the `questionPanel` in the `BoderLayout.CENTER`, which will retrieve and display the questions for the user to answer.

BoxLayout

The `BoxLayout` manager arranges components horizontally from left to right, or vertically from top to bottom, without the wraparound capability in the `FlowLayout` manager. Implementation of the `BoxLayout` manager warrants the instantiation of the `BoxLayout` class with two parameters, the first being the Container panel that will be displayed, followed by an integer axis value that indicates the placement of the components on the panel. An axis value of `Boxlayout.X_AXIS` indicates left-to-right layout management, whereas a value of `BoxLayout.Y_AXIS` signifies a top-to-bottom layout.

The following BoxLayout example will apply the Decorator pattern in its implementation so that users can add behavior dynamically through drag-and-drop operations. Figure 4-3 provides a model of the application and how the different image components occupy the BoxLayout panel real estate.

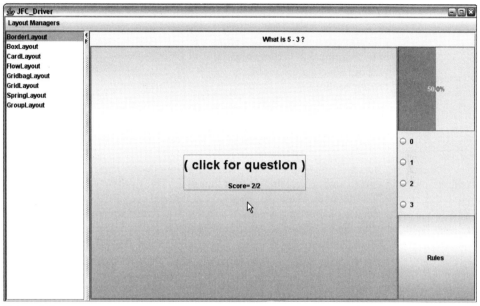

Figure 4-2

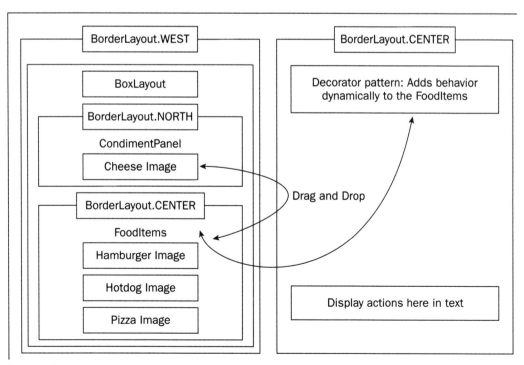

Figure 4-3

Dynamic behavior transfer occurs when a user drags the Cheese condiment image onto one of the three food item images on the left panel. Some of the benefits of the `Decorator` pattern are defined in the following table.

Pattern	Benefits	Consequences
Decorator	Can add or remove responsibilities of individual objects dynamically without affecting other objects during runtime. A class can be wrapped in another object to provide added functionalities.	Generates a lot of similar objects.

The `FoodComponent` interface allows the `BoxLayout` application to dynamically add behaviors to the three different food items (Hamburger, Hotdog, and Pizza) during runtime when the Cheese object is dragged and dropped on that item. The `FoodComponent` interface allows behaviors to be defined across the class hierarchy of the `BoxLayout` sample application with private implementations to address individual user needs, specifically the retrieval methods to collect relevant data for presentation purposes:

```
[FoodComponent.java]
package com.boxlayout;
interface FoodComponent {
    String getDescription();
    float getCost();
    float getTotalCost();
    FoodGraphic getGraphic();
}
```

The `FoodGraphic` class controls the user events associated with the three different food images, and the `FoodImage` class handles image files affiliated with the different food items. The `paintComponent (Graphics g)` method ensures that image files are drawn properly throughout the lifetime of the `JPanel` component `FoodImage`:

```
[FoodGraphic.java]
// package name and import statements omitted

public class FoodGraphic extends JPanel implements DropTargetListener,
MouseListener {

    // declarations omitted for the sake of brevity [Please check download code]
    private class FoodImage extends JPanel {
        private Image image = null;
        public FoodImage(String imageFile) {
            super();
            URL url = FoodImage.class.getResource(imageFile);
            image = Toolkit.getDefaultToolkit().getImage(url);
        }
        public void paintComponent(Graphics g) {
            super.paintComponent(g);
```

```
        g.drawImage(image, 0, 0, this);
    }
}

public FoodGraphic(FoodComponent foodcomponent, String imageFile, int weight, int
height, boolean tipsFlag) {
    this(foodcomponent, imageFile, width, height);
    updateTips = tipsFlag;
}
```

Retrieval of handler object references occurs from the FoodComponent class, which allows food item descriptions and costs to be collected for display. A new object reference is created with the DropTarget class to tell the application that the individual food item objects are willing to accept drops during operations, while the DropTargetListener interface performs callback notifications on registered subjects to signal event changes on the target being dropped on:

```
public FoodGraphic(FoodComponent foodcoomponent, String imageFile, int width, int
height) {
    super();
    handler = foodcomponent;

    dropTarget = new DropTarget(this, DnDConstants.ACTION_COPY_OR_MOVE, this);
    setBackground(Color.white);
    name = handler.getDescription();

    image = new FoodImage(imageFile);
    image.setPreferredSize(new Dimension(width,height));
    image.setMaximumSize(new Dimension(width,height));
    image.setMinimumSize(new Dimension(width,height));
    image.setAlignmentX(CENTER_ALIGNMENT);

    label = new JLabel(name,SwingConstants.CENTER);
    label.setPreferredSize(new Dimension(width,25));
    label.setMaximumSize(new Dimension(width,25));
    label.setMinimumSize(new Dimension(width,25));
    label.setAlignmentX(CENTER_ALIGNMENT);

    setLayout(new BoxLayout(this, BoxLayout.Y_AXIS));
    setBorder(BorderFactory.createLineBorder(Color.blue, 2));

    add(image);
    add(label);
    setToolTipText(name);
    addMouseListener(this);
}
```

A method summary of the DropTargetListener interface class and its methods is illustrated in the following table.

Method	Description
`void dragEnter(DropTargetDragEvent d)`	Method called when the mouse pointer enters the operable part of the drop site for the target registered with a listener.
`void dragExit(DropTargetEvent d)`	Method called when the mouse pointer has exited the operable part of the drop site for the target registered with a listener.
`void dragOver(DropTargetDragEvent d)`	Method called when the mouse pointer is still over the operable part of the drop site for the target registered with a listener.
`void drop(DropTargetDropEvent d)`	Method called when the drag operation has terminated with a drop on the operable part of the drop site for the target registered with a listener.
`void dropActionChanged (DropTargetDragEvent d)`	Method called if the user has modified the current drop gesture.

Conveyance of food item descriptions and costs are performed through the `DataFlavor` class implementation. The `drop(DropTargetDropEvent e)` method determines the behavior transferred through the `Transferable` interface and because there is only one condiment type, Cheese, that will be the behavior passed into this method. The `dragEnter` and `dragExit` methods are used to color the borders of the items being dragged and dropped in the GUI presentation:

```java
public void drop(DropTargetDropEvent e) {
    try {
        DataFlavor stringFlavor = DataFlavor.stringFlavor;
        Transferable tr = e.getTransferable();
        if (e.isDataFlavorSupported(stringFlavor)) {
            String behavior = (String)tr.getTransferData(stringFlavor);
            e.acceptDrop(DnDConstants.ACTION_COPY_OR_MOVE);
            e.dropComplete(true);

            DisplayPanel.writeLine(handler.getDescription() + " " +
handler.getTotalCost());

            if (handler != null && updateTips) {
                setToolTipText(handler.getDescription());
            }
        } else {
            e.rejectDrop();
        }
    } catch (Exception ex) {}
        setBorder(BorderFactory.createLineBorder(Color.blue, 2));
}

public void dragEnter(DropTargetDragEvent e) {
    setBorder(BorderFactory.createLineBorder(Color.red, 3));
}
```

```
    public void dragExit(DropTargetEvent e) {
       setBorder(BorderFactory.createLineBorder(Color.blue, 2));
    }
    public void dragOver(DropTargetDragEvent e){}
    public void dropActionChanged(DropTargetDragEvent e) { }

    public void setHandler(FoodComponent handler) {
       this.handler = handker;
    }

    public void setBorderColor(Color col) {
       setBorder(BorderFactory.createLineBorder(col, 2));
    }
```

Data retrieval routines are implemented through the `FoodComponent` interface with the assistance of mouse event listeners so that user clicks on the individual food items result in text renderings in the display panel that indicate which item was selected by the user:

```
    public void mouseClicked(MouseEvent e) {
       if (clickHandler != null) {
          DisplayPanel.writeLine(handler.getDescription() + " selected. That'll cost
you " + handler.getCost());      }
    }

    public void mouseEntered(MouseEvent e) {}
    public void mouseExited(MouseEvent e) {}
    public void mousePressed(MouseEvent e) {}
    public void mouseReleased(MouseEvent e) {}
}
```

The `CondimentPanel` class generates a decorator object for the Cheese item and associates a coin value with that object so that it can be passed along to the food item it is decorated with. A hamburger costs $1.35 alone, but will add to, or decorate, that cost by 10 cents if cheese is appended to it. The panel layout consists of a combination `GridLayout` manager called `pictures`, with the cheese image and label, added to a `BoxLayout` manager that combines this panel with a label component for presentation in the GUI display above the three different food items:

```
    [CondimentPanel.java]
    // package name and import statements omitted

    public class CondimentPanel extends JPanel {

       JPanel pictures = null;
       GridLayout pictureLayout = null;
       public HashMap<String,FoodComponent> condimentPrices = new
    HashMap<String,FoodComponent>();

       public CondimentPanel(String title) {
          super();
          setBackground(Color.white);

          pictures = new JPanel();
          pictureLayout = new GridLayout(1, 1);
```

```
    pictures.setLayout(pictureLayout);
    pictures.setAlignmentX(CENTER_ALIGNMENT);
    pictures.setBorder(BorderFactory.createLineBorder(Color.red));

    pictures.add(new FoodDecoratorGraphic("Cheese", "resources/Cheese.gif",
0.35f));
    condimentPrices.put("Cheese", new Cheese());

    JLabel label = new JLabel(title, SwingConstants.CENTER);
    label.setPreferredSize(new Dimension(200, 25));
    label.setMinimumSize(new Dimension(200, 25));
    label.setMaximumSize(new Dimension(200, 25));
    label.setAlignmentX(CENTER_ALIGNMENT);

    setLayout(new BoxLayout(this, BoxLayout.Y_AXIS));

    add(label);
    add(pictures);
  }
}
```

Three individual classes were crafted to represent the different food items (Hamburger, Hotdog, and Pizza) on the food court display. The Hamburger class is similar to the other two food classes in structure but differs in cost and graphic icon representation. All of the food classes extend the Decorator class so that they can dictate their own individual behaviors:

```
package com.boxlayout;
class Hamburger extends Decorator
{
    private float cost = 1.15f;
    private String description = "Hamburger";
    private String graphic = "resources/Hamburger1.gif";

    public Hamburger(FoodComponent component)
    {
        super(component);
    }
    public String getDescription()
    {
        return description;
    }
    public float getCost()
    {
        return cost;
    }
    public float getTotalCost()
    {
        return component.getTotalCost() + cost;
    }
    public FoodGraphic getGraphic()
    {
        return new FoodGraphic(this, graphic, 100, 35);
    }
}
```

The final class discussed for the `BoxLayoutPanel` application is the `FoodItems` class. `FoodItems` implements its layout in a similar fashion to the `CondimentPanel` class. A `GridLayout` manager is crafted to accommodate the food item images, which is then added to a `BoxLayout` manager for the final presentation. The static helper component named `Box.createVerticalGlue` lets the application adjust when the parent container is resized by the user so that the box layout maintains its spacing:

```
[FoodItems.java]
// package name and import statements omitted
public class FoodItems extends JPanel {

    private static JPanel pictures = null;
    private static GridLayout pictureLayout = null;
    private static JPanel imagePanel = null;
    private Map<String,FoodComponent> members = null;
    private BoxLayoutPanel panel = null;
    private HashMap<String,FoodComponent> condimentPrices = new
HashMap<String,FoodComponent>();
    public FoodItems(BoxLayoutPanel panel, Hashtable condimentPrices) {
        super();

        this.panel = panel;
        members = new HashMap<String,FoodComponent>();

        setBackground(new Color(204,204,102));

        pictures = new JPanel();
        pictureLayout = new GridLayout(3, 2);
        pictureLayout.setHgap(5);
        pictureLayout.setVgap(5);
        pictures.setLayout(pictureLayout);
        pictures.setAlignmentX(CENTER_ALIGNMENT);

        imagePanel = new JPanel();
        imagePanel.setBackground(Color.white);
        imagePanel.setLayout(new BoxLayout(imagePanel, BoxLayout.X_AXIS));

        JLabel label = new JLabel("", SwingConstants.CENTER);
        label.setAlignmentX(CENTER_ALIGNMENT);
        label.setPreferredSize(new Dimension(200,20));
        label.setMinimumSize(new Dimension(200,20));
        label.setMaximumSize(new Dimension(200,20));

        setLayout(new BoxLayout(this, BoxLayout.Y_AXIS));

        Component padding = Box.createRigidArea(new Dimension(100, 1));
```

The following code segment illustrates how the individual food items are "decorated" by the cheese object where the cost of cheese is appended to the food object. Once the food item has the cost of cheese added to its own cost, the object is passed to the `addMember` method where it's added to the hashtable named `members` for future retrieval and to the `pictures` panel for visual rendering:

```
        FoodComponent fc = null;
        fc = new Hamburger(new Cheese());
        addMember(fc);
```

```
        fc = new Hotdog(new Cheese());
        addMember(fc);
        fc = new Pizza(new Cheese());
        addMember(fc);

        add(label);
        add(padding);
        add(pictures);
        add(Box.createVerticalGlue());
    }

    public void addMember(FoodComponent food) {
        if (!members.containsKey(food.getDescription())) {
            members.put(food.getDescription(), food);
            pictures.add(food.getGraphic());
        }
    }
}
```

Figure 4-4 represents the GUI that is displayed when the user executes the BoxLayout application. As stated previously, users can drag and drop the cheese condiment on the three different food items to determine the total cost of the two products combined. This cost aggregation occurs because the Decorator pattern implementation allows item costs to be dynamically appended to one another during run time with public interface components and private implementations. Additionally, users can click the individual food items to determine the cost of that single item. All events that are generated by mouse clicks or drag-and-drop operations are tracked by listener classes and logged to the food court text area display to monitor user navigation activities.

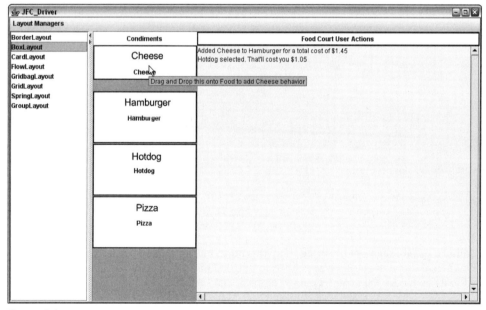

Figure 4-4

172

FlowLayout

The `FlowLayout` manager arranges components from left to right in the Container space; if the space on a line is exhausted, the components that are part of this manager will flow to the next line. By default, all components of the `FlowLayout` manager are centered in a horizontal fashion on each line. Three different constructors can be invoked to instantiate a `FlowLayout` manager object. The first constructor requires no parameters, and the second constructor requires an integer alignment value that indicates how components will be justified during construction. The last constructor method uses an integer alignment value like the aforementioned method, but also requires two integer values that specify horizontal and vertical gap values for pixel spacing.

The following `FlowLayout` example accepts a dollar value from the user and calculates the coin distribution using the Chain of Responsibility pattern. Figure 4-5 provides a high-level view of the `FlowLayoutPanel` application and how the Swing components are positioned on the `FlowLayout` panel.

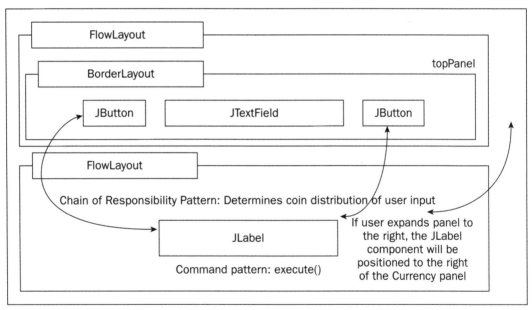

Figure 4-5

Request processing in the `FlowLayputPanel` application is handled with the Chain of Responsibility pattern that accepts the dollar amount from the user and cascades downward from the four different coin handlers (`QuarterHandler`, `DimeHandler`, `NickelHandler`, `PennyHandler`) until all the coins have been accounted for in the dollar amount specified by the user.

Pattern	Benefits	Consequences
Chain of Responsibility	Reduces coupling by allowing several objects the opportunity to handle a request. Distributes responsibilities among objects.	Requests can go unhandled with improper chain configuration.

The following `FlowLayoutPanel` class illustrates how the `FlowLayout` manager can be implemented. This sample application implements the `JFormattedTextField` class to dictate how the data must be input by the user and the `NumberFormat` class to establish what that format will be. Two buttons are created as extensions to the `JButton` class, one for kicking off the Chain of Responsibility pattern named `"Determine Coins"` and the other for clearing the text in the coin display panel:

```
[FlowLayoutPanel.java]
// package name and import statements omitted

public class FlowLayoutPanel extends JPanel implements ActionListener,
PropertyChangeListener {

  private JFormattedTextField amountField;
  private NumberFormat amountDisplayFormat;
  private NumberFormat amountEditFormat;
  // some GUI component initializations/declarations omitted for the sake of
brevity
  private JButtonCoins coinButton = new JButtonCoins("Determine Coins");
  private JButtonClear clearButton = new JButtonClear("Clear");

  private QuarterHandler quarterHandler;
  private DimeHandler dimeHandler;
  private NickelHandler nickelHandler;
  private PennyHandler pennyHandler;

  public FlowLayoutPanel() {
    setSize(700, 150);

    // Coin Button
    coinButton.setActionCommand("Coins");
    coinButton.addActionListener(this);

    // Clear button
    clearButton.setActionCommand("clear");
    clearButton.addActionListener(this);
```

The `FlowLayoutPanel` constructor establishes the currency display format using the `NumberFormat` class, which is the abstract base class for all number formats. The `setMinimumFractionDigits(int newValue)` method sets the minimum number of digits permitted in the fraction portion of a number. Once the format styles have been created, they can then be applied to the `JFormattedTextField` class used for rendering the dollar amount specified by the user. The `PropertyChangeListener` interface forces the application to deploy the `propertyChange` method (`PropertyChangeEvent evt`) to handle events when the dollar amount has been modified. The `BorderLayout` manager is applied to the `topPanel` component that organizes the `coinButton`, `amountField`, and `clearButton` components, which is added to the `FlowLayout` manager of the overall application by default:

```
amountDisplayFormat = NumberFormat.getCurrencyInstance();
amountDisplayFormat.setMinimumFractionDigits(0);
amountEditFormat = NumberFormat.getNumberInstance();

amountField = new JFormattedTextField(new DefaultFormatterFactory
                (new NumberFormatter(amountDisplayFormat),
                 new NumberFormatter(amountDisplayFormat),
                 new NumberFormatter(amountEditFormat)));
amountField.setValue(new Double(amount));
amountField.setColumns(10);
amountField.addPropertyChangeListener("value", this);

topPanel.add(coinButton);
topPanel.add(amountField);
topPanel.add(clearButton);

messageText = new JLabel("Coin Amounts");
results.add(messageText);
results.setPreferredSize(new Dimension(400, 100));
results.setBorder(BorderFactory.createLineBorder (Color.blue, 2));
results.setBackground(DIGIT_COLOR);

JPanel borderPanel = new JPanel(new BorderLayout());
borderPanel.setBorder(new TitledBorder("Formatted Currency"));
borderPanel.add(topPanel, BorderLayout.CENTER);
borderPanel.setSize(200,200);

add(borderPanel);
add(results);
```

The following code section implements the coin handlers that implement the Chain of Responsibility pattern to process all of the coins that are derived from the amount specified by the user in the GUI panel. The `setSuccessor(TestHandler successor)` method is used to specify the successor object along the chain of objects:

```
// setup chain of responsibility pattern implementation
try {
   quarterHandler = new QuarterHandler();
   dimeHandler = new DimeHandler();
   nickelHandler = new NickelHandler();
   pennyHandler = new PennyHandler();

   quarterHandler.setSuccessor( dimeHandler );
   dimeHandler.setSuccessor( nickelHandler );
   nickelHandler.setSuccessor( pennyHandler );
} catch( Exception e ) {
   e.printStackTrace();
}
}

public void propertyChange(PropertyChangeEvent e) {
   Object source = e.getSource();
   amount = ((Number)amountField.getValue()).doubleValue();
```

```
    }

    public void actionPerformed(ActionEvent e) {
        Command obj = (Command)e.getSource();
        obj.execute();
    }
```

The `JButtonCoins` method implements the `Command` interface to invoke the `execute()` method of the class when the user clicks the Determine Coins button. The dollar amount is read from the `amountField` component and passes that value to the `quarterHandler` object for coin processing. When all of the coins have been accounted for, the coin distribution will be displayed in the `messageText` component:

```java
class JButtonCoins extends JButton implements Command {

    public JButtonCoins(String caption) { super(caption); }
    public void execute() {

        amountField.setValue(new Double(amount));

        int coinAmount = (int)(amount * 100);
        quarterHandler.handleRequest(coinAmount);
        messageText.setText(" QUARTERS= " + quarterHandler.getCount() +
                            " DIMES= " + dimeHandler.getCount() +
                            " NICKELS= " + nickelHandler.getCount() +
                            " PENNIES= " + pennyHandler.getCount());
    }
}

class JButtonClear extends JButton implements Command {

    public JButtonClear(String caption) { super(caption); }
    public void execute() {
        amountField.setValue(new Double(0));
        messageText.setText("User cleared text: ");
    }
}

public interface Command {
    public void execute();
}

}
```

Individual coin handlers inherit the `TestHandler` class so get/set successor methods can be used to determine the successor objects that are implemented along the chain of coin handlers:

```java
[TestHandler.java]
// package name and import statements omitted
public class TestHandler {

    private TestHandler successor;

    public void setSuccessor( TestHandler successor ) { this.successor = successor; }
    public TestHandler getSuccessor() { return successor; }

    public void handleRequest(int coinAmount)
```

```
    { successor.handleRequest(coinAmount); }
}
```

The `QuarterHandler` class inherits the successor classes from its superclass `TestHandler` and takes the coin amount to determine how many quarters can be found in the dollar total. The modulus operator (`%`) divides the coin amount by 25 to determine the number of quarters in the sum, and takes the remainder and passes it along the chain of coin handlers for dimes, nickels, and pennies. For all of the handlers, if a remainder of zero is discovered, the chain processing is halted:

```
[QuarterHandler.java]
// package name and import statements omitted
public class QuarterHandler extends TestHandler {
    private int count;
    public void handleRequest(int coinAmount) {
        int numberQuarters = coinAmount / 25;
        coinAmount %= 25;
        this.count = numberQuarters;
        if (coinAmount > 0) getSuccessor().handleRequest(coinAmount);
    }
    public int getCount() {
        return this.count;
    }
}
```

Figure 4-6 represents the finished product of the `FlowLayoutPanel` application. When users add a dollar amount in the text field of the GUI application and click the Determine Coins button, the coin distribution will be displayed in the panel below the Formatted Currency panel. With the Chain of Responsibility pattern implementation, the coins are handled sequentially from quarters to dimes to nickels to pennies until all coins have been accounted for. An important point to take away from the Chain of Responsibility pattern is that rather than calling a single method to satisfy a request, multiple methods in a chain have a chance to fulfill that request.

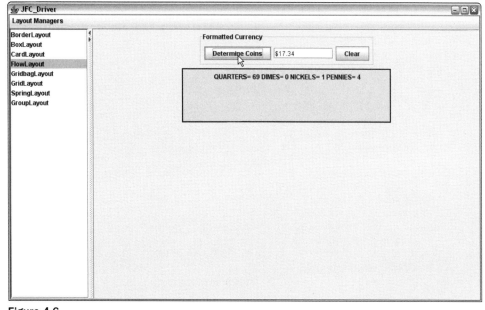

Figure 4-6

GridLayout

The `GridLayout` manager arranges its components in a rectangular, gridlike fashion. When components are added to the `GridLayout` manager, rows are populated first.

The following `GridLayout` example processes mouse events on buttons generated with Java 2D classes. Figure 4-7 shows how the buttons are organized on the `GridLayoutPanel` display.

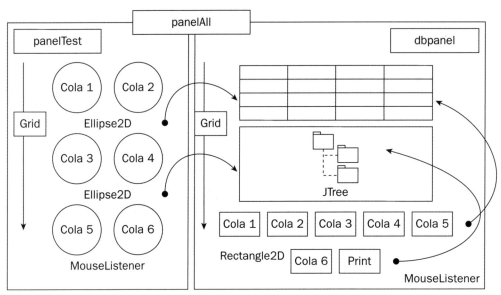

Figure 4-7

```
[GridLayoutPanel.java]
// package name and import statements omitted

public class GridLayoutPanel extends JPanel {

    // declarations omitted for the sake of brevity [Please check download code]
    public GridLayoutPanel() {

        JPanel panelAll = new JPanel(new GridLayout(0,2,5,5));

        DBPanel dbPanel = new DBPanel();
        Java2DPanel buttonPanel = new Java2DPanel(dbPanel);

        Java2DPanelMouseoverCola1 mouseButtonPanel = new
Java2DPanelMouseoverCola1(dbPanel);
        Java2DPanelMouseoverCola2 mouseButtonPane2 = new
Java2DPanelMouseoverCola2(dbPanel);
        Java2DPanelMouseoverCola3 mouseButtonPane3 = new
Java2DPanelMouseoverCola3(dbPanel);
        Java2DPanelMouseoverCola4 mouseButtonPane4 = new
Java2DPanelMouseoverCola4(dbPanel);
```

```
        Java2DPanelMouseoverCola5 mouseButtonPane5 = new
Java2DPanelMouseoverCola5(dbPanel);
        Java2DPanelMouseoverCola6 mouseButtonPane6 = new
Java2DPanelMouseoverCola6(dbPanel);
        Java2DPanelMouseclickPrint mouseclickPrint = new
Java2DPanelMouseclickPrint(dbPanel);

        JPanel panelTest = new JPanel(new GridLayout(0,1,5,5));
        dbPanel.add(mouseButtonPanel);
        dbPanel.add(mouseButtonPane2);
        dbPanel.add(mouseButtonPane3);
        dbPanel.add(mouseButtonPane4);
        dbPanel.add(mouseButtonPane5);
        dbPanel.add(mouseButtonPane6);
        dbPanel.add(mouseclickPrint);

        panelTest.add(dbPanel);
        panelAll.add(buttonPanel);
        panelAll.add(dataPanel);

        add(panelAll);
        setVisible(true);

    }
}
```

The Java2DPanel class implements the Rectangle2D class to create buttons to obtain information concerning six different Cola selections. These buttons are attached to a mouseListener handler to determine if a user has clicked the mouse inside one of those buttons. The setPreferredSize method allows the constructor class for Java2DPanel to set the panel display to a desired dimension using height and width values:

```
[Java2Dpanel.java]
// package name and import statements omitted

public class Java2DPanel extends JPanel implements MouseListener {

    DBPanel dbRef;
    Ellipse2D.Double circ1, circ2, circ3, circ4, circ5, circ6;

  public Java2DPanel(DBPanel db) {

      dbRef = db;
      // dark olive green outer circle
      circ1 = new Ellipse2D.Double(25, 25, 100, 100);
      circ2 = new Ellipse2D.Double(150, 25, 100, 100);

      circ3 = new Ellipse2D.Double(25, 150, 100, 100);
      circ4 = new Ellipse2D.Double(150, 150, 100, 100);

      circ5 = new Ellipse2D.Double(25, 275, 100, 100);
      circ6 = new Ellipse2D.Double(150, 275, 100, 100);
```

```
        this.addMouseListener(this);

        setBackground(Color.white);
        setPreferredSize(new Dimension(300, 200));
    }
```

When the `paintComponent(Graphics g)` method is invoked, six different circular buttons are drawn
on the user display to shadow the independent button drawings. These circular components are constructed by instantiating `Ellipse2D` class objects and filling them with the `Graphics2D fill(Shape s)`
method:

```
    public void paintComponent(Graphics g) {
        clear(g);

        Graphics2D g2 = (Graphics2D) g;
        g2.setRenderingHint(RenderingHints.KEY_ANTIALIASING,
RenderingHints.VALUE_ANTIALIAS_ON);

        // background lime green circle
        Ellipse2D.Double circle1 = new Ellipse2D.Double(35, 40, 100, 100);
        Ellipse2D.Double circle2 = new Ellipse2D.Double(160, 40, 100, 100);
        Ellipse2D.Double circle3 = new Ellipse2D.Double(35, 165, 100, 100);
        Ellipse2D.Double circle4 = new Ellipse2D.Double(160, 165, 100, 100);
        Ellipse2D.Double circle5 = new Ellipse2D.Double(35, 290, 100, 100);
        Ellipse2D.Double circle6 = new Ellipse2D.Double(160, 290, 100, 100);

        g2.setPaint(new Color(204, 255, 153));
        g2.fill(circle1);
        g2.fill(circle2);
        g2.fill(circle3);
        g2.fill(circle4);
        g2.fill(circle5);
        g2.fill(circle6);

        g2.setColor(new Color(123,123,45));

        g2.fill(circ1);
        g2.fill(circ2);
```

Now that the six different background buttons have been created and filled, the foreground buttons are
created by using the `Graphics2D drawstring(String str, int x, int y)` method to place string
text on the button display and the `fill(Shape s)` method to draw the circular button shape:

```
        g2.setColor(Color.black);
        g2.setFont(new Font("Serif", Font.BOLD, 18));

        g2.drawString("Cola 1", (float)(circ1.getX())+25,
(float)(circ1.getY()+circ1.getHeight()/2));
        g2.drawString("Cola 2", (float)(circ2.getX())+25,
(float)(circ2.getY()+circ2.getHeight()/2));

        g2.setColor(new Color(123,123,45));
        g2.fill(circ3);
```

```
    g2.fill(circ4);

    g2.setColor(Color.black);
    g2.setFont(new Font("Serif", Font.BOLD, 18));

    g2.drawString("Cola 3", (float)(circ3.getX())+25,
(float)(circ3.getY()+circ3.getHeight()/2));
    g2.drawString("Cola 4", (float)(circ4.getX())+25,
(float)(circ4.getY()+circ4.getHeight()/2));

    g2.setColor(new Color(123,123,45));
    g2.fill(circ5);
    g2.fill(circ6);

    g2.setColor(Color.black);
    g2.setFont(new Font("Serif", Font.BOLD, 18));

    g2.drawString("Cola 5", (float)(circ5.getX())+25,
(float)(circ5.getY()+circ5.getHeight()/2));
    g2.drawString("Cola 6", (float)(circ6.getX())+25,
(float)(circ6.getY()+circ6.getHeight()/2));
    }
```

User mouse events are verified by the `mousePressed(MouseEvent e)` method to see if the user clicked the mouse inside one of the Rectangle2D button shapes. If the application detects a click inside the button display area, the data values associated with that button will be set in the `JTree` and `JTable` components:

```
  public void mousePressed(MouseEvent e) {
      if ( insideCircle(e.getX(), e.getY(), circ1.getX(), circ1.getY(),
circ1.getWidth(), circ1.getHeight()) ) {
          dbRef.setRow(0);
          dbRef.addTreeData(0);
      }
      if ( insideCircle(e.getX(), e.getY(), circ2.getX(), circ2.getY(),
circ2.getWidth(), circ2.getHeight()) ) {
          dbRef.setRow(1);
          dbRef.addTreeData(1);
      }
      if ( insideCircle(e.getX(), e.getY(), circ3.getX(), circ3.getY(),
circ3.getWidth(), circ3.getHeight()) ) {
          dbRef.setRow(2);
          dbRef.addTreeData(2);
      }
      if ( insideCircle(e.getX(), e.getY(), circ4.getX(), circ4.getY(),
cir4.getWidth(), circ4.getHeight()) ) {
          dbRef.setRow(3);
          dbRef.addTreeData(3);
      }
      if ( insideCircle(e.getX(), e.getY(), circ5.getX(), circ5.getY(),
circ5.getWidth(), circ5.getHeight()) ) {
          dbRef.setRow(4);
          dbRef.addTreeData(4);
      }
```

```
        if ( insideCircle(e.getX(), e.getY(), circ6.getX(), circ6.getY(),
    circ6.getWidth(), circ6.getHeight()) ) {
            dbRef.setRow(5);
            dbRef.addTreeData(5);
        }
    }
```

Boolean values, true or false, are returned by the insideCircle method based on user navigations and mouse clicks inside the independent cola button shapes on the panel display. Each button maintains a mapped area marked by height and width coordinates that can be used to acknowledge if a user is within the button bounds. Coordinates passed into insideCircle represent the mouse positioning in the user display:

```
    public boolean insideCircle(int xMouse, int yMouse, double x, double y, double
    width, double height) {
        if((xMouse >= x && xMouse <= x+width) && (yMouse >= y && yMouse <= y+height))
        {
            return true;
        }
        return false;
    }

    protected void clear(Graphics g) {
        super.paintComponent(g);
    }

    public void mouseDragged(MouseEvent e) {}
    public void mouseReleased(MouseEvent e) {}
    public void mouseMoved (MouseEvent e) {}
    public void mouseEntered (MouseEvent e) {}
    public void mouseExited (MouseEvent e) {}
    public void mouseClicked (MouseEvent e) {}

}
```

The Java2DPanelMouseoverCola1 component, like the other mouse-over classes, generates a square button that acts differently than the larger, elliptical Java2DPanel buttons in that user mouse-overs will automatically set cola values in the JTree and JTable data stores. The Java2DPanel application requires that a user click inside the button display area to emulate the same behavior:

```
[Java2DPanelMouseoverCola1.java]
// package name and import statements omitted

public class Java2DPanelMouseoverCola1 extends JPanel {

    // declarations omitted for the sake of brevity [Please check download code]
    public Java2DPanelMouseoverCola1(DBPanel dbRef) {

        this.dbRef = dbRef;
        setPreferredSize(new Dimension(100, 100));
        setSize(100,100);
        this.mouseOverColor = new Color(123,123,45);
```

```
      this.normalColor = new Color(204, 255, 153);
      this.paintColor = normalColor;
```

The addMouseListener method is used to track the individual mouse movements of the user across the panel component. When the user enters the button space with the Cola 1 label, the mouseOverColor will displace the normalColor value and the JTable and JTree components will point to the data associated with the Cola1 item using the displayTableRow1() method:

```
      this.addMouseListener(new MouseListener() {
         public void mouseEntered(MouseEvent e) {
            displayTableRow1();
            paintColor = mouseOverColor;
            repaint();
         }
         public void mouseExited(MouseEvent e) {
            paintColor = normalColor;
            repaint();
         }
         public void mouseDragged(MouseEvent e) {}
         public void mouseClicked(MouseEvent e) {}
         public void mousePressed(MouseEvent e) {}
         public void mouseReleased(MouseEvent e) {}
      });
   }

   public void displayTableRow1() {
     dbRef.setRow(0);
     dbRef.addTreeData(0);
   }
```

Appropriate paint colors are applied to the independent Java2D buttons by the paintComponent (Graphics g) method using the color value stored in the paintColor variable. The MouseEntered method sets the paintColor to the mouseOverColor value and when the user exits the button space, it is reset to the normalColor value:

```
   public void paintComponent(Graphics g) {

      Graphics2D g2d = (Graphics2D) g;

      g2d.setRenderingHint(RenderingHints.KEY_ANTIALIASING,
   RenderingHints.VALUE_ANTIALIAS_ON);
      Dimension d = this.getSize();

      g2d.clearRect(0, 0, d.width, d.height);

      int centerX = d.width / 2;
      int centerY = d.height / 2;

      int xOffset = d.width / 2 - 3;
      int yOffset = d.height / 2 - 3;

      g2d.setColor(this.paintColor);
```

```
        g2d.fillRect(0, 0, 100, 100);

        g2d.setColor(Color.black);
        g2d.setFont(new Font("Serif", Font.BOLD, 18));
        g2d.drawString("Cola 1", 25, 50);


    }
}
```

Six different cola values are stored in the JTable component that resides in the DBPanel container where user mouse clicks on the Java 2D button components dynamically set row selections inside the populated table. The DBPanel constructor method is called when the class is first invoked, where an object reference of the MyTableModel class, named mtm, invokes the populateTable(String[] s) method to initialize the table values to empty strings prior to establishing the layout managers needed to place the visual components on. Three different GridLayout managers are instantiated, and two of those—panelData and panelTree—are placed inside the panelAll layout panel:

```
[DBPanel.java]
// package name and import statements omitted

  public class DBPanel extends JPanel implements PropertyChangeListener,
TableModelListener {
      // declarations omitted for the sake of brevity [Please check download code]
      public DBPanel() {
          JPanel panelAll = new JPanel(new GridLayout(0,1,5,5));
          JPanel panelData = new JPanel(new GridLayout(0,1,5,5));
          panelData.add(panelTable());

          setPreferredSize(new Dimension(300, 450));
          String[] s = { "", "", "", "" };
          mtm.populateTable(s);
          addTableData();

          panelAll.add(panelData);

          JPanel panelTree = new JPanel(new GridLayout(0,1,5,5));
          panelTree.add(treePanel());

          panelAll.add(panelTree);
          addTreeData(0);

          add(panelAll);
          setBackground(Color.white);
      }
```

The addTableData() method populates the array of string values called *s* with the four different Cola attributes (Brand, Cost, Calories, and Size) and passes that array to the populateTable method for display. The addTree(int row) method allows users to add the Cola data to the row value passed into the method:

```
      public void addTableData() {
          String[] s = { "", "", "", "" };
          for (int i=0; i < tableData.length; i++) {
```

```
            s[0]=tableData[i][0]; s[1]=tableData[i][1]; s[2]=tableData[i][2];
    s[3]=tableData[i][3];
            mtm.populateTable(s);
        }
    }

    public void addTreeData(int row) {
        root = new DefaultMutableTreeNode("Cola Attributes");
        tree = new JTree(root);
        DefaultMutableTreeNode items;

        items = new DefaultMutableTreeNode("Cola " + (row+1));
        root.add(items);
        items.add(new DefaultMutableTreeNode("Brand= " + tableData[row][0]));
        items.add(new DefaultMutableTreeNode("Cost= " + tableData[row][1]));
        items.add(new DefaultMutableTreeNode("Calories= " + tableData[row][2]));
        items.add(new DefaultMutableTreeNode("Size= " + tableData[row][3]));
        scrollPane.getViewport().add( tree );
        tree.expandRow(0);
    }
```

The `panelTable()` method creates a new `MyTableModel` object reference and adds it to a `JTable` object called `tree`, which in turn is placed inside a scroll pane component so that users can navigate up and down in the table when cola data attributes are added to the table component. The `ListSelectionModel` interface is implemented to maintain the tables' row selection state. The `addListSelectionListener` method monitors the list so changes to that list are reflected in the GUI representation:

```
    public JPanel panelTable() {

        JPanel tablePanel = new JPanel(new GridLayout(0,1,5,5));

        mtm = new MyTableModel();
        table = new JTable(mtm);
        table.setPreferredScrollableViewportSize(new Dimension(250, 70));
        JScrollPane scrollPane = new JScrollPane(table);

        tablePanel.add(scrollPane);

        table.setSelectionMode(ListSelectionModel.SINGLE_SELECTION);
        ListSelectionModel rowSM = table.getSelectionModel();
        rowSM.addListSelectionListener(new ListSelectionListener() {
            public void valueChanged(ListSelectionEvent e) {
                //Ignore extra messages.
                if (e.getValueIsAdjusting()) return;

                lsm = (ListSelectionModel)e.getSource();
                if (lsm.isSelectionEmpty()) {
                    //no rows are selected
                } else {
                    selectedRow = lsm.getMinSelectionIndex();
                }
            }
        });
```

```
            // titledBorder logic omitted for the sake of brevity

        return tablePanel;
    }
```

The `treePanel()` method establishes a new `GridLayout` manager so a `JTree` structure can be embedded within a scroll pane, which will allow the user to vertically scroll up and down the tree structure. The `BorderFactory` class is implemented so that a compound border titled Tree Information frames the tree component:

```
    public JPanel treePanel() {
        JPanel tablePanel = new JPanel(new GridLayout(0,1,5,5));

        scrollPane = new JScrollPane();
        scrollPane.setVerticalScrollBarPolicy(
        JScrollPane.VERTICAL_SCROLLBAR_ALWAYS);
        scrollPane.setPreferredSize(new Dimension(250, 150));
        scrollPane.setBorder(
        BorderFactory.createCompoundBorder(BorderFactory.createCompoundBorder(
        BorderFactory.createTitledBorder("Tree Information"),
        BorderFactory.createEmptyBorder(5,5,5,5)),
        scrollPane.getBorder()));

        root = new DefaultMutableTreeNode("Annotations");
        tree = new JTree(root);
        scrollPane.getViewport().add( tree );

        tablePanel.add(scrollPane);
        return tablePanel;
    }

    public void propertyChange( PropertyChangeEvent e ) {}
    public void tableChanged(TableModelEvent e) {}
```

The `MyTableModel` class handles all of the table data for the six different Cola types through its method implementations. The `setValueAt` method stores an individual object value at a designated row and column value:

```
    class MyTableModel extends AbstractTableModel {
        String[] columnNames= { "Brand", "Cost", "Calories", "Size" };
        private Object[][] data;
        public int getColumnCount() { return columnNames.length; }
        public int getRowCount() { return (data == null) ? 0 : data.length; }
        public String getColumnName(int col) { return columnNames[col]; }
        public Object getValueAt(int row, int col) { return data[row][col]; }
```

```
        // addRow() and deleteRow(int row) methods were omitted for sake of brevity

        public void setValueAt(Object value, int row, int col) {
            data[row][col] = value;
        }
```

The `populateTable` method receives a string array of table data that relates to the Cola button selection so it can be added to the `JTable` component for observation. Once the table has been populated, then the `fireTableDataChanged()` method is invoked so these table changes are updated in the GUI view:

```
        public void populateTable(String[] s) {
            // if data exists in table, rewrite table for new entry
            int rowCount = getRowCount();
            if (rowCount != 0) {
                // add another row
                Object[][] temp = data;
                data = new Object[rowCount+1][getColumnCount()];
                // copy old items into new structure
                for (int i=0; i < temp.length; i++) {
                    data[i][0] = temp[i][0];
                    data[i][1] = temp[i][1];
                    data[i][2] = temp[i][2];
                    data[i][3] = temp[i][3];
                }
                for (int i=0; i < getColumnCount(); i++)
                    setValueAt(s[i], rowCount-1, i);
            } else {
                data = cData;
                for (int i=0; i < getColumnCount(); i++)
                    setValueAt(s[i], 0, i);
            }
            fireTableDataChanged();
        }
    }

    public void setRow(int row) {
        table.setRowSelectionInterval(row, row);
    }

}
```

Figure 4-8 represents the `GridLayoutPanel` application defined in the previous source code. When users click the Java 2D button images, proper Cola values will be highlighted in the Swing components on the right side of the GUI display.

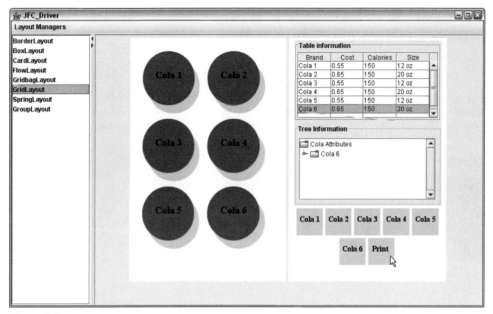

Figure 4-8

The `Java2DPanelMouseclickPrint` class allows users to print the cola attributes of the `JTable` component residing in the `DBPanel` object. When users employing the `GridLayout` model mouse over the Print icon and click it, a print dialog will pop up on the user's display so selections can be made as to how and where the table will be printed:

```
package com.gridlayout;

public class Java2DPanelMouseclickPrint extends JPanel {
    DBPanel dbRef;

    public Java2DPanelMouseclickPrint(final DBPanel dbRef)
    {
        this.dbRef = dbRef;
        setPreferredSize(new Dimension(50, 50));
        setSize(50,50);

        this.mouseOverColor = new Color(123,123,45);
        this.normalColor = new Color(204, 255, 153);
        this.paintColor = normalColor;

        this.addMouseListener(new MouseListener() {
            public void mouseEntered(MouseEvent e) {}
            public void mouseExited(MouseEvent e) {}
            public void mouseDragged(MouseEvent e) {}
            public void mouseClicked(MouseEvent e) {
                try {
                    MessageFormat headerFormat = new MessageFormat("Page {0}");
                    MessageFormat footerFormat = new MessageFormat("- {0} -");
                    dbRef.getTable().print(JTable.PrintMode.FIT_WIDTH,
headerFormat, footerFormat);
```

```
                } catch (Exception pe) {
                    System.err.println("Error printing: " + pe.getMessage());
                }
            }
        public void mousePressed(MouseEvent e) {}
        public void mouseReleased(MouseEvent e) {}
    });
    }
    public void paintComponent(Graphics g) { ... }
```

GridBagLayout

The GridBagLayout manager manages its components both vertically and horizontally by maintaining a rectangular grid of cells in its display area. Components are manipulated through constraint parameters using the GridBagConstraints class. These constraints specify where a component's display area should be positioned on the grid and its size using minimum and preferred size attributes.

The table here describes some attributes that can be implemented to position the GridBagLayout manager on a user display.

Instance Variables	Description
gridx, gridy	Specifies the cells containing the leading corner of the component's display area, where the cell at the origin of the grid has address x = 0 degrees and y = 0 degrees. For applications that have horizontal left-to-right layouts, the leading corner is on the upper left. For applications that have horizontal right-to-left layouts, the leading corner is on the upper right.
weightx, weighty	Used to determine how to distribute space for resizing. All components are placed together in the middle of a container unless a weightx or weighty value is specified. The GridBagLayout manager appends additional space between its cells and the container edges when the default weight is initialized to zero.
insets	Specifies the component's padding, which amounts to the minimum space available between the component and the display area edges.
fill	Implemented when the component's display area is larger than the component's requested size to determine whether (and how) to resize the component. GridBagConstraints.NONE (the default) GridBagConstraints.HORIZONTAL — Enables the component to fill its display area horizontally, not vertically. GridBagConstraints.VERTICAL — Allows the component to fill its display area vertically, not horizontally. GridBagConstraints.BOTH — Allows the component to fill its display area both vertically and horizontally.

The following GridBagLayout example applies both the Command and Visitor patterns to handle user events and message generation from Swing component activities. Figure 4-9 provides a model of the application and the component distribution on the GridBagLayout and their listeners.

GridBagLayout

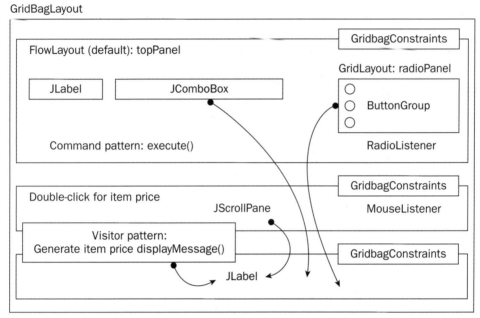

Figure 4-9

The GridBagLayoutPanel application will incorporate the Command and Visitor patterns to handle button requests for answers to the questions selected by the user in the different question components. Some of the benefits and shortcomings of these patterns are shown in the following table.

Pattern	Benefits	Consequences
Visitor	Separates operations from the objects that perform operations on it. Objects of the primary type *accept* the visitor and then call the visitor's dynamically bound method in a process referred to as *double dispatch.* Adding new operations is facilitated, no need for recompilation.	Difficult to maintain. Forces you to provide public operations that access internal state data, which may break encapsulation.

The `GridBagLayoutPanel` class incorporates the `GridBagLayout` manager, which allows for the placement of GUI components in a grid formation of rows and columns. The width and height of the rows and columns do not necessarily have to be the same size throughout a panel display, but this sample application maintains consistency across rows and columns for its GUI components:

```
[GridBagLayoutPanel.java]
// package name and import statements omitted

public class GridBagLayoutPanel extends JPanel implements ActionListener {
    // declarations omitted for the sake of brevity [Please check download code]
    private String[] data = {"Cranberry Muffin",
                             "Orange Sherbert",
                             "Potato Chips"};
```

The `GridBagLayoutPanel` constructor method declares and initializes the Swing components used for the food market application. First a `JComboBox` component is created with a list of food items that can be selected from the drop-down list. Next, a group of radio buttons is created, grouped together, and registered to the application using the `RadioListener` class. Those radio buttons are grouped vertically and appended to the `radioPanel`, while the drop-down list and the radio buttons are appended to the `topPanel` display for user interaction. Lastly, the same food items are added to a `JScrollPane` component and registered with a `MouseListener` so cost values are displayed when a user double-clicks a question in the list:

```
public GridBagLayoutPanel() {

    setSize(200, 150);
    cbQuestion = new JComboQuestion();
    cbQuestion.addActionListener(this);

    label = new JLabel("Food item: ");
    label.setFont(messageFont);

    RadioListener radioListener = new RadioListener();
    buttonCranberryMuffin.addActionListener(radioListener);
    buttonOrangeSherbert.addActionListener(radioListener);
    buttonPotatoChips.addActionListener(radioListener);
    buttonCranberryMuffin.setMnemonic('1');
    buttonOrangeSherbert.setMnemonic('2');
    buttonPotatoChips.setMnemonic('3');

    group.add(buttonCranberryMuffin);
    group.add(buttonOrangeSherbert);
    group.add(buttonPotatoChips);

    JPanel radioPanel = new JPanel();
    radioPanel.setLayout(new GridLayout(0, 1));
    radioPanel.add(buttonCranberryMuffin);
    radioPanel.add(buttonOrangeSherbert);
    radioPanel.add(buttonPotatoChips);
```

In the following code snippet, a `JList` component is instantiated and attached to a mouse listener so user clicks are detected upon that list. If a user double-clicks a list item, the `displayMessage()` method will be invoked with the cost of that item in the list:

```java
final JList list = new JList(data);
MouseListener mouseListener = new MouseAdapter() {
    public void mouseClicked(MouseEvent e) {
        if (e.getClickCount() == 2) {
            logger.info("Double clicked: " + list.locationToIndex(e.getPoint()));
            displayMessage();
        }
    }
};
list.setFont(listFont);
list.addMouseListener(mouseListener);
JScrollPane listScroller = new JScrollPane(list);
listScroller.setPreferredSize(new Dimension(100, 125));
listScroller.setBorder(new TitledBorder("Double-click query for item value"));
topPanel.add(label);
topPanel.add(cbQuestion);
topPanel.add(radioPanel);
topPanel.setBorder(new TitledBorder("Supermarket"));

messageText = new JLabel("Please pick a food item...
messageText.setFont(messageFont);
results.add(messageText);
results.setPreferredSize(new Dimension(400, 50));
results.setBorder(BorderFactory.createLineBorder (Color.blue, 2));
results.setBackground(Color.yellow);
```

The following code segment demonstrates how the components are rendered using the `GridBagLayout` manager. The `GridBagConstraints` class is instantiated so that constraints can be specified for the GUI components in the application using the `GridBagLayout` manager:

```java
setLayout(new GridBagLayout());

GridBagConstraints c = new GridBagConstraints();
c.gridx = 0;
c.gridy = 0;
c.weightx = 0.5;
c.insets = new Insets( 2, 2, 2, 2 );
c.fill = GridBagConstraints.BOTH;
add(topPanel, c);

c.gridy = 1;
c.weightx = 0.5;
c.gridwidth = 1;
c.fill = GridBagConstraints.HORIZONTAL;
add(listScroller, c);

c.gridx = 0;
c.gridy = 2;
c.weightx = 0.0;
c.insets = new Insets( 50, 50, 0, 0 );
c.fill = GridBagConstraints.NONE;
```

```
      add(results, c);
   }

   public void actionPerformed(ActionEvent e) {
      JComboQuestion cb = (JComboQuestion)e.getSource();
      Command obj = (Command)e.getSource();
      String question = (String)cb.getSelectedItem();
      if (!question.equals("Pick a food item?")) {
         obj.execute();
      }
   }
}
```

The JComboQuestion class implements the Command pattern interface so the GridBagLayoutPanel class can invoke its execute() method when a user clicks the combo box affiliated with a food list reference qbQuestion. The Command pattern increases reuse by decoupling the interface from the implementation, which means that all GUI components in the GridBagLayoutPanel class can use the public execute() method interface to serve as a gateway to private implementations associated with them:

```
class JComboQuestion extends JComboBox implements Command {

   public JComboQuestion() {
      this.addItem("Pick a food item?");
      this.addItem("Cranberry Muffin");
      this.addItem("Orange Sherbert");
      this.addItem("Potato Chips");
      setFont(messageFont);
   }
   public void execute() {
      displayMessage();
   }
}
```

The displayMessage() method selects a random number between one and three and uses that number to generate a fortune using the Visitor pattern. The Visitor pattern implementation polymorphically determines the proper accept method to call during operations:

```
public void displayMessage() {
   MessageText mt = new MessageText();
   if (msg.equals("Cranberry Muffin"))
      ((SuperMarket)new CranberryMuffin()).accept(text);
   else if (msg.equals("Orange Sherbert"))
      ((SuperMarket)new OrangeSherbert()).accept(text);
   else if (msg.equals("Potato Chips"))
      ((SuperMarket)new PotatoChips()).accept(text);
   messageText.setFont(messageFont);
   messageText.setText(text.getCost());
   results.add(messageText);
}

public interface Command {
   public void execute();
}

class RadioListener implements ActionListener {
```

```
    public void actionPerformed(ActionEvent e) {
        displayMessage();
    }
}

static public void main(String argv[]) {
    JFrame frame = new JFrame("GridBagLayout");
    frame.addWindowListener(new WindowAdapter() {
        public void windowClosing(WindowEvent e) {System.exit(0);}
    });
    frame.getContentPane().add(new GridBagLayoutPanel(), BorderLayout.CENTER);
    frame.pack();
    frame.setVisible(true);
}

}
```

Figure 4-10 shows the visual representation of the GridLayoutPanel application. Item prices will be generated by the Visitor pattern implementation when the user selects a particular item from the different JRadioButton, JComboBox, and JScrollPane components.

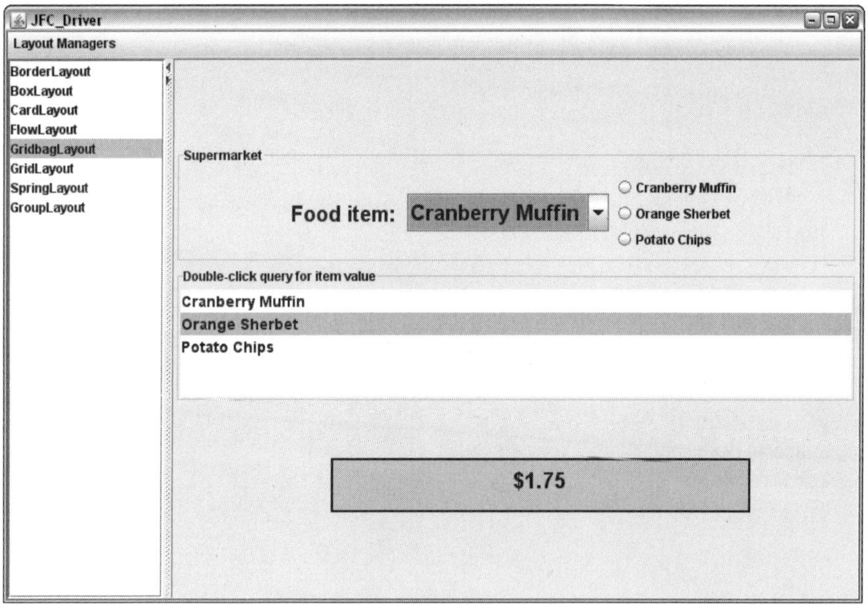

Figure 4-10

SpringLayout

The SpringLayout manager lays out its Container components according to user-specified constraint parameters. Each constraint, represented by a Spring object, controls the vertical or horizontal distance between two component edges. The edges can belong to any child of the container or to the container itself.

The SpringLayout manager does not set the location of its components automatically like some of the other layout managers. Component locations need to be initialized through constraint parameters so that minimum, maximum, and preferred lengths can be contained and bound. The following are some of the fields used to describe the constraints for component placement.

Field	Description
static String EAST	Right edge of component
static String NORTH	Top edge of component
static String SOUTH	Bottom edge of component
static String WEST	Left edge of component

The following SpringLayout example allows users to generate log entries for their triathlon events using a simple form display. Simple checks will be performed on the data prior to submission to ensure that all of the relevant data has been entered by the user. When the user saves that event, it will be stored in a JTable component for review. Figure 4-11 demonstrates what the SpringLayout application will look like. Only one tabbed panel will be on display at a time, which will be dictated by the user navigations from the button components at the bottom of the application.

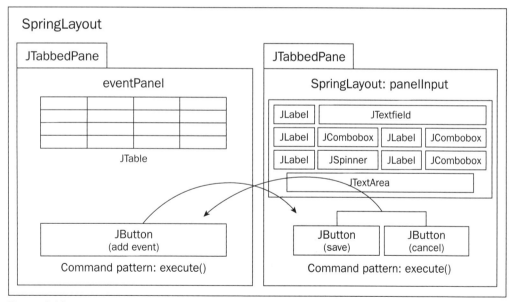

Figure 4-11

195

The following code segment outlines in code how the model in Figure 4-11 will be realized:

```
[SpringLayoutPanel.java]
// package name and import statements omitted

public class SpringLayoutPanel extends JPanel implements ActionListener {

  // declarations omitted for the sake of brevity [Please check download code]
  public SpringLayoutPanel(String name) {
    initComponents();
  }

  private void initComponents() {
    tabPanel = new JTabbedPane();

    eventPanel = new JPanel();
    eventPanel.setLayout(new BorderLayout());
    eventPanel.setPreferredSize(new Dimension(350, 400));
    eventPanel.setToolTipText("Event");
    eventPanel.add("Center", EventPanel());

    tabPanel.addTab("Triathlon Record Log", eventPanel);
    add(tabPanel, BorderLayout.CENTER);
  }
```

The `EventPanel()` method initializes many of the Swing components in the SwingLayoutPanel application and combines `BorderLayout` and `GridLayout` manager panels to obtain its visualization needs:

```
public JPanel EventPanel() {
    JPanel ePanel = new JPanel(new GridLayout(0, 1, 5, 5));
    ePanel.setMaximumSize(new Dimension(350, 400));
    ePanel.setMinimumSize(new Dimension(350, 400));
    ePanel.setPreferredSize(new Dimension(350, 400));

    eventPanel = new JPanel();
    eventButtonPanel = new JPanel();
    addEventButton = new JAddEventButton();

    eventPanel.setLayout(new BorderLayout());
    eventPanel.setMinimumSize(new Dimension(350, 400));
    eventPanel.setPreferredSize(new Dimension(350, 400));

    gridPanel = new JPanel(new GridLayout(0, 1, 5, 5));
    gridPanel.add(panelTable());

    eventButtonPanel.setLayout(new GridLayout(1, 2));

    addEventButton.setText("Add New Event");
    addEventButton.setToolTipText("Add New Event");
    addEventButton.addActionListener(this);
    eventButtonPanel.add(addEventButton);
    eventButtonPanel.setPreferredSize(new Dimension(350, 30));
    eventPanel.add(eventButtonPanel, BorderLayout.SOUTH);
```

```
        eventPanel.add(gridPanel, BorderLayout.NORTH);

        String[] s = { "", "", "", "" };
        mtm.populateTable(s);

        ePanel.add(eventPanel);

        return ePanel;
    }
```

The `panelTable` method implements a `GridLayout` manager to accommodate the inclusion of a `JTable` component that will store the different triathlon log entries. A `ListSelectionListener` is instantiated to handle user events that affect the table:

```
    public JPanel panelTable() {

        JPanel tablePanel = new JPanel(new GridLayout(0, 1, 5, 5));

        mtm = new MyTableModel();
        table = new JTable(mtm);
        table.setPreferredScrollableViewportSize(new Dimension(250, 70));
        JScrollPane scrollPane = new JScrollPane(table);
        tablePanel.add(scrollPane);

        table.setSelectionMode(ListSelectionModel.SINGLE_SELECTION);
        ListSelectionModel rowSM = table.getSelectionModel();
        rowSM.addListSelectionListener(new ListSelectionListener() {
            public void valueChanged(ListSelectionEvent e) {
                if (e.getValueIsAdjusting()) return;

                lsm = (ListSelectionModel) e.getSource();
                if (lsm.isSelectionEmpty()) {
                    //no rows are selected
                } else {
                    selectedRow = lsm.getMinSelectionIndex();
                    logger.info("selectedRow= " + selectedRow);
                }
            }
        });
        return tablePanel;
    }
```

The `formPanel()` method implements a `SpringLayout` manager where all of the log entry components are placed so user training activities can be tracked. Two Swing library layout managers, `BorderLayout` and `GridLayout`, are combined so a `SpringLayout` manager that holds the triathlon training attributes can be placed above the Save and Cancel buttons:

```
    public JPanel formPanel() {

        springLayout = new SpringLayout();
        panelInput = new JPanel(springLayout);
```

```
        panelInput.setMinimumSize(new Dimension(350, 370));
        panelInput.setPreferredSize(new Dimension(350, 370));

        eventPanel = new JPanel();
        eventPanel.setLayout(new BorderLayout());
        eventPanel.setPreferredSize(new Dimension(350, 400));

        panelButton = new JPanel();
        panelButton.setLayout(new GridLayout(1, 4));

        panelButton.setMinimumSize(new Dimension(350, 30));
        panelButton.setPreferredSize(new Dimension(350, 30));

        textareaDescription = new JTextArea();

        buttonSave = new JButtonSave();
        buttonCancel = new JButtonCancel();

        comboboxTime = new JComboBox();

        trainingLength = new String[] { "15 min", "30 min", "45 min", "1 hr", "2 hrs"
};
        comboboxLength = new JComboBox(trainingLength);
        textfieldTitle = new JTextField();
        category = new String[] { "Swim", "Bike", "Run", "Other" };
        comboboxCategory = new JComboBox(category);

        model = new SpinnerDateModel();
        model.setCalendarField(Calendar.WEEK_OF_MONTH);
        spinner = new JSpinner(model);
        JSpinner.DateEditor editor =
            new JSpinner.DateEditor(spinner, "MMMMM dd, yyyy");
        spinner.setEditor(editor);
        ChangeListener listener = new ChangeListener() {
            public void stateChanged(ChangeEvent e) {
                SpinnerModel source = (SpinnerModel) e.getSource();
                System.out.println("The value is: " + source.getValue());
            }
        };
        model.addChangeListener(listener);

        // label declarations and initializations for Title, Date, Category, Time,
    Duration, and Description omitted for better clarity
```

The subsequent code segment establishes two button components and a text area display for the triathlon entry form. The text area named `textareaDescription` is enabled and has an etched border frame to surround it. Minimum and maximum size constraints are defined as well as column values and line wrapping so that text entered by a user remains in sight of that user. Buttons for both the save and cancel operations have text labels attached to them with new font declarations and tool tip text for mouse-over pop-ups that indicate what purpose those buttons serve:

```
textareaDescription.setEnabled(true);
textareaDescription.setBorder(BorderFactory.createEtchedBorder());
textareaDescription.setMinimumSize(new Dimension(85, 51));
textareaDescription.setPreferredSize(new Dimension(85, 51));
textareaDescription.setText("");
textareaDescription.setColumns(25);
textareaDescription.setLineWrap(true);

buttonSave.setText("Save event");
buttonSave.setFont(new java.awt.Font("Dialog", 1, 12));
buttonSave.addActionListener(this);
buttonSave.setToolTipText("Save event.");
buttonSave.setPreferredSize(new Dimension(58, 25));

buttonCancel.setText("Return to event list.");
buttonCancel.setFont(new java.awt.Font("Dialog", 1, 12));
buttonCancel.addActionListener(this);
buttonCancel.setToolTipText("Return to event list.");
buttonCancel.setPreferredSize(new Dimension(58, 25));
```

The following code segment dictates how to implement `SpringLayout` constraints to achieve the look and feel of the disparate Swing components for tracking. The `Constraints` object of the `SpringLayout` manager positions the edges of the children in the container object through vertical and horizontal values:

```
//Add the components to the panel using SpringLayout.
panelInput.add(labelTitle,new
SpringLayout.Constraints(Spring.constant(15),Spring.constant(21)));
panelInput.add(textfieldTitle,new
SpringLayout.Constraints(Spring.constant(45),Spring.constant(17)));
panelInput.add(labelTime,new
SpringLayout.Constraints(Spring.constant(13),Spring.constant(69)));
panelInput.add(comboboxTime,new
SpringLayout.Constraints(Spring.constant(45),Spring.constant(63)));
panelInput.add(labelLength,new
SpringLayout.Constraints(Spring.constant(190),Spring.constant(69)));
panelInput.add(comboboxLength,new
SpringLayout.Constraints(Spring.constant(250),Spring.constant(63)));
panelInput.add(labelCategory,new
SpringLayout.Constraints(Spring.constant(190),Spring.constant(115)));
panelInput.add(comboboxCategory,new
SpringLayout.Constraints(Spring.constant(250),Spring.constant(109)));
panelInput.add(labelDate,new
SpringLayout.Constraints(Spring.constant(15),Spring.constant(115)));
panelInput.add(spinner,new
SpringLayout.Constraints(Spring.constant(45),Spring.constant(111)));
panelInput.add(textareaDescription,new
SpringLayout.Constraints(Spring.constant(10),Spring.constant(217)));
panelInput.add(labelDescription,new
SpringLayout.Constraints(Spring.constant(11),Spring.constant(201)));

for (int i = 0; i < 24; i++) {
    timeString = Integer.toString(i);
    if (timeString.length() == 1)
```

```
                timeString = "0" + timeString;
            if (i != 0) {
                comboboxTime.addItem(timeString + "00");
                comboboxTime.addItem(timeString + "15");
                comboboxTime.addItem(timeString + "30");
                comboboxTime.addItem(timeString + "45");
            }
        }
        comboboxTime.addItem("2400");
        comboboxTime.setSelectedItem("0930");

        eventPanel.add(BorderLayout.CENTER, panelInput);
        eventPanel.add(BorderLayout.SOUTH, panelButton);

        JPanel ePanel = new JPanel(new BorderLayout());
        ePanel.add(eventPanel, BorderLayout.CENTER);

        panelButton.add(buttonSave);
        panelButton.add(buttonCancel);

        return ePanel;
    }
```

The `JAddEventButton` class handles mouse events on the first tabbed pane display that occur when the user clicks the Add Event button on the bottom of the display. The application polymorphically invokes the `execute()` method, which removes all of the current panel components with the `removeAll()` method, and then creates a new layout so the `SpringLayout` manager can be applied from the `formPanel()` method:

```
class JAddEventButton extends JButton implements Command {
    public JAddEventButton() {
        super();
    }
    public void execute() {
        logger.info("[JAddEventButton:execute]");
        eventPanel.removeAll();
        eventPanel.setLayout(new BorderLayout());
        eventPanel.add(formPanel());
        eventPanel.requestFocusInWindow();
        eventPanel.validate();
    }
}
```

The `JButtonSave` component handles user events that occur when the user clicks the Save Event button. A cursory data check is performed on the title field to ensure that a proper title has been entered by the user prior to moving back to the initial tabbed panel screen with the user entry displayed in a `JTable` component:

```
class JButtonSave extends JButton implements Command {
    public JButtonSave() {
        super();
    }
```

```
        public void execute() {
            if (textfieldTitle.getText().length() == 0 || textfieldTitle.getText() ==
null) {
                Toolkit.getDefaultToolkit().beep();
                JOptionPane.showMessageDialog(null, "Please Enter Event Title",
                                        "Error", JOptionPane.ERROR_MESSAGE);
                textfieldTitle.requestFocusInWindow();
                textfieldTitle.selectAll();
                return;
            }

            JOptionPane.showMessageDialog(null, "Event saved.",
                                        "Operation Completed",
                                        JOptionPane.INFORMATION_MESSAGE);

            restoreLogPanel();
            String[] s = { "", "", "", "" };
            s[0] = (String) comboboxCategory.getSelectedItem();
            s[1] = textareaDescription.getText();
            s[2] = (String) comboboxTime.getSelectedItem();
            mtm.populateTable(s);
        }
    }

    class JButtonCancel extends JButton implements Command {
        public JButtonCancel() {
            super();
        }
        public void execute() {
            logger.info("[JButtonCancel:execute] date = " + getDate());
            restoreLogPanel();
        }
    }
```

The getDate() method returns a string value from the JSpinner component that represents the date affiliated with the triathlon event. The restoreLogPanel() method invokes the removeAll() method to clear the panel display, establishes a new BorderLayout presentation panel, and initializes that new panel with the triathlon event components for logging operations. The requestFocusInWindow() method is called to request that the panel component gets the input focus. Lastly, the validate() method is implemented to cause the container to lay out its subcomponents again:

```
    public String getDate() {
        return ((JSpinner.DateEditor) spinner.getEditor()).getTextField().getText();
    }

    public void restoreLogPanel() {
        removeAll();
        setLayout(new BorderLayout());
        initComponents();
        requestFocusInWindow();
        validate();
    }

    public void actionPerformed(ActionEvent e) {
```

```
        Command obj = (Command) e.getSource();
        obj.execute();
    }
    // main method omitted for beter clarity
}
```

Figure 4-12 represents the `SpringLayoutPanel` tabbed panel application that appears on the user display when a user invokes the Add Event button. The form display performs a cursory check on the data to ensure proper data is entered by the user when the Save Event button is clicked. The `SpringLayout` manager distributes `JTextField`, `JComboBox`, `JSpinner`, and `JTextArea` components using constraint values positioning.

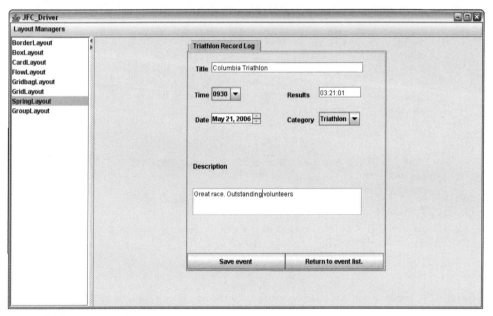

Figure 4-12

CardLayout

The `CardLayout` manager organizes its components as a stack of cards, where components are displayed one at a time. This allows components to be easily swapped in and out like a slide show presentation. The following `CardLayout` example employs the `Command` and `Strategy` patterns to encapsulate behavior that will be applied to the user text. Figure 4-13 shows the `CardLayout` model and the different Swing components applied to that layout manager panel.

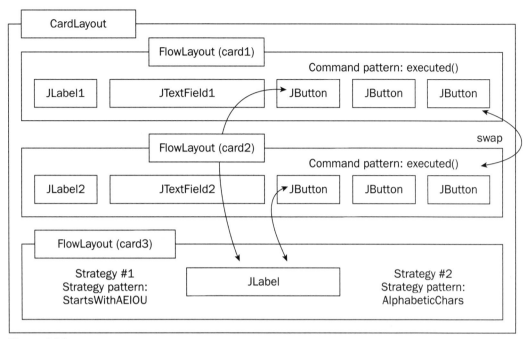

Figure 4-13

The CardLayoutPanel application utilizes the Strategy pattern to apply different algorithms to user-specified text. The Command pattern is used to polymorphically determine what strategy to apply during runtime. Some of the benefits and drawbacks of these two patterns are shown in the following table.

Pattern	Benefits	Consequences
Strategy	Decouples algorithms so programs can be more flexible in their execution of logic and behavior. Reduces multiple conditional statements.	Increases number of objects.

The CardLayoutPanel source code follows to demonstrate how the model in Figure 4-13 can be developed. The CardLayoutPanel constructor lays out the manager for the two card panels, card1 and card2. The card1 panel contains two independent buttons that implement the Strategy pattern on user-specified text. The card2 panel reveals the text that results from the State pattern algorithm application. The JButtonStrategy1 class applies the Pig-Latin algorithm to the user text when solicited by the user. The `JButtonStrategy2` button converts the user text to uppercase text by applying the AlphabeticChars algorithm in its operations:

```
[CardLayoutPanel.java]
// package name and import statements omitted

public class CardLayoutPanel extends JPanel implements ActionListener, ItemListener
{
  public CardLayoutPanel() {

      setSize(700, 150);
      cards = new JPanel(new CardLayout());
      card1 = new JPanel();
      card2 = new JPanel();
      card3 = new JPanel();

      // swap buttons
      swapButton1.addActionListener(this);
      swapButton1.setActionCommand("Swap to Strategy 2");
      swapButton2.addActionListener(this);
      swapButton2.setActionCommand("Swap to Strategy 1");

      // Strategy Buttons
      strategyButton1.setActionCommand("Strategy #1");
      strategyButton1.addActionListener(this);
      strategyButton2.setActionCommand("Strategy #2");
      strategyButton2.addActionListener(this);

      // Clear button
      clearButton1.setActionCommand("clear");
      clearButton1.addActionListener(this);
      clearButton2.setActionCommand("clear");
      clearButton2.addActionListener(this);

      topPanel1.add(labelText1);
      topPanel1.add(textfield1);
      topPanel1.add(strategyButton1);
      topPanel1.add(clearButton1);
      topPanel1.add(swapButton1);

      topPanel2.add(labelText2);
      topPanel2.add(textfield2);
      topPanel2.add(strategyButton2);
      topPanel2.add(clearButton2);
      topPanel2.add(swapButton2);

      messageText = new JLabel("Enter messages");
      results.add(messageText);
      results.setPreferredSize(new Dimension(700, 100));
      results.setBorder(BorderFactory.createLineBorder (Color.blue, 2));
      results.setBackground(DIGIT_COLOR);

      card1.add(topPanel1);
      card2.add(topPanel2);

      cards.add(cardText[0], card1);
```

```
        cards.add(cardText[1], card2);

        card3.add(results, "Results Panel");

        add(cards);
        add(card3);
    }
```

The `CardLayoutPanel` class implements the `ActionListener` interface so component objects created with that class can be registered using the `addActionListener(ActionListener l)` method shown in the previous code segment. The `actionPerformed(ActionEvent e)` method then processes the requests registered through the action listener. All of the `JButton` components in `CardLayoutPanel` implement the `Command` pattern interface method named `execute()` so the appropriate button control method logic is executed when the user clicks that component. This is feasible because the application uses the object reference to that `execute()` method for execution. If one of the swap buttons is selected, the sample application will alternate between strategy operations. The `cardLayout.next` method is implemented to swap operations, but alternative code that performs that same operation using the `swapNumber` token and the `cardLayout.show` method also demonstrates how to swap layouts:

```java
public void actionPerformed(ActionEvent e) {
    if (e.getActionCommand.startsWith("Swap")) {
        CardLayout cardLayout = (CardLayout)(cards.getLayout());
        // ++swapNumber;
        // cardlayout.show(cards, cardText[swapNumber%2]);
        cardLayout.next(cards);
    } else {
        Command obj = (Command)e.getSource();
        obj.execute();
    }
}
```

The `testStrategy(TestStrategy strategy, String m)` method allows the application to send in the appropriate Strategy algorithm class along with a String variable that will be applied to that algorithm. The object reference, called `strategy`, invokes the `test()` method in the `TestStrategy` interface:

```java
public boolean testStrategy(TestStrategy strategyApproach, String s) {
    return strategyApproach.test(s);
}
```

The `JButtonStrategy1` class invokes the `execute()` method when the user clicks the Strategy #1 button on the GUI panel. The text specified in the text field is stripped into individual tokens that are passed into the `StartsWithAEIOU` strategy class to return a Boolean value, true or false, if the token starts with either an a, e, i, o, or u. Strings that satisfy this test are converted to Pig-Latin by appending the word *way* to the end of the string. Tokens that don't match that test have their initial consonant value stripped from the start of the word and appended to the end along with the letters *ay*:

```java
class JButtonStrategy1 extends JButton implements Command {

    public JButtonStrategy1(String caption) { super(caption); }
    public void execute() {
        String s = textfield1.getText();
        String[] sArray = s.split("[ ,]+");
        StringBuffer sb = new StringBuffer();
```

```
            sb.append("PIG-LATIN: ");

            for (int i=0; i < sArray.length; i++) {
               if (testStrategy(new StartsWithAEIOU(), sArray[i])) {
                  sb.append(sArray[i] + "way ");
               } else {
                  sb.append(sArray[i].replaceAll("^([^aeiouAEIOU])(.+)", "$2$1ay "));
               }
            }
            messageText.setText(sb.toString());
         }
      }
```

The `JButtonStrategy2` class invokes the `execute()` method when the user clicks the Strategy #2 button on the GUI panel. The text specified in the text field is stripped into individual tokens that are passed into the `AlphabeticChars` strategy class to determine if they can be properly converted to uppercase lettering:

```
class JButtonStrategy2 extends JButton implements Command {

   public JButtonStrategy2(String caption) { super(caption); }
   public void execute() {
      String s = textfield2.getText();
      String[] sArray = s.split("[ ,]+");
      StringBuffer sb = new StringBuffer();
      sb.append("UPPERCASE: ");

      for (int i=0; i < sArray.length; i++) {
         if (testStrategy(new convertUppercase(), sArray[i])) {
            sb.append(sArray[i].toUpperCase());
            sb.append(" ");
         }
      }
      messageText.setText(sb.toString());
   }
}

class JButtonClear extends JButton implements Command {

   public JButtonClear(String caption) { super(caption); }
   public void execute() {
      textfield1.setText("");
      textfield2.setText("");
      messageText.setText("User cleared text: ");
   }
}

public void itemStateChanged(ItemEvent evt) {
   CardLayout cl = (CardLayout)(cards.getLayout());
   cl.show(cards, (String)evt.getItem());
```

```
    }

    public interface Command {
        public void execute();
    }
```

The `TestStrategy` interface is implemented by the `StartsWithAEIOU` and `AlphabeticChars` classes so the `CardLayoutPanel` application can apply different string algorithms to the user-specified text. Regular expression constructs are used to determine the patterns of the strings passed into the test method:

```
    public interface TestStrategy {
        public boolean test(String s);
    }

    public class StartsWithAEIOU implements TestStrategy {
        public boolean test(String s) {
            if( s == null || s.length() == 0) return false;
            return (s.toUpperCase().charAt(0) == 'A' ||
                        s.toUpperCase().charAt(0) == 'E' ||
                        s.toUpperCase().charAt(0) == 'I' ||
                        s.toUpperCase().charAt(0) == 'O' ||
                        s.toUpperCase().charAt(0) == 'U'
                    );
        }
    }

    public class convertUppercase implements TestStrategy {
        public boolean test(String s) {
            if( s == null || s.length() == 0 ) return false;
            Pattern pattern = Pattern.compile("[a-zA-Z]");
            Matcher match = pattern.matcher(s);
            if (!match.find()) {
                return false;
            } else {
                return (true);
            }
        }
    }

    // main routine omitted for brevity

}
```

Figure 4-14 represents the `CardLayoutPanel` application modeled in the previous source code. Users can enter text in the card layout shown in the top panel and click either strategy pattern button to apply the appropriate Strategy algorithm to that text. Results of those actions will be rendered in the card layout below. All of the button components employ the `Command` pattern to allow the application to determine at runtime the proper `execute()` method to invoke based on the user's navigations.

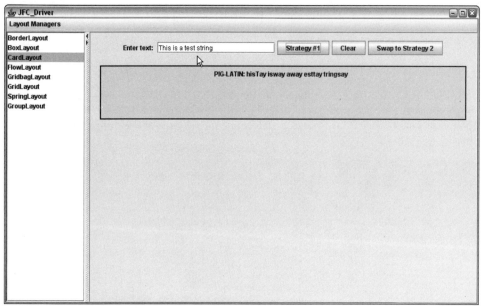

Figure 4-14

GroupLayout

The GroupLayout manager is a component of the NetBeans framework that is being considered for inclusion in the SE 6 Java framework. The GroupLayout manager is important in that it allows for horizontal and vertical layout positioning in an independent, flexible manner. With this manager, layout groups can be formed in both a sequential and parallel fashion. Sequentially, they are placed one after another, and in parallel, they are placed on top of one another and are aligned with a common reference axis.

A sample pizza delivery placement component design is shown in Figure 4-15. This model incorporates GroupLayout manager classes to position components on the user view. With this application, a user specifies his or her name, the toppings desired, and the size of the pizza for delivery. When the user makes the proper selections and clicks the order button, a receipt is generated with the user preferences.

All of the Swing components are instantiated and initialized at the onset of the GroupLayoutPanel class so they can be easily referenced by the GroupLayoutPanel method for display rendering. All of the user-selected data will be managed with a JTree object:

```
package com.grouplayout;

import java.util.logging.Logger;
import java.awt.*;
import java.awt.event.*;
import javax.swing.*;
import javax.swing.tree.DefaultMutableTreeNode;
import org.jdesktop.layout.*;

public class GroupLayoutPanel extends JPanel implements ActionListener {
```

```
    private JRadioButton largePizzaButton = new JRadioButton("Large");
    private JRadioButton mediumPizzaButton = new JRadioButton("Medium");
    private JRadioButton smallPizzaButton = new JRadioButton("Small");
    private JLabel label = new JLabel("Name:");;
    private JTextField textField = new JTextField();
    private JCheckBox anchoviesCheckBox = new JCheckBox("Anchovies");
    private JCheckBox mushroomsCheckBox = new JCheckBox("Mushrooms");
  private JCheckBox onionsCheckBox = new JCheckBox("Onions");
    private JCheckBox greenpeppersCheckBox = new JCheckBox("Green Peppers");
    private JCheckBox sardinesCheckBox = new JCheckBox("Sardines");
    private JCheckBox pepperoniCheckBox = new JCheckBox("Pepperoni");
    private JButtonOrder orderButton = new JButtonOrder("Order");
    private JButtonAllToppings allToppingsButton = new JButtonAllToppings("All
Toppings");
    private JPanel results = new JPanel();

    private JScrollPane scrollPane;
    private JTree tree;
    private DefaultMutableTreeNode root;
```

GroupLayout

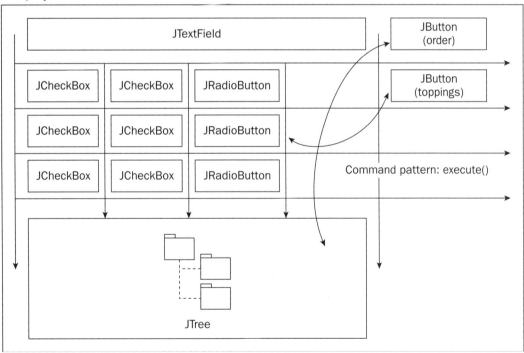

Figure 4-15

Results selected by the user will be reflected in a scroll pane to indicate all of the different dimensions and toppings the user has chosen for the pizza delivery:

```
public GroupLayoutPanel() {
    anchoviesCheckBox.setBorder(BorderFactory.createEmptyBorder(0, 0, 0, 0));
    mushroomsCheckBox.setBorder(BorderFactory.createEmptyBorder(0, 0, 0, 0));
    onionsCheckBox.setBorder(BorderFactory.createEmptyBorder(0, 0, 0, 0));
    greenpeppersCheckBox.setBorder(BorderFactory.createEmptyBorder(0, 0, 0,
0));
    sardinesCheckBox.setBorder(BorderFactory.createEmptyBorder(0, 0, 0, 0));
    pepperoniCheckBox.setBorder(BorderFactory.createEmptyBorder(0, 0, 0, 0));

    results.setLayout(new GridLayout(0,1));
    results.setPreferredSize(new Dimension(75, 75));
    results.setBorder(BorderFactory.createLineBorder (Color.blue, 2));
    results.setBackground(new Color(255, 255, 100));

    scrollPane = new JScrollPane();
    scrollPane.setVerticalScrollBarPolicy(
        JScrollPane.VERTICAL_SCROLLBAR_ALWAYS);
        scrollPane.setSize(75, 75);
        scrollPane.setPreferredSize(new Dimension(75, 75));
        scrollPane.setBorder(
            BorderFactory.createCompoundBorder(
                BorderFactory.createCompoundBorder(
                    BorderFactory.createTitledBorder("Pizza Order"),
                    BorderFactory.createEmptyBorder(5,5,5,5)),
                    scrollPane.getBorder()));

    root = new DefaultMutableTreeNode("Pizza Order");
    tree = new JTree(root);
    scrollPane.getViewport().add( tree );
    results.add(scrollPane);
```

Here is where the GroupLayout manager is instantiated and constructed to place the different Swing components for display rendering. Notice that horizontal groups are established and embedded on one another to get the grouping effect desired for presentation:

```
GroupLayout layout = new GroupLayout(this);
setLayout(layout);
layout.setAutocreateGaps(true);
layout.setAutocreateContainerGaps(true);

layout.setHorizontalGroup(layout.createSequentialGroup()
    .add(label)
    .add(layout.createParallelGroup(GroupLayout.LEADING)
        .add(textField)
        .add(layout.createSequentialGroup()
            .add(layout.createParallelGroup(GroupLayout.LEADING)
                .add(anchoviesCheckBox)
                .add(onionsCheckBox)
                .add(pepperoniCheckBox))
            .add(layout.createParallelGroup(GroupLayout.LEADING)
```

```
                    .add(mushroomsCheckBox)
                    .add(greenpeppersCheckBox)
                    .add(sardinesCheckBox))
                .add(layout.createParallelGroup(GroupLayout.LEADING)
                    .add(largePizzaButton)
                    .add(mediumPizzaButton)
                    .add(smallPizzaButton))) //)
            .add(results))
        .add(layout.createParallelGroup(GroupLayout.LEADING)
            .add(orderButton)
            .add(allToppingsButton))
    );
```

Vertical groups are established with the `setVerticalGroup` method so they can be aligned properly with previous horizontal group designations:

```
layout.linkSize(new Component[] { orderButton, allToppingsButton },
                GroupLayout.HORIZONTAL);
layout.setVerticalGroup(layout.createSequentialGroup()
    .add(layout.createParallelGroup(GroupLayout.BASELINE)
        .add(label)
        .add(textField)
        .add(orderButton))
    .add(layout.createParallelGroup(GroupLayout.LEADING)
        .add(layout.createSequentialGroup()
            .add(layout.createParallelGroup(GroupLayout.BASELINE)
                .add(anchoviesCheckBox)
                .add(mushroomsCheckBox)
                .add(largePizzaButton))
            .add(layout.createParallelGroup(GroupLayout.BASELINE)
                .add(onionsCheckBox)
                .add(greenpeppersCheckBox)
                .add(mediumPizzaButton))
            .add(layout.createParallelGroup(GroupLayout.BASELINE)
                .add(pepperoniCheckBox)
                .add(sardinesCheckBox)
                .add(smallPizzaButton)))
        .add(allToppingsButton))
        .add(layout.createParallelGroup(GroupLayout.BASELINE)
            .add(results))
    );
```

Now that all of the layout positions have been defined, the listeners associated with the individual components can be defined to track user event selections:

```
orderButton.addActionListener(this);
allToppingsButton.addActionListener(this);
largePizzaButton.addActionListener(this);
largePizzaButton.setActionCommand("large pizza");
mediumPizzaButton.addActionListener(this);
mediumPizzaButton.setActionCommand("medium pizza");
smallPizzaButton.addActionListener(this);
```

```
            smallPizzaButton.setActionCommand("small pizza");

            setBorder(BorderFactory.createLineBorder (Color.blue, 2));
    }

    class JButtonOrder extends JButton implements Command {

        public JButtonOrder(String caption) {
            super(caption);
        }
```

Polymorphic behavior is performed with the execute() method defined in the Command pattern interface
to finalize the user selections. With the Command pattern, additional execute() method implementations
could be defined later to add behaviors needed to perform operations for your application because operations are decoupled from objects that invariably know which operations need to be executed when invoked:

```
        public void execute() {
            String s = "Name: (empty)";

            tree = new JTree(root);
            DefaultMutableTreeNode items;

            if (!textField.getText().equals(""))
                s = textField.getText();
            items = new DefaultMutableTreeNode(s);
            root.add(items);

            s = "Size: None selected";
            if (largePizzaButton.isSelected())
                s = "Size: Large  pizza";
            else if (mediumPizzaButton.isSelected())
                s = "Size: Medium pizza";
            else if (smallPizzaButton.isSelected())
                s = "Size: Small pizza";
            items.add(new DefaultMutableTreeNode(s));

            if (anchoviesCheckBox.isSelected()) items.add(new
    DefaultMutableTreeNode("anchovies"));
            if (mushroomsCheckBox.isSelected()) items.add(new
    DefaultMutableTreeNode("mushrooms"));
            if (onionsCheckBox.isSelected()) items.add(new
    DefaultMutableTreeNode("onions"));
            if (greenpeppersCheckBox.isSelected()) items.add(new
    DefaultMutableTreeNode("peppers"));
            if (sardinesCheckBox.isSelected()) items.add(new
    DefaultMutableTreeNode("sardines"));
            if (pepperoniCheckBox.isSelected()) items.add(new
    DefaultMutableTreeNode("pepperoni"));

            scrollPane.getViewport().add( tree );
            tree.expandRow(0);
            results.add(scrollPane);
        }
    }
```

In the following code, the Command pattern is revealed in all its glory to dictate behavior associated with the All Toppings button. When the user clicks that button in the user display, the program knows that it must invoke the `execute()` method here to enable all of the checkbox components without explicitly stating so. During run time, the application retrieves the proper object reference so the `execute()` method associated with that reference will be called:

```java
class JButtonAllToppings extends JButton implements Command {

  public JButtonAllToppings(String caption) {
      super(caption);
  }

  public void execute() {
      anchoviesCheckBox.setSelected(true);
      mushroomsCheckBox.setSelected(true);
      onionsCheckBox.setSelected(true);
      greenpeppersCheckBox.setSelected(true);
      sardinesCheckBox.setSelected(true);
      pepperoniCheckBox.setSelected(true);
  }
}

public interface Command {
    public void execute();
}
```

Action events are monitored in the code that follows, in the `actionPerformed` method, to determine pizza dimension selections from the size radio buttons or to execute the Command pattern interface reference based on the user selection:

```java
public void actionPerformed(ActionEvent e) {

    if (e.getActionCommand().equals("large pizza")) {
        logger.info("Large pizza. Mama mia.");
        mediumPizzaButton.setSelected(false);
        smallPizzaButton.setSelected(false);
    } else if (e.getActionCommand().equals("medium pizza")) {
        logger.info("Want a drink with that? Big or Large?");
        largePizzaButton.setSelected(false);
        smallPizzaButton.setSelected(false);
    } else if (e.getActionCommand().equals("small pizza")) {
        logger.info("Take your pizza and go you cheapa-skate!");
        largePizzaButton.setSelected(false);
        mediumPizzaButton.setSelected(false);
    } else {
        Command obj = (Command)e.getSource();
        obj.execute();
    }
}

public static void main(String args[]) {
  JFrame frame = new JFrame("GroupLayoutPanel");

  frame.addWindowListener(new WindowAdapter() {
```

```
        public void windowClosing(WindowEvent e) {System.exit(0);}
        });

        frame.getContentPane().add(new GroupLayoutPanel(), BorderLayout.CENTER);
        frame.pack();
        frame.setVisible(true);
    }
}
```

Figure 4-16 represents a sample visualization of the pizza delivery placement application. In it, the user has placed selections for desirable toppings and size needs. Both the Order and All Toppings buttons implement the Command pattern interface so specific behaviors can be invoked when selected to call proper execute() method implementations.

With the GroupLayout manager, arrangements occur both sequentially and in parallel to form hierarchical presentations. Components arranged in parallel are stacked on top of one another along a common axis, whereas sequentially arranged components are placed after one another. Each dimension is defined independently and can operate without consideration to the other dimensions. The only deficiency associated with GroupLayout usage is that each component needs to be defined twice in the layout during implementation.

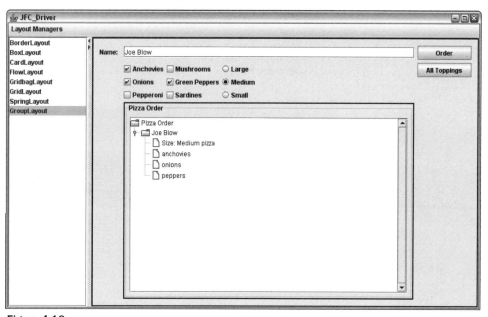

Figure 4-16

Mustang Release Desktop Enhancements

This chapter addresses a few of the new Java 6 SE Mustang features, namely system attribute collection, splash screen inclusion, and AWT modifications that are part of new modality modes. Improved drag-and-drop support and JTable sorting were shown in earlier sections of this chapter.

The following table outlines the four new AWT modality models introduced with the Java Mustang release.

Modal Type	Description
Mode-less	Does not block any other window while it's rendered on the user display.
Document-modal	Blocks all windows from the same document with the exception of those windows from its child hierarchy.
Application-modal	Blocks all windows from the same application with the exception of those windows from its child hierarchy.
Toolkit-modal	Blocks all windows from the same toolkit with the exception of those toolkits from its child hierarchy.

The following example demonstrates the mode-less type of dialog creation, which means that the dialog box does not block any other window rendered on the user display. The intent of this new modality inclusion is to scope dialog box displays so they cannot block operations from one another during program operations.

The new Tray feature provides a shortcut capability that allows users to quickly invoke their applications for deployment from the desktop tray. Figure 4-17 is deployed when the desktop icon is clicked. Along with the system tray integration, this application demonstrates the inclusion of several new capabilities included in the Mustang release, specifically a splash screen pop-up, new Modal APIs, the ability to obtain file system attributes, perform authentication operations upon invocation, and to append Java components to a tabbed display.

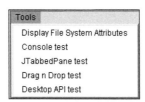

Figure 4-17

This code segment is kicked off when the user clicks the icon in the desktop tray. New Modal capabilities are demonstrated with the Frame and Dialog components. The new Dialog class allows developers to limit a dialog's blocking capability when rendered. This feature circumvents previous versions of Java that blocked input to other top-level windows that were part of an application and were not created with the dialog box as its parent. Now dialog boxes can have a null parent that limits the scope of a dialog box's modality:

```
package tray;

import java.awt.*;
import java.awt.datatransfer.*;
import java.io.*;
import java.sql.*;
```

```
import java.util.*;
import java.awt.event.*;

import javax.swing.*;
import javax.swing.text.*;
import javax.swing.event.*;

public class TrayDemo
{
    private static Frame frame;
    private Font labelFont = new Font("Arial", 18, Font.PLAIN);
    private Dialog dialog = new Dialog(frame, "Modeless Dialog");
    private Dialog dialog2 = new Dialog(frame, "Document-modal Dialog",
Dialog.ModalityType.DOCUMENT_MODAL);
    private JPanel tab, tab2;
    private JLabel[] label = { new JLabel("Question 1"), new JLabel("Question 2"),
new JLabel("Question3") };
    private JTabbedPane tabbedPane;
    private Dialog dialogConsole = new Dialog(frame, "Modeless Dialog");
    private static Vector<String> v = new Vector<String>();
    private JTextField urlTextfield = new JTextField(30);
    private JTextField emailTextfield = new JTextField(30);
    private JButton btnBrowser = new JButton();
    private JButton btnEmail = new JButton();
    private String username = "", password ="";
```

Once the `TrayDemo` constructor attempts to invoke the splash screen pop-up by executing the get SpashScreen() method from the `SplashScreen` class, a check is performed to ensure that the system tray can be placed on the system desktop. Passage through this check will allow the application to retrieve an icon and place it in the system tray so users can invoke the application with the new desktop icon. A `MouseListener` class is initialized and instantiated so the application can be popped up when a mouse click event on the desktop icon is detected:

```
public TrayDemo() {
    final TrayIcon trayIcon;
    final SplashScreen splash = SplashScreen.getSplashScreen();
    if (splash == null) {
        System.out.println("SplashScreen.getSplashScreen() returned null");
    }
    if (SystemTray.isSupported()) {
        SystemTray tray = SystemTray.getSystemTray();
        Image image = Toolkit.getDefaultToolkit().getImage("tray.gif");

        MouseListener mouseListener = new MouseListener() {

            public void mouseClicked(MouseEvent e) {
                System.out.println("Tray Icon - Mouse clicked!");
                frame = new Frame("SDK 6 - Modal implementation");

                JTextComponent textComp = createTextComponent();
                textComp.setBorder(
                BorderFactory.createCompoundBorder(
                BorderFactory.createCompoundBorder(
                BorderFactory.createTitledBorder("Text"),
                BorderFactory.createEmptyBorder(5,5,5,5)),
```

```
                    textComp.getBorder())));
                     textComp.setEditable(false);

                frame.add(textComp, BorderLayout.CENTER);
                frame.addWindowListener(closeWindow);
                frame.setSize(700, 500);
                frame.setMenuBar(createMenuBar());
                frame.setVisible(true);
            }
        public void mouseEntered(MouseEvent e) {
            System.out.println("Tray Icon - Mouse entered!");
        }
        public void mouseExited(MouseEvent e) {
            System.out.println("Tray Icon - Mouse exited!");
        }
        public void mousePressed(MouseEvent e) {
            System.out.println("Tray Icon - Mouse pressed!");
        }
        public void mouseReleased(MouseEvent e) {
            System.out.println("Tray Icon - Mouse released!");
        }
    };

    ActionListener exitListener = new ActionListener() {
        public void actionPerformed(ActionEvent e) {
            System.out.println("Exiting...");
            System.exit(0);
        }
    };
```

The PopupMenu class is instantiated so it can be passed to the trayIcon object that is attached to the ActionListener object that tracks events from the application. Additionally, the trayIcon object is attached to the mouseListener object so events can be tracked from the desktop view:

```
PopupMenu popup = new PopupMenu();
MenuItem defaultItem = new MenuItem("Exit");
defaultItem.addActionListener(exitListener);
popup.add(defaultItem);

trayIcon = new TrayIcon(image, "Tray Demo", popup);

ActionListener actionListener = new ActionListener() {
    public void actionPerformed(ActionEvent e) {
        trayIcon.displayMessage("Action Event",
            "An Action Event Has Been Peformed!",
            TrayIcon.MessageType.INFO);
    }
};

trayIcon.setImageAutoSize(true);
trayIcon.addActionListener(actionListener);
trayIcon.addMouseListener(mouseListener);

try {
    tray.add(trayIcon);
} catch (AWTException e) {
```

```
                  System.err.println("TrayIcon could not be added.");
            }
        } else {
            System.err.println("System tray is currently not supported.");
        }
    }

    protected JTextComponent createTextComponent() {
        JTextArea ta = new JTextArea();
        ta.setLineWrap(true);
        return ta;
    }

    private static WindowListener closeWindow = new WindowAdapter() {
        public void windowClosing(WindowEvent e) {
            e.getWindow().dispose();
        }
    };
```

All of the menu bar options are constructed in the createMenuBar method for presentation to the user.
First, the menu items must be instantiated and initialized so that listener objects can be attached to them.
These listeners track system events triggered by the user to enable operations for execution:

```
    protected MenuBar createMenuBar() {
        MenuBar menubar = new MenuBar();
        Menu menu = new Menu("Tools");
        menubar.add(menu);
        MenuItem displayAttributes = new MenuItem("Display File System
Attributes");
        MenuItem consoleTest = new MenuItem("Console test");
        MenuItem tabTest = new MenuItem("JTabbedPane test");
        displayAttributes.addActionListener(new ActionListener() {
            public void actionPerformed(ActionEvent e) {
                dialog.setBounds(132, 132, 300, 200);
                dialog.addWindowListener(closeWindow);
                dialog.setLayout(new BorderLayout());

                java.util.List<String> diskspace = new ArrayList<String>();
                DefaultListModel listModel = new DefaultListModel();
                JList list = null;

                File[] roots = File.listRoots();
                for (int i=0; i < roots.length; i++) {
                    diskspace.add(("root>" + roots[i] + "  Free space: " +
roots[i].getFreeSpace() + " bytes"));
                    diskspace.add(("root>" + roots[i] + "  Usable space: " +
roots[i].getUsableSpace() + "bytes"));
                }

                for (String s : diskspace) {
                    listModel.addElement(s);
                }
                list = new JList(listModel);
                JScrollPane listScrollPane = new JScrollPane(list);

                dialog.add(listScrollPane, BorderLayout.CENTER);
```

```
                dialog.setVisible(true);
        }
    });
    menu.add(displayAttributes);

    consoleTest.addActionListener(new ActionListener() {
        public void actionPerformed(ActionEvent e) {
            dialogConsole.setBounds(132, 132, 300, 200);
            dialogConsole.addWindowListener(closeWindow);
            dialogConsole.setLayout(new BorderLayout());
            login();
            //dialogConsole.add( , BorderLayout.CENTER);
            dialogConsole.setVisible(true);
        }
    });
    menu.add(displayAttributes);
    menu.add(consoleTest);
```

Figure 4-18 demonstrates a new Mustang enhancement to allows GUI developers to append Java components to a tab display. Previously, users were only allowed to implement icons and text items to a tab. The following sample display allows users to answer Yes or No for questions on the first two tabbed panes from drop-down menus and to select answers from checkboxes on the last tabbed component.

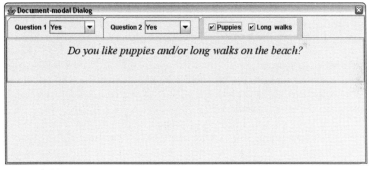

Figure 4-18

Implementation of the tab menu item is demonstrated in the following code snippet. The `tabTest` component establishes the tabbed pane panel along with the questions and the drop-down menus and checkboxes with the possible answers to those questions:

```
    tabTest.addActionListener(new ActionListener() {
            public void actionPerformed(ActionEvent e) {
                JPanel testPanel = new JPanel(new BorderLayout());
                testPanel.setBounds(0, 0, 700, 300);

                dialog2.setBounds(100, 100, 700, 300);
                dialog2.addWindowListener(closeWindow);
                dialog2.setLayout(new BorderLayout());

                tabbedPane = new JTabbedPane();

                String[] questions = { "Did you like this race?",
```

```
                                          "Have you run a triathlon before?",
                                          "Do you like puppies and/or long walks on
    the beach?" };

                    String[] answers = { "Yes", "No", "Undecided" };

                    // Create a combobox
                    JComboBox combo = new JComboBox();
                    combo.setBounds( 20, 35, 100, 20 );
                    for( int iCtr = 0; iCtr < answers.length; iCtr++ )
                       combo.addItem( answers[iCtr] );

                    JComboBox combo2 = new JComboBox();
                    combo2.setBounds( 20, 35, 100, 20 );
                    for( int iCtr = 0; iCtr < answers.length; iCtr++ )
                       combo2.addItem( answers[iCtr] );

                    JComboBox combo3 = new JComboBox();
                    combo3.setBounds( 20, 35, 160, 20 );
                    for( int iCtr = 0; iCtr < answers.length; iCtr++ )
                       combo3.addItem( answers[iCtr] );

                    JPanel tab1 = new JPanel();
                    tab1.add(label[0], BorderLayout.WEST);
                    tab1.add(combo, BorderLayout.EAST);
                    tabbedPane.addTab("Tab1", null, makeTextPanel(questions[0]),
    "Tab1");
```

New capabilities of the `setTabComponent` method are manifested in the following code segment, where drop-down menus are used for both the tab1 and tab2 panels, and the tab2 panel implements the `longwalksButton` checkbox along with the `puppiesButton` so users can select either or both of the answers in response to the panel question:

```
                    tabbedPane.setTabComponentAt(0, tab1);

                    JPanel tab2 = new JPanel();
                    tab2.add(label[1], BorderLayout.WEST);
                    tab2.add(combo2, BorderLayout.EAST);
                    tabbedPane.addTab("Tab2", null, makeTextPanel(questions[1]),
    "Tab2");
                    tabbedPane.setTabComponentAt(1, tab2);

                    JPanel tab3 = new JPanel();
                    tab3.add(label[2], BorderLayout.WEST);
                    tab3.add(combo3, BorderLayout.EAST);
                    JCheckBox puppiesButton = new JCheckBox("Puppies");
                    puppiesButton.setSelected(false);
                    JCheckBox longwalksButton = new JCheckBox("Long  walks");
                    longwalksButton.setSelected(false);
                    JPanel checkPanel = new JPanel();
                    checkPanel.add(puppiesButton, BorderLayout.WEST);
                    checkPanel.add(longwalksButton, BorderLayout.EAST);
```

```
                    tabbedPane.addTab("Tab3", null, makeTextPanel(questions[2]),
    "Tab3");

                    tabbedPane.setTabComponentAt(2, checkPanel);

                    testPanel.add(tabbedPane, BorderLayout.NORTH);

                    dialog2.add(testPanel, BorderLayout.CENTER);
                    dialog2.setVisible(true);
            }
        });
        menu.add(tabTest);
```

Here, new drag-and-drop functionality is implemented so users can add text to a `JTextField` component and drag that text to a `JScrollPane` drop area. Four different drop modes are listed in commented
text to outline what capabilities are available to users for drag-and-drop implementations, but the
`TrayDemo` application uses the `DropMode.INSERT` to enable text conveyance:

```
        dndTest.addActionListener(new ActionListener()
        {
            public void actionPerformed(ActionEvent e) {
                System.out.println("DnD test...");

                JPanel testPanel = new JPanel(new BorderLayout());
                testPanel.setBounds(0, 0, 700, 300);

                dialog2 = new Dialog(frame, "Document-modal Dialog",
    Dialog.ModalityType.DOCUMENT_MODAL);
                dialog2.setBounds(0, 0, 700, 300);
                dialog2.addWindowListener(closeWindow);
                dialog2.setLayout(new BorderLayout());
                dialog2.setSize(700, 300);

                final JList listDND = new JList();
                listDND.setModel(new DefaultListModel());
                // Drop modes:
                // 1. DropMode.USE_SELECTION
                // 2. DropMode.ON
                // 3. DropMode.INSERT
                // 4. DropMode.ON_OR_INSERT
                listDND.setDropMode(DropMode.INSERT);
```

With the Java Mustang release, a new `TransferHandler.TransferInfo` inner class can be implemented to capture the details of every transfer during drag-and-drop activities. The `canImport` method
determines whether or not drag-and-drop operations can occur with a component. Data import operations are enabled with the `importData` method:

```
                listDND.setTransferHandler(new TransferHandler() {
                    public boolean canImport(TransferHandler.TransferSupport
    support)
                    {
                        if (!support.isDataFlavorSupported(DataFlavor.stringFlavor)
    || !support.isDrop())
```

```
                               return false;

                        JList.DropLocation dropLocation =
        (JList.DropLocation)support.getDropLocation();

                        return dropLocation.getDropPoint() != null;
                    }

                    public boolean importData(TransferHandler.TransferSupport
        support) {
                        if (!canImport(support))
                            return false;

                        JList.DropLocation dropLocation =
        (JList.DropLocation)support.getDropLocation();
                        Transferable transferable = support.getTransferable();

                        String transferData;
                        try {
                            transferData =
        (String)transferable.getTransferData(DataFlavor.stringFlavor);
                        } catch (Exception e) {
                            e.printStackTrace();
                            return false;
                        }
```

When a user marks code in the textfield area, and drags it to the pane drop area, this code adds that text to a vector collection and uses the `setListData` method for data inclusion in the visualization component:

```
                        v.addElement(transferData);
                        listDND.setListData(v);
                        return true;
                    }
                });

                JLabel dragLabel = new JLabel("Drag me:");
                JScrollPane pane = new JScrollPane(listDND);
                final JTextField textfield = new JTextField();
                textfield.setDragEnabled(true);
                testPanel.add(dragLabel, BorderLayout.WEST);
                testPanel.add(textfield, BorderLayout.CENTER);
                testPanel.add(pane, BorderLayout.SOUTH);

                dialog2.add(testPanel, BorderLayout.NORTH);
                dialog2.setVisible(true);
            }
        });
        menu.add(dndTest);
```

In this section of the source code, new Desktop API classes and methods are implemented to read textfield data that is transferred to desktop classes for browser and email application invocation. The `isDesktopSupported` method ensures that the Desktop API is available so the application can retrieve an instance for method execution:

```
        deskTest.addActionListener(new ActionListener() {
            public void actionPerformed(ActionEvent e) {
                System.out.println("deskTest selected...");

                dialog2 = new Dialog(frame, "Document-modal Dialog",
Dialog.ModalityType.DOCUMENT_MODAL);
                dialog2.setBounds(0, 0, 600, 100);
                dialog2.addWindowListener(closeWindow);
                dialog2.setLayout(new GridLayout(0,1));

                JPanel desktopPanel = new JPanel(new GridLayout(0,3));
```

A button is enabled here to launch the user's browser with the url text specified by the user in the browser textfield:

```
                btnBrowser.setText("Browser");
                btnBrowser.addActionListener(new ActionListener() {
                    public void actionPerformed(ActionEvent evt) {
                        if (Desktop.isDesktopSupported()) {
                            Desktop desktop = Desktop.getDesktop();
                            URI uri = null;
                            try {
                                uri = new URI(urlTextfield.getText());
                                desktop.browse(uri);
                            } catch(Exception e) {
                                e.printStackTrace();
                            }
                        }
                        else
                            System.out.println("Desktop not supported");
                    }
                });
```

An email button launches the host's default email client with the text specified in the email textfield:

```
                btnEmail.setText("Email");
                btnEmail.addActionListener(new ActionListener() {
                    public void actionPerformed(ActionEvent evt) {
                        if (Desktop.isDesktopSupported()) {
                            Desktop desktop = Desktop.getDesktop();
                            String mailTo = emailTextfield.getText();
                            URI uri = null;
                            try {
                                if (mailTo.length() > 0) {
                                    uri = new URI("mailto", mailTo, null);
                                    desktop.mail(uri);
                                }
                            } catch(Exception e) {
                                e.printStackTrace();
                            }
                        }
                        else
```

```
                              System.out.println("Desktop not supported");
                    }
              });

              JLabel urlLabel = new JLabel("URL:");
              JLabel emailLabel = new JLabel("Email:");
              desktopPanel.add(urlLabel);
              desktopPanel.add(urlTextfield);
              desktopPanel.add(btnLaunchBrowser);
              desktopPanel.add(emailLabel);
              desktopPanel.add(emailTextfield);
              desktopPanel.add(btnLaunchEmail);
              dialog2.add(desktopPanel);
              dialog2.setVisible(true);
          }
      });
      menu.add(deskTest);

      return menubar;
  }
```

The login() method demonstrates new security capabilities introduced with the Mustang release so developers can affiliate username/password schemes with Swing applications. If the user enters an inappropriate username/password combination, a modal display will not be rendered to the user invoking that component:

```
    public void login() {
        Console console = System.console ();
        if (console == null) {
            System.err.println ("console procurement unsuccessful.");
            return;
        }

        // Obtain username.
        username = console.readLine ("Enter username: ");

        // Obtain password.
        password = new String (console.readPassword ("Enter password: "));

        try {
            System.out.println("username, password= " + username + ", " +
password);
        }
catch (Exception e) {
            System.out.println("Exception detected: " + e.toString());
        }
    }

    public static void main(String[] args) {
        TrayDemo main = new TrayDemo();
    }

}
```

Managing Navigation Flows in Swing Applications

Installation wizards are common Swing applications to consign software applications and their libraries to their file systems during their development or deployment tasks. Wizards typically perform initialization activities, gather user directory designations, and perform post-installation tasks for clean-up actions by leading users through a series of requests to ensure that applications and their libraries are configured properly for operations. This last segment of the chapter demonstrates how an InstallationWizard application can be developed using the State Pattern, a GoF behavioral pattern, to delegate behaviors across objects during user navigations at runtime. Each state, or step, of the wizard is encapsulated as an object, which is affiliated to a subclass of an abstract class for proper state management. This same application could have easily been developed with the `CardLayout` manager using its `first()`, `last()`, `previous()`, and `next()` methods, but the intent was to show how you could manage those flows in a different fashion.

The following table outlines some of benefits and drawbacks of implementing both patterns in your applications.

Pattern	Benefits	Consequences
Singleton	Direct control over how many instances can be created. Ensures that a class has only one instance and enforces controlled access to the sole instance.	Inability to subclass an application that implements it, which prevents extendability.
State	Allows an object to modify its behavior when its state changes internally. Localizes all behavior of a particular state in a single object. Polymorphically defines behaviors and states of an object.	Preponderance of classes to support the different states of an application.

The individual panel display components represent state-specific behaviors that are derived from the abstract `State` class. The application maintains a pointer to the current state position in the installation process and reacts to changes by the user as navigation is performed in a forward and backward direction using the Previous and Next buttons on the GUI display (see Figure 4-19).

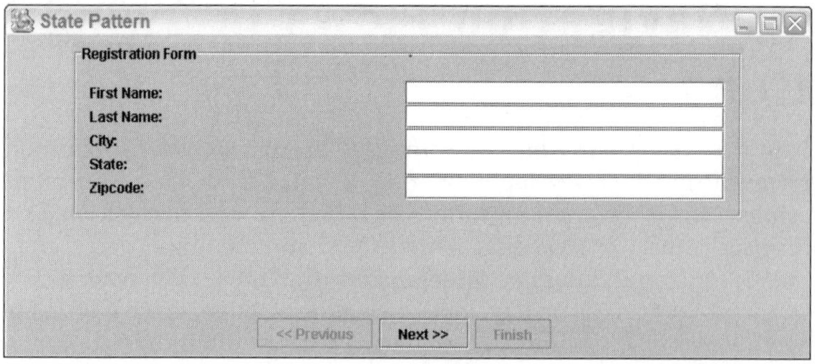

Figure 4-19

The InstallationWizard application implements two `JPanel` components, `componentPanel` and `buttonPanel`, to display the individual Swing visualizations for user input and the buttons used for previous/next operations, respectively:

```java
// [InstallationWizard.java]
// package name and import statements omitted

public class InstallationWizard implements ActionListener {

    private static Logger logger = Logger.getLogger("InstallationWizard");

    private static Frame frame;
    private JPreviousButton previousButton = new JPreviousButton("<< Previous");
    private JNextButton nextButton = new JNextButton("Next >>");
    private JFinishButton finishButton = new JFinishButton("Finish");
    private JPanel componentPanel;
    private JPanel buttonPanel;
    private Context context = new Context();

    private static WindowListener closeWindow = new WindowAdapter() {
        public void windowClosing(WindowEvent e) {
            e.getWindow().dispose();
        }
    };

    InstallationWizard() {
        frame = new Frame("Installation Wizard");
        frame.setBounds(32, 32, 300, 200);
        frame.addWindowListener(closeWindow);
        frame.setSize(700,300);
        frame.setLayout(new BorderLayout());
```

The application establishes a context reference that the application uses to determine proper panel visualization flows. The `FlowLayout` manager is used with the `buttonPanel` to position the buttons used for directing the wizard flow. The context reference invokes the `getColor()` method to set the background color of the panel component (the default color is Yellow) with the `setBackground(Color bg)` method. Additionally, the `previousButton` and `finishButton` components are disabled by the `setEnabled(Boolean b)` method:

```
        context = new Context();
        componentPanel = new JPanel();
        previousButton.addActionListener(this);
        nextButton.addActionListener(this);
        finishButton.addActionListener(this);

        buttonPanel = new JPanel();
        buttonPanel.setLayout(new FlowLayout());
        buttonPanel.add(previousButton);
        buttonPanel.add(nextButton);
        buttonPanel.add(finishButton);

        getContentPane().add(componentPanel, BorderLayout.CENTER);
        getContentPane().add(buttonPanel, BorderLayout.SOUTH);

        // default is yellow
        componentPanel.setBackground(context.getColor());
        previousButton.setEnabled(false);
        finishButton.setEnabled(false);
        componentPanel.add(context.getPanel(), BorderLayout.CENTER);
        componentPanel.setBackground(context.getColor());
        componentPanel.validate();

        frame.setVisible(true);
    }

    public void actionPerformed(ActionEvent e) {
        Command obj = (Command)e.getSource();
        obj.execute();
    }

    public interface Command {
        public void execute();
    }
```

The JPreviousButton component manages all user requests when the user clicks the Previous button. The execute() method uses the application's context reference to invoke the previous() and getState() methods to set the application to its previous state. The removeAll() method of the Container class is then used to remove all of the components from the container so the appropriate panel display will be positioned in the user visualization:

```
class JPreviousButton extends JButton implements Command {

    public JPreviousButton(String caption) { super(caption); }
    public void execute() {
        context.previous();
        context.getState();

        componentPanel.removeAll();
        componentPanel.add(context.getPanel(), BorderLayout.CENTER);
        componentPanel.setBackground(context.getColor());
        componentPanel.validate();

        nextButton.setEnabled(true);
```

```
            finishButton.setEnabled(false);
            if (context.getColor() == Color.yellow) {
                previousButton.setEnabled(false);
            } else {
                previousButton.setEnabled(true);
            }
        }
    }
}
```

The `JNextButton` component implements the same methods as the `JPreviousButton` component to render the appropriate user display when the installation invokes the Next button on the GUI presentation. When the user invokes the Next button, all of the components on the panel display will be removed using the `removeAll()` method. Once the remove operation has been executed, the next color panel will be discovered by using the reference state of the application using the context reference:

```
class JNextButton extends JButton implements Command {

    public JNextButton(String caption) { super(caption); }
    public void execute() {
        context.next();
        context.getState();

        componentPanel.removeAll();
        componentPanel.add(context.getPanel(), BorderLayout.CENTER);
        componentPanel.setBackground(context.getColor());
        componentPanel.validate();

        previousButton.setEnabled(true);
        if (context.getColor() == Color.blue) {
            nextButton.setEnabled(false);
            finishButton.setEnabled(true);
        } else {
            nextButton.setEnabled(true);
            finishButton.setEnabled(false);
        }
    }
}
```

The `FinishButton` class is enabled when the user has reached the final panel display in the series of four panel components:

```
class JFinishButton extends JButton implements Command {

    public JFinishButton(String caption) { super(caption); }
    public void execute() {
        System.exit(1);
    }
}

public static void main(String s[]) {
    InstallationWizard st = new InstallationWizard();
}
```

The abstract State class is a generalized class used by the Context class to establish a blueprint needed to describe the methods needed to handle the state flows in the wizard across the different panel displays. Two get methods, getColor() and getPanel(), are used to retrieve color and panel values of the individual JPanel components implemented for display:

```
[State.java]
public abstract class State {
    public abstract void handlePrevious(Context c);
    public abstract void handleNext(Context c);
    public abstract Color getColor();
    public abstract JPanel getPanel();
}
```

The Context class sets the initial state to yellow, so the YellowState application will start the installation program and create objects for the four color applications: Blue, Green, Orange, and Yellow:

```
// [Context.java]
// package name and import statements omitted

public class Context {

    private State state = null;
    public BlueState blueState;
    public GreenState greenState;
    public OrangeState orangeState;
    public YellowState yellowState;

    public Context(State state) { this.state = state; }
    public Context() {
        // get instances for all panels
        blueState = new BlueState();
        greenState = new GreenState();
        orangeState = new OrangeState();
        yellowState = new YellowState();

        state = getYellowInstance();
    }
    public State getState() { return state; }
    public void setState(State state) { this.state = state; }
    public void previous() { state.handlePrevious(this); }
    public void next() { state.handleNext(this); }
    public Color getColor() {
        return state.getColor();
    }
    public JPanel getPanel() {
        return state.getPanel();
    }
}
```

The following methods are used to return references to the object instances of the four different panel displays:

```
    public BlueState getBlueInstance() {
        return blueState.getInstance();
```

```
        }

        public GreenState getGreenInstance() {
            return greenState.getInstance();
        }

        public OrangeState getOrangeInstance() {
            return orangeState.getInstance();
        }

        public YellowState getYellowInstance() {
            return yellowState.getInstance();
        }

    }
```

The `YellowState` class is the first panel display invoked by the Installation Wizard to start the install process. The `YellowState` constructor method initializes all of the different textfield components that are used for data collection. The `getInstance()` method creates a new `YellowState` instance for reference by other objects if the reference has not been created. If a reference value has already been established, the reference will be returned to the object that references it:

```
// [YellowState.java]
// package name and import statements omitted

public class YellowState extends State {

    // component declarations and initialization omitted for better clarity

    static private YellowState _instance = null;

    public YellowState() {
        firstName = "";
        lastName = "";
        city = "";
        state = "";
        zipcode = "";
        generatePanel();
    }

    static public YellowState getInstance() {
        if(null == instance) {
            instance = new YellowState();
        }
        return instance;
    }
```

The `handlePrevious(Context c)` and `handleNext(Context c)` methods invoke the `setValues()` method to persist the values entered into the form display by the user. Once the data has been saved off the local instance variables, the context reference is implemented to obtain the reference to the next panel display. The `get<color>Instance()` method acquires the Singleton instance generated in the individual panel components:

```
    public void handlePrevious(Context c) {
       setValues();
       c.setState(c.getBlueInstance());
    }

    public void handleNext(Context c) {
       setValues();
       c.setState(c.getOrangeInstance());
    }

    public Color getColor() { return (Color.yellow); }

    public JPanel getPanel() {
       return panelYellow;
    }

    public void generatePanel() {
       log.info("[YellowState:generatePanel]");
       panelYellow = new JPanel(new GridLayout(0,1));
       panelYellow.setSize(200,200);

       formPanel.add(fnameLabel);
       formPanel.add(fnameTextfield);
       formPanel.add(lnameLabel);
       formPanel.add(lnameTextfield);
       formPanel.add(cityLabel);
       formPanel.add(cityTextfield);
       formPanel.add(stateLabel);
       formPanel.add(stateTextfield);
       formPanel.add(zipcodeLabel);
       formPanel.add(zipcodeTextfield);

       Border etchedBdr = BorderFactory.createEtchedBorder();
       Border titledBdr = BorderFactory.createTitledBorder(etchedBdr, "Registration
Form");
       Border emptyBdr  = BorderFactory.createEmptyBorder(15,15,15,15);
       Border compoundBdr=BorderFactory.createCompoundBorder(titledBdr, emptyBdr);
       formPanel.setBorder(compoundBdr);

       getValues();

       panelYellow.add(formPanel);
    }
```

The getValues() method sets the text in the various textfield components using the setText methods that are part of the JTextField class. The setValues() method retrieves the text from the textfield components and saves them to the various instance variables associated with the panel display:

```
    public void getValues() {
       fnameTextfield.setText(firstName);
       lnameTextfield.setText(lastName);
       cityTextfield.setText(city);
       stateTextfield.setText(state);
```

```
                    zipcodeTextfield.setText(zipcode);
        }

    public void setValues() {
        firstName = fnameTextfield.getText();
        lastName = lnameTextfield.getText();
        city = cityTextfield.getText();
        state = stateTextfield.getText();
        zipcode = zipcodeTextfield.getText();
    }

}
```

Lastly, the `OrangeState` class simulates a license viewer that enables an acknowledgment radio button when the user moves the scroll pane knob to the bottom of the license viewer:

```
package com.wizard;

import java.awt.*;
import java.awt.event.*;
import javax.swing.*;
import javax.swing.border.*;
import java.util.logging.Logger;

public class OrangeState extends State {

    private static Logger log = Logger.getLogger("OrangeState");
    private JPanel panelOrange;
    static private OrangeState _instance = null;
    private JRadioButton ackButton = new JRadioButton("Accept");
    private JScrollPane scrollingArea = null;
    private JTextArea resultArea = null;
    private int scrollValue = 0;

    private JPanel formPanel = new JPanel(new GridLayout(0,1));

    public OrangeState() {
        log.info("[OrangeState:constructor()]");
        generatePanel();
    }

    static public OrangeState getInstance() {
        log.info("[OrangeState:getInstance()]");
        if(null == _instance) {
            _instance = new OrangeState();
        }
        return _instance;
    }
```

To override or dictate the behavior of the `State` class, the `handlePrevious` and `handleNext` methods need to be implemented. The `OrangeState` class passes object references through these methods so user navigation flows can be processed through the `State` pattern implementation:

```
    public void handlePrevious(Context c) {
        log.info("[OrangeState:handlePrevious]");
        c.setState(c.getYellowInstance());
    }

    public void handleNext(Context c) {
        log.info("[OrangeState:handleNext]");
        c.setState(c.getGreenInstance());
    }

    public Color getColor() { return (Color.orange); }

    public JPanel getPanel() {
        log.info("[OrangeState:getPanel]");
        return panelOrange;
    }
```

Rendering of the license agreement is performed by the `generatePanel` method by populating the scroll pane with some dummy text. The sample text is stuffed into a stringbuffer that is added to the `JTextArea` component. The fabricated listener, `MyAdjustmentListener`, is attached to the scroll pane so events performed by the user can be monitored and tracked:

```
    public void generatePanel() {
        log.info("[OrangeState:generatePanel]");
        panelOrange = new JPanel(new GridLayout(0,1));
        panelOrange.setSize(400,400);

        Border etchedBdr = BorderFactory.createEtchedBorder();
        Border titledBdr = BorderFactory.createTitledBorder(etchedBdr, "License
Agreement");
        Border emptyBdr  = BorderFactory.createEmptyBorder(10,10,10,10);
        Border compoundBdr=BorderFactory.createCompoundBorder(titledBdr, emptyBdr);
        panelOrange.setBorder(compoundBdr);

        resultArea = new JTextArea(5, 30);
        resultArea.setLineWrap(true);

        String blah = "blah ";
        StringBuffer sb = new StringBuffer();
        for (int i=0; i < 300; i++)
            sb.append(blah);

        resultArea.setText(sb.toString());
        resultArea.setCaretPosition(0);

        scrollingArea = new JScrollPane(resultArea);
        AdjustmentListener listener = new MyAdjustmentListener();
        scrollingArea.getVerticalScrollBar().addAdjustmentListener(listener);

        ackButton.setSelected(false);
        formPanel.add(ackButton);
        panelOrange.add(scrollingArea);
        panelOrange.add(formPanel);
    }
```

Events are traced through the MyAdjustmentListener method, which implements the AdjustmentListener listener interface for receiving adjustment events. If the user scrolls past a specific numeric value (275) with the scroll pane knob, the acknowledgment button is enabled, indicating that the user has read most of the license agreement:

```java
class MyAdjustmentListener implements AdjustmentListener {
    public void adjustmentValueChanged(AdjustmentEvent evt) {

        Adjustable source = evt.getAdjustable();
        if (evt.getValueIsAdjusting()) {
            // The user is dragging the knob
            return;
        }
        scrollValue = evt.getValue();
        System.out.println("scrollValue = " + scrollValue);
        if (scrollValue > 275)
            ackButton.setSelected(true);
    }
}
```

Figure 4-20 represents the Orange stage of the Installation Wizard that renders the license agreement so that the user can read the text and accept its scope by clicking the Accept radio button. The Accept button is automatically enabled when the user slides the scroll pane knob to the bottom of the text display.

Figure 4-20

An important object-oriented (OO) concept to remember is that the Installation Wizard uses object composition to alter the behavior of the objects during runtime. The wizard application delegates behavior to a known interface and varies the implementation details for the different installation panels.

Summary

This chapter covered a tremendous amount of ground regarding all of the JFC components. All of the Swing top-level containers were discussed (`JFrame`, `JDialog`, and `JPanel`), as well as many of the other Swing visualization components (`JButton`, `JLabel`, `JSpinner`, `JTextField`, `JTextArea`, and others). Lastly, Swing listener and layout managers were implemented along with GoF design patterns to craft effective user interface displays. All of the sample applications should help developers address complex GUI development activities and influence designers with their modeling conceptualizations.

The difficulty in explaining the Java Foundation Class (JFC) libraries is that they're broad and varied. The complexities of their implementation can be overcome, as with many things in software development, by actually employing them. With a better understanding of what is possible with JFC packages, a developer can approach a task with greater confidence that their desktop visualizations can be realized.

Persisting Your
Application Using Files

The previous chapter discussed building user interfaces and stand-alone Java applications using the Java Foundation Classes (JFC). A key feature of many applications is the ability to save its state off to a file. Image manipulation programs need to read and write images to disk. Word processing and other office-productivity applications need to read and write spreadsheets, presentations, and text-based documents. Essentially, to do any of these save operations, an application must take its in-memory representation of its state, and write it to disk. Later on, this file can be read back into memory, putting the application back to exactly where the user had left using it.

Different applications need to save different pieces of information to disk. Some applications really only need to save their configuration to disk, because they may save their other data to a database (the subsequent chapter shows you how to persist your application's data to a database). A typical single-user application such as a word processor or image manipulation program will need to save its state to files. Java provides a couple of built-in mechanisms for saving or serializing data to disk. The two major APIs in the JDK for persisting application data to disk are the Java Serialization API for generic serialization and the XMLEncoder/Decoder API for serializing JavaBean components.

This chapter looks at the Java Serialization API, the XMLEncoder/Decoder API, and the Java API for XML Binding (JAXB). JAXB provides mechanisms to read and write to user-defined XML file formats. Each of these three APIs has different approaches to serialization and as such should be used in different circumstances. This chapter looks at the Serialization API first, followed by the XMLEncoder/Decoder API, and finishes with JAXB.

Application Data

Every application has some sort of in-memory data structure from which to retrieve its data. Besides data structures like maps, lists, sets, and trees, custom data structures are often built. For an application to save its data, the data in these structures must be saved to disk, and then at a later time, loaded back into the same data structure. Web browsers, for example, create what's called a Document Object Model (DOM) in memory for every web page that is loaded. It is their internal data structure for displaying HTML pages. Word processors also keep some sort of document object model as well — some way to represent the fact that certain pieces of text are aligned to the right, or possibly that other paragraphs of text are highlighted in a particular color. These custom data structures are necessary for the application to display the data properly to the user.

Applications like web browsers essentially read files and display them to the user. A web browser first reads HTML files over a network or from a disk, and parses the data into its internal in-memory data, the DOM. Now that the data is in the web browser's data structure, its functions can properly display the page to the user. Image viewing programs are similar; they read an image into their internal data structure representing images, and then display that image to the user. Other types of applications, though, also allow the user to manipulate the data. Word processors, in addition to reading files into their internal data structures and displaying them, also must allow the user to manipulate the data, and therefore the internal data structure, and then write it back to disk.

Many of these other applications that must allow the user to manipulate data follow the Model-View-Controller (MVC) design pattern (see Chapter 3 more for information on design patterns). The internal data structures of the application are its *data model*. This data model is contained in structures that are separate from UI components and UI-related data structures. In Java-based applications, the data model usually consists of JavaBeans, along with other data storage and collection classes. These data classes are manipulated and modified by UI controller classes (such as events generated by buttons, menus, and so forth), and presented in a view by other UI components. A simple MVC diagram is shown in Figure 5-1, illustrating how only the data model of an MVC-based application needs to be saved to restore the state of the application. Swing or other UI toolkit/utility classes would be in both the view and controller areas, whereas the internal data model specific to the domain of the application would be contained in the data model. This step of separating domain data from UI components simplifies the process of saving and loading the data from disk because the data is all in one place, the model.

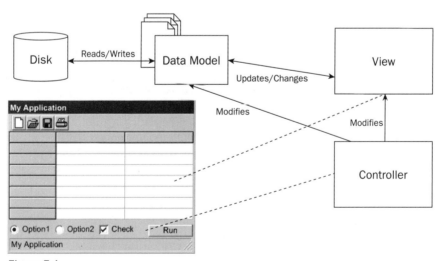

Figure 5-1

Once all the domain data is contained in its own model, separate from the UI components, the parts of the data model that need to be persisted can be identified. Some pieces of an internal data structure need not necessarily be saved. Some parts of the data structure in an application will not change from time to time, or can be re-created given that certain other aspects of the data structure exist. Developers wishing to save the state of their application must look carefully at the data they hold in memory in their model, identify the pieces that must be saved, and then write routines for saving and loading the data from the data structure to and from disk.

Saving Application Data

Now that application data structures have been discussed in a general sense, it is time to move to something a little more tangible and realistic. How exactly do Java applications store their data model in memory? Because Java is an object-oriented language, most applications have a set of data classes (which is the application's data model). Instances of these data classes reside in memory and the viewer and controller components (the UI) of the application interact with them to produce the functionality of the application.

Any Java class that has attributes (or *properties* in JavaBean terms) is a data structure. A simple data structure could be a `Person` class with two `String` attributes, for first name and last name. More complex classes that contain references to other classes, effectively form an *object graph*. An object graph is a graph where objects are the nodes in the graph and the connections are references from one instance of an object to another. The notion of object graphs is important because when you want to serialize the information contained in a class, you must also consider what data the class relies on in *other* classes and their dependencies and so on. The next section outlines a sample data model for a generic application's configuration, and you will view an example object graph.

Sample Configuration Data Model for an Application

Throughout this chapter you will be using a sample application and persisting its configuration using Java Serialization, the XMLEncoder/Decoder APIs, and JAXB. The application is fairly generic (and many applications could have similar configurations). Think of this example application as some sort of image editing/drawing program that includes a canvas with tool and palette windows. Different users of the application will undoubtedly have different preferences for some of the settings the application supports. At a high level, this user-preference or configuration information you want to persist includes the following:

❏   Location of the user's home directory or default directory to load and save files

❏   A list of recent files loaded or saved by the user

❏   Whether or not the application should use a tabbed windowed interface or a multiple document interface (MDI) with child windows

❏   Foreground and background colors last used (for drawing or painting operations)

❏   The positions of the tool and palette windows within the application when the application was last closed

In a full-fledged paint or photo editing application, there would probably be many more configuration options that users could potentially persist to a file. However, the process is the same, and can also be applied to how to save application data such as a custom image format, or reading and writing other image formats into your application's structure. Persisting information in Java objects to the file system is the same whether it is application configuration data or simply application data itself. Figure 5-2 shows the data model structure, and Figure 5-3 shows an example object graph of an instance of the data model.

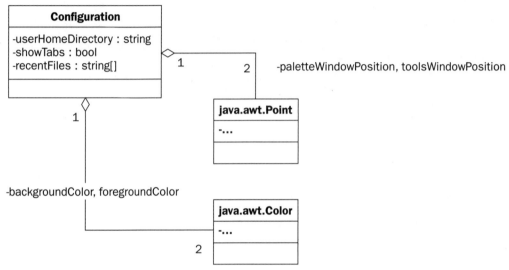

Figure 5-2

Configuration is the root object. It uses classes from java.awt to represent colors and points. In the object graph shown in Figure 5-3, you can see that an instance of configuration also contains references to instances of java.awt.Color and java.awt.Point. When you persist the information in a Configuration instance to disk, you must also save the information contained in the Color and Point instances (and any other class instances *they* may also reference), if you want to be able to re-create the Configuration object at a later point in time.

You will design Configuration using the JavaBeans architecture (getXXX and setXXX for all properties in your class). The application itself will read the configuration settings from this class and appropriately apply them throughout the application. It is typical to use JavaBeans conventions to store data in Java-based data models. Using the JavaBeans standard allows the designer to use many tools that are based on those standards such as XMLEncoder/Decoder. Other tools that utilize JavaBeans conventions are object-relational-mapping tools, which allow the developer to map Java objects to a database. Most of Java's third-party serialization tools require classes to use JavaBeans conventions. It is just good practice and design.

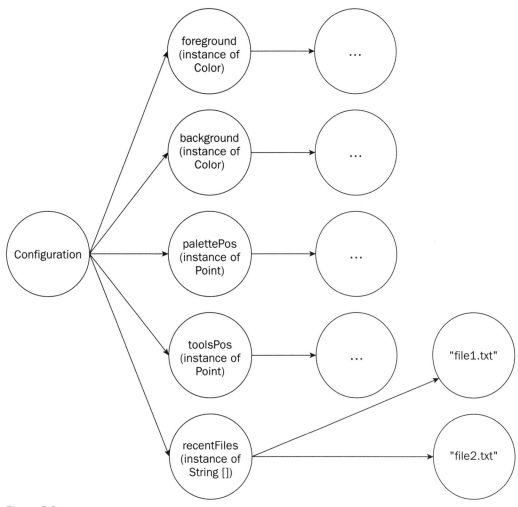

Figure 5-3

Java Serialization: Persisting Object Graphs

The Java Serialization API takes one approach to saving a data model. It writes all of the object instances in the data model's graph to disk. To reconstruct the saved object graph, it reads the saved class instances from disk back into memory. *Serializing* an object instance is the process of writing its data members to disk. *Deserializing* an object instance is the process of reconstructing the instance from the data members written to disk. Suppose you have a simple class MyPoint:

```
package book;

public class MyPoint {
  public int x;
```

```
      public int y;

      public void doSomething() { ... }
   }
```

To save an instance of `MyPoint` to disk, you simply need to write its two data members to disk. Saving x and y allows you to create a new instance of `MyPoint` at a later time and set its x and y values to the ones saved to disk — effectively re-creating the original instance. The method `doSomething()` is already specified in the compiled class file, and there is no need to store any method information in the serialization process. All a class instance is in memory is the values for all of its attributes. To serialize an instance to disk, all of its data members must be saved. What if the data member is a reference to another object instance? The reference itself is just a memory address and would be meaningless to save. The object instance the reference points to also would need to be saved as well. Suppose you add a color attribute to `MyPoint`:

```
package book;

import java.awt.Color;

public class MyPoint {
   public int x;
   public int y;

   private Color pointColor;

   public void doSomething() { ... }
}
```

The data members of the instance of `java.awt.Color` must now also be saved. As you can see, the entire object graph of an object instance must be saved when it is serialized to disk. If you only saved x and y from `MyPoint` and then subsequently re-created `MyPoint` at a later time, its color information would be lost. So how is an external API able to access all of the fields of a particular class? Java's reflection mechanism allows the dynamic ability to find out the fields and field values of any class, whether those fields are marked `public` or `private`. Thankfully, the Java Serialization API takes care of all these details for you, and it is easy to serialize object instances to disk.

It is important to note that the file format used by the Java Serialization API is a special binary file format developed specifically for Java Serialization and therefore not human-readable. It is an efficient format, but also specific to Java.

Key Classes

The Java Serialization API hides most of the complexity required to save object graphs to disk (such as circular references and multiple references to the same object). There are really only two interfaces and two classes that need to be learned in order to use the API. `ObjectInputStream` and `ObjectOutputStream` are two stream classes that can be wrapped around any type of `java.io.InputStream` or `java.io.OutputStream`, respectively, making it possible to send serialized objects over the network or simply save them to disk. The two interfaces, `Serializable` and `Externalizable`, allow for implementing classes to be serialized. If a class does not implement one of these two interfaces, it cannot be serialized using the

API. This means that if a class that *does* implement either `Serializable` or `Externalizable` contains a reference to a class that *does not* implement that interface somewhere in its object graph, it cannot be serialized successfully without some modification (this is discussed later on in this chapter).

Following is a table of the Serializable and Externalizable classes:

Class or Interface (from java.io)	Function
`Serializable`	Interface for marking the fact that a class supports serialization
`ObjectInputStream`	Input stream used to read object instances that were written by an `ObjectOutputStream`
`ObjectOutputStream`	Output stream used to write object instance data that can later be read by an `ObjectInputStream`
`Externalizable`	Interface that extends `Serializable` to give a class complete control over how it is read and written to streams

Serializing Your Objects

Performing the actual serialization of objects is straightforward. There are four main steps:

1. Make sure your class has a default constructor (takes no arguments).

2. Implement the `Serializable` or `Externalizable` interface to mark your class as supporting serialization.

3. Use `ObjectOutputStream` to serialize your object.

4. Use `ObjectInputStream` to read a serialized object back into memory.

Classes you wish to serialize must have default constructors. This is because the serialization API needs to create blank instances of the class when it re-creates object instances saved to disk — it does so by calling the default constructor. After it creates the new class it populates the data members of the class via reflection (meaning accessor and mutator methods are not required for private data members). The class must also be marked as serializable by implementing the `Serializable` interface. The `Serializable` interface contains no method definitions; it is simply a marker to the serialization API to indicate that the class is indeed serializable. Not all classes store their data — for example, the classic example is a `java.sql.ResultSet` object, which is used in the Java DataBase Connectivity API (JDBC) to access data from a database. The `ResultSet` object is querying the database for data when its methods are called and hence does not store the information it returns. Because it is a mediator between the client and the database, it has no information to serialize! It would be incorrect to serialize an instance of `ResultSet` and expect to later on deserialize it and access the results of a database query, because the query results exist in the database and not in the `ResultSet`. The `Serializable` interface exists to give developers the ability to mark certain classes as potentially serializable — essentially meaning the author of a particular class planned for the fact that his class may be saved to disk. The `Externalizable` interface gives developers more control over the actual serialization process and is discussed in more detail later on in this chapter.

Configuration Example: Saving Your App's Configuration to Disk

Earlier in this chapter, you developed the high-level data model for a sample configuration for a generic image manipulation application. Suppose now you want to develop that data model and the UI components to save and read it from disk. The first step is translating your data model into code. You will have one class, `Configuration`, represent the application's configuration. You will model it using the JavaBeans conventions, implicitly provide it a default constructor (by having no constructors), and implement the `Serializable` interface. The two classes referenced in `Configuration`, `java.awt.Point` and `java.awt.Color`, also both implement `Serializable`, so the entire graph is guaranteed to serialize. The code for `Configuration` is as follows:

```java
package book;

import java.awt.Color;
import java.awt.Point;
import java.io.Serializable;

public class Configuration implements Serializable {

    private String userHomeDirectory;

    private Color backgroundColor;
    private Color foregroundColor;

    private boolean showTabs;

    private Point paletteWindowPosition;
    private Point toolsWindowPosition;

    private String[] recentFiles;

    public Color getBackgroundColor() {
        return backgroundColor;
    }

    public void setBackgroundColor(Color backgroundColor) {
        this.backgroundColor = backgroundColor;
    }

    public Color getForegroundColor() {
        return foregroundColor;
    }

    public void setForegroundColor(Color foregroundColor) {
        this.foregroundColor = foregroundColor;
    }

    public Point getPaletteWindowPosition() {
        return paletteWindowPosition;
    }

    public void setPaletteWindowPosition(Point paletteWindowPosition) {
```

```java
        this.paletteWindowPosition = paletteWindowPosition;
    }

    public String[] getRecentFiles() {
      return recentFiles;
    }

    public void setRecentFiles(String[] recentFiles) {
      this.recentFiles = recentFiles;
    }

    public boolean isShowTabs() {
      return showTabs;
    }

    public void setShowTabs(boolean showTabs) {
        this.showTabs = showTabs;
    }

    public Point getToolsWindowPosition() {
      return toolsWindowPosition;
    }

    public void setToolsWindowPosition(Point toolsWindowPosition) {
        this.toolsWindowPosition = toolsWindowPosition;
    }

    public String getUserHomeDirectory() {
      return userHomeDirectory;
    }

    public void setUserHomeDirectory(String userHomeDirectory) {
        this.userHomeDirectory = userHomeDirectory;
    }
}
```

Writing the Configuration to Disk

Now that you have your configuration data model, you can write the code to serialize and deserialize instances of `Configuration`. Saving an instance of `Configuration` is almost too easy. First, create an `ObjectOutputStream` object, and because you want to save your instance of `Configuration` to a file, wrap it around a `FileOutputStream`:

```java
ObjectOutputStream out = new ObjectOutputStream(
                                new FileOutputStream("appconfig.config"));
```

Now create an instance of `Configuration` and save it to the file `appconfig.config`:

```java
Configuration conf = new Configuration();
// ... set its properties

out.writeObject(conf);
```

Now all you have to do is close the stream:

```
out.close();
```

Multiple object instances (and of potentially differing types) can be written to the same `ObjectOutputStream`. *Simply call* `writeObject()` *more than once, and the next object is appended to the stream. Also note the file extension,* `config`, *appended to the file was arbitrarily chosen.*

Reading the Configuration from Disk

Deserializing objects back into memory is as easy as serializing them. To read your configuration data model from disk, create an `ObjectInputStream` wrapped around a `FileInputStream` (because in this case you saved your `Configuration` to a file):

```
ObjectInputStream in = new ObjectInputStream(
                              new FileInputStream("appconfig.config"));
```

The counterpart to `ObjectOutputStream`'s `writeObject()` is `readObject()` in `ObjectInputStream`. If more than one object was explicitly written with a call to `writeObject()`, `readObject()` can be called more than once. The method `readObject()` returns an `Object` that needs to be cast the proper type—so the developer must know some of the details about the order in which object instances were saved to the stream. In addition to potentially throwing a `java.io.IOException` if the stream was corrupted or other I/O error, `readObject()` can throw a `java.lang.ClassNotFoundException`. The `ClassNotFoundException` occurs if the VM cannot find the class for the type of the object instance being deserialized. The following line of code reads the `Configuration` object back into memory:

```
Configuration conf = (Configuration) in.readObject();
```

After reading the object back in, you can use it as you would use any normal Java object. After you are done with the `ObjectInputStream`, close it like you would any other subclass of `InputStream`:

```
in.close();
```

As you can see, reading and writing objects using `ObjectInputStream` and `ObjectOutputStream` is a simple process with powerful functionality. Later, this section discusses customizing and extending the serialization process as well as some of the pitfalls that can occur along the way.

Wrapping Your Serialization and Deserialization Code Inside Swing Actions

Now that you have seen how to create and store data models, it is time to see your configuration data model serialization and deserialization code in the context of a real application. Because your application is a JFC-based Swing application, you will integrate your code to serialize and deserialize `Configuration` into the UI framework via Swing's `javax.swing.Action` interface. Actions are a useful way to generalize UI commands—such as a save or open command. These commands usually appear in multiple places in a UI; in the case of save and open, usually in the File menu and on the application's toolbar. Swing components such as menus and toolbars allow actions to be added and they create the necessary events and properties to control them. Actions abstract some of the UI code away, and allow the developer to concentrate on the logic of an action, like saving a file to disk. Your actions will need a reference to your application, to get and set its configuration before it serializes or deserializes the Configuration instance. Your actions will inherit from the class javax.swing.AbstractAction, because that class takes care of all of the methods in the Action interface except for the event method actionPerformed(). The class diagram shown in Figure 5-4 illustrates where your actions, LoadConfigurationAction and SaveConfigurationAction, fit with respect to Action and AbstractAction.

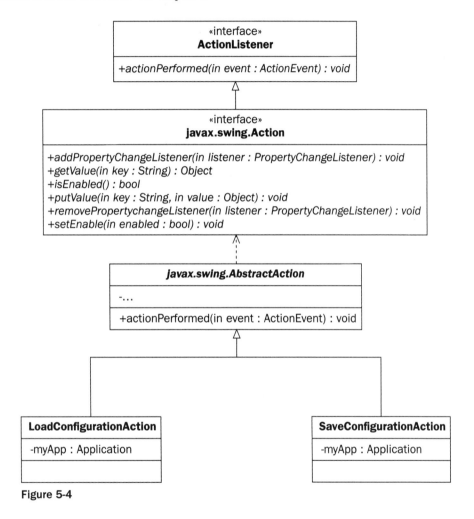

Figure 5-4

All of the code for both of these actions will reside in the event-driven method, actionPerformed(). When the user of the application clicks the save configuration menu item or button, this code will be invoked. The same goes for the action to load the application's configuration.

Implementing the Save Configuration Action

The main area of interest in any `Action` implementation is the `actionPerformed()` method. This method is called when a user clicks the menu item or button containing the `Action`. For your save action, you want the user to be first prompted to choose a file location, and then save the application's `Configuration` object instance to that file location. The implementation is fairly straightforward. Display a file chooser first, and if the user selects a file, the application's `Configuration` instance is retrieved:

```
public void actionPerformed(ActionEvent evt) {
    JFileChooser fc = new JFileChooser();
    if (JFileChooser.APPROVE_OPTION == fc.showSaveDialog(myApp)) {
      try {
        Configuration conf = this.myApp.getConfiguration();
```

Now that you know the file location, simply serialize the `Configuration` object to disk:

```
        ObjectOutputStream out = new ObjectOutputStream(
                            new FileOutputStream(fc.getSelectedFile()));

        out.writeObject(conf);

        out.close();

      } catch (IOException ioe) {
        JOptionPane.showMessageDialog(this.myApp, ioe.getMessage(), "Error",
                          JOptionPane.ERROR_MESSAGE);

        ioe.printStackTrace();

      }
    }
  }
```

Implementing the Load Configuration Action

The load action is similar to the save action. First, the user is prompted for a file. If the user selects a file, you will try to open it:

```
public void actionPerformed(ActionEvent evt) {
    JFileChooser fc = new JFileChooser();
    if (JFileChooser.APPROVE_OPTION == fc.showOpenDialog(myApp)) {
      try {
        ObjectInputStream in = new ObjectInputStream(
                            new FileInputStream(fc.getSelectedFile()));
```

If the user selects a file that is not a serialized instance of `Configuration`, an `IOException` will be thrown. If the instance of `Configuration` is successfully read, load it into your application via the application's `setConfiguration()` method:

```
Configuration conf = (Configuration) in.readObject();

in.close();

myApp.setConfiguration(conf);
} catch (IOException ioe) {
JOptionPane.showMessageDialog(this.myApp,
                    "File is not a configuration file!", "Error",
                    JOptionPane.ERROR_MESSAGE);

ioe.printStackTrace();

} catch (ClassNotFoundException clEx) {
JOptionPane.showMessageDialog(this.myApp,
                    "Classpath incorrectly set for application!",
                    "Error", JOptionPane.ERROR_MESSAGE);

clEx.printStackTrace();
}
}
}
```

Giving Your Application a Time-Based License Using Serialization

Serialization can be used to solve a variety of problems. It is easy to save JavaBeans and the data models for various kinds of application data as you saw in the last example. Serialization is not limited to simply saving objects to disk. Because `ObjectInputStream` and `ObjectOutputStream` are subclasses of `InputStream` and `OutputStream`, respectively, they can be used in any situation a normal stream could be. Objects can be serialized over the network, or read from a JAR file. Serialization is a fundamental aspect of Java's Remote Method Invocation (RMI) — it is the technology behind passing objects by value in RMI method calls.

To continue with the drawing application example, suppose you want to give it a time-based license. For the demo version of the application, you only want the application to be fully active for 30 days. After 30 days, you will require users to purchase a full license to use the product. There are many ways to do this, but using the serialization API could be an effective way to produce a time-based license file. The biggest challenge to creating time-based licenses is making it difficult for users to overcome the license, either by setting their computer's clock at an incorrect time, or by modifying whatever license file gets distributed (or registry key for some Windows-based applications and so on). Because Java's serialization produces a binary format that is unfamiliar to anyone except Java developers, it will make a good format for your application's license file. You will also need some mechanism to guard against users setting the incorrect date on their computer clock to give them a longer license. To do so, you will require them to authenticate against a timeserver on your network. The high-level design looks like Figure 5-5.

The next step in the design is to model the license file. Because you are using Java Serialization, all you need to do is produce a class that implements `Serializable` and contains the necessary fields to do license validation against the timeserver. The `License` class will look like Figure 5-6.

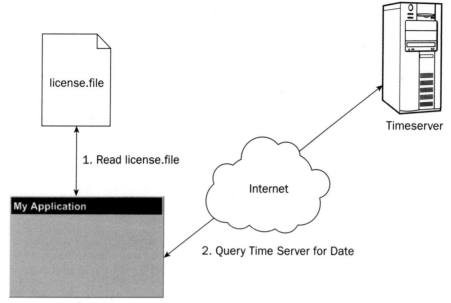

3. If server date is after the date in license.file, start the application

Figure 5-5

License
-expirationDate : Calendar -timeServerHost : URL
+isValid() : boolean

Figure 5-6

Implementing the License

The license file will consist of a serialized instance of the `License` class. The two data attributes it contains are `expirationDate`, which is the date when the license expires (stored in a `java.util.Calendar` instance), and `timeServerHost`, which is the `java.net.URL` representing the Internet address of your timeserver. Save the address as well as the expiration date to prevent tampering with the URL. The `isValid()` method gets the current date from the timeserver and checks to see if the expiration date is before the date returned from the timeserver. If it is, the license is valid. Actually implementing, the `License` yields the following code listing:

```
package book;

import java.io.IOException;
import java.io.ObjectInputStream;
import java.io.Serializable;
import java.net.URL;
```

```
import java.util.Calendar;

public class License implements Serializable {
  private Calendar expirationDate;

  private URL timeServerHost;

  public boolean isValid() throws IOException, ClassNotFoundException {
    ObjectInputStream in = new ObjectInputStream(timeServerHost.openStream());

    Calendar serverDate = (Calendar) in.readObject();

    in.close();

    return serverDate.before(expirationDate);
  }

  public Calendar getExpirationDate() {
    return expirationDate;
  }

  public void setExpirationDate(Calendar expirationDate) {
    this.expirationDate = expirationDate;
  }

  public URL getTimeserverHost() {
    return timeServerHost;
  }

  public void setTimeServerHost(URL timeServerHost) {
    this.timeServerHost = timeServerHost;
  }
}
```

Look into the implementation for isValid(). One thing not yet discussed in detail is the protocol you need to define between the timeserver and the License. How does the isValid() method get the current date from the timeserver? A normal HTTP GET request is sent to a URL on the timeserver, and instead of it returning an HTML page, it will return an instance of java.util.Calendar. Using the timeServerHost URL object, you open an ObjectInputStream via an HTTP request over the network:

```
ObjectInputStream in = new ObjectInputStream(timeServerHost.openStream());
```

From here, you simply read in a Calendar object just like any other object in Java serialization. After the object is read in, compare the expirationDate to see if it is before or after the date returned from the timeserver:

```
Calendar serverDate = (Calendar) in.readObject();

in.close();

return serverDate.before(expirationDate);
```

Serialization can make complex tasks very straightforward. Java programmers can serialize and deserialize information without ever really leaving the Java environment because actual class instances can be serialized. Rather than creating your own date format on the server, you simply returned an instance of `Calendar`. All the low-level details of marshalling information over the network and finding a format you can use for date information were all taken care of by Java Serialization and the `URL` class.

Implementing the Timeserver

Now that you know what the timeserver is supposed to do, you must actually implement it. The timeserver will run as a Java web application (see Chapters 7 and 8 for much more detailed information on web applications). All you need is a simple servlet. The servlet will take care of the HTTP request and response, and allow you to write a `Calendar` object out to the client. Here is the servlet code that runs on the timeserver:

```java
package book;

import java.io.IOException;
import java.io.ObjectOutputStream;
import java.util.Calendar;
import java.util.GregorianCalendar;
import java.util.logging.Logger;

import javax.servlet.ServletConfig;
import javax.servlet.ServletException;
import javax.servlet.http.HttpServlet;
import javax.servlet.http.HttpServletRequest;
import javax.servlet.http.HttpServletResponse;

public class ServerDate extends HttpServlet {

  private Logger logger;

  public void init(ServletConfig config) throws ServletException {
    logger = Logger.getLogger(ServerDate.class.getName());
  }

  public void doGet(HttpServletRequest req, HttpServletResponse resp)
                    throws IOException, ServletException {

    logger.info("Received date request");

    ObjectOutputStream out = new ObjectOutputStream(resp.getOutputStream());
    Calendar calendar = new GregorianCalendar();

    out.writeObject(calendar);

    out.close();

    logger.info("Wrote the date: " + calendar.getTime());
  }
}
```

By implementing the `doGet()` method, the servlet handles `HTTP GET` requests (which you are expecting from your `License` clients). The method is straightforward. All you do is wrap an `ObjectOutputStream` around the normal `ServletOutputStream`:

```
ObjectOutputStream out = new ObjectOutputStream(resp.getOutputStream());
```

Once you have your output stream back to the client, simply write a new instance of `Calendar` (which corresponds to the current date and time):

```
Calendar calendar = new GregorianCalendar();

out.writeObject(calendar);

out.close();
```

The `License` class and `ServerDate` servlet take care of the actual license file, and the means to validate the date it stores. In the next section, you see how to integrate the components in this example, with your configuration data model and Swing actions, into an actual Swing application.

Tying Your Serialization Components into the Application

You have developed Swing actions that load and save your configuration data model. You wrote a licensing system that uses serialization to specify both the license file format and the date and time format of your simple timeserver. Actually tying these pieces into your application is not very difficult, but helps to paint the larger picture of how serialization can fit into a real application design.

The first task your application does at startup is load the license file and verify that the date contained therein is before the date returned on the timeserver. The `license.file` is read in from the application's Java ARchive file (JAR) and then the validity of the license is verified against the timeserver found at the URL in the serialized license:

```
try {
    ObjectInputStream in = new ObjectInputStream(
                    Application.class.getResourceAsStream("license.file"));

    License license = (License) in.readObject();

    in.close();

    if (!license.isValid()) {
      JOptionPane.showMessageDialog(this, "Your license has expired",
                                "License", JOptionPane.ERROR_MESSAGE);
      System.exit(1);
    }

} catch (Exception ex) {
    JOptionPane.showMessageDialog(this, ex.getMessage(), "License",
                                JOptionPane.ERROR_MESSAGE);
    System.exit(1);
}
```

Notice how the license file, license.file, is loaded as a resource. Your application assumes that the license was packaged into the same JAR file as the application. This means that there must be some sort of license managing utility to put the license.file into the same JAR file as the application. That utility is not discussed, however, because it is irrelevant to this example. Getting the license.file from the JAR reduces the risk of a user attempting to tamper with its contents to gain a longer license. The Java Serialization API is a binary format that is not human-readable, but could potentially be recognized by another Java developer. If you really cared an awful lot about no one tampering with your license .file, you could always encrypt it using the Java Cryptography Extension (JCE) API. JCE allows you to encrypt any OutputStream and hence you could encrypt (and later decrypt) an ObjectOutputStream.

Adding your Swing actions to the File menu looks like this:

```
fileMenu.add(new JMenuItem(new LoadConfigurationAction(this)));
fileMenu.add(new JMenuItem(new SaveConfigurationAction(this)));
```

Now you have tied in all of your components based on serialization. The following is a stripped-down code listing for your basic application. Look at the setConfiguration(), loadConfiguration(), and getConfiguration() methods, because these are what your Swing actions interact with:

```
package book;

import java.awt.Color;
import java.awt.GridLayout;
import java.awt.event.ActionEvent;
import java.awt.event.ActionListener;
import java.io.IOException;
import java.io.ObjectInputStream;

import javax.swing.*;

public class Application extends JFrame {

    private Configuration configuration = new Configuration();

    private JButton hdButton;

    private JButton bcButton;
    private JButton fgButton;
    private Color defaultColor;

    private JCheckBox showTabsCheckBox;

...

    public Application() {
        this.setDefaultCloseOperation(JFrame.EXIT_ON_CLOSE);
        this.setTitle("My Application Serializes");

        try {
            ObjectInputStream in = new ObjectInputStream(
```

```
                            Application.class.getResourceAsStream("license.file"));

   License license = (License) in.readObject();

   in.close();

   if (!license.isValid()) {
     JOptionPane.showMessageDialog(this, "Your license has expired",
                                "License", JOptionPane.ERROR_MESSAGE);
     System.exit(1);
   }

 } catch (Exception ex) {
   JOptionPane.showMessageDialog(this, ex.getMessage(), "License",
                                        JOptionPane.ERROR_MESSAGE);
   System.exit(1);
 }

...

  JMenuBar menu = new JMenuBar();
  JMenu fileMenu = new JMenu("File");
  fileMenu.add(new JMenuItem(new LoadConfigurationAction(this)));
  fileMenu.add(new JMenuItem(new SaveConfigurationAction(this)));
  fileMenu.addSeparator();
...
  this.pack();
  this.setVisible(true);
}

private JPanel createConfigDisplayPanel() {
...
  return panel;
}

private void loadConfiguration() {
  hdButton.setText(this.configuration.getUserHomeDirectory());

  Color bcColor = this.configuration.getBackgroundColor();
  if (bcColor != null) {
    bcButton.setBackground(bcColor);
    bcButton.setText(null);
  } else {
    bcButton.setText("<No color set>");
    bcButton.setBackground(this.defaultColor);
  }

  Color fgColor = this.configuration.getForegroundColor();
  if (fgColor != null) {
    fgButton.setBackground(fgColor);
    fgButton.setText(null);
```

```
    } else {
      fgButton.setText("<No color set>");
      fgButton.setBackground(this.defaultColor);
    }

    showTabsCheckBox.setSelected(this.configuration.isShowTabs());
  }

  public Configuration getConfiguration() {
    return configuration;
  }

  public void setConfiguration(Configuration configuration) {
    this.configuration = configuration;

    this.loadConfiguration();
  }

  public static void main(String[] args) {
    Application app = new Application();
  }
}
```

Figure 5-7 shows the application editing part of the configuration data model. To get to this point means that the application was able to verify the license. Notice in the `loadConfiguration()` method in the previous code listing how the color buttons are set, the checkbox is checked, and the user's home directory is placed on the first button when a configuration is loaded. Users can then change these options, which modifies the application's `Configuration` object.

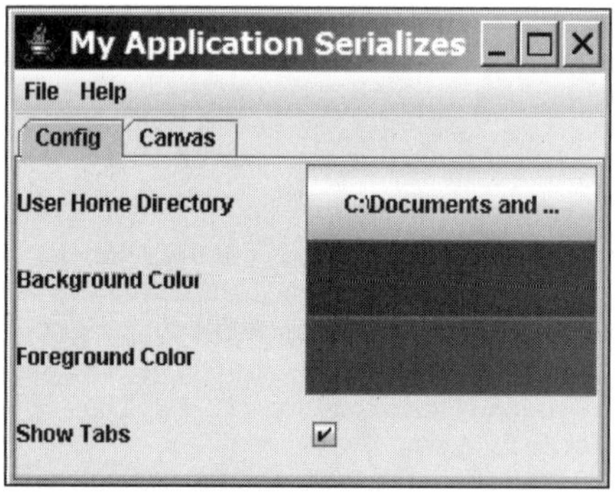

Figure 5-7

Once the `Configuration` object is changed, it can be saved back to disk. Because the whole configuration data model is contained in the `Configuration` object, all you need to do is export it to disk using your action, as shown in Figure 5-8.

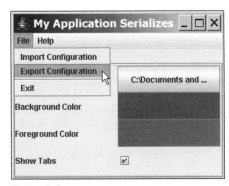

Figure 5-8

Extending and Customizing Serialization

Though most of the time the Java Serialization API provides enough functionality out of the box, there are some cases where a greater level of control is necessary for the developer. Sometimes you will not want every field of a class serialized to disk. Other times, you may want to append additional information not included in class fields into the stream — or maybe modify some of the class's members before serialization occurs. A very common case for customizing serialization occurs when a class definition is modified (in other words, the code is changed and the class recompiled) — that is, fields are renamed, or other fields added and others removed; classes serialized prior to these changes will have errors upon deserialization. This section discusses some of the commonly used mechanisms for customizing and extending Java Serialization.

The Transient Keyword

The `transient` keyword in the Java language is used for Java Serialization. Any field marked `transient` will not be saved to disk. This is useful when a class contains a reference to another object that does not implement `Serializable`, but you still would like to persist a class instance to disk. Sometimes certain fields are runtime-dependent and should not be persisted. Suppose in your `Configuration` object you wanted to additionally store a reference to your application (for callbacks perhaps). When you saved your application to disk, you would certainly not want to persist the application and every object associated with it on its object graph (even if all its objects implemented `Serializable`). To mark a field `transient`, simply put the keyword before the definition of the object or primitive:

```
private transient Application application;
```

The `transient` keyword is an easy way to quickly mark which fields of your class you would like the Serialization API to skip over and not save.

However, when a class is reconstructed after being serialized these fields marked `transient` *will be* `null` *(or if they are primitives, their default value), unless they are given a default value, or set in the default constructor of the class.*

257

Customizing the Serialization Format

Sometimes there is a need to perform additional operations either right before an object is serialized or right after it is deserialized. This need could arise if a class must retrieve data stored externally, such as on a server or in a cache, right before it is serialized. Objects may wish to verify some of their fields right after deserialization and fill in or create some of the fields marked `transient`. There are two methods you can add to a class to add behavior to the serialization and deserialization process, `writeObject()` and `readObject`. These methods are not part of any interface, and for them to be called by the Java serialization engine, they must have the exact signature as shown in the following listing:

```
private void writeObject(ObjectOutputStream out) throws IOException {
    // can do things like validate values, get data from an external source, etc

    out.defaultWriteObject(); // invokes normal serialization process on this object
}

private void readObject(ObjectInputStream in) throws IOException,
ClassNotFoundException {
    in.defaultReadObject(); // invokes normal deserialization process on this object

    // can do things like validate values, produce new values based on data, etc
}
```

The method `writeObject()` is called right before a class is serialized. The user can control when the class is actually serialized by calling `defaultWriteObject()` on the `ObjectOutputStream` as shown in the previous code. Doing so invokes the normal Java Serialization process on the current object. Before or after the object is written to the stream, though, values to current data members could be changed or updated. Additional information can also be written to the `ObjectOutputStream`. The `ObjectOutputStream` also implements the `java.io.DataOutput` interface, which includes methods for writing primitives (and `Strings`).

The `readObject()` method is called right before an object is deserialized. It is the natural counterpart to `writeObject()`. Similarly, the user can control when the object is deserialized by calling `defaultReadObject()` on the `ObjectInputStream`. After an object is deserialized, fields that did not have values could be assigned default values, or the values that were assigned could be checked. If any extra data was written to the `ObjectOutputStream` in `writeObject()` it *must* be read back in the `readObject()` method. For example, if the user wrote `java.util.Date` object to the stream before writing the current object (to signify when the object was serialized), the `Date` object would have to be read in *before* `defaultReadObject()` was called, or the stream would be in the incorrect place to read the instance in using `defaultReadObject()`, and an exception would occur.

Verification and Validation for Configuration

One example of how implementing `writeObject()` and `readObject()` could be useful to your `Configuration` object is data verification and validation. Your `Configuration` object stores the user's home directory and a list of recently accessed files. Between the time when a `Configuration` instance is serialized and later deserialized, these files and directory may not exist (they could have been moved or deleted). When your `Configuration` instance is deserialized, you want to remove the references to the directory or files that no longer exist where they originally did. To do this, implement the `readObject()` method as shown in the following code. After calling `defaultReadObject()` to populate the current instance of the object, you can go through the `userHomeDirectory` field and the `recentFiles` field to check if the files (and directory) exist. If a file or directory does not exist, simply set it to `null`:

```
    private void writeObject(ObjectOutputStream out) throws IOException {
      out.defaultWriteObject();
    }

    private void readObject(ObjectInputStream in) throws IOException,
  ClassNotFoundException {
      in.defaultReadObject();

      if (this.userHomeDirectory != null) {
        File f = new File(this.userHomeDirectory);
        if (!f.exists())
          this.userHomeDirectory = null;
      }

      if (this.recentFiles != null) {
        List list = new LinkedList();
        Collections.addAll(list, this.recentFiles);

        ListIterator it = list.listIterator();
        while (it.hasNext()) {
          String curr = (String) it.next();
          File f = new File(curr);
          if (!f.exists()) {
            it.remove();
          }
        }

        this.recentFiles = new String[list.size()];
        list.toArray(this.recentFiles);
      }
    }
```

The Externalizable Interface

Besides implementing readObject() and writeObject(), there is also an interface that extends
Serializable that allows for greater customization of serialization and deserialization. The java.io
.Externalizable interface allows more control of the serialization format than readObject() and
writeObject(). It exists to allow developers to write their own custom formats for a class. With
Externalizable, only the class identity is written to the stream by the Java Serialization API; the rest
is left for the developer. The Externalizable interface looks like this:

```
  public interface java.io.Externalizable extends java.io.Serializable {
    public void readExternal(java.io.ObjectInput in) throws java.io.IOException,
      java.lang.ClassNotFoundException { }

    public void writeExternal(java.io.ObjectOutput out) throws java.io.IOException
      { }
  }
```

The methods writeExternal() and readExternal() are public instead of private like readObject()
and writeObject(). Other classes can call these methods to read and write a class to disk without
specifically invoking Java Serialization. Externalizable is not generally used very often, because
normally when you want to save a class to disk, there is no need to completely customize the format.
However, there may be times when Externalizable could come in handy. If you wanted to serialize a

class that represented an image, and the in-memory representation was huge because it represented every pixel (like a bitmap), the `Externalizable` interface could be used to write the image in a different and compressed format (such as JPEG). The same could be done with `readObject()` and `writeObject()`, but these methods are not public, and in the case of your image-saving class, you may also want to save your image to disk outside of a serialization stream.

Versioning

The biggest stumbling block most developers run into with serialization is versioning. Many times classes will be serialized to disk, and then the definition of the class will change as source code is modified and the class recompiled. Maybe a field gets added, or one gets taken away. Design decisions could force the change of some internal data structures — for example, from lists to maps or trees. Any change to a class, by default, results in no other previously serialized instance to be deserialized — a version error results. Serialization versioning works by hashing a class based on its fields and class definition. Even if one of the field *names* is changed (but not its data type), previously serialized instances will not deserialize — the hash for the class has changed. Sometimes when the definition of a class changes, there would be no way to retain backward compatibility with previously saved instances. With smaller changes, especially things like name changes, or the addition or removal of one field, you probably would want to retain backward compatibility.

The Java Serialization API provides a way to manually set the hash of a class. The following field must be specified exactly as shown to provide the hash of the class:

```
private static final long serialVersionUID = 1L;  // version 1 of our class
```

If the `serialVersionUID` is specified (and is `static` and `final`), the value given will be used as the version for the class. This means that if you define a `serialVersionUID` for your class, you will not get versioning errors when deserializing instances of previous class definitions. The Serialization API provides a best-effort matching algorithm to try to best deserialize classes saved with an older class definition against a newer definition. If a field was added since a class was serialized, upon deserialization, that field will be `null`. Fields whose names have changed or whose types have changed will be `null`. Fields removed will not be set. You will still need to account for these older versions, but by setting the `serialVersionUID`, you are given a chance to do so, rather than just have an exception be thrown right when the deserialization process is attempted. It is recommended to set a `serialVersionUID` for a class that implements `Serializable`, and to change it only when you want previously serialized instances to be incompatible.

Say you have previously serialized class instances and want to change a field or add another. You did not set a `serialVersionUID`, so *any* change you make will render it impossible to deserialize the old instances. The JDK provides a tool to identify a class's hash that did not have a `serialVersionUID` field. The `serialver` tool identifies the JVM's current hash of a compiled class file. Before you modify your class, you can find the previous version's hash. For the `Configuration` object, for example, you did not previously define a `serialVersionUID` field. If you add a field, you will not be able to deserialize old instances. *Before* modifying the class, you need to find the hash. By running the `serialver` tool, you find the hash by:

```
serialver book.Configuration
```

`Serialver` *is located in the* \bin *directory of your JDK.*

`Configuration` must be on the classpath for the `serialver` tool to work. The output of the tool looks like Figure 5-9.

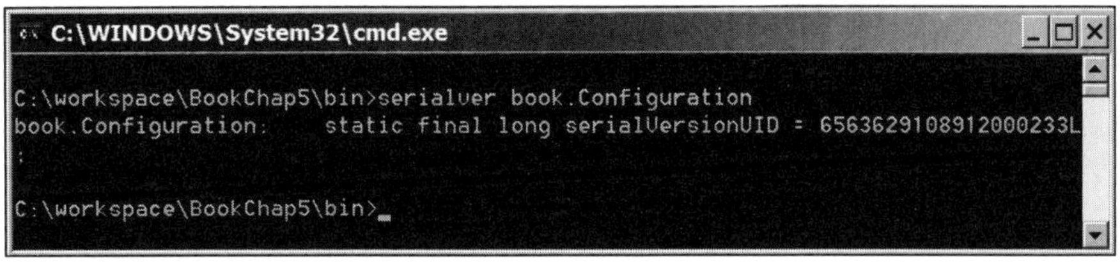

Figure 5-9

Now you can add this `serialVersionUID` value to your `Configuration` class:

```
private static final long serialVersionUID = 6563629108912000233L;
```

You can now add new fields and still deserialize your older instances. Versioning is such an issue with serialization that you should *always* set a `serialVersionUID` for any class that implements `Serializable` right off the bat. This is especially important if your class is to be serialized and deserialized on JVMs from different vendors, because the default hashing algorithm to find a class's `serialVersionUID` is implementation dependent.

When to Use Java Serialization

Java Serialization is a simple but very powerful API. It is easy to use and can serialize most any type of data your application could have. Its main strengths are:

❑   Can serialize complex Java class structures with little code from the developer

❑   An efficient binary file format

The file format defined by the Serialization API is usually what determines its suitability for an application. It is a fairly efficient file format, because it is binary as opposed to XML or other text file format. However, the file format also produces the following weaknesses (though potentially not weaknesses depending on your application's requirements):

❑   Not human-readable

❑   Only Java-based applications can access the serialized data

Because the data is in a binary format, it cannot be edited with simple text editors. Your application's configuration from the example could only be modified from the application. The data was not in an XML format (or other text format) where you could edit it in both the application or in an external editor. Sometimes this is important, but certainly not always. The key downside to Java Serialization is that only Java-based applications can access the serialized data. Because the serialization format is storing actual Java class instances, in a file specification particular to Java, no parsers have been written in other languages for parsing data serialized with the Java Serialization API.

The Java Serialization API is most useful when developing data models for Java applications and persisting them to disk. If your application needs a common file format with other applications not written in Java, serialization is the wrong design choice. If the files do not need to be human-readable, and the only applications written for reading them will be in Java, serialization can be a great design choice.

Serialization can sometimes be a good temporary solution. Every Java application will have some sort of in-memory data model. Certain classes will store data in memory for the application to use. These classes could be persisted to disk, or populated from reading some other file format. Serialization could be initially used to save and restore these class instances. Later on though, as the need for a common file format between non-Java-based applications arises, routines could be written to take the data in those classes and persist it to another format. In other words, the same classes would still be used for the application's internal memory model, just the load and save routines would have to change. You will see in the next sections how you can serialize your application's configuration data in other formats and still retain the use of `Configuration` as your in-memory way of representing that data. Only the load and save code will need to change — not the actual data model.

JavaBeans Long-Term Serialization: XMLEncoder/Decoder

The XMLEncoder/Decoder API is the new recommended persistence mechanism for JavaBeans components starting from the 1.4 version of the JDK. It is the natural progression from serialization in many respects, though it is not meant to replace it. Like Java Serialization, it too serializes object graphs. XMLEncoder/Decoder came around in response to the need for long-term persistence for Swing toolkit components. The Java Serialization API was only good for persisting Swing components in the short-term because it was only guaranteed to work for the same platform and JDK version. The reason for this is that some of the core UI classes that Swing depends on must be written in a platform-dependent manner. Their private data members may not always match up — leading to problems with the normal Serialization API. The Swing API also has had a lot of fluctuation in its implementation. Classes like `JTable` used to take up 30MB of memory alone. As the implementation has improved, the internal implementations of many of these Swing classes have drastically changed. A new serialization API was developed in response to the challenge of true portability between different implementations and versions of the JDK for Swing/JFC classes. XMLEncoder/Decoder thus has a different set of design criteria than the original Java Serialization API. It was designed for a different usage pattern. Both APIs are necessary, with XMLEncoder/Decoder filling in some of the gaps of the Java Serialization API. XMLEncoder is a more robust and resilient API for long-term serialization of object instances, but is limited to serializing only JavaBeans components, and not any Java class instance.

Design Differences

Because the XMLEncoder/Decoder API is designed to serialize only JavaBeans components, the designers had the freedom to make XMLEncoder/Decoder more robust. Version and portability problems were some of the key issues many developers had with the original Java Serialization API. The XMLEncoder/Decoder API was written in response to these issues. The XMLEncoder/Decoder API serializes object instances without *any* knowledge of their private data members. It serializes based upon the object's methods, its JavaBean properties, exposed through the JavaBeans convention of getters and setters (`getXXX` and `setXXX`). By storing an object based upon its public properties rather than its underlying private data members, the underlying implementation is free to change without affecting previously serialized instances (as long as the public properties remain the same). This supports more robust, long-term persistence, because a class's internal structure could be completely rewritten, or differ across platforms, and the serialized instance would still be valid. A simple example of a JavaBean follows:

```java
public class MyBean {
  private String myName;

  public String getMyName() { return this.myName; }

  public void setMyName(String myName) { this.myName = myName; }
}
```

Internal data members could be added, the field `myName` could be changed to a character array or `StringBuffer`, or some other mechanism of storing a string. As long as the methods `getMyName()` and `setMyName()` did not change, the serialized instance could be reconstructed at a later time regardless of other changes. You will notice that `MyBean` does not implement `Serializable`. XMLEncoder/Decoder does not require classes it serializes to implement `Serializable` (or any other `interface` for that matter). Only two requirements are levied upon classes for XMLEncoder/Decoder to serialize:

1. The class must follow JavaBeans conventions.

2. The class must have a default constructor (a constructor with no arguments).

In the upcoming "Possible Customization" section, you will see how both these requirements can be side-stepped, but at the expense of writing and maintaining additional code to plug into the XMLEncoder/Decoder API.

XML: The Serialization Format

The XMLEncoder/Decoder API lives true to its name and has its serialization format based in XML text, in contrast to the binary format used by Java Serialization. The format is a series of processing instructions telling the API how to re-create a given object. The processing instructions instantiate classes, and set JavaBean properties. This idea of serializing *how* to re-create an object, rather than every private data member of an object, leads to a robust file format capable of withstanding any internal class change. This section does not get into the nitty-gritty details of the file format. It is helpful, though, to see the result of serializing a JavaBean using the XMLEncoder/Decoder API. The following code listing is the output of an instance of the `Configuration` object, serialized using the XMLEncoder/Decoder API. Because `Configuration` follows JavaBeans conventions, no special code additions were necessary to serialize an instance using XMLEncoder/Decoder. Notice how the whole object graph is again saved like the Java Serialization API, and because `java.awt.Color` and `java.awt.Point` follow JavaBeans conventions, they are persisted as part of the graph. XMLEncoder/Decoder also optimizes what information is saved — if the value of a bean property is its default value, it does not save the information:

```xml
<?xml version="1.0" encoding="UTF-8"?>
<java version="1.6.0-beta2" class="java.beans.XMLDecoder">
 <object class="book.Configuration">
  <void property="recentFiles">
   <array class="java.lang.String" length="3">
    <void index="0">
     <string>c:\mark\file1.proj</string>
    </void>
    <void index="1">
     <string>c:\mark\testproj.proj</string>
    </void>
    <void index="2">
     <string>c:\mark\final.proj</string>
```

```
      </void>
     </array>
    </void>
    <void property="userHomeDirectory">
     <string>C:\Documents and Settings\Mark\My Documents</string>
    </void>
    <void property="showTabs">
     <boolean>true</boolean>
    </void>
    <void property="foregroundColor">
     <object class="java.awt.Color">
      <int>255</int>
      <int>255</int>
      <int>51</int>
      <int>255</int>
     </object>
    </void>
    <void property="backgroundColor">
     <object class="java.awt.Color">
      <int>51</int>
      <int>51</int>
      <int>255</int>
      <int>255</int>
     </object>
    </void>
   </object>
  </java>
```

One key point about the XML file format used by XMLEncoder/Decoder is that even though an XML parser in any language could read the file, the file format is still specific to Java. The file format encodes processing instructions used to re-create serialized JavaBean class instances, and is therefore not directly useful to applications written in other languages. It would be possible to implement a reader in another language that read some data from this file format, but it would be a large and fairly difficult task. The other language would also need to have some sort of notion of JavaBeans. Think of this format as a Java-only file format and do not rely on it for transmitting data outside of the Java environment. Later this chapter discusses the Java API for XML Binding (JAXB), which is far more suited to exporting data to non-Java consumers.

Because XML is human-readable, it is possible to save class instances to disk and then edit the information with a text editor. Editing the previous XML document would not be for the casual user; it would be more useful to a developer because some knowledge of how the XMLEncoder/Decoder API stores information is necessary to understand *where* to modify the file. If you wanted users to be able to save the Configuration object to disk and then edit it outside of the application, you probably would not choose the XMLEncoder/Decoder XML file format. In the previous file, for example, java.awt.Color was persisted using four integer values, described only by int for each one. What user would know that they correspond to the red, blue, green, and alpha channels of a color, and that they can range from 0–255? A descriptive configuration file format in XML would probably be a task for JAXB, as discussed later in the chapter. The file format used by XMLEncoder/Decoder is Java-specific and is also not well suited for general hand editing like many XML formats are. XML was simply the storage mechanism chosen — why define a new file type when you can use XML?

Key Classes

Using the XMLEncoder/Decoder API is similar to using the Java Serialization API. It was developed to have the same core methods and such that `java.beans.XMLEncoder` and `java.beans.XMLDeocoder` could literally be substituted for `ObjectOutputStream` and `ObjectInputStream`, respectively. `XMLEncoder` and `XMLDecoder` are the only classes needed for normal JavaBean serialization. The "Possible Customization" section briefly discusses some other classes needed to serialize JavaBeans that do not completely follow JavaBeans conventions. Following is a table of the classes needed to use XMLEncoder/Decoder:

Class (from java.beans)	Function
XMLEncoder	Class that takes an instance of a JavaBean and writes the corresponding XML representation of it to the `java.io.OutputStream` it wraps
XMLDecoder	Class that reads a `java.io.InputStream` and decodes XML formatted by `XMLEncoder` back into instances of JavaBeans

Serializing Your JavaBeans

The process of serializing JavaBeans using XMLEncoder/Decoder is almost exactly like the process of serializing a Java class using normal Java Serialization. There are four steps to serialization:

1. Make sure the class to be serialized follows JavaBeans conventions.
2. Make sure the class to be serialized has a default (no argument) constructor.
3. Serialize your JavaBean with `XMLEncoder`.
4. Deserialize your JavaBean with `XMLDecoder`.

To save an instance of the `Configuration` object to disk, simply begin by creating an `XMLEncoder` with a `FileOutputStream` object:

```
XMLEncoder encoder = new XMLEncoder(
                        new FileOutputStream("config.bean.xml"));
```

Then, write an instance of `Configuration`, `conf`, to disk and close the stream:

```
encoder.writeObject(conf);

encoder.close();
```

Reading the serialized instance of `Configuration` back in is just as simple. First the `XMLDecoder` object is created with a `FileInputStream` this time:

```
XMLDecoder decoder = new XMLDecoder(
                        new FileInputStream("config.bean.xml"));
```

Next, read in the object, much as you did with `ObjectInputStream`, and then close the stream:

```
Configuration config = (Configuration) decoder.readObject();

decoder.close();
```

On the surface, XMLEncoder/Decoder works much like Java Serialization. The underlying implementation though, is much different, and allows for the internal structure of classes you serialize to change drastically, yet still work and be compatible with previously saved instances. XMLEncoder/Decoder offers many ways to customize how it maps JavaBeans to its XML format, and some of those are discussed in the "Possible Customization" section.

Just like the Java Serialization API, multiple objects can be written to the same stream. `XMLEncoder`'s `writeObject()` *method can be called in succession to serialize more than one object instance. When instances are deserialized, though, they must be deserialized in the same order that they were written.*

Robustness Demonstrated: Changing a Configuration's Internal Data

Suppose you want to change the way the `Configuration` object stores the references to the user's recently accessed files of your application. They were stored previously in the string array bean property, `recentFiles`, and accessed with the normal bean getter/setter pair, `getRecentFiles()` and `setRecentFiles()`. The `Configuration` object looked like this:

```java
package book;

import java.awt.Color;
import java.awt.Point;
import java.beans.XMLDecoder;
import java.io.File;
import java.io.FileInputStream;
import java.util.ArrayList;
import java.util.List;

public class Configuration {

...

  private String[] recentFiles;

  public String[] getRecentFiles() {
    return recentFiles;
  }

  public void setRecentFiles(String[] recentFiles) {
    this.recentFiles = recentFiles;
  }

...

}
```

Now you would like to store them as a `java.util.List` full of `java.io.File` objects. If you do not change the signature of `getRecentFiles()` and `setRecentFiles()`, you can do whatever you like with the underlying data structure. The modified `Configuration` class illustrates changes to the storage of recent files to a `List` without changing the method signatures for the `recentFiles` bean property:

```
package book;

import java.awt.Color;
import java.awt.Point;
import java.beans.XMLDecoder;
import java.io.File;
import java.io.FileInputStream;
import java.util.ArrayList;
import java.util.List;

public class Configuration {

...

  private List recentFiles;

  public String[] getRecentFiles() {
    if (this.recentFiles == null || this.recentFiles.isEmpty())
      return null;

    String[] files = new String[this.recentFiles.size()];

    for (int i = 0; i < this.recentFiles.size(); i++)
      files[i] = ((File) this.recentFiles.get(i)).getPath();

    return files;
  }

  public void setRecentFiles(String[] files) {
    if (this.recentFiles == null)
      this.recentFiles = new ArrayList();

    for (int i = 0; i < files.length; i++) {
      this.recentFiles.add(new File(files[i]));
    }
  }

...

}
```

Notice how in the `setRecentFiles()` method you convert an array of `String` objects to a `List` of `File` objects. In the `getRecentFiles()` method you convert the `List` of `File` objects into an array of `String` objects. This conversion is the key to the information hiding principle that XMLEncoder/Decoder uses to serialize and deserialize object instances. Because XMLEncoder/Decoder only works with the operations of a class, the private data members can be changed. By keeping the interface the same, the `Configuration` class can undergo all kinds of incremental changes and improvements under the hood without affecting previously saved instances. This is the key benefit of XMLEncoder/Decoder that provides its ability to serialize instances not just in the short-term, but also in the long-term, by weathering many types of changes to a class's internal implementation.

The `main()` method shown in the following code demonstrates `XMLDecoder` deserializing an instance of `Configuration` previously saved with the older version of `Configuration` that stored the `recentFiles` property as a `String` array. The file this method is loading is the one shown previously in this section as sample output for XMLEncoder/Decoder (see the previous section "XML: The Serialization Format").

```
public static void main(String[] args) throws Exception {
  XMLDecoder decoder = new XMLDecoder(
               new FileInputStream("config.bean.xml"));

  Configuration conf = (Configuration) decoder.readObject();

  decoder.close();

  String[] recentFiles = conf.getRecentFiles();
  for (int i = 0; i < recentFiles.length; i++)
    System.out.println(recentFiles[i]);
}
```

As you can see, the output from the `main()` method confirms that not only was the old `Configuration` instance successfully read, but the new `List` of `File` objects is working properly, and populated with the correct objects:

```
c:\workingdir\file1.proj
c:\workingdir\testproj.proj
c:\workingdir\final.proj
```

Possible Customization

XMLEncoder/Decoder supports serialization of JavaBeans out of the box, but it can also be customized to serialize any class — regardless of whether or not it uses JavaBeans conventions. In fact, throughout the Swing/JFC class library, you will find classes that do not fully conform to JavaBeans conventions. Many types of collection classes do not; some Swing classes have other ways of storing data besides getters and setters. The following XML file is a serialized instance of a `java.util.HashMap`, and a `javax.swing.JPanel`. Both of these classes have their data added to them by methods that do not follow the JavaBeans convention:

```
<?xml version="1.0" encoding="UTF-8"?>
<java version="1.6.0-beta2" class="java.beans.XMLDecoder">
 <object class="java.util.HashMap">
  <void method="put">
   <string>Another</string>
   <string>AnotherTest</string>
  </void>
  <void method="put">
   <string>Mark</string>
   <string>Test</string>
  </void>
 </object>
 <object class="javax.swing.JPanel">
  <void method="add">
   <object class="javax.swing.JLabel">
    <void property="text">
     <string>Mark Label</string>
    </void>
```

```
      </object>
    </void>
  </object>
</java>
```

Note how data is added to a `HashMap` by its `put()` method, and components are added to `JPanels` by its `add()` method. How does the XMLEncoder/Decoder API know how to look for this—or even find the data that should be inserted via those methods? Because its file format is a series of processing instructions, XMLEncoder/Decoder can serialize the information necessary to make method calls to disk. This generic capability lets XMLEncoder/Decoder do any kind of custom initialization or setting of data that a class may require. Just because the file format supports this type of generic processing instructions, though, does not mean that the XMLEncoder automatically knows how to use them. The solution is the API's `java.beans.PersistenceDelegate` class.

Persistence Delegates

Every class serialized and deserialized has an instance of `java.beans.PersistenceDelegate` associated with it. It may be the default one included for classes following the JavaBeans conventions, or it could be a custom subclass of `PersistenceDelegate` that writes the processing instructions needed to re-create a given instance of a class. Persistence delegates are responsible only for writing an object to disk—*not* reading them. Because all objects are written in terms of known processing instructions, these instructions can be used to re-create the object. Reading an object consists solely of executing the processing instructions as they were written—independent of whether these instructions were written using a custom `PersistenceDelegate`. How to write a custom persistence delegate is a fairly complex topic that is out of the scope of this section.

For detailed information on how to use and create custom persistence delegates, visit `http://java.sun.com/products/jfc/tsc/articles/persistence4/` to read an article written by Philip Mine, the designer and author of XMLEncoder/Decoder API.

When to Use XMLEncoder/Decoder

Use of the XMLEncoder/Decoder API over the Java Serialization API is generally preferred when one is serializing object graphs consisting of JavaBeans and Swing components. It was designed precisely for that purpose and fixes the more generic Java Serialization API's shortcomings with respect to both JavaBeans, but especially Swing components. Prior to the XMLEncoder/Decoder API there was no built-in mechanism for the long-term serialization of Swing components. XMLEncoder/Decoder has only been in the JDK since version 1.4; if you must support any JDK released before 1.4 you cannot use XMLEncoder/Decoder.

Thinking in more general terms, and assuming your application has a data model you wish to persist to disk, XMLEncoder/Decoder has the following advantages:

- ❑ Can serialize complex Java class structures with little code from the developer

- ❑ You can add properties and remove properties from your JavaBeans class definitions without breaking previously serialized instances

- ❑ The internal private data structure of your beans can change without breaking previously serialized instances

- ❑ Instances are saved in XML, making the resulting files human-readable

Some of the potential downsides to choosing the XMLEncoder/Decoder for serializing your object graph of JavaBeans are:

❑ Even though the file format is human-readable, it is editable in the real world only by developers

❑ Even though the file format is XML, it is still Java-specific — it would take great effort to allow a non-Java-based application to read the data

❑ Every piece of data you want persisted in the class must be a JavaBean property (or customized with a special persistence delegate)

The XMLEncoder/Decoder API is perfect for what it is designed for — the long-term serialization of JavaBeans components for use later on by Java-based applications. Because it is so customizable, it can often be used for a variety of other purposes, and serialize a lot of data beyond ordinary JavaBeans. Generally though, its main advantage over normal Java Serialization is its robustness through even class definition changes. Apart from that, however, it still has the same limitations of the Java Serialization API. When you have an internal data model based with JavaBeans, XMLEncoder/Decoder makes sense. Once you would like your application's file formats to be read by other applications — other non-Java applications — eventually you will have to specify some other custom file format or write to an existing standard.

Flexible XML Serialization: Java API for XML Binding (JAXB)

Like both the Java Serialization API and the XMLEncoder/Decoder API, the Java API for XML Binding (JAXB) is a serialization framework for Java objects. It serializes and deserializes object graphs to and from an XML representation. The XML representation is flexible, and differs per Java class type being serialized. It is defined by mapping Java class members and bean properties to various XML elements or attributes. The mapping can be defined by either an XML Schema document or by simply using Java annotations to annotate Java classes, instructing the JAXB framework where a bean property or field member maps to which XML element or attribute in an XML document.

> The XML Schema language is the World Wide Web Consortium's standard for specifying the XML structure for a particular XML file format. Think of XML Schema as being to XML what a database schema is to a relational database — it defines the blueprints and data storage for a particular domain of data. It is a widely accepted standard and already maps many primitive data types to XML. XML Schemas also let XML parsers validate an XML instance document to verify conformance to the schema's requirements. This can greatly reduce the time it takes to write code that must read XML because it does a lot of the validation for you. View the XML Schema specification at the following URL: www.w3.org/TR/xmlschema-0/.

Because JAXB lets the user actually define the mapping (or binding) between an XML representation and a Java object, the developer has control of the serialization file format. This flexibility allows the JAXB framework to read and write to third-party XML formats, as well as custom XML formats — allowing for much easier data interchange with other applications than data saved with either the Java Serialization API or the XMLEncoder/Decoder API, because both of these are dependent on Java (and having access to the particular classes used for serialization).

The original JAXB 1.0 specification mainly addressed these data interchange possibilities. As XML Schema has matured, it has become an increasingly popular way of specifying file formats. Many publicly open file formats publish an XML Schema defining the format, allowing third-party applications to easily read and write data defined in that format. For example, the Open Financial Exchange format (OFX) is a format many financial institutions use for exchanging data. Many banks with online access support downloading account information in this format. Third-party financial software can then import the account data. Because JAXB allows the creation of JavaBeans based on an XML schema, JAXB can generate JavaBeans that will read and write this format (the OFX specification is available at `www.ofx.net/ofx/de_spec.asp`). JAXB is the perfect API to use for reading and writing these different standard file formats defined in XML Schema.

Starting with version 6, the JAXB 2.0 framework is now included with the JDK. Unlike JAXB 1.0, it now takes full advantage of Java annotations. Previously, JAXB 1.0 only allowed the generation of JavaBeans from an XML schema. These generated JavaBeans could then be used to serialize data to the XML format defined by the original XML schema. It was a useful framework if one was required to read and write a particular XML format defined by an XML schema (such as the OFX format). With the addition of new annotations to the framework, JAXB has increased its scope to now serializing potentially any Java object. Now Java classes can be annotated to let the JAXB framework know how to serialize a particular instance of a class to a custom-defined XML format.

In the overview of JAXB presented in the remainder of this chapter, two use cases for JAXB are discussed. For both, you will continue to utilize the configuration data model example in this chapter for the hypothetical image manipulating application. First, you will create an XML schema to allow JAXB to generate a set of JavaBean classes used to serialize and deserialize data, illustrating both a high-level overview of XML Schema, as well as the process you would take to import a third-party schema. The second use case will illustrate the ease and benefits of simply annotating an existing set of Java classes, an application's data model, to serialize and deserialize it to an XML format suitable for interchange with other applications.

Sample XML Document for the Configuration Object

Suppose you want to take your `Configuration` data model and define an XML schema to represent it. You will not be able to write an XML schema that maps directly to the already-existing `Configuration` class, but you can write an XML schema that saves all the necessary data attributes to re-create the `Configuration` instance. To refresh your memory on what data attributes are stored in `Configuration`, refer to Figure 5-2.

You need to store data to represent a color, a point, a directory and file locations, and a Boolean variable. XML Schema is more than equipped to handle this — you just have to actually define it. Following is an XML instance document that contains all of the information you would need to re-create the `Configuration` object. Notice how it is not only human-readable in the sense that it is text, but also conceivably modifiable by a user. Colors are obviously defined, and the user's home directory element is easily modified. The following XML is far more readable than the output from the XMLEncoder/Decoder API:

```xml
<?xml version="1.0" encoding="UTF-8" standalone="yes"?>
<configuration xmlns="http://book.org/Configuration">
    <user-settings>
        <user-home-directory>C:\Documents and Settings\Mark\My Documents</user-home-
directory>

        <recent-files>
```

```
            <recent-file>c:\mark\file1.proj</recent-file>

            <recent-file>c:\mark\testproj.proj</recent-file>

            <recent-file>c:\mark\final.proj</recent-file>
        </recent-files>
    </user-settings>

    <ui-settings>
        <palette-window-position>
            <x-coord>5</x-coord>

            <y-coord>5</y-coord>
        </palette-window-position>

        <tools-window-position>
            <x-coord>10</x-coord>

            <y-coord>10</y-coord>
        </tools-window-position>

        <background-color>
            <red>51</red>

            <green>51</green>

            <blue>255</blue>

            <alpha>255</alpha>
        </background-color>

        <foreground-color>
            <red>255</red>

            <green>255</green>

            <blue>51</blue>

            <alpha>255</alpha>
        </foreground-color>

        <show-tabs>true</show-tabs>
    </ui-settings>
</configuration>
```

Note, though, that this XML file is *not* the XML schema; it is a document that conforms to the XML schema you will define in the next section. JAXB will generate Java classes that read and write files like the preceding XML. It will give you JavaBean-like access to all of the data contained in the document.

Defining Your XML Format with an XML Schema

Now that you have looked at a sample XML instance document containing a sample set of `Configuration` data for your data model, you can look under the hood and see how to specify the schema. This section goes through the various data types for configuration and looks at how they can be defined in a schema. The following list reiterates what data needs to be stored in the configuration data model:

❑ The user's home directory, a String value

❑ A flag whether or not to use a tabbed interface, a Boolean value

❑ A list of recently accessed files by the user, an array of String values

❑ Two colors, foreground and background, for drawing operations, color values

❑ Two points, for the last position of the tool and palette windows, point values

Though this section is not a thorough guide to using XML Schema, it does go through how to define the data bullets listed. First, though, XML Schema must be discussed. XML Schema is a simple but powerful language for defining and specifying what types various XML elements can be, and where they can appear in a document. There are two types of XML elements you can define with XML Schema: simple elements and complex elements. Simple elements have no attributes and contain only text data — they also have no child elements. Any example of a simple element would be:

```
<hello>world</hello>
```

Complex elements can have attributes, child elements, and potentially mix their child elements with text. An example of a complex element is:

```
<complex c="12">
    <hello>world</hello>
</complex>
```

XML Schema is fairly intuitive, and a full and thorough coverage of it is outside the scope of this book. You can find a great introductory tutorial at www.w3schools.com/schema/default.asp.

Defining Your Data: Configuration.xsd

To define your data, you will be using both simple and complex elements. Looking back at the bullet list of data points you will need — both the user's home directory and your tabbed interface flag (the first two bullets), can probably be modeled with simple elements. Here is how they will be modeled in XML Schema:

```
<xs:element name="user-home-directory" type="xs:string" />
<xs:element name="show-tabs" type="xs:boolean" />
```

You are defining elements, and requiring that the text within those elements be of the type specified. An instance example of both of these elements is:

```
<user-home-directory>c:\my-home-directory</user-home-directory>
<show-tabs>true</show-tabs>
```

273

Your string array of recent files is slightly more complex to model. You are going to model it as a complex element, with a child element for each individual recent file. First, define the complex type:

```
<xs:complexType name="recentFilesType">
   <xs:sequence>
      <xs:element name="recent-file" type="xs:string" maxOccurs="unbounded" />
   </xs:sequence>
</xs:complexType>
```

After defining your complex type, which is a sequence of `recent-file` elements, define the element that uses your custom XML type. Note how the `type` attribute in the following element definition corresponds to the `name` attribute in the preceding complex type definition:

```
<xs:element name="recent-files" type="recentFilesType" minOccurs="0" />
```

An example instance of the `recent-files` element looks like this:

```
<recent-files>
   <recent-file>c:\workingdir\file1.proj</recent-file>

   <recent-file>c:\workingdir\testproj.proj</recent-file>

   <recent-file>c:\workingdir\final.proj</recent-file>
</recent-files>
```

Defining colors presents an interesting challenge. You must make sure you have enough information specified in the XML file to construct a `java.awt.Color` object. If you specify in the XML file the `red`, `green`, `blue`, and `alpha` components of a color, you will have enough information to construct a `java.awt.Color` instance. Model your color type in the schema as follows:

```
<xs:complexType name="colorType">
   <xs:sequence>
      <xs:element name="red" type="xs:int" />

      <xs:element name="green" type="xs:int" />

      <xs:element name="blue" type="xs:int" />

      <xs:element name="alpha" type="xs:int" default="255" />
   </xs:sequence>
</xs:complexType>
```

As you can see, the complex type, `colorType`, contains child elements for the RGBA components. These components are integer values and if the `alpha` component is not specified, it defaults to 255 (a totally opaque color). You define two elements that take your newly defined type, `colorType`: the foreground and background colors for your application's configuration data model:

```
<xs:element name="background-color" type="colorType" minOccurs="0" />
<xs:element name="foreground-color" type="colorType" minOccurs="0" />
```

An example instance of a `foreground-color` element is shown here:

```
      <foreground-color>
         <red>255</red>

         <green>255</green>

         <blue>51</blue>

         <alpha>255</alpha>
      </foreground-color>
```

The last major custom type you must define is the type for point objects. This type must have enough information encoded in the XML to construct a `java.awt.Point` instance. All you essentially need are integer values representing the x and y coordinates of a point. The last two element definitions are also listed that use the new XML type for points, `pointType`. These elements represent the position of the palette window and the tool window of your application:

```
      <xs:complexType name="pointType">
         <xs:sequence>
            <xs:element name="x-coord" type="xs:int" />

            <xs:element name="y-coord" type="xs:int" />
         </xs:sequence>
      </xs:complexType>

   <xs:element name="palette-window-position" type="pointType" minOccurs="0" />
   <xs:element name="tools-window-position" type="pointType" minOccurs="0" />
```

Now that you have defined all the basic types in your schema, they can be organized around other elements for better readability of your XML instance documents. The actual schema listed at the end of this section will have more elements and complex type definitions to account for document readability. The next step is to generate JAXB classes from your schema to start reading and writing XML documents that conform to your schema.

The full XML Schema Definition (XSD) file for your configuration data model, `configuration.xsd`, is listed here:

```
<?xml version="1.0" encoding="utf-8" ?>
<xs:schema targetNamespace="http://book.org/Configuration"
elementFormDefault="qualified" xmlns="http://book.org/Configuration"
xmlns:xs="http://www.w3.org/2001/XMLSchema">
   <xs:complexType name="configurationType">
      <xs:sequence>
         <xs:element name="user-settings" type="user-settingsType" />

         <xs:element name="ui-settings" type="ui-settingsType" />
      </xs:sequence>
   </xs:complexType>

   <xs:complexType name="recentFilesType">
      <xs:sequence>
         <xs:element name="recent-file" type="xs:string" maxOccurs="unbounded" />
      </xs:sequence>
```

```
      </xs:complexType>

      <xs:complexType name="pointType">
         <xs:sequence>
            <xs:element name="x-coord" type="xs:int" />

            <xs:element name="y-coord" type="xs:int" />
         </xs:sequence>
      </xs:complexType>

      <xs:complexType name="colorType">
         <xs:sequence>
            <xs:element name="red" type="xs:int" />

            <xs:element name="green" type="xs:int" />

            <xs:element name="blue" type="xs:int" />

            <xs:element name="alpha" type="xs:int" default="255" />
         </xs:sequence>
      </xs:complexType>

      <xs:complexType name="ui-settingsType">
         <xs:sequence>
            <xs:element name="palette-window-position" type="pointType" minOccurs="0"
            />

            <xs:element name="tools-window-position" type="pointType" minOccurs="0" />

            <xs:element name="background-color" type="colorType" minOccurs="0" />

            <xs:element name="foreground-color" type="colorType" minOccurs="0" />

            <xs:element name="show-tabs" type="xs:boolean" />
         </xs:sequence>
      </xs:complexType>

      <xs:complexType name="user-settingsType">
         <xs:sequence>
            <xs:element name="user-home-directory" type="xs:string" />

            <xs:element name="recent-files" type="recentFilesType" minOccurs="0" />
         </xs:sequence>
      </xs:complexType>

      <xs:element name="configuration" type="configurationType" />

   </xs:schema>
```

Generating JAXB Java Classes from Your Schema

New in JDK 6, the tools for generating JAXB classes from an XML schema are now included in the JDK. Previously they were available as part of the Java Web Services Development Pack (JWSDP). To use the XML schema compiler, you must make sure your PATH environment variable includes the /<JDK 6 home>/bin directory. The xjc command in the JDK bin directory invokes the schema compiler. You saved your schema to the file `configuration.xsd`. To compile the schema, simply type at the command prompt, in the same directory as the schema, the following:

```
xjc -d gen configuration.xsd
```

The `-d` option simply tells the compiler in which directory to put the generated Java source files. In this case, you have a directory under the main project specifically for generated source files, `gen`, so if you modify the schema, you can easily regenerate the files to this same location. After running the `xjc` compiler, the following Java source files were generated:

```
org\book\configuration\ColorType.java
org\book\configuration\ConfigurationType.java
org\book\configuration\ObjectFactory.java
org\book\configuration\PointType.java
org\book\configuration\RecentFilesType.java
org\book\configuration\UiSettingsType.java
org\book\configuration\UserSettingsType.java
org\book\configuration\package-info.java
```

JAXB 1.0-generated sources are not compatible with the JAXB 2.0 runtime. You can, however, simply include the JAXB 1.0 runtime on your classpath to use older generated classes (or simply generate new classes to use the 2.0 runtime). In 2.0, the older impl package classes are no longer generated (the JAXB runtime includes all the necessary runtime support in 2.0).

Generated JAXB Object Graphs

JAXB-generated classes follow certain conventions corresponding to how an XML schema is written. For every top-level XML schema complex type defined, JAXB generates a class corresponding to that type. In this configuration example, for instance, you defined the following complex types in your XML schema: `configurationType`, `recentFilesType`, `pointType`, `colorType`, `ui-settingsType`, and `user-settingsType`. Respectively corresponding to each of these XML schema types are the following generated JAXB classes: `ConfigurationType`, `RecentFilesType`, `PointType`, `ColorType`, `UiSettingsType`, and `UserSettingType`. The Java package where each of the generated classes is placed depends on the XML namespace assigned to its type. In this example, all of the complex types defined were in the `http://book.org/Configuration` XML namespace. JAXB placed all of your types, therefore, on the `org.book.configuration` package.

For each generated class, JAXB creates JavaBean properties based on the contents of the corresponding XML schema complex type. If a complex type contains complex sub-elements, JAXB will generate bean properties to other JAXB classes, representing those complex types. See Figure 5-10 for a class diagram of your generated classes.

Notice in `ConfigurationType` that there are two bean properties: `uiSettings` and `userSettings`. The types for these correspond to `UiSettingsType` and `UserSettingsType`, respectively, matching the definition in your XML schema. Looking into `ColorType` and `PointType` in more detail (see Figure 5-11) shows how JAXB maps a complex element definition to a generated Java class.

As you can see from Figure 5-11, JAXB maps XML elements and attributes of complex types to JavaBean properties. The complex type `colorType` in the schema had four sub-elements, `red`, `blue`, `green`, and `alpha`. These were all mapped to JavaBean `int` properties. They were mapped to `int` because that was the type specified in their element definitions. Note that this type could be another generated class type, if the element definition specified another XML schema complex type.

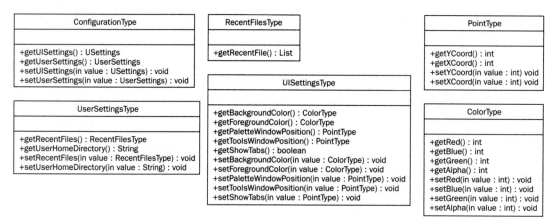

Figure 5-10

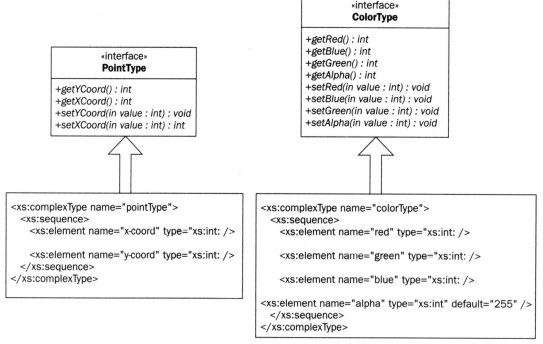

Figure 5-11

Because XML documents are hierarchical in nature, the structure of the generated JAXB classes is also hierarchical. JAXB serializes and deserializes root elements in an XML document. This root element is the beginning of an object graph. The XML complex type `pointType`, for instance, has sub-elements `x-coord` and `y-coord`; they are therefore properties of `pointType`. In the generated JAXB class, these coordinates become properties of the `PointType` interface. Figure 5-12 shows the generated JAXB object graph from the root element of the configuration data model, `configuration`.

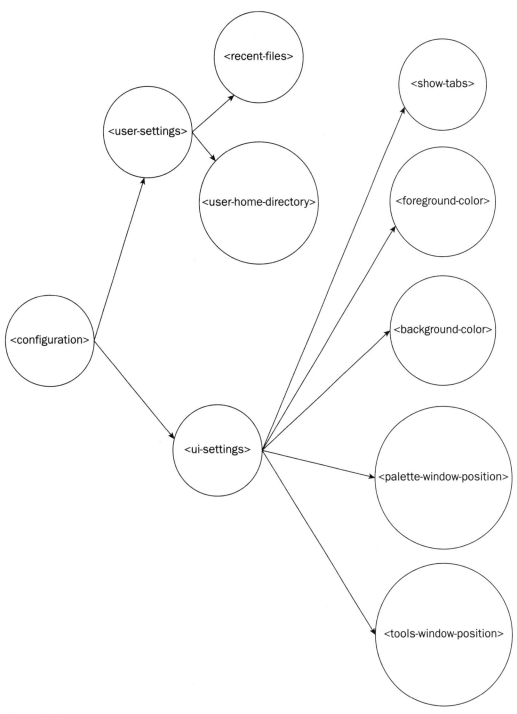

Figure 5-12

In XML Schema, elements that will be the root of an XML document must be specified as a top-level element definition in an XML schema. For this configuration example, the `configuration` element is the root element, and it is defined in XML schema as follows:

```
<xs:element name="configuration" type="configurationType" />
```

Because `configuration` is a top-level element and will be serialized as the root of an XML document, JAXB handles it a little differently. `ConfigurationType` is no different in structure than other JAXB-generated classes, but how it is serialized is different. This is where the `ObjectFactory` class generated by JAXB comes into play. JAXB uses the factory design pattern to create instances of its generated classes. For every set of classes it generates, it also generates a corresponding `ObjectFactory` class. This class contains methods to create instances of every Java type it generates. The `ObjectFactory` harkens back to the JAXB 1.0 days, when each complex type had both a Java `interface` and corresponding implementation class generated. The factory still serves a useful purpose, even when now in JAXB 2.0 all generated resources are actual concrete Java classes. This purpose is to wrap complex types *to be serialized as the root element of an XML document* in an instance of `javax.xml.bind.JAXBElement`.

Objects to be serialized as the root of an object graph *must* be wrapped in an instance of `javax.xml.bind.JAXBElement`. The generated `ObjectFactory` class makes this simple. When it comes time to serialize an instance of `ConfigurationType`, the `ObjectFactory` provides a clean and simple way to wrap the instance within a `JAXBElement` instance:

```
ConfigurationType ct = factory.createConfigurationType();
... set data properties...

JAXBElement<ConfigurationType> rootElement = factory.createConfiguration(ct);
```

The `rootElement` object is the one you will actually serialize and deserialize via JAXB. This is counter-intuitive when you're used to either the Java Serialization API or the XMLEncoder/Decoder API. With those APIs you just pass the actual Java object that is to be the root of the graph serialized — there is no need for a wrapper object. In the section "Annotating Existing Java Classes for Use with JAXB" you will see how wrapping an instance in `JAXBElement` can be circumvented to serialize it as root (through the use of the new annotations introduced with JAXB 2.0).

If you look at the source for any classes generated by JAXB, you will notice that all of the classes are annotated using the new annotations package in JAXB 2.0, `javax.xml.bind.annotation`. These annotations are discussed in the "Annotating Existing Java Classes for Use with JAXB" section of this chapter.

JAXB API Key Classes

While thus far this chapter has discussed the classes JAXB generates based on an XML schema, these generated classes are different from the classes used to actually serialize and deserialize them to and from XML. The JAXB runtime provides a couple of interfaces to perform the actual serialization operations, or conversion of Java class instances to their XML representation — `Marshaller` and `Unmarshaller`, both retrieved from the `JAXBContext`. `JAXBContext` instances must be set up using the Java class and package data of those classes to be serialized. From this information, the `JAXBContext` can create `Marshaller`s and `Unmarshaller`s that know the mapping between a particular set of Java classes and XML. `JAXBElement` must be used to wrap the root Java object being serialized or deserialized (unless you're using the XmlRootElement annotation—see the section "Annotating Existing Java Classes for Use with JAXB" for more information).

Class or Interface (from javax.xml.bind)	Function
JAXBContext	The JAXBContext is the initial class in which you create Marshaller and Unmarshaller classes for various JAXB-generated types
JAXBElement<T>	Used to represent a root element to be serialized, necessary to use if the root Java class of type T to be serialized is not marked with the annotation XmlRootElement
Marshaller	Interface that allows for the marshalling of JAXB-generated objects to XML in various formats (stream, DOM nodes, SAX events, and so forth)
Unmarshaller	Interface that allows for the unmarshalling of various XML representations (from a stream, a DOM tree, or SAX events), to populate instances of JAXB-generated classes

Marshalling and Unmarshalling XML Data

The process of marshalling and unmarshalling data to and from JAXB classes all occurs through three classes, JAXBContext, Marshaller, and Unmarshaller. Both Marshaller and Unmarshaller are created from an instance of JAXBContext, and they do the actual work of marshalling and unmarshalling the data. JAXBContext objects are configured upon creation, with the Java types that will be marshaled and unmarshaled. This allows the JAXBContext to set up the Marshaller and Unmarshaller objects with the particular schema rules and constraints for those classes that will be serialized. From the Java types passed in to configure the JAXBContext, the other dependent Java types will be automatically configured by the context (as long as they can be loaded by the same classloader)—therefore, only the root object of an object graph is necessary to configure the context. There are three steps to unmarshalling XML instance data conforming to a schema into your JAXB-generated object graph:

1. Retrieve an instance of JAXBContext specific the Java class(es) to be unmarshaled as the root of an XML document.

2. Create an Unmarshaller object from the JAXBContext instance.

3. Use the Unmarshaller to unmarshal XML data into instances of the generated JAXB classes.

Now you can unmarshal XML data conforming to the configuration.xsd schema into the generated JAXB classes. First, retrieve the JAXBContext, passing in ConfigurationType.class because that is the root Java object you are deserializing (meaning all other Java types being deserialized can be inferred from that type):

```
JAXBContext ctx = JAXBContext.newInstance(ConfigurationType.class);
```

Then create the Unmarshaller from the context:

```
Unmarshaller u = ctx.createUnmarshaller();
```

Now that you have an `Unmarshaller`, you can pass various streams, readers, and so forth, to access XML data to transform into an instance of the JAXB-generated object graph. In this example, you will pass it a `FileInputStream` corresponding to an XML file saved on disk that conforms to your schema. Notice how you cast the resulting `java.lang.Object` returned from the call to `unmarshal()` to `JAXBElement`. Using that object you can then get the `ConfigurationType` instance:

```
JAXBElement rootElement = (JAXBElement)
                             u.unmarshal(new FileInputStream("configuration.xml"));

org.book.configuration.ConfigurationType conf =
            (org.book.configuration.ConfigurationType)
                  rootElement.getValue();
```

Now you have the JAXB-generated `ConfigurationType` object, which represents the root node of your XML file, and is the root of your object graph. You can now use the data as necessary in your application. Marshalling data back into XML is just as simple as unmarshalling. The three steps to marshal the data mirror the three steps to unmarshal it:

1. Retrieve an instance of `JAXBContext` specific the Java class or classes to be marshaled as the root of an XML document.

2. Create a `Marshaller` object from the `JAXBContext` instance.

3. Use the `Marshaller` to marshal XML data into instances of the generated JAXB classes.

Now you can marshal instances of `org.book.configuration.ConfigurationType` back to disk (or to DOM representations or SAX events). Just like before, you get the `JAXBContext` particular for your package of JAXB-generated classes:

```
JAXBContext ctx = JAXBContext.newInstance(ConfigurationType.class);
```

Then you create the `Marshaller` from the context:

```
Marshaller m = ctx.createMarshaller();
```

Now you can use the `Marshaller` instance to serialize the information in the `conf` instance of `org .book.configuration.Configuration` to a `FileOutputStream`. Use the generated `ObjectFactory` class in `org.book.configuration` to create the `JAXBElement` wrapper for the root `ConfigurationType` object:

```
m.marshal(factory.createConfiguration(conf),
        new FileOutputStream("configuration.xml");
```

That's all there is to marshalling and unmarshalling data. As you can see, the difficult part is writing the schema.

> *If the* `org.book.configuration.Configuration` *type is not populated with all the data the schema requires, the instance might be marshaled incorrectly to XML, meaning it will not be able to be unmarshaled back by JAXB. Exceptions will be thrown and the XML document will have to be fixed.*

Creating New XML Content with JAXB-Generated Classes

You have looked at how to load XML data into a JAXB object graph. You have looked into saving an existing JAXB object graph back into XML. How would you create a new JAXB graph and populate it programmatically? Unfortunately, this is one area where JAXB can become a little unwieldy. In JAXB, every set of generated classes comes with an `ObjectFactory` class at the root package of the generated classes. You may have noticed the class `org.book.configuration.ObjectFactory` back when you generated the set of classes for the `configuration.xsd` schema. This is the class you would use to create every JAXB object. The example that follows shows the creation and population of an `org.book.configuration.Configuration` instance:

```
ObjectFactory factory = new ObjectFactory();

ConfigurationType configType = factory.createConfiguration();
UiSettingsType uiSettingsType = factory.createUiSettingsType();
UserSettingsType userSettingsType = factory.createUserSettingsType();

configType.setUiSettings(uiSettingsType);
configType.setUserSettings(userSettingsType);
ColorType fgColorType = factory.createColorType();
fgColorType.setRed(255);
fgColorType.setBlue(255);
fgColorType.setGreen(0);

uiSettingsType.setForegroundColor(fgColorType);

uiSettingsType.setShowTabs(true);

userSettingsType.setUserHomeDirectory(conf.getUserHomeDirectory());

... // continue on as such, populating the entire object graph
```

One thing to take into consideration when manually populating JAXB object graphs, though, is completeness and conformance to the schema. Although it is easy to populate JAXB objects, and use the data in a Java application, if you want to save the data you are populating out to disk (or somewhere else) as XML, every schema-required piece of data must exist in your newly created object graph. In the preceding example, if you did not create a `UserSettingsType` instance and set it on the `Configuration` instance, you would get JAXB exceptions thrown if, after marshalling the data, you tried to unmarshal it back into your Java object.

Using JAXB-Generated Classes in Your Application

One of the potential issues that arise whenever information is saved and loaded from a file is that the information must be turned into objects used by the application. The nice thing about the Java Serialization API and XMLEncoder/Decoder is that they save the actual Java class instances used by an application, so there is no need to transform the data loaded into a format used by the application — it is already in the format used by the application. The classes that JAXB generates can be used as the in-memory data model for your application, but generally there is a need to perform at least some transformations. The Java classes in the JDK are rich and full of functionality — it would be wasteful to ignore it. Why store URLs as Strings? Why store File objects as Strings? Why not represent a color with a java.awt.Color object? Because it makes sense to use the classes in the JDK, a lot of the time you will find yourself taking data from the

JavaBeans generated by JAXB, and putting them into your own data structures. You'll find yourself adding JAXB classes to your own lists, maps, trees, and other data structures. This is the added burden of using JAXB with an existing schema over using Java Serialization or XMLEncoder/Decoder. In the example configuration data model used throughout this chapter, you used an instance of `book`
`.Configuration` to represent the model. It contained Java representations of points and colors. To use the JAXB-generated configuration data model in your application, you will have to transform it to and from the `book.Configuration` data model. It's not a difficult task, but must be done for things like color and point representations to have any meaning to your application. The diagram in Figure 5-13 illustrates where transformations fit into the bigger picture of your application.

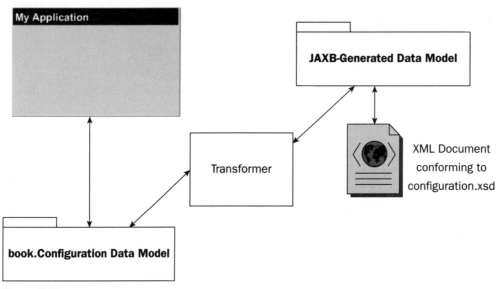

Figure 5-13

In the original `Configuration` data model example, you wrapped your serialization code into Swing actions. This let you easily add code to save and load configuration data to menus and buttons in your application. You will do the same for code to save and load configuration data, this time with the XML format based on the `configuration.xsd` schema file. The key difference, though, will be that you need to integrate transformation functionality into these actions, because a conversion needs to be done between the JAXB-generated data model, and the original `Configuration` data model (as shown in Figure 5-13). Other than this transformation, the new XML save and load Swing actions will be very similar in structure and nature to the older actions.

Implementing the Save Action

The save action's `actionPerformed()` method will start out the same way as the original save action — by prompting the user for a file in which to save the configuration information:

```
package book;

...

import org.book.configuration.ColorType;
```

```
import org.book.configuration.ConfigurationType;
import org.book.configuration.ObjectFactory;
import org.book.configuration.PointType;
import org.book.configuration.RecentFilesType;
import org.book.configuration.UiSettingsType;
import org.book.configuration.UserSettingsType;

public class SaveXMLConfigurationAction extends AbstractAction {

  private Application myApp;

  public SaveXMLConfigurationAction(Application app) {
    super("Export XML Configuration");

    this.myApp = app;
  }

  public void actionPerformed(ActionEvent arg0) {
    JFileChooser fc = new JFileChooser();
    if (JFileChooser.APPROVE_OPTION == fc.showSaveDialog(myApp)) {
      try {
```

If the user chooses a file to save the configuration to, you get the application's `book.Configuration` object, and begin the process of transforming it to a `org.book.configuration.Configuration` object. Notice where the `JAXBContext` is created — it is created by programmatically getting the package name from `ConfigurationType` (which is in the `org.book.configuration` package). This is another method of creating a `JAXBContext`. By passing in the `String` for a Java package name, JAXB will keep all of the classes in the package in its context. Create the `ObjectFactory`, and then begin creating the `ConfigurationType` and mapping the information in the original `book.Configuration` object to the new JAXB `ConfigurationType`:

```
Configuration conf = this.myApp.getConfiguration();

JAXBContext ctx = JAXBContext.newInstance(
                      ConfigurationType.class.getPackage().getName());

Marshaller m = ctx.createMarshaller();
ObjectFactory factory = new ObjectFactory();

ConfigurationType configType = factory.createConfigurationType();
UiSettingsType uiSettingsType = factory.createUiSettingsType();
UserSettingsType userSettingsType = factory.createUserSettingsType();

configType.setUiSettings(uiSettingsType);
configType.setUserSettings(userSettingsType);

Color fgColor = conf.getForegroundColor();
if (fgColor != null) {
  ColorType fgColorType = factory.createColorType();
  fgColorType.setRed(fgColor.getRed());
  fgColorType.setBlue(fgColor.getBlue());
  fgColorType.setGreen(fgColor.getGreen());
```

```
      fgColorType.setAlpha(fgColor.getAlpha());

    uiSettingsType.setForegroundColor(fgColorType);
}

Color bgColor = conf.getBackgroundColor();
if (bgColor != null) {
  ColorType bgColorType = factory.createColorType();
  bgColorType.setRed(bgColor.getRed());
  bgColorType.setBlue(bgColor.getBlue());
  bgColorType.setGreen(bgColor.getGreen());
  bgColorType.setAlpha(bgColor.getAlpha());

    uiSettingsType.setBackgroundColor(bgColorType);
}

Point ppPoint = conf.getPaletteWindowPosition();
if (ppPoint != null) {
  PointType ppPointType = factory.createPointType();
  ppPointType.setXCoord(ppPoint.x);
  ppPointType.setYCoord(ppPoint.y);

    uiSettingsType.setPaletteWindowPosition(ppPointType);
}

Point tpPoint = conf.getToolsWindowPosition();
if (ppPoint != null) {
  PointType tpPointType = factory.createPointType();
  tpPointType.setXCoord(tpPoint.x);
  tpPointType.setYCoord(tpPoint.y);

    uiSettingsType.setToolsWindowPosition(tpPointType);
}

uiSettingsType.setShowTabs(conf.isShowTabs());

userSettingsType.setUserHomeDirectory(conf.getUserHomeDirectory());
String[] recentFiles = conf.getRecentFiles();
if (recentFiles != null) {
  RecentFilesType rFilesType = factory.createRecentFilesType();

    Collections.addAll(rFilesType.getRecentFile(), recentFiles);

    userSettingsType.setRecentFiles(rFilesType);
}
```

Finally, after you finish mapping the data, marshal it to the file specified by the user:

```
    m.marshal(factory.createConfiguration(configType),
                      new FileOutputStream(fc.getSelectedFile())));

} catch (IOException ioe) {
  JOptionPane.showMessageDialog(this.myApp, ioe.getMessage(), "Error",
```

```
                                        JOptionPane.ERROR_MESSAGE);

        ioe.printStackTrace();

    } catch (JAXBException jaxbEx) {
        JOptionPane.showMessageDialog(this.myApp, jaxbEx.getMessage(), "Error",
                                JOptionPane.ERROR_MESSAGE);

        jaxbEx.printStackTrace();
    }
  }
 }
}
```

Note how you must catch JAXBException in the preceding code. Most JAXB operations can throw a JAXBException — when saving it can mean that you did not populate all the information that was required in the generated object structure.

Implementing the Load Action

The load action is, of course, similar to the original load action — and probably most actions that load files. The user is prompted for a file from which to load the configuration:

```
package book;

...

import javax.xml.bind.JAXBContext;
import javax.xml.bind.JAXBException;
import javax.xml.bind.Unmarshaller;

import org.book.configuration.ColorType;
import org.book.configuration.ConfigurationType;
import org.book.configuration.PointType;
import org.book.configuration.RecentFilesType;

public class LoadXMLConfigurationAction extends AbstractAction {

  private Application myApp;

  public LoadXMLConfigurationAction(Application app) {
    super("Import XML Configuration");
    this.myApp = app;
  }

  public void actionPerformed(ActionEvent evt) {
    JFileChooser fc = new JFileChooser();
    if (JFileChooser.APPROVE_OPTION == fc.showOpenDialog(myApp)) {
      try {
```

Once the user has picked the file, begin the process of unmarshalling the XML data contained in the file to the JAXB-generated data model. Once the data has been unmarshaled, you can begin the process of mapping the data from the JAXB model to the book.Configuration model. This is essentially the reverse process of what you did in the save action. You are converting things like the JAXB `ColorType` back into a form you can display in the Swing user interface, the `java.awt.Color` object. Other mappings are not quite as important, because in theory if the application had originally been built to use the JAXB data model instead of the `book.Configuration` model, you could access the user's home directory and other Java-primitive–based properties directly from the JAXB model. Unfortunately, you would still lose some benefit — the `java.io.File` class would better represent files than a `String`, and so forth. Some degree of this type of mapping will almost always be required when using any sort of generated code:

```java
JAXBContext ctx = JAXBContext.newInstance(ConfigurationType.class
                                  .getPackage().getName());

Unmarshaller u = ctx.createUnmarshaller();

JAXBElement rootElement = (JAXBElement)
                  (JAXBElement) u.unmarshal(fc.getSelectedFile());

org.book.configuration.Configuration configType =
                  (org.book.configuration.Configuration)
                  rootElement.getValue();

Configuration conf = new Configuration();

ColorType bgColorType = configType.getUiSettings().getBackgroundColor();
if (bgColorType != null) {
  Color bgColor = new Color(bgColorType.getRed(),
                    bgColorType.getGreen(), bgColorType.getBlue(),
                    bgColorType.getAlpha());

  conf.setBackgroundColor(bgColor);
}

ColorType fgColorType = configType.getUiSettings().getForegroundColor();
if (fgColorType != null) {
  Color fgColor = new Color(fgColorType.getRed(),
                    fgColorType.getGreen(), fgColorType.getBlue(),
                    fgColorType.getAlpha());

  conf.setForegroundColor(fgColor);
}

PointType ppPointType = configType.getUiSettings()
                    .getPaletteWindowPosition();

if (ppPointType != null) {
  Point ppPoint = new Point(ppPointType.getXCoord(),
                        ppPointType.getYCoord());

  conf.setPaletteWindowPosition(ppPoint);
}

PointType tpPointType = configType.getUiSettings()
```

```
                                        .getToolsWindowPosition();

            if (tpPointType != null) {
              Point tpPoint = new Point(tpPointType.getXCoord(),
                                        tpPointType.getYCoord());

              conf.setToolsWindowPosition(tpPoint);
            }

            conf.setShowTabs(configType.getUiSettings().isShowTabs());

            conf.setUserHomeDirectory(
                        configType.getUserSettings().getUserHomeDirectory());

            RecentFilesType rFilesType =
                            configType.getUserSettings().getRecentFiles();

            if (rFilesType != null) {
              List recentFileList = rFilesType.getRecentFile();
              if (recentFileList != null) {
                String[] recentFiles = new String[recentFileList.size()];

                recentFileList.toArray(recentFiles);

                conf.setRecentFiles(recentFiles);
              }
            }


        myApp.setConfiguration(conf);
      } catch (JAXBException jaxb) {
        JOptionPane.showMessageDialog(this.myApp, jaxb.getMessage(), "Error",
                                      JOptionPane.ERROR_MESSAGE);

        jaxb.printStackTrace();

      }
    }
  }
}
```

Similar to the save action, you must also catch JAXBException. If an error occurs while loading the file — for example, it does not conform to the configuration.xsd schema, or the file could not be found — the exception will be thrown.

The Swing actions you just developed get integrated into your application the same way the previous ones did. Your application now has two mechanisms for persisting its configuration data model. One is user-friendly to edit, the other one cannot be edited outside of the application. The updated application is shown in Figure 5-14.

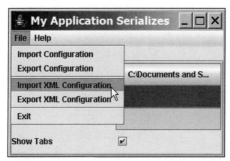

Figure 5-14

Annotating Existing Java Classes for Use with JAXB

As you can probably see from the previous example, the classes JAXB generates for you from an existing XML schema are not always that friendly to use within your application. Many times this is the case when working with a generated data model — there will always be some part of the data model generated that will need to be transformed into some more useful format, either for more efficient data traversal, or cases where conversion to some other type used in third-party libraries is necessary, like converting color values into the object actually used within AWT/Swing, `java.awt.Color`. These types of conversions can be tedious, and in the worst case, an application must work with two entirely separate in-memory object graphs, one to serialize and deserialize, and the other to actually use throughout the application. JAXB 2.0's annotations bridge this gap tremendously. By annotating existing Java objects, JAXB's scope widens significantly to include potentially any Java object for serialization. This is the best of both worlds in some respects — similar ease of serialization is like the Java Serialization API, but also the power to customize the output format.

A Simple Case

JAXB can handle the serialization of many existing Java classes, straight out of the box, without any annotation. For an object to be serialized as the root of an object graph, it must satisfy one of the following criteria:

❑ The class `javax.xml.bind.JAXBElement` must be used to wrap the object

❑ The class declaration must have the annotation `javax.xml.bind.annotation.XmlRootElement`

Looking back at the simple `MyPoint` class, both methods of serialization will be illustrated. Notice that the actual serialization code is identical to the previous JAXB classes, and similar to the API patterns found in the Java Serialization API and XMLEncoder/Decoder. The class `MyPoint`, without any JAXB annotations, is shown here:

```
package book;

public class MyPoint {
  public int x;
  public int y;
}
```

Because there is no `XmlRootElement` annotation on the class, it must be wrapped with `JAXBElement` to serialize properly. By simply creating a parameterized `JAXBElement`, you can assign the element name and namespace, and marshal the object to XML:

```
JAXBContext ctx = JAXBContext.newInstance(MyPoint.class);

Marshaller m = ctx.createMarshaller();
m.setProperty("jaxb.formatted.output", true);

MyPoint p = new MyPoint();
p.x = 50;
p.y = 75;

JAXBElement<MyPoint> root = new JAXBElement<MyPoint>
                                (new QName("my-point"),
                                 MyPoint.class, p);

m.marshal(root, System.out);
```

The second option to serialize the class would be to add the `XmlRootElement` annotation to the class declaration. Doing so allows instances of the class to be serialized using JAXB without using a `JAXBElement` wrapper if it is to be the root element. If you attempt to serialize a class that does not have the `XmlRootElement` annotation as the root element, JAXB will throw an exception and the serialization will not occur. Here is the slightly modified `MyPoint` class, annotated with `XmlRootElement`:

```
package book;

import javax.xml.bind.annotation.XmlRootElement;

@XmlRootElement(name="my-point")
public class MyPoint {
  public int x;
  public int y;
}
```

Serialization follows exactly as illustrated in the previous JAXB example, without the need to use an instance of `JAXBElement` for the root element:

```
JAXBContext ctx = JAXBContext.newInstance(MyPoint.class);

Marshaller m = ctx.createMarshaller();
m.setProperty("jaxb.formatted.output", true);

MyPoint p = new MyPoint();
p.x = 50;
p.y = 75;

m.marshal(p, System.out);
```

If you wanted to serialize `MyPoint` as part of another class — for example, it was a field or JavaBean property in another class — it would not have to be wrapped in `JAXBElement` nor have an `XmlRootElement` annotation. Also note the `jaxb.formatted.output` property; when set to `true`, the `Marshaller` object formats the XML with indentions and line breaks, making it more human-readable.

The XML generated is the same for both simple examples and looks like the following:

```
<?xml version="1.0" encoding="UTF-8" standalone="yes"?>
<my-point>
    <x>50</x>
    <y>75</y>
</my-point>
```

JAXB API Key Annotations

With other JAXB annotations, the XML output can be customized. Some annotations can only be placed on a class declaration, such as XmlType and XmlRootElement. Annotations like XmlAttribute and XmlElement can only be placed on fields or JavaBean properties. The annotations map directly to XML Schema constructs, and an understanding of XML Schema is required to fully understand how all of the annotations in the javax.xml.bind.annotation package should be used. The annotations listed in the following table, though, can be understood enough without in-depth knowledge of XML Schema to be used in applications requiring simple XML serialization.

Annotations (from javax.xml.bind.annotation)	Function
XmlAttribute	Maps a field or JavaBean property to an XML attribute. Note that the Java type of the field or property being annotated must correspond to an XML schema simple type — a Java String, Boolean, integer, and so on — or a Java class annotated to make it map to a simple type.
XmlElement	Maps a non-static and non-transient field or JavaBean property to an XML element. If the Java type of the field or JavaBean property is another Java class, that class must be serializable by JAXB (annotated appropriately if necessary).
XmlElementWrapper	Can be used on any field or JavaBean property where XmlElement can be used. It works with XmlElement usually, but can also work with XmlJavaTypeAdapter. XmlElementWrapper puts another XML element around whatever element the field or property maps to (wrapping the element). It is mainly intended for use when serializing a field or property representing a collection of elements (such as a List).
XmlID	Can only be used on a field or bean property of type java.lang.String. It signifies the key field of an XML element, used when referring back to an element using the XmlIDREF annotation (XML schema ID and IDREF concept).
XmlIDREF	Placed on a field or bean property and changes how the Java type is serialized. Instead of serializing the whole type, only the key field (specified on that class via XmlID) is serialized — allowing the same instance of an object to be serialized multiple times in the document, but only listing the entire element once, with subsequent elements simply referring back to the original via the XmlIDREF annotation.

Annotations (from javax.xml.bind.annotation)	Function
XmlJavaTypeAdapter	Used on a class declaration, or a field or bean property declaration. It is used when the Java type to be serialized by JAXB does not meet the minimum requirements for serialization and must be adapted (by an adapter class). Every class serialized by JAXB must have a default no-arg constructor, or classes that do not match well to serialization will have to be adapted for use with JAXB.
XmlRootElement	Any class that is to be serialized as the root XML element must have the XmlRootElement annotation on its class declaration, or be serialized through the use of JAXBElement.
XmlTransient	By annotating a field or JavaBean property with XmlTransient, that field will not be serialized by JAXB (analogous to the Java transient keyword used in Java Serialization).
XmlType	Used to annotate a class declaration. It is used to annotate a class as being a complex type in XML Schema. Here the serialization order of fields can be specified (XML Schema's sequence), or simple anonymous types can be declared (when used in conjunction with the XmlValue annotation).
XmlValue	Used to represent the XML element content of an XML schema simpleContent type. Only one field or bean property can be annotated with XmlValue in a class, and the only other annotation allowed on other fields or bean properties is XmlAttribute (and any fields or bean properties not marked with XmlAttribute should be marked XmlTransient).

Annotating the Data Model

Using JAXB's powerful annotations, you can annotate the existing configuration data model. By annotating this data model, your application can avoid the problem of having two separate data models. The same data model used throughout the application can simply be serialized without the need to transform it to a different set of classes essentially used only for JAXB. Annotating existing Java classes is a great way to generate XML application configuration files. Just by annotating whatever Java classes hold the data for an application's configuration with JAXB annotations, you can easily create XML configuration files without the need for writing SAX handlers or traversing DOM trees with lower level XML APIs. Annotating the book.Configuration class yields the following:

```
... (imports) ...

@XmlRootElement(name="configuration", namespace="http://book.org/Configuration")
@XmlType(name="configurationType", namespace="http://book.org/Configuration",
    propOrder={"showTabs","backgroundColor","foregroundColor","recentFiles"})
@XmlAccessorType(value=XmlAccessType.PUBLIC_MEMBER)
```

```java
public class Configuration {

  ... (un-annotated private fields)

  private List<File> recentFiles;

  @XmlAttribute(name="user-home-directory",
      namespace="http://book.org/Configuration")
  public String getUserHomeDirectory() {
    return userHomeDirectory;
  }

  public void setUserHomeDirectory(String userHomeDirectory) {
    this.userHomeDirectory = userHomeDirectory;
  }

  public boolean isShowTabs() {
    return showTabs;
  }

  @XmlElement(name="show-tabs",
      namespace="http://book.org/Configuration")
  public void setShowTabs(boolean showTabs) {
    this.showTabs = showTabs;
  }

  @XmlElementWrapper(name="recent-files",
      namespace="http://book.org/Configuration")
  @XmlElement(name="file",
      namespace="http://book.org/Configuration")
  public String[] getRecentFiles() {
...
  }

  public void setRecentFiles(String[] files) {
...
  }

  public Color getBackgroundColor() {
    return backgroundColor;
  }

  @XmlElement(name="background-color",
      namespace="http://book.org/Configuration")
  @XmlJavaTypeAdapter(value=ColorAdapter.class)
  public void setBackgroundColor(Color backgroundColor) {
    this.backgroundColor = backgroundColor;
  }

  @XmlElement(name="foreground-color",
      namespace="http://book.org/Configuration")
  @XmlJavaTypeAdapter(value=ColorAdapter.class)
  public Color getForegroundColor() {
    return foregroundColor;
```

```
    }

    public void setForegroundColor(Color foregroundColor) {
      this.foregroundColor = foregroundColor;
    }

    @XmlTransient
    public Point getPaletteWindowPosition() {
      return paletteWindowPosition;
    }

    public void setPaletteWindowPosition(Point paletteWindowPosition) {
      this.paletteWindowPosition = paletteWindowPosition;
    }


    @XmlTransient
    public Point getToolsWindowPosition() {
      return toolsWindowPosition;
    }

    public void setToolsWindowPosition(Point toolsWindowPosition) {
      this.toolsWindowPosition = toolsWindowPosition;
    }
  }
```

The Class Declaration: XmlRootElement, XmlType, and XmlAccessorType

Now after seeing the newly annotated `book.Configuration` class all at once, you can analyze the various annotations present. Start with the annotations on the class declaration. Previously, this chapter discussed the `XmlRootElement` attribute. It is necessary to annotate a class or interface declaration with `XmlRootElement` if you want to serialize instances of the class as the root object of the object graph. It is possible to marshal a class as the root of a serialization, without `XmlRootElement`, just by wrapping the instance to serialize as root within the parameterized-type `JAXBElement`:

```
@XmlRootElement(name="configuration", namespace="http://book.org/Configuration")
@XmlType(name="configurationType", namespace="http://book.org/Configuration",
    propOrder={"showTabs","backgroundColor","foregroundColor","recentFiles"})
@XmlAccessorType(value=XmlAccessType.PUBLIC_MEMBER)
public class Configuration {
```

Note the two values passed in to the `XmlRootElement` annotation, `name` and `namespace`. They represent the element name and its corresponding namespace for the class when it is serialized as the root element. If `name` and `namespace` are not specified, the default XML namespace will be used, and the name of the element will follow JavaBeans conventions and be generated from the Java class name. The name and namespace can change if the class is serialized in other places besides the root element, as you will see, because name and namespace can also be specified in the `XmlElement` attribute.

Many annotations in JAXB are implicit if they are not specified. `XmlType` is one of them. Every Java type to be serialized is automatically assumed to be annotated as an `XmlType`. `XmlType` maps the Java type to the two different XML schema types, simple or complex. In this example, you specify the name of the complex XML schema type you are generating, its namespace, and its property order (via the `propOrder` value). The `propOrder` value takes an array of `Strings`, representing the names of the field names and bean property names in the class. The order in which these names appear in the `propOrder` value dictates the order in which they appear in the output XML (creating a sequence in XML Schema). Sample XML output from serializing an instance of this class looks like the following:

```
<?xml version="1.0" encoding="UTF-8" standalone="yes"?>
<configuration xmlns="http://book.org/Configuration" user-home-
directory="C:\Documents and Settings\Mark\My Documents">
    <show-tabs>true</show-tabs>
    <background-color>
        <red>204</red>
        <green>0</green>
        <blue>153</blue>
        <alpha>255</alpha>
    </background-color>
    <foreground-color>
        <red>51</red>
        <green>51</green>
        <blue>51</blue>
        <alpha>255</alpha>
    </foreground-color>
    <recent-files>
        <file>test.xml</file>
        <file>test2.xml</file>
    </recent-files>
</configuration>
```

As you can see, the order of the XML elements in this sample output matches the order specified in the `XmlType` annotation's `propOrder` value. The namespace of the entire document is the same, and JAXB gave it the default XML prefix for the document.

> `XmlType` **can represent both simple and complex XML schema types. When one field or bean property in the class has the** `XmlValue` **attribute, the** `XmlType` **declaration automatically assumes an XML schema simple content type (and the property marked with** `XmlValue` **is the content). When** `XmlValue` **is used, no other field or bean property can be marked as an** `XmlElement`, **only with** `XmlAttribute`. `XmlType` **can represent other complex element declarations — see its JavaDoc for more information.**

Now to talk about the annotation you noticed on the class declaration, which was strangely absent from the previous table of key JAXB annotations — the `XmlAccessorType` annotation. This is an important annotation, but one you will probably find yourself rarely using. Its value takes the `XmlAccessType` enumeration. The values for this enumeration are FIELD, NONE, PROPERTY, and PUBLIC_MEMBER. These values define the scope of JAXB serialization for the class. `XmlAccessorType` is an optional annotation, and it defaults to PUBLIC_MEMBER if it is not specified. It is redundantly specified in `book.Configuration` class to aid in its explanation. For the PUBLIC_MEMBER `XmlAccessType`, JAXB serializes all public fields and JavaBean properties (even if they are not explicitly annotated). That is why the `MyPoint` class serialized the way it did; with no annotations whatsoever, it was using the default PUBLIC_MEMBER `XmlAccessType`. The other `XmlAccessType` values are straightforward. FIELD specifies that every non-static, non-transient field will be serialized (including private and protected fields). NONE indicates fields or bean properties to be serialized must be explicitly annotated. Finally, the PROPERTY value indicates that all JavaBean properties will be serialized by default. Note that the XmlAccessorType annotation merely tells JAXB which fields and properties to serialize by default — fields or bean properties explicitly marked for serialization will always be serialized.

XmlElement and XmlAttribute

The next couple annotations are the simplest, and probably the ones you will find yourself most often using. The following code segment shows XmlAttribute and XmlElement in action:

```
@XmlAttribute(name="user-home-directory",
    namespace="http://book.org/Configuration")
public String getUserHomeDirectory() {
  return userHomeDirectory;
}

public void setUserHomeDirectory(String userHomeDirectory) {
  this.userHomeDirectory = userHomeDirectory;
}

public boolean isShowTabs() {
  return showTabs;
}

  @XmlElement(name="show-tabs",
    namespace="http://book.org/Configuration")
public void setShowTabs(boolean showTabs) {
  this.showTabs = showTabs;
}
```

Notice how only one of the getter/setter pairs is actually annotated for each JavaBean property, userHomeDirectory and showTabs. To annotate JavaBean properties, either the getter or the setter can be annotated, but not both. XmlAttribute and XmlElement have the name and namespace values. These correspond to the XML element's local name and namespace (just as they did in the XmlRootElement attribute). Note that for XmlAttribute, the Java type of the field or bean property must be an XML schema simple type (because it must fit into an XML attribute). The XmlElement annotation does not have this limitation, and can be placed on any Java type valid for JAXB.

XmlElementWrapper

Java collection classes can also be serialized by JAXB. The most common case for collection class serialization is a list or array. In the book.Configuration class, you store a list of the most recent files the user has last accessed while using your application. Annotating this for serialization in JAXB looks like the following:

```
@XmlElementWrapper(name="recent-files",
    namespace="http://book.org/Configuration")
@XmlElement(name="file",
    namespace="http://book.org/Configuration")
public String[] getRecentFiles() {
...
```

```
    }

    public void setRecentFiles(String[] files) {
...
    }
```

When `XmlElement` is applied to a collection, JAXB applies it to every object in the collection. When applied to the `String` array for example, each `String` in the array is represented as an XML element, with the name of `"file"`. Often when serializing a list of similar items in XML, convention is to wrap all of the similar elements in one larger element, increasing the readability of the document. The `XmlElementWrapper` is precisely for this purpose. It wraps the entire collection in one element; in this case, `recent-files`. Output XML from using the `XmlElementWrapper` looks like the following:

```
    <recent-files>
        <file>test.xml</file>
        <file>test2.xml</file>
    </recent-files>
```

XmlJavaTypeAdapter

Sometimes JAXB cannot serialize a particular Java type. Classes to be serialized must have a default constructor. Other times classes such as `java.util.HashMap` do not serialize naturally. The `XmlJavaTypeAdapter` annotation allows for custom marshalling and can be applied at the field or bean property level, the class level, or even the package level. `XmlJavaTypeAdapter` maps a Java class to another Java class, one that does serialize well under JAXB. Note how this process is similar to the data transformation discussed previously, when you converted the `book.Configuration` data model to an entirely separate data model, the one generated by JAXB. One advantage to `XmlJavaTypeAdpater` over such a strategy is that your data model transformations can be fine grained, at the object level (and not the entire data model). Maybe one class in an otherwise huge data model does not properly serialize. You would only have to use `XmlJavaTypeAdapter` for that one class, and not transform your entire model:

```
    public Color getBackgroundColor() {
      return backgroundColor;
    }

    @XmlElement(name="background-color",
        namespace="http://book.org/Configuration")
    @XmlJavaTypeAdapter(value=ColorAdapter.class)
    public void setBackgroundColor(Color backgroundColor) {
      this.backgroundColor = backgroundColor;
    }
```

The `XmlJavaTypeAdapter` annotation takes as its value a `Class` type. The class passed in must extend `javax.xml.bind.annotation.adapters.XmlAdapter`. The type passed in that extends `XmlAdapter` does the work of transforming an object of whatever type the `XmlJavaTypeAdapter` was placed on (in this example, `java.awt.Color`), to a type JAXB can serialize. In this example, you chose to use `XmlJavaTypeAdapter` on `java.awt.Color` because `Color` has no default constructor. The parameterized class `XmlAdapter<ValueType, BoundType>` has two abstract methods that must be overridden:

```
    ValueType marshal(BoundType b)
    BoundType unmarshal(ValueType v)
```

The `BoundType` refers to the Java class that cannot be serialized, the one that is being bound to XML—in this case it is `java.awt.Color`. The `ValueType` refers to the type you will transform the bound type to and from, the type that JAXB can understand and properly serialize. As you can see, these two methods you must implement give you a lot of freedom of how to serialize a particular Java type to XML. It is a more fine-grained method of data model transformation to a format more suitable for serialization. There will always be those times where a particular class has a data structure well suited to memory access that is simply incompatible with serialization. The code for the custom `ColorAdapter` class is as follows:

```java
package jaxb2;

import java.awt.Color;
import javax.xml.bind.annotation.adapters.XmlAdapter;
import org.book.configuration.ColorType;

public class ColorAdapter extends XmlAdapter<ColorType,Color> {

  @Override
  public Color unmarshal(ColorType ct) throws Exception {
    return new Color(ct.getRed(), ct.getGreen(), ct.getBlue(), ct.getAlpha());
  }

  @Override
  public ColorType marshal(Color c) throws Exception {
    ColorType ct = new ColorType();

    ct.setAlpha(c.getAlpha());
    ct.setBlue(c.getBlue());
    ct.setGreen(c.getGreen());
    ct.setRed(c.getRed());

    return ct;
  }

}
```

Notice the use of `org.book.configuration.ColorType` for the JAXB-suitable `ValueType`. The code was generated for it from the previous example of generating JAXB classes from an XML schema. You could have just as easily created it yourself, though, for this one small use. The code for `ColorType` is properly annotated, and the class has a default constructor:

```java
... (imports) ...

@XmlAccessorType(XmlAccessType.FIELD)
@XmlType(name = "colorType", propOrder = {
    "red",
    "green",
    "blue",
    "alpha"
})
public class ColorType {

    @XmlElement(namespace = "http://book.org/Configuration", type = Integer.class)
    protected int red;
    @XmlElement(namespace = "http://book.org/Configuration", type = Integer.class)
```

```
    protected int green;
    @XmlElement(namespace = "http://book.org/Configuration", type = Integer.class)
    protected int blue;
    @XmlElement(namespace = "http://book.org/Configuration", type = Integer.class,
defaultValue = "255")
    protected int alpha;

... (Java Bean properties for the above fields) ...

}
```

In the JAXB-suitable `ColorType` class you have defined all the attributes necessary to reproduce a `java.awt.Color` object—its RGBA values. When the `java.awt.Color` object is to be marshaled to XML, the `marshal(BoundType b)` method is called, and the `ColorAdapter` class creates a new, JAXB-suitable `ColorType` instance, and sets the appropriate RGBA values. The process is reversed during unmarshalling. The XML generated from the `ColorType` class looks like the following:

```
<background-color>
    <red>204</red>
    <green>0</green>
    <blue>153</blue>
    <alpha>255</alpha>
</background-color>
```

Notice how the name of the element is determined by the `XmlElement` annotation placed on the bean property (the `backgroundColor` property in this case). `XmlJavaTypeAdapter` does not determine the name of the element or the namespace—that is all determined by the `XmlElement` attribute, just as with any non-adapted bean property or field.

XmlTransient

`XmlTransient` is used much like the `transient` keyword in Java. Fields or bean properties marked with `XmlTransient` will be ignored by JAXB. In this example, you marked the `paletteWindowPosition` and the `toolsWindowPosition` bean properties as `XmlTransient`. In the output XML, these properties did not appear:

```
@XmlTransient
public Point getPaletteWindowPosition() {
  return paletteWindowPosition;
}

public void setPaletteWindowPosition(Point paletteWindowPosition) {
  this.paletteWindowPosition = paletteWindowPosition;
}


@XmlTransient
public Point getToolsWindowPosition() {
  return toolsWindowPosition;
}

public void setToolsWindowPosition(Point toolsWindowPosition) {
  this.toolsWindowPosition = toolsWindowPosition;
}
```

One of the reasons you chose to mark your properties of type `java.awt.Point` with `XmlTransient` is because `java.awt.Point` must be adapted to serialize properly. If you wanted to serialize `java.awt` `.Point` you would have had to create an `XmlJavaTypeAdapter` annotation on these properties, and create another subclass of `XmlAdapter` just like with `java.awt.Color`. The reason `java.awt.Point` cannot be serialized by JAXB is that one of its bean properties refers to itself (see `Point.getLocation()`), which creates an infinite loop during JAXB marshalling.

Generating an XML Schema from JAXB Annotated Classes

Now that the `book.Configuration` data model is annotated, you can generate its corresponding XML schema. You can distribute the generated schema to third parties who need to read the data you will be serializing to that format. Third parties then have a blueprint of the XML document type — they can either write an XML parser to parse it, or use a mechanism like JAXB for their programming language and platform (.NET, for instance, comes with an XML schema tool that generates classes from a schema). The JAXB `schemagen` tool generates XML schemas from a Java class and can be found in the `<JDK 6 Home>/bin` directory. Its usage is simple (assuming your classpath is correctly set up to find all the classes referenced by `book.Configuration`):

```
schemagen book.Configuration
```

Running this command creates two schemas:

```
schema1.xsd:

<?xml version="1.0" encoding="UTF-8" standalone="yes"?>
<xs:schema version="1.0" targetNamespace="http://book.org/Configuration"
xmlns:xs="http://www.w3.org/2001/XMLSchema">

  <xs:import schemaLocation="schema2.xsd"/>

  <xs:element name="alpha" type="xs:int"/>

  <xs:element name="blue" type="xs:int"/>

  <xs:element name="green" type="xs:int"/>

  <xs:element name="red" type="xs:int"/>

  <xs:element name="configuration" type="ns1:configurationType"
xmlns:ns1="http://book.org/Configuration"/>

  <xs:complexType name="configurationType">
    <xs:sequence>
      <xs:element name="show-tabs" type="xs:boolean" form="qualified"/>
      <xs:element name="background-color" type="colorType" form="qualified"
minOccurs="0"/>
      <xs:element name="foreground-color" type="colorType" form="qualified"
minOccurs="0"/>
      <xs:element form="qualified" name="recent-files" minOccurs="0">
        <xs:complexType>
          <xs:sequence>
            <xs:element name="file" type="xs:string" form="qualified"
maxOccurs="unbounded" minOccurs="0"/>
```

```
            </xs:sequence>
          </xs:complexType>
        </xs:element>
      </xs:sequence>
      <xs:attribute name="user-home-directory" type="xs:string" form="qualified"/>
    </xs:complexType>

    <xs:attribute name="user-home-directory" type="xs:string"/>
  </xs:schema>

schema2.xsd:

<?xml version="1.0" encoding="UTF-8" standalone="yes"?>
<xs:schema version="1.0" xmlns:ns1="http://book.org/Configuration"
xmlns:xs="http://www.w3.org/2001/XMLSchema">

  <xs:import namespace="http://book.org/Configuration"
schemaLocation="schema1.xsd"/>

  <xs:complexType name="colorType">
    <xs:sequence>
      <xs:element ref="ns1:red" minOccurs="0"/>
      <xs:element ref="ns1:green" minOccurs="0"/>
      <xs:element ref="ns1:blue" minOccurs="0"/>
      <xs:element ref="ns1:alpha" minOccurs="0"/>
    </xs:sequence>
  </xs:complexType>
</xs:schema>
```

These schemas could now be given to a third party to read the `book.Configuration` file format.

JAXB Pitfalls

There are a couple things to be wary of when annotating your classes with JAXB annotations. Usage of JAXB can be similar to usage of the Java Serialization API or the XMLEncoder/Decoder API, and this can lead to misconceptions of the capabilities of JAXB.

JAXB Serializes by Value

By default, all objects in an object graph are serialized by value. This is very different from the Java Serialization API and the XMLEncoder/Decoder API, which keep the referential integrity of an object graph being serialized by serializing multiple references to the same object only once. In these APIs, when two copies of the same object instance are saved, the object is only actually saved the first time, and all other references pointing back to that instance are saved as references, not as another duplicate copy of the object. When deserializing object graphs from the Java Serialization API or the XMLEncoder/Decoder API, multiple references to the same object instance will be returned as such and the original referential integrity of the object graph will be kept intact. Just as a simple demonstration of these concepts, serialize a slightly modified version of `MyPoint`, which has been changed to make its public fields private, and make them accessible via getters/setters to follow JavaBeans conventions, allowing XMLEncoder/Decoder to property serialize them. Serialize the following class, `PointContainer`, using both JAXB and XMLEncoder/Decoder:

```java
@XmlRootElement(name="point-container")
public static class PointContainer {
  private MyPoint pointA;
  private MyPoint pointB;

  public MyPoint getPointA() {
    return pointA;
  }
  public void setPointA(MyPoint pointA) {
    this.pointA = pointA;
  }
  public MyPoint getPointB() {
    return pointB;
  }
  public void setPointB(MyPoint pointB) {
    this.pointB = pointB;
  }
}
```

The serialization code will set the same `MyPoint` instance to both of `PointContainer`'s bean properties, `pointA` and `pointB`:

```java
JAXBContext ctx = JAXBContext.newInstance(MyPoint.class, PointContainer.class);

Marshaller m = ctx.createMarshaller();
m.setProperty("jaxb.formatted.output", true);

MyPoint p = new MyPoint();
p.setX(50);
p.setY(75);

PointContainer c = new PointContainer();
c.setPointA(p);
c.setPointB(p);

m.marshal(c, System.out);

XMLEncoder encoder = new XMLEncoder(System.out);
encoder.writeObject(c);

encoder.close();
```

The XML output for JAXB looks like the following:

```xml
<?xml version="1.0" encoding="UTF-8" standalone="yes"?>
<point-container>
    <pointA>
        <x>50</x>
        <y>75</y>
    </pointA>
    <pointB>
        <x>50</x>
        <y>75</y>
    </pointB>
</ point-container >
```

303

Notice how in JAXB the MyPoint instance is serialized by value twice in the output, when it is actually the same instance in the previous serialization code. If you were to deserialize this XML using JAXB, you would actually get two separate distinct instances of MyPoint, one for the pointA property and one for the pointB property. XMLEncoder/Decoder, on the other hand, produces the following XML output:

```
<?xml version="1.0" encoding="UTF-8"?>
<java version="1.6.0-beta2" class="java.beans.XMLDecoder">
 <object class="book.MyPoint$PointContainer">
  <void property="pointA">
   <object id="MyPoint0" class="book.MyPoint">
    <void property="x">
     <int>50</int>
    </void>
    <void property="y">
     <int>75</int>
    </void>
   </object>
  </void>
  <void property="pointB">
   <object idref="MyPoint0"/>
  </void>
 </object>
</java>
```

In the XML output, the second reference to the same instance of MyPoint, pointB, simply refers to the already serialized pointA MyPoint instance (because they were the same instance in the serialization code). Both XMLEncoder/Decoder and the Java Serialization API handle this appropriately: they keep the object graph's referential integrity intact. JAXB does not do this by default, because it is not intended to exactly save Java object graphs, but merely bind them to and from an XML representation based on XML Schema. It is possible to keep the referential integrity intact, though, if your application requires it. To keep an object graph's referential integrity intact using JAXB requires some manual work, using the XML schema constructs of XML ID and XML IDREF. The main strategy with using ID and IDREF is to first serialize the full XML output for a given element, and then later on in the XML document, refer to that element by its ID. By manually forcing your JAXB classes into this model, you can enforce referential integrity for those areas of your object graph that require it. Modifying the MyPoint class and the PointContainer class, you can make the pointA and pointB fields of PointContainer serialize by reference and not by value. By annotating pointA and pointB with XmlIDREF, they will be serialized only by their key. The XmlID annotation identifies the key in the given type. In the code that follows, MyPoint.key is your key. Whatever key values pointA and pointB have must exist somewhere else in your XML document for proper deserialization to occur. Serialization will still occur if pointA and pointB have key values referring to nonexistent elements in your XML document. In this case though, pointA and pointB will not deserialize properly; they will only have their key field set (because the element they refer to does not exist in the document). In this code example, all points will first be added to be serialized by value in the pointList field. Then pointA and pointB will reference points in the list:

```
@XmlRootElement
public class MyPoint {
  public int x;
  public int y;

  @XmlID
  public String key;
```

```
    }

    @XmlRootElement(name="point-container")
    public class PointContainer {
        @XmlElementWrapper(name="all-points")
        @XmlElement(name="point")
        public List<MyPoint> pointList = new ArrayList<MyPoint>();

        @XmlIDREF
        public MyPoint pointA;

        @XmlIDREF
        public MyPoint pointB;
    }
```

Note that the XmlID tag can only be applied to a field or property of the String data type. Now you can serialize pointA and pointB by reference with the following code:

```
    JAXBContext ctx = JAXBContext.newInstance(MyPoint.class, PointContainer.class);

    Marshaller m = ctx.createMarshaller();
    m.setProperty("jaxb.formatted.output", true);

    MyPoint p = new MyPoint();
    p.key = "MyPointKey:1";
    p.x = 50;
    p.y = 75;

    PointContainer c = new PointContainer();
    c.pointList.add(p);
    c.pointA = p;
    c.pointB = p;

    m.marshal(c, System.out);
```

The XML output uses the key field from MyPoint in the serialization of pointA and pointB:

```
<?xml version="1.0" encoding="UTF-8" standalone="yes"?>
<point-container>
    <all-points>
        <point>
            <key>MyPointKey:1</key>
            <x>50</x>
            <y>75</y>
        </point>
    </all-points>
    <pointA>MyPointKey:1</pointA>
    <pointB>MyPointKey:1</pointB>
</point-container>
```

There are still dangers in relying on XmlID and XmlIDREF to enforce referential integrity of an object graph. JAXB will not check to make sure the object referred to by an XmlIDREF actually exists in the document. If it does not, when the object is deserialized, it will only have its key set! Because referential integrity is enforced via the XmlID tag (whatever it annotates becomes the key), it is still up to the client programmer to keep track of the keys and make sure they all match up correctly.

XmlJavaTypeAdapter as the Root of Serialization

When `XmlJavaTypeAdapter` is applied to a class definition, JAXB serializes all instances of the class using the adapter, with one notable exception. When the root object to be serialized is adapted with `XmlJavaTypeAdapter`, JAXB will not use the adapter — and will error out if the object by default will not serialize with JAXB (if the class does not have a default `no-arg` constructor, for example). To serialize these objects as the root of a serialization graph, you must manually call the `XmlAdapter` subclass defined in the `XmlJavaTypeAdapter`, both for marshalling and unmarshalling. The following example illustrates this problem:

```
... (imports) ...

@XmlRootElement
@XmlJavaTypeAdapter(value=AdaptedExample.MyAdapter.class)
public class AdaptedExample {

  public String toAdapt = "Test";



  @XmlRootElement(name="root-element")
  public static class MyJAXBFriendlyType {
    @XmlAttribute(name="id")
    public String adapted;
  }

  public static class MyAdapter
          extends XmlAdapter<MyJAXBFriendlyType, AdaptedExample> {

    @Override
    public AdaptedExample unmarshal(MyJAXBFriendlyType v) throws Exception {
      AdaptedExample a = new AdaptedExample();
      a.toAdapt = v.adapted;

      return a;
    }

    @Override
    public MyJAXBFriendlyType marshal(AdaptedExample v) throws Exception {
      MyJAXBFriendlyType t = new MyJAXBFriendlyType();
      t.adapted = v.toAdapt;

      return t;
    }

  }
}
```

In this example, you want the serialization of `AdaptedExample` to be done by the `XmlAdapter` subclass, `MyAdapter`. `MyAdapter` adapts `AdaptedExample` to and from `MyJAXBFriendlyType`. However, when serializing an instance of `AdaptedExample` as the root of serialization, the adapter is ignored (had it been serialized anywhere else in the object graph it would have been used, but not at the root). Serializing as the root with the code:

```
m.marshal(new AdaptedExample(), System.out);

... yields the following output ...

<?xml version="1.0" encoding="UTF-8" standalone="yes"?>
<adaptedExample>
    <toAdapt>Test</toAdapt>
</adaptedExample>
```

The preceding XML has not been adapted. Therefore, whenever you serialize an object whose class is marked with XmlJavaTypeAdapter as root, you have to manually perform the transformation:

```
MyAdapter adapter = new MyAdapter();
m.marshal(adapter.marshal(new AdaptedExample()), System.out);

... yields the following output ...

<?xml version="1.0" encoding="UTF-8" standalone="yes"?>
<root-element id="Test">
</root-element>
```

You will have to know which objects you are serializing as root are marked with XmlJavaTypeAdapter, and manually use the adapter on both ends of serialization — during marshalling as shown previously, as well as during unmarshalling.

When to Use JAXB

JAXB is fundamentally different from either the Java Serialization API or the XMLEncoder/Decoder API. In the Java Serialization and XMLEncoder/Decoder APIs, the developer designs Java classes and does not worry about the serialization file format — that is taken care of by the APIs. However, it has the unfortunate disadvantage of limiting the use of the serialized objects to Java-based applications. With JAXB, you can either generate Java data classes from an XML schema, or annotate existing Java classes to customize and create a new XML file format. JAXB is ideal for reading and writing a third-party XML schema, or creating an XML schema for other third parties to use. Advantages to using JAXB include:

❑   Existing objects can be annotated to quickly allow for serialization to a custom-defined XML format

❑   XML file formats defined by JAXB can by read by other applications written in any language

❑   The XML structure of serialized documents is completely customizable via XML Schema

❑   Fast way to read XML data based on an XML schema — uses less memory to represent an entire XML document in memory than a DOM tree

Its disadvantages are namely:

❑   Requires more development effort — sometimes you need to manage *two* data models, one your application can use, and the JAXB-generated data model

❑   Difficult to ensure referential integrity across an object graph

❑   Working with JAXB-generated objects can be unwieldy because they are generated — things like naming and object creation are more tedious to develop with than custom Java classes

JAXB should be used when you want a human-readable file format that can be edited by users. It should be used when you are developing a file format you wish non-Java–based applications to be able to read. It can be used in conjunction with other XML technologies, and to read third-party XML documents based on third-party XML schemas. Because of the ease of annotating classes, JAXB becomes ideal for quick application configuration files — simply annotate the config classes you already have and read and write to disk.

Where JAXB Fits in the JDK

JAXB is one of the new additions to JDK 6. It is one of the core technologies supporting another new JDK feature: Web Services. As discussed in Chapter 11, the JDK now includes tools to automatically publish and import Web Services. These tools use JAXB to generate classes based on the Web Services Definition Language (WSDL). JAXB now fits cleanly into the Web Services stack, and is an integral part of both publishing and importing Web Services. For publishing Web Services, JAXB is used to generate XML schemas to put into WSDL based on the methods of a class that are published as Web Services. JAXB generates these schemas based on the parameters and return types of the methods being published. As you have seen in this chapter, JAXB is useful from a file and third-party schema perspective, but in the bigger picture, it is also a key technology enabling Java Web Services. See Chapter 11 for more information on how Web Services are now integrated into JDK 6.

Summary

Saving the state of an application to a file is saving all of the pieces of its in-memory data model necessary to reconstruct it exactly as it was at a later point of time. Most object-oriented applications store their data model as a set of data storage classes. In Java, it is standard practice to have the data model represented as a series of classes following the JavaBeans conventions and utilizing collection classes where necessary (such as lists, maps, trees, sets, and so on). In applications that have graphical user interfaces, it is best to separate the in-memory data structure from the GUI toolkit classes as much as possible. The standard Java GUI toolkit, Swing, follows the Model-View-Controller design pattern to accomplish this separation. This way, to persist the state of an application, *only* the data model needs to be written to disk — the GUI is simply a transient aspect of the state of the application. Normally, when you say you want to be able to save an application's state, you are referring to saving some sort of file an application produces, whether an image file, a word processing document, or a spreadsheet. These types of files are simply a data model persisted to disk. By keeping your data model separate from your GUI classes, it is easier to save it off to a file. This chapter looked at the Java Serialization API and the XMLEncoder/Decoder API. These APIs take a set of Java classes, and persist enough information to disk to reconstruct the actual object instances as they used to look in memory. This methodology makes adding serialization capabilities to an application easy, but at the cost of limiting the use of the serialized information to Java-based applications.

The JAXB API takes a fundamentally different approach, and bases all of its serialization and deserialization on XML Schema. The file formats read and saved by JAXB are all based on XML Schema and can be completely customized, unlike XMLEncoder/Decoder. JAXB data models can be generated from existing XML schema documents or existing data models can be annotated with JAXB annotations to create custom XML formats. XML schemas can then be generated from these annotated data models to allow third parties access to the blueprints of the file format, making it easier for them to interoperate with your data. JAXB is ideal for data interoperability, and XMLEncoder/Decoder and the Java Serialization API are ideal for saving exact Java object graphs (they enforce object graph referential integrity).

Both the JAXB API and the XMLEncoder/Decoder API persist their information in XML — but the XML produced by the XMLEncoder/Decoder API can only be used by Java-based applications. The Java Serialization API serializes its information in a Java-specific binary format that is much more efficient than XML but also is only useful by Java applications and is not human-readable, not to mention presents versioning problems across different versions of the classes serialized. Persisting your applications using files can require as little design and development time as you give it. If you use JAXB it takes a little more time. Your application's in-memory data model is one of the most important aspects of your data design. Once that exists, the various serialization and persistence strategies found in this chapter can all be applied. The next chapter talks about how to serialize your application's data model using a database, which is usually necessary for multi-user systems.

6

Persisting Your Application Using Databases

In the previous chapter, you learned about how to persist the state of your application using file-based mechanisms. This is a useful way to handle things in a single-user model, but when multiple users need to share the same data, databases are the solution. In this chapter, you learn about how to persist your application to a database.

Java is an object-oriented programming language. Database programming and object-oriented design can feel like oil and water. Because of this difference between the two technologies, there are two schools of thought for database development in an object-oriented environment. The first is that the database is just a resource, like any other, and the API that communicates with the database needs to have robust tools related to working tabular data. The second school of thought is that the objects in the application represent the data, there is no separation; therefore, the access should be seamless.

This chapter is organized around those two thoughts. The first section explores the JDBC 4.0 API, which provides robust tools for dealing with tabular relational data. In my view, JDBC is one of the most highly used and significant APIs developed for the Java platform. It's one of the reasons Java is portable across platform and database alike.

The second section of the chapter explores the Object Relational Mapping (ORM) approach. An ORM framework is used to abstract data access. This allows your application to communicate directly with objects, instead of relational table structures.

Database access has always required effort, regardless of your development language. Java has been making substantial leaps in this area and has come a long way in making the task much easier with its addition of the JDBC 4.0 API. This chapter discusses how to persist your application's data to a database using features of the JDBC 4.0 API. JDBC has undergone major improvements building upon JDK 5's introduction of Annotations. JDK 1.6 and JDBC 4.0 have made it easier to do database development.

Java and its open source community are becoming extremely aware of the importance of data persistence, especially for a developer in the J2EE architecture. Therefore they continue to enhance the JDBC API to support the ever-growing needs of its developers.

JDBC API Overview

The JDBC API provides a simple way for Java applications to access data from one or more relational data sources. A Java developer can use the JDBC API to do the following things:

- ❑ Connect to a data source
- ❑ Execute complex SQL statements
- ❑ Persist changes to a data source
- ❑ Retrieve information from a data source
- ❑ Interact with legacy file systems

The JDBC API is based on the specification X/Open SQL Call Level Interface (CLI), which provides an application with an alternative method for accessing databases with embedded SQL calls. This specification has been accepted by the International Organization for Standards (ISO) as an international standard. ODBC is also based on this standard, and the JDBC API can interface with ODBC through JDBC-ODBC bridge drivers.

The JDBC API makes it relatively simple to send SQL statements to databases, and it doesn't matter what platform, what database vendor, or what combination of platform and vendor you choose to use. It's all done through one common API layer for all platforms. This is what makes Java the front-runner of programming languages in today's market. Although different vendors are creating their own drivers, they all must follow the JDBC 4.0 specification. With that said, all drivers fit into four categories.

Driver Type	Description
JDBC-ODBC Bridge Driver	JDBC driver used to bridge the gap between JDBC and ODBC. It allows them to communicate and is mostly used in three-tier architectures. This is not a pure Java solution.
Native API/Part Java Driver	Specific to a DBMS (Database Management System) and converts JDBC calls to specific client calls for the DBMS being used. This type of driver is usually operating-system specific and is also not a pure Java solution.
JDBC-Net Pure Java Driver	Uses net server middleware for connecting Java clients to DBMS. It converts the JDBC calls into an independent protocol that can then be used to interface with the DBMS. This is a pure Java solution with the main drawback being security.
Native-Protocol Pure Java Driver	Provided by the database vendor, and its main purpose is to convert JDBC calls into the network protocol understood by the DBMS. This is the best solution to use and is pure Java.

The first two driver-type options are usually temporary solutions to solve the problem, where the JDBC driver for the particular DBMS (Database Management System) in use does not exist. The third and fourth driver-type options represent the normal, preferred usage of JDBC because they keep the platform-independent fundamentals in place. If you would like to find out if your DBMS vendor supports a particular version of the JDBC API, please check out the following web site for details: `http://servlet .java.sun.com/products/jdbc/drivers`.

The JDBC API is contained in two Java packages — `java.sql` and `javax.sql`. The first package, `java.sql`, contains the original core APIs for JDBC. The second package, `javax.sql`, contains optional, more advanced features such as row sets, connection pooling, and distributed transaction management. It is important to determine your application's data access needs and architecture ahead of time to properly assess which packages you need to import.

Setting Up Your Environment

To use the JDBC API and its advanced features, it is recommended that you install the latest Java 2 SDK Standard Edition. The JDBC API is currently shipping with both Java 2 SDK SE and Java 2 SDK Enterprise Edition (the latter is a must if you are doing server-side development).

You will also need to install a JDBC driver that implements the JDBC 4.0 features. Your driver vendor may not support all the features that are in the `javax.sql` package, so you should check with them first.

Finally, you will need access to a Database Management System that is supported by your driver. You can find further information on JDBC support at `http://java.sun.com/products/jdbc/`.

This chapter uses Apache Derby because it is being bundled with JDK 1.6 and renamed java db. If you download JDK 1.6 after build 88, its already installed! Look for the database in `%JAVA_HOME%\db`.

JDBC API Usage in the Real World

The JDBC API is most commonly used by applications to access data in two main models: the two-tier model and three-tier model, both of which are covered in the following paragraphs.

Understanding the Two-Tier Model

The two-tier model is the simplest of the models. It comprises a *client layer* and a *server layer*. The client layer interacts directly with the server layer, and no middleware is used. The business logic, application/presentation layer, transaction management, and connection management are all handled by the client layer. The server layer contains only the data source and doesn't manage anything that the client is doing, except for user access and rights. Figure 6-1 illustrates the two-tier model.

This is a good design for small applications but would present a scalability dilemma for larger applications requiring more robust connection and transaction management.

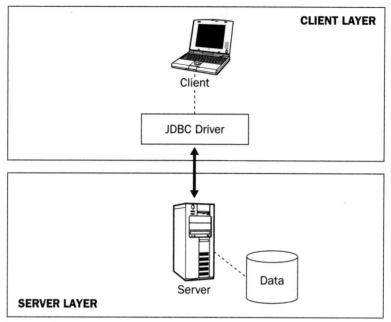

Figure 6-1

Understanding the Three-Tier Model

The three-tier model is the most complex and the most scalable of the models. It removes the business logic and adds a layer of abstraction to the data sources. This model is shown in Figure 6-2.

The *client layer* in this model is a thin client layer that contains only very lightweight presentation layers that will run on web browsers, Java Programs, PDAs, Tablet PCs, and so forth. It does not handle business logic, methods of accessing the data sources, the drivers used to provide access, or the methods in which data is saved.

The *middle layer* is where the core of the functionality exists in the three-tier model. The thin clients interact with applications that support the business logic and interactions with data sources. Connection pools, transaction management, and JDBC drivers can all be found here. This is the layer that adds increased performance and scalability compared to the two-tier model.

The *server layer* is where the data sources such as database management systems and files exist. The only interaction that occurs here is from the middle layer to the server layer through a JDBC driver.

The main benefit of the three-tier model is the fact that it adds layers of abstraction that can be scaled, removed, added, and improved upon. It also adds extra performance benefits when simultaneously accessing multiple data sources. The main drawback is that it can be expensive, depending on the choices made for the application server software and the hardware to run the system.

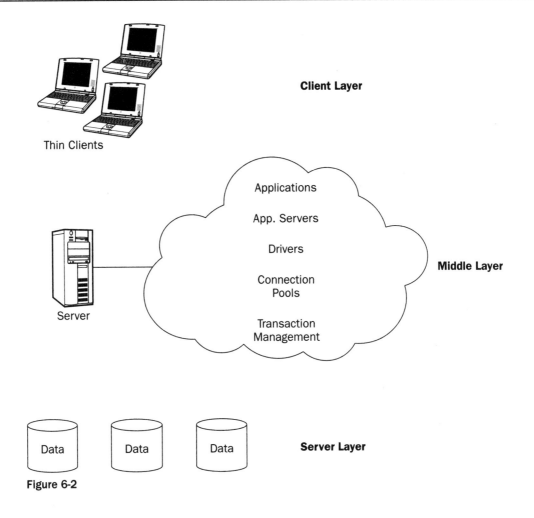

Figure 6-2

Effectively Using JDBC 4.0

This part of the chapter explores the main usage of the JDBC API before moving on to more advanced topics, such as connection pooling, Annotations, and managing transactions to ensure that you have a solid foundation with which to start your JDBC API journey.

Overview

There are basically three interfaces that collaborate that allow the Java developer access to data in a relational database:

❏   Connection

❏   Statement

❏   ResultSet

315

The basics are that the connection is the physical link or path to the database system. The Statement interface encapsulates all the commands that a relational database can process, such as executing an SELECT, INSERT, UPDATE, DELETE, in addition to modifying the underling database schema. And finally, the ResultSet is the tabular results of executing a database query. There are a number of ways to vary the behavior of these interfaces, and that is the subject of this section of this chapter.

Figure 6-3 displays the calling sequence associated with database programming.

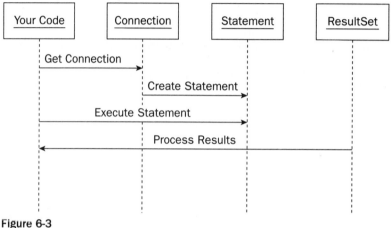

Figure 6-3

Connection resources are very expensive because they have external dependencies that add latency. JDBC 4.0 has associated with it a number of performance enhancements targeted at the Driver level to be taken advantage of in a three-tier or enterprise environment. The next section looks that the connection process and discuses two methods for obtaining a connection to a relational database server.

Managing Connections

A Java application can establish a connection to a data source via a JDBC API-enabled driver. Connections are maintained in code by the Connection object. A Java application can have multiple connections to multiple data sources at the same time using multiple Connection objects. A Connection object can be obtained by a Java application in two ways: through a DriverManager class or through an implementation of the DataSource interface.

DriverManager

Prior to the release of the JDBC 4.0 specification, the client application needed to load the Driver class via the command

```
Class.forName("org.apache.derby.jdbc.ClientDriver");
```

However, you no longer have to fulfill this requirement; the new specification requires vendors to mark the driver class within the implementing jar in a file called META-INF.services\java.sql.Driver. In this text file there is a line specifying the class that implements the java.sql.Driver interface. The DriverManager handles the registration for you.

You can take a look at this structure by unzipping the `derbyclient.jar`, the database driver provided for Derby. Derby is now packaged as part of the Java 1.6 JDK and is located in the `%java_home%\db\lib` directory. The traditional method to establish a connection is to use the `DriverManager` class and then make the connection:

```
String sURL     = "jdbc:derby//localhost:1527/wrox";
String sUsername = "APP";
String sPassword = "password";

try {

   // Obtain a connection
   Connection cConn = DriverManager.getConnection(sURL, sUsername, sPassword);
} catch (...) {
} finally {
   if (cConn != null) {
      cConn.close(); // Close the connection
   }
}
```

A `Connection` object is obtained by a static `DriverManager` API call, `getConnection(JDBCURL, Username, Password)`. A connection is now established. The driver itself views the `Connection` object as the user's session.

DataSource

The preferred method to establish a connection is to use the `DataSource` interface. The `DataSource` interface is preferred because it makes the code more portable, it allows for easier program maintenance, and it permits the `Connection` object to participate in distributed transaction management as well as transparent connection pooling. Connection pooling is a great idea when performance is the primary goal for your application. The ability to reuse `Connection` objects eliminates the need to constantly create a new physical connection every time a connection request is made. Distributed transactions allow you to create applications that work well in robust enterprise architectures where an enormous amount of concurrent database tasks are likely to occur.

The `DataSource` interface utilizes the Java Naming and Directory Interface (JNDI) to store a logical name for the data source instead of using the fully qualified driver name to connect to the data source. This type of usage aids in code portability and reusability. One of the very neat features of a `DataSource` object is that it basically represents a physical data source; if the data source changes, the changes will be automatically reflected in the `DataSource` object without invoking any code.

Using JNDI, a Java application can find a remote database service by its logical name. For the application to use the logical name, it must first be registered with the JNDI naming service. The following code shows an example of how to register a data source with the JNDI naming service. This is not the application developer's responsibility. Most application servers register their configured data sources at startup.

```
VendorDataSource vdsDataSource = new VendorDataSource();
vdsDataSource.setServerName("localhost");
vdsDataSource.setDatabaseName("wrox");
vdsDataSource.setDescription("example wrox database");

// Get the initial context
```

317

```
Context ctx = new InitialContext();

// Create the logical name for the data source
ctx.bind("jdbc/wroxDB", vdsDataSource);
```

If JNDI is new to you, it can best be thought of as a directory structure like that of your file system that provides network-wide naming and directory services. However, it is independent of any naming or directory service. For more information on JNDI, please visit http://java.sun.com/products/jndi/.

Once registered, the data source is available via the Context's lookup method:

```
Context ctx = InitialContext();

// Look up the registered data source from JNDI
DataSource dsDataSource = (DataSource) ctx.lookup("jdbc/wroxDB");

// Obtain a Connection object from the data source
Connection cConn = dsDataSource.getConnection("username", "password");

// Close the connection
cConn.close();
```

Now that you have established a connection, there are a couple of things that can occur that are transparent to the developer. The first thing is that the data source's properties that you are connected to can change dynamically. These changes will be automatically reflected in the DataSource object. The second thing that could occur, which is very nice, is that the middle tier managing the connections could seamlessly switch the data source to which you are connected, without your knowledge. This is definitely a benefit for fail-over, clustered, and load-balanced enterprise architectures.

Understanding Statements

Statements are essential for communicating with a data source using embedded SQL. There are three main types of statements. The first one is the Statement interface. When objects are created from Statement interface implementations, they are generally used for executing generic SQL statements that do not take any parameters. The second type of statement is the PreparedStatement, which inherits from the Statement interface. PreparedStatement objects are useful when you need to create and compile SQL statements ahead of time. PreparedStatement objects also accept IN parameters, which are discussed further in this section under the title "Setting IN Parameters." The final type of statement is the CallableStatement. The CallableStatement inherits from the PreparedStatement and accepts both IN and OUT parameters. Its main purpose is to execute stored database procedures.

Investigating the Statement Interface

The basic Statement object can be used to execute general SQL calls once a connection has been established and a Connection object exists:

```
Connection cConn = dsDataSource.getConnection("username", "password");

Statement sStatement = cConn.createStatement();

// Execute the following SQL query
```

```
ResultSet rsResults = sStatement.executeQuery("SELECT * FROM PLAYERS");

while (rsResults.next()) {
        // Perform operations
}
```

You can see from the previous code that once you establish a connection, creating a `Statement` object is trivial. The main area of importance is the `Statement` execution method, called `executeQuery`, which executes the given SQL command with the data source.

The following table describes the different execution methods that can be used with a `Statement` object.

Method	Description
`boolean execute(String sql)`	Use this method to execute a generic SQL request. It may return multiple results. Use `getResultSet` to retrieve the `ResultSet`.
`boolean execute(String sql, int autoGenKeys)`	Executes the SQL request and also notifies the driver that auto-generated keys should be made accessible.
`boolean execute(String sql, int [] columnIndexes)`	Allows you to specify, via the array, which auto-generated keys should be made accessible.
`boolean execute(String sql, String [] columnNames)`	Allows you to specify, via the array, which auto-generated keys should be made accessible.
`int [] executeBatch()`	Executes a batch of database commands and returns an array of update counts.
`ResultSet executeQuery(String sql)`	Executes the SQL string and returns a single `ResultSet` object.
`int executeUpdate(String sql)`	Executes a SQL string, which must be an INSERT, UPDATE, DELETE, or a statement that doesn't return anything.
`int executeUpdate(String sql, int autoGeneratedKeys)`	Executes a SQL string, which must be an INSERT, UPDATE, DELETE, or a statement that doesn't return anything. It will also allow you to notify the driver that auto-generated keys should be made accessible.
`int executeUpdate(String sql, int[] columnIndexes)`	Executes a SQL string, which must be an INSERT, UPDATE, DELETE, or a statement that doesn't return anything. It will also allow you to specify, via the array, which auto-generated keys should be made accessible.
`int executeUpdate(String sql, String[] columnNames)`	Executes a SQL string, which must be an INSERT, UPDATE, DELETE, or a statement that doesn't return anything. It will also allow you to specify, via the array, which auto-generated keys should be made accessible.

In general, you do not use statements unless the SQL statement is static. If it contains parameters, you should use the prepared statement interface discussed next.

Exploring the PreparedStatement Interface

If you need to execute a SQL statement many times, the PreparedStatement is the perfect choice for the task because it increases program efficiency and performance. The PreparedStatement is the logical name choice for the interface because it contains a SQL statement that has been previously compiled and sent to the DBMS of choice, hence the term *prepared*. The PreparedStatement is a subclass of the Statement interface; therefore, it inherits all of the functionality listed in the previous "Investigating the Statement Interface" section, with a few exceptions. When using the execute methods with a PreparedStatement object, you should never attempt to pass parameters to the methods execute(), executeQuery(), or executeUpdate(). These methods have been modified to be parameterless for the PreparedStatement interface and should be called without parameters.

Setting IN Parameters

The PreparedStatement also gives the developer the ability to embed IN parameters in the SQL statement contained in the PreparedStatement object. These IN parameters are denoted in the SQL statement by the question mark symbol. Anywhere in the SQL statement where an IN parameter occurs, you must have your application fill in a value for the IN parameter using the appropriate setter method before executing the PreparedStatement. The most common setter methods are listed in the following table.

There are many more setter methods from which to choose than those listed in this table. These are just the ones that are most commonly used.

Method	Description
void setBoolean(int paramIndex, boolean x)	Sets the IN parameter to a Boolean value.
void setDate(int paramIndex, Date x)	Sets the IN parameter to a java.sql .Date value.
void setDouble(int paramIndex, double x)	Sets the IN parameter to a Double value.
void setFloat(int paramIndex, float x)	Sets the IN parameter to a Float value.
void setInt(int paramIndex, int x)	Sets the IN parameter to an Int value.
void setLong(int paramIndex, long x)	Sets the IN parameter to a Long value.
void setString(int paramIndex, String x)	Sets the IN parameter to a String value.
void clearParameters()	Clears the parameter values set by the setter methods.

The next example shows a typical usage of the PreparedStatement interface. A table called CAR is defined as follows:

```
CREATE TABLE CAR (
  ID INTEGER NOT NULL,
  MODEL VARCHAR(28),
  MODEL_YEAR VARCHAR(10)
  );
```

And a corresponding `Car` class with similar properties:

```
public class Car {

Long id;

String model;
String year;
// access set & get methods omitted
}
```

Next, create a method that will execute a query and return the collection of cars that match your selection criteria. The method signature takes a parameter year:

```
public Collection<Car> getAllCars( String year) {

    Collection<Car> cars = new ArrayList<Car>( );
    Connection con = null;
    PreparedStatement stmt = null;
    ResultSet rs = null;
    try {
       String url = "jdbc:derby://localhost:1527/wrox;create=true";
       con = DriverManager.getConnection(url , "APP", "password");

       String sql = "SELECT ID, MODEL, MODEL_YEAR FROM CAR WHERE MODEL_YEAR= ?";
       stmt = con.prepareStatement(sql);
       stmt.setString(1, year);
       rs = stmt.executeQuery();
```

Loop through the results of the query, pulling by name the columns in the select statement and return them as an object collection. This is preferred in a multi-threaded environment. It shortens the life of the `ResultSet` object and frees the resources held open by the database:

```
       while ( rs.next() ) {
          System.out.println(" result");
          Car car = new Car( );
          long id = rs.getLong("ID");
          String model = rs.getString("MODEL");
          String modelyear = rs.getString("MODEL_YEAR");

          car.setId( id) ;
          car.setModel( model);
          car.setYear(modelyear);
          cars.add(car);
       }
    } catch (SQLException e) {
```

New in JDBC 4.0, you can now navigate through the exception chain:

```
       while(ex != null) {
             System.out.println("SQLState:" + ex.getSQLState());
             System.out.println("Error Code:" + ex.getErrorCode());
             System.out.println("Message:" + ex.getMessage());
```

```
          Throwable t = ex.getCause();
          while(t != null) {
              System.out.println("Cause:" + t);
              t = t.getCause();
          }
          ex = ex.getNextException();
      }
```

It is important to place the `ResultSet`, `Statement`, and `Connection` `close()` calls in a `finally` clause. If an exception is thrown, the final statement lets you return the connection to the connection pool:

```
  } finally {
    try {
      if ( rs != null ) rs.close();
      if ( stmt != null ) stmt.close();
      if ( con != null ) con.close();
    } catch (SQLException e) { }


  }
  return cars;
}
```

This code can become very tedious and repetitive. Annotation and Hibernate — two approaches discussed later in this chapter — help reduce this repetitive code. Next, look as some specific hang-ups regarding prepared statements.

IN Parameter Pitfalls

Certain pitfalls can occur when setting parameters with the setter methods that may not be obvious to you. Anytime you set a parameter and then execute the `PreparedStatement` object, the JDBC driver will convert the Java type into a JDBC type that the DBMS understands. For instance, if you were to set a parameter to a Java float type and pass it to a DBMS that is expecting an `INTEGER` JDBC type, you could run into serious problems: potential data loss or exceptions, depending on how the DBMS handles the situation. Trying to write code that is portable to different vendors is possible, but it definitely requires knowledge of the mappings that occur between Java types and JDBC types. The following table lists the most commonly used Java types and their mappings to JDBC types.

Java Object/Type	JDBC Type
Int	INTEGER
Short	SMALLINT
Byte	TINYINT
Long	BIGINT
Float	REAL
Double	DOUBLE
java.math.BigDecimal	NUMERIC
Boolean	BOOLEAN or BIT

Java Object/Type	JDBC Type
String	CHAR, VARCHAR, or LONGVARCHAR
Clob	CLOB
Blob	BLOB
Struct	STRUCT
Ref	REF
java.sql.Date	DATE
java.sql.Time	TIME
java.sql.Timestamp	TIMESTAMP
java.net.URL	DATALINK
Array	ARRAY
byte[]	BINARY, VARBINARY, or LONGVARBINARY
Java class	JAVA_OBJECT

Specifying JDBC Types with setObject

A way around the potential mapping pitfalls of using IN parameters is by using the PreparedStatement .setObject() method for setting IN parameters:

```
void setObject(int paramIndex, Object x, int targetSqlType)
```

The setObject method allows you to pass a Java object and specify the targeted JDBC type. This method will ensure that the conversion from the Java type to the JDBC type occurs as you intend. Here is an example using setObject to specify a JDBC type:

```
PreparedStatement psStatement = cConn.prepareStatement("SELECT * FROM PLAYERS WHERE
TEAM=?");

// Set the IN parameter to Titans using setObject
psStatement.setObject(1, "Titans", java.sql.Types.VARCHAR);

// Execute the statement
ResultSet rsResults = psStatement.executeQuery();

// Clear parameters
psStatement.clearParameters();
```

User Defined Types (UDT), which are classes that implement the SQLData interface, can also be used as a parameter for the setObject method. All of the conversion details are kept from the programmer, so it is important to use the following form of the setObject method rather than the previous form, which explicitly maps the Java types to JDBC types:

```
void setObject(int paramIndex, Object x)
```

The difference between the two `setObject` methods is that this form intentionally omits the parameter for specifying the target JDBC type. Another valuable method that requires mentioning is the `setNull` method, which allows you to send a NULL for a specific JDBC type to the DBMS:

```
void setNull(int paramIndex, int sqlType)
```

Even though you are sending a NULL value to the DBMS, you still must specify the JDBC type (`java.sql.Types`) for which the NULL will be used.

Exploring the CallableStatement Interface

Occasionally you may run into to a situation where you will need to execute stored procedures on a Remote Database Management System (RDBMS). The `CallableStatement` provides a standard way to call stored procedures using the JDBC API stored procedure SQL escape syntax. The SQL escape syntax supports two forms of stored procedures. The first form includes a result parameter known as the OUT parameter, and the second form doesn't use OUT parameters. Each form may have IN parameters. The IN parameters were discussed in depth earlier in the "Exploring the PreparedStatement Interface" section of this chapter. The syntax of the two forms is listed as follows:

```
This form does not return a result.
{call <procedure name>[(?,?, ...)]}
This form does return a result.
{? = call <procedure name>[(?,?, ...)]}
```

The `CallableStatement` interface extends `PreparedStatement` and therefore can use all of the methods contained in the `PreparedStatement` interface. As a result, IN parameters are handled the same way as in the `PreparedStatement`; however, OUT parameters must be handled differently. They must be registered before the `CallableStatement` object can be executed. Registration of the OUT parameters is done through a method contained in the `CallableStatement` object called `registerOutParameter`. The intent is to register the OUT parameters with the appropriate JDBC type (`java.sql.Types`), not the Java type. Here is the `registerOutParameter` method in its simplest form:

```
void registerOutParameter (int paramIndex, int sqlType) throws SQLException
```

One more type of parameter hasn't yet been discussed, and it is called the INOUT parameter. This simply means that an IN parameter that you are passing in will also have a new value associated with it on the way out. These must also be registered as OUT parameters with the `registerOutParameter` method. Listed as follows are code examples that show how to prepare a callable statement, and they also illustrate all three parameter types (IN, OUT, and INOUT).

❑   `CallableStatement` using an IN parameter:

```
CallableStatement cStatement = cConn.prepareCall(
                        "{CALL setPlayerName(?)}";

cStatement.setString("John Doe");

cStatement.execute();
```

❑ `CallableStatement` using an `OUT` parameter:

```
CallableStatement cStatement = cConn.prepareCall(
                    "{CALL getPlayerName(?)}";

cStatement.registerOutParameter(1, java.sql.Types.STRING);

cStatement.execute();

// Retrieve Player's name
String sName = cStatement.getString(1);
```

❑ `CallableStatement` using an `INOUT` parameter:

```
CallableStatement cStatement = cConn.prepareCall(
                    "{CALL getandsetPlayersName(?)}";

cStatement.setString("John Doe");
cStatement.registerOutParameter(1, java.sql.Types.STRING);
cStatement.execute();

// Retrieve Player's name
String sName = cStatement.getString(1);
```

There is another escape syntax that has not been discussed because it may be supported differently by different vendors. It is the escape syntax for *scalar functions* and its form is as follows:

```
{ fn <function name> (?, ...)}
```

To figure out which scalar functions your DBMS uses, the JDBC API provides several methods in the `DatabaseMetaData` class for retrieving a comma-separated list of the available functions. These methods are shown in the following table.

Method	Description
`String getNumericFunctions()`	Returns a comma-separated list of math functions available for the given database. Example: POWER(number, power)
`String getStringFunctions()`	Returns a comma-separated list of string functions available for the given database. Example: REPLACE(string)
`String getSystemFunctions()`	Returns a comma-separated list of system functions available for the given database. Example: IFNULL(expression, value)
`String getTimeDateFunctions()`	Returns a comma-separated list of time and date functions available for the given database. Example: CURTIME()

The `DatabaseMetaData` class contains an enormous amount of useful functions for retrieving meta data about a database. This is discussed later in this chapter. However, two other methods of the `DatabaseMetaData` class are worth mentioning here because they relate to stored procedures: the supportsStoredProcedures and getProcedures methods. The supportsStoredProcedures method returns true if the DBMS supports stored procedures. The getProcedures method returns a description of the stored procedures available in a given DBMS.

Utilizing Batch Updates

To improve performance, the JDBC API provides a batch update facility that allows multiple updates to be submitted for processing at one time. Statement, PreparedStatement, and CallableStatement all support batch updates. Imagine a case where you have to input 100 new changes to a database using single calls to it. Wouldn't it be easier if you could just send the request at one time instead of making 100 calls to the database? Well, that is exactly the type of functionality that batch updates provide. This portion of the chapter explains how to create batch updates for the Statement, PreparedStatement, and CallableStatement objects.

Creating Batch Updates Using a Statement Object

The Statement object can submit a set of updates to a DBMS in one single execution; however, statement objects are initially created with empty batch command lists. Therefore you must invoke the Statement.addBatch method to add SQL commands to the Statement object. The SQL commands must return an update count and are not allowed to return anything else, like ResultSets. If a return value other than that of an update count is returned, a BatchUpdateException is thrown and must be processed. An application can determine why the exception occurred by calling the BatchUpdateException.getUpdateCounts method to retrieve an integer array of update counts, which allows you to determine the cause of the failure.

To properly process batch commands, you should always set auto-commit to false so the DBMS's driver will not commit the changes until you tell it to do so. This will give you a chance to catch exceptions and clear the batch list, if necessary. To clear a batch list that has not been processed, use the Statement.clearBatch method. This will clear the Statement object's batch list of all commands. If a batch is successfully processed, it is automatically cleared.

When a Statement.executeBatch is successful, it will return an array of update counts that are in the same order as the commands were when added to the batch of the Statement. Each entry in the array will contain one of the following:

❑ A value that is 0 or greater, which means the command was processed successfully. If the value is greater than 0, the number signifies the number of rows that were affected when the command was executed.

❑ A Statement.SUCCESS_NO_INFO signifies that the particular command was processed successfully; however, it did not contain any information about the number of rows that were affected by the command.

In the event of a failure during the execution of the batch command, a BatchUpdateException will be thrown. Certain drivers may continue with the execution of the batch commands, and others will stop execution altogether. If the batch command fails and the driver stops processing after the first failure, it will return the number of update counts via the BatchUpdateException.getUpdateCounts. If the batch command fails and the driver continues to process other commands in the batch list, it will return in its update counts array a value of Statement.EXECUTE_FAILED for the command or commands that failed during the batch execution. You can determine which type of driver you have by checking to see whether an error occurs and whether the size of the returned array from `BatchUpdateException` `.getUpdateCounts` is equal to the same number of commands submitted.

JDBC drivers do not have to support batch updates. Typically, you will know if your driver supports batch updates via its documentation. If you don't know, you can always detect it in code using the `DatabaseMetaData.supportsBatchUpdates` method.

The following is an example of creating a batch update to enter five new team members into a TEAMS table and checking to make sure that the database driver supports batch updates:

```java
try {
    // Make sure that autocommit is off
    cConn.setAutoCommit(false);

    // Retrieve metadata info about the data source
    DatabaseMetaData dbmData = cConn.getMetaData();

    // Make sure our driver supports batch updates
    if (dbmData.supportsBatchUpdates()) {

        Statement sStatement = cConn.createStatement();

        // Add batch commands
        sStatement.addBatch("INSERT INTO TEAMS VALUES ("'Tom')");
        sStatement.addBatch("INSERT INTO TEAMS VALUES ('Roger')");
        sStatement.addBatch("INSERT INTO TEAMS VALUES ('Jon')");
        sStatement.addBatch("INSERT INTO TEAMS VALUES ('Julia')");
        sStatement.addBatch("INSERT INTO TEAMS VALUES ('George')");

        int []uCounts = sStatement.executeBatch();

        // Commit the changes
        cConn.commit();
    } else {
        System.err.print("Your driver does not support batch updates!");
    }
} catch(BatchUpdateException batchEx) {
    int []uCounts = batchEx.getUpdateCounts();
    for (int i = 0; i < uCounts.length; i ++) {
        System.err.print("Count #" + i + "=" + uCounts[i] + "\n");
    }
    // Handle errors further here if necessary
}
```

Creating Batch Updates Using a PreparedStatement Object

The `PreparedStatement` object batch updates follow mostly the same method of operations as the `Statement` object batch updates, with the exception that you now have to deal with parameterized SQL statements and setting each parameter before adding a batch command. So for each command you will need to set the necessary IN parameter before issuing a `PreparedStatement.addBatch` call. The following code example shows how to correctly add batch commands to a `PreparedStatement` object:

```
try {
  // Make sure that autocommit is off
  cConn.setAutoCommit(false);

  // Retrieve metadata info about the data source
  DatabaseMetaData dbmData = cConn.getMetaData();

  // Make sure our driver supports batch updates
  if (dbmData.supportsBatchUpdates()) {
    PreparedStatement psStatement = cConn.prepareStatement(
          "INSERT INTO TEAMS VALUES (?)");

    // Set the IN parameter
    psStatement.setString(1, "Jennie Vitale");

    // Add batch command
    psStatement.addBatch();

    // Set the IN parameter for the next command
    psStatement.setString(1, "Andrew Vitale");

    // Add batch command
    psStatement.addBatch();

    int []uCounts = psStatement.executeBatch();

    // Commit the changes
    cConn.commit();
  } else {
    System.err.print("Your driver does not support batch updates!");
  }
} catch(BatchUpdateException batchEx) {
}
```

The key point to note from the preceding code is where the `PreparedStatement.addBatch` methods occur. They occur after the IN parameters are set, so you simply change the IN parameters for each batch command you wish to execute.

Utilizing Result Sets

In simple terms, a `ResultSet` object is a Java object that is created to contain the results of a SQL query that has been executed. The results are in table row fashion, meaning they contain column headers, types, and values. All this information can be obtained through either the `ResultSet` object or the `ResultSetMetaData` object.

`ResultSet` objects are very common, and you will interface with them on a continuous basis when doing JDBC programming, so it is important to understand the different types of `ResultSet` objects that are available for you to exploit. Understanding how `ResultSet` objects are created and manipulated is crucial when you are designing different algorithms, especially with regard to performance. So find the best possible option for executing a query, and manipulate its results for your particular situation.

Investigating Types of Result Sets

There are two main areas of interest when dealing with result sets of which you must be aware. The first area of interest is the concentration on how the cursor in a result set can be exploited. Cursors can be limited to only moving forward, or they can be allowed to move in both forward and backward directions. The second area of interest is how changes in the data source affect the result set. You can instruct a result set to be aware of changes that occur in an underlying data source and have a `ResultSet` object reflect those changes.

Three types of result sets warrant explanation. Each of these types will be scrollable or non-scrollable, sensitive or insensitive. Scrollable means that the cursor in the result set can move both forward and backward. Non-scrollable signifies that the cursor can only move in one direction: forward. If the result set is sensitive to change, it will reflect changes that occur while the result set is open. If the result set is insensitive to change, it will usually remain fixed with no change to its structure, even if the underlying data source changes. The following is a list of constants in the `ResultSet` interface that you can use to specify a result set type:

❏ `TYPE_FORWARD_ONLY` — The result set cursor can only be moved forward from the beginning to the end. It cannot move backward. Also, the result set is not sensitive to change from the data source.

❏ `TYPE_SCROLL_INSENSITIVE` — The result set cursor can move forward and backward and jump to rows specified by the application. Also, the result set is not sensitive to change from the data source.

❏ `TYPE_SCROLL_SENSITIVE` — The result set cursor can move forward and backward and jump to rows specified by the application. This time the result is sensitive to changes to the data source while the result set is open. This provides a dynamic view to the data.

Setting Concurrency of Result Sets

Result sets have only two levels of concurrency: *read-only* and *updatable*. To find out if your driver supports a specific concurrency type, use the `DatabaseMetaData.supportResultSetConcurrency` method to find out. The following is a list of constants that are in the `ResultSet` interface that you can use to specify a result set concurrency type:

❏ `CONCUR_READ_ONLY` — Specify this constant when you want your result set to be read-only, meaning it cannot be updated programmatically.

❏ `CONCUR_UPDATABLE` — Specify this constant when you want your result set to be updatable, meaning it can be updated programmatically.

Setting Holdability of Result Sets

Result sets are generally closed when a transaction has been completed. This means that a `Connection.commit` has been called, which in turn closes any related result sets. In special cases, this may not be the desired behavior that you were hoping for. It is possible to hold a result set open and keep its cursor position in the result set after a `Connection.commit` has been called by creating your statements with the following `ResultSet` interface constants present:

❏ `HOLD_CURSORS_OVER_COMMIT` — Specifies that a `ResultSet` object will not be closed when a `Connection.commit` is called. Instead, it will remain open until the program calls the method `ResultSet.close`. If you are interested in better performance, this is usually *not* the best option.

❏   `CLOSE_CURSORS_AT_COMMIT` — Specifies that a `ResultSet` object will be closed when a `Connection.commit` occurs. This is the best performance option.

Another interesting point to note is that the default holdability is determined by the DBMS that you are interfacing with. In order to determine the default holdability, use the `DatabaseMetaData` `.getResultSetHoldability` method to retrieve the default holdability for the DBMS.

Using Result Sets

Now that you know the different types of result sets that exist and the concurrency and holdability levels, it is time to see what a result set looks like in action. The following code shows how to create a statement that is scrollable, updatable, insensitive to data source changes, and closes the cursor when a commit occurs:

```
// Look up the registered data source from JNDI
DataSource dsDataSource = (DataSource) ctx.lookup("jdbc/wroxDB");

// Obtain a Connection object from the data source
Connection cConn = dsDataSource.getConnection("APP", "password");

Statement sStatement = cConn.createStatement(
          ResultSet.CONCUR_UPDATABLE,
          ResultSet.TYPE_SCROLL_INSENSITIVE,
          ResultSet.CLOSE_CURSORS_AT_COMMIT
);

ResultSet rsResults = sStatement.executeQuery("SELECT NAME, TEAM FROM PLAYERS");

// Though we have not done anything to warrant a commit we put this here to show
where the ResultSet would be closed
cConn.commit();

// Close the connection
cConn.close();
```

Navigating Result Sets

The `ResultSet` interface of the JDBC API provides a rich set of methods for navigating through `ResultSet` objects. If your `ResultSet` object is scrollable, you can easily jump to different rows in the `ResultSet` object with little effort. Here is a list of the main methods provided in the `ResultSet` interface for navigation with a `ResultSet` object.

Method	Description
First	Moves the cursor to the first row in the `ResultSet` object. Returns `true` if successful. Returns `false` if there are no rows in the `ResultSet` object.
Last	Moves the cursor to the last row in the `ResultSet` object. Returns `true` on success. Returns `false` if there are no rows in the `ResultSet` object.
Next	Moves the cursor one row forward in the `Result` object. It will return `true` if successful and `false` if the cursor has been moved past the last row.

Method	Description
Previous	Moves the cursor one row backward in the Result object. It will return true if successful and false if the cursor has been moved past the first row.
absolute(int)	Moves the cursor to the row specified by the int parameter. The first row is represented by the number 1. If you send a 0 as a parameter, the cursor is moved just before the first row. If the integer specified is a negative number, it will move the number of rows specified backward from the end of the ResultSet object.
BeforeFirst	Moves the cursor to the beginning of the ResultObject just before the first row.
AfterLast	Moves the cursor to the end of the ResultObject just after the last row.
relative(int)	Depending on whether the integer specified is negative or positive, this method will move the cursor the number of rows specified from its current position. A positive value signifies a forward movement. A negative value signifies a backward movement. A zero signifies that the cursor remains in the same position.

Manipulating Result Sets

The ResultSet interface has an enormous number of methods that can be used for updating a ResultSet object. The majority of the methods are prefixed with the word *update*. In order to be able to update a ResultSet object, it must have a concurrency of type CONCUR_UPDATABLE. If a ResultSet object is updatable, its columns can be altered, its rows can be deleted, new rows can be added, and its data can be changed. The following code example shows several ways to manipulate a ResultSet object:

```
Statement sStatement = cConn.createStatement(
            ResultSet.CONCUR_UPDATABLE,
            ResultSet.TYPE_SCROLL_INSENSITIVE,
            ResultSet.CLOSE_CURSORS_AT_COMMIT
);

ResultSet rsResults = sStatement.executeQuery("SELECT NAME, TEAM, AGE, " +
                                             "RANK FROM PLAYERS");

// Move to the last row
rsResults.last();

// Update specific data in the row
rsResults.updateString(2, "Hornets");
rsResults.updateInt(3, 27);
rsResults.updateLong(4, 5021);

// Commit the changes to the row
rsResults.updateRow();
cConn.commit();

// Close the connection
cConn.close();
```

The following example shows you how to insert and delete rows. Inserting rows is not a difficult process but it does require a bit of know-how because it is not initially intuitive. To insert a row into a ResultSet object, you must first make a call to ResultSet.moveToInsertRow. This may seem confusing, but the JDBC API defines a concept of an insert row in the ResultSet object. When you call ResultSet .moveToInsertRow, this essentially allows you to remember your current cursor position, move to a temporary area in memory, perform the creation of your new row, and call ResultSet.insertRow to insert the newly created row into the ResultSet object at the cursor position you were at before calling ResultSet.moveToInsertRow.

Deleting a row is much more trivial than inserting a row. To delete a row, you simply move to the row you want to delete and call ResultSet.deleteRow. The following code demonstrates how to delete and insert a row using the methods that were just described:

```
Statement sStatement = cConn.createStatement(ResultSet.CONCUR_UPDATABLE);

ResultSet rsResults = sStatement.executeQuery("SELECT NAME, TEAM, AGE," +
                                              "RANK FROM PLAYERS");

// Move to the fourth row
rsResults.absolute(4);

// Delete the fourth row
rsResults.deleteRow();

// Now let's insert a new row
rsResults.moveToInsertRow();

// Build data for new row
rsResults.updateString(1, "Ken Pratt");
rsResults.updateString(2, "Tigers");
rsResults.updateInt(3, 32);
rsResults.updateLong(4, 7521);

// Add the new row to the ResultsSet
rsResults.insertRow();

// Move the cursor back the original position
rsResults.moveToCurrentRow();

// Commit changes
cConn.commit();

// Close the connection
cConn.close();
```

Closing Result Sets

If the Statement object that created the ResultSet object is not yet closed, you can use the ResultSet .close method to close a ResultSet object and free its resources. If you specified the HOLD_CURSORS_ OVER_COMMIT flag when you created the Statement object, then you will also need to call the ResultSet .close method when you are done with the ResultSet object. Otherwise it would remain open even if a Connect.commit is called. However, if the Statement object that created the ResultSet object is closed, the ResultSet object would be closed as well even if the HOLD_CURSORS_OVER_COMMIT was specified during creation.

Advanced Concepts

This section addresses some of the advanced data management concepts starting with a new annotations capability added to the JDBC 4.0 specification.

Annotations

Annotations were introduced into the language with JDK 1.5, and now they are making an impact with JDBC 4.0. An annotation is a declarative programming model where comments, associated with a code element, are used to inject code at runtime.

The `PreparedStatement` example in this chapter can be re-written as an annotation, greatly reducing the amount of code required by the application developer.

The annotation solution consists of two elements. The first is the declaration of a Query Interface , extending an interface `BaseQuery` in the `java.sql.` package. And the second element is a `QueryObject` used to execute the query.

Start by declaring the interface. You will not have to implement the interface; that will be done for you based on the declared annotation. The annotation is a `@Select`, it takes the SQL statement as a parameter and maps the parameter of the method with the `?#` IN parameter on the statement. Note that unlike the `ResultSet` object returned in the previous example, the `DataSet` collection is typed with your user-defined class `Car`:

```
package wrox.ch6.jdbc;

import java.sql.BaseQuery;
import java.sql.DataSet;
import java.sql.Select;

public interface QueryAnnotationExample extends BaseQuery {

  @Select(sql="SELECT ID, MODEL, MODEL_YEAR FROM CAR WHERE MODEL_YEAR = ?1")
  public DataSet<Car> getCarsModelYear( String year );

}
```

Next, use the object factory to create and execute this statement. That is, by passing the query interface as a parameter, all the work was done for you, and the results are mapped to the collection of objects you specified in the interface:

```
public void testQueryAnnotation(  ) {
  QueryAnnotationExample qae = null;
  try {
    String url = "jdbc:derby://localhost:1527/wrox;create=true";
    Connection con = DriverManager.getConnection(url , "APP", "password");
    qae = con.createQueryObject(QueryAnnotationExample.class);
  } catch (SQLException e) {
    e.printStackTrace();
  }
  Collection<Car> cars = qae.getCarsModelYear("1999");
```

Here is a simple loop to print out the results of the query:

```
for ( Car c : cars) {
    System.out.println(" car id=" + c.getId() +
                        " model="+c.getModel() +" year="+ c.getYear() );
}
}
```

When this query executes the output will be:

```
car id=1 model=Honda Accord year=null
```

You might be thinking, "The year parameter couldn't have been null. I was filtering on 1999. Why is the year parameter returning null from the query?"

The answer relates back to the Car class definition. The annotation API maps the columns to properties by name. So ID mapped ID, model mapped to model, but year didn't map to MODEL_YEAR as it was declared in the database. The solution is to either change the parameter to be the same name as the database columns or add a column name annotation to the Car class. @ResultColumn(name= "MODEL_YEAR") tells the annotation API the name of the column to which to map the year field.

```
import java.sql.ResultColumn;
public class Car {

Long id;
String model;

@ResultColumn(name="MODEL_YEAR")
String year;
```

If you re-execute the example the model year will be populated with the correct information from the statement. A huge time saver compared to working with traditional PreparedStatement.

The next section discusses supporting database transactions.

Managing Transactions

Transaction management is extremely important when dealing with data sources. Transaction management ensures data integrity and data consistency; without it, it would be very easy for applications to corrupt data sources or cause problems with the synchronization of the data. Therefore, all JDBC drivers are required to provide transaction support.

What Is a Transaction?

To explain transactions best, take using an ATM as an example. The steps to retrieve money are as follows:

1. Swipe your ATM card.
2. Enter your PIN.
3. Select the withdrawal option.
4. Enter the amount of money to withdraw.

5. Agree to pay the extremely high fee.

6. Collect your money.

If anything was to go wrong along the way and you didn't receive your money, you would definitely not want that to reflect on your balance. So a transaction encompasses all the preceding steps and has only two possible outcomes: *commit* or *rollback*. When a transaction commits, all the steps had to be successful. When a transaction fails, there should not be any damage done to the underlying data source. In this case, the data that stores your account balance!

Standard Transactions

JDBC transactions are extremely simple to manage. Transaction support is implemented by the DBMS, which eliminates your having to write anything — code-wise — that would be cumbersome. All the methods you need are contained in the `Connection` object. There are two main methods you need to be concerned about: `Connection.commit` and `Connection.rollback`. There isn't a begin transaction method because the beginning of a transaction is implied when the first SQL statement is executed.

JDBC 3.0 introduced a concept called a *savepoint*. Savepoints allow you to save moments in time inside a transaction. For example, you could have an application that sends a SQL statement, then invokes a savepoint, tries to send another SQL statement, but a problem arises and you have to rollback. Now instead of rolling back completely, you can choose to rollback to a given savepoint. The following code example demonstrates JDBC transactions and the new savepoint method, `Connection.setSavepoint`:

```
Statement stmt = cConn.createStatement();

int nRows = stmt.executeUpdate("INSERT INTO PLAYERS (NAME) " +
                                        VALUES ('Roger Thomas')");

// Create our save point
Savepoint spOne = cConn.setSavepoint("SAVE_POINT_ONE");

nRows = stmt.executeUpdate("INSERT INTO PLAYERS (NAME) " +
                                    VALUES ('Jennifer White')");

// Rollback to the original save point
cConn.rollback(spOne);

// Commit the transaction.
cConn.commit();
```

From this example, the second SQL statement never gets committed because it was rolled back to `SAVE_POINT_ONE` before the transaction was committed.

This concludes the use of the JDBC 4.0 API. The next section explores Hibernate, to map Java objects to persistent data within a relational database.

Hibernate

Hibernate is an open-source framework for integrating an Object Oriented Domain Model with a relational database. This is a specific implementation of Object Relational Mapping or ORM.

In this section you learn how to create persistent Java objects, map these objects to database tables, set up your environment, and use the Hibernate API. In sections that follow you create an example domain model and use Hibernate to manipulate your persistent object data.

When you work with relational databases a majority of your application is dedicated to writing SQL in your application. There are a number of disadvantages to this approach:

❑ The relational database model works with tabular results, not objects; therefore it is difficult to take advantage of object-oriented features such as inheritance and polymorphism.

❑ SQL is compiled at runtime, making type conversion and null point errors common.

❑ Data access code is very redundant; developers spend a significant amount of time writing basic data access code.

❑ Database changes can have a ripple effect causing errors and rework through your application.

Hibernate eliminates these limitations when working with database systems. With Hibernate you can isolate your data access code as part of your application design. Figure 6-4 shows an example of where Hibernate fits in application design.

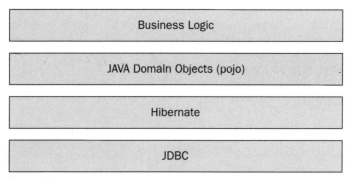

Figure 6-4

The business logic communicates with a Java *domain model*. A *domain model* is a set of Java objects that represent the abstraction of your application. The business logic then communicates with the Hibernate API to save and retrieve parts of your domain model. Hibernate handles all the data access code based on how the configuration has been defined in the persistence mapping.

In a later section you walk through the steps of building a domain model of a book club and using Hibernate to save your domain model to a relational database. But first it's necessary to discuss the components of a Hibernate solution.

Hibernate Components

There are four major components required for developing a Hibernate solution. Once you understand how these pieces fit together you will be able to create your own solutions using Hibernate.

Component	Role
Persistent Java Object	These are the java classes that represent your domain abstractions. Each object will map to one or more rows of data in a relational database.
Hibernate Configuration File	The `hibernate.cfg.xml` file is for configuring global parameters of the ORM framework. This includes the database information and information affecting all persistent classes.
Hibernate Mapping File	Each class that Hibernate persists needs an associated mapping file to describe the property-to-column mapping, and relationships defined between the classes.
Hibernate API	Your application uses the Hibernate API to perform all data access. Hibernate translates those API calls into the correct `INSERT`, `DELETE`, `UPDATE`, and `SELECT` statements based on your configuration settings.

Now that you know the components involved, look closer at each one.

Persistent Java Object

One of the reasons that Hibernate is so popular in the Java community is that there are very small requirements for what can be considered a persistent object. This Plain Old Java Object (POJO) approach means that your application will not be tightly bound to a framework. This was one of the significant limiting factors of the initial EJB specification, where persistent entity beans needed to extend a base class, and be deployed to an EJB container. None of those requirements are true for Hibernate.

For this example, you will use a persistent class called `Book`. There are three significant things about the following class declaration for `Book`. The first is the properties id, title, and created, as well as the access methods defined. They define the persistent data that will be saved to the database. Second, there is a public no-parameter constructor declared. Hibernate uses reflection to instantiate these objects. Third, this class has overridden the `equals()` and `hashcode()` methods. This is not required but a good practice when dealing with persistent classes. This is covered in more detail during discussion of object identity within a collection such as a Set or Map:

```
package wrox.ch6.dm;

import java.util.Date;

public class Book {

  private long id;
  private String title;
  private Date created = new Date();

  public Book() {

  }

  public long getId() {
    return id;
```

```
   }

   public void setId(long id) {
     this.id = id;
   }

   public String getTitle() {
     return title;
   }

   public void setTitle(String title) {
     this.title = title;
   }
   public boolean equals(Object obj) {

     if ( obj == this) return true;
     if ( !( obj instanceof Book)) return false;
     Book b = (Book) obj;
     if ( this.title.equals(b.title) ) return true;
     return false;
   }

   public int hashCode() {
     return this.title.hashCode();
   }
   }
```

Just to reiterate, there is no reference to Hibernate at all in your domain model. Next, look at a `Book` `.hbm.xml`. This will define how Hibernate will save this object to the database.

Hibernate Mapping File

To review, the Hibernate Mapping File is an XML document that tells the Hibernate API how to persist a Java class to a relational database. There are four core elements to a mapping file:

❑   The class-to-table mapping

❑   An `id` element to identify the primary key of the table

❑   Property-to-column mapping

❑   Relationships with other persistent objects

The XML file contains a document type definition (DTD) that specifies the required and optional methods of the file:

```
<?xml version="1.0" encoding="UTF-8"?>
<!DOCTYPE hibernate-mapping PUBLIC
"-//Hibernate/Hibernate Mapping DTD 3.0//EN"
"http://hibernate.sourceforge.net/hibernate-mapping-3.0.dtd" >
<hibernate-mapping>
```

The `class` element maps the class name with the database table name:

```
<class name="wrox.ch6.dm.Book" table="BOOK">
```

The `id` element is required for the mapping because all classes require an ID. Hibernate can determine an object's identity, so for example, Hibernate can look at the ID value and determine whether an update or insert statement needs to be run for this object. You also need to specify how the ID value is obtained. Native, specified in the mapping, means to use the default based on the database, but there are a number of options Hibernate provides and you will look at those when you configure the database in the next section:

```
<id name="id" column="BOOKID">
  <generator class="native"></generator>
  </id>
```

The next part of the mapping file is the persistent property-to-column mapping:

```
<property name="title" column="TITLE" type="string"></property>
  <property name="created" column="CREATEDON" type="timestamp" update="false" />
</class>
</hibernate-mapping>
```

The only part missing from this example is the fourth item: relationships with other persistent objects. This includes common database relationships such as many-to-one, one-to-many, and many-to-many, and are discussed later. For now you have a simple class-to-table mapping with no relationships defined. This definition would read as:

"Class Book is mapped to table BOOK with an ID property id corresponding primary key column BOOKID in the BOOK table. Two persistent properties created and title map to CREATEDON and TITLE within the BOOK table".

The next section looks at that the `hibernate.cfg.xml` file, where you specify global properties with Hibernate.

Hibernate Configuration File

There is typically only one `hibernate.cfg.xml` file in your application. There are several options in the configuration file. A complete listing is available at `www.hibernate.org`. In general, the configuration defines the mapped files, the database connection information, and which database dialect to use when generating SQL. SQL syntax varies depending on the RDMS. The `Dialect` class encapsulates these differences. For example, to get the first ten rows from a query in Oracle the `SELECT` statement would be:

```
SELECT * FROM BOOK where rownum < 10
```

But in Microsoft SQLServer:

```
SELEC TOP 10 * from BOOK
```

There are dialects defined for a majority of commercial and open-source database systems. This example utilizes the APACHE DerbyDialect and provides database connection information in the Hibernate configuration file. Derby is being used because it's distributed as part of the JAVA 1.6 JDK. Derby is a pure Java relational database and is a good workgroup-level RDBMS.

There are several other properties to highlight. `show_sql` will print to the standard output, all the SQL being executed. `hibernate.hbm2ddl.auto` will automatically create the database tables based on the mapping files defined. This option is just for development! Having Hibernate create the database definition is a good way to learn how to build relational mappings:

```
<!DOCTYPE hibernate-configuration PUBLIC
  "-//Hibernate/Hibernate Configuration DTD 3.0//EN"
  "http://hibernate.sourceforge.net/hibernate-configuration-3.0.dtd">
<hibernate-configuration>
  <session-factory>
   <property name="show_sql">true</property>
   <property name="hibernate.dialect" >org.hibernate.dialect.DerbyDialect
 </property>
   <property name="hibernate.connection.driver_class">
   org.apache.derby.jdbc.ClientDriver
 </property>
   <property name="hibernate.hbm2ddl.auto">create-drop</property>
   <property name="hibernate.connection.username">APP</property>
   <property name="hibernate.connection.password">password</property>

   <property name="hibernate.connection.url">
     jdbc:derby://localhost:1527/wrox;create=true
 </property>
```

Finally, specify the mapped resource, in this case the location of the `Book.hbm.xml` mapping file you defined in the previous section.

```
<mapping resource="wrox/ch6/dm/Book.hbm.xml"/>
  </session-factory>
</hibernate-configuration>
```

Hibernate API

The Hibernate API contains all the resources required to support persistence, implementing the mappings, database transaction, as well as two robust query models. This section highlights a few of the classes used in most persistence scenarios. These resources reside in the `org.hibernate.*` package.

Class / Interface	Description
SessionFactory	Contains the database metadata and Java class information for performing persistent operations. The session factory is typically created at startup based on the `hibernate.cfg.xml` file stored either as a single static class reference or bound to a JNDI object registry.
Session	The entry point for all persistent operations. It has simple methods for loading and saving objects as well as responsibility as a factory method for creating the `Transaction`, `Query` and `Criteria` interfaces. The `Session` is designed to be short lived, created and destroyed per request.
Transaction	Interface that ensures that a database operation happens within a designated transaction.
Query	Interface that retrieves objects using a SQL-like language call Hibernate Query Language (HQL).
Criteria	Interface that is more object-oriented than the `Query` interface. Both have slightly differing behavior and preference might dictate which you gravitate toward. The `Criteria` API is very effective at creating dynamic SQL requests at runtime.

This concludes the section for introducing Hibernate. The following section provides an example that displays common functionality used in everyday Hibernate development.

Hibernate Example

This example builds upon your understanding of the core Hibernate components. It begins by setting up the environment including the Hibernate dependencies and the new Java database, formerly known as Apache Derby. Then you will build your domain model in this chapter by adding other classes and relationships to the Book Club domain model. Finally, you'll see various methods of retrieving objects via the `Query` and `Criteria` APIs discussed in the previous section.

Setup

Setup involves configuring the database server and database connection in Hibernate.

Apache Derby, the database used for the following examples, is now bundled with JDK1.6 starting with build number 88. All you need to do to get up and running is start the database server:

```
set JAVA_HOME=C:\Program Files\Java\jdk1.6.0
set DERBY_INSTALL=%JAVA_HOME%\db
set
CLASSPATH=%CLASSPATH%;%DERBY_INSTALL%\lib\derby.jar;%DERBY_INSTALL%\lib\derbytools.
jar;%DERBY_INSTALL%\lib\derbynet.jar;
cd %DERBY_INSTALL%\frameworks\NetworkServer\bin
startNetworkServer.bat
```

You should see the message in Figure 6-5.

Figure 6-5

Now that your database server is up and running you can connect to it via Hibernate. As you recall the `Hibernate.cfg.xml` specified the Derby connection information and pointed to the mapped class `Book`. Next, create a class to handle the creation of your `SessionFactory`.

HibernateUtil

This example uses a utility class to create and store the `SessionFactory`. The application will share a static `SessionFactory`:

```
package wrox.ch6.util;

import org.hibernate.Session;
import org.hibernate.SessionFactory;
```

```
import org.hibernate.cfg.Configuration;

public class HibernateUtil {
private static SessionFactory sf;
```

When you run `configure().buildSessionFactory()`, Hibernate looks for a `hibernate.cfg.xml` file within the root of your application's classpath. You can specify a different location as parameter. This will cause the mapping information specified in the configuration file to be loaded into the `SessionFactory`. The application calls `currentSession()` to save and load objects via Hibernate:

```
static {
  sf = new Configuration().configure().buildSessionFactory();
}

public static Session currentSession() {
  return sf.openSession();
}

public static void close(Session session) {
  session.close();
}
}
```

In the next section you create a class called `BookManager` to handle all of Hibernate's API calls.

Book Manager

The book manager class will encapsulate calls to the Hibernate API:

```
package wrox.ch6.example;

import java.util.Date;

import org.hibernate.HibernateException;
import org.hibernate.Session;
import org.hibernate.Transaction;
import wrox.ch6.dm.Book;
import wrox.ch6.util.HibernateUtil;

public class BookManager {
  Session s = HibernateUtil.currentSession();

  public void save(Book book) {

    try {
      Transaction tx = s.beginTransaction();
      s.saveOrUpdate(book);
      tx.commit();
    } catch (HibernateException e) {

      e.printStackTrace();
```

```
    }
  }
  public static void main(String[] args) {
    Book book = new Book();
    book.setTitle("Lucas: nine months and counting.");
    book.setCreated(new Date());

    BookManager manager = new BookManager();
    manager.save(book);
  }
}
```

The following output was produced after running the example. It's been filtered so you are only looking at some key logging statements. The first line indicates that Hibernate has found the mapping file and is mapping the Book class to the BOOK table. The second line shows that the property hibernate .hbm2ddl.auto caused Hibernate to create the BOOK table in Derby. And the third shows Hibernate created the insert statement for the book object you created:

```
INFO: Mapping class: wrox.ch6.dm.Book -> BOOK
...
Aug 4, 2006 3:49:47 PM org.hibernate.tool.hbm2ddl.SchemaExport execute
INFO: schema export complete
...
Hibernate: insert into BOOK (TITLE, CREATED, BOOKID) values (?, ?, ?)
```

If you browse the database with an administrative tool, you will see that the Book object was inserted as a record with an auto-generated primary key of one, shown in Figure 6-6.

BOOKID [BIGINT]	TITLE [VARCHAR(255)]	CREATED [TIMESTAMP]
	Lucas: nine months and counting.	8/4/06 3:36:19 PM

Figure 6-6

Consider this question: "What if you were to change the title and save it again? Would Hibernate insert another record or update the existing one?"

First, add a load to retrieve Book from the database via the primary key:

```
public Book load(Long id) {
    Book book = null;

    try {
      Transaction tx = s.beginTransaction();
      book = (Book) s.load(Book.class, id);
      tx.commit();
    } catch (HibernateException e) {

      e.printStackTrace();
    }
    return book;
  }
```

Then load the object and update the title property and save again:

```
. . .
book = manager.load(new Long(1) );
book.setTitle("Lucas: Born Oct 30 2005 ");
manager.save( book);
```

The console output shows an update instead of an insert. Because the id field was not null, Hibernate knew to update an existing row. Also note: the created property was not in the update statement because it was mapped with update="false" in the Book.hbm.xml file:

```
Hibernate: update BOOK set TITLE=? where BOOKID=?
```

That was a simple example of creating persistent objects. The real strength of an ORM solution is mapping the relationships between data associations. In the next section, you build a domain model to illustrate relationship mapping.

Hibernate Example

In this section you build your domain model by adding persistent classes and adding relationships to the existing Book class. The abstraction will be of a Book Club so you will add Member, Review, Address, and Genre to the domain model. Figure 6-7 shows the domain model in UML notation.

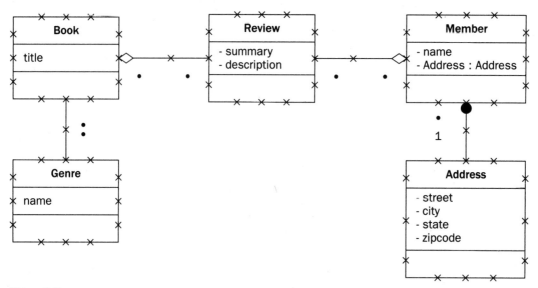

Figure 6-7

These classes will map to the relational database tables specified in Figure 6-8.

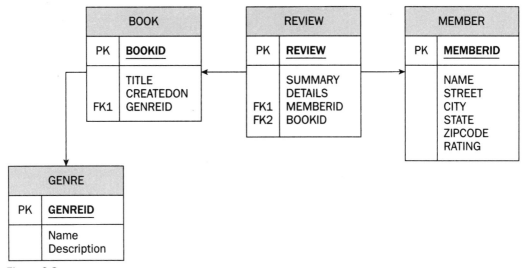

Figure 6-8

To make the modifications, first create the Genre and data properties with the same steps used to create the `Book` class:

❑ Define the Java class with persistent properties.

❑ Create the mapping file specifying the id entity as well as the name and description properties.

❑ Add the new `Genre.hbm.xml` file to the `hibernate.cfg.xml`.

Now create a many-to-one association between the Genre and Book as described by the model.

Many-to-One

A many-to-one relationship between Book and Genre states that a Book can have only one Genre association. For that reason a Book instance will have a reference to a single Genre object, and the BOOK table will have a foreign key defined that references the GENREID id.

First, add the association to the `Book` class:

```
public class Book {

    private long id;
    private String title;
    private Date created = new Date();
    private Genre genre;

    public Genre getGenre() {
        return genre;
    }
```

```
    public void setGenre(Genre genre) {
        this.genre = genre;
    }
// other methods omitted for brevity
}
```

Next, modify the `Book.hbm.xml` file to declare the many-to-one association:

```
<?xml version="1.0" encoding="UTF-8"?>
<!DOCTYPE hibernate-mapping PUBLIC
"-//Hibernate/Hibernate Mapping DTD 3.0//EN"
"http://hibernate.sourceforge.net/hibernate-mapping-3.0.dtd" >
<hibernate-mapping>
  <class name="wrox.ch6.dm.Book" table="BOOK">
  // omitted previous mapping

    <many-to-one name="genre" column="GENREID"
      class="wrox.ch6.dm.Genre" />
</class>
</hibernate-mapping>
```

The name references the name of the property and the column references the foreign key column in the BOOK table. Hibernate will assign the foreign key automatically.

Modify the test code to save the Book object:

```
    Genre genre = new Genre( );
    genre.setName("Children's");
    Book book = new Book();
    book.setTitle("Lucas: nine months and counting.");
    book.setCreated(new Date());
    book.setGenre(genre);
    BookManager manager = new BookManager();
    manager.save(book);
```

If you run this as-is, an exception will occur:

```
org.hibernate.TransientObjectException: wrox.ch6.dm.Genre
  at org.hibernate.engine.ForeignKeys.getEntityIdentifierIfNotUnsaved(ForeignKeys
.java:216)
  at org.hibernate.type.EntityType.getIdentifier(EntityType.java:108)
...
```

Hibernate couldn't figure out the foreign key for the Book class. This is because the Genre had not been saved. You could either explicitly `save()` and `load()` the genre class, or you could update the mapping and set the cascade property to `cascade="save-update"`.

Modifying the mapping looks like this:

```
    <many-to-one name="genre" column="GENREID" cascade="save-update"
      class="wrox.ch6.dm.Genre" />
```

With this change, the code will execute successfully, ordering the insert statements appropriately:

```
Hibernate: insert into GENRE (name, description, GENREID) values (?, ?, ?)
Hibernate: insert into BOOK (TITLE, CREATED, GENREID, BOOKID) values (?,?, ?, ?)
```

In the next section, you map the Member class using the components.

Mapping Components

The class Member has a component called Address but there is no associated Address table in the database. The address columns are part of the MEMBER table. The component mapping provides the ability to have fine-grain control over the object model and doesn't require a strict table-to-object mapping policy.

First, define the Member and Address classes done previously for Book and Genre. Next, add the mapping for Member. You do not need a mapping file for Address because it will be contained within the Member mapping file as a component declaration.

The Member class needs the object association Address:

```java
package wrox.ch6.dm;

public class Member {
    long id;
    String name;
    Address address;

    public Member() {

    }
    public long getId() {
        return id;
    }
    public void setId(long id) {
        this.id = id;
    }

    public Address getAddress() {
        return address;
    }

    public void setAddress(Address address) {
        this.address = address;
    }

}
```

Next, declare the component in the Member.hbm.xml file:

```xml
<class name="wrox.ch6.dm.Member" table="MEMBER">
  <id name="id" column="MEMBERID">
    <generator class="native"></generator>
  </id>
```

```
            <component name="address" class="wrox.ch6.dm.Address">
                <property name="street" />
                <property name="city" />
                <property name="state" />
                <property name="zipcode" />
            </component>
    <!--  other mappings omitted -->
    </class>
```

Also note that you did not declare the column or type attributes in the mapping, because these are optional for both classes and component properties. Hibernate will use reflection to figure out the default data types and column names.

Mapping Collections

So far you've created associations that relate one object to another. This section discusses mappings that relate one object to a collection of other objects.

Before doing that, Figure 6-9 illustrates the "instance view" of the objects in your domain model. Each book can be associated with one or more reviews and each member can write one or more reviews.

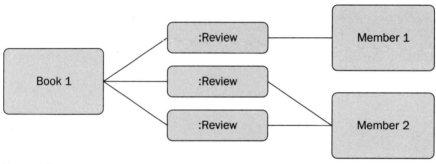

Figure 6-9

The steps to add this to the domain model are:

❑   Update the Book and Member class definitions to support a Set attribute.

❑   Declare the <set> element within the Mapping file.

The book class needs a collection to reference the Review objects. This example uses a Set because each review is unique. Hibernate supports several collection types: List, Bag, and Map. Each has its own restrictions based on the Collection contract. For example, a List would need to be ordered. The add method makes sure that the association between Book and Review will be bi-directional.

The Member class will mirror the Book class. The Book class now looks like the following:

```
public class Book {

    private long id;
    private String title;
```

```
        private Date created = new Date();
        private Genre genre;

        private Set<Review> reviews = new HashSet<Review>();

        public Book() {

        public Set<Review> getReviews() {
          return reviews;
        }
        public void setReviews(Set<Review> reviews) {
          this.reviews = reviews;
        }
```

Within the `Book` class you have defined a bi-directional link between Review and Book. Then you added a convenience method to make sure the links are in both the `Book` and the `Review` classes.

```
        public void addReview( Review review){
          review.setBook(this);
          reviews.add(review);
        }
}
```

For this to be complete, add many-to-one relationships to the `Review` class for both `Book` and `Member`:

```
<?xml version="1.0" encoding="UTF-8"?>
<!DOCTYPE hibernate-mapping PUBLIC "-//Hibernate/Hibernate Mapping DTD 3.0//EN"
"http://hibernate.sourceforge.net/hibernate-mapping-3.0.dtd" >
<hibernate-mapping>
<class name="wrox.ch6.dm.Review" table="REVIEW" >

<id name="id" column="REVIEWID" >
  <generator class="native"></generator>
</id>
<many-to-one name="book" class="wrox.ch6.dm.Book"  >
  <column name="BOOKID" />
</many-to-one>

<many-to-one name="member" class="wrox.ch6.dm.Member" >
  <column name="MEMBERID" />
</many-to-one>
</class>
```

The next step is to update the Book mapping file. The set elements reference the set property by name. The key column is the foreign key in the review table:

```
<?xml version="1.0" encoding="UTF-8"?>
<!DOCTYPE hibernate-mapping PUBLIC
"-//Hibernate/Hibernate Mapping DTD 3.0//EN"
"http://hibernate.sourceforge.net/hibernate-mapping-3.0.dtd" >
<hibernate-mapping>
  <class name="wrox.ch6.dm.Book" table="BOOK">
    <id name="id" column="BOOKID">
      <generator class="native"></generator>
```

```
        </id>
<!—omitted other methods -!>
        <set name="reviews" lazy="true" inverse="true" cascade="all-delete-orphan" >
            <key column="BOOKID" />
            <one-to-many class="wrox.ch6.dm.Review" />
        </set>
</class>
```

The three properties `lazy="true"`, `inverse="true"`, and `cascade="all-delete-orphan"` are all important and worth mentioning. Cascade was discussed previously when looking at inserting the `Genre` and `Book` records. The behavior you want is that if a review is added to a book, the review is saved when the book is saved. But, you also would like the `Review` deleted if the `Book` is deleted. This is determined by how you design ownership within the Domain model. The inverse attribute is like a hint; it tells Hibernate that you have declared a bi-directional relationship. The problem is that if you add a Review to a book, the object reference to Book is detected as changed in two places, the book collection and the review association. Hibernate cannot tell that they are two ends of the same associated record. The inverse flag tells Hibernate to create only one UPDATE statement.

And finally, the `lazy` attribute has to do with object retrieval. When you request a Book from the database, Hibernate will not automatically populate the reviews for the database. It will select all the reviews once you request the first review. If you would have set `lazy` to `false`, then Hibernate would have created an outer join between Book and Review and retrieved all the objects with a single SELECT statement:

```
SELECT b.*, r.* from BOOK b OUTER JOIN REVIEW r on r.bookid – b.bookid
```

Hibernate maps the tabular SQL query result to an object graph, deleting the duplicate book information. Mapping as lazy is a good practice because you can change the behavior at runtime using the query APIs.

In this example you can now add reviews to a book, save books, and have the changes persisted to the database:

```
        Review review = new Review();
        review.setSummary("Outstanding");
        review.setDetails("The best I've read all day.");
        review.setRating(5);
        review.setMember(lucas);

        Review r2 = new Review ();
        r2.setSummary("Great.");
        r2.setRating(5);
        r2.setMember(heather);

        book.addReview(review);
        book.addReview(r2);
        manager.save(book);
```

Adding Review to the Set in the book is why it is important to declare the `equals()` and `hashcode()` methods.

This concludes mapping collections. The next section examines and builds queries against the domain model using the `Criteria` and `Query` interfaces provided by Hibernate.

Criteria Interface

The `Criteria` interface is for querying objects by object property. The `Criteria` interface is extremely powerful at building dynamic SQL. In the next example you build a dynamic `Criteria` method for looking up books called `findBooks`.

`findBooks()` takes a series of parameters as restrictions. This first step is to create a `Criteria` object from the Hibernate session using `Book` as the object you would like to return.

Then, based on the method parameters, you can limit each property by adding Restrictions:

```
public Collection<Book> findBooks(String title, Date start, Date end,
    Integer rating, String genre, int rows) {
  List l = null;

  try {
    Criteria c = s.createCriteria(Book.class);
```

Title is a simple property of a book. The `ilike` function will translate into `%title%` for wildcard searching:

```
    if (title != null) {
      c.add(Restrictions.ilike("title", title, MatchMode.ANYWHERE ));
    }
    if (start != null && end != null) {
      Restrictions.between("created", start, end);
    }
```

By limiting books by genre, you are performing an implicit join on the GENRE table, just like it was any other property:

```
    if ( genre != null ) {
      c.add( Restrictions.eq("genre.name", genre));
    }
```

This example will also limit by rating because rating is a property in the review table, and there is a one-to-many association with reviews. You would create an alias to join the review and book tables, and then you could reference the review properties based on your alias.

This is similar to writing SQL:

```
SELECT b.* FROM BOOK b JOIN Review rev on b.bookid = rev.bookid WHERE rev.RATING
= ?
    if (rating != null) {
      c.createAlias("reviews", "rev");
      c.add(Restrictions.eq("rev.rating", rating));
    }
    l = c.setMaxResults(rows).list();

  } catch (HibernateException e) {
```

```
        e.printStackTrace();
    }
    return 1;
}
```

For convenience, you can also limit the results returned using the `setMaxResults()` method.

Now, if you run this example, there is some behavior you might not expect. `displayBooks` is an example of setting restrictions on title, rating, and genre:

```
public void displayBooks( ) {
  Collection <Book> books = findBooks("months", null, null,5, null, 25);
  for ( Book b : books ) {
    System.out.println(" books title [" +b.getTitle()+"]" );
    Collection<Review> reviews = b.getReviews();
    for ( Review r : reviews) {
      System.out.println(" review summary ["+ r.getSummary() +"] rating [" +
r.getRating() +"]" );

    }
  }
}
```

This is the output:

```
books title [Lucas: nine months and crawling.]
  review summary [Great.] rating [5]
  review summary [Outstanding] rating [5]
books title [Lucas: nine months and crawling.]
  review summary [Great.] rating [5]
  review summary [Outstanding] rating [5]
```

You were looking for a list of books with a rating of five, but you have one book with two separate reviews with a rating of five. So you have two of the same book returned in the results because of the SQL join! What you wanted was a distinct list of books that matched your `Criteria`. Modify the `Criteria` object to return a distinct set of `Book` objects:

```
          l = c.setMaxResults(rows)
        .setResultTransformer(Criteria.DISTINCT_ROOT_ENTITY)
        .list();
    } catch (HibernateException e) {
      e.printStackTrace();
    }
Re-executing the method produced the desired results. The matching Book is only
returned once as part of the results::books title [Lucas: nine months and
crawling.]
  review summary [Great job..] rating [5]
  review summary [Outstanding..] rating [5]
```

This concludes the example using the `Criteria` interface. The next section focuses on the second object retrieval interface Hibernate supports, the `Query` interface.

Query Interface

The `Query` interface provides similar functionality to the `Criteria` interface, except the syntax is closer to traditional SQL. The `Query` interface uses Hibernate Query Language or HQL. The following code listing shows an example HQL query:

```
FROM Member where address.zipcode in (:zips )
```

There are a few things to note, however. First of all, there is no SELECT clause. The SELECT clause is optional in HQL because the API will return objects of type `Member`. Secondly, note the use of named parameters within the HQL statement. Standard JDBC parameters are marked by question marks (?) and referenced by numeric location. In HQL you can reorder the where clause elements without affecting the results. And lastly, the `zipcode` parameter is not a single value but a list:

```
public Collection<Member> findMembers( List<String> zipcodes  ) {

    List l = null;
    String hql = "FROM Member where address.zipcode in (:zips ) ";

    try {
      Query q = s.createQuery(hql);
      q.setParameterList("zips", zipcodes);
      l = q.list();
    } catch (HibernateException e) {

      e.printStackTrace( );
    }
    return l;
  }
```

If there are two zipcodes in the parameter list, this roughly translates into SQL as:

```
SELECT * from MEMBER where zipcode in (? , ? );
```

The two strengths of the HQL language are that it's familiar to those who are comfortable working with SQL and it allows the developer to make use of SQL-style joins to limit results based on related table restrictions.

To rewrite the previous `Criteria` query for `Book` classes in HQL, use the following:

```
FROM Book book join book.reviews r where r.rating = :rating
```

In this case, the join is caused by the relationship mapped between the `Book` and `Review` classes. But HQL can create a Cartesian join, relating properties that are not mapped as a relationship. This is something that cannot be done with the `Criteria` interface.

For example, there is no relationship defined between the `Member` class and the book's author. If you need to find out that a book club member is also an author you would build a Cartesian join using the HSQL API:

```
FROM Book book, Member member where member.name = book.author.name
```

353

This has only scratched the surface of what is possible with HQL, but it should give you a feel for querying for objects from an Object domain model.

Summary

This chapter examined two distinct approaches to saving persistent data to a relational database. The first section looked at JDBC 4.0 for executing database commands and manipulating tabular result sets. The second section looked at mapping object data to relational tables and using an ORM tool to persist object data on your behalf. Both solutions should warrant careful consideration when designing database applications.

The next chapter switches gears and focuses on developing user interfaces for web-based applications using the Model 1 development architecture.

7

Developing Web Applications Using the Model 1 Architecture

Look into any web application, and you should recognize the presence of some web navigation scheme that dictates how pages should flow along with the data that needs to be processed with them. Some applications employ Model 1 Architecture practices that hard code these flows in the pages that comprise their web applications, whereas others use Model 2 practices that embed flow attributes in an external file so that maintenance and navigation paths can be handled outside the code itself. Inevitably, speculations during the design phase of your program will have to be made as to which method will be put into practice prior to software deployment. Outside influences, like experimentation and lessons learned from previous engagements ("been there, done that, got the T-shirt"), could be used in your decision making, but more likely, delivery timelines, staff maturity, and scheduling constraints will affect this decision.

This chapter demonstrates how you can overcome speculation over how to construct a web application using the Model 1 Architecture by constructing a hands-on Contact Management Tool. Two different types of Java syntax, JSTL 1.1 and JSP 2.0, will be utilized to craft the sample GUI component that will allow users to manage contact information through upload and query activities. The sample application's use of Model 1 was chosen to suit design and implementation needs for a quick prototype that can be implemented by novice Java Web developers in an easy fashion, and to demonstrate some of the new Java language enhancements that were delivered with the JSTL 1.1 and JSP 2.0 specifications.

Additionally, consideration is shown for the very popular AJAX technology and some language extensions that circumvent traditional request/response operations accompanying web page submission and refresh activities.

What Is Model 1? Why Use It?

The Model 1 Architecture is a *page-centric* approach where page flows are handled by individual web components. This means that request and response processing are hard-coded into pages to accommodate user navigations in a web application. With Model 2 Architecture, navigation flows are generally handled by a servlet controller that works in conjunction with configuration files to dictate page renderings during application operations.

Naturally, this presents maintenance problems when logic modifications are needed to accommodate changes in requirements and end-user needs. Those changes would oblige developers to comb through code to ensure that all logic flows are properly handled as users navigate through a web application. Along with the responsibilities of maintaining navigation flow in Model 1 deployments is the need to manage concerns regarding security and application state.

Model 1 Architecture concerns are certainly difficult design decisions to tackle at the inception of a project, but limitations in your team's development expertise, the scope of your application, and time to delivery might persuade you to adopt this development philosophy to get your project going. Adoption of the Model 1 philosophy is not necessarily a bad decision depending on your predicament and your estimation of what and how your team will deliver in an allotted delivery schedule. Model 2 implementations would most likely help you overcome maintenance issues in the long run, so it is paramount that your team overcomes its deficiencies by practicing with Model 2 frameworks and their configurations to better understand their intricacies so that your earlier Model 1 applications can be migrated fairly easily.

Figure 7-1 provides a high-level overview of a Model 1 template used for the sample Contact Management application that will be built to demonstrate web application assembly combining JSP and JSTL technologies. Notice the individual JSP components (`header`, `leftNav`, `content`, and `footer`) that are all aggregated in the home page. As a user navigates the taxonomy in the application, indexes are established and passed along all of the individual pages so that operations can be performed inside those pages based on those indexes.

On many web application components, content is typically retrieved from JavaBean components that persist data on the back-end tier of an enterprise system for visualization on the client tier. The sample application modeled in Figure 7-1 aggregates content from a MySQL database by using indexes from the left panel drill-down to determine proper page inclusion demonstrated in the following `content.jsp` code. When a user clicks the initial Tasks link in the left panel, three navigation links will be presented (Add Profile, Add Contact, and View Contacts) so contact names can be saved and queried:

```
<!--content.jsp -+
<%@ taglib prefix="c" uri="http://java.sun.com/jstl/core" %>

<link href="CMS.css" rel="stylesheet" type="text/css">

<c:if test="${param.taxonomyIndex == '101'}">
    <jsp:include page="addProfile.jsp"/>
</c:if>

<c:if test="${param.taxonomyIndex == '102'}">
    <jsp:include page="addContact.jsp"/>
</c:if>

<c:if test="${param.taxonomyIndex == '103'}">
    <jsp:include page="viewContacts.jsp"/>
</c:if>
```

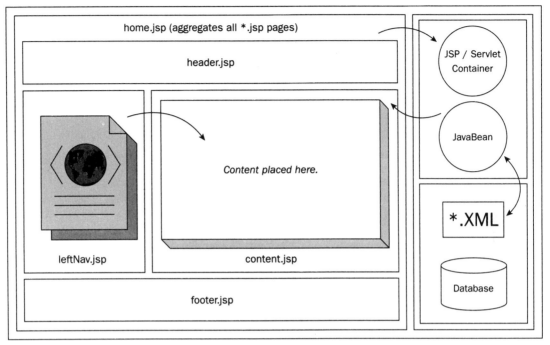

Figure 7-1

The Expression Language (EL) construct `<c:if>` is used in `content.jsp` to evaluate the three different test conditions so that the appropriate JSP script will be included, which will in turn collect the proper content for visualization.

Java Server Page (JSP) 2.0 and Java Standard Template Library (JSTL) 1.1 are both important web application components for constructing dynamic content on J2EE platforms. JSP 2.0 scripts can easily construct HTML content and access JavaBean properties through Expression Language libraries. JSTL components encapsulate functionalities that allow developers to iterate through data, perform XSLT transform operations, and access both database and object data. Both technologies can be combined to craft presentation-tier components to display and interact with back-end data models.

This section discusses JSP 2.0 and JSTL 1.1 technologies by presenting overviews of their capabilities followed by some individual components of their libraries and demonstrates their usage in figures and source code listings.

JSP 2.0 Overview

The viability of the Model 1 Architecture depends heavily on a number of the new features in the JSP 2.0 specification. In this section you learn about the following:

❏ Servlet 2.4 specification support

❏ Expression Language (EL) support

❏ Code reuse with .tag and .tagx files

❑   JSP page extensions (.jspx)

❑   Simple Invocation Protocol

The introduction of these new script language constructs with the JSP 2.0 and JSTL 1.1 specifications was meant to eliminate the need to include Java expressions in script code, which would result in scriptless page development. These enhancements will certainly provide more controlled interactions and flexibility with other components as well as reusability among common actions.

Servlet 2.4 Support

The JSP 2.0 specification uses the Servlet 2.4 specification for its syntax, which allows applications to handle Expression Language (EL) expressions as native syntax.

The following table describes some of the ServletRequest methods that were introduced with the Servlet 2.4 specification to determine client connection attributes.

Method	Description
getRemotePort()	Method that returns the IP address of the port that sent a request
getLocalName()	Method that returns the hostname of the IP address from which the request was received
getLocalAddr()	Method that returns the IP address from which the request was received
getLocalPort()	Method that returns the IP port number from which the request was received

This code segment illustrates how these methods can be implemented to realize these client connection values:

```
<html>
<head>
<title>Servlet 2.4 Features</title>
</head>
<body>
<h2>Servlet 2.4 Features</h2>
<%
out.println("Remote Port : " + request.getRemotePort() + "<br>");
out.println("Local Name : " + request.getLocalName() + "<br>");
out.println("Local Address : " + request.getLocalAddr() + "<br>");
out.println("Local Port : " + request.getLocalPort() + "<br>");
%>
</body>
</html>
```

After this code snippet is executed, the four different system parameters will be rendered to the user display. In addition to these capabilities, the new Servlet 2.4 feature support includes the introduction of new features for the RequestDispatcher and ServletRequest listener classes, as well as login operations related to the HttpSession class.

Expression Language Support

The Expression Language (EL) implementation in JSP 2.0 allows easy access to data from JSP script components. Language enhancements allow developers to avoid writing scriptlets inside their pages, which should result in cleaner and more readable JSP pages.

EL syntax is purported to be more user-friendly than Java and was introduced to encourage its use for accessing data over Java language implementations. The power of EL constructs is that they allow users to embed Java code in a Java Server Page through scripting elements. Three types of scripting elements are shown in the following table.

Scripting Element	Example
Expressions	`<jsp:expression> objectRef.loadValues()` `</:jsp:expression>`
Scriptlets	`<% for (int increment = 0; increment < 25;` `increment++) { }`
Declarations	`<%! boolean firstPass = true; %>`

The following JSP and JavaBean components use EL features to perform Pig Latin word translations and string replacement operations. The tag library prefix `test` is used to access the `pigLatin` and `dw Replacement` methods to perform string operations on user-specified text that is saved in the `sample Text` parameter. For those not familiar with Pig Latin, it can be described as a silly word twisting exercise that takes words starting with consonants and moves that letter to the end of the word and adds "ay" to that consonant, and words that start with a vowel have "ay" appended to them on the back end:

```
<%-- index.jsp --%>
<%@ taglib prefix="test" uri="/WEB-INF/el-taglib.tld"%>

<html>
  <head>
    <title>Expression Language Examples</title>
  </head>
  <body>
  <h1>Expression Language Examples</h1>

  <form action="functions.jsp" method="GET">
  sampleText = <input type="text" name="sampleText"value="${param['sampleText']}">
        <input type="submit">
  </form>

  <table border="0">
  <tr>
    <td bgcolor="#ffff99">Pig-Latin = </td>
    <td bgcolor="#ffff99">${test:pigLatin(param["sampleText"])} </td>
  </tr>
  <tr>
    <td bgcolor="#ffff99">Dirty Word Replacement = </td>
    <td bgcolor="#ffff99">${test:dwReplacement(param["sampleText"])} </td>
  </tr>
```

```
    </table>

  </body>
</html>
```

The following Java method performs regular expression string manipulation operations on the text expressions specified by the user in the text field components of index.jsp. For the pigLatin method, a check is performed on the first character of the string passed in to see if that character is a vowel; if so, the string will be returned with the word "way" appended to the end of it. Strings that start with consonants will have their first character moved to the end of the string and then have "ay" added to the end of string:

```java
// [StringMethods.java]
package examples.el;

import java.util.*;
import java.util.regex.*;

public class StringMethods {

    public static String pigLatin( String text) {
        // works for one word ONLY
        Pattern pattern = Pattern.compile("^([aeiouAEIOU])");
        Matcher matcher = pattern.matcher(text);
        if (matcher.find())
            return text+"way";
        else
            return text.replaceAll("^([^aeiouAEIOU])(.+)", "$2$1ay");
    }

    public static String dwReplacement( String text ) {
        Pattern pattern = Pattern.compile("(darn|damn|stupid|dummy)");
        Matcher matcher = pattern.matcher(text);
        text = matcher.replaceAll("#%&@");
        return text;
    }
}
```

This tag library definition file defines the two different text functions, pigLatin and dwReplacement, that are invoked in the index.jsp file and defined in StringMethods.java:

```xml
<!-- el-taglib.tld -->
<?xml version="1.0" encoding="UTF-8" ?>

<taglib xmlns="http://java.sun.com/xml/ns/j2ee"
    xmlns:xsi="http://www.w3.org/2001/XMLSchema-instance"
    xsi:schemaLocation="http://java.sun.com/xml/ns/j2ee web-jsptaglibrary_2_0.xsd"
    version="2.0">

    <description>Function Examples</description>
    <tlib-version>1.0</tlib-version>
    <short-name>Function Examples</short-name>
    <uri>/el</uri>

    <function>
```

```
      <description>PIG-Latin</description>
            <name>pigLatin</name>
      <function-class>examples.el.StringMethods</function-class>
      <function-signature>
         java.lang.String pigLatin( java.lang.String )
      </function-signature>
      </function>
      <function>
      <description>Dirty Word Replacement</description>
            <name>dwReplacement</name>
      <function-class>examples.el.StringMethods</function-class>
      <function-signature>
         java.lang.String dwReplacement( java.lang.String )
      </function-signature>
      </function>

</taglib>
```

As this example demonstrates, EL library extensions are powerful features that strengthen developer's capabilities for web development. The function methods described here are easily mapped to public static methods in Java classes that can be accessed by EL constructs throughout your web application.

Code Reuse with .tag and .tagx Files

The implementation of .tag and .tagx file syntax delivered with JSP 2.0 implementations allows for better code reuse by enabling developers to encapsulate common behavior that can be easily shared across components. Those familiar with older code conventions used to craft custom tag libraries should recognize this and embrace these amendments for defining reusable custom actions with great enthusiasm.

The following code snippet demonstrates how tag files can be implemented for reuse by other web applications. In this example, a portlet-like visualization component is crafted using a tagged file named portlet.tag. Two parameters, title and color, are passed into the portlet tag file to dynamically alter those properties in the component display:

```
<%@ taglib prefix="tags" tagdir="/WEB-INF/tags" %>
<html>
<head><title>tagx test</title>
</head>
<body>
<table width="100%"><tr><td>
   <tags:portlet title="Portlet" color="#0000ff"> Test 1 </tags:portlet>
</td></tr></table>
</body>
</html>
```

The portlet.tag file encapsulates the portlet component and renders the title and color features passed into the file by the preceding script:

```
<!--portlet.tag -->
<%@ attribute name="title" required="true" %>
<%@ attribute name="color" required="true" %>

<table width="250" border="1" cellpadding="2" cellspacing="0">
  <tr bgcolor="${color}" color="#ffffff">
```

```
    <td nowrap>
      ${title}
    </td>
  </tr>
  <tr>
    <td valign="top">
      &#149;  <a href="">Test1</a><br>
      &#149;  <a href="">Test2</a><br>
    </td>
  </tr>
</table>
```

After this code is run, a simple portlet-like component is displayed with two test references embedded in it. What the reader should take away from this is how easily this syntax can be implemented to generate custom tags and share them across a project's code base. Consideration might be given for implementing tag files in header and footer implementations that contain common information that can be easily propagated to the other web pages with their inclusion.

JSP Page Extensions (.jspx)

Java Server Page 2.0 syntax has included .jspx extensions that are meant to advocate the use of XML syntax to generate XML documents in JSP 2.0-compliant web containers. The following code describes how .jspx files can be implemented when you develop web applications to generate user displays:

```
<!--forms.jspx -->
<?xml version="1.0"?>
<tags:test xmlns:tags="urn:jsptagdir:/WEB-INF/tags"
           xmlns:jsp="http://java.sun.com/JSP/Page"
           xmlns:c="http://java.sun.com/jsp/jstl/core"
           xmlns="http://www.w3.org/1999/xhtml">
<jsp:directive.page contentType='text/html'/>
<head><title>Form Test</title></head>
<body>
  <c:choose>
  <c:when test='${param.name == null} and ${param.address == null}'>
     <form action="form.jspx">
        Please enter your name and address:<br/>
        <input name="name" size="40"/><br/>
        <input name="address" size="40"/><br/>
        <input type="submit"/>
     </form>
  </c:when>
  <c:otherwise>
User entered name=${param.name}, address=${param.address}<br/>
  </c:otherwise>
  </c:choose>
</body>
</tags:test>
```

The following test.tag file is used to invoke the JSP fragment using the <jsp:doBody> standard action. After the script has been run, a form will be rendered so that name and address can be entered by the user and captured by the script for execution:

```
<!DOCTYPE html PUBLIC "-//W3C//DTD XHTML Basic 1.0//EN"
"http://www.w3.org/TR/xhtml-basic/xhtml-basic10.dtd">
<html xmlns="http://www.w3.org/1999/xhtml">
<jsp:doBody/>
</html>
```

As the JSP 2.0 specification indicates, web applications that contain files with an extension of .jspx will have those files interpreted as JSP documents by default.

Simple Invocation Protocol

This API enhancement was developed to exploit the use of scriptless pages among web developers using JSP libraries in their development activities for implementing tag files.

In the following code example, the `<lottery:picks/>` tag file invocation demonstrates how simple it is to incorporate logic into a web page using tag libraries:

```
<%@ taglib uri="/WEB-INF/tlds/lottery.tld" prefix="lottery" %>
<html>
<head>
<title>Lottery Picks</title>
</head>
<body>
<h2>Lottery Picks</h2>
Lottery number generated is...<lottery:picks/>
</body>
</html>
```

The lottery tag library descriptor file, `lottery.tld`, outlines the lottery tag file application invoked from the preceding web application:

```
<!--lottery.tld -->
<?xml version="1.0" encoding="UTF-8" ?>
<taglib xmlns="http://java.sun.com/xml/ns/j2ee"
    xmlns:xsi="http://www.w3.org/2001/XMLSchema-instance"
    xsi:schemaLocation="http://java.sun.com/xml/ns/j2ee/web-jsptaglibrary_2_0.xsd"
    version="2.0">

    <description>
     Lottery picks
    </description>
    <jsp-version>2.0</jsp-version>
    <tlib-version>1.0</tlib-version>
    <short-name>picks</short-name>
    <uri></uri>

  <tag>
     <name>picks</name>
     <tag-class>lottery.LotteryPickTag</tag-class>
     <body-content>empty</body-content>
     <description>Generate random lottery numbers</description>
  </tag>
</taglib>
```

The `LotteryPickTag` application illustrates how the `SimpleTagSupport` class can be extended to allow developers to craft tag handlers. The `doTag()` method is invoked when the end element of the tag is realized. In the sample Lottery application, the `getSixUniqueNumbers()` method is called from the `doTag()` method, which in turn displays the string output of six unique lottery numbers generated in random fashion:

```java
package lottery;

import java.io.*;
import java.util.*;
import javax.servlet.jsp.*;
import javax.servlet.jsp.tagext.SimpleTagSupport;

public class LotteryPickTag extends SimpleTagSupport {

    public LotteryPickTag(){}
    public void doTag() throws JspException, IOException {
        getJspContext().getOut().write("Random #'s =" + getSixUniqueNumbers());
    }

    public String getSixUniqueNumbers() {
        StringBuffer sb = new StringBuffer();
        int count = 0, number = 0;
        int numbers[] = {0,0,0,0,0,0,0};
        boolean found;

        while (count < 6) {
            number = (int)(Math.random()*59) + 1;
            found = false;
            for (int i=0; i < numbers.length; i++)
                if (numbers[i] == number) found = true;
            if (!found) {
                if (count != 0) sb.append(" - ");
                sb.append(number);
                numbers[count++] = number;
            }
        }
        return sb.toString();
    }
}
```

JSP tag files are converted into Java code by the JSP container in the same fashion that JSP scripts are translated into servlets. It should be fairly evident from this example how easily tag files can be constructed for deployment in web components for enterprise systems because they hide the complexity of building custom JSP tag libraries, which makes them easier to maintain in the long run.

Figure 7-2 outlines visually some of the enhancements of the JSP 2.0 specification along with some of the backwards compatibility issues that are addressed in the JSP 2.0 specification.

Certainly, the JSP 2.0 upgrade, with its ready-made Expression Language implementations, along with improvements in Java Server Pages Standard Tag Libraries, will enhance developer's abilities to build cohesive and robust web components.

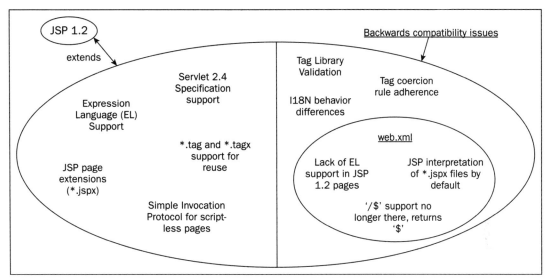

Figure 7-2

Integrated Expression Language (EL)

The following section concentrates on the Expression Language (EL) and its implementation in JSP applications. Certainly, there is ample content in the JSP 2.0 specification to discuss and demonstrate, especially some of the Servlet 2.4 features that were discussed briefly earlier, but this section concentrates on EL implementations because they are exploited prominently in the Contact Management Tool. Some of the other aspects of that specification are fairly involved and extend beyond the scope of this chapter.

EL expressions can be used with three different attribute values. First, they can be applied when an attribute value has a single expression; second, they can be used when the attribute value contains one or more expressions surrounded or separated by text; and lastly, they can be used when the attribute value contains only text. The following table shows how these operations can be implemented.

EL Expressions	Implementation
Single expression	`<xyz.tag value="${expression}"/>`
One or more expressions	`<xyz.tag value="abc${expression}text${expression}"/>`
Text only	`<xyz.tag value="abc text"/>`

JSP 2.0 scripts allow EL expressions to perform conditional operations on your web page variables. An example of this follows:

```
<c:if test="${param.Comments > 250}">
</c:if>
```

365

The parameter `param.Comments` is checked to see if it is greater than 250; if so, the logic that lies between the `if` statement is executed.

The JSTL core tag libraries can also be used for variable output. Here is an example of this:

```
<c:out value="${testELexpression}"/>
```

JSP 2.0 pages implement several different implicit objects through EL expressions; the table that follows lists some examples.

Implicit Object	Description
pageContext	Accesses the `PageContext` object, which provides access to all the namespaces associated with a JSP page
pageScope	A Map that contains page-scoped attribute names and values
requestScope	A Map that contains request-scoped attribute names and values
sessionScope	A Map that contains session-scoped attribute names and values
applicationScope	A Map that contains application-scoped attribute names and values
param	A Map that correlates parameter names to single `String` parameter values
paramValues	A Map that correlates parameter names to a `String[]` of all values of that parameter
header	A Map that contains header names in a `String`
headerValues	A Map that contains header names in a `String` array component
cookie	A Map that contains web cookie objects
initParam	A Map that holds context initialization parameter names and their values

Implicit objects (for example, objects that don't need to be declared and are declared automatically) allow developers to access web container services and resources.

JSTL 1.1 Overview

Capabilities of the Java Standard Template Library (JSTL 1.1) specification are too numerous to elaborate in great depth, so this chapter concentrates on two tag library capabilities that are helpful in the sample Contact Management Tool (CMT). The CMT application persists data in a MySQL database during storage and retrieval operations so the SQL Actions libraries are implemented and the Function Tag Library operations are used for string manipulation. The latter is discussed as well.

Function Tag Library

The Function Tag Library capabilities were introduced with the JSP 2.0 specification to allow developers to extend EL functionalities with string manipulation libraries. The JSTL 1.1 specification outlines these functions as follows. The following table demonstrates some of the new method functions available as part of the expression language support in JSP 2.0.

Function [fn:]	Description of Function
fn:contains (string, substring)	If the substring exists in a specified string value, true will be returned to the user, otherwise false. Example, fn:contains("independence", "depend") returns true.
fn:containsIgnoreCase (string, substring)	Ignoring case differences, if a substring exists in a specified string value, true will be returned to the user, otherwise false. Example, fn:containsIgnoreCase("independence", "DEPEND") returns true.
fn:endsWith(string, suffix)	Tests the end of a string with the suffix specified to determine if there is a match. Example, fn:endsWith("whirlyjig', "jag") returns false.
fn:escapeXml(string)	Escape characters that might be XML. Example, fn.escapeXml("<test>yea</test>") returns converted string.
fn:indexOf(string, substring)	Returns integer value of the first occurrence of the specified substring in a string. Example, fn:indexOf("democratic", "rat") returns 6
fn:join(array, separator)	Joins elements from an array into a string with a specified separator. Example, array[0]="X", array[1]="Y" fn:join(array,";") returns String = "X;Y"
fn:length(item)	Returns a collection count or the number of characters in a string as an integer value. Example, fn.length("architecture") returns 12.
fn:replace (string, before, after)	Returns a new string after replacing all occurrences of the before string with the after string. Example, fn:replace("downtown", "down", "up") returns uptown.
fn:split(string, separator)	Returns an array where all the items of a string are added based on a specified delimiter. Example, fn:split("how now brown cow"," ") returns array[0]="how", array[1]="now", array[2]="brown", array[3]="cow"
fn:startsWith(string, prefix)	Returns a Boolean value (true/false) depending on whether or not a string contains a specified prefix value. Example, fn:startsWith("predicament", "pre") returns true.

Table continued on following page

Function [fn:]	Description of Function
`fn:substring` `(string, begin, end)`	Returns a substring of a string based upon specified index values. Example, `fn:substring("practical", 2,5)` returns `act`.
`fn:substringAfter` `(string, substring)`	Returns a string value that follows a specified substring. Example, `fn:substringAfter("peppermint", "pepper")` returns `mint`.
`fn:substringBefore` `(string, substring)`	Returns a string value that precedes a specified substring value. Example, `fn:substringBefore("peppermint", "mint")` returns `pepper`.
`fn:toLowerCase(string)`	Converts all the characters of a specified string to lowercase. Example, `fn:toLowerCase("Design Patterns")` returns `design patterns`.
`fn.toUpperCase(string)`	Converts all the characters of a specified string to uppercase. Example, `fn:toUpperCase("Patterns")` returns `PATTERNS`.
`fn:trim(string)`	Eliminates leading and trailing white space from a specified string. Example, `fn:trim(" almost done ")` returns `"almost done"`.

Because text manipulation is so prevalent in web applications, these function libraries are invaluable components for your development and deployment operations. Many of these functions mirror the same APIs that the Java String class possesses, so they should be learned fairly easily.

SQL Actions

A general rule of thumb for SQL transactions on enterprise systems is to handle database operations within business logic operations (as demonstrated with the Add Contact web application in Figure 7-6, later in this chapter). But sometimes you might want to perform those activities with the SQL tag libraries that are part of the JSTL 1.1 libraries.

JSTL SQL Actions allow developers to interact with databases on the presentation layer. An overview of its capabilities include the ability to perform queries through SELECT statements, database updates with insert, update, and delete operations, and transactional activities that allow the aggregation of database operations.

The following table illustrates the SQL Action tags for establishing a data source.

Tag	Description

<sql:setDataSource>	This tag exports a data source.
	<sql:setDataSource
	    {datasource="dataSource" |
	    url = "jdbcUrl"
	    [driver = "driverClassName"]
	    [user = "userName"]
	    [password = "password"] }
	    [var="varName"]
	    [scope="{page | request | session | application}"]/>

The following table illustrates the SQL Action tags for query operations.

Tag	Description

<sql:query>	This tag queries the database.
	Without body content
	<sql:query sql="queryString"
	    var="varName"
	    [scope="{page | request | session | application}"]
	    [maxRows="maxRows"]
	    [startRow="startRow"] />
	With a body for query parameters
	<sql:query sql="queryString"
	    var="varName"
	    [scope="{page | request | session | application}"]
	    [maxRows="maxRows"]
	    [startRow="startRow"]
	  <sql:param> actions
	 </sql:query>
	With a body for query parameters and options
	<sql:query sql="queryString"
	    var="varName"
	    [scope="{page | request | session | application}"]
	    [maxRows="maxRows"]
	    [startRow="startRow"]
	  query optional
	  <sql:param> actions
	 </sql:query>

The following table illustrates the SQL Action tags for update operations.

Tag	Description

<sql:update>	This tag executes an INSERT, UPDATE, or DELETE statement. Without body content
	<sql:update sql="updateString"
	     [datasource="datasource"]
	     [var="varName"]
	     [scope="{page | request | session | application}"]/>
	With a body for query parameters
	<sql:update sql="updateString"
	     [datasource="datasource"]
	     [var="varName"]
	     [scope="{page | request | session | application}"]
	  <sql:param> actions
	 </sql:update>
	With a body for query parameters and options
	<sql:update sql="updateString"
	     [datasource="datasource"]
	     [var="varName"]
	     [scope="{page | request | session | application}"]
	  update statement optional
	  <sql:param> actions
	 </sql:update>

The SQL Action tags elaborated in the preceding tables certainly are powerful mechanisms to perform SQL transactions inside your JSP web components without having to worry about back-end JavaBean applications to perform the same duties. Ultimately, developers must decide during their coding operations if they opt to perform script or JavaBean queries in their deployments. Fortunately, the Contact Management Tool illustrates both to facilitate your design decisions.

Developing Your Web Application Visualizations with JSTL 1.1

The following code example demonstrates the use of SQL actions mentioned previously. The first course of action in your code is to establish a data source object that will allow the application to connect to the *picture* database so queries can collect data for visualization on your JSP page:

```
<%@ page language="java"
    contentType="text/html"
    import="java.util.*,java.lang.*,java.io.*" %>

<%@ taglib prefix="c" uri="http://java.sun.com/jstl/core_rt" %>
<%@ taglib prefix="sql" uri="http://java.sun.com/jstl/sql" %>

<link href="CMT.css" rel="stylesheet" type="text/css">

<sql:setDataSource
```

```
            var="pictures"
            driver="org.gjt.mm.mysql.Driver"
            url="jdbc:mysql://localhost/picture"
            user=""
            password=""
            scope="page"/>
```

After the data source has been established, a query is performed using the database reference
${pictures} where the result set is stored in the results variable:

```
<sql:query var="results" dataSource="${pictures}">
    select * from picture
</sql:query>
```

The result set variable called results is then used to iterate through the individual database entries so
they can be shown on the user display:

```
<table cellSpacing=0 cellPadding=4 align=center><tr><td bgColor=#7b849c>
    <table border="0"><tr><td>
        <c:forEach var="row" items="${results.rows}" varStatus="counter">
            <tr class="row1">
            <td>
            <table cellSpacing="0" cellPadding="0" border="0">
                <td valign="top"><b>${counter.count}.</b></td>
                <td>
                <table width="500" border="0">
                    <tr>
                        <td class="smallblue" noWrap align="middle">
                             
                        </td>
                        <td>
                            <u>Attributes:</u>
                        </td>
                    </tr>
                    <tr>
                        <td align="middle">
                         <a href="">
                            <img src="./images/${row.name}" width=50 border=0>
                         </a>
                        </td>
                        <td>
                        <table>
                        <tr>
                          <td>Phone Number:</td>
                          <td>${row.telephone_num}</td>
                        </tr>
                        <tr>
                          <td>Comments:</td>
                          <td>${row.comments}</td>
                        </tr>
                        </table>
                        </td>
                    </tr>
                </table>
```

```
                </td>
            </table>
          </td>
        </tr>
      </c:forEach>
    </td></tr></table>
  </td></tr></table>
  <br>
  <br>
```

The resulting display is demonstrated in Figure 7-3. The JSP script culls the picture database for the image and metadata associated with that image for rendering. The person marked in the file text is hyperlinked so users can click it and obtain more information about the selected contact.

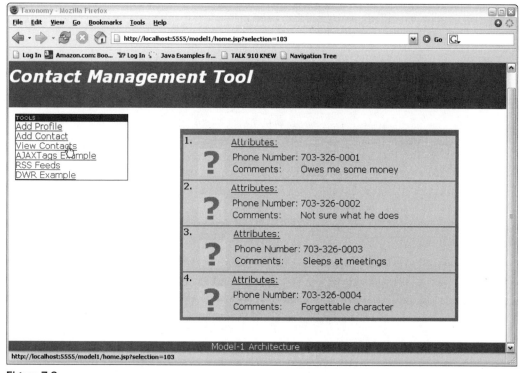

Figure 7-3

The addProfile.jsp application uses both the core tag libraries for logic operations and the SQL actions to perform form processing actions on the Add Profile page. Once the form has been properly filled out, checks will be done to ensure that required fields have been entered. Once those checks have been performed, and the application has determined that the form entries can be pushed to the back-end database, the application will send the data to the registration database for storage and subsequent retrievals:

```
<!--addProfile.jsp -->
<%@ taglib prefix="c" uri="http://java.sun.com/jstl/core" %>
<%@ taglib prefix="fmt" uri="http://java.sun.com/jstl/fmt" %>
<%@ taglib uri="http://java.sun.com/jstl/sql_rt" prefix="sql" %>

<script language="JavaScript">
function textCounter(field, countfield, maxlimit) {
    if (field.value.length > maxlimit) {
        field.value = field.value.substring(0, maxlimit);
    } else {
        countfield.value = maxlimit - field.value.length;
    }
}
</script>
```

The JSTL 1.1 core library tags are used in the following code to perform logic operations on the form entries specified by the user. If either firstName, lastName, or email is empty, the application will not allow the form to pass the data to the back-end registration database:

```
<c:if test="${param.submitted}">

  <c:if test="${empty param.firstName}" var="noFirstName" />
  <c:if test="${empty param.lastName}" var="noLastName" />
  <c:if test="${empty param.email}" var="noEmail" />

  <c:if test="${not (noFirstName or noLastName or noEmail)}">
    <c:set value="${param.firstName}" var="firstName" scope="request"/>
    <c:set value="${param.lastName}" var="lastName" scope="request"/>
    <c:set value="${param.email}" var="email" scope="request"/>
```

Once the user has entered the proper form entries, the data source will be established with the SQL action tags by passing familiar JDBC driver, url, user, and password parameters to the library to create a connection. After the connection has been created, the SQL update tag <sql:update> can be used to perform an insert operation on the registration database using a prepared statement construct:

```
<sql:setDataSource
    var="datasource"
    driver="org.gjt.mm.mysql.Driver"
    url="jdbc:mysql://localhost/registration"
    user=""
    password=""
    scope="page"/>

<sql:update dataSource="${datasource}">
    INSERT INTO registration (registration_id, first_name, last_name, email)
VALUES(?, ?, ?, ?)
    <sql:param value="${param.firstName}" />
    <sql:param value="${param.lastName}" />
    <sql:param value="${param.email}" />
</sql:update>

</c:if>
</c:if>
```

The following code represents the registration form and its components that will be used to register contacts in the Contact Management Tool. EL constructs, such as `${param.lastName}`, are used to represent and persist data items entered by the form user:

```
<form method="post">

<table border="0" cellpadding="0" cellspacing="0">

<tr valign="bottom">
<td nowrap="nowrap">

<table cellspacing="2" cellpadding="2" bgcolor="#336699">
<tbody>
   <tr>
      <td nowrap="nowrap" colspan="2">Registration</td>
   </tr>
   <tr>
      <td nowrap="nowrap" class="mandatory">First Name: (required)</td>
      <td class="value">
      <input name="firstName" value="${param.firstName}" size="25" maxlength="50">
      <c:if test="${noFirstName}">
         <small><font color="red">
         Please enter a First Name
         </font></small>
      </c:if>
      </td>
   </tr>
   <tr>
      <td nowrap="nowrap" class="mandatory">Last Name: (required)</td>
      <td class="value">
      <input name="lastName" value="${param.lastName}" size="25" maxlength="50">
      <c:if test="${noLastName}">
         <small><font color="red">
         Please enter a Last Name
         </font></small>
      </c:if>
      </td>
   </tr>

   <!-- Email, Gender, Marital Status, Date of Birth, Country, Zip Code, Age,
Place of Birth, Occupation and Interests components were omitted for the sake of
brevity -- >

   <tr>
      <td align="left" nowrap="nowrap" class="field" colspan="2">
      Characters remaining: 
      <input readonly="readonly" type="text" name="inputcount" size="5"
maxlength="4" value="" class="text">
      <br>
      <script language="JavaScript">
      document.form1.inputcount.value = (200 -
document.form1.interests.value.length);
```

```
      </script>
      </td>
    </tr>

    <tr>
      <td nowrap="nowrap" class="field" align="middle" colspan="2">
      <input type="hidden" name="submitted" value="true" />
      <input type="submit" value="Register" />
      </td>
    </tr>

  </tbody>
  </table>

  </form>
```

The form visualization (see Figure 7-4) is the result of the code fragments in the addProfile.jsp script described previously. Some JavaScript code was used for the comments section to provide client-side validation, which ensures that the user does not enter more than 200 characters.

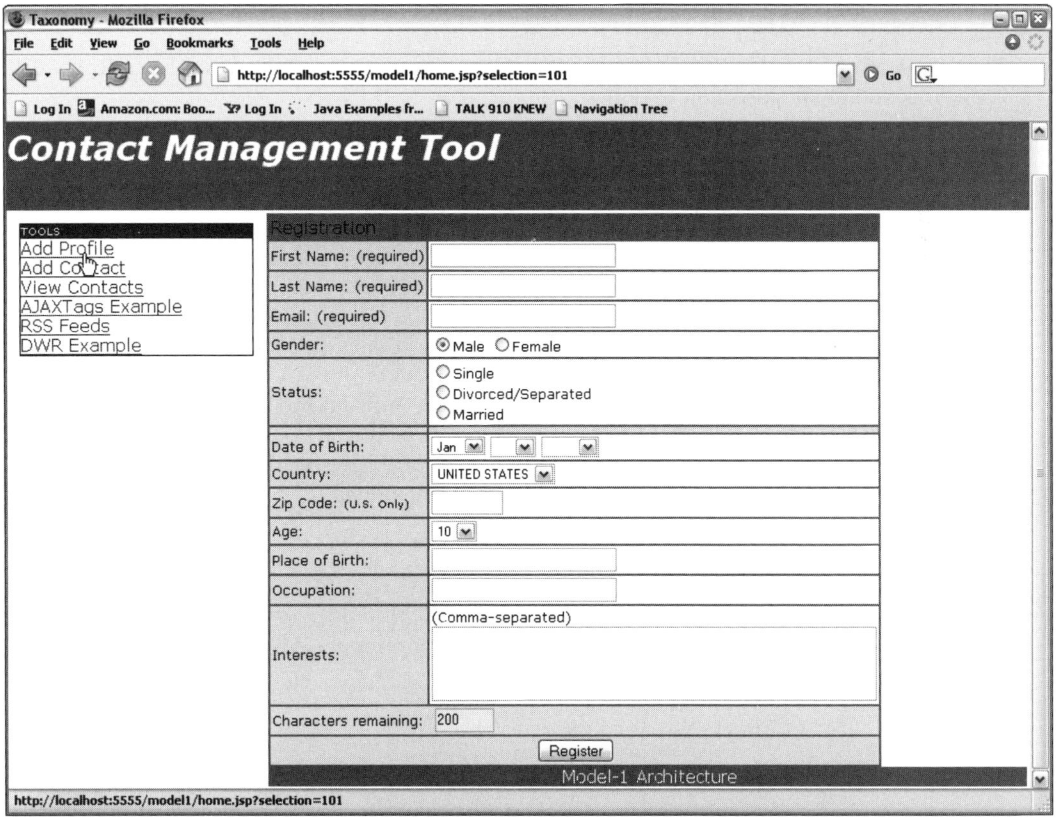

Figure 7-4

Developing Your Web Application Visualizations with JSP 2.0

Java Server Pages (JSPs) are generally implemented in distributed systems to aggregate content with back-end components for user visualizations. When application servers first receive a request from a JSP component, the JSP engine compiles that page into a servlet. Additionally, when changes to a JSP occur, that same component will be recompiled into a servlet again where it will be processed by a class loader so it can restart its life cycle in the web container.

A general best practice for developing web components is to use JSPs for display generation and servlets for processing requests. The idea is to encapsulate complicated business logic in JavaBean components written in Java that are entirely devoid of scriptlet syntax so display scripts are not obfuscated with complicated logic that might make your code hard to decipher for maintenance purposes. Naturally, your JavaBean code artifacts will transfer across platforms because they are written in Java, which accommodates reuse in your overall development operations.

The benefits of JSP technology include the following points:

❑ **Code reuse across disparate platforms.** Components and tag libraries can be shared in development operations and among different tools.

❑ **Separation of roles.** Web designers can work presentation scripts and developers can work back-end data transaction activities.

❑ **Separation of content.** Both static and dynamic content can be "template-tized," which inevitably facilitates coding operations.

A JSP page has two distinct phases during operations: *translation* and *execution*. During translation, the web container validates the syntax of a JSP script. The web container manages the class instances of a JSP during the execution phase as user requests are made for it.

Figure 7-5 conceptualizes how a web page can be constructed using the Model 1 Architecture.

In the GUI presentation shown in Figure 7-6, when a user attempts to add a new contact to the Contact Management Tool, a form will be presented to the user for a picture and metadata that will be associated with that picture. The web application uses JSP 2.0 EL features to present data, and JavaBean components to persist and manipulate contact data for retrieval and storage.

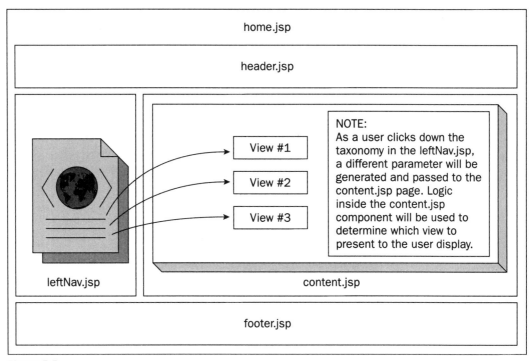

Figure 7-5

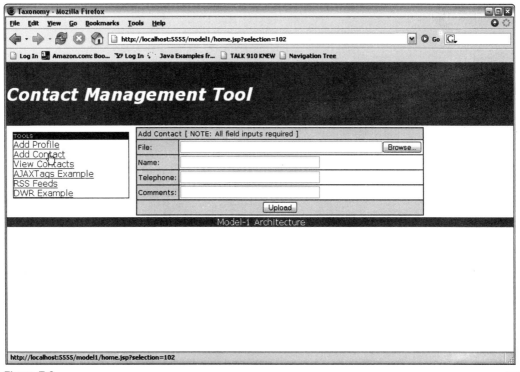

Figure 7-6

The following form application code utilizes Jakarta Commons Upload libraries to capture user-specified entries for back-end database publishing. If the form is properly filled out, meaning all entries are populated, the application will use the `FileManager` bean to upload the designated image file for upload and insert the metadata associated with that image into the picture database for future retrieval:

```java
<%@ page language="java" contentType="text/html"
import="java.util.*,java.lang.*,java.io.*,com.model1.*,org.apache.commons
.fileupload.*"  %>

<%@ taglib uri="http://java.sun.com/jsp/jstl/core" prefix="c" %>
<%@ taglib uri="http://java.sun.com/jsp/jstl/functions" prefix="fn" %>
<jsp:useBean id="fm" class="com.model1.FileManager" scope="request"/>

<title>Insert Contact</title>
<%
boolean validEntry = false;
if(!FileUpload.isMultipartContent(request)) {
    System.out.println("Request is not multipart!");
} else {
    DiskFileUpload fileUpload = new DiskFileUpload();
    List items = fileUpload.parseRequest(request);
    if (items.size() > 0) {
        String tempName = "", tempTelephone = "", tempComments = "", tempFilename =
"";
        Iterator iter = items.iterator();
        FileItem item;
        while(iter.hasNext()) {
            item = (FileItem) iter.next();
            if(item.isFormField()) {
                if (item.getFieldName().equals("name")) tempName = item.getString();
                if (item.getFieldName().equals("telephone")) tempTelephone =
item.getString();
                if (item.getFieldName().equals("comments")) tempComments =
item.getString();
            } else {
                if(item.getSize() > 0) {
                    File fullFile = new File(item.getName());
                    tempFilename = fullFile.getName();
                    File savedFile = new
File(getServletContext().getRealPath("/images/"), fullFile.getName());
                    item.write(savedFile);
                }
            }
        }
        if ( !tempName.equals("") && !tempTelephone.equals("") &&
!tempComments.equals("") && !tempFilename.equals("") ) {
            fm.addMetadata(tempName, tempTelephone, tempComments);
            validEntry = true;
        }
    }
    else
        System.out.println("item.size() = 0");
}
%>
```

The form applications requirement for uploading image files that will be attached to contact metadata requires the inclusion of the `enctype` tag, which will dictate how the form data should be encoded for transmission. Whenever data is broadcast across a network, an agreement needs to be made as to how that data will be represented. For file uploads, the HTML `Input` tag needs to be set to `file` to instruct the browser to prepare to read and transmit a file from a user's system to a remote server. Setting the `ENCTYPE FORM` attribute to `multipart/form-data` tells the server that the form submission contains an uploaded file. The problem with implementing this form attribute is that the `getParameter(String)` method of the `HttpServletRequest` class returns null values when the content type is `multipart/form-data`. To adjust for this, the Jakarta Commons FileUpload library uses the `FileItem` class to parse those form elements so the data associated with them can be collected:

```
<form name="formUpload" method="post" action="home.jsp?selection=102"
enctype="multipart/form-data">

<table border="0" cellpadding="0" cellspacing="0" bgcolor="#336699"><tbody>
<tr valign="bottom"><td nowrap="nowrap">
<table cellspacing="2" cellpadding="2">
<tbody>
   <tr>
      <td nowrap="nowrap" class="mandatory" colspan="2">
      Add Contact [ NOTE: All field inputs required ]
       <% if (validEntry) out.println("<font color=\"#ff0000\">Successful
entry</font>"); %>
      </td>
   </tr>
   <tr>
      <td nowrap="nowrap" class="mandatory">File:</td>
      <td class="value">
      <input type="file" size="60" name="filename" value="${fm.filename}">
      </td>
   </tr>
   <tr>
      <td nowrap="nowrap" class="mandatory">Name:</td>
      <td class="value">
      <input name="name" value="${fm.name}" size="40" maxlength="50">
      </td>
   </tr>
   <tr>
      <td nowrap="nowrap" class="mandatory">Telephone:</td>
      <td class="value">
      <input name="telephone" value="${fm.telephone}" size="40" maxlength="50">
      </td>
   </tr>
   <tr>
      <td nowrap="nowrap" class="mandatory">Comments:</td>
      <td class="value">
      <input name="comments" value="${fm.comments}" size="40" maxlength="50">
      </td>
   </tr>
   <tr>
     <td align="middle" class="mandatory" colspan="2">
     <input type="submit" name="UploadFile" value="Upload">
     </td>
```

```
        </tr>
    </tbody>
    </table>
    </td></tr>
    </tbody>
    </table>
    </form>
```

The `FileManager` bean performs simple publication operations on the metadata associated with the uploaded image file designated in the data submission form. A prepared statement is invoked to pass the user-specified content to the back-end picture data store. Java Naming and Directory Interface (JNDI) method calls are implemented to retrieve user login attributes from the `web.xml` deployment descriptor file to connect to the database for data insertion:

```java
package com.model1;

import java.io.*;
import java.net.*;
import java.sql.*;
import java.util.*;
import java.util.logging.*;;
import javax.naming.*;

public class FileManager {
    private static Logger log = Logger.getLogger("FileManager");
    private Connection conn;
    private PreparedStatement pstmt;
    private String dbDriver = "";
    private String dbUrl = "";
    private String dbUser = "";
    private String dbPass = "";

    // form entries
    private String filename;
    private String name;
    private String telephone;
    private String comments;

    public FileManager() throws SQLException {
```

The new J2EE 5 libraries enable users to inject resources with the `@Resource` annotation. The idea behind dependency injection is that each application declares what type of service object it requires and then the container resolves the dependency between application components, instantiates service objects, and finally injects service stubs into the component at runtime with Java Bean accessor method calls or by direct data field assignment:

```java
        /*  new changes with JSP 2.1 allow users to inject resources as needed
            @Resource(name="jdbc/test") javax.sql.DataSource testDB;
            public FileManager() throws SQLException {
                Connection conn = testDB.getConnection();
            }
        */
        try {
```

```
                    InitialContext ic = new InitialContext();
                    Context ctx = (Context)ic.lookup("java:comp/env");
                    dbDriver = (String)(ctx.lookup("dbDriver"));
                    dbUrl = (String)(ctx.lookup("dbUrl"));
                    dbUser = (String)(ctx.lookup("dbUser"));
                    dbPass = (String)(ctx.lookup("dbPass"));
                    Class.forName(dbDriver);
                    conn = DriverManager.getConnection( dbUrl, dbUser, dbPass);
            } catch (Exception e) {
                    log.info("[FileManager()] EXCEPTION. " + e.toString());
            }
        }

    public void addMetadata(String name, String telephone, String comments) {
            String sqlQuery = "INSERT INTO picture (name, telephone_num, comments,
ignore) VALUES (?, ?, ?, 'N')";
            if (conn != null) {
                    try {
                            pstmt = conn.prepareStatement(sqlQuery);
                            pstmt.setString(1, name);
                            pstmt.setString(2, telephone);
                            pstmt.setString(3, comments);
                            pstmt.execute();
                    } catch (Exception e) {
                            log.info("Exception: " + e.toString());
                    }
            }
            else
                    System.out.println("conn is NULL");
    }

    // getters/setters for: filename, name, telephone, comments omitted below
}
```

The `FileManager` bean application demonstrates how Java components can be constructed with robust libraries to facilitate form processing and data persistence activities. The keys to good bean development are to migrate common methods with one another for easy maintenance and to provide simple interfaces to data so users will be more likely to incorporate them into their presentation code. Granted, the file upload logic in the JSP that interfaces with the bean could easily be added to the bean component, but were not for demonstration purposes and the need to avoid a lengthy bean component that might be difficult to comprehend.

AJAX

Although this chapter was written primarily to demonstrate Model 1 Architecture concepts through simple source code implementations, you should consider a popular new web page technology called Asynchronous JavaScript and XML (AJAX) when making design decisions for web deployments that aggregate disparate web applications in a single unified view for presentation.

Of course, this would apply to many portal implementations that commonly aggregate back-end data from distinct data sources for user presentation. The collection of data for user display typically takes some time to refresh a browser page with new content predicated on user selections from the user front-end component. Caching of content would allow for quicker view presentations, but the query being cached must be performed first in order for it to be persisted.

The AJAX technology was established to satisfy this problem where user needs for quicker front-end responses and more natural (quicker) data presentations are required. With AJAX, back-end queries appear a lot less obvious in a user's browser view because the request/response action that occurs when a user clicks a submit button or hyperlinked item in a web page is supplanted by an `HTTPXMLRequest` object that performs asynchronous data processing and marshalling between client and server applications. This means that a page does not need to wait for a request to come back for a page to be rendered in a browser view and data content can be fed back to a view in a continuous, free-flowing manner.

The purpose of the remaining text in this chapter is to juxtapose the request/response features demonstrated in the web applications shown in earlier sections with new AJAX script components that behave in a different fashion than older, more established web components when processing user requests. Two different AJAX library extensions, AJAXTags and DWR, are discussed and exhibited through simple web applications so their differences become more obvious and tangible as complementary technologies to existing Model 1 web application deployments.

What Is AJAXTags? Why Use It?

The AJAXTags libraries were created primarily as an alternative technology to JavaScript for client-side web development. Although AJAX is rooted in JavaScript, it supercedes JavaScript's functionality when performing form updates in that AJAX interacts asynchronously with back-end components, which JavaScript cannot.

The example implementation in Figure 7-7 demonstrates a tabbed display that generates random lottery numbers from a JavaBean for rendering in the individual tab displays. The interaction occurs through the AJAXTags library in an asynchronous manner using a back-end servlet delivery mechanism.

Figure 7-7

The following code implements the AJAXTags library and associates the individual tag content values using through the `test.jsp` scripts:

```
<%@ page language="java" contentType="text/html; charset=ISO-8859-1"
pageEncoding="ISO-8859-1"%>
<%@ taglib uri="http://ajaxtags.org/tags/ajax" prefix="ajax" %>
<jsp:include page="header.jsp" flush="true" />
<h1>Do You Feel Lucky?</h1>
<script type="text/javascript">

function initProgress() {
  Element.show('progressMsg');
}

function resetProgress(request) {
  Effect.Fade('progressMsg');
}

function reportError() {
  $('errorMsg').innerHTML = "Tab panel busted!";
  Element.show('errorMsg');
  setTimeout("Effect.DropOut('errorMsg')", 2500);
}
</script>

<div id="tabPanelWrapper">

<ajax:tabPanel panelStyleId="tabPanel"
               contentStyleId="tabContent"
               currentStyleId="ajaxCurrentTab">
  <ajax:tab caption="Lottery - VA"
baseUrl="${contextPath}/test.jsp?stateLottery=Lottery-VA" defaultTab="true"/>
  <ajax:tab caption="Lottery - NY"
baseUrl="${contextPath}/test.jsp?stateLottery=Lottery-NY"/>
  <ajax:tab caption="Lottery - DE"
baseUrl="${contextPath}/test.jsp?stateLottery=Lottery-DE"/>

</ajax:tabPanel>

</div>

<jsp:include page="footer.jsp" flush="true" />
```

The `Test.java` bean component creates an `ArrayList` of six randomly generated numbers that can be retrieved with the `getData()` method:

```
package com.ajax;
import java.util.*;
public class Test
{
    private ArrayList<Integer> list = new ArrayList<Integer>();
    private final int NUMBERS = 6;
    public Test() {}
    public String getData()
    {
```

```
            Random rand = new Random();
            for (int i=0; i < NUMBERS; i++) {
                list.add((1 + (int)(Math.random() * 60)));
            }
            StringBuffer sb = new StringBuffer();
            for (int i=0; i < NUMBERS; i++) {
                sb.append(list.get(i) + " ");
            }
            return sb.toString();
        }
    }
```

The AJAXTags open source offering satisfies several client-side needs such as form auto-completion, interactive selection box population, form field refreshment, and popup generation. Users should consider implementing AJAXTags because of its rich example base, as well as its implementation ease, but more importantly because of its capability to serve content from back-end data stores in a rewarding manner.

What Is DWR? Why Use It?

Anyone who has engaged in large enterprise web deployments and has experienced request-driven latency issues with back-end components knows how frustrating operations can be when trying to perform simple query requests or publication tasks. Often the web experience is so dissatisfying that end users would threaten to quit their jobs rather than use that agonizing application. Rather than suffering an outflow of end users who might hit the road if forced to suffer through that experience, consideration might be given to an alternative open source web technology called Direct Web Remoting (DWR) crafted by a small consultancy group called Getahead.

DWR functions by dynamically generating JavaScript components from Java classes to overcome cumbersome page refresh operations that occur with large server-side data retrieval and presentation activities by incorporating JavaScript XMLHttpRequest objects. This activity prevents long delays that might occur while a web page is collecting back-end data and reformatting it into HTML for presentation. Because requests are sent asynchronously across the network with DWR, page components can be refreshed seamlessly with new content without the appearance of breaks that some web applications cause inside web browsers during request operations.

With DWR, a back-end servlet processes user requests and marshals responses back to the browser, while client-side JavaScript components send user requests and dynamically process and render content for presentation in the browser view. The magic that allows web content to be refreshed without having page refreshes in the browser occurs because JavaScript interface components are dynamically generated from Java applications during operations. The interfaces that are crafted with DWR libraries allow for asynchronous data communication to occur between client and server programs.

The sample DWR application that follows reads a MySQL database that collects and disseminates contact information through DWR interfaces and allows users to ignore items for display through the implementation of checkbox selections (see Figure 7-8). When a user checks an item for omission by clicking the Omit Checked Items button, the request is sent to the server where a flag is set so future data viewings omit those items. Alternatively, the Renew Results button allows users to reset the ignore flag attribute in the database so that previously marked items can be viewed again.

Figure 7-8

The following code sample incorporates DWR library scripts so that the JSP page can communicate with the back-end database where data is collected and aggregated as web content in the user display in a seamless fashion. The `engine.js` script facilitates communication from the dynamically generated `javascript` function interfaces. The `util.js` script consists of helpful utility functions that are designated to accommodate web page refresh activities with JavaScript data.

The `omitCheckedItems` function determines what individual items will be marked for display omission and passes those items to the `getContactData` bean residing on the server back-end. Once that operation completes, the DWR library functions will receive the data that will be rendered to the display from that same bean. The `renewResults` function performs the same back-end data communication through DWR interfaces, but refreshes the `ignoreflag` attribute for all of the items in the picture database so they will be eligible for display when data is passed back to the presentation tier:

```
<%@ page language="java" import="java.util.*" %>
<%@ page language="java" import="com.dwr.*" %>

<html>
<head>
<title>DWR Example</title>
<meta http-equiv="Content-Type" content="text/html; charset=iso-8859-1">

<script src='dwr/interface/ContactMgmtToolDAO.js'></script>
<script type='text/javascript' src='dwr/engine.js'></script>
```

```
<script type='text/javascript' src='dwr/util.js'></script>

<script>
function omitCheckedItems() {
    txt="";
    omit="Y";
    count = 0;
    while(check = document.getElementById("item" + count))
    {
        if (check.checked)
        {
            txt=txt + check.value + ","
        }
        count++;
    }
    DWRUtil.removeAllRows("mgrbody");
    ContactMgmtToolDAO.getContactData(fillTable, txt, omit);
    $("resultTable").style.display = '';
}

function renewResults() {
    txt="Y";
    omit="N";
    DWRUtil.removeAllRows("mgrbody");
    ContactMgmtToolDAO.getContactData(fillTable, txt, omit);
    $("resultTable").style.display - '';
}
```

The checkAll and uncheckAll functions allow users to check and uncheck all of the items returned from the back-end query through client-side operations. This means that a page refresh is avoided so users can view an uninterrupted display of these items in the user view:

```
function checkAll() {
    count=0;
    while (check = document.getElementById("item" + count)) {
        check.checked = "true";
        count++;
    }
}

function uncheckAll() {
    count=0;
    while (check = document.getElementById("item" + count)) {
        check.checked = "";
        count++;
    }
}
```

The following code outlines how DWR returns data from server-side queries. The individual database attribute mappings will be populated with content for rendering on the user display as they are returned from to the back-end bean component through the JavaScript interface to the fillTable function. The mgrBody object will be used to reference the content later in the script for display. Header rows are grouped with the THEAD tag, which enables browsers to support scrolling of table bodies independently of the table header and footer:

```
var getPictureId = function(unit) { return unit.pictureId };
var getName = function(unit) { return unit.name };
var getTelephone = function(unit) { return unit.telephone };
var getComments = function(unit) { return unit.comments };
var getIgnoreThis= function(unit) { return unit.ignoreThis };

function fillTable(mgr) {
    DWRUtil.addRows("mgrbody", mgr, [ getPictureId, getName, getTelephone,
getComments, getIgnoreThis ]);
}
</script>
</head>

<body onload="omitCheckedItems();" bgcolor="#FFFFFF" leftmargin="0" topmargin="0"
leftmargin="0" rightmargin="0">

<form name="test">
<table border="0" cellspacing="0" cellpadding="0" height="50%">
  <tr>
    <td valign="top">
    <table border="1">
    <tr>
        <td>
            <div id="resultTable">
                <thead>
                    <tr>
                        <th>Picture ID</th>
                        <th>Name</th>
                        <th>Telephone</th>
                        <th>Comments</th>
                        <th>Omit</th>
                    </tr>
                </thead>
                <tbody id="mgrbody">
                </tbody>
            </div>
        </td>
    </tr>
```

The following table row item uses JavaScript to execute functions that check and uncheck checkbox items without refreshing the user display. When the Renew Results link is clicked, the `renewResults` JavaScript function will invoke the DWR servlet and the back-end `ContactMgmtToolDAO` JavaBean to reset the `ignoreflag` in the picture database to `N` for No so all items previously ignored will be rendered on the user display again:

```
    <tr>
        <td colspan="5">
        <input type="button" onclick="omitCheckedItems();" value="Omit Checked
items">
         
        <span style="text-decoration:underline"
onMouseover="this.style['color']='red';" onMouseout="this.style['color']='black';"
onClick="checkAll()">Check all items</span>
         
```

```
            <span style="text-decoration:underline"
onMouseover="this.style['color']='red';" onMouseout="this.style['color']='black';"
onClick="uncheckAll()">Uncheck all items</span>
         
        <input type="button" onclick="renewResults();" value="Renew Results">
        </td>
    </tr>
    </table>
    </td>
  </tr>
</table>

</form>
```

The `ContactMgmtToolDAO` JavaBean manages the contact information that is rendered to the user display. The `getConnection` method invokes the JDBC driver libraries to create a new connection that will be passed back to the calling routine so that data can be updated and retrieved and passed back to the presentation tier through the getter/setter functions in the `ContactMgmtTool` JavaBean, which interfaces with the JavaScript implementation `ContactMgmtToolDAO.js`:

```
package com.dwr;

import java.sql.*;
import java.util.*;
import java.util.logging.*;
import java.io.*;

public class ContactMgmtToolDAO
{
    private static Logger logger = Logger.getLogger("ContactMgmtToolDAO");
    private static Collection<Object> list = null;
    private Connection conn = null;
    private PreparedStatement pstmt = null;

    public getConnectionn() {
        conn = null;
        try {
            Class.forName("org.gjt.mm.mysql.Driver");
            conn = DriverManager.getConnection("jdbc:mysql://localhost/picture",
"root", "");
        } catch (Exception e) {
            logger.info("[ContactMgmtToolDAO:] EXCEPTION " + e.toString());
        }
        return conn;
    }
```

The `getContactData` method populates a vector object with contact data where the `ignorethis` attribute is not `Y`. Once all of the appropriate data has been collected, it will be returned through the interface specified in the `dwr.xml` configuration file placed in the `web.xml` deployment descriptor:

```
    public Collection getContactData(String filename, String omitItems) {
        list = new Vector<Object>();

        pstmt = null;
```

```
            conn = getConnection();

        if (conn != null) {
            try {
                if (omitItems.equals("Y"))
                    eraseItems(filename);
                else
                    renewItems(filename);

                String sqlQuery = "select * from PICTURE where ignorethis = ?";
                pstmt = conn.prepareStatement(sqlQuery);
                pstmt.setString(1, "N");
                ResultSet rslt = pstmt.executeQuery();

                int count = 0;
                while(rslt.next()) {
                    ContactMgmtTool mgr = this.getContactMgmtTool(rslt, count);
                    list.add(mgr);
                    count++;
                }
            } catch (Exception e) {
                logger.info("[ContactMgmtToolDAO:getContactData] EXCEPTION " +
e.toString());
            } finally {
                try {
                    if (pstmt != null) pstmt.close();
                    if (conn != null) conn.close();
                } catch(Exception e) {
                    e.printStackTrace();
                }
            }
        }
        else
            logger.info("[ContactMgmtToolDAO:getContactData] conn is NULL");
        return list;
    }
```

The getContactMgmtTool method creates ContactMgmtTool objects from the result set passed into it. The count parameter is used to set the ID of the checkbox items so the checkAll and uncheckAll JavaScript methods can retrieve them with the getElementById method:

```
    public ContactMgmtTool getContactMgmtTool(ResultSet rs, int count) throws
SQLException
    {
        ContactMgmtTool mgr = new ContactMgmtTool();
        mgr.setPictureId(rs.getLong("picture_id"));
        mgr.setName(rs.getString("name"));
        mgr.setTelephone(rs.getString("telephone_num"));
        mgr.setComments(rs.getString("comments"));
        mgr.setIgnoreThis("<center><input type=\"checkbox\" id=\"item" +
String.valueOf(count) + "\" value=\"" + rs.getLong("picture_id") + "\"></center>");
        return mgr;
    }
```

The `eraseItems` method performs a simple query to update the ignore flag for individual members using a SQL prepared statement invocation. Once this flag has been set, the item affiliated with that flag will not be rendered to the user view when the data is passed back to the presentation tier:

```
public void eraseItems(String filenames) {

    if (filenames.equals("")) return;

    pstmt = null;
    try {
        String sqlQuery = "update picture set ignorethis = 'Y' where picture_id
in (" + (filenames.substring(0, filenames.lastIndexOf(','))) + ")";
        pstmt = conn.prepareStatement(sqlQuery);
        pstmt.executeUpdate();
        pstmt.close();
    } catch(Exception e) {
        logger.info("[ContactMgmtToolDAO:eraseItems] EXCEPTION " +
e.toString());
    }
}
```

The `renewItems` method refreshes the picture database by toggling all of the items flagged as `ignore` to N so they will displayed on the user display for inspection:

```
public void renewItems(String omit) {
    pstmt = null;

    try {
        pstmt = null;
        String sqlQuery = "update picture set ignorethis = ? where ignorethis =
?";
        pstmt = conn.prepareStatement(sqlQuery);
        pstmt.setString(1, "N");
        pstmt.setString(2, omit);
        pstmt.executeUpdate();
        pstmt.close();
    } catch(Exception e) {
        logger.info("[ContactMgmtToolDAO:renewItems] EXCEPTION " +
e.toString());
    }
}
```

The `dwr.xml` file illustrates how DWR generates interfaces to the back-end JavaBean DAO components. The `ContactMgmtToolDAO` class is defined here within the `<create>` tag so the front-end JavaScript component can communicate with it. The `<convert>` tag is implemented so the `ContactMgmtTool` Plain Old Java Object (POJO) can be transformed into JavaScript associative arrays for data marshalling operations:

```
<?xml version="1.0" encoding="UTF-8"?>
<!DOCTYPE dwr PUBLIC "-//GetAhead Limited//DTD Direct Web Remoting 1.0//EN"
"http://www.getahead.ltd.uk/dwr/dwr10.dtd">

<dwr>
```

```
    <allow>
      <create creator="new" javascript="ContactMgmtToolDAO">
        <param name="class" value="com.dwr.ContactMgmtToolDAO"/>
        <include method="getContactData"/>
      </create>
      <convert converter="bean" match="com.dwr.ContactMgmtTool"/>
    </allow>
  </dwr>
```

This example elucidates how DWR library inclusion can improve your front-end presentation needs. The strength of DWR lies in its ability to generate interface objects between front-end pages and server-side business objects.

Summary

This chapter has demonstrated several different implementations to enable database transactions using tag libraries, JNDI lookups, Resource Injection, and JavaBean components with the Contact Management Tool while incorporating the Model 1 Architecture approach. Page flows were hard-coded to accommodate user navigations from hyperlinks with the assistance of core tag library logic operators, data was published and collected using JavaBean database persistence methods, and lastly, content was uploaded with the implementation of Jakarta Commons FileUpload libraries. Naturally, not all of the features of the JSP 2.0 and JSTL 1.1 specifications and API libraries could be discussed in this chapter alone, but the sample web applications constructed here should provide ample knowledge on how to craft J2EE web components with useful capabilities for professional presentation tier needs.

Truth be told, software design and modeling activities typically involve difficult decision-making speculations that are made from experience and the constraints that are placed on a project by scheduling timelines. But, those decisions can be facilitated by eliminating ambiguous or murky conceptualizations in your development operations by understanding different modeling architectures and philosophies. The key is to embrace some of the advice elaborated in Chapter 2 concerning agile software development by experimenting and enhancing existing web components so future design decisions can be determined more intelligently and expediently. The examples that accompany this chapter are fairly simple but can be challenging and should serve as important reference resources in your web page development discovery.

Developing Web Applications Using the Model 2 Architecture

In the previous chapter, you learned about building web applications using the Model 1 Architecture, which is heavily dependent on a page-centric development focus. In this chapter, you review and apply a prominent pattern in software development known as Model-View-Controller (MVC) to build web applications in a more modular and componentized manner. You learn a little about the Model 2 Architecture, particularly a framework known as WebWork, and its use of a concept known as Inversion of Control. You will see an example of how componentized development with WebWork provides a tremendous advantage to you as a web developer, as it saves you time in having to rebuild the same components over and over in your application.

The Problem

Imagine your office needed a centralized contact manager for referencing people that could be used for given projects. You know that such functionality would be useful, but are worried about trying to do something too ad hoc and inflexible, leading to it being quickly thrown away.

You need something quick, but flexible. You need something where you can reuse a lot of components to build your solution. You need to look at a Model 2 Architecture framework.

What Is Model 2?

To understand Model 2, you should review the Model-View-Controller paradigm, which you examined in depth in Chapter 3. As you saw in Chapter 3, MVC is often described in the context of Swing, so you may be wondering, "But these are web applications, how could they have much to do with each other?" So, you should remember that the MVC Architecture simply refers to breaking your system into distinct components to satisfy three concepts:

❑ The *Model* refers to the real-world representation of your domain. For example, if you have a golf scoring system, you would have objects to represent things like a golf hole, a score, and so on.

❑ The *View* refers to the ways that you view the data you are managing. For example, you may have a view of every player on a given hole, or you may have a scorecard for a given player over the whole course.

❑ The *Controller* refers to the actual discrete actions that the system can perform. For example, "enter a score," "generate a leaderboard," and so on.

Of course, there are wide debates about where the divisions really exist — is your model just data objects and does your controller handle the business logic? For purposes of this book, just simplify it down to three basic concepts: The model is "what it is"; the view is "what it looks like"; and the controller is "what it does."

So, how does the Model 2 Architecture actually work? Figure 8-1 demonstrates the Model 2 Architecture in action.

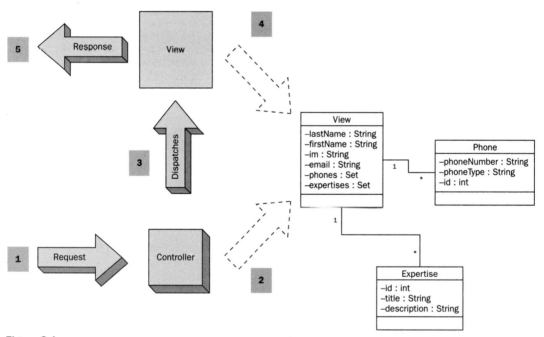

Figure 8-1

The Model 2 Architecture works like this:

1. The Request comes into the Controller.

2. The Controller performs a given action with the provided parameters.

3. The Controller forwards control to the View in order to give the response.

4. The View refers to the domain model to build the presentation.

5. The View is passed back in the Response to the user.

A critical thing that is usually missed by a lot of people who look at this diagram is the concept of "scope." Think of it like this: There are objects that are along for the ride, whether they are along for the duration of the request, the session, or the application.

Those are the key principles of Model 2 Architectures; next you learn why the Model 2 Architecture is good for use in web applications.

Why Use Model 2?

Now that you have a good sense of what the Model 2 Architecture is, you may be asking, "Why do I need this?" or "Isn't that a lot of effort for a web page?" There are a number of significant advantages to the Model 2 Architectures, particularly in large-scale applications. Here are several of the advantages of the Model 2 Architecture:

Advantage	Description
Flexibility	Model 2 is flexible because it separates your application into components by their relevant piece of what they do. This allows you to plug in new views or actions as needed without having to rewrite everything. You can even reuse your components in other application platforms like Swing.
Reuse	Because Model 2 is componentized by definition, you can reuse a framework to provide a lot of the glue that holds your application together. A couple of examples of Model 2 frameworks are Apache Struts and OpenSymphony's WebWork.
Scalability	Because you have separated out the components, it is easy to add more components where necessary. Plus, you can cache your data components more easily because of the separation of concerns — your view doesn't care if it is handling a cached version of an object or a real version.
Security	By handling all actions through a central controller, you can easily configure and manage access control to your data and actions.

However, there is no perfect solution. The disadvantages of using the Model 2 Architecture are illustrated in the following table.

Disadvantage	Description
Learning curve	You cannot use the Model 2 Architecture if you do not understand it. Furthermore, if you want to reuse a framework, you must learn the particulars of that application. Of course, you are reading this chapter, so this should be fairly well mitigated after you read all about WebWork.

Table continued on following page

Disadvantage	Description
Complexity	There are many things to learn about Model 2 Architecture in order to use it effectively. Learning curves are different, but compared to JSP, it can be quite intimidating to the average web developer who has been building page-centric database-driven web applications for quite a while.
Programming versus scripting	Many web developers are used to developing their applications interactively — as if they were scripting their web site. The concept of compiling and dependencies is simply something foreign to them, particularly if they came to web development out of graphical design rather than programming. Now, you can still separate responsibilities among the team and allow these scripters to handle the views of the application, which are still conventional JSP.

The critical concept in deciding whether to go with Model 2 is to decide whether or not it is overkill. A rule of thumb could be that if you have more than five or six pages in your web application, you really should use Model 2 Architecture. Note that this assumes that you will *never* have more than five or six pages, or that you are building a throwaway application.

The example application in this chapter deals directly with this issue of Model 1 versus Model 2. Too many explanations of Model 2 find it necessary to describe a system sufficiently complex to demonstrate the utility of Model 2, while ignoring the fact that the bigger the scope, the harder it is to wrap your mind around it. This application, a contact manager, would probably be a good candidate for Model 1, if it were not going to change or grow.

That is the fundamental distinction between Model 1 and Model 2 — "Pay me now or pay me later." Either way you are not really saving any effort with Model 1 unless you intend not to be around later — because the project is not expected to undergo further development (as opposed to some untimely demise).

Now that you understand the concepts, advantages, and disadvantages of the Model 2 Architecture, you will want to look at an implementation of a Model 2 Architecture. This chapter shows you a simple example of building a Model 2 application using the popular web application framework called WebWork.

Developing an Application with WebWork

Building applications with the Model 2 Architecture is not very helpful if you have to build all of this additional glue code that provides the framework that implements the architecture. It is far better if you use a framework like Struts to implement Model 2. In this chapter, you will see one of the more popular emerging frameworks known as WebWork, or more specifically, WebWork2. WebWork is a web application framework built upon a generic command framework that provides for modularizing code through a concept known as *Inversion of Control* (IoC). Though WebWork could be used to build a Model 1 web application, it is really geared toward being a great Model 2 framework.

What Is Inversion of Control and Why Is it Useful?

To explain Inversion of Control, you should be familiar with a couple of concepts that are widely used by software and system architects to categorize components and services of a bigger system. These categories are as follows:

❑ **Vertical:** When a component or service is referred to as being vertical, it is focused on a business process. For example, a billing application would be a vertical application.

❑ **Horizontal:** Conversely, a component or service that is horizontal provides something that is relevant to all of the vertical services and components. A security manager and database connection pool are examples of horizontal components.

What has become increasingly painful in developing enterprise applications, that is, vertical components, is interfacing to horizontal services and components. Outside of the obvious performance benefit, how much better is it to have to do a custom, configurable lookup of a database connection pool than just creating the connection yourself? Furthermore, you don't want to have to account for all the horizontal services in all your application components, so you end up creating another layer of indirection on top of the horizontal service in order to provide the role for that service in your application.

Here is what that would look like in code:

```java
package org.advancedjava.ch08;
import javax.naming.Context;
import javax.naming.InitialContext;
import javax.naming.NamingException;
import javax.sql.DataSource;
public class LookupMethod {
  private DataSource ds;
  public LookupMethod() {
    try {
      Context initCtxt = new InitialContext();
      ds = (DataSource) initCtxt.lookup("/jdbc/DS");
    } catch (NamingException e) {
      e.printStackTrace();
    }
  }
  /**
   * @return
   */
  public DataSource getDs() {
    return ds;
  }
  /**
   * @param source
   */
  public void setDs(DataSource source) {
    ds = source;
  }
}
```

Note in the constructor how you must go to the trouble to look up a component using the Java Naming and Directory Interface — and you tie yourself to that name. This wouldn't be such a big problem in such a limited circumstance, but consider that this class is not the start point for your application; rather, it is just a component of the application. You may have many of these components, all looking things up for themselves.

What if you inverted the whole equation and you simply declared your need for a given horizontal service? This is what Inversion of Control does; it allows you to develop your application components independent of how they will actually be provided. You simply declare the need for a given component, and allow the framework to inject the dependency — that is, provide the needed component at runtime for you.

Instead, you could write it as what they call a Plain Old Java Object (POJO), which simply declares a member variable for the needed dependency and leaves the how and where of satisfying that dependency to the framework that runs it. So, your class would look something like this:

```
package org.advancedjava.ch08;
import javax.sql.DataSource;
public class InjectorMethod implements Injector {
  private DataSource ds;
  public InjectorMethod() {
  }
  /**
   * @return
   */
  public DataSource getDs() {
    return ds;
  }
  /**
   * @param source
   */
  public void setDs(DataSource source) {
    ds = source;
  }
}
```

Note how you have implemented an interface known as `Injector`, to declare the method through which you expose your dependency. Here is what that interface looks like:

```
package org.advancedjava.ch08;

import javax.sql.DataSource;
public interface Injector {
  public void setDs(DataSource ds);
}
```

By doing this, you are keeping your objects based more purely on solving the domain problems of your application, and deferring the context (setting up resources and finding them, and so on) to another part of the application. You have inverted the control, that is, let the infrastructure call your code to do its specific part, rather than having your code and every other piece of code call the infrastructure to suit their needs.

Before you stop reading under the pressure of having to understand every nuance of all these complex pieces and abstract concepts, realize that you are learning these things as the background to understanding how things work under the hood. The nice thing about frameworks is that they handle a lot of the heavy lifting for you.

Now that you have learned the foundation concepts of WebWork — Inversion of Control and Model 2 Architecture — next you get some background in the WebWork framework in particular.

Architecture

You don't need to know every intricacy of WebWork in order to use it, but this text provides you with some of the fundamental concepts so that you understand how it all fits together. Figure 8-2 demonstrates how the framework fits together.

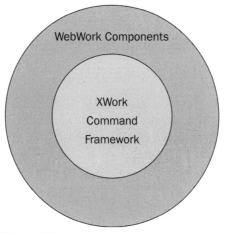

Figure 8-2

Note how the WebWork components (JSP tags, servlets, listeners, and servlet filters) are really just web extensions to the generic command pattern framework known as XWork. In fact, you could easily wrap your exact same XWork Actions with RMI or Web Service interfaces, or even embed them within a Swing application. That is the key concept; you are only applying the web context to your core POJOs that represent your domain.

The essence of WebWork (and XWork) is that you write basic Java objects called Actions, and then allow the framework to inject the dependencies that you need. By configuring interceptors, you can inject the dependencies that your Java object requires. Figure 8-3 shows how the request-response flow works in WebWork.

The request comes into the interceptor stack and is processed in the order of the interceptors until it gets to your developed `Action` class. Then, in reverse sequence, it makes its way back out through the response processing. This allows you to configure interceptors to provide facilities that are independent of the domain action, and you can thus inject those dependencies, without burdening your `Action` with unneeded code.

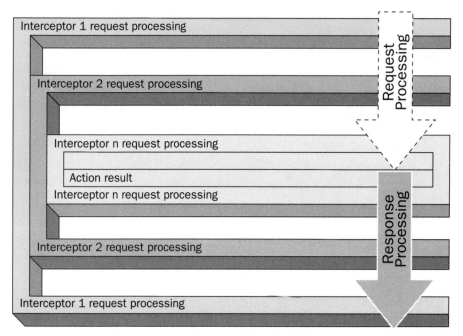

Figure 8-3

Interceptors

Several interceptors come with the WebWork framework; here is what each of them provides:

Interceptor	Description
LoggingInterceptor	Provides a logging statement before and after the execution of an action. Helpful for tracing through the application.
TimerInterceptor	Tracks the time taken to execute a given action. Useful for isolating bottlenecks, particularly in multiple action chains.
StaticParametersInterceptor	Maps the configuration parameters provided in your xwork.xml to the Action.
ParametersInterceptor	Populates the Action with the parameters passed in with the request.
ModelDrivenInterceptor	Unlike the other parameter interceptors, which only apply parameters directly to the member variables in the Action, this interceptor will allow you to map them into more complex domain objects in your action.
ChainingInterceptor	Applies the result of the previous action to the next action, useful for tying together multiple actions to form a useful composite. For example, you may have an action for calculating the sales tax, which is chained to an action that handles the totaling of the whole bill.

Interceptor	Description
DefaultWorkflowInterceptor	If the Action implements Validateable, it will call validate(). If the Action implements ValidationAware, it will call hasErrors() to see if there are any registered error messages; if there are, it will return the INPUT status. If neither of these occur, it will invoke the Action execute method.

Of course, you can implement your own interceptors, and you see this in action later in the chapter, as it is used to provide support for Hibernate.

ValueStack

Remember how you learned earlier in the chapter about how your domain-specific objects are "along for the ride?" The ValueStack is where they ride. Much like Java uses a stack to hold the relevant objects it uses within a given method or code block, XWork uses the ValueStack to accumulate the results of what has happened through your request's life cycle. This is useful because the View components can simply build themselves using JSP (or Velocity) tags that interact with the ValueStack.

The way that your views interact with the ValueStack is through something called the Object Graph Navigation Language (OGNL).

OGNL

OGNL, pronounced as it would sound if you tried to say it, provides you with a useful and easy way to express how you retrieve objects from an object graph. It also does things like automatic type conversion. (You think to yourself, "Sure, the request sends all of its parameters as String objects and yes, the domain object takes an int, so why do I have to always tell it to execute Integer.parseInt()?") In effect, it is very useful for providing simple expressions for manipulations of objects that otherwise take several lines of code.

Not only does the WebWork tag library make great use of OGNL for traversing the ValueStack, but WebWork also uses it to populate Action objects from request parameters.

Components

As you learned earlier, WebWork is built upon IoC. The first way that IoC is used is in injecting dependencies into Actions. However, WebWork also provides the ability to use a Component to inject resources into various scopes. You can configure your WebWork application to inject components into three different scopes:

1. **Request.** The Component will be attached to every user request, making it accessible to each Action.

2. **Session.** The Component will be attached when each new user session is created.

3. **Application.** The Component will exist throughout the life cycle of the application.

However, a practical example would probably make it easier to understand how components are used. Next, you see how Hibernate is configured as a set of WebWork components to provide a complementary solution for persisting your objects.

Extending the Framework to Support Hibernate

The nice thing about Model 2 Architecture frameworks in general and WebWork in particular is that they are easily componentized and extended. One of the more exciting open source tools available online is the Hibernate tool, which provides object/relational persistence. Put more simply, it allows you to persist your objects more easily to a relational database than conventional SQL. For more discussion of the problem that Hibernate seeks to address, see Chapter 6.

The genius behind Hibernate is a guy named Gavin King. King wanted to demonstrate how easily Hibernate pulled into a Model 2 framework, so he created a sample application to provide user and role administration for Tomcat by linking Hibernate to WebWork.

To make it more focused, King's example has been stripped down to the point that it would probably not be recognizable to him, but he still deserves credit for the concepts. Plus, you can refer to his application if you want to see a more sophisticated use of these techniques. You can download it at `http://hibernate.org`.

The fundamental component in building your Hibernate applications is the `HibernateFactory` object. This object performs the setup and configuration of Hibernate, and then provides `Session` objects for users to interact with the framework. As you might imagine, you only need one of these for your application; any more would be excessive and inefficient.

What if you could create one at startup time and share it among all of your applications? That is where WebWork components come into play. As demonstrated in Figure 8-4, WebWork will initialize a `HibernateFactory` at startup and inject that dependency into your application's context.

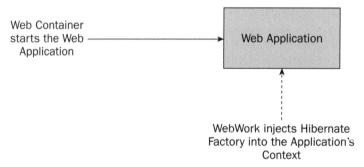

Figure 8-4

But WebWork doesn't stop with just injecting a `HibernateFactory` into your application; it also provides the ability to inject a Hibernate `Session` object into every user request. Figure 8-5 demonstrates how a `Session` object is injected into the request object that is created to service a given request.

Now that you have learned how WebWork components inject Hibernate into your Model 2 Architecture application, next you see how that comes in very useful.

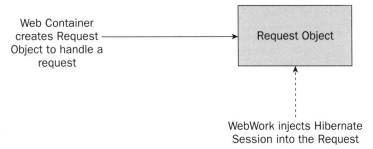

Figure 8-5

Preventing the Hanging Session

A tough problem in matching up Model 2 Architecture applications with object/relational mapping tools is that they tend to have two common operating models that can work against each other:

❑ A Model 2 application wants to conduct an action to retrieve a given graph of objects in the domain model and then forward it along to the view. In effect, it wants to disconnect from the database to prevent unnecessary binding. Also, it allows for clear packaging and handling of unanticipated actions in processing, namely exceptions and errors. Model 2 wants to consider the View part of the model to be about rendering data, independent of where it comes from.

❑ An ORM tool (like Hibernate) tends to prefer deferring initializing all of the objects on a given graph until they are needed, to avoid performance problems, data latency issues, and so on. Basically, the more data you pull, the slower and less efficient your application can become. Furthermore, the longer it is disconnected, the less likely it is to be current.

Now, before you start dismissing the two models as inconsistent, realize that this is a hiccup in two otherwise very compatible techniques. So, there is clearly a motivation to try to make the two work together more cleanly.

This is where the `HibernateInterceptor` comes into play. The short answer to what it does is allow you to maintain an open Hibernate session during the rendering of your view, because it intercepts the request model going out and closes the session cleanly.

Here is what the `HibernateInterceptor` looks like:

```
package org.advancedjava.ch08.interceptor;
import org.hibernate.HibernateException;
import org.apache.commons.logging.Log;
import org.apache.commons.logging.LogFactory;
import org.advancedjava.ch08.HibernateAction;
import org.advancedjava.ch08.component.HibernateSession;
import com.opensymphony.xwork.Action;
import com.opensymphony.xwork.ActionInvocation;
import com.opensymphony.xwork.interceptor.Interceptor;
public class HibernateInterceptor implements Interceptor {
  private static final Log LOG =
    LogFactory.getLog(HibernateInterceptor.class);
```

```
    public void destroy() {
    }
    public void init() {
    }
    public String intercept(ActionInvocation invocation)
      throws Exception {
      Action action = invocation.getAction();
      if (!(action instanceof HibernateAction))
        return invocation.invoke();
      HibernateSession hs =
        ((HibernateAction) action).getHibernateSession();
      try {
        return invocation.invoke();
      }
      // Note that all the cleanup is done
      // after the view is rendered, so we
      // have an open session in the view
      catch (Exception e) {
        hs.setRollBackOnly(true);
        if (e instanceof HibernateException) {
          LOG.error("HibernateException in execute()", e);
          return Action.ERROR;
        } else {
          LOG.error("Exception in execute()", e);
          throw e;
        }
      } finally {
        try {
          hs.disposeSession();
        } catch (HibernateException e) {
          LOG.error("HibernateException in dispose()", e);
          return Action.ERROR;
        }
      }
    }
  }
}
```

This brings the discussion back to the aforementioned `HibernateAction` class. Simply extending this class will allow your other actions to use these advantages rather transparently:

```
package org.advancedjava.ch08;
import org.hibernate.HibernateException;
import org.hibernate.Session;

import org.advancedjava.ch08.component.HibernateSession;
import org.advancedjava.ch08.component.HibernateSessionAware;
import org.apache.commons.logging.Log;
import org.apache.commons.logging.LogFactory;

import com.opensymphony.xwork.ActionSupport;

public abstract class HibernateAction
  extends ActionSupport
```

```
  implements HibernateSessionAware {
  private static final Log LOG =
    LogFactory.getLog(HibernateAction.class);
  private HibernateSession session;
  public String execute() throws Exception {
    if (hasErrors()) {
      LOG.debug("action not executed, field or action errors");
      LOG.debug("Field errors: " + getFieldErrors());
      LOG.debug("Action errors: " + getActionErrors());
      return INPUT;
    }
    LOG.debug("executing action");
    return go();
  }
  protected abstract String go() throws HibernateException;
  public void setHibernateSession(HibernateSession session) {
    this.session = session;
  }
  public HibernateSession getHibernateSession() {
    return session;
  }
  /**
   * Get the Hibernate Session instance
   */
  protected Session getSession() throws HibernateException {
    return session.getSession();
  }
  protected void setRollbackOnly() {
    session.setRollBackOnly(true);
  }
}
}
```

Now that you have seen all that the WebWork2 and Hibernate frameworks have to offer, it is time to move on to a more concrete example of using them — your contact manager.

Defining Your Domain Model

One of the first things you will do in your project is get your hands around what things your system will manage. Whether you call them entities or objects, and no matter where you store them (in a database or file system), there is still a set of conceptual classes that holds your system (and your business) together.

When it comes to defining your domain model, you have three things to consider:

❑   What domain objects already exist in the form of databases, documents, and so on?

❑   If you don't have them, what is available to help you make them up?

❑   What if your domain already exists, but is unsatisfactory for the users?

In essence, you generally fall into one of these two scenarios: Either you already are managing this data, in which case you are probably already in possession of a database, or you are starting from something new. The third way, having something already and needing something new, is the most painful.

405

Because data modeling and data migration are beyond the scope of this chapter (and book), the focus is limited to a very basic domain model. Figure 8-6 demonstrates the conceptual classes for your small contact management system.

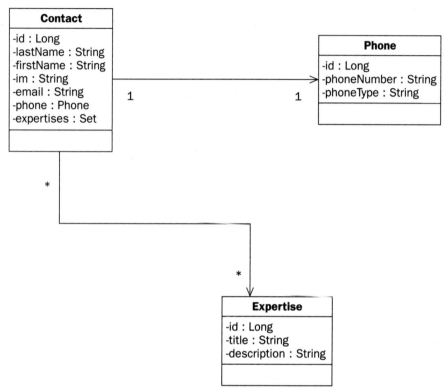

Figure 8-6

This model provides you with a basic capability to track a person and their relevant phone number and expertise. A person can be related to many expertise objects, but only one phone number, as well as the inverse being true. There are many experts in Java, and someone can be an expert in many things.

No methods are represented in this diagram, although you could assign behaviors to domain objects if they were to make sense. An example of where you may want to capture a behavior would be something like a calculator object where you would have obvious domain behaviors. The diagram in Figure 8-6 demonstrates what is the primary domain of this application — storing information on contacts and their expertise.

Models really embody the core concept behind object-oriented programming, creating software objects that represent the system-relevant attributes and behaviors of a real-world object.

Now, the model is turned into a set of JavaBeans, with accessor and mutator methods (the "getters and setters"). For the sake of brevity, you will not have to look through all of them here, but instead they are provided with the source on the companion web site.

Hibernate is going to handle object persistence to a database, so you should take a look at the Hibernate mapping file to see how the object and the database model are resolved. In this first section, you declare the mapping package, and the first part of the first class, `Contact`. In there you define your basic properties and to which columns they bind. An interesting thing to note here: You are letting the database handle creating unique IDs for your contact objects, so you should leave the `id` property alone in your code. It will be null until the database assigns it an identifier:

```xml
<?xml version="1.0"?>
<!DOCTYPE hibernate-mapping PUBLIC
    "-//Hibernate/Hibernate Mapping DTD 3.0//EN"
    "http://hibernate.sourceforge.net/hibernate-mapping-3.0.dtd">
<hibernate-mapping package="org.advancedjava.ch08.model">
    <class name="Contact" table="contacts">
        <id name="id" column="ID"
            unsaved-value="null">
            <generator class="increment"/>
        </id>
        <property name="firstName" column="FIRST_NAME" />
        <property name="lastName" column="LAST_NAME"/>
        <property name="email" column="EMAIL"/>
        <property name="im" column="IM"/>
```

In this next section of code, you are mapping the set of `Expertise` objects for a given `Contact`. Note how it specifies your conventional many-to-many join table, with the key column referring to the key of the containing object and the many-to-many column referring to the key of the related class:

```xml
        <set name="expertises"
            table="contact_expertise"
            cascade="save-update">
            <!-- the foreign key of the Contact -->
            <key column="CONTACT_ID"/>
            <many-to-many column="EXPERTISE_ID"
                class="Expertise"/>
        </set>
```

The last section of code shows an example of mapping a complex type with a one-to-one relationship (phone) and then gives the mapping definitions for the other classes in your domain model. Note that generally mappings are defined each in their own file, but for brevity, they are defined together here. It is important to recognize that you must not define the same class twice:

```xml
        <one-to-one name="phone" cascade="all"/>
    </class>

    <class name="Expertise" table="expertise">
        <id name="id" column="ID"
            unsaved-value="null">
            <generator class="increment"/>
        </id>
        <property name="title" column="TITLE" />
        <property name="description" column="DESCRIPTION"/>
    </class>

    <class name="Phone" table="phone">
```

```
        <id name="id" column="ID"
              unsaved-value="null">
              <generator class="increment"/>
        </id>
        <property name="phoneNumber" column="PHONENUMBER" />
        <property name="phoneType" column="PHONETYPE"/>
    </class>
</hibernate-mapping>
```

Wait a second! You may be thinking that now you have to go and create the database, being careful to set everything up to match this mapping file. You may also be thinking: "There is no way I am going to do this myself for this little sample application. Where is the SQL script to load this database?"

Not so fast. Now that you have defined the semantics of how the database should look, you can just use Hibernate's `SchemaExport` tool to create the database for you!

Hibernate has a tools project that provides both plug-ins for Eclipse and a set of Ant tasks. Here is a sample build file that uses the Ant tasks:

```
<?xml version="1.0" encoding="UTF-8" ?>
<project name="hibernate" default="schemaExport">
  <taskdef name="hibernatetool"
classname="org.hibernate.tool.ant.HibernateToolTask">
    <classpath>
      <pathelement location="WEB-INF\classes"/>
      <fileset dir="toolsjars">
        <include name="**/*.jar"/>
      </fileset>
    </classpath>
  </taskdef>
  <target name="schemaExport" >
    <hibernatetool destdir="">
      <configuration
        configurationfile="WEB-INF\classes\hibernate.cfg.xml"
        propertyfile="WEB-INF\classes\hibernate.properties" >
      </configuration>
      <hbm2ddl drop="true" create="true" export="true" update="false" />
    </hibernatetool>
  </target>
  <target name="schemaUpdate" >
    <hibernatetool destdir="">
      <configuration
          configurationfile="WEB-INF\classes\hibernate.cfg.xml"
          propertyfile="WEB-INF\classes\hibernate.properties" >
      </configuration>
      <hbm2ddl drop="false" create="false" export="true" update="true" />
    </hibernatetool>
  </target>
</project>
```

Note that it looks for a `hibernate.properties` file to tell it how to configure Hibernate for your purposes. The one that comes with the Hibernate distribution has a tremendous number of options and examples, so this one is simplified for your purposes. Here is what that properties file will look like for your MySQL implementation:

```
hibernate.query.substitutions true 1, false 0, yes 'Y', no 'N'
hibernate.dialect org.hibernate.dialect.MySQLDialect
hibernate.connection.driver_class com.mysql.jdbc.Driver
hibernate.connection.url jdbc:mysql:///contact
hibernate.connection.username root
hibernate.connection.password
hibernate.connection.pool_size 5

#Comment this out as soon as you have seen the SQL
hibernate.show_sql true

hibernate.jdbc.batch_size 0
hibernate.jdbc.use_streams_for_binary true
hibernate.max_fetch_depth 1

#If you are having Hibernate problems, set this to true
#very helpful for debug.
#hibernate.cglib.use_reflection_optimizer false
hibernate.cache.use_query_cache true
hibernate.cache.provider_class org.ehcache.hibernate.Provider
```

Of course, most of the examples for other databases have been taken out for the sake of brevity, but you could easily substitute another database for this one. You will reuse this properties file later to configure your web application:

```
<!DOCTYPE hibernate-configuration PUBLIC
    "-//Hibernate/Hibernate Configuration DTD//EN"
    "http://hibernate.sourceforge.net/hibernate-configuration-3.0.dtd">

<hibernate-configuration>
    <session-factory>
        <mapping resource="org/advancedjava/ch08/model/Model.hbm.xml"/>
    </session-factory>
</hibernate-configuration>
```

It is very interesting to see what happens when you run the `SchemaExport` utility, because it offers much insight into how Hibernate operates. In this first section, Hibernate does its setup and configuration:

```
C:\AdvancedJavaBook\JDK6Edition\Ch08\contact>ant
Buildfile: build.xml

schemaExport:
[hibernatetool] Executing Hibernate Tool with a Standard Configuration
[hibernatetool] 1. task: hbm2ddl (Generates database schema)
[hibernatetool] Feb 5, 2006 10:40:02 PM org.hibernate.cfg.Environment <clinit>
[hibernatetool] INFO: Hibernate 3.1.2
```

```
[hibernatetool] Feb 5, 2006 10:40:02 PM org.hibernate.cfg.Environment <clinit>
[hibernatetool] INFO: loaded properties from resource hibernate.properties: {hib
ernate.connection.driver_class=com.mysql.jdbc.Driver, hibernate.cglib.use_reflec
tion_optimizer=true, hibernate.cache.provider_class=org.hibernate.ehcache.hibern
ate.Provider, hibernate.cache.use_query_cache=true, hibernate.max_fetch_depth=1,
 hibernate.dialect=org.hibernate.dialect.MySQLDialect, hibernate.jdbc.use_stream
s_for_binary=true, hibernate.jdbc.batch_size=0, hibernate.query.substitutions=tr
ue 1, false 0, yes 'Y', no 'N', hibernate.connection.username=root, hibernate.co
nnection.url=jdbc:mysql://localhost:3307/contact, hibernate.connection.password=
****, hibernate.connection.pool_size=5}
[hibernatetool] Feb 5, 2006 10:40:02 PM org.hibernate.cfg.Environment <clinit>
[hibernatetool] INFO: using java.io streams to persist binary types
[hibernatetool] Feb 5, 2006 10:40:02 PM org.hibernate.cfg.Environment <clinit>
[hibernatetool] INFO: using CGLIB reflection optimizer
[hibernatetool] Feb 5, 2006 10:40:02 PM org.hibernate.cfg.Environment <clinit>
[hibernatetool] INFO: using JDK 1.4 java.sql.Timestamp handling
[hibernatetool] Feb 5, 2006 10:40:02 PM org.hibernate.cfg.Configuration configure
[hibernatetool] INFO: configuring from file: hibernate.cfg.xml
[hibernatetool] Feb 5, 2006 10:40:02 PM org.hibernate.cfg.Configuration addResource
```

Now that it has configured the environment, it starts picking up the mapping files or, in this case, the
only mapping file. On the first pass, it maps all of the entities, and then it does a second pass to map the
relationships and constraints:

```
[hibernatetool] INFO: Reading mappings from resource: org/advancedjava/ch08/mode
l/Model.hbm.xml
[hibernatetool] Feb 5, 2006 10:40:02 PM org.hibernate.cfg.HbmBinder bindRootPers
istentClassCommonValues
[hibernatetool] INFO: Mapping class: org.advancedjava.ch08.model.Contact -> cont
acts
[hibernatetool] Feb 5, 2006 10:40:02 PM org.hibernate.cfg.HbmBinder bindCollecti
on
[hibernatetool] INFO: Mapping collection: org.advancedjava.ch08.model.Contact.ex
pertises -> contact_expertise
[hibernatetool] Feb 5, 2006 10:40:02 PM org.hibernate.cfg.HbmBinder bindRootPers
istentClassCommonValues
[hibernatetool] INFO: Mapping class: org.advancedjava.ch08.model.Expertise -> ex
pertise
[hibernatetool] Feb 5, 2006 10:40:02 PM org.hibernate.cfg.HbmBinder bindRootPers
istentClassCommonValues
[hibernatetool] INFO: Mapping class: org.advancedjava.ch08.model.Phone -> phone
[hibernatetool] Feb 5, 2006 10:40:02 PM org.hibernate.cfg.Configuration doConfig
ure
[hibernatetool] INFO: Configured SessionFactory: null
[hibernatetool] Feb 5, 2006 10:40:02 PM org.hibernate.dialect.Dialect <init>
[hibernatetool] INFO: Using dialect: org.hibernate.dialect.MySQLDialect
```

Here it sets up its database connection by using the specified parameters (this is a good place to check if
your database isn't where you expect it):

```
[hibernatetool] Feb 5, 2006 10:40:03 PM org.hibernate.tool.hbm2ddl.SchemaExport
execute
[hibernatetool] INFO: Running hbm2ddl schema export
[hibernatetool] Feb 5, 2006 10:40:03 PM org.hibernate.tool.hbm2ddl.SchemaExport
execute
[hibernatetool] INFO: exporting generated schema to database
[hibernatetool] Feb 5, 2006 10:40:03 PM org.hibernate.connection.DriverManagerCo
nnectionProvider configure
[hibernatetool] INFO: Using Hibernate built-in connection pool (not for producti
on use!)
[hibernatetool] Feb 5, 2006 10:40:03 PM org.hibernate.connection.DriverManagerCo
nnectionProvider configure
[hibernatetool] Feb 5, 2006 10:40:03 PM org.hibernate.connection.DriverManagerCo
nnectionProvider configure
[hibernatetool] INFO: autocommit mode: false
[hibernatetool] Feb 5, 2006 10:40:03 PM org.hibernate.connection.DriverManagerCo
nnectionProvider configure
[hibernatetool] INFO: using driver: com.mysql.jdbc.Driver at URL: jdbc:mysql://l
ocalhost:3307/contact
[hibernatetool] Feb 5, 2006 10:40:03 PM org.hibernate.connection.DriverManagerCo
nnectionProvider configure
[hibernatetool] INFO: connection properties: {user=root, password=****}
```

Finally, it spits out the SQL that it will execute and reports on its success with the export. It then reports that it is cleaning up after itself:

```
[hibernatetool] alter table contact_expertise drop foreign key FK750E78B228D1E6B4;
[hibernatetool] alter table contact_expertise drop foreign key FK750E78B2381FFE94;
[hibernatetool] drop table if exists contact_expertise;
[hibernatetool] drop table if exists contacts;
[hibernatetool] drop table if exists expertise;
[hibernatetool] drop table if exists phone;
[hibernatetool] create table contact_expertise (CONTACT_ID bigint not null, EXPE
RTISE_ID bigint not null, primary key (CONTACT_ID, EXPERTISE_ID));
[hibernatetool] create table contacts (ID bigint not null, FIRST_NAME varchar(25
5), LAST_NAME varchar(255), EMAIL varchar(255), IM varchar(255), primary key (ID
));
[hibernatetool] create table expertise (ID bigint not null, TITLE varchar(255),
DESCRIPTION varchar(255), primary key (ID));
[hibernatetool] create table phone (ID bigint not null, PHONENUMBER varchar(255)
, PHONETYPE varchar(255), primary key (ID));
[hibernatetool] alter table contact_expertise add index FK750E78B228D1E6B4 (CONT
ACT_ID), add constraint FK750E78B228D1E6B4 foreign key (CONTACT_ID) references c
ontacts (ID);
[hibernatetool] alter table contact_expertise add index FK750E78B2381FFE94 (EXPE
RTISE_ID), add constraint FK750E78B2381FFE94 foreign key (EXPERTISE_ID) referenc
es expertise (ID);
[hibernatetool] Feb 5, 2006 10:40:05 PM org.hibernate.tool.hbm2ddl.SchemaExport
execute
[hibernatetool] INFO: schema export complete
[hibernatetool] Feb 5, 2006 10:40:05 PM org.hibernate.connection.DriverManagerCo
nnectionProvider close
[hibernatetool] INFO: cleaning up connection pool:
jdbc:mysql://localhost:3307/contact
```

In this case, you are using the MySQL database, so you can execute the `Show Tables` command and view that they were actually created:

```
mysql> show tables;
+-------------------+
| Tables_in_contact |
+-------------------+
| contact_expertise |
| contacts          |
| expertise         |
| phone             |
+-------------------+
5 rows in set (0.01 sec)
```

Now that you have handled the domain model for this application, it is time to bring this application to life and actually do something by implementing your `Action` classes.

Implementing Your Use Cases with Actions

So now what is it that your system does? Your use cases describe what a user hopes to achieve through interacting with your system. They describe the behavior of your system, or the actions that your system can provide. The chicken and egg argument is only slightly older than the old software argument concerning whether you should describe your system's behavior or structure first. In this case, you have described the structure first for two reasons:

❑   This sample is an overwhelmingly data-centric application.

❑   Because it is a data-centric application, the easiest way to restrict the scope is to define the data first.

Now, you develop the use cases that comprise this application. Here is a set of use cases for the system:

Use Case	Description
Browse Contacts	If you specify a given expertise, it will display the contacts that have that expertise.
Add Contact	Gather the relevant information to add a contact to the contact manager.
Remove Contact	Remove a contact from the contact manager.

Each of these use cases maps into an XWork Action. Here is the XWork Action used to handle the Browse Contacts use case. The interesting points about it are

❑   It is just one Plain Old Java Object; its simplicity is that it has methods for accessing and mutating its member variables and a go method to handle executing its intended function.

❑   It extends `HibernateAction` providing easy access to the Hibernate framework.

❑   It takes only a handful of lines of code to implement the use case. Even novice developers could start doing the basics very quickly. In this case, you execute a query based on the `Id` of the expertise for which you seek to find `Contacts`, and assign it to your `List` of contacts. Simply return `SUCCESS`; if anything should fail in terms of the database, query, and so on, it will be handled by the `HibernateInterceptor`:

```java
package org.advancedjava.ch08;
import java.util.List;
import org.hibernate.HibernateException;
import org.hibernate.Query;
public class BrowseContactAction extends HibernateAction {
  private Integer expertiseId;
  private List contacts;
  public String go() throws HibernateException {
    Query q =
      getSession().createQuery(
        "select con from Contact con  join con.expertises as exp where exp.id =
:ids");
    q.setParameter("ids", expertiseId);
    contacts = q.list();
    return SUCCESS;
  }
  /**
   * @return
   */
  public List getContacts() {
    return contacts;
  }
  /**
   * @return
   */
  public Integer getExpertiseId() {
    return expertiseId;
  }
  /**
   * @param list
   */
  public void setContacts(List list) {
    contacts = list;
  }
  /**
   * @param integer
   */
  public void setExpertiseId(Integer integer) {
    expertiseId = integer;
  }
}
```

Of course, there is nothing to browse if you do not add contacts to the database. The following code shows the `Action` that adds a `Contact` into the database. Note a couple of interesting things here:

❑ You are not handling the individual form elements or parameters and mapping them into the domain objects. WebWork is doing that for you, along with the tedious type conversion code.

❑ Because you only got the `Ids` for the types of expertise, you need to pull the actual objects from the database and assign them as a set to your `Contact` object.

```
package org.advancedjava.ch08;
import java.util.HashSet;
import org.hibernate.HibernateException;
import org.hibernate.Query;
import org.advancedjava.ch08.model.Contact;
import org.advancedjava.ch08.model.Phone;
public class AddContactAction extends HibernateAction {
  private Integer[] selectedExpertises;
  private Contact contact;
  private Phone phone;
  public AddContactAction() {
    contact = new Contact();
    phone = new Phone();
  }
  public String go() throws HibernateException {
    Query q =
      getSession().createQuery(
        "from Expertise exp where exp.id in (:ids)");
    q.setParameterList("ids", selectedExpertises);
    contact.setExpertises(new HashSet(q.list()));
    contact.setPhone(phone);
    getSession().save(contact);
    return SUCCESS;
  }
}
```

The remainder of this code demonstrates just the conventional accessor and mutator methods of the object. Though frequently overlooked, and rarely considered very seriously, you must not forget them when they are necessary, and with two frameworks like Hibernate and WebWork that make such extensive use of reflection, they are very often necessary:

```
/**
 * @return
 */
public Contact getContact() {
  return contact;
}
/**
 * @return
 */
public Phone getPhone() {
  return phone;
}
/**
 * @return
 */
public Integer[] getSelectedExpertises() {
  return selectedExpertises;
}
/**
 * @param contact
 */
public void setContact(Contact contact) {
  this.contact = contact;
```

```
    }
    /**
     * @param phone
     */
    public void setPhone(Phone phone) {
      this.phone = phone;
    }
    /**
     * @param integers
     */
    public void setSelectedExpertises(Integer[] integers) {
      selectedExpertises = integers;
    }
}
```

Of course, note that you could have written validation rules in your code, but instead it is easier to leverage XWork's validation framework. Here is the validation XML file for this `Action`. It is pretty straightforward; you specify the types of validators that you wish to apply to each field, as well as a message if it fails. You can consult XWork's documentation for all of its validation features:

```
<!DOCTYPE validators
    PUBLIC "-//OpenSymphony Group//XWork Validator 1.0//EN"
    "http://www.opensymphony.com/xwork/xwork-validator-1.0.dtd">

<validators>
    <field name="contact.firstName">
        <field-validator type="requiredstring">
            <message>You must enter a first name.</message>
        </field-validator>
    </field>
    <field name="contact.lastName">
        <field-validator type="requiredstring">
            <message>You must enter a last name.</message>
        </field-validator>
    </field>
    <field name="contact.email">
        <field-validator type="email">
            <message>Please correct the e-mail address.</message>
        </field-validator>
        <field-validator type="required">
            <message>Please enter an e-mail address.</message>
        </field-validator>
    </field>
</validators>
```

These `Action` classes provide the core business logic of your application, but no application would be complete without considering the user interface.

Developing Your Views

Now it is time to specify what the users will see as they traverse through the web application. You will now describe your system's user interface. Given different actions, what will the user see? In Figure 8-7, you have a drawing of how this web application flows.

415

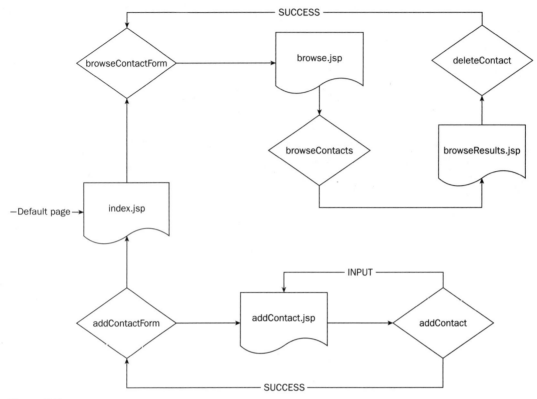

Figure 8-7

The flow starts with the default page of the web application (specified just like any other J2EE web application, in the `web.xml` file) — `index.jsp`. This page just serves as the front page for the application, which gives you links to your two major branches of the application: browsing contacts and adding contacts. Figure 8-8 shows you the simplicity of this page.

As you start to mock up your view elements, it becomes obvious that you will need to pull expertise data in order to populate the lists of expertise available in order to assign to a given contact, or by which to browse your contacts. Thus, based on these views, you have now derived two use cases in support of them:

Derived Use Case	Description
Browse Contact Form	This action will retrieve the relevant domain information required to build the browse contact view. In this case, it will just be a list of types of expertise.
Add Contact Form	In the same way, you will need to gather that expertise list in order to provide the user with the ability to assign which types of expertise a contact brings.

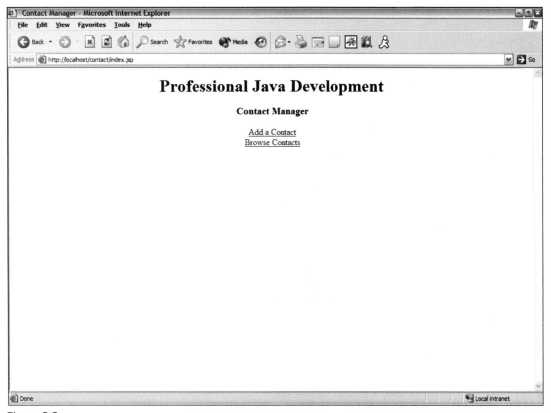

Figure 8-8

Often in situations like this one, where you have use cases specified simply to build the view, you will make a small departure from Model 2 purity and allow these pages to call their own application code specific to just building the view. WebWork provides the capability to reference its Actions and framework from within its WebWork JSP custom tags. However, for the sake of this chapter, because you used JSP custom tags extensively in the previous chapter, you will use the pure approach.

Adding Contacts to the System

To browse the contacts in the system, first you must add some contacts to the system. Following the Add a Contact link on the web application's homepage leads you to the screen displayed in Figure 8-9.

Following is addContact.jsp, which renders the input form. The important point to take away from this important form is how it maps onto your Action class, right down to the internal attributes of its domain objects (like Contact and Phone):

```
<%@ taglib prefix="ww" uri="webwork" %>
<jsp:include page="index.jsp"/>
<table cellspacing="0" cellpadding="0" border="0">
    <tr>
        <th>Enter Contact:</th>
```

417

```
    </tr>
    <tr>
        <td class="mask">
  <ww:form name="'createContactForm'"
            action="'addContact.action'" method="'POST'">
<ww:textfield label="'First Name'" name="'contact.firstName'"/>
<ww:textfield label="'Last Name'" name="'contact.lastName'"/>
<ww:textfield label="'Email'" name="'contact.email'"/>
<ww:textfield label="'IM'" name="'contact.im'"/>
<ww:textfield label="'Phone Number'" name="'phone.phoneNumber'"/>
<ww:textfield label="'Phone Type'" name="'phone.phoneType'"/>
  <ww:select label="'Expertise'" name="'selectedExpertises'"
                listKey="id"
                listValue="title"
                list="expertises"
                multiple="true"
            />
<ww:submit value="'CREATE'" />
  </ww:form>
        </td>
    </tr>
  </table>
```

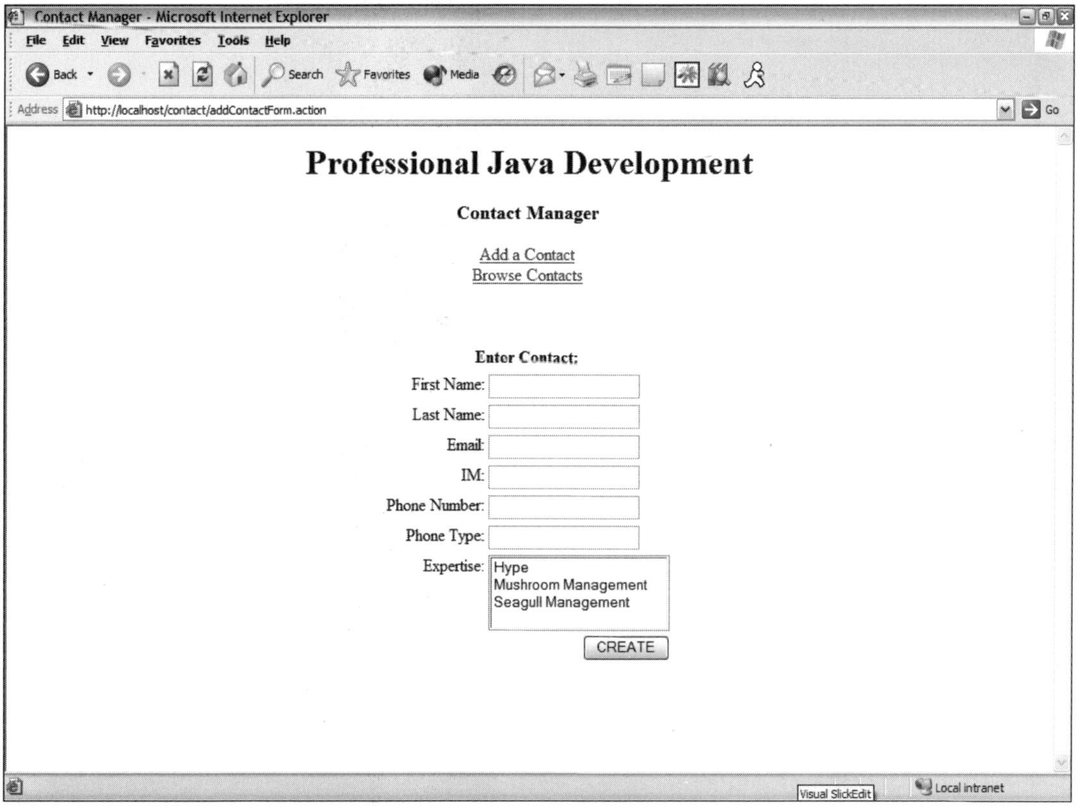

Figure 8-9

Of course, after you submit your new `Contact`, it brings you right back to the same page, with the form already filled in. This would be an ill-advised thing in production, but for a personal use system, it would probably save some data entry. Either way, in this case, you are just doing this to reduce the scope of the application so it can focus on the critical concepts of Model 2.

Browsing Contacts

Now that you have contacts, you can browse through them based on their expertise. Clicking Browse Contacts leads you to the screen displayed in Figure 8-10.

Figure 8-10

This page was built by using the Browse Contact Form use case, which provides an opportunity to demonstrate how to map the domain object into a Select box. Following is the code for `browse.jsp`. Note how the WebWork `select` tag maps to the `List` of `Expertise` objects that this page renders. The `listKey` attribute provides the value for each of the options within the HTML `select`, and the `listValue` provides the display value:

```
<%@ taglib prefix="ww" uri="webwork" %>
<jsp:include page="index.jsp"/>
<table cellspacing="0" cellpadding="0" border="0">
    <tr>
```

```
                <th>Select an expertise:</th>
        </tr>
        <tr>
            <td class="mask">
        <ww:form name="'browseContactForm'"
                    action="'browseContacts.action'" method="'POST'">
        <ww:select label="'Expertise'" name="'expertiseId'"
                    listKey="id"
                    listValue="title"
                    list="expertises"
                />
        <ww:submit value="'BROWSE'" />
        </ww:form>
            </td>
        </tr>
    </table>
```

When you submit this page, you get a table of contacts (see Figure 8-11) with their relevant information.

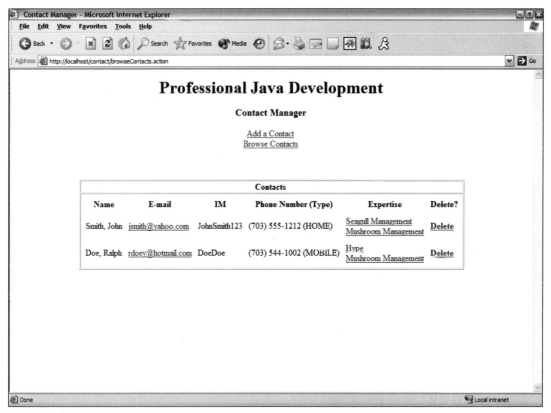

Figure 8-11

This screen is rendered by `browseContacts.jsp`. In it you see the use of the WebWork `iterator` tags to traverse the list of contacts and print out the relevant details about each contact:

```
<%@ taglib prefix="ww" uri="webwork" %>
<jsp:include page="index.jsp"/>
<table cellspacing="1" cellpadding="1" border="">
  <tr>
    <th>Contacts</th>
  </tr>
  <tr>
    <td class="mask">
      <table cellspacing="4" cellpadding="4">
        <tr>
          <th>Name</th>
          <th>E-mail</th>
          <th>IM</th>
          <th>Phone Number (Type)</th>
          <th>Expertise</th>
          <th>Delete?</th>
        </tr>
        <ww:iterator id="curContact" value="contacts">
        <tr>
          <td>
            <ww:property value="firstName"/>, <ww:property value="lastName"/>
          </td>
          <td><a href="mailto:<ww:property value="email"/>"/>
            <ww:property value="email"/>
            </a></td>
          <td>
            <ww:property value="im"/>
          </td>
          <td>
            <ww:property value="phone.phoneNumber"/>
            (
            <ww:property value="phone.phoneType"/>
            )</td>
          <td>
            <ww:iterator id="expertiseCur" value="expertises">
            <a href="browseContacts.action?expertiseId=<ww:property value="id"/>">
            <ww:property value="title"/>
            <br>
            </a>
            </ww:iterator>
          </td>
          <td><a href="deleteContact.action?selectedContact=<ww:property
value="id"/>">
            <b>Delete</b></a></td>
        </tr>
        </ww:iterator>
      </table>
    </td>
  </tr>
</table>
```

Of course, the link to Delete will remove a given `Contact` from the database, but it returns the user to the Browse Contacts screen, so it is unnecessary to review again.

Now that you have put together all of the components of a WebWork application, you need to review how to configure all of them to work together.

Configuring Your Application

In putting together all of these components you have built using the WebWork framework, the first thing to remember is that WebWork is a J2EE web application first and foremost. Therefore, it is useful to start with the web application deployment descriptor, commonly called the `web.xml`:

```xml
<?xml version="1.0" encoding="ISO-8859-1"?>

<!DOCTYPE web-app
    PUBLIC "-//Sun Microsystems, Inc.//DTD Web Application 2.3//EN"
    "http://java.sun.com/dtd/web-app_2_3.dtd">

<web-app>
  <display-name>Contact manager</display-name>
  <description>Example of Model 2 using Hibernate</description>
    <filter>
        <filter-name>container</filter-name>
        <filter-class>com.opensymphony.webwork.lifecycle.RequestLifecycleFilter
</filter-class>
    </filter>
    <filter>
        <filter-name>webwork</filter-name>
        <filter-class>com.opensymphony.webwork.dispatcher.FilterDispatcher</filter-
class>
    </filter>
    <filter-mapping>
        <filter-name>webwork</filter-name>
        <url-pattern>/*</url-pattern>
    </filter-mapping>
    <filter-mapping>
        <filter-name>container</filter-name>
        <url-pattern>/*</url-pattern>
    </filter-mapping>
    <listener>
        <listener-
class>com.opensymphony.webwork.lifecycle.ApplicationLifecycleListener</listener-
class>
    </listener>
    <listener>
        <listener-class>com.opensymphony.webwork.lifecycle.SessionLifecycleListener
</listener-class>
    </listener>
    <welcome-file-list>
        <welcome-file>index.jsp</welcome-file>
    </welcome-file-list>
    <taglib>
        <taglib-uri>webwork</taglib-uri>
```

```
            <taglib-location>/WEB-INF/webwork.tld</taglib-location>
        </taglib>
    </web-app>
```

Note that the WebWork wrapper to XWork is composed of a servlet filter, a listener, two servlets, and a tag library. You could always modify the mappings as you see fit — for example, if you prefer to make your actions more like those of Struts and end in `.do`, rather than `.action`.

The XWork framework, of course, defines the flow of the application, and that is defined within the `xwork.xml` file:

```
<!DOCTYPE xwork
    PUBLIC "-//OpenSymphony Group//XWork 1.0//EN"
    "http://www.opensymphony.com/xwork/xwork-1.0.dtd">
<xwork>
    <include file="webwork-default.xml"/>
    <package name="default" extends="webwork-default">
        <default-interceptor-ref name="defaultStack"/>
        <action name="browseContactForm"
class="org.advancedjava.ch08.BrowseContactFormAction">
            <result name="success" type="dispatcher">
                <param name="location">/browse.jsp</param>
            </result>
            <interceptor-ref name="defaultStack"/>
        </action>
        <action name="addContactForm" class="org.advancedjava.ch08
.AddContactFormAction">
            <result name="success" type="dispatcher">
                <param name="location">/addContact.jsp</param>
            </result>
            <interceptor-ref name="defaultStack"/>
        </action>
        <action name="addContact" class="org.advancedjava.ch08.AddContactAction">
            <result name="input" type="dispatcher">
                <param name="location">/addContact.jsp</param>
            </result>
            <result name="success" type="chain">
                <param name="actionName">addContactForm</param>
            </result>
            <interceptor-ref name="defaultStack"/>
            <interceptor-ref name="validation"/>
        </action>
        <action name="browseContacts" class="org.advancedjava.ch08
.BrowseContactAction">
            <result name="success" type="dispatcher">
                <param name="location">/browseResults.jsp</param>
            </result>
            <interceptor-ref name="defaultStack"/>
        </action>
        <action name="deleteContact" class="org.advancedjava.ch08
.DeleteContactAction">
            <result name="success" type="chain">
                <param name="actionName">browseContactForm</param>
            </result>
            <interceptor-ref name="defaultStack"/>
```

```
            </action>
        </package>
</xwork>
```

As you learned earlier in the chapter, WebWork provides the capability to inject dependencies into a web application, which was used to strap Hibernate into the application. In the `components.xml`, you specify the components and the enabler interfaces:

```
<components>
    <component>
        <scope>request</scope>
        <class>org.advancedjava.ch08.component.HibernateSession</class>
        <enabler>org.advancedjava.ch08.component.HibernateSessionAware</enabler>
    </component>
    <component>
        <scope>application</scope>
        <class>org.advancedjava.ch08.component.HibernateSessionFactory</class>
        <enabler>org.advancedjava.ch08.component.HibernateSessionFactoryAware
</enabler>
    </component>
</components>
```

Now that you have built the components and configured the application, you are ready to deploy and use your application.

Adapting to Changes

Now that the contact manager is up and running, what if you wanted to add an attribute to your `Contact` object? Since your application has become so wildly successful, you have forgotten who all of these contacts are and need to add a description to your contact. To accomplish this, you changed the UML diagram in Figure 8-6 to look like Figure 8-12, by adding a `description` attribute to the `Contact` object.

Of course, you would have to modify the Hibernate mapping file to accommodate the change to the domain model. Here is the change to `Model.hbm.xml`:

```
<?xml version="1.0"?>
<!DOCTYPE hibernate-mapping PUBLIC
    "-//Hibernate/Hibernate Mapping DTD 3.0//EN"
    "http://hibernate.sourceforge.net/hibernate-mapping-3.0.dtd">
<hibernate-mapping package="org.advancedjava.ch08.model">
    <class name="Contact" table="contacts">
        <id name="id" column="ID"
            unsaved-value="null">
            <generator class="increment"/>
        </id>
        <property name="firstName" column="FIRST_NAME" />
        <property name="lastName" column="LAST_NAME"/>
        <property name="email" column="EMAIL"/>
        <property name="description" column="DESCRIPTION"/>
        <property name="im" column="IM"/>
```

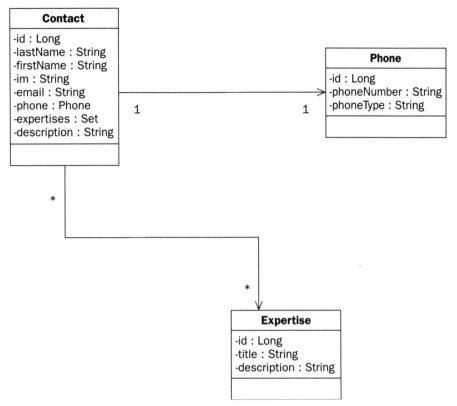

Figure 8-12

Now that you have added your description column, you could do one of two things: You can modify the database schema by hand, or you can run Hibernate's `SchemaUpdate` tool to resynchronize your database with your Hibernate mappings.

Once you have gotten your database and mappings back up to date, you will need a place to enter the data. This is the change to your `addContact.jsp` file:

```
<%@ taglib prefix="ww" uri="webwork" %>
<jsp:include page="index.jsp"/>
<table cellspacing="0" cellpadding="0" border="0">
    <tr>
        <th>Enter Contact:</th>
    </tr>
    <tr>
        <td class="mask">
  <ww:form name="'createContactForm'"
            action="'addContact.action'" method="'POST'">
    <ww:textfield label="'First Name'" name="'contact.firstName'"/>
    <ww:textfield label="'Last Name'" name="'contact.lastName'"/>
    <ww:textfield label="'Email'" name="'contact.email'"/>
    <ww:textfield label="'IM'" name="'contact.im'"/>
```

```
        <ww:textfield label="'Description'" name="'contact.description'"/>
        <ww:textfield label="'Phone Number'" name="'phone.phoneNumber'"/>
        <ww:textfield label="'Phone Type'" name="'phone.phoneType'"/>
         <ww:select label="'Expertise'" name="'selectedExpertises'"
                        listKey="id"
                        listValue="title"
                        list="expertises"
                        multiple="true"
                    />
        <ww:submit value="'CREATE'" />
         </ww:form>
           </td>
        </tr>
    </table>
```

Other than the obvious change to your `Contact.java`, that is all you need to do to add an attribute to your model. This is the key point in using the Model 2 Architecture: Modularity allows flexibility.

Summary

You have built a contact manager using the Model 2 Architecture leveraging WebWork framework (and Inversion of Control) to add support for the Hibernate Object persistence framework. Although the application is simplified to keep the examples easy to understand, it clearly demonstrates how you can easily adapt your application to new requirements.

In this chapter, you learned the following things:

❑　Web applications do not have to be developed using a page-centric approach, but rather there is an approach toward building modular web applications known as the Model 2 Architecture.

❑　In a popular web application framework called WebWork, the Model 2 Architecture is combined with a concept known as Inversion of Control, to allow Plain Old Java Objects (POJOs) to implement your functionality independent of the burdens of configuring external components.

❑　The modularity of WebWork allows you to plug in useful tools like Hibernate to build very streamlined applications that focus directly on your business domain.

The next chapter discusses how to leverage code developed in other languages through the Java Native Interface.

9

Interacting with C/C++ Using Java Native Interface

This chapter discusses connecting Java programs to programs written in C/C++. Java Native Interface (JNI) provides a sophisticated mechanism for invoking routines written in native code, and also provides a mechanism for native code to call routines that are written in Java.

A First Look at Java Native Interface

Creating a Java program that uses native code is fundamentally simple. First, you write the Java code and mark certain methods as `native` and leave the method unimplemented (as if you were writing an abstract method). Next, you run a utility that comes with the JDK to create a C/C++ header file. The native methods are then implemented in C/C++, with signatures matching the version in the generated header file. The Java code must then load this library in order to obtain access to the native routines. This process is illustrated in Figure 9-1.

To get a basic idea of how to write a program using JNI, create a small library of math routines implemented in C++ and invoke this from Java.

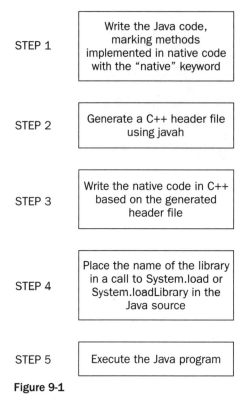

Figure 9-1

Creating the Java Code

The Java code is straightforward. Two methods are created, `addTwoNumbers` and `multiplyTwoNumbers`. These methods have no method bodies and are marked with the `native` keyword:

```java
public class JNIMathClient {
    public native int addTwoNumbers(int one, int two);
    public native int multiplyTwoNumbers(int one, int two);

    static {
        System.loadLibrary("MathLibrary");
    }

    public static void main(String args[])
    {
```

```
            JNIMathClient client = new JNIMathClient();

        int num1, num2;

        num1 = 5;
        num2 = 100;
        System.out.println(num1 + " + " + num2 + " = " +
                           client.addTwoNumbers(num1, num2));
        System.out.println(num1 + " * " + num2 + " = " +
                           client.multiplyTwoNumbers(num1, num2));
    }
}
```

The rest of the Java program is written as expected. The native methods are called as if they were normally implemented routines in Java. The static initializer is used to ensure the native library is loaded before it can be used inside the program. The discussion of the loadLibrary call is saved for the next section because it requires details of the native library.

Creating the Native Code and Library

In order to write the code in C++, javah — a tool that comes with the JDK — must be used to generate a header file. This header file contains the prototypes for the functions that must be implemented in C++. The Java code is first compiled and then this tool is executed on the class file. You execute javah by specifying the name of the class (not a filename) as the first parameter. The output of javah is a header file that has the same name as the class, and h as the file extension.

The resulting header file after executing javah JNIMathClient is JNIMathClient.h:

```
/* DO NOT EDIT THIS FILE - it is machine generated */
#include <jni.h>
/* Header for class JNIMathClient */

#ifndef _Included_JNIMathClient
#define _Included_JNIMathClient
#ifdef __cplusplus
extern "C" {
#endif
/*
 * Class:     JNIMathClient
 * Method:    addTwoNumbers
 * Signature: (II)I
 */
JNIEXPORT jint JNICALL Java_JNIMathClient_addTwoNumbers
  (JNIEnv *, jobject, jint, jint);

/*
 * Class:     JNIMathClient
 * Method:    multiplyTwoNumbers
 * Signature: (II)I
 */
```

```
JNIEXPORT jint JNICALL Java_JNIMathClient_multiplyTwoNumbers
  (JNIEnv *, jobject, jint, jint);


#ifdef __cplusplus
}
#endif
#endif
```

Each native method declaration is translated into a counterpart in C++. Each function always takes as its first two parameters a handle to the Java VM environment and a handle to the object that called the native method. Each parameter after those are the parameters specified in the original declaration of the function in the Java code.

> **Prototypes, also known as function signatures, follow a specific naming convention. The full package name comes first (following the prefix `_Java`) with each dot replaced with an underscore, then the name of the class, another underscore, then the name of the method. A native method named `addNumbers` defined in a package named `com.mathlib` and inside a class named `Math` becomes `_Java_com_mathlib_Math_addNumbers` in the header file.**

After creating the header file, it can then be used in a C++ project. Using Visual Studio 2005, create a simple DLL project and include this header file. Implementing the functions is a simple matter of copying the function signatures and filling in the bodies.

Select File⇨New and navigate to the Projects tab. Choose Win32 Dynamic-Link Library and give it a name. Figure 9-2 shows an example. On the first step of the wizard, choose A Simple DLL Project in order to already have the boilerplate code for a DLL. Click Finish and then OK. Look at Figure 9-2 to see these options chosen in the Visual C++ wizard.

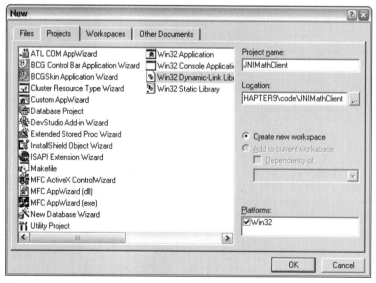

Figure 9-2

Continuing this example, the routines in the source file `MathLibrary.cpp` will be filled in. Don't forget to include the generated header file at the top of the source file:

```cpp
// MathLibrary.cpp : Defines the entry point for the DLL application.
//

#include "stdafx.h"
#include "..\JNIMathClient.h"

JNIEXPORT jint JNICALL Java_JNIMathClient_addTwoNumbers
  (JNIEnv *, jobject, jint one, jint two)
{
    return(one + two);
}

JNIEXPORT jint JNICALL Java_JNIMathClient_multiplyTwoNumbers
  (JNIEnv *, jobject, jint one, jint two)
{
    return(one * two);
}

BOOL APIENTRY DllMain( HANDLE hModule,
                       DWORD  ul_reason_for_call,
                       LPVOID lpReserved
                     )
{
    return TRUE;
}
```

After the native methods are implemented in C++, build the project. If there are no errors, you end up with a DLL file. This is the native library that then must be referenced in a call to `System.load` or `System.loadLibrary`. The library must be in the same directory as the Java program, or found somewhere in the paths specified in the system property `java.library.path`. If you use `System.loadLibrary`, specify only the base name of the native library—don't include the extension or a path. If you use `System.load`, you can specify a full path and must specify the extension of the library. The name of the library has nothing to do with the routines inside it, so feel free to name this file anything you want, but preserve the extension.

Executing the Code

If all is configured correctly, executing the Java code loads the native library, calls the routines, and uses the returned results. Executing the preceding Java code provides the following output:

```
5 + 100 = 105
5 * 100 = 500
```

If the library (`MathLibrary.dll`) is not found, you will end up with the following error:

```
java.lang.UnsatisfiedLinkError: no MathLibrary in java.library.path
    at java.lang.ClassLoader.loadLibrary(ClassLoader.java:1644)
    at java.lang.Runtime.loadLibrary0(Runtime.java:817)
    at java.lang.System.loadLibrary(System.java:986)
    at JNIMathClient.<clinit>(JNIMathClient.java:7)
Exception in thread "main"
```

You will also get this error if you try to use the native routines before you've called `System.load` or `System.loadLibrary`. By placing this call in the static initializer, you ensure the native library will be loaded well before it is needed.

Java Native Interface

JNI provides many functions, such as string and array handling, and a complete set of functions to create and use Java objects. These functions all take a pointer to the Java environment as the first parameter. However, in order to simplify programming, these functions all have an alias that is defined in the JNIEnv structure. This means you can invoke any JNI function by calling it through the pointer to the JNI environment. The rest of this chapter describes functions that are defined using the corresponding alias, that is, not the full versions that include this first parameter. Each function's declaration will precede its explanation throughout the rest of this chapter.

Data Types

The most important aspect of interfacing with other languages is the treatment of various data types such as strings. Different languages store strings in different ways. For example, character array strings in C and C++ are null-terminated. Strings in Java store the length separately, but are also zero-indexed. JNI provides a number of functions to manipulate strings, described in detail later. The primitive data types are provided with natural analogs on the native side. Consult the following table to see how data types in Java translate to types in C++.

Primitive Type (Java)	Native Type (C++)	Size (Bits)
boolean	jboolean	8, unsigned
byte	jbyte	8
char	jchar	16, unsigned
short	jshort	16
int	jint	32
long	jlong	64
float	jfloat	32
double	jdouble	64
void	void	n/a

Strings in JNI

The `jstring` data type is used to handle Java strings in C/C++. This type should not be used directly. If you try to use it in a call to `printf` (a C function to output text to the screen), for example, you run the risk of crashing the Java virtual machine. The `jstring` must first be converted to a C-string using one of several string conversion functions that JNI provides.

Java passes strings to the native environment in a slightly modified UTF-8 format, a multibyte way to encode Unicode strings. Take a look at Figure 9-3 to see how UTF-8 encoding is organized in memory. If the high bit is set for a particular byte, the byte is part of a multibyte character. This means that ASCII characters from value 1 to 127 stay the same, and though you can't count on it, if all the characters in the `jstring` are in this range, you can use the `jstring` directly in C/C++ code. Java does not use UTF-8 encoding longer than three bytes, and the NULL character (ASCII 0) is represented by two bytes, not one. This means you will never have a character that has all its bits set to 0.

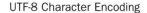

UTF-8 Character Encoding

A single byte accounts for characters in the range \u0001 to \u007F. The high bit is always 0.

Two bytes account for characters in the range \u0080 to \u07FF, and the null character, \u0000

Three bytes account for characters in the range \u0800 to \uFFFF

Figure 9-3

There are also routines that work with 2-byte encoded Unicode strings. If you're writing a program that uses localized strings, always handle your strings in Unicode because UTF-8 does not support internationalization. There are five functions that work with UTF-8 encoded strings, and each has a counterpart for Unicode strings that use 2-byte encoding. Two additional functions round out the set of string functions. These last two functions obtain a lock or release a lock on the string for purposes of synchronizing strings when in a threaded environment. Each string function takes as its first parameter a pointer to the Java environment. This is already passed in when a native function is called, so this is easily available. Take a closer look at these functions:

```
jstring NewString(const jchar *unicodeChars, jsize len);
jstring NewStringUTF(const char *bytes);
```

The first version of `NewString` takes a sequence of characters (`jchar`, which is two bytes) and the length in number of characters (not number of bytes). The UTF version takes a sequence of bytes. Each byte may form part of a one-, two- or three-byte character, and the end of the string is marked by a two-byte NULL character.

```
jsize GetStringLength(jstring string);
jsize GetStringUTFLength(jstring string);
```

Both versions of `GetStringLength` take a `jstring` and return its size in number of characters. These two `GetStringChars` functions return a pointer to the sequence of characters in a specified `jstring`:

```
const jchar *GetStringChars(jstring string, jboolean *isCopy);
const char *GetStringUTFChars(jstring string, jboolean *isCopy);
```

These are the main functions used to take a `jstring` and turn it into a string that can be easily used in native code. The pointer is valid until the accompanying version of `ReleaseStringChars` is invoked. The first version returns a pointer to `jchar`, and the UTF version returns a pointer to `jbyte`. The `isCopy` parameter is set to `JNI_TRUE` if a copy of the string is made, or set to `NULL` or `JNI_FALSE` if no copy is made.

Invoking one of the `ReleaseStringChars` functions tells the VM that the native code no longer needs to use the memory obtained in the call to the accompanying version of `GetStringChars`:

```
void ReleaseStringChars(jstring string, const jchar *chars);
void ReleaseStringUTFChars(jstring string, const char *utf);
```

The pointer to the characters is no longer valid after this function is called. The original string must be passed in along with the pointer obtained from the `GetStringChars` call. The `GetStringRegion` functions transfer a substring of the string `str` to a character buffer:

```
void GetStringRegion(jstring str, jsize start, jsize len, jchar *buf);
void GetStringUTFRegion(jstring str, jsize start, jsize len, char *buf);
```

The substring starts at position `start` and stops at `len-1` (therefore transferring `len` number of characters). This may throw a `StringIndexOutOfBoundsException`. The `GetStringCritical` function returns a pointer to the characters in the specified string:

```
const jchar *GetStringCritical(jstring string, jboolean *isCopy);
```

If necessary, the characters are copied and the function returns with `isCopy` set to `JNI_TRUE`. Otherwise, `isCopy` is `NULL` or set to `JNI_FALSE`. After this function is invoked, and up to the point `ReleaseStringCritical` is invoked, the functions used cannot cause the current thread to block.

```
void ReleaseStringCritical(jstring string, const jchar *carray);
```

The `ReleaseStringCritical` function releases the pointer obtained from the call to `GetStringCritical`.

Here's an example of implementing a string replace function in native code. The function `replaceString` takes a source string and replaces a string inside of the source string with another, then returns the new string. The Java code sets up what is needed on the native side:

```
public class StringExamples {
    public native String replaceString(String sourceString, String strToReplace,
                                        String replaceString);

    static {
        System.loadLibrary("StringLibrary");
    }

    public static void main(String args[])
    {
        StringExamples ex = new StringExamples();
        String str1 = "";
        String str2 = "";

        str1 = "Sky Black";
        str2 = ex.replaceString(str1, "Black", "Blue");
        System.out.println("The string before: " + str1);
        System.out.println("The string after: " + str2);
    }
}
```

The C++ implementation of the `replaceString` method, shown next, makes use of the string functions that you just learned:

```
JNIEXPORT jstring JNICALL Java_StringExamples_replaceString
  (JNIEnv *env, jobject obj,
   jstring _srcString, jstring _strToReplace, jstring _replString)
{
    const char *searchStr, *findStr, *replStr, *found;
    jstring newString = NULL;
    int index;

    searchStr = env->GetStringChars(_srcString, NULL);
    findStr = env->GetStringChars(_strToReplace, NULL);
    replStr = env->GetStringChars(_replString, NULL);

    found = strstr(searchStr, findStr);

    if(found != NULL) {
        char *newStringTemp;

        index = found - searchStr; // Calculate index to searchStr
        newStringTemp =
            new char[strlen(searchStr) + strlen(replStr) + 1];

        strcpy(newStringTemp, searchStr);
        newStringTemp[index] = 0;
```

435

```
        strcat(newStringTemp, replStr);
        strcat(newStringTemp, &searchStr[index+strlen(findStr)]);

        newString = env->NewString((const char*)newStringTemp);
        delete[] newStringTemp;
    }

    env->ReleaseStringChars(_srcString, searchStr);
    env->ReleaseStringChars(_strToReplace, findStr);
    env->ReleaseStringChars(_replString, replStr);

    return(newString);
}
```

The `GetStringChars` function is used to convert the string to a string usable in native code. The code within the `if` clause performs the search and replace, and finally allocates a new string with the affected string. This reference is returned, so it is the only reference not released using `ReleaseStringChars`.

Arrays in JNI

JNI supports the use of both arrays of primitive types and arrays of objects. Each primitive type has an array type counterpart. These array types are listed in the following table.

Name of Primitive Data Type (Java)	Array Type (For Use in C/C++ Code)
boolean	jbooleanArray
byte	jbyteArray
char	jcharArray
short	jshortArray
int	jintArray
long	jlongArray
float	jfloatArray
double	jdoubleArray

How Arrays Can and Cannot Be Used

Much like strings in JNI, arrays cannot be used directly. JNI provides a complete set of functions to access, get information about, create, and synchronize both arrays of objects and arrays of primitive data types. The following is an example of how Java arrays should *not* be used in C/C++:

```
JNIEXPORT jint JNICALL
int findNumber(JNIEnv *env, jobject obj, jintArray intArray,
              jint arraySize, jint numberToFind)
{
    int i;

    for(i=0; i<arraySize; i++) {
```

```
        if(intArray[i] == numberToFind) {
            return(i);
        }
    }

    return(-1);
}
```

This piece of code does not take into account any of the functions provided by JNI for processing arrays. JNI has a function to get the length of an array, and functions to access the array elements because the elements cannot be accessed directly. If you attempt to compile and execute the preceding code, it will crash the VM.

Array Functions

This section separates the array functions into those that work with arrays of objects and those that work with arrays of primitive data types. The function GetArrayLength works with any array:

```
jsize GetArrayLength(jarray array);
```

The GetArrayLength function returns the length of the array. This is the same value you get when accessing the length property of the array in Java code.

Functions for Arrays of Objects

Three functions are provided for working with arrays of Java objects in native code. These are NewObjectArray, GetObjectArrayElement, and SetObjectArrayElement. The NewObjectArray function creates a new object array of size length that holds objects of type elementClass:

```
jobjectArray NewObjectArray(jsize length, jclass elementClass,
                            jobject initialElement);
```

All elements in the array are set to initialElement, thus providing an easy way to initialize the entire array to null (or to another value). The GetObjectArrayElement function retrieves an object inside the array at the index specified by index:

```
jobject GetObjectArrayElement(jobjectArray array, jsize index);
```

If the index is out of bounds, an IndexOutOfBoundsException is thrown. The SetObjectArrayElement function sets the array element inside array at position index to value:

```
void SetObjectArrayElement(jobjectArray array, jsize index, jobject value);
```

If the index is out of bounds, an IndexOutOfBoundsException is thrown.

Functions for Arrays of Primitive Types

There are five core functions for use with each primitive data type. There is one version of each function for each primitive data type. Because there are so many functions, this section uses an abbreviation for each function. Certain information must be replaced with correct data types. In the following list of functions, the [Type] is replaced with the exact name of a primitive type from the first column in the following table. The [ArrayType] is replaced with the exact name of the array data type from the second column in the table. The [NativeType] is replaced with the exact name of the native data type from column three in the table. For example, to create a new integer array, you use the function NewIntArray that returns jintArray.

Name of Primitive Data Type	Array Type((For Use in C/C++ Code)	Primitive Type (For Use in C/C++ Code)
boolean	jbooleanArray	jboolean
byte	jbyteArray	jbyte
char	jcharArray	jchar
short	jshortArray	jshort
int	jintArray	jint
long	jlongArray	jlong
float	jfloatArray	jfloat
double	jdoubleArray	jdouble

The NewArray function returns a newly created Java array that is length elements in size:

```
[ArrayType] New[Type]Array(jsize length);
```

The GetArrayElements function returns a pointer to an array of the native type that corresponds to the Java data type:

```
[NativeType] *Get[Type]ArrayElements([ArrayType] array, jboolean *isCopy);
```

The parameter isCopy is set to JNI_TRUE if the memory returned is a copy of the array from the Java code, or JNI_FALSE if the memory is not a copy. The ReleaseArrayElements function releases the memory obtained from the call to Get[Type]ArrayElements:

```
void Release[Type]ArrayElements([ArrayType] array, [NativeType] *elems, jint mode);
```

If the native array is not a copy, the mode parameter can be used to optionally copy memory from the native array back to the Java array. The values of mode and their effects are listed in the following table.

Value of Mode	Description
0	Copies the memory from the native array to the Java array and deallocates the memory used by the native array.
JNI_COMMIT	Copies the memory from the native array to the Java array, but does *not* deallocate the memory used by the native array.
JNI_ABORT	Does not copy memory from the native array to the Java array. The memory used by the native array is still deallocated.

The `GetArrayRegion` function operates much like `Get[Type]ArrayElements`. However, this is used to copy only a subset of the array:

```
void Get[Type]ArrayRegion([ArrayType] array, jsize start, jsize len,
                          [NativeType] *buf);
```

The parameter `start` specifies the starting index to copy from, and `len` specifies how many positions in the array to copy into the native array. The `SetArrayRegion` is the counterpart to `Get[Type]Array Region`. This function is used to copy a segment of a native array back to the Java array:

```
void Set[Type]ArrayRegion([ArrayType] array, jsize start, jsize len,
                          [NativeType] *buf);
```

Elements are copied directly from the beginning of the native array (index 0) but are copied into the Java array starting at position `start` and `len` elements are copied over. The `GetPrimitiveArrayCritical` function returns a handle to an array after obtaining a lock on the array:

```
void *GetPrimitiveArrayCritical(jarray array, jboolean *isCopy);
```

If no lock could be established, the `isCopy` parameter comes back with a value `JNI_TRUE`. Otherwise, `isCopy` comes back `NULL` or as `JNI_FALSE`. The `ReleasePrimitiveArrayCritical` releases the array previously returned from a call to `GetPrimitiveArrayCritical`:

```
void ReleasePrimitiveArrayCritical(jarray array, void *carray, jint mode);
```

Look at the next table to see how the mode parameter affects the `array` and `carray` parameters.

Value for Mode	Meaning
0	Copies the values from `carray` into `array` and frees the memory associated with `carray`.
JNI_COMMIT	Copies the values from `carray` into `array` but does not free the memory associated with `carray`.
JNI_ABORT	Does not copy the values from `carray` to `array`, but does free the memory associated with `carray`.

Here's an example of implementing a sort routine in native code. To keep things simple, the insertion sort is used. The Java code, as usual, is fairly simple. The native method is declared, then the library is statically loaded, and the native method is invoked in the main method:

```
public class PrimitiveArrayExample {
    public native boolean sortIntArray(int[] numbers);

    static {
        System.loadLibrary("PrimitiveArrayLibrary");
    }

    public static void main(String args[])
    {
```

```
            PrimitiveArrayExample pae = new PrimitiveArrayExample();
            int numberList[] = {4, 1, 2, 20, 11, 7, 2};

            if(pae.sortIntArray(numberList)) {
                System.out.print("The sorted numbers are: ");
                for(int i=0; i<numberList.length; i++) {
                    System.out.print(numberList[i] + " ");
                }
                System.out.println();
            } else {
                System.out.println("The sort operation failed because " +
                                   "the array memory could not be allocated.");
            }
        }
    }
```

The native code uses the array functions to work with an array of integers:

```
JNIEXPORT jboolean JNICALL Java_PrimitiveArrayExample_sortIntArray
              (JNIEnv *env, jobject obj, jintArray intArrayToSort)
{
    jint *intArray;
    jboolean isCopy;
    int i, j, num;

    intArray = env->GetIntArrayElements(intArrayToSort, &isCopy);

    if(intArray == NULL) {
        return(JNI_FALSE);
    }

    for(i=1; i<env->GetArrayLength(intArrayToSort); i++) {
        num = intArray[i];

        for(j=i-1; j >= 0 && (intArray[j] > num); j--) {
            intArray[j+1] = intArray[j];
        }

        intArray[j+1] = num;
    }

    env->ReleaseIntArrayElements(intArrayToSort, intArray, 0);
    return(JNI_TRUE);
}
```

This sortIntArray function uses the GetIntArrayElements in order to work with the array in a native form. The GetArrayLength function is used to know how many elements are in the array, and finally, ReleaseIntArrayElements is used to both save the changed memory to the Java array and deallocate the memory.

As one final example of arrays, create an array of strings and then implement a find function that returns the index to the string:

```
public class ObjectArrayExample {
    public native int findString(String[] stringList, String stringToFind);

    static {
        System.loadLibrary("ObjectArrayLibrary");
    }

    public static void main(String args[])
    {
        ObjectArrayExample oae = new ObjectArrayExample();
        String[] colors = {"red","blue","black","green","grey"};
        int foundIndex;

        System.out.println("Searching for 'black'...");
        foundIndex = oae.findString(colors, "black");

        if(foundIndex != -1) {
            System.out.println("The color 'black' was found at index "
                                + foundIndex);
        } else {
            System.out.println("The color 'black' was not found");
        }
    }
}
```

An array of strings is created and passed to the native method `findString`. If the string is not found, the method returns `-1` and otherwise returns the index to the string from the array:

```
JNIEXPORT jint JNICALL Java_ObjectArrayExample_findString
  (JNIEnv *env, jobject obj, jobjectArray strList, jstring strToFind)
{
    const char *findStr;
    int i;
    int arrayLen;

    arrayLen = env->GetArrayLength(strList);
    findStr = env->GetStringChars(strToFind, NULL);

    if(findStr == NULL) {
        return(-1);
    }

    for(i=0; i<arrayLen; i++) {
        jstring strElem = (jstring)env->GetObjectArrayElement(strList, i);

        if(strElem != NULL) {
            const char *strTemp = env->GetStringChars(strElem, NULL);

            if(strcmp(strTemp, findStr) == 0) {
                env->ReleaseStringChars(strElem, strTemp);
                env->ReleaseStringChars(strToFind, findStr);
                env->DeleteLocalRef(strElem);
```

```
                    break;
            }

            env->ReleaseStringChars(strElem, strTemp);
            env->DeleteLocalRef(strElem);
        }

        env->ReleaseStringChars(strToFind, findStr);
    }

    if(i == arrayLen) {
        return(-1);
    } else {
        return(i);
    }
}
```

The GetArrayLength function is used to retrieve the length of the object array. The object array is then accessed using the GetObjectArrayElement function to retrieve a specific element. Note that the object is then cast to a jstring in order to get a handle to the array element's specific type. Also note that because the GetObjectArrayElement function returns a local reference, the reference is freed using DeleteLocalRef. As is explained in the local reference section, this call to DeleteLocalRef isn't necessary in this case, but it introduces the fact that many native functions return a local reference that should be cleaned up.

Working with Java Objects in C/C++

Java Native Interface also provides a set of functions to manipulate Java objects (using methods/fields), handle exceptions, and synchronize data for threads. These functions provide greater access to Java objects on the native side, allowing for more sophisticated applications. One way that these functions can be used is to make callbacks to Java methods, perhaps to communicate information. You see this in action in the mail client example at the end of this chapter.

Accessing Fields in JNI

There are two types of member variables in Java classes — static fields, which belong to classes, and non-static fields, which belong to individual objects. In order to gain access to a field, you must pass a field descriptor and the name of the field to GetFieldID or GetStaticFieldID. A field descriptor is one or more characters that fully describe a field's type. For example, the field int number has as its field descriptor I. Consult the next table for a full list of descriptors for primitive types. The descriptor for an array type is prefixed with the character [for each dimension of the array. Therefore, the type int[] numbers is described by [I, and int[][] numbers is [[I. For reference types, the fully qualified name of the class is used but the dots are replaced with a forward slash and the descriptor is surrounded by an L at the beginning and a semicolon at the end. For example, the type java.lang.Integer is described by Ljava/lang/Integer;.

Primitive Type (Java)	Field Descriptor
boolean	Z
byte	B
char	C
short	S
int	I
long	J
float	F
double	D

Much like the variety of functions for use with arrays of primitive types, each primitive type has its own Get and Set function for fields. This section also uses the abbreviated version for compactness. The [NativeType] is replaced by a string from the first column of the next table, and [Type] is replaced by the corresponding string from the second column in the table.

Name of Primitive Data Type (Java)	Primitive Type (For Use in C/C++ Code)
boolean	jboolean
byte	jbyte
char	jchar
short	jshort
int	jint
long	jlong
float	jfloat
double	jdouble

Here are the functions that are provided to access fields inside Java classes:

```
jfieldID GetFieldID(jclass clazz, const char *name, const char *sig);
```

The GetFieldID function returns a handle to the specified field for use in the Get and Set functions. The GetObjectClass function (described later) can be used to get a jclass suitable for the first parameter to this function. The name is the name of the field, and the sig parameter is the field descriptor. If this function fails, it returns NULL.

443

The `GetField` function returns the value of a particular field specified by `fieldID` that belongs to the Java object `obj`:

```
[NativeType] Get[Type]Field(jobject obj, jfieldID fieldID);
```

The `SetField` function sets the value of a particular field specified by `fieldID` that belongs to the Java object `obj` to the value `val`:

```
void Set[Type]Field(jobject obj, jfieldID fieldID, [NativeType] val);
```

The `GetStaticFieldID` function works the same as `GetFieldID` but is used for getting a handle to a static field:

```
jfieldID GetStaticFieldID(jclass clazz, const char *name, const char *sig);
```

The `GetStaticField` function returns the value of a static field specified by the `fieldID` handle and belonging to the class described by `clazz`:

```
[NativeType] GetStatic[Type]Field(jclass clazz, jfieldID fieldID);
```

The `SetStaticField` function sets the value of a static field specified by the `fieldID` that belongs to the class described by `clazz`:

```
void SetStatic[Type]Field(jclass clazz, jfieldID fieldID, [NativeType] value);
```

Here's an example of accessing fields on an object. The Java code defines a `Point` class and the native code performs some transformation on that point:

```
class Point {
    public int x, y, z;

    public String toString()
    {
        return("(" + x + ", " + y + ", " + z + ")");
    }
}

public class FieldAccessExample {
    public native void transformPoint(Point p);

    static {
        System.loadLibrary("FieldAccessLibrary");
    }

    public static void main(String args[])
    {
        FieldAccessExample fae = new FieldAccessExample();
        Point p1 = new Point();

        p1.x = 17;
        p1.y = 20;
        p1.z = 10;
        System.out.println("The point before transformation: " + p1);
```

```
            fae.transformPoint(p1);
            System.out.println("The point after transformation: " + p1);
        }
    }
```

The native library is loaded as usual. An instance of the Point class is created and set up, then the native function is called. The native code accesses the fields in the Point object and modifies these fields. Note that the object passed in isn't a copy — any changes done to it in native code take effect in the Java code when the native function returns. The GetObjectClass function is used to get a handle to the class behind a specified object:

```
JNIEXPORT void JNICALL Java_FieldAccessExample_transformPoint
  (JNIEnv *env, jobject obj, jobject thePoint)
{
    jfieldID x_id, y_id, z_id;
    jint x_value, y_value, z_value;
    jclass cls;

    cls = env->GetObjectClass(thePoint);

    x_id = env->GetFieldID(cls, "x", "I");
    y_id = env->GetFieldID(cls, "y", "I");
    z_id = env->GetFieldID(cls, "z", "I");

    x_value = env->GetIntField(thePoint, x_id);
    y_value = env->GetIntField(thePoint, y_id);
    z_value = env->GetIntField(thePoint, z_id);

    x_value = x_value;
    y_value = 10*y_value + 5;
    z_value = 30*z_value + 2;

    env->SetIntField(thePoint, x_id, x_value);
    env->SetIntField(thePoint, y_id, y_value);
    env->SetIntField(thePoint, z_id, z_value);
}
```

In this case, GetObjectClass returns a handle to the Point class. Each field is an integer, so the field descriptor used is simply I. After the field IDs are retrieved, accessing the value of the field happens through GetIntField and the field values are written back using SetIntField.

Invoking Java Methods Using JNI

Just like fields, there are static and nonstatic methods in Java. JNI provides functions to execute methods on Java objects and also static methods on Java classes. Much like accessing fields, the name and a descriptor for the method are used in order to get a handle to a specific Java method. Once you have this handle, you pass it to one of the CallMethod functions along with the actual parameters for the method. There are actually a number of CallMethod functions — one for each possible return type from a method. Consult the previous table for a listing of the various return types.

The method descriptor is formed by placing all the method's parameter types inside a single set of parentheses, and then specifying the return type after the closing parenthesis. Types for parameters and return type use the field descriptor described in the previous section. If the method returns void, the descriptor is simply V. If the method does not take any parameters, the parentheses are left empty. The method descriptor for the main method that you are familiar with is `([Ljava/lang/String;)V`. The parameters to `main` are placed inside the parentheses. A single open square bracket is used for each dimension of an object array, in this case a single one for a one-dimensional array of String, which is specified immediately after the bracket. Outside the parentheses is a single V because `main` has `void` as its return type. If you wish to invoke the constructor, use the method name `<init>`, and for static constructors, use the name `<clinit>`.

A shortcut to deriving field and method descriptors can be found in the `javap` **utility that comes with the JDK. By passing the command-line option** `-s` **to** `javap`**, you get a listing of the descriptors for the methods and fields of a class. For example, running** `javap` **on the** `Point` **class generates the following output:**

```
H:\CHAPTER9\code>javap -s Point
    Compiled from FieldAccessExample.java
    class Point extends java.lang.Object {
        public int x;
            /*    I    */
        public int y;
            /*    I    */
        public int z;
            /*    I    */
        Point();
            /*    ()V    */
        public java.lang.String toString();
            /*    ()Ljava/lang/String;    */
    }
```

Both field descriptors and method descriptors are output. You can copy these descriptors directly into the calls to the `GetFieldID` **or** `GetMethodID` **functions instead of figuring the descriptors out manually.**

Following is a list of functions for use when invoking methods on Java objects. The various `CallMethod` functions have versions for each data type, much like the functions for accessing fields, so the abbreviation is also used here. Replace the `[NativeType]` with a native data type, and replace the `[Type]` with the type name to finish the name of the function.

The `GetObjectClass` function returns a `jclass` that represents the class of the Java object `obj` that is passed in:

```
jclass GetObjectClass(jobject obj);
```

The `GetMethodID` and `GetStaticMethodID` functions return a handle to the specified method for use in the various `CallMethod` functions:

```
jmethodID GetMethodID(jclass clazz, const char *name, const char *sig);
jmethodID GetStaticMethodID(jclass clazz, const char *name, const char *sig);
```

The GetObjectClass function can be used to get a jclass suitable for the first parameter to this function. The name is the name of the method, and the sig parameter is the method descriptor. If this function fails it returns NULL.

The CallMethod functions (and variants) are used to invoke an instance method on a Java object:

```
[NativeType] Call[Type]Method (jobject obj, jmethodID methodID, ...);
[NativeType] Call[Type]MethodV(jobject obj, jmethodID methodID, va_list args);
[NativeType] Call[Type]MethodA(jobject obj, jmethodID methodID,
                        const jvalue *args);
```

The first two parameters to these functions are a handle to the object that has the method, and the handle to the specific method to invoke. The other parameters are the actual parameters to the Java method about to be invoked. The first function accepts a variable number of arguments and passes these arguments directly to the Java method. The second function accepts the list of arguments as a va_list structure that is prepackaged with the list of arguments. The third function accepts the method arguments as an array of jvalue. The jvalue type is a union made up of all the native Java data types, including jobject. Thus, each instance of a jvalue represents a single Java native type. If you wish to invoke a constructor or a private method, the method ID has to be obtained based on the actual class of the object, not one of the object's superclasses.

The CallNonvirtual functions also invoke an instance method of an object, but which Java method to invoke is based on the clazz parameter:

```
[NativeType] CallNonvirtual[Type]Method(jobject obj, jclass clazz,
                                    jmethodID methodID, ...);
[NativeType] CallNonvirtual[Type]MethodV(jobject obj, jclass clazz,
                                    jmethodID methodID, va_list args);
[NativeType] CallNonvirtual[Type]MethodA(jobject obj, jclass clazz,
                                    jmethodID methodID,
                                    const jvalue *args);
```

These enable you to invoke a specific method somewhere in the hierarchy of the object's class instead of invoking a method based on just the object's class. Just like the normal CallMethod functions, these allow you to pass in arguments to the Java method in the same three different ways.

The CallStaticMethod functions (and variants) invoke a static method belonging to the class clazz that is passed in:

```
[NativeType] CallStatic[Type]Method(jclass clazz, jmethodID methodID, ...);
[NativeType] CallStatic[Type]MethodV(jclass clazz, jmethodID methodID,
                                    va_list args);
[NativeType] CallStatic[Type]MethodA(jclass clazz, jmethodID methodID,
                                    const jvalue *args);
```

Use GetStaticMethodID to obtain a handle to the specific method to invoke. Arguments to the method can be passed in to this function in the same three ways as described previously.

Along with showing how to invoke Java methods, the following example shows the relationship of the Call and CallNonvirtual functions to combinations of an object and a handle to a class and a handle to a method:

```
class InvokeMethodParentClass {
    public void printMessage()
    {
        System.out.println("Inside InvokeMethodParentClass");
    }
}

public class InvokeMethodExample extends InvokeMethodParentClass {
    public native void execMethods();

    static {
        System.loadLibrary("InvokeMethodLibrary");
    }

    public void printMessage()
    {
        System.out.println("Inside InvokeMethodExample");
    }

    public static void main(String args[])
    {
        InvokeMethodExample ime = new InvokeMethodExample();

        ime.execMethods();
    }
}
```

The Java source defines a parent and a child class and both classes define the same method. The execMethods native method invokes the Call and CallNonvirtual functions in a variety of ways:

```
JNIEXPORT void JNICALL Java_InvokeMethodExample_execMethods
  (JNIEnv *env, jobject obj)
{
    jclass childClass, parentClass;
    jmethodID parent_methodID, child_methodID;

    childClass = env->GetObjectClass(obj);
    parentClass = env->FindClass("InvokeMethodParentClass");

    if(childClass == NULL || parentClass == NULL) {
        printf("Couldn't obtain handle to parent or child class");
        return;
    }

    parent_methodID = env->GetMethodID(childClass, "printMessage", "()V");
    child_methodID = env->GetMethodID(parentClass, "printMessage", "()V");

    if(parent_methodID == NULL || child_methodID == NULL) {
        printf("Couldn't obtain handle to parent or child method");
```

```
        return;
    }

    // These two calls invoke the method on the child class
    env->CallVoidMethod(obj, parent_methodID);
    env->CallVoidMethod(obj, child_methodID);

    // These two calls invoke the method on the parent class
    env->CallNonvirtualVoidMethod(obj, childClass, parent_methodID);
    env->CallNonvirtualVoidMethod(obj, parentClass, parent_methodID);

    // These two calls invoke the method on the child class
    env->CallNonvirtualVoidMethod(obj, childClass, child_methodID);
    env->CallNonvirtualVoidMethod(obj, parentClass, child_methodID);
}
```

Here's the output from this example:

```
Inside InvokeMethodExample
Inside InvokeMethodExample
Inside InvokeMethodParentClass
Inside InvokeMethodParentClass
Inside InvokeMethodExample
Inside InvokeMethodExample
```

Using the regular version, `CallVoidMethod`, the child's method is always invoked, regardless of which method ID is used (the one for the parent class or the one for the child). The `CallNonvirtualVoid Method` must be used to cause the method of the parent class to execute. Note that regardless of which class type is passed in, the determining factor for which method to execute is the method ID that is passed in.

Handling Java Exceptions in Native Code

JNI provides hooks to the Java exception mechanism in order to handle exceptions that are thrown in the course of executing methods that are implemented in Java code, or native methods written to throw Java exceptions. This mechanism has no bearing on standard error handling for regular functions implemented in C/C++. JNI provides a set of functions for checking, analyzing, and otherwise handling Java exceptions in native code. This section explores these functions and shows how to go about handling Java exceptions in native code in order to maintain Java's approach to exception handling.

The `ExceptionCheck` function returns `JNI_TRUE` if an exception has been thrown, or `JNI_FALSE` if one hasn't:

```
jboolean ExceptionCheck();
```

The `ExceptionOccurred` function retrieves a local reference to an exception that is being thrown. The native code or the Java code must handle this exception:

```
jthrowable ExceptionOccurred();
```

The `ExceptionDescribe` function prints information about the exception that was just thrown to the standard error output. This information includes a stack trace:

```
void ExceptionDescribe();
```

The `ExceptionClear` function clears an exception if one was just thrown:

```
void ExceptionClear();
```

The `Throw` function throws an exception that has already been created. If the exception was successfully thrown, 0 is returned; otherwise, a negative value is returned:

```
jint Throw(jthrowable obj);
```

The `ThrowNew` function creates an exception based on `clazz`, which should inherit from `Throwable`, with the exception text specified by `msg` (in UTF-8 encoding). If the construction and throwing of the exception is successful, this function returns 0; otherwise, a negative value is returned:

```
jint ThrowNew(jclass clazz, const char *msg);
```

The `FatalError` function causes the signaling of a fatal error. A fatal error is only for situations where recovery is not possible. The VM is shut down upon calling this function:

```
void FatalError(const char *msg);
```

You should always check for exceptions that might occur in the course of executing native code. If an exception is left unhandled, it will cause future calls to most JNI functions to fail. Here's a simple scenario using the `FindClass` function to try to find a class that isn't there and then handle the exception:

```
JNIEXPORT void JNICALL Java_ExceptionExample_testExceptions
  (JNIEnv *env, jobject obj)
{
    // Try to find a class that isn't there to trigger an exception
    env->FindClass("NoSuchClass");

    // If an exception happened, print it out and then clear it
    if(env->ExceptionCheck()) {
        env->ExceptionDescribe();
        env->ExceptionClear();
    }
}
```

The first statement in the function triggers a `NoClassDefFoundError` exception. When running this native function, the following output is generated:

```
java.lang.NoClassDefFoundError: NoSuchClass
        at ExceptionExample.testExceptions(Native Method)
        at ExceptionExample.main(ExceptionExample.java:13)
Exception in thread "main"
```

The exception details are printed, specifying which exception was thrown, extra information (in this case, the name of the class passed to `FindClass`), and the stack trace showing the method calls up to the native method, where the exception was thrown. The stack trace doesn't include line numbers in the native code, because Java does not have native code line number information immediately available to it.

Working with Object References in Native Code

JNI provides sets of functions to utilize Java objects in native code, as you've seen with strings, arrays, and general objects. This raises an important question that you may have already considered — how are references to objects handled? More specifically, how does the garbage collector handle object references and know when to collect garbage? JNI provides three different types of references:

❑ **Local references:** For use only in a single native method.

❑ **Global references:** For use across multiple invocations of native methods.

❑ **Weak global references:** Just like global references, but these do not prevent the object from being garbage collected.

The following sections describe these references in detail.

Local References

Local references are explicitly created using the `NewLocalRef` function, though a number of JNI functions return a local reference. These references are intended only for use while a native function executes and disappear when that function returns. Local references should not be cached on the native side (such as in a local static variable) because they are not valid across multiple calls to the native method. As soon as the native function returns, any local references that existed are now eligible for garbage collection. If you want to deallocate the local reference before the function returns, you can explicitly deallocate the local reference using the `DeleteLocalRef` function. Local references are also only valid in the thread that created them, so don't try to store a local reference and use it in a different thread.

The following functions are available to explicitly create and destroy local references.

The `NewLocalRef` function returns a new local reference to the object reference passed in. If `NULL` is passed in, the function returns `NULL`:

```
jobject NewLocalRef(jobject ref);
```

The `DeleteLocalRef` function deallocates the local reference that is passed in:

```
void DeleteLocalRef(jobject obj);
```

All local references are available for garbage collection when a native function returns. Local references are created by many JNI functions, such as `GetStringChars`. Most local references are created and cleaned up automatically. Because local references are so common, look at the example a bit later in this section to see an example of explicitly accounting for local references.

Because Java is a platform that manages your memory for you, when working with native code you raise the possibility of leaking memory because the memory is outside the scope of Java's memory management. You must be conscious of how many local references are currently in use because many functions return local references. JNI only allows for a set maximum number of local references. Also, if you create references to large objects, you run the risk of exhausting the available memory. The following functions are provided for management of local references:

```
jint EnsureLocalCapacity(jint capacity);
```

This function ensures that at least `capacity` number of local references can be created. The VM ensures that at least 16 local references can be created when a native method is called. If you try to create more local references than are available, `FatalError` is invoked. This function returns 0 on success and a negative number on failure along with throwing an `OutOfMemoryException`. The `PushLocalFrame` is a useful function to create a new scope of local references:

```
jint PushLocalFrame(jint capacity);
```

This function makes it simple to release all local references allocated in this frame by using the `PopLocalFrame` function. When this is called, at least `capacity` number of local references can be created in this frame, provided there is enough memory. This function returns 0 on success and a negative number on failure along with throwing an `OutOfMemoryException`. The `PopLocalFrame` function releases all local references in the current frame (pops up a level):

```
jobject PopLocalFrame(jobject result);
```

Because storing the result of this function (the return value) might cause a local reference creation in the about-to-be-popped frame, this function accepts a parameter that causes the reference creation to happen in the topmost frame after the current one is popped. This ensures you maintain a reference that stores the result of this function.

Here's an example showing the usage of the local reference management functions:

```
JNIEXPORT void JNICALL Java_LocalRefExample_testLocalRefs
  (JNIEnv *env, jobject obj)
{
    jint count;

    // Let's figure out just how many local references
    // we can create
    for(count=16; count<10000; count++) {
        if(env->EnsureLocalCapacity(count+1)) {
            break;
        }
    }

    printf("I can create up to %d local references\n", count);

    // Now let's create a few...
    jcharArray charArray;
    jintArray intArray;
```

```
    jstring str;

str = env->NewString("This is a test");

if(env->PushLocalFrame(10)) {
    charArray = env->NewCharArray(13);

    if(charArray == NULL) {
        printf("Failed to create character array\n");
        return;
    }

    if(env->PushLocalFrame(10)) {
        intArray = env->NewIntArray(14);

        if(intArray == NULL) {
            printf("Failed to create integer array\n");
            return;
        }

        // intArray created. Use PopLocalFrame to free all allocated
        // references in this scope level, in this case just intArray
        env->PopLocalFrame(NULL);
    }

    // charArray created. Use PopLocalFrame to free all allocated
    // references in this scope level, in this case just charArray
    env->PopLocalFrame(NULL);
}

// 'str' is freed after this function exits
}
```

After running this function, it printed that it can allocate 4,096 local references. The Java VM only guarantees 16 local references, so always call the EnsureLocalCapacity function if you need a large number of local references. Each call to PushLocalFrame allocates a new scope level for allocating local references. All local references that are allocated are automatically freed when PopLocalFrame is called. Only intArray is freed when the first PopLocalFrame is called, and only charArray is freed when the second call to PopLocalFrame happens.

Global and Weak Global References

Global references are meant for use across different invocations of a native method. They are created only by using the NewGlobalRef function. Global references can also be used across separate threads. Because global references give you these added benefits, there is a trade-off: Java cannot control the lifetime of a global reference. You must determine when the global reference is no longer needed and deallocate it manually using the DeleteGlobalRef function. Weak global references are much like global references, but the underlying object might be garbage collected at any time. JNI provides a special invocation of IsSameObject for finding out if the underlying object is still valid.

The following functions are used for creating and destroying global references. NewGlobalRef creates a new global reference and returns it, and NewWeakGlobalRef creates and returns a new weak global reference:

```
jobject NewGlobalRef(jobject lobj);
jweak NewWeakGlobalRef(jobject obj);
```

The parameter to these functions is the class of the object to create. If you don't have a handle to a class, you can obtain one by invoking the FindClass function. If you try to create a reference to the null object, or the object cannot be created, these functions return NULL. If the reference cannot be created due to no more available memory, an OutOfMemoryException is thrown.

The DeleteGlobalRef and DeleteWeakGlobalRef functions deallocate the global (or weak global) reference that was previously allocated in a call to NewGlobalRef or NewWeakGlobalRef:

```
void DeleteGlobalRef(jobject gref);
void DeleteWeakGlobalRef(jweak ref);
```

Here's an example of how to cache a class for use across multiple calls to the NewGlobalRef native function:

```
JNIEXPORT void JNICALL Java_GlobalRefExample_testGlobalRef
    (JNIEnv *env, jobject obj)
{
    static jstring globalString = NULL;
    const char *gStr;

    if(globalString == NULL) {
        // First time through, create global reference
        jstring localStr;

        localStr = env->NewString("This is a string");

        if(localStr == NULL) {
            return;
        }

        printf("Global reference does not exist, creating...\n");
        globalString = (jstring)env->NewGlobalRef(localStr);
    }

    gStr = env->GetStringChars(globalString, NULL);

    printf("The contents of globalString: %s\n", gStr);
    fflush(stdout);

    env->ReleaseStringChars(globalString, gStr);
}
```

The globalString is marked static so it is preserved across multiple calls to the function. The global String reference must be created using NewGlobalRef so that the underlying object is also preserved across multiple calls to this function. The first time this is invoked, a local reference to a string is created.

This local reference is then used to create a global reference, which is then stored in globalString. The output from the preceding function, invoked twice, shows how the globalString is created only the first time through:

```
--- FIRST TIME CALLING ---
Global reference does not exist, creating...
The contents of globalString: This is a string
--- SECOND TIME CALLING ---
The contents of globalString: This is a string
```

Don't forget to build in code to deallocate the global reference. This example shows only how to create a global reference. When to call DeleteGlobalRef depends on your application design.

Comparing References

JNI provides a special function, IsSameObject, in order to test whether the object behind two references is the same. In C++, the keyword NULL corresponds to a null object in Java. Thus, you can pass NULL as a parameter to IsSameObject or compare an object reference directly to NULL. The IsSameObject function has the following prototype:

```
jboolean IsSameObject(jobject obj1, jobject obj2);
```

The IsSameObject function returns JNI_TRUE if the objects are the same, and JNI_FALSE otherwise. If you attempt to compare a weak global reference to NULL using IsSameObject, it returns JNI_TRUE if the underlying object hasn't been garbage collected, and JNI_FALSE if the object has.

Advanced Programming Using JNI

JNI provides several other capabilities to the programmer of native routines. Because Java is a multi-threaded environment, routines related to threading are available on the native side. JNI also supports a way of exposing native routines to Java code singly, rather than making all native functions immediately available through a call to System.load or System.loadLibrary. In addition to these features, Java exposes the reflection library natively.

Java Threading

Because Java is a multithreaded environment, it is possible that one or more threads in a system will invoke native methods. This makes it important to know how native methods and other entities in native libraries, such as global references, relate to threading in Java. The pointer to the Java environment is thread specific, so don't use one thread's environment pointer in another thread. If you plan to pass a local reference from one thread to another, convert it to a global reference first. Local references are also thread specific.

Native code can interact with Java's threading mechanisms — most important, thread synchronization. JNI provides two native functions for synchronizing objects: MonitorEnter and MonitorExit. These are the only threading functions that are exposed directly at the native level because these are time-critical functions. Other functions such as wait and notify should be invoked using the method invocation functions described in an earlier section.

Invoking the `MonitorEnter` function is equivalent to using `synchronized(obj)` in Java:

```
jint MonitorEnter(jobject obj);
```

The current thread enters the specified object's monitor, unless another thread has a lock on the object, in which case the current thread pauses until the other thread leaves the object's monitor. If the current thread already has a lock on the object's monitor, a counter is incremented for each call to this function for the object. The `MonitorEnter` function returns a 0 on success, or a negative value if the function failed.

The `MonitorExit` function decrements the object's monitor counter by 1, or releases the current thread's lock on the object if the counter reaches 0:

```
jint MonitorExit(jobject obj);
```

The `MonitorExit` function returns a 0 on success, or a negative value if the function failed.

Native NIO Support

Introduced to JNI in the 1.4 version of Java are three functions that work with NIO direct buffers. A direct byte buffer is a container for byte data that Java will do its best to perform native I/O operations on. JNI defines three functions for use with NIO. Based on a pointer to a memory address and the length of the memory (capacity), the `NewDirectByteBuffer` function allocates and returns a new `java.nio.ByteBuffer`:

```
jobject NewDirectByteBuffer(void* address, jlong capacity);
```

Returns NULL if this function is not implemented for the current Java virtual machine, or if an exception is thrown. If no memory is available, an `OutOfMemoryException` is thrown. The `GetDirectBufferAddress` function returns a pointer to the address referred to by the `java.nio.ByteBuffer` object that is passed in:

```
void *GetDirectBufferAddress(jobject buf);
```

Returns NULL if the function is not implemented, if the `buf` is not an object of the `java.nio.ByteBuffer` type, or if the memory region is not defined. The `GetDirectBufferCapacity` function returns the capacity (in number of bytes) of a `java.nio.ByteBuffer` object that is passed in:

```
jlong GetDirectBufferCapacity(jobject buf);
```

Returns –1 if the function is not implemented or if the `buf` is not an object of the `java.nio.ByteBuffer` type.

Manually Registering Native Methods

JNI provides a way to register native methods at runtime. This dynamic registration is especially useful when a native application initiates an instance of the virtual machine at runtime. Native methods in this application cannot be loaded by the VM (because they aren't in a native library), but can still be used by the Java code after the functions have been manually registered. It is also possible to register a native function multiple times, changing its implementation at runtime. The only requirement for native functions is that they follow the JNICALL calling convention. In this section you see how to utilize these functions to perform more sophisticated coding tasks using JNI. The next function is used to perform this registration.

The `RegisterNatives` function is used to register one or more native methods. It returns 0 if successful, or a negative value otherwise:

```
jint RegisterNatives(jclass clazz, const JNINativeMethod *methods,
                     jint nMethods);
```

The parameter `clazz` is a handle to the Java class that contains the native methods about to be registered. The `nMethods` parameter specifies how many native methods are in the list to register. The methods parameter is a pointer to a list of native methods (can be one or more methods). Each element of the methods array is an instance of the `JNINativeMethod` structure. The `JNINativeMethod` structure is shown here:

```
typedef struct {
    char *name;
    char *signature;
    void *fnPtr;
} JNINativeMethod;
```

The strings are UTF-8 encoded strings. The `name` member contains the name of the native method to register (from the Java class) and `signature` is the method descriptor that fully describes the method's type. The `fnPtr` member is a function pointer that points to the C function to register. The function behind this pointer must adhere to the following prototype:

```
[ReturnType] (*fnPtr)(JNIEnv *env, jobject objectOrClass, ...);
```

The `[ReturnType]` must be one of the native equivalents of the Java data types. The first two parameters, as in all native method implementations, are a pointer to the Java environment and a reference to the class or object invoking the native method. The variable argument list is used to pass in the expected parameters to the method.

The `UnregisterNatives` function should not be used except in highly specialized situations:

```
jint UnregisterNatives(jclass clazz);
```

This function unregisters all native methods registered with the class passed in. This function returns 0 on success and a negative value otherwise.

Here's an example of manually registering a native method. The Java code defines two native functions, one that is used to select which sort routine to use, and the other to perform the sort. The `sortNumbers` method has no implementation when the library is loaded. The `setSort` function uses an input parameter to know which sort routine to manually register:

```
import java.io.*;

public class RegisterNativeExample {
    public native boolean sortNumbers(int strList[]);
    public native void setSort(int whichSort);

    static {
        System.loadLibrary("RegisterNativeLibrary");
    }

    public static void main(String args[])
```

```
{
    RegisterNativeExample rne = new RegisterNativeExample();
    int sortType = 1;
    int nums[] = {23, 1, 6, 1, 2, 7, 3, 4};

    try {
        BufferedReader br = new BufferedReader(
                                new InputStreamReader(System.in));

        System.out.println("Choose a sort routine");
        System.out.println("   1. Bubble");
        System.out.println("   2. Insertion");
        System.out.print("% ");
        sortType = Integer.parseInt(br.readLine());
        rne.setSort(sortType);
        rne.sortNumbers(nums);
        System.out.print("Sorted numbers are: ");
        for(int i=0; i<nums.length; i++) {
            System.out.print(nums[i] + " ");
        }
        System.out.println("");
    } catch(IOException ioe) {
        System.out.println("IOException occurred");
        ioe.printStackTrace();
    }
}
}
```

Much like the example of using primitive arrays, the list of numbers is hard-coded. The user is asked to choose which sort to use, and the setSort function manually registers the chosen sort routine.

Here's the native code. The sort routines are what you would expect, so just their signatures are listed here, along with the setSort function. The full code is available online.

```
jboolean JNICALL bubbleSort(JNIEnv *env, jobject obj, jintArray intArrayToSort)
{ /* ... */ }

jboolean JNICALL insertionSort(JNIEnv *env, jobject obj, jintArray intArrayToSort)
{ /* ... */ }

JNIEXPORT void JNICALL Java_RegisterNativeExample_setSort
  (JNIEnv *env, jobject obj, jint which)
{
    JNINativeMethod sortMethod;

    sortMethod.name = "sortNumbers";
    sortMethod.signature = "([I)Z";

    if(which == 1) {
        sortMethod.fnPtr = bubbleSort;
    } else {
        sortMethod.fnPtr = insertionSort;
    }

    env->RegisterNatives(env->GetObjectClass(obj), &sortMethod, 1);
}
```

The name of the sort method in the Java code is `sortNumbers` and its signature is `([I)Z`; that is, it takes an array of integers and returns a Boolean. The final member of the `JNINativeMethod` structure is the function pointer and is set to either `bubbleSort` or `insertionSort`. Finally the `RegisterNatives` function is called to register the single method that was just configured. After this call, the `sortNumbers` method can be invoked in the Java code.

Reflection

JNI provides a set of reflection functions that mirror those in the Java API. Using these functions makes it possible to discover information about classes such as a class's superclass or whether one type can be cast to another. Functions are also provided to convert `jmethodID` and `jfieldID` types to and from their corresponding method or field. The `FindClass` function searches all classes and JAR files found in the CLASSPATH for the class name passed in:

```
jclass FindClass(const char *name);
```

If the class is found, a handle to that class is returned. The name is a UTF-8 encoded string that includes the full package name and class name, but the dots are replaced with forward slashes. If the class is not found, NULL is returned and one of the following exceptions is thrown:

❑ **ClassFormatError:** The class requested is not a valid class.

❑ **ClassCircularityError:** The class or interface is its own superclass or superinterface.

❑ **OutOfMemoryError:** There is no memory for the handle to the class.

The `GetObjectClass` function returns a handle to the class of the object passed in:

```
jclass GetObjectClass(jobject obj);
```

The `GetSuperclass` function returns a handle to the superclass of the class passed in. If `java.lang.Object` is passed in, or an interface is passed in, this function returns NULL:

```
jclass GetSuperclass(jclass sub);
```

The `IsAssignableFrom` function is used to determine if an object of the class described by `sub` can be successfully cast to the class described by `sup`:

```
jboolean IsAssignableFrom(jclass sub, jclass sup);
```

Returns `JNI_TRUE` if `sub` and `sup` are the same classes, if `sub` is a subclass of `sup`, or if `sub` implements the interface `sup`. Returns `JNI_FALSE` otherwise.

The `IsInstanceOf` function returns `JNI_TRUE` if `obj` is an instance of `clazz`, and `JNI_FALSE` otherwise:

```
jboolean IsInstanceOf(jobject obj, jclass clazz);
```

Passing in NULL for `obj` causes the function to always return `JNI_TRUE` because null objects can be cast to any class.

The `FromReflectedMethod` function accepts a handle to an object of the `java.lang.reflect.Method` and returns a `jmethodID` suitable for use in the functions that require a `jmethodID`:

```
jmethodID FromReflectedMethod(jobject method);
```

The `ToReflectedMethod` function accepts a handle to a Java class and a handle to a specific method (which might be a constructor) and returns a `java.lang.reflect.Method` object corresponding to that method:

```
jobject ToReflectedMethod(jclass cls, jmethodID methodID, jboolean isStatic);
```

Set `isStatic` to `JNI_TRUE` if the method is a static method, and `JNI_FALSE` (or 0) otherwise. If the function fails, it returns NULL and throws an `OutOfMemoryException`.

The `FromReflectedField` function accepts a handle to an object of the `java.lang.reflect.Field` and returns a `jfieldID` suitable for use in the functions that require a `jfieldID`:

```
jfieldID FromReflectedField(jobject field);
```

The `ToReflectedField` function accepts a handle to a Java class and a handle to a specific field and returns a `java.lang.reflect.Field` object corresponding to that field:

```
jobject ToReflectedField(jclass cls, jfieldID fieldID, jboolean isStatic);
```

Set `isStatic` to `JNI_TRUE` if the field is a static field, and `JNI_FALSE` (or 0) otherwise. If the function fails, it returns NULL and throws an `OutOfMemoryException`.

Developing an Email Client

To wrap up this chapter, look at a full-blown program that will retrieve information stored in MS Outlook. This example is based on a project I worked on and provides a way to bring different aspects of JNI together to show what a real-world application of JNI looks like. The email client will provide a user interface to check mail and send mail. This is displayed in a Swing user interface. The mail and mail folder information is accessed using the MAPI routines through COM. The JNI portion is the most important, so the complete user interface code is not included here (but is available in the code online for this chapter). In order to retrieve email on the client side, CDO (Collaborative Data Objects) is used, so this example assumes you are running Outlook and it is configured to send mail. Note that due to security updates in Outlook, you might be presented with a dialog cautioning you that an external program is attempting to access information from Outlook or attempting to send mail.

System Design

Take a look at Figure 9-4 to see how the Java code relates to the native code. The `MailClient` contains the user interface (using Swing). The `MailClient` class communicates with the `JNIMailBridge`, which has the native functions to invoke the send and check email native functions. The native library then uses COM to access the information stored in Outlook.

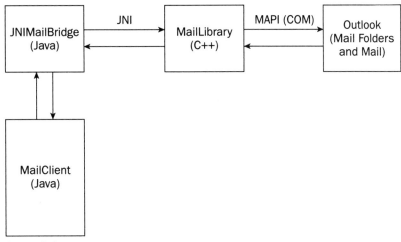

Figure 9-4

User Interface

The following two figures, Figures 9-5 and 9-6, are screenshots of the actual mail client. In the first screenshot, the Mail Folders tree contains all the folders beneath the top folder from Outlook. The table in the top-right shows all the messages in the Example folder (shown after double-clicking Example). The bottom-right contains the body of the message (shown after double-clicking a specific message in the table).

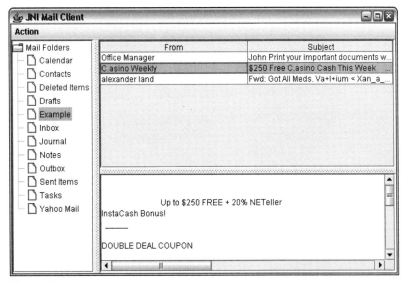

Figure 9-5

This second screenshot contains a basic set of fields to address an email, write the email, and send it (after clicking the Send Mail button).

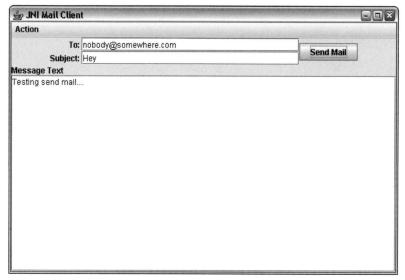

Figure 9-6

The `JNIMailBridge` class contains all the code related to the retrieval and storage of messages from Outlook. The native code uses the method-calling functions in order to pass data back to the Java application. Two helper classes are defined as follows in order to store the folder and email information:

```java
class MailMessage {
    public String fromAddress;
    public String subject;
    public String body;

    public MailMessage(String from, String subj, String b)
    {
        fromAddress = from;
        subject = subj;
        body = b;
    }

    public String toString()
    {
        return("FROM: " + fromAddress + "  SUBJECT: " + subject);
    }
}

class MailFolder {
    String folderName="";
    ArrayList<MailMessage> messageList;

    public MailFolder(String name)
```

```
    {
        setFolderName(name);
        messageList = new ArrayList<MailMessage>();
    }

    public String getFolderName()
    {
        return(folderName);
    }

    public void setFolderName(String name)
    {
        folderName = name;
    }

    public int getMessageCount()
    {
        return(messageList.size());
    }

    public MailMessage getMessage(int index)
    {
        if(index < 0 || index >= messageList.size()) {
            return(null);
        }

        return((MailMessage)messageList.get(index));
    }

    public void addMessage(MailMessage msg)
    {
        messageList.add(msg);
    }

    public void clearMessages()
    {
        messageList = new ArrayList<MailMessage>();
    }

    public String toString()
    {
        return(folderName);
    }
}
```

The `MailMessage` class stores basic information about a single email message. The `MailFolder` class stores a collection of these `MailMessage` objects in an `ArrayList` and allows for ease of saving and retrieving email messages. The real work on the Java side happens in the `JNIMailBridge` class:

```
public class JNIMailBridge {
    ArrayList<MailFolder> mailFolders;

    public native void sendMail(String profile, String to,
                                String subject, String body);
```

```
public native void getFolderContents(String profile,
                                    String topFolderName, String folderName);
public native void getFolderList(String profile, String topFolderName);

static {
    System.loadLibrary("MailLibrary");
}
```

These methods establish the functions that will be implemented on the native side. The `sendMail` method sends an email from the user associated with the profile. The `getFolderContents` returns a list of all pieces of mail inside a specified folder. The `getFolderList` returns a list of all folders within a top-level folder. The following methods are used to store and retrieve lists of folders and mail messages:

```
public void clearFolderList()
{
    mailFolders = new ArrayList<MailFolder>();
}

public void addFolder(String folderName)
{
    mailFolders.add(new MailFolder(folderName));
}

public int getFolderCount()
{
    return(mailFolders.size());
}

public MailFolder getFolder(int index)
{
    if(index < 0 || index >= mailFolders.size()) {
        return(null);
    }

    return(mailFolders.get(index));
}

public MailFolder findFolder(String folderName)
{
    int index;
    MailFolder folder;

    for(index=0; index<mailFolders.size(); index++) {
        folder = mailFolders.get(index);

        if(folder.getFolderName().equals(folderName)) {
            return(folder);
        }
    }

    return(null);
}

public void clearMessageList(String folderName)
```

```
    {
        MailFolder folder;

        folder = findFolder(folderName);

        if(folder != null) {
            folder.clearMessages();
        }
    }

    public void addMessage(String folderName, String from,
                            String subj, String body)
    {
        MailFolder folder;
        MailMessage msg;

        folder = findFolder(folderName);

        if(folder != null) {
            msg = new MailMessage(from, subj, body);
            folder.addMessage(msg);
        }
    }
}
```

The `JNIMailBridge` class defines three native functions. The `profile` parameter is used to select a specific profile in Outlook. Each user generally has one profile for storing mail and other data in Outlook. The other parameters to `sendMail` are the address to send the mail message to and the subject and text of the mail message. The `getFolderContents` method transfers messages from a specified folder in Outlook (using the two parameters' top folder; that is, the folder that contains other folders, and the individual folder that has the messages) to the `JNIMailBridge` class using the `clearMessageList` and `addMessage` methods. The `getFolderList` method transfers all folders that are located beneath the top folder. For purposes of this example, Outlook has the set of standard folders beneath the folder named *Top of Personal Folders* and the profile name is *Outlook*.

The code on the native side performs the necessary communication with Outlook. The three native functions are implemented using COM to utilize the MAPI routines. MAPI provides an interface to access mail data and send mail through Outlook:

```
JNIEXPORT void JNICALL Java_JNIMailBridge_getFolderList
  (JNIEnv *env, jobject obj, jstring _profile, jstring _topFolder)
{
    const char *folderName = env->GetStringChars(_topFolder, 0);
    const char *profile = env->GetStringChars(_profile, 0);

    _SessionPtr pSession("MAPI.Session");

    // Log on with a specific profile.
    // If this isn't specified a logon box would pop up.
    pSession->Logon(profile);

    InfoStoresPtr pInfoStores;
    InfoStorePtr pInfoStore;
    FolderPtr pTopFolder;
```

```
FoldersPtr pPSTFolders;
long l;

pInfoStores = pSession->GetInfoStores();

if(pInfoStores == NULL) {
    env->ThrowNew(env->FindClass("java/lang/Exception"),
        "Can't obtain handle to InfoStores");
    return;
}

// Search for the specific folder name
for(l=1; l <= (long)(pInfoStores->GetCount()); l++) {
    pInfoStore = pInfoStores->GetItem(l);
    pTopFolder = pInfoStore->GetRootFolder();

    _bstr_t fName = folderName;
    _bstr_t compName = (_bstr_t)pTopFolder->GetName();

    if(fName == compName) {
        // We've found it, exit the loop
        break;
    }
}

if(pTopFolder == NULL || l==(long)pInfoStores->GetCount()) {
    env->ThrowNew(env->FindClass("java/lang/Exception"),
        "Can't obtain handle to top folder");
    return;
}

pPSTFolders = pTopFolder->GetFolders();

if(pPSTFolders == NULL) {
    env->ThrowNew(env->FindClass("java/lang/Exception"),
        "Can't obtain handle to PST folders");
    return;
}
```

This block of code will look familiar to you shortly. This code establishes a connection to the data stored in Outlook via the MAPI object. The `InfoStores` contains all top-level folders. This collection is searched for the top-level folder that contains the various mail folders:

```
jclass cls = env->GetObjectClass(obj);
jmethodID clearFolderID =
    env->GetMethodID(cls, "clearFolderList", "()V");
jmethodID addFolderID =
    env->GetMethodID(cls, "addFolder", "(Ljava/lang/String;)V");
```

This code establishes handles to the `clearFolderList` and `addFolder` methods defined in the Java code. These handles are then used to invoke the methods on the Java side in order to communicate data back to the Java object.

```
    // First reset the list of folders
    env->CallVoidMethod(obj, clearFolderID);

    // Loop over all available folders
    for(l=1; l <= (long)(pPSTFolders->GetCount()); l++) {
        FolderPtr tempFolder = pPSTFolders->GetItem(l);

        _bstr_t pstName = tempFolder->GetName();

        // Add folder. Remember that the string must be transformed
        // into a Java string using NewString.
        env->CallVoidMethod(obj, addFolderID,
                            env->NewString((char *)pstName));
    }

    env->ReleaseStringChars(_topFolder, folderName);
    env->ReleaseStringChars(_profile, profile);
}
```

The `getFolderList` function retrieves the list of folders beneath a specified top folder. Note how the strings are allocated and released at the end. The method invocation functions are used to make callbacks to the Java code in order to first re-initialize the list of folders (invoking `clearFolderList`) and then adding each folder to the collection in Java by invoking `addFolder`. The `getFolderContents` function, listed next, performs a retrieval of email messages in a specified folder using similar callback semantics to `getFolderList`. Take a look at this function piece by piece:

```
JNIEXPORT void JNICALL Java_JNIMailBridge_getFolderContents
  (JNIEnv *env, jobject obj,
   jstring _profile, jstring _folderName, jstring _searchName)
{
    jclass mapiSupportClass;
    jmethodID mAddMessage, mClearMessages;

    const char *folderName = env->GetStringChars(_folderName, 0);
    const char *searchName = env->GetStringChars(_searchName, 0);
    const char *profile = env->GetStringChars(_profile, 0);

    mapiSupportClass = env->GetObjectClass(obj);

    if(mapiSupportClass == NULL) {
        env->ThrowNew(env->FindClass("java/lang/Exception"),
                    "Can't obtain class handle from object passed in");
        return;
    }

    _SessionPtr pSession("MAPI.Session");

    // Log on with a specific profile.
    // If not specified a logon box would pop up.
    pSession->Logon(profile);
```

The three `jstrings` that are passed in must first get converted to strings suitable for use in the native code. Next, because methods will be invoked on a Java object, a handle to the Java object must be obtained. This happens via the call to `GetObjectClass`. Next, a pointer to the `MAPI.Session` object is obtained and then `Logon` is called in order to work with the MAPI object because it requires authentication.

```
InfoStoresPtr pInfoStores;
InfoStorePtr pInfoStore;
FolderPtr pTopFolder;
FoldersPtr pPSTFolders;
long l;

pInfoStores = pSession->GetInfoStores();

if(pInfoStores == NULL) {
    env->ThrowNew(env->FindClass("java/lang/Exception"),
                "Handle to info stores is invalid");
    return;
}

// First we search for the correct collection of folders.
for(l=1; l <= (long)(pInfoStores->GetCount()); l++) {
    pInfoStore = pInfoStores->GetItem(l);
    pTopFolder = pInfoStore->GetRootFolder();

    _bstr_t fName = folderName;
    _bstr_t compName = (_bstr_t)pTopFolder->GetName();

    if(fName == compName) {
        break;
    }
}

if(l > (long)pInfoStores->GetCount() || pTopFolder==NULL) {
    env->ThrowNew(env->FindClass("java/lang/Exception"),
                "Can't get pointer to top folder");
    return;
}

pPSTFolders = pTopFolder->GetFolders();

if(pPSTFolders == NULL) {
    env->ThrowNew(env->FindClass("java/lang/Exception"),
                "Can't create global reference to Java class");
    return;
}
```

The `InfoStores` collection contains all the top-level folders. This loop executes in order to find the root folder of the mail folders. If at any point an object is NULL, an exception is thrown.

```
// Second we need a handle to the correct folder,
// so search for folderName.
for(l=1; l <= (long)(pPSTFolders->GetCount()); l++) {
    FolderPtr tempFolder = pPSTFolders->GetItem(l);
```

```
        _bstr_t pstName = tempFolder->GetName();

        _bstr_t compSearchName = searchName;

        if(pstName == compSearchName) {
            break;
        }
    }

    if(1 > (long)pPSTFolders->GetCount()) {
        env->ThrowNew(env->FindClass("java/lang/Exception"),
                    "Could not find folder name");
        return;
    }

    // Get a handle to the first message (after getting
    // a handle to the folder, then the folder's
    // message collection)
    FolderPtr pFoundFolder = pPSTFolders->GetItem(1);

    if(pFoundFolder == NULL) {
        env->ThrowNew(env->FindClass("java/lang/Exception"),
                    "Folder requested was not found");
        return;
    }

    MessagesPtr pMessages = pFoundFolder->Messages;

    if(pMessages == NULL) {
        env->ThrowNew(env->FindClass("java/lang/Exception"),
                    "Can't obtain handle to message collection");
        return;
    }

    MessagePtr pMessage = pMessages->GetFirst();

    if(pMessage == NULL) {
        env->ThrowNew(env->FindClass("java/lang/Exception"),
                    "Can't obtain handle to first message in collection");
        return;
    }
```

After obtaining a handle to the correct top-level folder, its contents are searched to obtain a handle to the mail folder. A `MessagePtr` is then configured to point to the first message in this folder.

```
    mAddMessage = env->GetMethodID(mapiSupportClass,
        "addMessage",
        "(Ljava/lang/String;Ljava/lang/String;"
        "Ljava/lang/String;Ljava/lang/String;)V");

    mClearMessages = env->GetMethodID(mapiSupportClass,
        "clearMessageList",
```

```
                 "(Ljava/lang/String;)V");

    if(mAddMessage == NULL || mClearMessages == NULL) {
        printf("Can't obtain handle to class\n");
        env->ThrowNew(env->FindClass("java/lang/Exception"),
                     "Can't obtain handle to addMessage"
                     " or clearMessageList Java method");
        return;
    }
```

These two calls to `GetMethodID` return handles to the Java methods that will soon get called in order to pass information back to the Java object. If either of these handles are NULL, an exception is thrown.

```
    // Call the clearMessageList method to reset the
    // message collection
    env->CallVoidMethod(obj, mClearMessages, _searchName);

    // Loop through all messages in the folder, using the
    // addMessage method to store each message
    while(pMessage != NULL) {
        _bstr_t subject, sender, text, sent;
        subject = pMessage->GetSubject();

        sender = pMessage->GetSender();
        text = pMessage->GetText();

        jstring jsSubject, jsSender, jsText;

        jsSubject = env->NewString((char *)subject);
        jsSender = env->NewString((char *)sender);
        jsText = env->NewString((char *)text);

        env->CallVoidMethod(obj, mAddMessage, _searchName,
                           jsSender, jsSubject, jsText);

        pMessage = NULL;
        pMessage = pMessages->GetNext();
    }
```

The first `CallVoidMethod` is invoked to cause the `clearMessageList` method to execute. This resets the collection of messages inside the Java object, allowing multiple calls to this function, each returning a different set of messages. For each message in the folder, the appropriate information (subject, sender, and recipient information) is converted to a `jstring` via `NewString` and then passed to `addMessage` via the `CallVoidMethod` invocation. This sends basic information about each message, one message at a time, to the Java code for storage and later processing.

```
    pFoundFolder = NULL;
    pMessages = NULL;
    pMessage = NULL;

    // Release the strings
    env->ReleaseStringChars(_searchName, searchName);
    env->ReleaseStringChars(_folderName, folderName);
}
```

The Java code and C++ code work together to create a miniature email client. The Java code is responsible for the user interface and storing the message and folder information. The C++ code is responsible for using COM to access the folders and email in MS Outlook. Java Native Interface is the technology that allows Java code to work with C++ code with a minimum of hassle to you, the developer. This application demonstrates many elements of JNI that were discussed in this chapter and should serve as an instructive example of using JNI to solve real problems.

Summary

Java Native Interface is a powerful mechanism for writing advanced systems in Java. Linking Java to native code enables a developer to leverage functionality provided by the operating system, such as utilizing COM in Windows or perhaps using a native user interface library (presenting speed improvements over Swing). This chapter has given you a lot of information about how to utilize JNI, presenting you with plenty of examples that demonstrate common constructs on both the native and Java side. You should now be able to judge if, when, and where to use JNI in your projects.

10

EJB 3 and the Java Persistence API

Many developers were introduced to the promise of Enterprise JavaBeans (EJBs) eight years ago during the dotcom era where mad speculation about what was necessary to be successful in business with new technologies relied more on hype than reality for normal business operations. On effort after effort people were convinced that large solutions implemented with EJBs would solve all problems when most were easily handled by simple web applications accompanied by other services (security, caching, and so forth).

More often than not, complexities of the EJB architecture necessitated the development of bloated models too cumbersome to deploy and maintain on software deployments. XML deployment descriptor requirements for individual EJBs and extraneous callback method generation, along with difficult EJB Query Language constructs, all contributed to an unpleasant development experience that forced developers to seek alternative technologies for their enterprise implementations. Also, EJBs promoted non-object-oriented-like code generation that dictated the use of parameter passing constructs to marshal data collections across the network.

But the biggest reason why EJBs were a problem in the past was how entity beans gave rise to latency issues on the systems they ran on when those systems performed lots of transactions. In earlier releases, entity beans were individual resources, shared by both session and thread processes, that were always accessed within transactions. This access meant that a bean was dedicated to that transaction until that process was either rolled back or committed, causing other processes that wanted access to that entity to queue up for it. As the number of entity beans being accessed grew on a system, so did the performance problems.

During the past few years, the introduction of two new Object-Relational Mapping (O/RM) libraries, Hibernate and TopLink, were widely accepted because they allowed developers to strap their infrastructure to their code rather than forcing them to write their code to the infrastructure like EJB components did.

Thankfully, the latest EJB 3 specification contributors have learned to evolve and leverage the best practices of previous efforts, which have resulted in large number of necessary improvements that should assist developers in crafting purposeful applications for their enterprise deployments by co-locating data and the operations performed on that data, and eliminating superfluous interface components that had been previously required for implementation. Now, session beans are Plain Old Java Objects (POJOs) managed by the EJB container. Once the session bean is deployed into the EJB container, a stub object is created, and it is registered in the server's Java Naming Directory Interface (JNDI) registry. Client code components now obtain a stub of the bean using the class name of the interface in the JNDI. This new concept called Inversion of Control allows developers to craft their application components independently of how they will be created.

This chapter focuses on high-level concepts that apply to the new features of the EJB 3 and Java Persistence API (JPA) specifications, but more importantly on the introduction and implementation of Interceptors, Resource Injection capabilities, JPA libraries, and EJB 3 annotations with relevant working applications and web components to facilitate user understandings and their deployment in enterprise applications.

New Features

The EJB 3 and Java Persistence API specifications have introduced some new and important modifications to J2EE framework. Specifically, these updates include the following:

❑   A query language for Java Persistence that is an extension to EJB QL

❑   An interceptor facility for session beans and message-driven beans

❑   Java Language Metadata Annotations

❑   Simplification of Enterprise Bean Types

❑   Elimination of the requirements for EJB component interfaces/Home interfaces for session beans

❑   Simplification of entity persistence through the Java Persistence API. Support for lightweight domain modeling, including inheritance and persistence

The new EJB 3 framework attempts to fuse application services to POJOs by injecting service objects or intercepting the execution contexts during runtime. Framework class interaction is avoided so that inheritance structures can be crafted for applications in a more flexible manner. Declarative services are implemented by using annotation markings in Java code.

The Dependency Injection (DI) pattern is implemented so that applications can remain loosely coupled from one another. This functionality allows service objects to be generated by object factory classes as dictated by runtime configurations so that they can be injected to POJOs during runtime.

Java Persistence API (JPA)

The EJB 3 specification has introduced new data persistence mechanisms, referred to as Java Persistence APIs (JPA), to provide Plain Old Java Object (POJO) modeling of Java objects predicated on database entities. The Java Persistence API has the following key features:

❑ **Named queries:** Named queries are static queries expressed in metadata. This means that they have flexibility built in to be used as both native and JPA queries.

❑ **POJO entities:** Entities are now independent modules not beholden to rigid component structures required in past versions.

❑ **Standardized O/R mappings:** Mapping constructs adhere to the non-proprietary format of the Java Persistence API specification.

❑ **EntityManager API:** The EntityManager performs standard database create, read, and update activities on entities.

This section elaborates on some of the basic features of the Java Persistence API with a simple database add and delete application, and delves into three different scenario applications that incorporate JPA capabilities further.

Entities

An entity is basically a lightweight persistent domain object that is managed by helper classes to maintain the state of data for that object. With EJB 3, entities must be annotated with the `@Entity` annotation or specified in the deployment descriptor as such. Instance variables represent the persistent state of entities that correlate with JavaBean properties. Accessibility of instance variables occurs from within the methods of the entity and their visibility, or scope, are dictated by private, protected, and public access modifiers.

Entities are objects that exist and are distinguishable from other objects that typically possess relationships, or associations, with other entities.

Query Language

The Java Persistence query language was introduced to define queries for entities independent of SQL constructs normally implemented to query and publish data content from a backend database. The query language uses SQL-like syntax to select items based on abstract schema types and relationships among them. Java Persistence query language statements can be one of three different types of operations: select, update, or delete.

Typically, SELECT statements consist of the clauses outlined in this table:

SELECT	Determines the type of values desired for collection.
FROM	Declares domain(s) used by other clauses of query.
WHERE	Restricts result collections from query.
GROUP BY (optional)	Aggregates criteria for grouping results.
HAVING (optional)	Filters implemented over group aggregations.
ORDER BY (optional)	Performs collection result ordering operations.

Here is an example select statement that might be implemented with the new Java Persistence API (JPA) libraries:

```
SELECT d from DraftPicks d where d.salary < 20000.0 ORDER BY d.lastname, d.position
```

UPDATE and DELETE statements perform bulk operations over collections of entities with the WHERE clause to restrict the scope of their operations. Here are two samples of JPA delete and update constructs:

```
DELETE FROM Personnel p WHERE p.name = 'Player A';
UPDATE Players p SET p.moveup = 'YES' WHERE p.battingaverage > 300;
```

EntityManager

The entity manager is acquired from an entity manager factory so that a persistence context can be used to retrieve entity data. This procurement process typically occurs through JNDI or dependency injection in the application container, which in turn marshals interactions between applications and the factory object. Constraints are placed on entity managers so that they cannot be shared among concurrent threads leaving them to operate in a single-threaded fashion. The persistence.xml code that follows frames the connection properties that will be invoked when the entity manager in the League application performs transactions with the MySQL back-end database:

```
<persistence xmlns="http://java.sun.com/xml/ns/persistence" version="1.0">
    <persistence-unit name="test">

<provider>oracle.toplink.essentials.ejb.cmp3.EntityManagerFactoryProvider</provider>
        <class>entity.Team</class>
        <class>entity.Players</class>
        <properties>
            <property name="toplink.jdbc.driver" value="org.gjt.mm.mysql.Driver"/>
            <property name="toplink.jdbc.url" value="jdbc:mysql://localhost/ejb"/>
            <property name="toplink.jdbc.user" value="root"/>
            <property name="toplink.jdbc.password" value=""/>
        </properties>
    </persistence-unit>
</persistence>
```

Now, the League application operates by parsing command-line inputs that dictate which one of three operations (add, remove, find) will be performed on the EJB database using the testAdd, testDelete, and testFind methods:

```
package client;

import javax.persistence.EntityManager;
import javax.persistence.Persistence;
import javax.persistence.EntityManagerFactory;
import javax.persistence.Query;

import java.util.Collection;
import java.util.List;

import entity.Players;
```

```
import entity.Team;

public class League {

    private static EntityManagerFactory entityMgrFactory;
    private static EntityManager entityMgr;

    public static void main(String[] args) {

        if (args.length != 1)
        {
            System.out.println("USAGE: java League [add | remove | find]");
            System.exit(1);
        }

        entityMgrFactory = Persistence.createEntityManagerFactory("test");
        entityMgr = entityMgrFactory.createEntityManager();

        if (args[0].equalsIgnoreCase("remove"))
        {
            entityMgr.getTransaction().begin();
            Team t = findTeam("PW Cannons");
            System.out.println("Removing all... " + testDelete(t));
            entityMgr.getTransaction().commit();
        }
        else if (args[0].equalsIgnoreCase("add"))
        {
            entityMgr.getTransaction().begin();
            System.out.println("Inserting Team and Players... " + testAdd());
            entityMgr.getTransaction().commit();
        }
        else if (args[0].equalsIgnoreCase("find"))
        {
            Team t = testFind("PW Cannons");
        }
        entityMgr.close();
    }
```

Data insertion activities occur here in the `testAdd` method where specified text values are passed to set methods of the `Team` and `Players` domain objects that store them to the back-end tables with the persist method in the `EntityManager` class:

```
    private static String testAdd() {
        Team team0 = new Team();
        team0.setId(10000);
        team0.setName("PW Cannons");

        entityMgr.persist(team0);

        Players players1 = new Players();
        players1.setId(10011);
        players1.setName("Player #1");

        Players players2 = new Players();
        players2.setId(20011);
```

```
            players2.setName("Player #2");

            Players players3 = new Players();
            players3.setId(30011);
            players3.setName("Player #3");

            team0.getPlayers().add(players1);
            players1.setTeam(team0);

            team0.getPlayers().add(players2);
            players2.setTeam(team0);

            team0.getPlayers().add(players3);
            players3.setTeam(team0);

            return "OK";
        }
```

Delete and find activities occur here using the entity manager object reference produced earlier. The testFind method defines a query dynamically by passing a query string called name to the create Query method of the EntityManager interface:

```
        private static String testDelete(Team t) {
            Team t0 = entityMgr.merge(t);
            entityMgr.remove(t0);
            return "OK";
        }

        private static Team testFind(String name) {
            Query q = entityMgr.createQuery("select t from Team t where t.name =
:name");
            q.setParameter("name", name);
            return (Team)q.getSingleResult();
        }
```

An entity class for the Team database table is revealed in the Team application here with the @Entity annotation that marks the class for persistence. The @Id annotation marks the ID retrieved from the getId method as the primary key field. The @OneToMany annotation on the getPlayers method maps a one-to-many relationship with the Players table:

```
package entity;

import java.io.Serializable;
import javax.persistence.*;
import static javax.persistence.CascadeType.*;
import java.util.Collection;
import java.util.ArrayList;


@Entity
public class Team implements Serializable {

    private int id;
```

```
    private String name;
    private Collection<Players> players = new ArrayList<Players>();

    @Id
    public int getId() {
        return id;
    }

    public void setId(int id) {
        this.id = id;
    }

    public String getName() {
        return name;
    }

    public void setName(String name) {
        this.name = name;
    }

    @OneToMany(cascade=ALL, mappedBy="team")
    public Collection<Players> getPlayers() {
        return players;
    }

    public void setPlayers(Collection<Players> newValue) {
        this.players = newValue;
    }

}
```

In this example, the Players table is mapped by the `Players` class using the `@Table` annotation to establish the entity bean's persistence. `@Column` markings identify persistent columns in the database table. If Object-Relational (O/R) mappings are not defined with the `@Column` annotation, the persistence mechanism of the application server will try to save a columns state with the same name as the field or property name of the database:

```
package entity;

import javax.persistence.*;

@Entity
@Table(name="PLAYERS")
public class Players
{
    private int id;
    private String name;
    private Team team;

    @Id
    @Column(name="PLAYER_ID")
    public int getId() {
        return id;
```

```
        }

        public void setId(int id) {
            this.id = id;
        }

        @Column(name="NAME")
        public String getName() {
            return name;
        }

        public void setName(String name) {
            this.name = name;
        }

        @ManyToOne()
        @JoinColumn(name="TEAM_ID")
        public Team getTeam() {
            return team;
        }

        public void setTeam(Team team) {
            this.team = team;
        }
    }
```

This simple example demonstrates some important JPA and EJB 3 annotation and entity management capabilities that are useful in performing transactions with Java code. It is important to understand how these constructs are embedded in POJO components when defining properties that identify entity attributes and their relationships with database items, as well as how transactions are managed with new query language and persistence components.

What Are Session Beans? The Demise of Entity Beans?

Session beans generally characterize individual clients on the application server. This means that a session bean collects and publishes content with the back-end system through interactive interfaces in an individual fashion. When a client terminates control within a system, its session bean terminates its connection with the client application.

Session beans come in two different flavors: stateful and stateless. *Stateful* beans are managed individually by the server and are not shared between clients while their state is retained for the duration of the client-bean session. *Stateless* beans are not persistent, meaning they cease to exist when a client invocation terminates. In other words, stateless beans retain their state for the duration of the client-bean session and that same state disappears when a client ends its relationship with that bean.

As mentioned in the introduction of this chapter, the biggest issue on why EJBs were a problem in the past was how entity beans gave rise to latency issues on the systems they ran on when those systems performed lots of transactions. In earlier releases, entity beans were individual resources, shared by both session and thread processes, that were always accessed within transactions. This access meant that a bean was dedicated to that transaction until that process was either rolled back or committed causing other processes that wanted access to that entity to queue up for it. As the number of entity beans being accessed grew on a system, so did the performance problems.

These problems have led to the introduction of the new Java Persistence API (JPA). With JPA, developers can more easily manage transactions and object-relational mappings in their J2EE deployments using the POJO persistence model. With JPA, objects and data can retain values between sessions in an easier fashion than previous persistence models, which warranted more work for developers in their implementations.

Interceptors

When an EJB business process method is invoked by a calling event, the EJB container provides transaction management services prior to delegating control to that method so checks can be made on the presence of a new or existing transaction. At this time in the container process, interceptors can be run to perform operations on the data being passed into those business process methods.

Interceptor methods are typically defined in bean classes or in separate classes with the exception that there can only be one interceptor method per class. These methods are called upon when business method invocations are made on a bean that implements them.

The `@AroundInvoke` annotation marks interceptor methods with the format `Object <method>` `(javax.ejb.InvocationContext)`, so business method invocations know what code to process during operations. Alternatively, interceptors on individual or entire bean methods can be defined using the `@Interceptors` annotation.

`InvocationContext` references permit applications to propagate state across interceptor chains so that method and object references retrievals from beans can be attained, as well as accessor method (get/set) parameter items. If multiple interceptors are defined for an application, the conveyance of these components is determined by the order in which they were defined in the `@Interceptors` annotation. It is also possible to employ the deployment descriptor (`web.xml`) to specify the sequence of interceptor component invocations and to override metadata annotation specifications.

The methods provided by InvocationContext interface are outlined in the following table.

`Object getBean()`	Returns a reference to the bean.
`Method getMethod()`	Returns a reference to the invoked method.
`Object[] getParameters()`	Returns the parameters passed to the method.
`void setParameters(Object[] parameters)`	Sets the parameters.
`Map getContextData()`	Gets contextual data that can be shared in a chain.
`Object proceed()`	Proceeds to the next interceptor in the chain or the business method if it is the last interceptor.

InvocationContext instances are passed to each interceptor method for each business-tier method or life cycle event process.

Here are four different styles of describing Interceptors in the deployment descriptor (web.xml) as outlined in the EJB 3 specification.

This style of using the interceptor element syntax specifies a wildcard value for the ejb-name element, which earmarks all enterprise beans contained in the ejb-jar file with that interceptor component:

```
<interceptor-binding>
    <ejb-name>*</ejb-name>
    <interceptor-class>INTERCEPTOR</interceptor-class>
<interceptor-binding>
```

The following style defines class-level interceptors for specific enterprise bean classes:

```
<interceptor-binding>
    <ejb-name>EJBNAME</ejb-name>
    <interceptor-class>INTERCEPTOR</interceptor-class>
<interceptor-binding>
```

This next style is generally implemented to associate specific methods in enterprise beans to method-level interceptors:

```
<interceptor-binding>
    <ejb-name>EJBNAME</ejb-name>
    <interceptor-class>INTERCEPTOR</interceptor-class>
    <method-name>METHOD</method-name>
<interceptor-binding>
```

The fourth style is used to break down the application of interceptors to a single method within a set of methods:

```
<interceptor-binding>
    <ejb-name>*</ejb-name>
    <interceptor-class>INTERCEPTOR</interceptor-class>
    <method-name>METHOD</method-name>
    <method-params>
        <method-param>PARAM-1</method-param>
    </method-params>
<interceptor-binding>
```

Now that the configuration of Interceptor components has been outlined for the user, discussion now focuses on the implementation of them in application deployments. Here, the StatelessSessionApp Client application code demonstrates how Interceptor classes can be implemented to test different parameter values during runtime activities. Four different invocations of the testBattingAverage method are made with disparate batting average values to test the constraints of the different Interceptor methods:

```
package com.interceptor.interceptor_stateless_appclient;

import javax.ejb.EJB;
import com.interceptor.interceptor_stateless_ejb.*;

public class StatelessSessionAppClient
```

```
{
    @EJB
    private static StatelessSession stateless;

    public static void main(String args[])
    {
        testBattingAverage(246.0);
        testBattingAverage(274.2);
        testBattingAverage(505.0);
        testBattingAverage(-373.2);
    }

    private static void testBattingAverage(double battingAverage)
    {
        try {
            String scoutingReport = stateless.check(battingAverage);
            System.out.println("scoutingReport = " + scoutingReport);
        } catch (ImproperArgumentException improperEx) {
            System.out.println("Improper value found: " + battingAverage);
        } catch (Exception ex) {
            System.out.println("Exception: " + battingAverage);
        }
    }
}
```

Specification of the @Remote annotation in the StatelessSession interface allows accessibility of the classes' methods to a client application. In this example, the StatelessSessionAppClient application invokes the check method to ensure that the batting average parameter value passed into it resides within the constraints that are monitored by the Interceptor components:

```
package com.interceptor.interceptor_stateless_ejb;

import javax.ejb.Remote;

@Remote
public interface StatelessSession
{
    public String check(double val)
        throws ImproperArgumentException;
}
```

The StatelessSessionBean code implements the check method defined in the StatelessSession interface to perform checks on input data. Two interceptor classes, StatisticsTooLow and StatisticsTooHigh, are defined with the Interceptors annotation here so they can retrieve the check method operations during runtime:

```
package com.interceptor.interceptor_stateless_ejb;

import javax.ejb.Stateless;
import javax.interceptor.Interceptors;


@Stateless
```

```
@Interceptors( { StatisticsTooLow.class, StatisticsTooHigh.class })
public class StatelessSessionBean implements StatelessSession
{
    public String check(double val)
    {
        String report = "he's awesome";
        if (val < 300.0) report = "he's so-so";
        return report;
    }
}
```

Constraint checks on individual batting averages items are performed by the invocation of the StatisticsTooLow class. The @AroundInvoke annotation marks the checkIfTooLow method as an interceptor method that will be executed prior to and after any other bean method executes. If a batting average value passed into the check method is less than 0.0, an ImproperArgumentException object will be thrown indicating that the item possesses an invalid value:

```
package com.interceptor.interceptor_stateless_ejb;

import java.lang.reflect.Method;
import javax.interceptor.AroundInvoke;
import javax.interceptor.InvocationContext;

public class StatisticsTooLow
{
    @AroundInvoke
    public Object checkIfTooLow(InvocationContext ctx) throws Exception
    {
        Method method = ctx.getMethod();
        if (method.getName().equals("check"))
        {
            double param = (Double)(ctx.getParameters()[0]);
            if (param < 0.0)
            {
                throw new ImproperArgumentException("Illegal argument: < 0.0");
            }
        }
        // GOTO the next interceptor
        return ctx.proceed();
    }
}
```

The InvocationContext object produces metadata so interceptor methods can control the behavior of the invocation chain. Here, the StatisticsTooHigh interceptor method checks to see if the batting average value passed to it is greater than 500.0 indicating that the item is too high to be considered a legitimate value:

```
package com.interceptor.interceptor_stateless_ejb;

import java.lang.reflect.Method;
import javax.interceptor.AroundInvoke;
```

```
import javax.interceptor.InvocationContext;

public class StatisticsTooHigh
{
    @AroundInvoke
    public Object checkIfTooLow(InvocationContext ctx) throws Exception
    {
        Method method = ctx.getMethod();
        if (method.getName().equals("check"))
        {
            double param = (Double)(ctx.getParameters()[0]);
            if (param > 500.0)
            {
                throw new ImproperArgumentException("Illegal argument: > 500.0");
            }
        }
        // Proceed to the next interceptor
        return ctx.proceed();
    }
}
```

Interceptors share the same life cycle properties as the bean instances that implement them. Both the Interceptor and bean instance are activated before any `PostConstruct` and `PostActivate` callbacks are invoked. Callbacks for `PreDestroy` or `PrePassivate` are called prior to the execution of bean or Interceptor instances.

EJB 3 and Java Persistence API Web Component Examples

This section presents three different scenarios to demonstrate how EJB 3 components can be crafted to publish and retrieve data from back-end data stores during enterprise development.

Scenario 1

The first scenario attempts to satisfy the need to publish user-specified content through a web form that presents three different league attribute templates for data entry. After a user has properly entered player information, that data will be rendered beneath the input display. The intent here is to demonstrate simple EJB 3 persistence capabilities facilitated by new annotation markings. Figure 10-1 provides a conceptual view of the form publication and query implementation that will be demonstrated with the code that follows it.

Four database tables were created, Personnel, TeamA, TeamAA, and TeamAAA, to persist data collected from the different user views. After data has been properly entered by users, the data will be saved through `EntityManager` objects using the new Java Persistence API libraries and retrieved for web page rendering with Query Language constructs.

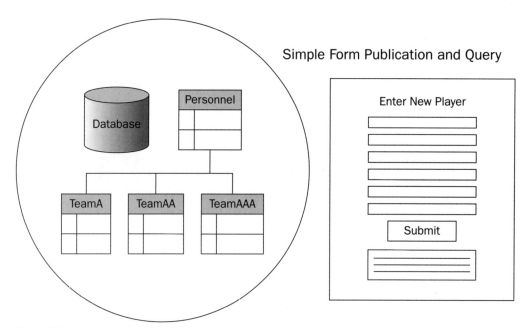

Figure 10-1

An interface object named `SessionStateLocal` was generated here with the `@Local` annotation to define the business interface for the web application. Three different method signatures were established to persist (save) and find data from the Personnel entity:

```
package com.scenario1.ejb.session;

import java.util.*;
import javax.ejb.Local;
import java.util.Collection;
import com.scenario1.persistence.*;

@Local
public interface SessionStatelessLocal
{
    public void persist(Object obj);
    public Personnel find(String acctNum);
    public List findAll();
}
```

Here, the `@Stateless` annotation is used to mark a stateless bean and business logic is developed for the "implement"-ed interface. Both find operations, one for all personnel and another for individual members, are implemented to collect `List` and `Personnel` object data along with the persist method that saves object references. The `@PersistenceContext` annotation marking expresses a dependency on a `Entity Manager` persistence context called `sampleEJB3Book` that is defined in the `persistence.xml` file.

The intent of Resource Injection was to simplify environment access and to offer an alternative to JNDI queries for information access. The injection process allows annotated instance variables and methods to be accessed prior to processing a method service request. Alternatively, an interface component named `EJBContext` can be used to perform runtime data lookups on annotations or XML files too. Here is a list of annotations that allow users to implement resource injection in their EJB beans:

`@PersistenceContext`	Expresses a dependency on a container-managed entity manager persistence context.
`@PersistenceContexts`	Defines multiple `@PersistenceContext` annotations.
`@PersistenceUnit`	Specifies a dependency on an entity manager factory.
`@PersistenceUnits`	Defines multiple `@PersistenceUnits` annotations.

Dependency Injection naturally results in cleaner code because resource creation constructs and lookup logic is no longer required in source code artifacts:

```
package com.scenario1.ejb.session;

import com.scenario1.persistence.*;
import javax.ejb.Stateless;
import javax.persistence.PersistenceContext;
import javax.persistence.EntityManager;
import javax.persistence.*;
import java.util.*;

@Stateless
public class SessionStateless implements SessionStatelessLocal {

    public SessionStateless() {
    }

    @PersistenceContext(unitName="sampleEJB3Book")
    private EntityManager em;

    public Personnel find (String acctNum) {
        return em.find(Personnel.class, acctNum);
    }

    public void persist(Object obj) {
        em.persist(obj);
    }

    public List findAll()
    {
        List list = em.createQuery("select p from Personnel
p").setMaxResults(10).getResultList();
        return list;
    }
}
```

The `Personnel` entity class maps the properties of the Personnel table used to capture attributes that describe player individuals. The `@Entity` annotation marks the class as a domain object that maps an the default inheritance strategy of `InheritanceType.SINGLE_TABLE`, which allows all entities in the hierarchy to map to a single table. In this example, the three different league components can map to the Personnel table. The @Discriminator annotation is specified here, at the top of the entity class hierarchy, to define the column used for the SINGLE_TABLE inheritance mapping strategy:

```java
package com.scenario1.persistence;

import javax.persistence.*;
import com.scenario1.common.*;

@Entity
@Inheritance(strategy=InheritanceType.SINGLE_TABLE)
@DiscriminatorColumn(name="DISCRIMINATORCOLUMN")

public abstract class Personnel extends BasePersonnel
{
 public enum Status { HEALTHY, INJURED}

 @Id
 private  String acctNum;
 private  String name;
 private  String created;
 private  Status status;
 private  float salary;
 private  String description;

    public Personnel(){}

    public String getName() {
        return name;
    }

    public void setName(String name) {
        this.name = name;
    }

    public String getCreated() {
        return created;
    }

    public void setCreated(String created) {
        this.created = created;
    }

    public Status getStatus() {
        return status;
    }

    public void setStatus(Status status) {
        this.status = status;
    }

    public float getSalary() {
        return salary;
    }

    public void setSalary(float salary) {
```

```
            this.salary = salary;
    }

    public String getDescription() {
        return description;
    }

    public void setDescription(String description) {
        this.description = description;
    }

    public String getAcctNum() {
        return acctNum;
    }

    public void setAcctNum(String acctNum) {
        this.acctNum = acctNum;
    }
}
```

A `@MappedSuperclass` annotation is implemented with the abstract `TeamAccount` class to allow all of the mapping information to be available to entities that use it for inheritance. The three individual league components (TeamA, TeamAA, and TeamAAA) all extend this class for team name collection purposes:

```
package com.scenario1.persistence;

import javax.persistence.*;

@MappedSuperclass
public abstract class TeamAccount extends Personnel {
    private String teamName;

    public TeamAccount() {}

    public String getTeamName() {
        return teamName;
    }

    public void setTeamName(String teamName) {
        this.teamName = teamName;
    }
}
```

Two remaining classes are defined here, `TeamA` and `TeamAA`, that extend the `Personnel` entity class with additional attributes to describe player personnel. The `highestBid` variable is used to specify the highest bid that should be made for this particular player:

```
package com.scenario1.persistence;

import javax.persistence.*;

@Entity
public class TeamA extends TeamAccount
{
```

489

```
    private float highestBid;

    public TeamA() {}

    public float getHighestBid() {
        return highestBid;
    }

    public void setHighestBid(float highestBid) {
        this.highestBid = highestBid;
    }

}
```

TeamAA uses the Boolean moveUp attribute to indicate if a particular player needs to be promoted to another team division. Again, like the TeamA class, this class extends the Player entity class to provide additional player attributes. The @AttributeOverride annotation is used to override the mapping of an Id property or field:

```
package com.scenario1.persistence;

import javax.persistence.*;

@Entity
@AttributeOverride(name="teamName", column=@Column(name="team_name"))
public class TeamAA extends TeamAccount
{
    private boolean moveUp;

    public TeamAA() {}

    public boolean getMoveUp() {
        return moveUp;
    }

    public void setMoveUp(boolean moveUp) {
        this.moveUp = moveUp;
    }

}
```

Figure 10-2 represents a visual presentation of the servlet code manifested here. The BaseballServlet component implements the @EJB annotation to inject EJB references, which means that when the instance is created, the EJB container will set the sessionStatelessLocal reference.

Figure 10-2

In this sample servlet application named `BaseballServlet`, query language constructs retrieve player information submitted from the form template application. Two actions, `createAccount` and `persistAccount`, are implemented to create simple player bios and save them to the database using the `Personnel` entity class:

```
package com.scenario1.servlet;

import javax.servlet.*;
import javax.servlet.http.*;
import javax.naming.*;
import java.util.*;
import java.io.*;
import com.scenario1.ejb.session.*;
import com.scenario1.persistence.*;
import javax.ejb.*;

public class BaseballServlet extends HttpServlet {
```

```
    private static final String CREATE_ORDER="createOrder";

    @EJB
    private SessionStatelessLocal sessionStatelessLocal;

    private InitialContext ctx;

    public BaseballServlet() {
        try {
            ctx = new InitialContext();
        } catch(Exception ex) {
            ex.printStackTrace();
        }
    }

    protected void doGet( HttpServletRequest request, HttpServletResponse response
) throws ServletException, IOException {
        processAction(request, response);
    }

    protected void doPost( HttpServletRequest request, HttpServletResponse response
) throws ServletException, IOException {
        processAction(request, response);
    }
```

All events that occur in the player publication web component are processed by the `processAction` method here. Once the user's action has been determined, the proper form display will be rendered so that the user can properly input player content for publication:

```
    private void processAction(HttpServletRequest request, HttpServletResponse
response) throws IOException {
        String action = request.getParameter("action");

        response.setContentType("text/html");
        ServletOutputStream out = response.getOutputStream();

        if(action == null || "".equals(action)) {
            response.sendRedirect("index.html");
        } else if("createAccount".equalsIgnoreCase(action)) {
            String accountType = request.getParameter("accountType");
            out.println("<html><head><title>Java Persistence
Example</title></head>");
            out.println("<body><form name=\"submitForm\"
action=\"/sampleEJB3Book/BaseballServlet\" method=\"post\">");
            out.println("<table border=\"1\" align=\"center\" width=\"75%\"
valign=\"center\">");
            out.println("<tr><td colspan=\"2\" align=\"center\"
bgcolor=\"#cccccc\"><h2><b>Enter New Player (" + accountType +
")</b></h2></td></tr>");

            out.println("<tr><td>Account Number</td><td><input type=\"text\"
name=\"acctNum\"></td></tr>");
            out.println("<tr><td>Name</td><td><input type=\"text\"
name=\"acctName\"></td></tr>");
```

```
        out.println("<tr><td>Status</td><td><select name=\"status\"><option
value=\"healthy\" selected=\"true\">Healthy</option><option
value=\"injured\">Injured</option></select></td></tr>");
        out.println("<tr><td>Description</td><td><input type=\"text\"
name=\"description\"></td></tr>");
        out.println("<tr><td>Salary</td><td><input type=\"text\"
name=\"salary\"></td></tr>");
        out.println("<tr><td>Team</td><td><input type=\"text\"
name=\"team\"></td></tr>");
```

Three different drop-down selections are used in this example to dictate different behaviors for the application view. Disparate user views are presented in the browser depending on these selections. The following code checks the accountType, which represents the different league divisions, and provides HTML components that are required for form submission to the database:

```
        if("TeamA".equalsIgnoreCase(accountType)) {
            out.println("<tr><td>Move up?</td><td><select
name=\"moveup\"><option value=\"yes\" selected=\"true\">Yes</option><option
value=\"no\">No</option></select></td></tr>");
            out.println("<tr><td colspan=\"2\" align=\"center\"> <input
type=\"hidden\" name=\"accountType\" value=\"TeamA\"></td></tr>");
        } else if("TeamAA".equalsIgnoreCase(accountType)) {
            out.println("<tr><td>Savings Rate</td><td><input type=\"text\"
name=\"savingsRate\"></td></tr>");
            out.println("<tr><td colspan=\"2\" align=\"center\"> <input
type=\"hidden\" name=\"accountType\" value=\"TeamAA\"></td></tr>");
        }
        out.println("<tr><td colspan=\"2\" align=\"center\"> <input
type=\"submit\" name=\"submit\" value=\"Submit\"></td></tr>");
        out.println("<tr><td colspan=\"2\" align=\"center\"> <input
type=\"hidden\" name=\"action\" value=\"persistAccount\"></td></tr>");
        out.println("<tr><td colspan=\"2\" align=\"center\"> <input
type=\"hidden\" name=\"accountType\" value=\"" + accountType+ "\"></td></tr>");
        out.println("</table>");
    }
```

Here, if the action is determined that all of the user-specified form items need to be persisted, the publication parameters will be collected, a Personnel object will be instantiated, and set methods on the individual elements of that object will be set:

```
        else if ("persistAccount".equalsIgnoreCase(action))
        {
            String accountType = request.getParameter("accountType");
            String acctNum = request.getParameter("acctNum");
            String name = request.getParameter("acctName");
            String salary = request.getParameter("salary");
            String description = request.getParameter("description");
            String status = request.getParameter("status");
            String team = request.getParameter("team");

            Personnel account = null;
            if("TeamA".equalsIgnoreCase(accountType)) {
                float fBid=0;
```

493

```
                    try {
                        String bid = request.getParameter("highestBid");
                        if ( (bid == null) || (bid.equals("")) )
                            fBid = 0;
                        else
                            fBid=Float.valueOf(bid);

                    } catch(Exception ex) {
                        ex.printStackTrace();
                    }

                    account = new TeamA();
                    ((TeamA)account).setHighestBid(fBid);
                    ((TeamA)account).setTeamName(team);
                }
                else if("TeamAA".equalsIgnoreCase(accountType))
                {
                    String moveUp = request.getParameter("moveUp");

                    account = new TeamAA();
                    ((TeamAA)account).setMoveUp("yes".equalsIgnoreCase(moveUp));

                    ((TeamAA)account).setTeamName(team);
                }
                else if("TeamAAA".equalsIgnoreCase(accountType))
                {
                    String moveUp = request.getParameter("moveUp");

                    account = new TeamAA();
                    ((TeamAAA)account).setMoveUp("yes".equalsIgnoreCase(moveUp));
                }

                float fSalary=0;
                try {
                    fSalary=Float.valueOf(request.getParameter("salary"));
                } catch(Exception ex) {
                    ex.printStackTrace();
                }

                String szStatus = request.getParameter("status");
```

At this point in the servlet, the persist method from the `sessionStatelessLocal` object will be used to pass the data to the back-end table for publication:

```
                account.setAcctNum(acctNum);
                account.setSalary(fSalary);
                account.setDescription(request.getParameter("description"));
                account.setName(name);

                if("injured".equalsIgnoreCase(szStatus))
                    account.setStatus(Personnel.Status.INJURED);
                else
```

```
                    account.setStatus(Personnel.Status.HEALTHY);

            sessionStatelessLocal.persist(account);

            out.println("<html><head><title>Test</title></head><body><form
name=\"submitForm\" action=\"/sampleEJB3Book/BaseballServlet\"
method=\"post\"><table cellspacing=\"3\" cellpadding=\"3\" align=\"center\"
width=\"50%\" valign=\"center\"><th>Test</th><tr><td> </td></tr>");
                    out.println("<tr><td colspan=\"2\" align=\"center\">Account information
was successfully saved.</td></tr>");
                    out.println("<tr><td colspan=\"2\" align=\"center\"> <input
type=\"submit\" name=\"submit\" value=\"Submit\"></td></tr>");
                    out.println("</form></body></html>");
        }

        out.println("<br><br>");
        out.println("<table border=\"1\" width=\"100%\">");
        out.println("<tr><td bgcolor=\"#cccccc\">#</td><td
bgcolor=\"#cccccc\">Account #</td><td bgcolor=\"#cccccc\">Name</td><td
bgcolor=\"#cccccc\">Description</td><td bgcolor=\"#cccccc\">Salary</td></tr>");
```

The remaining code here attempts to find all of the items currently available in the Personnel table for presentation on the user display. If results are discovered with the findAll() method, they will be output to the browser for user inspection:

```
        List list = sessionStatelessLocal.findAll();
        if ( (list == null) || (list.size() == 0) )
         out.println("<tr><td colspan=\"5\" align=\"center\"> No players
available</td></tr>");
        else
        {
            for (int i=0; i < list.size(); i++)
            {
                Personnel p = (Personnel)list.get(i);
                out.println("<tr>");
                out.println("<td>" + (i+1) + "</td>");
                out.println("<td>" + p.getAcctNum() + "</td>");
                out.println("<td>" + p.getName() + "</td>");
                out.println("<td>" + p.getDescription() + "</td>");
                out.println("<td>" + p.getSalary() + "</td>");
                out.println("</tr>");
            }
        }
        out.println("</table>");
    }

    }
```

This example demonstrates the new java2db feature that is bundled with the Derby database. To enable this functionality, the persistence.xml script must possess the following entries:

```
<persistence...>
  <persistence-unit name =...>
      <!-- the datasource affiliated with the bundled derby database -->
      <jta-data-source>jdbc/__default</jta-data-source>
      <properties>
        <!--Enable the java2db feature -->
        <property name="toplink.ddl-generation" value="drop-and-create-tables"/>
      </properties>
  </persistence-unit>
</persistence>
```

To enable java2db for an EJB 3.0 EAR archive, define the following properties for a persistence unit descriptor in the `persistence.xml`:

Property	Description
toplink.ddl-generation	Default none. Probable values are: "create-tables", "drop-and-create-tables", and "none"
toplink.create-ddl-jdbc-file-name	Name of creation table (jdbc ddl file).
toplink.drop-ddl-jdbc-file-name	Name of drop table (jdbc ddl file).
toplink.application-location	App-generated directory. Defines the location where jdbc ddl files would be stored.

Another example of a simple `persistence.xml` file using all of the aforementioned properties is:

```
<?xml version="1.0" encoding="UTF-8"?>
<persistence xmlns="http://java.sun.com/xml/ns/persistence">
    <persistence-unit name ="em1">
        <jta-data-source>jdbc/DataSource1</jta-data-source>
        <properties>
          <property name="toplink.ddl-generation" value="drop-and-create-tables"/>
          <property name="toplink.create-ddl-jdbc-file-name"
value="create_ora.jdbc"/>
          <property name="toplink.drop-ddl-jdbc-file-name" value="drop_ora.jdbc"/>
        </properties>
    </persistence-unit>
</persistence>
```

Scenario 2

The next scenario chronicles how a simple web component can be constructed with tables sharing a one-to-many database relationship using an application server's Container-Managed Persistence (CMP) mechanism (see Figure 10-3).

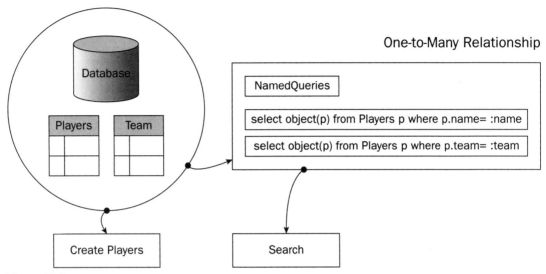

Figure 10-3

New persistence libraries will be implemented so named queries can be used to collect data from the Players table with both name and team attributes. Additionally, a form component will allow users to populate both the Team and Players entities using `EntityManager` objects:

```
package com.scenario2.ejb.session;

import javax.ejb.Local;
import com.scenario2.persistence.*;
import com.scenario2.common.*;
import java.util.List;

@Local
public interface PlayersSessionLocal
{
    public Players searchForPlayers(String id);
    public void persist(Object obj);
    public List findPlayersByName(String name);
    public List findPlayersByTeam(String team);
    public void remove(Object obj);
}
```

Notice how a stateless transaction boundary is established in the `PlayersSession` application using the `@Stateless` annotation, indicating that the application's state will not be retained across multiple client requests. The `@TransactionManagement` marking establishes whether or not a session bean performs container-managed or bean-managed transactions. By default, session beans maintain container-managed properties if the transaction management type is not specified:

```
package com.scenario2.ejb.session;

import javax.ejb.Stateless;
import javax.ejb.Stateful;
import javax.ejb.SessionContext;
import javax.persistence.*;
import javax.ejb.*;
import java.util.List;

import com.scenario2.persistence.*;
import com.scenario2.common.*;

@Stateless
@TransactionManagement(value=TransactionManagementType.CONTAINER)
```

Both the `PlayersSessionLocal` and `PlayersSessionRemote` interfaces are implemented by `PlayersSession` to retrieve data with the named queries crafted in the `Players` class:

```
public class PlayersSession implements PlayersSessionLocal, PlayersSessionRemote
{
    @javax.persistence.PersistenceContext(unitName="persistence_sample")
    private EntityManager em;

    public PlayersSession(){}

    public Players searchForPlayers(String id) {
        Players players = (Players)em.find(Players.class, id);
        return players;
    }

    @TransactionAttribute(TransactionAttributeType.REQUIRED)
    public void remove(Object obj) {
        Object mergedObj = em.merge(obj);
        em.remove(mergedObj);
    }

    public void persist(Object obj) {
        em.persist(obj);
    }
```

Both the `findPlayersByName` and `findPlayersByTeam` methods pass user-defined search attributes from presentation tier web components to named queries to retrieve data from the Players table. If a hit is made on a particular query, the result set is returned as a `List` component by the `getResultList()` method applied to the query object. The `findPlayersByName` method employs an `EntityManager` object to invoke the `createNamedQuery` method, but this operation could also be implemented using a JDBC-style query with the `createQuery(query language string)` method or with a native query using the `createNativeQuery(native sql string)` method:

```
    public List findPlayersByName(String name)
    {
        List players =
em.createNamedQuery("findPlayersByName").setParameter("name",
name).getResultList();
```

498

```
            return players;
    }

    public List findPlayersByTeam(String team)
    {
        List players =
em.createNamedQuery("findPlayersByTeam").setParameter("team",
team).getResultList();
        return players;
    }
}
```

Query and publication activities are performed by the `Players` domain object. Two named queries are created with the `@NamedQueries` annotation. The `@Entity` marking specifies that the `Players` class is an entity, meaning that it is part of a domain model that provides an object view of data in the database:

```
package com.scenario2.persistence;

import java.util.Vector;
import java.util.ArrayList;
import java.util.Collection;
import java.util.Iterator;
import javax.persistence.*;
import javax.persistence.OneToMany;

@Entity
@NamedQueries(
    value=
    {
    @NamedQuery(name="findPlayersByName", query="select object(p) from Players p
where p.name= :name"),
    @NamedQuery(name="findPlayersByTeam", query="select object(p) from Players p
where p.team= :team")
    }
)

public class Players implements java.io.Serializable
{
    private int playerId;
    private String name;
    private String team;
    private String position;
    private int teamId;

    public Players(int playerId, String name, String team, String position, int
teamId) {
        setPlayerId(playerId);
        setName(name);
        setTeam(team);
        setPosition(position);
        setTeamId(teamId);
    }
```

Specification of the primary key of the Players table is made with the @Id annotation. By default, the mapped column for the primary key of the entity is typically assumed to be the primary key of the primary table. If a column annotation is not established, the column name is presumed to be the name of the primary key property or field. The get and set accessor methods allow components to retrieve and set private variables through public methods:

```java
public Players() {}

@Id
@Column(name="playerId")
public int getPlayerId() {
    return playerId;
}

public void setPlayerId(int playerId){
    this.playerId = playerId;
}

public String getName() {
    return name;
}

public void setName(String name) {
    this.name = name;
}

public String getTeam() {
    return team;
}

public void setTeam(String team) {
    this.team = team;
}

public String getPosition() {
    return position;
}

public void setPosition(String position) {
    this.position = position;
}

public int getTeamId() {
    return teamId;
}

public void setTeamId(int teamId) {
    this.teamId = teamId;
}
```

Two callback methods, `PostPersist` and `PostRemove`, are invoked for an entity after the entity has been made persistent or removed. Both of these callbacks will be invoked on all entities to which these operations are cascaded and after database insert and delete transactions have been performed:

```
@PostPersist
public void postCreate () {
    System.out.println("Players::postCreate:");
}

@PostRemove
public void ejbRemove() {
    System.out.println("Players::postRemove");
}
}
```

Enterprise JavaBean (EJB) session declarations for the `PlayersSessionLocal` component are established in the following deployment descriptor (`web.xml`):

```
<?xml version="1.0" encoding="UTF-8"?>

<web-app xmlns="http://java.sun.com/xml/ns/j2ee"
        xmlns:xsi="http://www.w3.org/2001/XMLSchema-instance"
        xsi:schemaLocation="http://java.sun.com/xml/ns/j2ee
http://java.sun.com/xml/ns/j2ee/web-app_2_4.xsd"
    version="2.4">
    <session-config>
        <session-timeout>
            600
        </session-timeout>
    </session-config>
    <ejb-local-ref>
    <description> EJB Session</description>
    <ejb-ref-name>PlayersSessionLocal</ejb-ref-name>
    <ejb-ref-type>Session</ejb-ref-type>
    <local-home></local-home>
    <local> com.scenario2.ejb.session.PlayersSessionLocal</local>
    <ejb-link>PlayersSession</ejb-link>
    </ejb-local-ref>
    <welcome-file-list>
    <welcome-file>
        index.jsp
    </welcome-file>
    </welcome-file-list>
</web-app>
```

Visualization of the web tier presentation component to create players that will be persisted in the Players table is shown in Figure 10-4. Five individual text fields allow users to set the attributes for players drafted by the different teams in the baseball league.

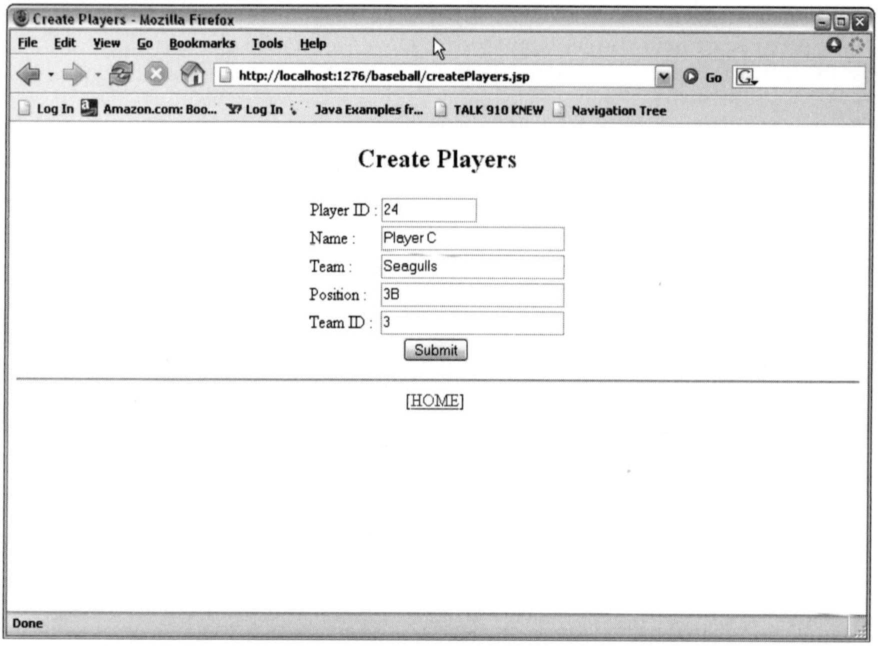

Figure 10-4

Player creation starts with the front-end component createPlayers.jsp that renders the Figure 10-4 display. The code at the beginning of the page establishes all of the form pieces for the user to add text for back-end data publication:

```
<%@ page language="java" %>
<%@ page import="javax.naming.InitialContext" %>
<%@ page import=" com.scenario2.persistence.Players" %>
<%@ page import=" com.scenario2.ejb.session.*" %>
<%@ page import='java.util.*' %>


<html>
<head><title>Create Players</title></head>

<body bgcolor="white">
<center>
<h2>Create Players</h2>

<form method="post" action="/baseball/createPlayers.jsp">
<table border="0">
  <tr>
    <td>Player ID : </td>
    <td><input type="text" name="playerId" size="11" value=""></td>
  </tr>
  <tr>
    <td>Name : </td>
    <td><input type="text" name="name" size="25" value=""></td>
  </tr>
```

```
      <tr>
        <td>Team : </td>
        <td><input type="text" name="team" size="25" value=""></td>
      </tr>
      <tr>
        <td>Position : </td>
        <td><input type="text" name="position" size="25" value=""></td>
      </tr>
      <tr>
        <td>Team ID : </td>
        <td><input type="text" name="teamId" size="25" value=""></td>
      </tr>
    </table>
    <input type="submit" name="submit" value="Submit">
    </form>
```

Player publication starts with business-tier logic that retrieves a JNDI context that uses a `PlayersSessionLocal` interface to retrieve an object reference that will be used to invoke the persist method to push the `Player` object to the back-end data store for publication:

```
<%
String playerId = request.getParameter("playerId");
String name = request.getParameter("name");
String team = request.getParameter("team");
String position = request.getParameter("position");
String teamId = request.getParameter("teamId");

if (playerId != null && !"".equals(playerId))
{
    try {
        InitialContext ic = new InitialContext();

        Object o = ic.lookup("java:comp/env/PlayersSessionLocal");
        PlayersSessionLocal playersSession = (PlayersSessionLocal) o;

        Players player = new Players(Integer.parseInt(playerId), name, team,
position, Integer.parseInt(teamId));
        playersSession.persist(player);
%>
New player created :
<b>
<%=player.getPlayerId()%>, 
<%=player.getName()%>, 
<%=player.getTeam()%>, 
<%=player.getPosition()%>, 
<%=player.getTeamId()%>
</b>
<%
    } catch(Exception e) {
        e.printStackTrace();
        out.println("EXCEPTION : " + e.toString());
    }
}
```

```
%>

<hr>
[<a href="/baseball/index.html">HOME</a>]
</center>
</body>
</html>
```

Retrieval of player items is performed through the search team GUI display in Figure 10-5. Users need to select a search criterion, either player or team, and enter a search value before clicking the Submit button to collect all of the items affiliated with the user-specified query.

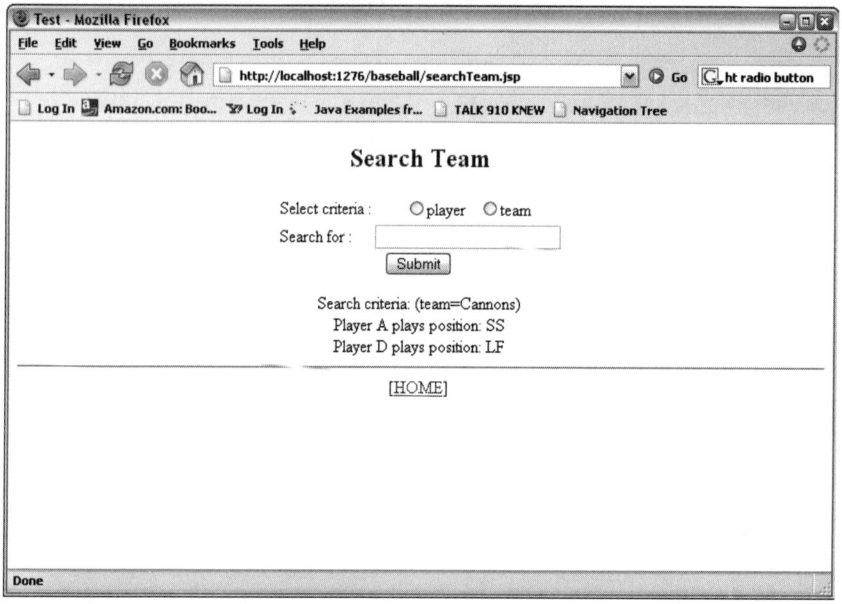

Figure 10-5

All of the business-tier logic needed to perform search activities for the Figure 10-5 presentation are shown in the code that follows. The domain object class `Players` is imported so the accessor methods can be used to collect data:

```
<%@ page language="java" %>
<%@ page import="java.util.ArrayList" %>
<%@ page import="java.util.Collection" %>
<%@ page import="javax.ejb.ObjectNotFoundException" %>
<%@ page import="javax.naming.InitialContext" %>
<%@ page import=" com.scenario2.persistence.Players" %>
<%@ page import=" com.scenario2.ejb.session.*" %>
<%@ page import='java.util.*' %>

<html>
<head><title>Test</title></head>
```

```
<body bgcolor="white">
<center>

<html>
<head><title>Search Team</title></head>
<body bgcolor="white">
<center>
<h2>Search Team</h2>

<form method="post" action="/baseball/searchTeam.jsp">
<table border="0">
  <tr>
    <td>Select criteria : </td>
    <td align="center">
        <input type="radio" name="criteria" value="player">player
         
        <input type="radio" name="criteria" value="team">team
    </td>
  </tr>
  <tr>
    <td>Search for : </td>
    <td><input type="text" name="searchString" size="25" value=""></td>
  </tr>
</table>
<input type="submit" name="submit" value="Submit">
</form>
```

Two request parameters, `criteria` and `searchString`, are retrieved from the form display to pass along to the `findPlayersByName` method if the player radio button was checked or to the `find PlayersByTeam` if the team radio button was selected. Back-end classes perform named queries with the user-specified `searchString` text and return `List` arrays of data that match the criteria if hits are made:

```
<%
String criteria = request.getParameter("criteria");
String searchString = request.getParameter("searchString");

if (searchString != null && !"".equals(searchString))
{
    try {

        InitialContext ic = new InitialContext();
        Object o = ic.lookup("java:comp/env/PlayersSessionLocal");
        PlayersSessionLocal playersSession = (PlayersSessionLocal) o;

        List players = new ArrayList();
        String label = "Search criteria: ";

        if (criteria.equals("player"))
        {
            label += ("(player=" + searchString + ")<br>");
            players = playersSession.findPlayersByName(searchString);
        }
```

```
        else if (criteria.equals("team"))
        {
            label += ("(team=" + searchString + ")<br>");
            players = playersSession.findPlayersByTeam(searchString);
        }


        out.println(label);
```

Data hits on the user-specified queries are performed here by checking the size of the Players object reference. Looping is performed to strip off the individual items for display from the list array returned from the query:

```
        if (players.size() > 0)
        {
            for (int i = 0; i < players.size(); i++)
            {
                Players p = (Players)(players).get(i);
                String pName = (String)p.getName();
                String pPosition = (String)p.getPosition();
                out.println(pName + " plays position: " + pPosition + "<br>");
            }
        }
    }
    catch(Exception e)
    {
        e.printStackTrace();
        out.println(e.toString());
    }
}
%>

<hr>
[<a href="/baseball/index.html">HOME</a>]
</center>
</body>
</html>
```

With NamedQuery annotations, the query must be unique and scoped to the persistence unit implementation. This example implements the NamedQuery feature to accommodate player queries with different criteria and to improve application performance by avoiding runtime parse operations on query language constructs.

Scenario 3

Scenario three attempts to summarize a web component deployment that manages different team owner draft pick selections with tables possessing a many-to-many relationship (see Figure 10-6). In this application, pre-loaded draft picks represent potential candidates for an owner in a drop-down HTML component. Owners also have the option of removing selections from their portfolios by checking off the players to discard and then clicking the Remove button in the web form to complete the remove transaction.

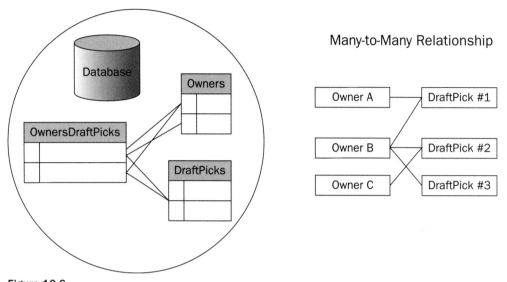

Figure 10-6

Many-to-many relationships cannot be directly characterized by relations in the same manner that one-to-many and one-to-one relations are, so a third relation needs to be developed to represent the relationship properly. The key for an intersection relation, in this case a table named OwnersDraftPicks, is always the combination of parent keys. With OwnersDraftPicks in Figure 10-6, a parent key is implemented for each key value.

The OwnerSessionLocal interface defines the method signatures that will be implemented in this example to perform database publication, search, and removal operations. Entity class references for the Owners and DraftPicks tables are used to manipulate the data that is marshaled between the abstraction layer that exists between the business tier and the database:

```
package com.scenario3.ejb.session;

import javax.ejb.Local;
import com.scenario3.persistence.*;

import java.util.List;

@Local
public interface OwnersSessionLocal
{
    public Owners searchForOwners(String id);
    public DraftPicks searchForDraftPicks(String id);
    public void persist(Object obj);
    public List findAllDraftPicks();
    public void remove(Object obj);
    public Owners removeOwnersDraftPicks(String ownr, String pick);
    public Owners addOwnersDraftPicks(String ownr, String pick);
}
```

`OwnerSession` is a stateless bean that implements the interface classes that are responsible for conveyance of data between the client application and the back-end database. Here, the `@Transaction Management` annotation declares that the `OwnersSession` class utilizes container-managed transactions and injects the `persistence_sample` resource described in the `persistence.xml` artifact:

```
package com.scenario3.ejb.session;

import javax.ejb.Stateless;
import javax.ejb.Stateful;
import javax.ejb.SessionContext;
import javax.persistence.*;
import javax.ejb.*;
import java.util.List;
import java.util.Collection;

import com.scenario3.persistence.*;

@Stateless
@TransactionManagement(value=TransactionManagementType.CONTAINER)

public class OwnersSession implements OwnersSessionLocal, OwnersSessionRemote {
    @javax.persistence.PersistenceContext(unitName="persistence_sample")
    private EntityManager em;

    public OwnersSession() {}

    public Owners searchForOwners(String id) {
        Owners owners = (Owners)em.find(Owners.class, id);
        return owners;
    }

    public DraftPicks searchForDraftPicks(String id) {
        DraftPicks draftPicks = (DraftPicks)em.find(DraftPicks.class, id);
        return draftPicks;
    }
```

The `@TransactionAttribute` marking specified that the EJB container will invoke the remove business method within a transaction context. The named query called `findAllDraftPicks` is invoked in a similarly named method that returns a `List` collection after applying the `getResultList` method on the query operation:

```
@TransactionAttribute(TransactionAttributeType.REQUIRED)
public void remove(Object obj) {
    Object mergedObj = em.merge(obj);
    em.remove(mergedObj);
}

public void persist(Object obj) {
    em.persist(obj);
}

public List findAllDraftPicks() {
    List draftPicks = em.createNamedQuery("findAllDraftPicks").getResultList();
    return draftPicks;
}
```

Draft pick removal occurs in the removeOwnersDraftPicks method by first querying the Owner and DraftPicks entities with the criteria specified by the user from the form display. Once these entity objects retrieve their result sets from their respective queries, a check is performed to ensure that a draft pick actually exists, before finalizing the transaction. Both entities invoke their remove methods, which in turn eliminate that particular draft pick reference from their tables:

```
public Owners removeOwnersDraftPicks(String ownr, String pick) {
    Owners owners = null;
    DraftPicks draftPicks = null;
    try {
        owners = (Owners)em.find(Owners.class, ownr);
        draftPicks = (DraftPicks)em.find(DraftPicks.class, pick);
        if(!owners.getDraftpicks().contains(draftPicks)) {
            System.out.println("remove: did not find a draft pick obj for :" +
draftPicks.getName());
        } else {
            owners.getDraftpicks().remove(draftPicks);
            draftPicks.getOwners().remove(owners);
        }
    } catch(Exception e) {
        e.printStackTrace();
    }
    return owners;
}

public Owners addOwnersDraftPicks(String ownr, String pick) {
    Owners owners = null;
    DraftPicks draftPicks = null;
    try {
        owners = (Owners)em.find(Owners.class, ownr);
        draftPicks = (DraftPicks)em.find(DraftPicks.class, pick);

        if(owners.getDraftpicks().contains(draftPicks)) {
            System.out.println("add: found an existing subscription obj for :"
+ draftPicks.getName());
        } else {
            owners.getDraftpicks().add(draftPicks);
            draftPicks.getOwners().add(owners);
        }
    } catch(Exception e) {
        e.printStackTrace();
    }
    return owners;
}

}
```

The DraftPicks entity described here maps to the DraftPicks table that persists the owners draft day selections. A named query called findAllDraftPicks performs a generic query that will retrieve all items from the DraftPicks table when invoked:

```
package com.scenario3.persistence;

import java.util.ArrayList;
import java.util.Collection;
```

509

```
import java.util.Iterator;
import javax.persistence.*;

@Entity
@NamedQuery(name="findAllDraftPicks", query="select d from DraftPicks d")

public  class DraftPicks implements java.io.Serializable {
    private String name;
    private String position;
    private Collection owners;

    public DraftPicks() {}

    @Id
    public String getName() { // primary key
        return name;
    }

    public void setName(String name) {
        this.name = name;
    }

    public String getPosition() {
        return position;
    }

    public void setPosition(String position) {
        this.position = position;
    }
```

A many-to-many relationship is defined here so that owner and draft pick entities remain in sync during transactional activities dictated by the web client application:

```
    @ManyToMany(mappedBy="draftpicks", targetEntity=
com.scenario3.persistence.Owners.class)
    public Collection<Owners> getOwners() {
        return owners;
    }

    public void setOwners(Collection owners) {
        this.owners = owners;
    }

    public DraftPicks(String name, String position) {
        _create(name, position);
    }

    private String _create(String name, String position) {
        setName(name);
        setPosition(position);
        return name;
    }
}
```

Here, the `Owner` entity maps to the Owners table that persists potential draft pick selections that are made by the individual owners. As shown by previous classes, the `@Entity` marks the class as a database entity and the `@Id` marking declares the primary key for that table; in this case, the primary key is named OWNERID:

```
package com.scenario3.persistence;

import java.util.ArrayList;
import java.util.Collection;
import java.util.Iterator;
import javax.persistence.*;
import javax.persistence.OneToMany;

@Entity
public class Owners implements java.io.Serializable
{
    private String ownerId;
    private String firstName;
    private String lastName;
    private Collection draftpicks;

    public Owners() {}

    @Id
    @Column(name="OWNERID")
    public String getOwnerId() {
        return ownerId;
    }

    public void setOwnerId(String ownerId) {
        this.ownerId = ownerId;
    }

    public String getFirstName() {
        return firstName;
    }

    public void setFirstName(String firstName) {
        this.firstName=firstName;
    }

    public String getLastName() {
        return lastName;
    }

    public void setLastName(String lastName) {
        this.lastName=lastName;
    }

    public Owners(String ownerId, String firstName, String lastName) {
        setOwnerId(ownerId);
        setFirstName(firstName);
        setLastName(lastName);
    }
```

Table entities are joined here in the `Owners` class through the `@ManyToMany` and `@JoinTable` annotations using the OWNERSDRAFTPICKS table relation. Join columns are specified for both the OWNERS and DRAFTPICKS tables so that operations on them will be properly synched:

```
@ManyToMany(targetEntity= com.scenario3.persistence.DraftPicks.class,
    fetch=FetchType.EAGER )
    @JoinTable(
            name="OWNERSDRAFTPICKS",
            joinColumns=@JoinColumn(name="OWNERS_OWNERS",
referencedColumnName="OWNERID"),
            inverseJoinColumns=@JoinColumn(name="DRAFTPICKS_NAME",
referencedColumnName="NAME")
    )

    public Collection<DraftPicks> getDraftpicks() {
        return draftpicks;
    }

    public void setDraftpicks (Collection draftpicks) {
        this.draftpicks=draftpicks;
    }
```

The `getDraftpicksList` method uses the `@Transient` annotation to indicate that the `getDraft picksList` method is not persistent, and will not be cached. The `@PostPersist` and `@PostRemove` markings designate callback methods for the application server's life cycle event activities. These annotations ensure that the `postCreate` and `ejbRemove` methods will be invoked for the Owners entity after it has been made persistent or removed:

```
@Transient
public ArrayList getDraftpicksList() {
    ArrayList list = new ArrayList();
    Iterator c = getDraftpicks().iterator();
    while (c.hasNext()) {
        list.add((DraftPicks)c.next());
    }
    return list;
}

@PostPersist
public void postCreate () {
    System.out.println("[Owners:postCreate]");
}

@PostRemove
public void ejbRemove() {
    System.out.println("[Owners:postRemove]");
}

}
```

Figure 10-7 exhibits the baseball draft web component that allows owners to select their potential draft picks from a drop-down list of players. A remove button that resides in the form display along with the owner's current selections allows for the removal of players that were previously selected.

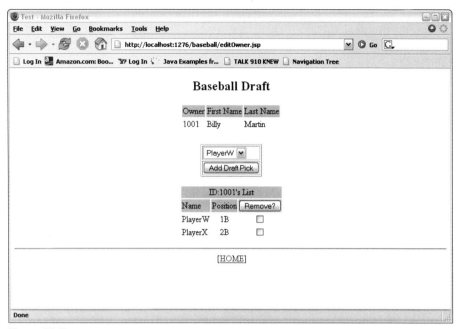

Figure 10-7

A Java Server Page (JSP) named editOwner.jsp is shown here to demonstrate how the EJB 3 components described previously are implemented to create the web presentation in Figure 10-7. Three parameters are passed among the web container (oid [owner ID], draftpicks, removeitem) so that users can dictate the behaviors that will be applied to the entity classes for transactions to the database:

```
<%@ page language="java" %>
<%@ page import="java.util.Collection" %>
<%@ page import="javax.naming.InitialContext" %>
<%@ page import=" com.scenario3.persistence.Owners" %>
<%@ page import=" com.scenario3.persistence.DraftPicks" %>
<%@ page import=" com.scenario3.ejb.session.*" %>
<%@ page import=" com.scenario3.common.*" %>
<%@ page import='java.util.*' %>

<html>

<head><title>Test</title></head>
<body bgcolor="white">
<center>
<h2>Baseball Draft</h2>

<%
System.out.println("getting params");
String oid = request.getParameter("oid");
String draftpicks = request.getParameter("draftpicks");
```

```java
String[] removeitem = request.getParameterValues("removeitem");

String name = "";
String position = "";
if (draftpicks != null) {
    String[] playerposition = draftpicks.split("[|]");
    if (playerposition.length == 2) {
        name = playerposition[0];
        position = playerposition[1];
    }
}
```

If the owner ID, named `oid`, is determined to be a legitimate value, meaning it's not null or empty, then a lookup will be performed using the `ownerSession`'s interface and the `searchForOwners` method to retrieve owner attributes from the database. Owner information collected from the `searchOwners` query will be published on the user display to specify which owner is actually drafting players:

```java
Owners owners = null;
OwnersSessionLocal ownersSession = null;

if ( (oid != null) && (!oid.equals("")) ) {
    try {
        InitialContext ic = new InitialContext();
        Object o = ic.lookup("java:comp/env/OwnersSessionLocal");
        ownersSession = (OwnersSessionLocal) o;
        owners = ownersSession.searchForOwners(oid);
    } catch(Exception e) {
        e.printStackTrace();
        out.println(e.toString());
    }

    if (owners != null) {
%>
<table border="0">
<tr bgcolor="#cccccc"><td>Owner</td><td>First Name</td><td>Last Name</td></tr>
<tr>
    <td><%=owners.getOwnerId()%></td>
    <td><%=owners.getFirstName()%></td>
    <td><%=owners.getLastName()%></td>
</tr>
<tr><td colspan="3"> </td></tr>
</table>
<%
}
```

In this code segment, removal operations are performed on draft picks that have been selected by the user to be removed from the owner's draft list. The `removeItem` variable is a string array that contains all of the players deemed removable. The `ownerSession` object reference is used to call the `removeOwnersDraftPicks` method for player removal using the remove methods that reside in both the Owners and DraftPicks entities:

```java
    if ( (removeitem != null) && (removeitem.length > 0) ) {
        for (int i=0; i < removeitem.length; i++) {
            try {
                System.out.println("removing oid, name= " + oid + ", " +
removeitem[i]);
                owners = ownersSession.removeOwnersDraftPicks(oid, removeitem[i]);
            } catch(Exception e) {
                e.printStackTrace();
            }
        }
    }

    String userSubmit = request.getParameter("submit");
    if ( (userSubmit != null && userSubmit.equals("Add Draft Pick")) &&
(!name.equals("")) ) {
        try {
            System.out.println("adding oid, name= " + oid + ", " + name);
            owners = ownersSession.addOwnersDraftPicks(oid, name);
        } catch(Exception e) {
            e.printStackTrace();
            out.println(e.toString());
        }
    }

    List allDraftPicks = null;
    try {
        allDraftPicks = ownersSession.findAllDraftPicks();
    } catch(Exception e) {
        e.printStackTrace();
        out.println(e.toString());
    }
```

Checks are used here in the JSP to ensure that the `allDraftPicks` list is populated with draft pick selections by the owner. If player items are discovered, they will be added to the drop-down list display component. Note that both the draft pick name and position are concatenated with a pipe (|) delimiter so both player attributes can be parsed above by the application for visual presentation in the owners list:

```jsp
%>
<form method="post" action="/baseball/editOwner.jsp">
<table border="1">
<%
if ( (allDraftPicks == null) || (allDraftPicks.size() == 0)) {
%>
    <tr>
        <td colspan="2">No draft picks found.</td>
    </tr>
<%
} else {
%>
    <tr>
```

```
            <td>
            <select name="draftpicks">
            <%
            for (int i = 0; i < allDraftPicks.size(); i++)
            {
                DraftPicks draftPicks = (DraftPicks)allDraftPicks.get(i);
            %>
                <option
value="<%=draftPicks.getName()%>|<%=draftPicks.getPosition()%>">
                <%=draftPicks.getName()%>
                </option>
            <%
            }
            %>
            </select>
            </td>
        </tr>
    <%
    }
    %>
    <tr>
        <td colspan="2" align="center">
            <input type="submit" name="submit" value="Add Draft Pick">
            <input type="hidden" name="oid" value="<%=oid%>">
        </td>
    </tr>

    </table>
    </form>
```

Lastly, in this segment of the JSP component, the owners draft pick list is rendered along with checkboxes that allow selections to be removed if warranted. The owners draft pick list is obtained from the owner reference procured from the `ownersSession.searchForOwners` lookup query:

```
    <form method="post" action="/baseball/editOwner.jsp">
    <table>
    <tr bgcolor="#cccccc"><td colspan="3" align="center">ID:<%=oid%>'s
List</td></tr>
    <tr bgcolor="#cccccc">
        <td>Name</td>
        <td>Position</td>
        <td><input type="submit" name="remove" value="Remove?"></td>
        <input type="hidden" name="oid" value="<%=oid%>">
        <input type="hidden" name="draftpicks" value="<%=draftpicks%>">
    </tr>
    <%
    if (owners != null) {
        List ownersList = owners.getDraftpicksList();
        if ( (ownersList != null) && (ownersList.size() > 0) ) {
            for (int i=0; i < ownersList.size(); i++) {
                DraftPicks draftPicks = (DraftPicks)ownersList.get(i);
```

```
                        %>
                        <tr>
                            <td><%=draftPicks.getName()%></td>
                            <td align="center"><%=draftPicks.getPosition()%></td>
                            <td align="center"><input type="checkbox" name="removeitem"
    value="<%=draftPicks.getName()%>"></td>
                        </tr>
                        <%
                    }
                }
            }%>
        </table>
        </form>
    <%
    }
    else
        out.println("No owner found with ID = " + oid);
    %>
    <hr>
    [<a href="/baseball/index.html">HOME</a>]
    </center>
    </body>
    </html>
```

This scenario tried to address many complex features that have been provided by the new EJB 3 persistence model libraries to perform transactions with enterprise-tier components from a web-tier JSP. The confluence of EJB libraries and their annotations in source code development is a daunting modeling task to undertake, but hopefully the code in this scenario will prove beneficial for readers in their development and deployment endeavors.

Summary

It should be noted that modifications in the EJB 3 and Java Persistence API specifications were developed so users would have to craft fewer classes in their implementations because more work is now performed by EJB/web containers that reside in application servers. EJB artifacts have shed the need for home and object interfaces that have been required in the past, resulting in the need for only a business interface. Annotation markings are now declared in EJB components forgoing previous release requirements that required deployment descriptor configurations which now allow the container to manage transactions. Lastly, the introduction of annotations in POJOs has allowed developers to map Java objects to relational data stores making O/R mapping much simpler for development and maintenance.

Developers who have developed enterprise bean components from previous releases should recognize how the new EJB 3 and persistence model libraries have streamlined deployment descriptor requirements with the introduction of annotations to generate artifacts, document code, and provide services for operations. These annotations now allow developers to define Web Services, map Java methods to operations and components to XML and database persistence mechanisms, as well as specify external dependencies to EJB applications in a more efficient manner than ever before.

11

Communicating between Java Components and Components of Other Platforms

Java is an ideal platform for server-side development. Many of the ongoing professional and open source Java development projects are for various server-side applications. Java EE (Enterprise Edition) dominates this Java server space, providing a strong open platform for many different types of server applications. One of the core principles and architectural themes in Java EE is the ability to segregate and distribute various *components* of the same software system to different machines. Remote communication between Java objects and components to other Java objects and components is at the heart of Java EE. Because Java EE is an open platform, it also defines how external objects and components in other applications (and other programming languages) communicate with Java EE components. In today's heterogeneous Internet-centric computing world, this cross-platform communication is absolutely essential.

> Component is an ambiguous term that can mean many different things to many different developers. In the context of this chapter, *component* refers to any software object or collection of objects that are network-aware, either sending information to other components or receiving it from the latter. For a high-level example, a web server could be considered a component. Web browsers and other client applications need to communicate with this component. More granular examples include Enterprise JavaBeans (EJBs; see Chapter 10), and Web Services.

In this chapter, you investigate the general high-level design of component-to-component communication as well as some concrete examples for coding the actual communication. The `java.net` package is looked at first for its sockets support, because sockets are the basic building block for all other communication technologies. Understanding protocols follows and an example partial implementation of HTTP is demonstrated. A brief discussion of Remote Method Invocation (RMI) and the Common Object Request Broker Architecture (CORBA) comes next. Concluding the chapter is information on how best to utilize the newest addition to JDK 6, Web Services.

The information regarding sockets and protocols will be trivial for the advanced developer but crucial for a developer with no distributed programming experience. If you are an advanced developer familiar with sockets, protocols, and understand the basic premises of RMI and CORBA, feel free to skip ahead to the "Web Services" section — you will probably find them too basic. Web Services are now a first-class citizen in the JDK and are rapidly becoming the cross-platform component technology of choice for new software projects.

Component Communication Scenarios

A few examples of where component-to-component communication takes place will aid the understanding of where sockets, CORBA, RMI, and Web Services fit into a given application's architecture. In each of the scenarios shown, almost any of these technologies *could* be used. Being equipped with more in-depth knowledge of these technologies later on in the chapter will allow software developers to weigh the pros and cons of each in their particular situation and pick the right technology for the job.

News Reader: Automated Web Browsing

Little software utilities can often eliminate tedious tasks such as constantly watching and monitoring particular web sites. Software can be developed to automate these tasks as much as possible. Developing an application for monitoring web sites would involve communicating with the remote web server to check various news sites for new stories and information on topics of interest every ten minutes. Whenever a new story popped up, fitting your criteria, the user would be notified, eliminating the need to constantly check and refresh certain web sites. Writing client components that monitor data sources for new information is a common task in distributed computing.

A Bank Application: An EJB/Java EE Client

Because of Java EE's component-based nature, existing systems can often be extended by simply adding new software components, without destroying their existing infrastructure. Suppose a bank wants to modernize the client software that its tellers use to access the banking infrastructure. The terminals the bank tellers use daily are all running Microsoft Windows 2000 and the application must run on this existing infrastructure. The bank already has a Java EE-based back-end to keep track of all banking data, and the application merely needs to interface with it. This Java EE system exposes a web front-end, which is good for personal use over the Internet by various members of the bank, but not for the heavy daily use necessary for tellers. A thick client is needed. The EJB components on the server will need to be accessed by the client. Writing client applications that access EJBs (or other Java EE components) is typical in professional Java development.

A *Portal: Integrating Heterogeneous Data Sources and Services*

Many web portals, such as Yahoo!, integrate various pieces of data such as stock tickers, sports scores, and news headlines. The software design of such a portal must be flexible enough to integrate many of these different pieces of data, oftentimes from many different locations. Many larger corporations have their own internal intranet portal. These portals need to access information from a variety of sources. Component-to-component communication is crucial to access the databases, files, and information from other software applications necessary for the functionality of the portal.

Overview of Interprocess Communication and Basic Network Architecture

In the development of these distributed software applications, it is often necessary for components running in one process to communicate with components running in another process. For instance, a database runs in one process on a server, and the client application that reads and writes information from and to this database runs in a separate process (and possibly on a different machine). There must be some mechanism through which these two processes communicate. Often, these other processes that your Java application must communicate with are not written in Java and are not running inside a virtual machine. Whether or not another process is running in a Java Virtual Machine, any communication between two processes must follow some sort of *protocol*. Protocols are the language two disparate components use to speak to one another. Your web browser speaks the HyperText Transfer Protocol (HTTP) to web servers to retrieve web content to your local machine. Your instant messaging client speaks a certain protocol back to its server and potentially to other users of an instant messaging service. Peer-to-peer file-sharing services speak protocols to allow the searching and sharing of files. (Gnutella is one popular example of a common protocol allowing many different file-sharing clients to communicate with each other.)

All of the applications and protocols mentioned can communicate over a network. They can also communicate to another process on the same machine. This is because these protocols have been abstracted from their transport. They could run locally, or over a TCP/IP network. In communicating between Java components and components of other platforms, you must always consider possible network transports. The Open Systems Interconnection (OSI) network architecture gives a high-level abstraction of some of the layers in any form of interprocess network communication. For the discussion in this chapter, you can think of an even higher-level architecture (derived from the OSI architecture) for understanding component-to-component communication. Figure 11-1 shows the derived architecture with three main layers: the application layer, the protocol layer, and the transport layer.

Two disparate components communicate by sending data through each of the layers as shown. The application layer represents high-level protocols such as HTTP or FTP. The protocol layer represents lower-level transport protocols such as TCP or UDP running over IP. The transport layer represents the actual physical transport, such as Ethernet, as its corresponding mechanisms for sending and retrieving data. For distributed components to communicate, they must speak the same protocol at the application level.

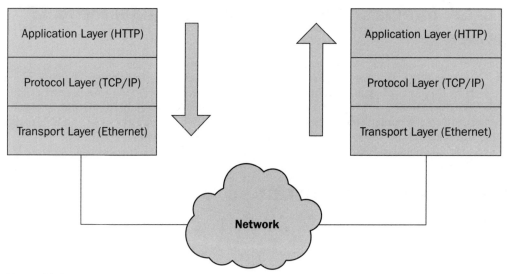

Figure 11-1

This chapter focuses on the application level; the lower-level hardware transport is out of the scope of this book. For most distributed application development, the application layer is most important to software developers. In web applications, for example, HTTP is the application-level protocol that dictates many of the application's design decisions. HTTP does not support stateful connections, and therefore the state of any user's session must be simulated by the use of session cookies or session identification parameters. Designing *any* network-aware application, or in other words, any application that must communicate between separate components, Java or non-Java, locally or remote, requires the knowledge of the limitations and features of the various application-level and transport-level protocols available to facilitate such communication.

> *Threads are a critical aspect of designing any good I/O-intensive application, especially I/O over a network and between two disparate processes.*

Sockets

Sockets are the basic mechanism for interprocess communication provided by the operating system. In most development projects, they will probably not have to be used explicitly, because they are fairly low-level. However, *any* type of interprocess communication is built on top of sockets, and in any type of network communication, sockets are used implicitly. Therefore, it would be prudent to understand just some simple background as to how they work. This section of the chapter provides a broad overview of sockets for the purposes of better understanding RMI, CORBA, and Web Services.

A *socket* is essentially a defined endpoint for communication between two processes. It provides a full duplex channel to two different parties (potentially more if it is multicasting) involved in communication — there are two separate data streams, one going in and one going out. There are two types of sockets:

❑ **User Datagram Protocol (UDP).** Sockets using UDP provide a *datagram* service. They receive and send discrete packets of data. UDP is a connectionless protocol, meaning that there is no connection setup time as there is in TCP. However, UDP is unreliable — packets are not guaranteed to be sent or received in the right order. UDP is mainly used for applications such as multimedia streaming and online gaming, where not all data is necessary, for which the UDP's best-effort service model is well suited.

❑ **Transmission Control Protocol (TCP).** Sockets using TCP provide a reliable byte-stream service. TCP guarantees delivery of all packets sent and the reception of them in the correct order. TCP is a connection-oriented protocol, which allows it to provide the byte-stream service. TCP is best suited for applications that cannot allow data transmitted to be lost, such as for file transfer, web browsing, or Telnet.

This section only considers using TCP sockets, because UDP is more for advanced network applications that require the development of their own low-level protocols or multimedia streaming algorithms, which are out of the scope of this book. For the purposes of this text, sockets simply allow you an input and output stream to another process, either running locally or remotely.

The Java Socket API

The Java Socket API is the core Java interface to network programming. As such, all of the core socket classes are found in the `java.net` package. Java implements the two types of sockets: TCP sockets, which communicate using the Transmission Control Protocol, and UDP sockets, which communicate via the Universal Datagram Protocol. In addition to the normal UDP socket implementation, Java also provides a UDP multicast socket implementation, which is a socket that sends data to multiple clients simultaneously. Because Java was built from the ground up as an object-oriented language, you will find that the socket library interacts heavily with the Java I/O libraries (both `java.io` and `java.nio`). If you need a refresher on some of the aspects of Java I/O and serialization, see Chapter 5. This section concentrates on TCP sockets throughout, because they are far more prevalent than UDP sockets in most client/server or distributed systems.

Key Classes

The following table shows the four major classes used for socket communication in Java. The `Socket` and `DatagramSocket` classes implement TCP and UDP, respectively. Both TCP and UDP use an IP address and port number as the demultiplexing key, or address, to another process. `InetSocketAddress` represents this address. Both `Socket` and `DatagramSocket` use an `InetSocketAddress` to locate the machine and process that should be the recipient of any data sent.

Class (From `java.net`)	Function
Socket	Class used to represent a client socket endpoint for sending and receiving data over TCP connections.
DatagramSocket	Both client and server class for sending and receiving data sent via UDP.

Table continued on following page

Class (From `java.net`)	Function
`ServerSocket`	Class used for TCP servers. Once a client connects, this class returns a Socket class to actually send and receive data.
`InetSocketAddress`	Represents an IP address (or hostname) along with a port number. For example, `InetSocketAddress` could represent `www.example.com:8080`.

Client Programming

The `Socket` and `InetSocketAddress` classes are used by a client to connect to a server running in another process (whether remote or local). Once a connection is set up, all communication takes place utilizing normal Java I/O classes. There is a stream of data coming in, and a stream of data going out. To set up a connection, first create the address object that defines which server and port to connect:

```
InetSocketAddress address = new InetSocketAddress("www.example.com", 80);
```

`InetSocketAddress` objects can also be created with an IP address:

```
InetSocketAddress address = new InetSocketAddress("127.0.0.1", 80);
```

Once the address of the remote endpoint has been defined, a connection can be attempted. Be sure to catch `java.io.IOException`, because this exception will be thrown if there are any problems connecting (such as the network is down, the server is busy, the server cannot be located, and so on). In network programming, it is important to pay extra attention to error-handling details, because communication problems aren't just a possibility — they are pretty much guaranteed to happen at some point. Now that you have defined an address, you can create a new `Socket` class to attempt a connection:

```
Socket socket = new Socket();
socket.connect(address);
```

If the connection succeeds, either Java I/O classes or NIO (`java.nio`) classes can be used to send and receive data. In these examples, you will use normal Java I/O because it is often easier to understand and provides better code readability. Once the socket is connected, both `InputStream` and `OutputStream` objects from the `java.io` package can be retrieved and communication can begin:

```
InputStream in = socket.getInputStream();
OutputStream out = socket.getOutputStream();
```

These objects are often wrapped around other higher-level and easier-to-use I/O classes just as they are in normal Java I/O programming. Suppose, for example, that all the communication you are going to send and receive over the socket is textual data. Java provides the `BufferedReader` and `PrintWriter` objects that can be wrapped around the input and output stream objects:

```
PrintWriter writer = new PrintWriter(out);
BufferedReader br  = new BufferedReader(new InputStreamReader(in));
writer.println("Hello, remote computer");
writer.flush();
String serverResponse = br.readLine();
```

The call to flush(). PrintWriter *and other I/O classes buffer data before writing them to their underlying output stream. To have the send take place immediately, you flush the underlying output stream so the data you have written to the* PrintWriter *is immediately written to the underlying output stream, in this case, the* OutputStream *from the* Socket, *which then sends the data over the network.* PrintWriter *can also be created to automatically flush any output written straight to the underlying output stream, at the disadvantage of losing the ability to buffer data before it is sent to optimize network performance.*

That's really all there is to sockets. The difficult aspect of sockets comes when determining and implementing the *protocol* by which two different processes agree to communicate. In the "Implementing a Protocol" section, the difficulties are explored, and a small portion of HTTP is implemented.

Server Programming

Programming server-side sockets with Java is just as easy as on the client side. The ServerSocket class is used to initiate a passive TCP connection. A passive TCP connection monitors a particular port on the host machine and waits for a remote client to connect. Once a connection is initiated by a client, the ServerSocket class dispatches a Socket class, which in turn can be used to get the input and output streams associated with the connection (as well as the hostname and address of the client machine). Certain ports on computers are generally associated with certain protocols—port 80 is HTTP, 23 is Telnet, 25 is SMTP, and so on. When picking a port to use for your application, the general rule of thumb is to keep it above 1000, because most common server applications do not use ports in this range. If a ServerSocket is created on a port that is already in use, an exception will be thrown, and the server socket will not be created. Only *one* application on a machine can use any given port at one time. The following code creates a ServerSocket and prepares it to accept incoming connections on port 1500:

```
ServerSocket serverSocket = new ServerSocket(1500);
Socket incomingClient = serverSocket.accept();
```

The accept() method blocks until a client connects. Once a client connects, a Socket instance is returned that represents the connection to the remote process. Input and output streams can be obtained to facilitate communication using the same mechanisms described in the preceding section. You do not have to call connect() on the incoming Socket though, because the connection setup has already occurred.

The previous code segment will accept one connection and one connection only. Server-side applications generally need to service more than one client simultaneously, however. Imagine if eBay or other popular web sites could only serve one client at a time! The accept() method on the ServerSocket negotiates another port on the server for the client's connection to move to, freeing up the original port the ServerSocket was created on for another incoming connection. You could call accept() again to wait for another connection. However convenient the behavior of accept() is though, it does not solve the problem of allowing multiple *simultaneous* connections. This is solved through the use of threads. The following code is a simple example of how a server could allow for multiple simultaneous connections:

```
boolean conditionToKeepRunning = true;

while (conditionToKeepRunning) {
    Socket client = serverSocket.accept();

Thread clientServiceThread = new Thread(new ClassThatImplementsRunnable(client));
    clientServiceThread.start();
}
```

Notice how every time your server receives a connection, it spawns off a worker thread to handle the incoming request. This allows the incoming request to be serviced *while* the server waits for another connection. Because each request receives its own thread, more than one request can also be processed at the same time.

> *This model of one thread per request is not the most efficient solution; it is used here for simplicity. Creation and destruction of threads is an expensive operation, and a thread pool would be a better solution. Keeping a fixed number of active threads and using them as they become available can keep the server from being overloaded, as well as virtually eliminating the cost of thread creation and destruction.*

Putting it All Together: An Echo Server

Writing a simple server application will demonstrate a full application using sockets. This cleverly named echo server will echo any text sent to it back to the client. Whenever a client connects, they will receive a welcome message, and after the message is sent, your server will simply begin its loop of echoing back to the client any text the client sends.

SocketEcho

Your server class, `SocketEcho`, will implement `java.lang.Runnable` because every instance you create of `SocketEcho` will be running in a separate thread, allowing you to process multiple simultaneous connections. All of the server logic will reside in the `SocketEcho.run()` method (for the threading). In its constructor, `SocketEcho` is passed a `Socket` with which it conducts all communications with its client in the `run()` method. The `run()` method is shown in the following code, and as you can see after the welcome message is printed, the application simply loops on receiving textual input from its client. Every time a new character is received, the server checks to see if it was the exit character (the ? in this case). If the exit character was received, the application breaks out of its loop and the socket is closed in the `finally` block. Any other character besides the exit character is sent back to the client:

```java
public void run() {
  try {
    BufferedReader br = new BufferedReader(new
                           InputStreamReader(socket.getInputStream()));
    PrintWriter out = new PrintWriter(socket.getOutputStream());

    // print a welcome message
    out.println("Hello, you've contacted the Echo Server.");
    out.println("\tWhatever you type, I will type back to you...");
    out.println("\tPress '?' to close the connection.");
    out.println();
    out.println();
    out.flush();

    int currChar = 0;
    while ((currChar = br.read()) != -1) {
      char c = (char) currChar;

      // if '?' is typed, close the connection
      if (c == '?')
        break;

      out.print(c);
```

```
        out.flush();
      }
    } catch (IOException ioe) {
      ioe.printStackTrace();
    } finally {
      try {
        if (socket != null) {
          socket.close();
        }
      } catch (IOException ex) {
        ex.printStackTrace();
      }
    }
  }
}
```

The `main()` function simply launches the server, using a `ServerSocket`. In here, the code for accepting client connections and spawning new threads is found. Every time a client connects, a new instance of `SocketEcho` is created with the client's corresponding `Socket` instance, and a thread to run it is produced. Once this new thread is started, the control flow for the client that connected goes to the `run()` method in `SocketEcho` (which is in a different thread). While one or many clients are connected, the server can still wait for new connections, because the server handles each client in a separate thread:

```
    try {
        ServerSocket serverSocket = new ServerSocket(port);

        System.out.println("Echo Server Running...");
        int counter = 0;
        while (true) {
          Socket client = serverSocket.accept();

          System.out.println("Accepted a connection from " +
                             client.getInetAddress().getHostName());

          // use multiple threads to handle simultaneous connections
          Thread t = new Thread(new SocketEcho(client));
          t.setName(client.getInetAddress().getHostName() + ":" + counter++);
          t.start(); // starts up the new thread and SocketEcho.run() is called
        }
    } catch (IOException ioe) {
      ioe.printStackTrace();
    }
```

The full listing of the code for `SocketEcho` is as follows:

```
package book;

import java.io.BufferedReader;
import java.io.IOException;
import java.io.InputStreamReader;
import java.io.PrintWriter;
import java.net.ServerSocket;
```

```java
import java.net.Socket;

public class SocketEcho implements Runnable {

  private Socket socket;

  public SocketEcho(Socket socket) {
    this.socket = socket;
  }

  public void run() {
    try {
      BufferedReader br = new BufferedReader(new
                          InputStreamReader(socket.getInputStream()));
      PrintWriter out = new PrintWriter(socket.getOutputStream());

      // print a welcome message
      out.println("Hello, you've contacted the Echo Server.");
      out.println("\tWhatever you type, I will type back to you...");
      out.println("\tPress '?' to close the connection.");
      out.println();
      out.println();
      out.flush();

      int currChar = 0;
      while ((currChar = br.read()) != -1) {
        char c = (char) currChar;

        // if '?' is typed, close the connection
        if (c == '?')
          break;

        out.print(c);
        out.flush();
      }
    } catch (IOException ioe) {
      ioe.printStackTrace();
    } finally {
      try {
        if (socket != null) {
          socket.close();
        }
      } catch (IOException ex) {
        ex.printStackTrace();
      }
    }
  }

  public static void main(String[] args) {
    // our default port
    int port = 1500;

    // use port passed in by the command line, if one was
    if (args.length >= 1) {
      try {
```

```
            port = Integer.parseInt(args[0]);
        } catch (NumberFormatException nfe) {
            System.out.println("Error: port must be a number -- using 1500 instead.");
        }
    }

    try {
        ServerSocket serverSocket = new ServerSocket(port);

        System.out.println("Echo Server Running...");
        int counter = 0;
        while (true) {
            Socket client = serverSocket.accept();

            System.out.println("Accepted a connection from " +
                                client.getInetAddress().getHostName());

            // use multiple threads to handle simultaneous connections
            Thread t = new Thread(new SocketEcho(client));
            t.setName(client.getInetAddress().getHostName() + ":" + counter++);
            t.start(); // starts up the new thread and SocketEcho.run() is called
        }
    } catch (IOException ioe) {
        ioe.printStackTrace();
    }
  }
}
```

Running the Echo Server

To start up the echo server, simply run it like any other Java application from the command prompt:

```
java book.SocketEcho
```

Once the server is started, it will begin accepting connections on port 1500 (or what was specified as a parameter in the command line). Whenever a connection is accepted, information about who connected is outputted to the screen as seen in Figure 11-2.

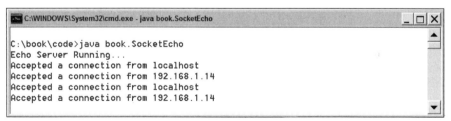

Figure 11-2

To connect to your client, run Telnet. Because you are running your server on a different port than Telnet's default, you have to specify the port to which you want Telnet to connect:

```
telnet localhost 1500
```

529

After connecting, the welcome message displays. Now anything you type will be sent to the server and then echoed back to your screen. If you press the ? character, the server closes the connection. Figure 11-3 shows an example conversion between the client and server.

```
Telnet localhost                                          _ □ ×
Hello, you've contacted the Echo Server.                    ▲
        Whatever you type, I will type back to you...
        Press '?' to close the connection.


TThhiiss  sshhoowwss  hhoowww  tthhee  eecchhoo  sseerrvvrr  rreessppoonnddss
bbaacckk  ttoo  mmee  wwhhaatteevveerr  II  ttyyppee  ttoo  iitt......

--TThhee  eennddd..?

Connection to host lost.

Press any key to continue...
                                                            ▼
```

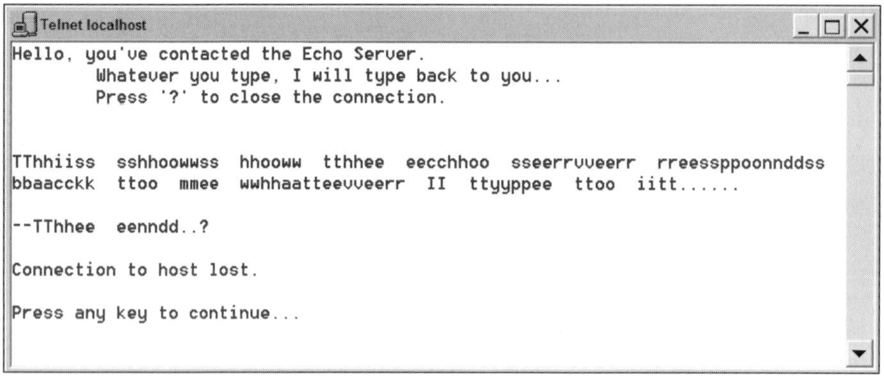

Figure 11-3

Note how the echo server will run continuously until CTRL+C is pressed in the command prompt. Normally, other mechanisms are used to stop the server. Some server-based software listens separately on another socket and waits for an authorized user or machine to connect to send a special shutdown message. Simple server applications like this one sometimes only rely on CTRL+C if no major cleanup is required on application shutdown, and one does not mind immediately disconnecting any clients.

Implementing a Protocol

Sockets provide the building blocks for developing communication languages, or protocols, between two separate applications. TCP sockets provide input and output streams, but any data sent on one end is simply bytes to the other end unless the other end understands its meaning. In the previous echo server example, the server did not *understand* any of the data sent to it. It only read the data, and passed it back to the client. In practice, applications such as these are really only good to test network connectivity. They can serve no other purpose. To have any sort of meaningful communication, both a client and server must talk the same language, or protocol. Implementing protocols is a difficult task. As you have seen previously, sockets in Java are not difficult to program — they are simply another way of reading from an input stream and writing to an output stream. Many of the hard tasks associated with socket programming are the same hard problems associated with reading certain types of files. Files are structured in some sort of meaningful way — for instance, HTML files are text files structured with a series of tags to indicate how content should be displayed. Web browsers can read and display HTML files because they understand how to *parse* the file format. Writing parsers for anything more involved than simple text commands can be a daunting task, and is out of the scope of this chapter. Implementing a protocol requires agreeing on some form of a contract (or file/data *format*) between the client and server. Once this protocol has been developed, clients and servers can then implement it to talk to each other. The protocol needs to be unambiguous for two separate implementations to work correctly with each other. *It is no trivial task to specify an unambiguous protocol and then have two separate implementations work with each other.* In this section, a simple implementation of one of the commands in the HTTP protocol is explored. By implementing just a minute fraction of a simple textual protocol like HTTP, you will appreciate the difficulty in writing and implementing more detailed protocols. Other options then follow that spare application programmers the need to re-create the wheel by writing new protocols for every application they develop.

Protocol Specification

During the development of an application that employs the use of sockets, there will be some point where either a custom protocol is defined, or the definition of an existing protocol is used as the foundation for the logic in all socket programming in the application. Only for the development of specialized applications is there ever a need to develop a custom protocol. For example, the communications modules of the Mars Landers from NASA probably have to use sockets to issue commands to the robot and receive its status (or if not sockets, some other software abstraction of communication for which you would develop your own protocol). A custom protocol would need to be specified and implemented for this unique set of commands for the Lander. In most applications though, there is probably a protocol out there that suits the application's needs. There are many different ways to write a protocol specification, and this chapter will not delve into such matters, because it is a large subject on its own. In this section, HTTP is used as a test case for implementing someone else's protocol. Only a small portion of the HTTP specification is looked at and a simple piece implemented.

Basic Elements of HTTP

HTTP follows the simple request/response paradigm. A client sends a request to an HTTP server, issuing a particular command. The server then returns a response to the client based upon what command was sent. HTTP is a stateless protocol, meaning that the HTTP server does not need to retain information about a particular client *across* different requests. Every request is treated the same, no matter what requests a client has previously made.

> *There are ways to simulate state over HTTP, and this is what all web applications do. They use session identifiers and cookies to retain information about a particular client across multiple requests. This is how sites like amazon.com can identify particular users and provide one of the building blocks necessary for e-commerce.*

HTTP was developed purposely to be a simple protocol and easy to implement. This is why things such as stateful-session support had to be built on top of HTTP later — HTTP was originally designed just to be a mechanism for transferring HTML pages across a network. In HTTP, a client merely connects to a port (usually 80) on a remote machine and issues an HTTP command. The main HTTP commands are:

❑ **GET.** Retrieves the content found at the URL specified.

❑ **POST.** Sends data to the HTTP server and retrieves the content found at the URL specified. Oftentimes the content the HTTP server passes back is based on the data sent in by the POST command (that is, form data passed to a server).

❑ **PUT.** Asks the HTTP server to store the data sent with the request to the URL specified.

❑ **HEAD.** Retrieves only the HTTP headers of a request, not the actual content.

❑ **DELETE.** Asks the HTTP server to delete the content found at the URL specified.

After receiving an HTTP command, an HTTP server returns a response. It returns a response code to indicate something about the response. I'm sure you have seen some of these response codes while simply browsing the Web. Depending on which response code is returned, content may be returned along with the response code. The client can then parse through the content and display it as necessary. Some of the more common HTTP response codes are:

- ❑ **200.** Response OK, the request was fulfilled.
- ❑ **404.** The requested URL could not be found.
- ❑ **403.** The request for the URL was forbidden.
- ❑ **500.** The server encountered an internal error that prevented it from fulfilling the request.

See the actual HTTP specification online at `www.w3.org/Protocols/HTTP/`.

It is detailed and precise, and gives a good idea of what a specification for even a protocol as simple as HTTP looks like. For this example, you are going to look at a simple implementation of GET, and how it is implemented.

A Simple Implementation of HTTP GET

By implementing a small portion of a protocol, the inherent complexity and difficulty of implementing a full protocol specification will be revealed. Writing custom protocols is no picnic, and often leads to hard-to-maintain systems. Open protocols such as HTTP, which are published, are among the easiest to implement. The source code to reference and sample implementations can often be found. Freely available test suites to test the validity of an implementation often exist for open protocols. In the next example, first some of the details of HTTP GET (though not all by any means) must be examined. Your implementation of a simple stripped-down version of GET can then commence, concluding with a look at some methods for testing the validity of the implementation.

Background on HTTP GET

HTTP GET is probably the most commonly used HTTP request operation. Anytime a user types a URL into the address bar of his or her browser and navigates to that URL, GET is used. GET simply asks the server to retrieve a particular file. The server returns a response code indicating whether or not it was successful and, if successful, returns the file. A sample HTTP GET request looks like this:

```
GET / HTTP/1.1
Accept: */*
Accept-Language: en-nz
Accept-Encoding: gzip, deflate
User-Agent: Mozilla/4.0 (compatible; MSIE 6.0; Windows NT 5.0; .NET CLR 1.1.4322)
Host: www.cnn.com
Connection: Keep-Alive
```

Notice the format of the request. First the HTTP command line is given:

```
GET / HTTP/1.1
```

GET signifies the HTTP GET command. The / signifies the file on the server (in this case the root file) — for example it could be /index.html, which would correspond to the URL http://www.cnn.com/index.html. The HTTP/1.1 signifies which version of HTTP is being used by this request — this request is using the 1.1 version of the protocol. HTTP/1.0 is the other valid entry in this field.

After the HTTP command line, HTTP headers follow. An HTTP header follows this format:

```
Key: Value
```

Headers are optional in HTTP 1.0, but in 1.1 certain headers are defined to be required, though most HTTP servers are lenient and do not enforce these requirements. Many of the optional features of HTTP are built on top of headers. Features such as compressing responses or setting cookies are all based on HTTP headers. This part of the book will not delve further into the meaning of individual HTTP headers because this simple implementation of HTTP GET will not make use of them. At the end of the headers, the request is ended by two line-feeds, or new line characters. This notifies the server that no more HTTP headers will be sent, and the server can begin sending the response.

An HTTP response is similar in structure to an HTTP request. The first line of a response contains the HTTP response status code. Headers follow, and then the content of the file requested (in the case of a successful HTTP GET). The response you receive from your request in the previous example looks like this:

```
HTTP/1.1 200 OK
Date: Sun, 06 Aug 2006 03:40:21 GMT
Server: Apache
Vary: Host
Content-Type: text/html; charset=ISO-8859-1
X-Cache: MISS from www.java.net
Connection: close

<!DOCTYPE HTML PUBLIC "-//W3C//DTD HTML 4.01 Transitional//EN"><html lang="en">
... (more html follows)
```

The first line of the response contains the HTTP protocol version, the status code of the response, and a brief textual message indicating the nature of the response code. Following are headers, and then the actual content of the page requested. An implementation of HTTP GET must be able to read the status code to determine and report back to the user the success or failure to retrieve a page.

HttpGetter: The Implementation

Your implementation of HTTP GET will be a simple command-line Java application. It will save a remote HTML file specified by the user to a local file. Your application will do four main tasks in a simple sequential order:

1. Parse URL and file location to save the remote file from the command-line parameters.

2. Set up the Socket and InetSocketAddress corresponding to the URL parsed from the command line, and connect to the remote host.

3. Write the HTTP GET request to the Socket's OutputStream.

4. Read the HTTP GET response from the server from the Socket's InputStream, and write the remote file to disk in the file location specified in the command line.

To parse the URL from the command line, you will use the `java.net.URL` class. This class breaks up a URL into its components, such as host, port, and file. The code to parse the URL and local filename to save the URL to disk from the command-line parameters is straightforward:

```
    URL url = new URL(args[0]);
  File outFile = new File(args[1]);
```

Persons experienced with the URL class will note that it already has HTTP protocol capabilities — you will not be using them, because the exercise is to show the HTTP protocol via sockets.

Now that the URL has been successfully parsed, the connection to the remote server can be set up. Using socket programming techniques learned from the previous section, the connection is set up as follows:

```
Socket socket = new Socket();

  int port = url.getPort();
  if (port == -1)
    port = url.getDefaultPort();

  InetSocketAddress remoteAddress = new InetSocketAddress(url.getHost(), port);
  socket.connect(remoteAddress);
```

One of the idiosyncrasies of the URL class is that if no port is explicitly set in the URL (like `http://www.example.com:1234`), `getPort()` returns `-1`, meaning you have to check for it. Once you have the port, you can create the `InetSocketAddress`, representing the endpoint on the remote server to connect, and then connect to it.

Now connected to the remote server, you simply write the request to the socket's output stream, and then read the HTTP server's response from the input stream. Because HTTP is a text-based protocol, `PrintWriter` is the perfect class to wrap your `Socket`'s `OutputStream` and use to send character data over the socket. Notice in the following code how the two HTTP headers, User-Agent and Host, are sent. User-Agent tells the HTTP server what client software is making the request. Because your client software is called `HttpGetter`, that is the value put in the header. This header is mainly a courtesy to the server, because many web servers return different content based on the value of User-Agent (that is, Netscape compatible pages or Internet Explorer compatible pages). The Host value is simply the hostname of the remote server to which you are connecting:

```
PrintWriter out = new PrintWriter(socket.getOutputStream());

// write our client's request
out.println("GET " + url.getFile() + " HTTP/1.0");
out.println("User-Agent: HttpGetter");
out.println("Host: " + url.getHost());
out.println();
out.flush();
```

After you send the request, you must now read the response. The first line of any HTTP response contains the status code for the request. That is the first thing you must check — if the response code is anything other than 200 (OK), you do not want to save the contents of the input to a file, because the only content that could be sent back would be some sort of error message. In the first line of the response, the status code is the second of the three groups of information:

```
HTTP/1.1 200 OK
```

You want to parse out the 200 in this case, because the 200 is HTTP OK, meaning your request was successfully processed and the content of the page you request will follow. In the following code, first use a `BufferedReader` to begin reading character data from the remote server. To parse the status code out of the first line, use a `StringTokenizer` to separate the three groups of values and then choose the second one to convert to an integer:

Because you are using a `BufferedReader`, you can only read character data from the remote server. This means that your implementation will not be able to request any file in your HTTP GET command that contains binary data (such as an image file, a zip file, and so on).

```
InputStream in = socket.getInputStream();
boolean responseOK = true;

BufferedReader br = new BufferedReader(new InputStreamReader(in));
String currLine = null;


// get http response code from first line of result
currLine = br.readLine();
if (currLine != null) {
  System.out.println(currLine);
  StringTokenizer st = new StringTokenizer(currLine, " \t");
  st.nextToken();
  String responseCode = st.nextToken();

  int httpResponseCode = Integer.parseInt(responseCode.trim());

  if (httpResponseCode != 200) {
    // response not OK
    responseOK = false;
  }
} else {
  System.err.println("Server returned no response!");
  System.exit(1);
}
```

The last step is to print out the headers, and then save the content of the request to the file specified at the command line by the user. The headers follow the status-code line of the response until a blank line is encountered. In the first loop in the following code, simply print the headers out on the standard output stream for the user to see until you encounter a blank line when you break out of your loop, knowing the content will immediately follow. If the status code previously parsed was 200, save the remaining content found in the `Socket`'s `InputStream` (which is wrapped in a `BufferedReader`) to the file specified by the user:

```
// read headers
  while ((currLine = br.readLine()) != null) {
    System.out.println(currLine);

    // done reading headers, so break out of loop
    if (currLine.trim().equals(""))
      break;
  }

  if (responseOK) {
```

```
      FileOutputStream fout = new FileOutputStream(outFile);

      int currByte;
      while ((currByte = br.read()) != -1)
        fout.write(currByte);

      fout.close();
      System.out.println("** Wrote result to " + args[1]);
    } else {
      System.out.println("HTTP response code not OK -- file not written");
    }
```

The following is the full listing for the code for `HttpGetter`:

```
package book;

import java.io.BufferedReader;
import java.io.File;
import java.io.FileOutputStream;
import java.io.IOException;
import java.io.InputStream;
import java.io.InputStreamReader;
import java.io.PrintWriter;
import java.net.InetSocketAddress;
import java.net.MalformedURLException;
import java.net.Socket;
import java.net.URL;
import java.util.StringTokenizer;

public class HttpGetter {
  public static void main(String[] args) {
    try {
      if (args.length < 2) {
        System.out.println("Usage");
        System.out.println("\tHttpGetter <Http URL> <file to save>");
        System.out.println
                    ("\tExample: HttpGetter http://www.google.com/ google.html");

        System.exit(1);
      }

      URL url = new URL(args[0]);
      File outFile = new File(args[1]);

      Socket socket = new Socket();

      int port = url.getPort();
      if (port == -1)
        port = url.getDefaultPort();

      InetSocketAddress remoteAddress = new
                              InetSocketAddress(url.getHost(), port);
      socket.connect(remoteAddress);
      PrintWriter out = new PrintWriter(socket.getOutputStream());

      // write our client's request
```

```java
out.println("GET " + url.getFile() + " HTTP/1.0");
out.println("User-Agent: HttpGetter");
out.println("Host: " + url.getHost());
out.println();
out.flush();

// read remote server's response
InputStream in = socket.getInputStream();
boolean responseOK = true;

BufferedReader br = new BufferedReader(new
                          InputStreamReader(in));
String currLine = null;


// get http response code from first line of result
currLine = br.readLine();
if (currLine != null) {
  System.out.println(currLine);
  StringTokenizer st = new StringTokenizer(currLine, " \t");
  st.nextToken();
  String responseCode = st.nextToken();

  int httpResponseCode =
                 Integer.parseInt(responseCode.trim());

  if (httpResponseCode != 200) {
    // response not OK
    responseOK = false;
  }
} else {
  System.err.println("Server returned no response!");
  System.exit(1);
}

// read headers
while ((currLine = br.readLine()) != null) {
  System.out.println(currLine);

  // done reading headers, so break out of loop
  if (currLine.trim().equals(""))
    break;
}

if (responseOK) {
  FileOutputStream fout = new FileOutputStream(outFile);

  int currByte;
  while ((currByte = br.read()) != -1)
    fout.write(currByte);

  fout.close();
  System.out.println("** Wrote result to " + args[1]);
} else {
  System.out.println("HTTP response code not OK -- file not written");
```

```
        }

        socket.close();
    } catch (MalformedURLException me) {
        me.printStackTrace();
    } catch (IOException ioe) {
        ioe.printStackTrace();
    }
  }
}
```

Congratulations — you have implemented part of a real protocol. There a couple of things to note about this simple implementation. First, as noted before, your implementation can only read text, not binary, which makes it not too robust, because images and other binary files are frequently served from HTTP servers. Secondly, it does not handle errors gracefully, and in reality would require more of a full-fledged parser than your handyman `java.io` usage. This implementation is a minimal amount of code and logic to implement HTTP GET.

The command-line screenshot in Figure 11-4 shows a user downloading the root web page of `http://java.net/` to `java.net.html`.

Figure 11-4

TCP Monitoring: Testing with Apache TCPMon

Testing and debugging protocol implementations is far more difficult and tedious than testing and debugging a standalone application. To make sure the protocol implementation you are developing is correct, it is extremely helpful to see what is being sent and received over the wire with the remote server. Utilities are available to do just that — view what is being sent and received over a TCP/IP socket connection. For `HttpGetter`, I used the Apache utility, TCPMon, to monitor my TCP/IP connection with remote web servers. Being able to read my request from the utility let me know that my request was following the HTTP specification. If there was any trouble parsing the response, I could look at exactly what was sent back from the server using the monitoring utility. Parsing the input from a socket is very similar to parsing a file — the data is in a certain format, and the code must read in that format. With sockets though, there is no file to view and test against. If there is a bug, it is difficult to see what problem in the transmission could be causing it. This is why the TCPMon utility is invaluable; it lets the developer look at the server's response as if it were a file on the local machine. It is useful for the implementation of any protocol based on TCP/IP, or during development with Web Services. This chapter also discusses using TCPMon in the "Web Services" section.

Getting and Running TCPMon

TCPMon originally was written as part of Apache AXIS, but now stands alone as a separate project. Originally written for debugging Web Service requests and responses, TCPMon can also be useful for socket development as well, especially when implementing a protocol. TCPMon can be downloaded from the following URL:

```
http://ws.apache.org/commons/tcpmon/
```

Simply run TCPMon by running the `tcpmon.bat` file found in the `build` directory of the distribution.

Using TCPMon

To have TCPMon be able to print out your requests and the server's responses, it must be set up as a middleman between your local machine and the remote server. To test your program, it will have to connect to TCPMon, which in turn connects it to the remote server. TCPMon relays whatever is sent to it to the remote server, and whatever the remote server sends it, it relays back to your application. To configure TCPMon in this manner, it must be set up as a `Listener`, and given a port number on the local machine. The screen in Figure 11-5 is the first screen and main configuration screen of TCPMon. The figure shows the configuration necessary for TCPMon to act as a `Listener` on port 8079. TCPMon will relay any connection made to port 8079 on the local machine to www.google.com, port 80 (the default HTTP port). Once the Add button is clicked, TCPMon will set up the relay.

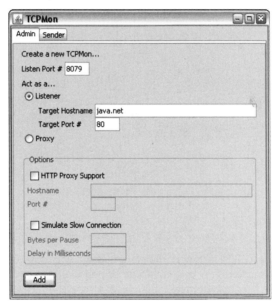

Figure 11-5

Now that the relay is running, `HttpGetter` can be tested by running this:

```
java book.HttpGetter http://localhost:8079/ tester.html
```

`HttpGetter` connects to TCPMon, which in turn, connects it to `java.net`. Going to the "Port 8079" tab on TCPMon yields a list of all connection attempts made to `java.net` in this session. Figure 11-6 shows each request and response in detail.

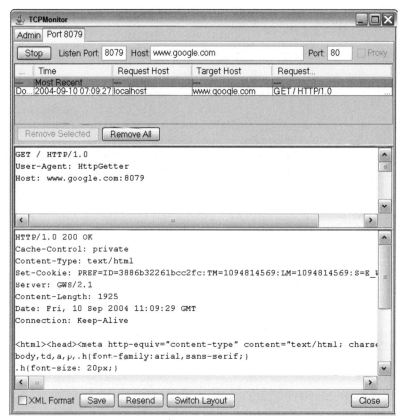

Figure 11-6

Debugging a protocol implementation is far easier with a utility such as Apache TCPMon, which allows the developer to view the data sent and received over a TCP/IP connection.

Proprietary Protocols and Reverse Engineering

Some protocols are not open. The internals of instant messaging protocols for AOL's Instant Messenger and Microsoft's Messenger clients are proprietary information that currently is not shared (although the FCC is trying to force an open instant messaging standard to allow various clients to interoperate). If your software must communicate with servers such as these, whose protocol is either unknown or proprietary, there are not a whole lot of options. One option is to attempt to reverse-engineer the protocol. In the case of AOL's Instant Messenger, there are now many instant messaging clients besides AOL's own that implement most of its proprietary protocol, OSCAR. Reverse engineering is normally done by monitoring the TCP connections and data sent between proprietary clients and servers. Sometimes portions of a protocol can be identified. When designing a proprietary protocol, taking into account how easy it would be to reverse-engineer is important (especially if security is a high priority). For extra security, some sort of encryption may be necessary for the protocol to avoid being reverse-engineered. Most of the time, protocols should be open. The specifications are generally easier for everyone to implement, because they have the advantage of being reviewed by many different sets of eyes. HTTP, for example, has undergone a number of performance-improving amendments from version 1.0 to 1.1. The most robust and stable implementations of protocols generally result from free and open protocols that have been in use for a while. High-quality reference implementations have been developed for protocols such as HTTP, TCP/IP, and X-Windows precisely because those protocols are open.

Utilizing Existing Protocols and Implementations

Developers will want to avoid designing and writing their own protocol if at all possible. Some existing protocol somewhere usually will fulfill the requirements of almost any application. There is no point in reinventing the wheel, and oftentimes using open protocols is a good avenue to ease the difficultly of interoperating with the outside world. If your app needs to interface to other applications, writing and designing a custom protocol has even more costs. Any other application that wishes to interface with your application must now implement a custom protocol. Getting two disparate implementations of a protocol to work robustly together is no easy task in itself, let alone in addition to normal application development. Many protocols out there already have high-quality implementations freely available to Java developers. The Jakarta Project from Apache hosts many open source projects. The Jakarta Commons Net package, for example, provides an API that implements FTP, NNTP, SMTP, POP3, Telnet, TFTP, and more. You can find more information about it at the following URL:

```
http://jakarta.apache.org/commons/net/
```

Even though in the `HttpGetter` example, you found that implementing one small section of HTTP was fairly simple, implementing the entire protocol with all of its optional components would be far more difficult. There are already optimized implementations of HTTP out there, and using one would be a far better design choice in *any application* that requires HTTP client support. The JDK provides limited support for HTTP via the `java.net.URL` class. It is good for simple HTTP operations, but sometimes more control over *how* HTTP is used is necessary. For example, to view and set HTTP headers, an HTTP client library that exposes more HTTP details than the `java.net.URL` class found in the JDK would be required. The HTTP Client project in the Jakarta Project provides a high-quality HTTP implementation. You can find more information on HTTP Client here:

```
http://jakarta.apache.org/commons/httpclient/
```

You have just looked at some freely available client libraries. There are also freely available libraries for servers. The Jakarta Project provides an HTTP server implementation with its servlet container, Tomcat. Implementations of POP3 mail servers are available. It should, almost 100 percent of the time, make sense to use an existing protocol in your application for communicating between your Java components and components on other platforms. You also should not have to implement the protocol yourself, because there are high-quality robust open source implementations available for almost all of the major open protocols in use today.

Some great resources for finding and aggregating open source Java projects into your application are listed in the following table.

Resource	URL
The Jakarta Project	`http://jakarta.apache.org`
OpenSymphony Quality Components	`www.opensymphony.com`
JBoss: Professional Open Source	`www.jboss.org`
The Apache XML Project	`http://xml.apache.org`
The Eclipse Project	`www.eclipse.org`

Remote Method Invocation

Remote Method Invocation (RMI) is the Java platform's standard for remote procedure calls (RPC). Remote procedure calls are abstractly the same concept as a normal procedure call within a program, except that the calls can happen over a network, and are between two separate processes. Different forms of RPC have been around for a while, but the concepts are similar. There is a client program and a server program, each running on separate machines (or at the very least, on two separate processes on the same machine). The client program calls a procedure (or in Java terminology, a method) on the server, and waits till the server returns the method result before continuing its normal execution (just like a normal local method call). Figure 11-7 illustrates a high-level view of object-to-object communication over a network in different JVMs. This chapter takes an abstract view of RMI and sees how it fits as a technology into distributed systems, and how it interacts with CORBA.

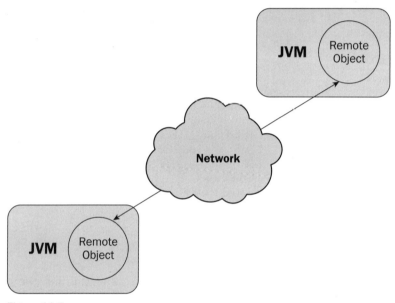

Figure 11-7

Core RPC/RMI Principles

The Java platform makes writing client/server programs fairly simple. In Java, you can call methods on an object, and not even necessarily *know* that the object resides on a remote machine. The code for the method call is no different than a normal local method call. In Java EE, you generally have to look up object instances from a naming service before using them. When you look up the object and receive a reference to it, it may be a local reference *or a remote reference*. The code does not change though, and it is one of the reasons Java is such a powerful server language — a lot of the complex details of technologies such as RMI have been abstracted away. Now, this does not mean developers can be completely oblivious to whether an object instance is remote or local. Remote objects have certain design trade-offs that must be taken into account. Method calls happen across a network, and thus are limited to the reliability and speed of the network. RMI is a powerful mechanism for writing distributed systems. The following sections look into the basic core principles common to almost all RPC mechanisms, and show how they relate to RMI.

In RPC, all method calls must be transformed into a format that can be sent over the network and understood by a remote process. In order to call methods on a remote object, three main steps occur:

1. **A *reference* to the remote object must be obtained.** The remote object must be looked up on the remote server.

2. **Marshalling and unmarshalling of parameters.** When a method is invoked on the remote reference, the parameters must be *marshaled* into a byte stream that can be sent over the network. On the server side, these parameters must be *unmarshaled* from the byte stream into their original values and then passed to the appropriate method.

3. **Transmission of data through a common protocol.** There must be a protocol defined for the transport and delivery of these method calls and returns. A standard format for parameters is necessary, along with standards to tell the server which method on which object is to be invoked.

To make the remote call appear like a local call, a local implementation exists with the same interface (*all RMI objects must be defined as Java interfaces*). This local implementation is called a *stub* and is essentially a proxy to the real implementation. Whenever a method is called on this local implementation or stub, the local implementation performs the operations necessary to send the method call to a remote implementation of the same interface on another server. The stub marshals the parameters and sends them over the network using a common RMI protocol. In turn, a stub on the server side implementing the same interface unmarshals the parameters and then passes them on to the actual remote object in a normal method call. This process is reversed for the return value; the stub on the server side marshals and sends it, and the stub on the client unmarshals and returns it to the original caller. Figure 11-8 displays this entire process graphically.

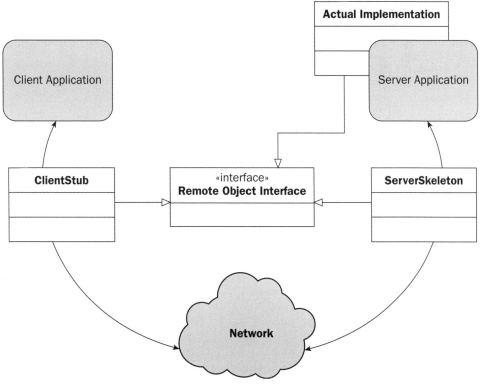

Figure 11-8

Marshalling and Unmarshalling

The parameters and method call must be flattened into a byte stream before they can be sent over the network. This process is called marshalling. The reverse is called unmarshalling, when the byte stream is decoded into the original parameters and method call information. After unmarshalling the parameters and method call, the server dispatches the method call to the appropriate object that actually implements the remote method and then marshals the return value back to the client. By serializing the parameters and method into a byte stream, RMI protocols can work on top of network protocols that provide a reliable byte stream, such as TCP/IP.

In RMI, two types of objects besides primitives can be passed as parameters: objects that implement the `java.rmi.Remote` interface or objects that implement the `java.io.Serializable` interface. These two interfaces do not contain any methods, instead they mark objects with a particular property. Java's RMI mechanism knows that `Remote` objects could be on another virtual machine, and will have stubs. Objects that implement `Serializable`, on the other hand, can be transformed into a byte stream (to save to disk, or in RMI's case, to send over a network). In RMI, objects that implement `Remote` are passed by reference, whereas objects that implement `Serializable` (and not `Remote`) are passed by value. When parameters are marshaled over the network and transformed into a byte stream, any object that must be passed via an RMI call must be `Serializable`. So now for the first time, objects in Java can be passed by value. This is not as confusing as it sounds—`Remote` objects are passed by reference and `Serializable` objects are passed by value. This helps reduce the number of network calls that must occur. If an object being passed contains a large number of properties that must be accessed through `getXXX` methods, there would be a large number of network calls taking place. By serializing the object, all these calls become local calls on the remote server and use up far less network bandwidth. Method calls on `Remote` objects passed in, on the other hand, will go over the network and must be taken into consideration.

Suppose this is an implementation of a method on a server that is being invoked remotely by a client:

```
public void myTestMethod(A a, B b) {
    a.remoteMethod();
    Data d = b.getData();
    ...
}
```

In this example, `A` implements `java.rmi.Remote`, and thus a call to `remoteMethod()` is a remote callback to your client. `B` implements `Serializable` and hence `getData()` is a local call to `b`, which was unmarshaled from its serialized state back into an object now running on the server.

> *Important:* **Any objects passed by value in RMI must be in the classpath of the JVM running on the remote server.**

See Chapter 5 for more information on `java.io.Serializable` *and serializing objects to disk.*

Protocols

In RPC, all method calls must be transformed into a standard format that can be sent over a network. In other words, two programs running on two separate processes must be able to read and write this same format. RPC mechanisms have their own protocols. Sometimes these protocols are built on top of

TCP/IP, or at other times they define their own transport protocol in addition to the RPC protocol, combining the transport layer and the application layer protocols for optimal performance. Operating systems sometimes provide system-level services in this manner.

RMI is implemented such that it can support more than one underlying transport protocol (though obviously only one protocol can be used between any two objects). There are two main choices as the transport protocol for RMI:

- ❑   Java Remote Method Protocol (JRMP)
- ❑   Internet InterORB Protocol (IIOP)

Either of these protocols could be used in a given system, and both have their trade-offs. IIOP offers compatibility with CORBA, which is discussed later in this chapter. IIOP, because it was not designed specifically for Java remote procedure calls, does not support some of the features JRMP supports, such as security and distributed garbage collection. Using IIOP as the underlying protocol for RMI makes it easy to integrate legacy objects written in other languages, however (discussed more in the "Common Object Request Broker Architecture" section of this chapter). JRMP is the default protocol for RMI. IIOP stubs differ from JRMP stubs and must be generated separately. See `rmic` tool documentation for more details.

RMI Registry

Object instances must be made available in a registry on the server before they can be used by remote clients. Clients obtain an instance by looking up a particular name—for example, the string "EmployeeData" might refer to a class containing the data for the employees of a particular company. When a server is starting up, it creates instances of the objects it wishes to be available, and registers them in a registry. Because these objects are globally available, they must be thread-safe (because their methods can be called at the same time by different threads). The code to look up a particular instance of a class is not very difficult, and uses the Java Naming and Directory Interface (JNDI) API (found in `javax.naming`). A small snippet of code to look up an object on a remote server follows:

```
import javax.naming.InitialContext;
...

InitialContext ctx = new InitialContext();

EmployeeData data = (EmployeeData) ctx.lookup("CompanyX\\MyEmployeeDataInstance");
...
```

JNDI is configured by setting certain Java system properties to tell it the location and protocol of the registry. This is how objects can be transparently remote or local. If the registry is configured locally, in the same JVM, then all calls to `data` will be local. If `data` is an instance on a remote server, all calls will go through RMI, using whatever protocol was specified.

See Chapter 10 for more detailed information on the mechanics and details of RMI.

Distributed Objects

RMI allows a developer to abstract away where objects physically reside from his application. Object-oriented applications can be transparently spread across multiple machines. Objects that do heavy processing or provide server-side functionality, such as mail services, transactional database services, or file

545

serving services, can be located on server-class machines. Typical desktop client applications can then access these objects as if they were local and part of the same object-oriented application. Location-independent objects are powerful because they can be dynamically moved around from machine to machine. If mail services' objects on a server become too bogged down, they can be spread across multiple machines, all transparently to the client applications using them. Java's platform independence adds even more value to its location-independent objects. Server objects could reside on a Unix-based operating system for example, and client objects on a Microsoft Windows platform. Figure 11-9 shows many objects communicating from different JVMs on different machines.

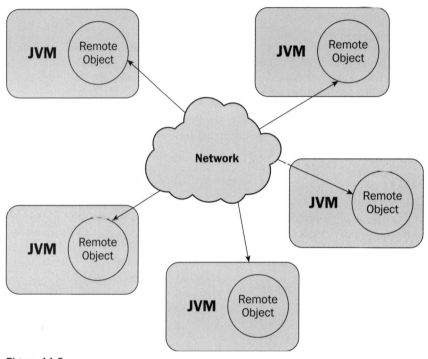

Figure 11-9

Middleware and Java EE

Most of time, the main reasons for distributing objects onto various machines is to give access to various services provided by these machines. Mail services, transactional-database services, and file-server services all can be encapsulated by various software components, or in this case, Java objects. By allowing all these objects to communicate in a standard, distributed way, server-side applications can be developed with ease. Location-independent objects allow for server applications to scale, because when one server no longer provides enough horsepower for a server application, you just add a couple more machines and spread the objects around.

Middleware is a software layer between various data sources and their client applications. RMI distributed objects is one way to implement middleware for different applications. Middleware abstracts away the details of the one-or-many data sources. RMI is the perfect building block for middleware because of its location and platform independence. Java is most prevalent in server-side applications and middleware because of the foundation it provides for building stable and reliable software systems.

The Java Enterprise Edition (Java EE) platform uses RMI as one of its core technologies. Java EE provides reliable messaging, rock-solid transactional storage capabilities, remote management and deployment, and frameworks for producing web-enabled server-side applications. Java EE is a standard platform for developing middleware and other server-side services. RMI enables Java EE to be location-independent and distributed. Rather than developing one's own middleware solely with RMI, it is far better to build on the Java EE standard for writing server-side applications.

Common Object Request Broker Architecture

The Common Object Request Broker Architecture, or CORBA for short, is a set of specifications by the Object Management Group (OMG) for language-independent distributed objects. It allows for objects written in a number of different programming languages to interoperate and communicate with one another. C++ classes can talk to Java classes. C# can talk to C++ or Java. Programs written in C are supported by some CORBA implementations, as well as even scripting languages such as Python. CORBA is similar to RMI conceptually, but supports more languages than simply Java. CORBA itself is a set of specifications, not an actual implementation. For it to be possible for a language to support CORBA and other CORBA objects, it must have an implementation in its native language (or somehow be bound to an implementation). For instance, the Java Development Kit (JDK) includes an implementation of the CORBA 2.3.1 specification. That means that, out of the box, Java supports CORBA implementations up to and including the 2.3.1 specification (the latest CORBA specification at the time of this writing is 3.02). Though there has been industry criticism for the age of the JDK's support for CORBA, 2.3.1 includes many of CORBA's modern features, and is certainly enough to implement and use most CORBA distributed objects. There are many implementations of CORBA that can be used with Java besides the implementation that comes with the JDK. You can find a list of free CORBA downloads (either trials of commercial implementations or free open-source implementations) on OMG's web site at `www.omg.org/technology/corba/corbadownloads.htm`.

CORBA is a massive set of specifications and has been an immense undertaking. CORBA has a history of having slow, bloated, and buggy implementations — on top of being extremely complex and difficult to develop with. Today though, because CORBA is a stable and mature technology, its implementations are much faster and reliable, and it is used in many mission-critical environments. CORBA is still complex and not as developer friendly as technologies such as RMI though, and usually for newer systems, Java EE-based servers are the best design choice if the Java platform is the primary development environment. This chapter briefly examines CORBA, though not in any depth worthy of its complexity.

CORBA Basics

There are four main concepts of the CORBA specification that define how distributed objects written in different languages communicate with one another. Like RMI, there is a naming service, where remote object references can be registered, to be retrieved at some point in time by one or more clients. The Internet InterORB Protocol (IIOP) is used for the communication between clients and servers. This is the protocol that is responsible for defining the format of the marshalling and unmarshalling of remote method invocations and parameter passing. Object Request Brokers (ORBs) are responsible for processing all remote method calls and dispatching them to the appropriate object, both on the client and server. Figure 11-10 demonstrates these CORBA concepts.

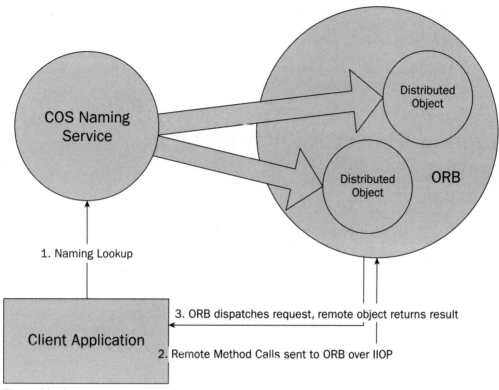

Figure 11-10

The paradigm for object-to-object communication is similar to RMI:

1. Remote object references are obtained using the COS Naming Service.

2. Method call information and parameters are marshaled into a byte stream to send over the network via the Internet InterORB Protocol (IIOP).

3. An Object Request Broker (ORB) receives incoming requests on the remote server, and dispatches them to the object implementing the CORBA interface called.

IDL: Interface Definition Language

The Interface Definition Language (IDL) is a CORBA specification for writing an interface. In CORBA, all distributed objects must implement a CORBA interface. These interfaces are similar to Java's concept of an interface — an interface allows for multiple implementations. CORBA interfaces though, can be implemented by any language that supports CORBA. Figure 11-11 shows a class diagram of a CORBA being implemented both in Java and C#.

Three things can be declared in CORBA interfaces:

❑ Operations (like Java methods)

❑ Attributes (like JavaBean properties, implemented by getXXX and setXXX methods)

❑ Exceptions

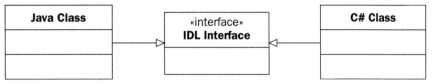

Figure 11-11

A CORBA interface for each distributed object allows IDL compilers to compile IDL to stub classes in an existing language. For instance, the JDK provides tools that map CORBA IDL types to Java types, and generate stub classes for any given IDL file. These stub classes allow Java programmers to see the CORBA object as a Java class, and call its methods with Java syntax just like any other Java class. IDL is the link between different languages — it provides the description of an interface that can be transformed into the corresponding class in a concrete programming language.

When using remote CORBA objects, the client programmer is using the *interface*, not the specific object implementing it. The ORB running on the remote machine resolves the request, and dispatches it to the correct implementation. The client never knows which language the remote object was written in; it is all transparent.

In the "Distributed File System Notifications: An Example CORBA System" section that follows at the end of this CORBA section, a CORBA interface called `FileNotification` is defined. Seeing the Java representation will help you understand the CORBA representation. Here is the Java representation of that interface:

```
package book;

public interface FileNotification
{
  public void fileModified (String fileName);
  public void fileDeleted (String fileName);
  public void fileCreated (String fileName);
}
```

The equivalent definition of this Java interface in IDL looks like this:

```
#include "orb.idl"

#ifndef __book_FileNotification__
#define __book_FileNotification__


module book {
    interface FileNotification {

        void fileModified(
            in ::CORBA::WStringValue fileName );
        void fileDeleted(
            in ::CORBA::WStringValue fileName );
        void fileCreated(
```

```
              in ::CORBA::WStringValue fileName );

    };

    #pragma ID FileNotification "RMI:book.FileNotification:0000000000000000"

    };

    #endif
```

If you have developed with C++ before, you will notice that the IDL syntax is similar to the C++ syntax, because C++ was the dominant language at the time of CORBA's inception. This chapter does not go heavily into the IDL syntax, because that is better left to books dedicated solely to CORBA. The main concept of IDL is simple: Separate the interface from the implementation. This principle applies to good software design in general, but is absolutely essential when an implementation could be written in more than one language. There would be no other way to have two disparate languages communicate with one another if not for a common interface.

ORB: Object Request Broker

The Object Request Broker is responsible for mediating incoming CORBA method invocations. ORBs are the core infrastructure of any CORBA implementation. They provide a common entry point for all CORBA requests to any given server. Many different method invocations on a number of CORBA objects go through the same entry point, the ORB. The ORB then dispatches the request to the correct CORBA object instance corresponding to the client's reference.

Common Object Service (COS) Naming

The Common Object Service (COS) Naming provides a registry to hold references to CORBA objects. It is similar in concept to the RMI registry. When a server wants to expose CORBA object instances to remote clients, it registers each instance with the naming service. Each instance gets a unique name on the server. Clients use the name to retrieve the reference and call its methods.

JNDI provides an InitialContext that can interact with COS Naming and look up various CORBA objects in the same fashion as one would look up an RMI object. As long as the correct stubs for IIOP are in place, setting the following system properties (which is the URI, containing the correct hostname and port for the remote COS Naming service), client Java programs can access CORBA objects transparently:

```
java.naming.factory.initial=com.sun.jndi.cosnaming.CNCtxFactory
java.naming.provider.url=iiop://hostname:1049
```

Once these properties are set (using the -D option at the command line is one way to set them), the JNDI lookup occurs normally.

> *Client programs can also use the* org.omg.CORBA *package to manually access CORBA references, and have all of the many intricacies of CORBA at their disposal.*

IIOP: Internet InterORB Protocol

The Internet InterORB Protocol is the protocol that CORBA ORBs use to communicate with one another over a network. All method calls and parameters are marshaled and unmarshaled over this protocol. It is an efficient binary protocol. JDK 1.5 supports version 2.3.1 of the IIOP specification.

RMI-IIOP: Making RMI Compatible with CORBA

RMI-IIOP combines some of the best aspects of RMI with the language independence of CORBA. RMI is far simpler for developers to use than CORBA. The main limitation of RMI is that it only supports the Java language. Though Java is platform independent, sometimes there are legacy components or systems written in other languages that must be interacted with. CORBA provides that channel of communication but can be a painful experience for developers. RMI-IIOP is Java RMI, but uses the IIOP protocol for communication, meaning normal RMI objects can be exposed as CORBA objects to external systems. By the same token, external CORBA objects can be accessed through the RMI APIs, again because of the use of IIOP as the underlying communication protocol.

It would be a perfect world if RMI-IIOP had exactly the same feature set as RMI over JRMP. IIOP was not designed for Java though. Objects passed by value over IIOP (ones that implement `java.io.Serializable` instead of `java.rmi.Remote` — see "Marshalling and Unmarshalling" in the RMI section of this chapter) get passed in the byte stream as Java objects. *This means that any parameters passed by value over RMI-IIOP can only be read by Java clients!* Fortunately, CORBA has a mechanism to deal with value types. It does, however, mean that the same interface of the value type must be implemented by the client. For example, suppose a Java RMI object returns a value type of `java.util.ArrayList`. A CORBA client cannot read this value type. The CORBA client application then must implement the interface for `ArrayList` (and make it compatible with the binary representation passed in!). Because of this large extra burden placed by objects passed by value on CORBA systems being communicated with using RMI-IIOP, it generally makes sense to try to make the interfaces pass only primitive types or objects by reference.

CORBA IDL unfortunately does not support method overloading. This, combined with the non-use of value types in passing parameters, can be a burden to designing a distributed system using RMI-IIOP. One design approach is to start thinking from the limiting IDL perspective when you are creating your Java interface for your remote object (if the system must communicate with CORBA clients). Your code may not be as clean using only primitive types, but the ease of interoperability makes it by far worth the price. The client-side development is tremendously simplified when value types do not have to be implemented also. Doing so is essentially implementing an object twice, once in Java and once in the CORBA client's language, and is asking for buggy and incompatible implementations, not to mention the synchronization nightmare of keeping their functionality and IDL up to date.

In most situations, though, RMI-IIOP makes CORBA programming far simpler, and is the preferred method of integrating with CORBA in Java if the advanced features of CORBA are not necessary. The programming model is the same as RMI, and allows the Java developer to easily integrate with other platforms.

How to Turn an RMI Object into an RMI-IIOP Object

To take an existing RMI object and expose it via RMI-IIOP requires a minimal amount of work. Suppose you have a simple RMI HelloWorld interface:

```
package simple.rmi;

import java.rmi.Remote;
import java.rmi.RemoteException;

public interface HelloWorld extends Remote {
    public void hello() throws RemoteException;
}
```

Normal RMI object implementations extend `java.rmi.UnicastRemoteObject`. Your simple `HelloWorldImpl` as a normal RMI object looks like this:

```
package simple.rmi;

import java.rmi.RemoteException;
import java.rmi.server.UnicastRemoteObject;

public class HelloWorldImpl extends UnicastRemoteObject implements HelloWorld {

  public HelloWorldImpl() throws RemoteException {
    super();
  }

  public void hello() throws RemoteException {
    System.out.println("Hello");
  }
}
```

Note that `UnicastRemoteObject` **is in context.**

To allow this object to be used over RMI-IIOP, the first step is to make the class extend `javax.rmi.PortableRemoteObject` instead of `java.rmi.UnicastRemoteObject`:

```
package simple.rmi;

import java.rmi.RemoteException;

import javax.rmi.PortableRemoteObject;

public class HelloWorldImpl extends PortableRemoteObject implements HelloWorld {

  public HelloWorldImpl() throws RemoteException {
    super();
  }

  public void hello() throws RemoteException {
    System.out.println("Hello");
  }
}
```

Now `HelloWorldImpl` is ready to be used over RMI-IIOP. The last step is to generate the IDL and IIOP stubs from your class. The IIOP stubs allow the object to be sent over the wire using IIOP. The IDL allows CORBA clients to generate the stubs necessary to use the class. To generate both the stubs and the IDL, use the `rmic` tool from the JDK (in the `bin` directory under the JDK home). Running `rmic` from the command line, make sure that `simple.rmi.HelloWorldImpl` is on the classpath:

```
rmic -iiop -idl simple.rmi.HelloWorldImpl
```

The last step is to write the main program that actually starts up the RMI-IIOP server. This book talks more about communicating with the Java ORB daemon included with the JDK, orbd, in the "Distributed File System Notifications: An Example CORBA System" section, including registering objects and communicating with remote CORBA ORBs.

When to Use CORBA

CORBA is a difficult platform on which to develop software. It is robust and successful in mission-critical software systems, but the learning curve is high and development costs can rise. CORBA is best used in distributed systems that must have components written in more than one language, or have the potential to be written in more than one language. Java EE is a more ubiquitous standard for server-side applications today. It also provides CORBA support for some of its components. If you are creating a new server-side application in Java, sticking with Java EE is most certainly your best choice. CORBA support can always be added on later should you need to support clients written in other languages. Here are a couple of good instances of where to add CORBA to your distributed system:

❑   When you have to integrate with legacy systems that support CORBA in your middleware

❑   When there are components written in other languages just not available in Java that are essential to your server-side application (and would require less effort to build a CORBA link than to rewrite the component in Java)

CORBA as a distributed technology is simply not used as much in industry practice as Java EE-based component technologies (or COM/COM+/DCOM). It is a solid platform because it has been around for about ten years. Most of the complaints CORBA developers had originally have been rectified. CORBA implementations are fast and efficient now, and more than robust enough to use in mission-critical applications. CORBA has a steep learning curve, and the only value it adds over Java EE component technology is the ability to write components in different languages than Java. If your system is all Java, it just does not make sense to use CORBA — especially because Java EE can expose Java components to CORBA systems already through RMI-IIOP. It is best to use CORBA when you must integrate with a system that supports it.

CORBA may be a good technology to use when integrating with the Microsoft .NET platform. There has recently been an open source project, IIOP.NET, which integrates .NET Remoting (.NET's equivalent to RMI) with IIOP. This product is becoming mature, and allows for easy integration between RMI-IIOP and .NET Remoting. This is a big step toward an easier integration between .NET and Java components. You can find the IIOP.NET project at the following URL:

```
http://iiop-net.sourceforge.net/
```

IIOP.NET provides an exciting new way to use CORBA. By integrating with .NET Remoting, it allows programmers in the .NET environment and the Java environment to use their remote objects seamlessly (with normal IIOP limitations, of course, with value types, and so on). You have already seen how you can expose a Java component to CORBA using RMI-IIOP; the process is quick and easy, and better yet, can be *automated*. The process on the .NET side is the same way. CORBA can be used in this manner to allow .NET and Java components to interact transparently. The following example examines such a system. A .NET component is wrapped with a CORBA interface and components in Java can access it like a normal Java component via RMI-IIOP.

Distributed File System Notifications: An Example CORBA System

Java does not contain any classes in the JDK to monitor for file system events. File system events occur when a file is deleted, modified, created, or renamed. These operations are platform specific and work different depending not only on the file system type, but on the host operating system. The only pure Java way to achieve this effect is to run a program that polls the file system and looks for updates — hardly an efficient mechanism of monitoring the file system. It would be far better if you could hook into the operating system and whenever a file system event occurred, be notified. Try to find a component that meets these needs and then provide a CORBA wrapper to access the component from your Java application.

Fortunately, one of the components of the .NET Framework fits your needs. The `FileSystemWatcher` class from the `System.IO` namespace hooks into the Windows operating system, and notifies the user of file system events. Because your application is written in Java, you need somehow to integrate this non-Java component into your application. CORBA is a fine choice in this case, especially because of the advent of IIOP.NET, which was discussed in the proceeding section. IIOP.NET allows .NET Remoting to run over IIOP, which basically means you can access .NET remote objects from Java's RMI-IIOP. For this example, you will wrap the `FileSystemWatcher` class in a .NET remote object, expose this object through CORBA, and then implement the Java client. This text does not go into any code details for the .NET side, because this is a Java book and not a C# book. However, the code for the .NET side can be downloaded from this book's Web site at www.wrox.com. Figure 11-12 is a high-level diagram of the architecture for the communication between .NET and Java.

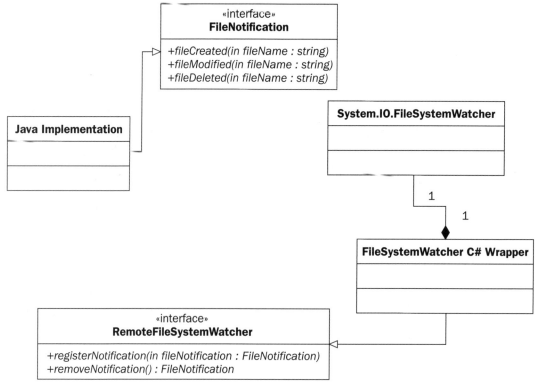

Figure 11-12

You have the IDL for the remote .NET components. The CORBA object that wraps the .NET component, `FileSystemWatcher`, has the following IDL:

```
#include "orb.idl"
#include "Predef.idl"

#include "FileNotification.idl"
#ifndef __ConsoleCorbaServer_RemoteFileSystemWatcher__
#define __ConsoleCorbaServer_RemoteFileSystemWatcher__
module ConsoleCorbaServer {

interface RemoteFileSystemWatcher {

void registerNotfication(in ::book::FileNotification notification) raises
(::Ch::Elca::Iiop::GenericUserException);
void removeNotification(in ::book::FileNotification notification) raises
(::Ch::Elca::Iiop::GenericUserException);
void setDirectory(in ::CORBA::WStringValue path) raises
(::Ch::Elca::Iiop::GenericUserException);
};

#pragma ID RemoteFileSystemWatcher
"IDL:ConsoleCorbaServer/RemoteFileSystemWatcher:1.0"

};

#endif
```

You can run `idlj`, the Java IDL compiler, to generate stub classes that will proxy your requests to these methods to the CORBA ORB running on the .NET platform's host machine. Notice how the IDL generated includes other IDL files, namely, `orb.idl`, `predef.idl`, and `FileNotification.idl`. These other files must be in the same directory when you run `idlj` for the compilation to work properly. The file `orb.idl` is the Java mapping definitions from IDL to Java specific types. The IIOP.NET provides `predef.idl` for some types specific to its .NET to CORBA mappings. The Java IDL compiler is included in JDK 5.0. Running the `idlj` compiler is simple:

```
idlj RemoteFileSystemWatcher.idl
```

By running `idlj` on the IDL, the following files were generated:

```
RemoteFileSystemWatcherStub.java
RemoteFileSystemWatcher.java
RemoteFileSystemWatcherHelper.java
RemoteFileSystemWatcherHolder.java
RemoteFileSystemWatcherOperations.java
GenericUserException.java
GenericUserExceptionHolder.java
GenericUserExceptionHelper.java
```

These are the stub and interfaces necessary to use the remote CORBA object, `RemoteFileSystemWatcher` (which wraps the .NET component, `FileSystemWatcher`). Note that because the IDL contained exceptions, exception classes were also generated. The `RemoteFileSystemWatcherOperations.java` defines the interface methods available to you:

```
package ConsoleCorbaServer;


/**
* ConsoleCorbaServer/RemoteFileSystemWatcherOperations.java .
* Generated by the IDL-to-Java compiler (portable), version "3.1"
* from RemoteFileSystemWatcher.idl
* Friday, June 11, 2004 5:56:29 PM EDT
*/

public interface RemoteFileSystemWatcherOperations
{
  void registerNotfication (book.FileNotification notification) throws
Ch.Elca.Iiop.GenericUserException;
  void removeNotification (book.FileNotification notification) throws
Ch.Elca.Iiop.GenericUserException;
  void setDirectory (String path) throws Ch.Elca.Iiop.GenericUserException;
} // interface RemoteFileSystemWatcherOperations
```

Notice how `registerNotification()` and `removeNotification()` have a `book.FileNotification` object as their parameter. `FileNotification` is the callback interface defined by `RemoteFileSystem Watcher`. `FileNotification` is defined in `FileNotification.idl`. You will have to generate Java stubs for this CORBA object as well. The difference, though, is that you will have to provide an implementation of `FileNotification` if you want to receive these file system events. By providing an implementation of `FileNotification`, you will be able to pass to the remote CORBA ORB a local instance that can receive events from the remote server. To implement `FileNotification`, you must run `idlj` with a different parameter, one to generate both the client stubs and the server stubs necessary for you to provide your own implementation. Here is the IDL for `FileNotification`:

```
#include "orb.idl"

#ifndef __book_FileNotification__
#define __book_FileNotification__


module book {

    interface FileNotification {
            void fileModified(
            in ::CORBA::WStringValue fileName );
        void fileDeleted(
            in ::CORBA::WStringValue fileName );
        void fileCreated(
```

```
            in ::CORBA::WStringValue fileName );

    };

#pragma ID FileNotification "RMI:book.FileNotification:0000000000000000"

};

#endif
```

Now run `idlj` to produce client and server stubs (to produce both client and server stubs, the `-fall` option is used):

```
idlj -fall FileNotification.idl
```

The following files were then generated:

```
FileNotificationStub.java
FileNotification.java
FileNotificationHelper.java
FileNotificationHolder.java
FileNotificationOperations.java
FileNotificationPOA.java
```

Notice how the only additional file generated with the `-fall` option was `FileNotificationPOA.java`. This is an abstract class that gives you the means to provide an implementation of `FileNotification`. By extending it and providing the implementation of the methods defined in the interface, you will have a CORBA Portable Object Adapter (POA) that can be connected to a running ORB. By connecting the POA to the ORB, the ORB will be able to route incoming requests for `FileNotification` to the correct instance.

The Implementation

Your implementation of `FileNotification` will extend `FileNotificationPOA`. Here you will have to provide simple implementations for the methods found in the file `FileNotificationOperations.java`, because `FileNotificationPOA` implements `FileNotificationOperations`. This chapter then goes through the code necessary to do the following:

1. Implement the `FileNotificationOperations` interface.

2. Connect to the local ORB.

3. Create a Portable Object Adapter for your implementation of `FileNotification`.

4. Connect the POA to the ORB's root POA.

5. Register your instance of `FileNotification` with the local COS Naming service.

6. Connect to the remote COS Naming service.

7. Obtain an instance of `RemoteFileSystemWatcher`.

8. Register your instance of `FileNotification` with `RemoteFileSystemWatcher` to receive the file system notification events.

9. Wait for file system events.

The key CORBA classes used in the example code are summarized in the following table. They are the minimal set of classes necessary to use a local ORB and COS Naming service to publish an instance of a CORBA object for use by remote clients.

Class	Function
org.omg.CORBA.Object	Class used to represent any CORBA remote object reference.
org.omg.CORBA.ORB	Class used to represent a CORBA ORB. This class provides the core CORBA infrastructure services, and brokers incoming and outgoing CORBA object method invocations.
org.omg.CosNaming.NamingComponent	Class used for representing a CORBA Name. Names refer to instances of a particular object running on a COS Naming service. With a name, a client can look up a particular object and receive a reference to it, and then begin to use the object.
org.omg.CosNaming.NamingContext	Class used to represent the actual COS Naming service. This class is used to perform the actual object lookups to receive references to remote CORBA objects.
org.omg.PortableServer.POA	Represents a Portable Object Adapter. Since JDK 1.4, the POA feature of the CORBA specification was added to the Java implementation. POAs allow for CORBA objects to be easily deployed on different implementations of CORBA ORBs. They connect a CORBA object reference to the ORB, allowing for incoming requests for that reference to be processed.

Your first task is to implement FileNotificationOperations in your class that extends the abstract class FileNotificationPOA that was generated by the idlj tool. Your implementation will simply print out what file system notifications were received to standard output:

```java
public class FileNotificationImpl extends FileNotificationPOA {

    public FileNotificationImpl() {
    }

    // next three methods are the implementation of FileNotification.idl
    public void fileModified(String fileName) {
        System.out.println(fileName + ": Modified");
    }

    public void fileDeleted(String fileName) {
        System.out.println(fileName + ": Deleted");
    }
```

```
        public void fileCreated(String fileName) {
            System.out.println(fileName + ": Created");
        }

    ...
```

These methods implement the CORBA interface found in the `FileNotification.idl` file. Now that you have the interface implemented, you must create the `main()` method that starts up your server, registers an instance of your `FileNotification` implementation with a local ORB, retrieves an instance of `RemoteFileWatcher`, and registers your instance of `FileNotification` with this remote instance to receive file system events.

Your main method begins by setting the properties necessary for the local ORB to find the COS Naming service daemon running in a separate process on your local machine. This is the naming service you will be using to register your instance of `FileNotification`. The `java.util.Properties` object in the following code stores where your ORB is running with its initial port. These parameters allow your ORB to connect to the COS Naming service running on port 1049:

```
        public static void main(String[] args) throws Exception {

            Properties props = new Properties();
            props.put("org.omg.CORBA.ORBInitialHost", "localhost");
            props.put("orb.omg.CORBA.ORBInitialPort", "1049");

            ORB orb = ORB.init(args, props);

            ...
```

Once you have your ORB instance, you must get the root Portable Object Adapter (POA). Every ORB has a root POA. From this POA, all additional POAs are attached in a treelike structure with the root POA being the root of the tree:

```
    POA rootPOA = POAHelper.narrow(orb.resolve_initial_references("RootPOA"));
```

You must activate the root POA so that the ORB will accept incoming requests:

```
    rootPOA.the_POAManager().activate();
```

Now that the root POA is active, you need to create the POA that contains your implementation of `FileNotification`. Once created, you connect your POA to the root POA so it can actively accept requests. To retrieve the actual CORBA reference of your implementation, you use the `File NotificationHelper` object. The `FileNotificationHelper` object was also generated by the `idlj` tool and the `narrow()` method was used to take an `org.omg.CORBA.Object reference` and cast it to a `FileNotification` object (with CORBA, a standard Java cast would not do the trick):

```
        FileNotificationPOA nPOA = new FileNotificationImpl();

        // attach File Notification POA to the root and register a reference
        org.omg.CORBA.Object ref = rootPOA.servant_to_reference(nPOA);
        FileNotification fileNotification = FileNotificationHelper.narrow(ref);
```

The next step is to bind your reference to the COS Naming service. You will name your reference `FileNotification`. You then bind your CORBA object reference `ref` to the naming service. Your `FileNotification` instance is now ready to receive incoming requests:

```
// bind the reference to the local cos naming server
    NamingContext ctx =
NamingContextHelper.narrow(orb.resolve_initial_references("NameService"));

NameComponent comp = new NameComponent("FileNotification", " ");

    ctx.rebind(new NameComponent[] {comp}, ref);
```

Now you must look up the remote CORBA object reference of the type `RemoteFileSystemWatcher`. This object allows you to register your local instance of `FileNotification` with it to receive file system events. The first step is to find the remote COS Naming service and lookup the object. To do this you must inform JNDI that you want to use a COS Naming context. The Java system property `java.naming.factory.initial` is set to reflect this. The `java.naming.provider.url` tells JNDI where to look for the remote COS Naming service (though in this example, the so-called remote COS Naming service is running on the local machine, and hence the hostname `localhost`). You then perform a normal JNDI lookup. However, because you are using IIOP for the underlying protocol with RMI, you cannot simply cast the object returned to the appropriate type. You must use the static `javax.rmi.PortableRemoteObject.narrow()` instead:

```
Hashtable env = new Hashtable();
env.put("java.naming.factory.initial", "com.sun.jndi.cosnaming.CNCtxFactory");
env.put("java.naming.provider.url", "iiop://localhost:1500");

// connect to the remote cos naming service and lookup the RemoteFileSystemWatcher
InitialContext remoteCtx = new InitialContext(env);
java.lang.Object fswRef = remoteCtx.lookup("FileSystemWatcher");

// register our File Notification reference to receive events from the watcher
RemoteFileSystemWatcher watcher = (RemoteFileSystemWatcher)
                PortableRemoteObject.narrow(fswRef, RemoteFileSystemWatcher.class);
```

Now that you have a reference to `RemoteFileSystemWatcher`, you can register your local reference of `FileNotification` and start receiving file system events. You tell the ORB to `run()` and your program blocks so you can receive file system events:

```
//remote call to register our local FileNotification instance on the remote server
watcher.registerNotfication(fileNotification);

System.out.println("File Notification registered on remote server.");
System.out.println("Waiting for file notification events...");
System.out.println();

// let our server run and wait for events
orb.run();
```

That is all there is to it. Your implementation is finished. You implemented a CORBA interface, `File Notification`, in Java. You produced stubs for another CORBA interface, `RemoteFileSystemWatcher`, to proxy requests to a remote implementation. You then set up a local ORB with your implementation of

FileNotification, looked up the remote instance of RemoteFileSystemWatcher, and then registered your reference of FileNotification with the remote CORBA object. The remote CORBA object now calls your local FileNotification reference whenever a file system event occurs.

The following is the full code listing for FileNotificationImpl.java:

```java
package book;

import java.util.Hashtable;
import java.util.Properties;

import javax.naming.InitialContext;
import javax.rmi.PortableRemoteObject;

import org.omg.CORBA.ORB;
import org.omg.CosNaming.NameComponent;
import org.omg.CosNaming.NamingContext;
import org.omg.CosNaming.NamingContextHelper;
import org.omg.PortableServer.POA;
import org.omg.PortableServer.POAHelper;

import ConsoleCorbaServer.RemoteFileSystemWatcher;


public class FileNotificationImpl extends FileNotificationPOA {

  public FileNotificationImpl() {
  }

  // next three methods are the implementation of FileNotification.idl
  public void fileModified(String fileName) {
    System.out.println(fileName + ": Modified");
  }

  public void fileDeleted(String fileName) {
    System.out.println(fileName + ": Deleted");
  }

  public void fileCreated(String fileName) {
    System.out.println(fileName + ": Created");
  }

  public static void main(String[] args) throws Exception {

    Properties props = new Properties();
    props.put("org.omg.CORBA.ORBInitialHost", "localhost");
    props.put("orb.omg.CORBA.ORBInitialPort", "1049");

    // connect to the local cos naming server, get and activate
    // the RootPOA
    ORB orb = ORB.init(args, props);
    POA rootPOA =
                POAHelper.narrow(orb.resolve_initial_references("RootPOA"));
```

```
rootPOA.the_POAManager().activate();
FileNotificationPOA nPOA = new FileNotificationImpl();

// attach File Notification POA to the root and register a reference
org.omg.CORBA.Object ref = rootPOA.servant_to_reference(nPOA);
FileNotification fileNotification = FileNotificationHelper.narrow(ref);

// bind the reference to the local cos naming server
NamingContext ctx =
        NamingContextHelper.narrow(orb.resolve_initial_references("NameService"));
NameComponent comp = new NameComponent("FileNotification", " ");

ctx.rebind(new NameComponent[] {comp}, ref);

System.out.println("File Notification bound to local ORB");


Hashtable env = new Hashtable();
env.put("java.naming.factory.initial",
                   "com.sun.jndi.cosnaming.CNCtxFactory");
env.put("java.naming.provider.url", "iiop://localhost:1500");

// connect to the remote naming service and lookup the RemoteFileSystemWatcher
InitialContext remoteCtx = new InitialContext(env);
java.lang.Object fswRef = remoteCtx.lookup("FileSystemWatcher");

// register our FileNotification reference to receive events from the watcher
RemoteFileSystemWatcher watcher = (RemoteFileSystemWatcher)
            PortableRemoteObject.narrow(fswRef, RemoteFileSystemWatcher.class);
watcher.registerNotfication(fileNotification);

System.out.println("File Notification registered on remote server.");
System.out.println("Waiting for file notification events...");
System.out.println();

// let our server run and wait for events
orb.run();
    }
}
```

Running the Example

To run your example, you first need to start up the remote CORBA server. You do this by running
ConsoleCorbaServer.exe (a compiled .NET binary):

```
ConsoleCorbaServer
```

This ConsoleCorbaServer creates a C# instance of RemoteFileSystemWatcher, and registers it for
use over IIOP via a COS Naming service. ConsoleCorbaServer.exe has the instance of RemoteFile
SystemWatcher set up by default to monitor the current working directory. This can be changed by calling its setDirectory() method (which is exposed via CORBA), but for the purposes of running the
example, the default is fine.

Next you must start up your local COS Naming service with which you will register your instance of `FileNotification`. The JDK provides a CORBA COS Naming service with its `orbd` tool. To start up the naming service, simply run `orbd` from the command line:

```
orbd
```

With no parameters specified, `orbd` runs on port 1049 (where your code will be looking for it). After `orbd` is running, you can now start your client program:

```
java book.FileNotificationImpl
```

The output screenshot in Figure 11-13 shows your program receiving some file system events after I created, modified, and deleted a text file in the `d:\book` directory.

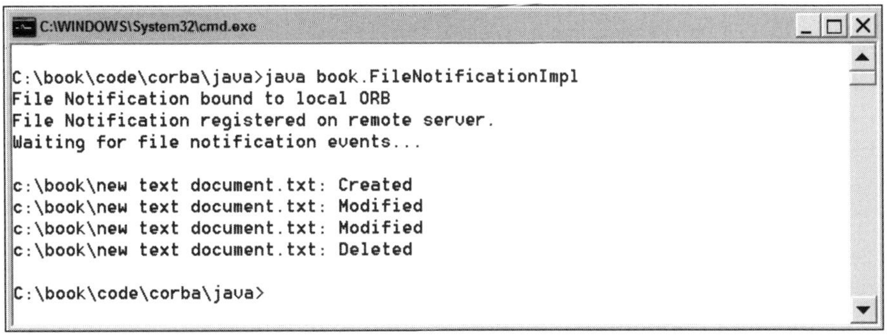

```
C:\WINDOWS\System32\cmd.exe

C:\book\code\corba\java>java book.FileNotificationImpl
File Notification bound to local ORB
File Notification registered on remote server.
Waiting for file notification events...

c:\book\new text document.txt: Created
c:\book\new text document.txt: Modified
c:\book\new text document.txt: Modified
c:\book\new text document.txt: Deleted

C:\book\code\corba\java>
```

Figure 11-13

Web Services

Over the past few years Web Services have emerged from the hype and are becoming the interoperable ubiquitous technology they have long been promised to be. Many major vendors are offering Web Service APIs to their services, from Amazon, to eBay, and Google. You can interact with Google Maps, search for books on Amazon, and query auctions on eBay, all from your own thick or thin custom clients. Programmatic access to services provided by web sites such as these has been the driving force behind Web Services. Web Services are a key enabler of the next-generation World Wide Web — the Semantic Web, in which content is not only human-readable (browser displayed HTML markup), but also machine-readable (API access to Google Maps). The other driving force behind Web Services is enabling business-to-business communication. Companies can share data, and integrate heterogeneous data and services — in one conglomerate Service Oriented Architecture (SOA). SOA is now the new buzzword, as Web Services have settled in as an accepted and interoperable technology.

Web Services enable remote procedure calls and asynchronous messaging. Web Services are generally implemented as XML messages over the HTTP protocol. There are numerous standards surrounding this simple definition, and this chapter delves into some of them later. There are a lot of things Web Services do not provide. They do not support sessions out of the box (though like HTTP, they can be simulated). They do not support distributed objects like CORBA or RMI. Until recently, there were no implementations of security standards for secure message passing or reliable transport. The number one goal of Web

Services is interoperability. The formation of the open industry organization, Web Services Interoperability Organization (WS-I) demonstrates the importance of interoperability as it is supported by many companies and exists for the sole purpose of defining interoperability standards.

Starting with Java 6, support for Web Services has been integrated into the core Java platform. Web Services can be used and even hosted using only the standard JRE. Though Web Services are not intended as replacements for RMI and CORBA, most distributed architectures are starting to use them as their interface with other distributed systems. Web Services will allow for a whole new generation of applications that can leverage many services already found on the World Wide Web.

Random-Weather.org

For the rest of this section, you will Web Service–enable a hypothetical web site, `random-weather.org`. Your random weather web application generates a random weather forecast based on a zip code. There is an HTML interface to the application and it is shown in Figure 11-14.

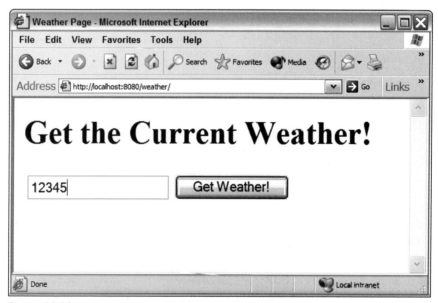

Figure 11-14

It is a simple site; users enter their zip code into the form and then receive their weather forecast—not all that different from real weather sites, except of course, that this one is hideous. This page is encoded in HTML, and works with the browser to send the web server whatever zip code was typed in (as with any web application). Here is the simple HTML of this page:

```
<html>
<head>
  <title>Weather Page</title>
</head>
<body>
```

```
<h1>Get the Current Weather!</h1>

<form method="get" action="weather.jsp">

<table border="0" cellspacing="2" cellpadding="2">
  <tr>
    <td><input name="zipcode" type="textbox"/></td>
    <td><input type="submit" value="Get Weather!"/></td>
  </tr>
</table>

</form>

</body>
</html>
```

Note that there are only a couple of input tags, and this is where the information is exchanged. Figure 11-15 shows what the resulting web page from this dynamic site looks like.

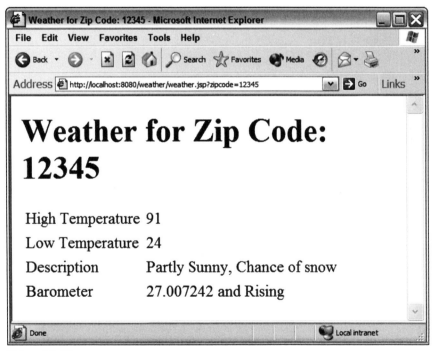

Figure 11-15

The HTML for this page shows where the actual weather information is encoded:

```
<html>
<head>
  <title>Weather for Zip Code: 12345</title>
```

```
    </head>

    <body>

      <h1>Weather for Zip Code: 12345</h1>

      <table border="0" cellspacing="2" cellpadding="2">
        <tr>
          <td>High Temperature</td>
          <td>93</td>
        </tr>
        <tr>
          <td>Low Temperature</td>
          <td>73</td>
        </tr>
        <tr>
          <td>Description</td>
          <td>Partly Cloudy</td>
        </tr>
        <tr>
          <td>Barometer</td>
          <td>26.11519 and Rising</td>
        </tr>
      </table>

    </body>
    </html>
```

Writing software to programmatically access this information from `random-weather.org` is a much more difficult task. The preceding HTML would have to be parsed by the software, and the relevant data (barometric pressure, high and low temperatures, and so on) would have to be extracted. Though this is possible, anytime `random-weather.org` changed its basic web site design (which would then change the HTML structure), it would potentially break the client software. If `random-weather.org` had a Web Service allowing access to random forecasts, you could easily code against it. The resulting data would be in a structured format, and not intermingled with its presentation.

Platform-Independent RPC

Web Services are an implementation of platform-independent remote procedure calls. Think of each individual Web Service as a remote method. An XML-encoded request is sent to a server, and an XML-encoded response is returned. Normally Web Services are sent over the HTTP protocol via the HTTP POST operation. XML is posted to the web server, and XML is returned from the HTTP POST operation. While the underlying RPC protocol itself is in XML, the application data passed to and from the server is also encoded in XML — and can be any valid XML described by XML Schema. A sample XML request/response posted via HTTP is diagrammed in Figure 11-16.

There are other advantages to implementing RPC via XML over HTTP. HTTP is a mature protocol and is implemented in many different languages. Piggybacking onto established protocols hastens the adoption and avoids some of the interoperability problems common to RPC specifications (in the early days of CORBA, different ORBs from different vendors did not always communicate). Debugging applications that use XML over HTTP is much simpler than debugging applications using binary protocols such as JRMP or IIOP. The plain text of the messages can be viewed with tools such as TCPMon as the data crosses the wire.

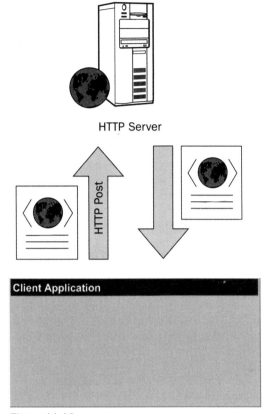

HTTP Server

Client Application

Figure 11-16

XML Web Services do not have certain features found in CORBA or RMI into them out of the box. They do not support sessions (because HTTP is a stateless protocol). They do not support procedure callbacks and there are no distributed objects. Security, transactions, and scalability are all follow-on standards and specifications that vary from implementation to implementation. Eventually these standards will become a cornerstone of making Web Services truly able to serve mission-critical applications. Web Services do enable current dynamic web sites to a new generation of applications.

WS-I Basic Profile

The Web Services Interoperability Organization's Basic Profile is a set of implementation guidelines for Web Services interoperability. The implementation of Web Services in Java 6, the Java APIs for XML Web Services (JAX-WS, formerly known as JAX-RPC), conforms to the WS-I Basic Profile, version 1.1. At the time of this writing, version 1.1 is the most current profile issued by WS-I, and there are other compatible implementations, such as the one in the Microsoft .NET Framework.

Though the WS-I Basic Profile references other specifications and protocols, it does not actually define any. The Simple Object Access Protocol (SOAP) is used for the Web Service message format and the Web Services Description Language (WSDL) is used to describe what is in a particular service's messages, and how to access them. Both SOAP and WSDL are flexible enough to be used in many different ways, and can produce different styles of SOAP services. The Basic Profile clarifies which of these styles should be used, defining how the message payload is formatted in SOAP and described in WSDL. For example, SOAP allows the encoding of the actual data payload to be done either with SOAP RPC encoding, or with plain XML Schema. The WS-I Basic Profile requires XML Schema to be used, called document style encoding, and *not* SOAP RPC encoding. Another example of how the basic profile clarifies how standards should be used is with HTTP. Though Web Services can be run over other transports besides HTTP, because HTTP is the most common transport, the Basic Profile specifies which HTTP codes should be returned under which circumstances, how errors should be handled, and so on.

The 1.0 version of the WS-I Basic Profile came about because of the interoperability issues between different Web Service toolkits. When looking to implement Web Services you should try to use toolkits conforming to the 1.1 Basic Profile, and make sure the toolkits you will be communicating with also conform to the 1.1 Basic Profile. As evidence of the older interoperability problems, Google, eBay, and Amazon, actually offer their own client Web Service SDKs written specifically to interoperate with their servers. Now that the WS-I Basic Profile is becoming better adopted, this should change in the future. Ideally, only publishing a service's description with WSDL should be enough for interoperability.

Web Services Description Language (WSDL)

The Web Services Description Language is the Web Services equivalent of CORBA IDL — in the sense that it is an interface document. It describes how to communicate with a particular Web Service. Some say you can be more descriptive with data you are passing; because all data is defined in XML, you are not limited to primitive data types and particular classes like you are in CORBA IDL. Web Services described in WSDL can have the following pieces of information attached to them:

- ❏ **Types.** The XML data types used in the services (XML Schema can be used here to describe the data, and in WS-I Basic Profile 1.1, is used as the mechanism for data definition — SOAP RPC encoding is no longer supported).

- ❏ **Messages.** The content each for Web Service defined (described with XML Schema data types, normally referenced from the **Types** section).

- ❏ **Port Types.** Specifies input and/or output messages for a particular operation or method.

- ❏ **Binding.** Specifies the underlying communications protocol and transport protocol the Web Services run over.

WSDL files themselves are XML and the complete specification for its format can be found at the following URL:

```
http://www.w3.org/TR/wsdl
```

Later on in this chapter you will build a Web Service for the random-weather.org site. The WSDL is shown here for a sampling of what a simple service looks like:

```xml
<?xml version="1.0" encoding="UTF-8"?>
<definitions xmlns="http://schemas.xmlsoap.org/wsdl/" xmlns:tns="http://book/"
xmlns:xsd="http://www.w3.org/2001/XMLSchema"
xmlns:soap="http://schemas.xmlsoap.org/wsdl/soap/" targetNamespace="http://book/"
name="WeatherGetterService">
  <types>
    <xs:schema xmlns:xs="http://www.w3.org/2001/XMLSchema"
```

```
                    targetNamespace="http://book/" version="1.0">

    <xs:element xmlns:ns1="http://book/" name="getWeather"
            type="ns1:getWeather"></xs:element>

    <xs:complexType name="getWeather">
      <xs:sequence>
        <xs:element name="zipcode" type="xs:int"></xs:element>
      </xs:sequence>
    </xs:complexType>

    <xs:element xmlns:ns2="http://book/" name="getWeatherResponse"
            type="ns2:getWeatherResponse"></xs:element>

    <xs:complexType name="getWeatherResponse">
      <xs:sequence>
        <xs:element xmlns:ns3="http://book/" name="return" type="ns3:weather"
            minOccurs="0"></xs:element>
      </xs:sequence>
    </xs:complexType>

    <xs:complexType name="weather">
      <xs:sequence>
        <xs:element name="barometer" type="xs:float"></xs:element>

        <xs:element name="barometer-description" type="xs:string"
                minOccurs="0"></xs:element>
        <xs:element name="general-description" type="xs:string"
                minOccurs="0"></xs:element>
        <xs:element name="high-temperature" type="xs:int"></xs:element>
        <xs:element name="low-temperature" type="xs:int"></xs:element>
      </xs:sequence>
    </xs:complexType>
  </xs:schema>
</types>
<message name="getWeather">
  <part element="tns:getWeather" name="parameters"></part>
</message>

<message name="getWeatherResponse">
  <part element="tns:getWeatherResponse" name="parameters"></part>
</message>
<portType name="WeatherGetter">
  <operation name="getWeather">
    <input message="tns:getWeather"></input>
    <output message="tns:getWeatherResponse"></output>
  </operation>
</portType>

<binding name="WeatherGetterPortBinding" type="tns:WeatherGetter">
  <soap:binding style="document"
        transport="http://schemas.xmlsoap.org/soap/http"></soap:binding>
  <operation name="getWeather">
    <soap:operation soapAction=""></soap:operation>
```

```
        <input>
           <soap:body use="literal"></soap:body>
        </input>
        <output>
           <soap:body use="literal"></soap:body>

        </output>
      </operation>
    </binding>
    <service name="WeatherGetterService">
      <port name="WeatherGetterPort" binding="tns:WeatherGetterPortBinding">
        <soap:address
             location="http://localhost:8080/services/weather"></soap:address>
      </port>
    </service>
</definitions>
```

Note how in the `<types>` section of the WSDL, XML Schema is used to define all of your data types. In the JAX-WS implementation in JDK 6, the Java API for XML Binding (JAXB) is used when defining the parameters and return types of Java Web Services to define their types in XML Schema — to conform to the document/literal encoding recommended in WS-I Basic Profile 1.1.

This chapter does not go into too much depth for the actual details of WSDL — that is better left to books or chapters dedicated solely to WSDL. In CORBA or RMI, one generates stub classes to use distributed objects transparently in code. WSDL allows the same sort of functionality for Web Services. There are toolkits and compilers for WSDL in a number of languages. Later, this chapter examines how to generate Java classes from WSDL and then use them in code using tools included with the JDK. You need never know what goes on under the hood, but it certainly helps in understanding. Because Web Services boiled down to their core are really just XML posted via HTTP, one could use an XML API and an HTTP API and write Web Services. Now that the WS-I Basic Profile 1.1 has been adopted by the major Web Service toolkits, it is normally best to let the toolkits generate and process WSDL.

Simple Object Access Protocol (SOAP)

Every RPC system needs a communications protocol. RMI uses either JRMP or IIOP. CORBA uses IIOP. Web Services use the Simple Object Access Protocol, or SOAP. SOAP is a message format defined in XML. SOAP is inherently platform independent because it is based entirely in XML. Like WSDL, SOAP is also a W3C standard, and its specification can be found at the following URL:

```
http://www.w3.org/TR/soap/
```

SOAP messages have the following structural attributes:

❑   **Envelope.** The entire XML message has as its root element the SOAP Envelope — all content of the message is contained here.

❑   **Headers.** XML data can be placed in the header of a SOAP message away from the actual content — keeping things like usernames and passwords (if required) separate from the actual content of the message.

❑   **Body.** The XML content delivered in a SOAP message is contained in the body.

SOAP is a fairly straightforward protocol, assuming you understand XML and XML namespaces. A sample SOAP request message from the `random-weather.org` Web Service looks like the following:

```
<soap:Envelope xmlns:soap="http://schemas.xmlsoap.org/soap/envelope/"
xmlns:xsi="http://www.w3.org/2001/XMLSchema-instance"
xmlns:xsd="http://www.w3.org/2001/XMLSchema">
  <soap:Body>
    <getWeather xmlns="http://book/">
      <zipcode xmlns="">12345</zipcode>
    </getWeather>
  </soap:Body>
</soap:Envelope>
```

The SOAP message response returned looks like this:

```
<?xml version="1.0" ?>
<soapenv:Envelope xmlns:soapenv="http://schemas.xmlsoap.org/soap/envelope/"
xmlns:xsd="http://www.w3.org/2001/XMLSchema" xmlns:ns1="http://book/">
  <soapenv:Body>
    <ns1:getWeatherResponse>
      <return>
        <barometer>30.623604</barometer>
        <barometer-description>Holding Steady</barometer-description>
        <general-description>Sunny</general-description>
        <high-temperature>23</high-temperature>
        <low-temperature>17</low-temperature>
      </return>
    </ns1:getWeatherResponse>
  </soapenv:Body>
</soapenv:Envelope>
```

Notice how both messages are rooted with the XML element envelope. There are no headers for these messages, and the `<Body>` for each is straightforward. This chapter does not go into any further depth describing SOAP. The exact syntax of SOAP is not as big of an issue, because most Web Service toolkits will handle it all for you (much the same way you wouldn't think of knowing how JRMP or IIOP work). Learning the ins and outs of WSDL is more worth your while, because some complex services can require the importing of other external XML schemas for data description of the payload.

Underlying Transport Protocols

SOAP can be transported over a variety of protocols. The normal course of action is over HTTP/HTTPS, which is over TCP/IP. However, SOAP messages can also be sent over the following:

❑   Straight TCP/IP (no HTTP/HTTPS)

❑   Simple Mail Transport Protocol (SMTP)

❑   Java Messaging Service Protocols

Over HTTP, Web Services are normal HTTP requests, and no new ports need to be opened on network firewalls—the standard HTTP and HTTPS ports still apply.

Weather Web Site Example

Going back to the `random-weather.org` site from before, this section takes a look under the hood of how it is currently implemented. After looking at its current implementation, you will enable it for Web Services. After being Web Service enabled, the local random weather forecast will not only be available from your web browser, but developers can also programmatically access this same information. The weather web site has a particular class that does most of the work, `WeatherGetter`. `WeatherGetter` randomly generates a weather forecast for a certain zip code. This forecast changes daily and randomly. If you ran a real web site, you could think of `WeatherGetter` as providing accurate weather information, maybe from a database, probably aggregated from local weather stations. The weather forecasts will consist of four items:

❑ High Temperature

❑ Low Temperature

❑ Weather Description

❑ Barometer and Description

The JavaBean, `Weather`, holds these properties:

```java
package book;

public class Weather {
  private String description;

  private int lowTemp;
  private int highTemp;

  private float barometer;
  private String barometerDescription;

  public float getBarometer() {
    return barometer;
  }

  public void setBarometer(float barometer) {
    this.barometer = barometer;
  }

  public String getBarometerDescription() {
    return barometerDescription;
  }

  public void setBarometerDescription(String barometerDescription) {
    this.barometerDescription = barometerDescription;
  }

  public String getDescription() {
    return description;
  }

  public void setDescription(String description) {
```

```
    this.description = description;
  }

  public int getHighTemp() {
    return highTemp;
  }

  public void setHighTemp(int highTemp) {
    this.highTemp = highTemp;
  }

  public int getLowTemp() {
    return lowTemp;
  }

  public void setLowTemp(int lowTemp) {
    this.lowTemp = lowTemp;
  }
}
```

The `WeatherGetter` class is also straightforward. This section does not go into detail explaining exactly how the forecasts are generated; if you are curious, though, look at the `java.util.Random` class in the JDK. The following code listing is important later on so you can see how to expose it as a Web Service:

```
package book;

import java.util.Calendar;
import java.util.GregorianCalendar;
import java.util.Random;

public class WeatherGetter {

  private Random random;

  public WeatherGetter() {
    this.random = new Random();
  }

  public Weather getWeather(int zipCode) {
    Calendar cal = new GregorianCalendar();
    // changes the weather value daily
    random.setSeed(zipCode + cal.get(Calendar.DAY_OF_YEAR) +
             cal.get(Calendar.YEAR));

    Weather w = new Weather();

    int x = random.nextInt(100);
    int y = random.nextInt(100);

    if (x >= y) {
      w.setHighTemp(x);
      w.setLowTemp(y);
    } else {
      w.setHighTemp(y);
```

```java
        w.setLowTemp(x);
    }

    w.setBarometer(25 + random.nextFloat() * 8);
    if (random.nextBoolean()) {
        if (random.nextBoolean()) {
            w.setBarometerDescription("Rising");
        } else w.setBarometerDescription("Falling");
    } else w.setBarometerDescription("Holding Steady");

    String adjective;
    String noun;

    if (random.nextBoolean()) {
        adjective = "Partly";
    } else adjective = "";

    if (random.nextBoolean()) {
        noun = "Sunny";
    } else noun = "Cloudy";

    if (("Partly".equals(adjective) || "Cloudy".equals(noun))
            && random.nextBoolean()) {
        noun += ", Chance of ";
        if (w.getLowTemp() < 32)
            noun += "snow";
        else noun += "rain";
    }

    w.setDescription((adjective + " " + noun).trim());

    return w;
    }
}
```

The weather web application is fairly straightforward. There is one Java Server Page (JSP) that handles incoming weather requests and outputs the current random forecast for that zip code (shown in the screenshots and HTML code from earlier). The JSP determines the forecast by using `WeatherGetter` and returns the result to the user. An end user's typical session on your web application would follow the flow shown here:

1. User requests `http://random-weather.org/weather/` from browser

2. `index.jsp` returns HTML form for inputting zip code

3. User inputs zip code, submits the form

4. `index.jsp` processes the request, and calls `WeatherGetter.getWeather(int zipcode)`, to retrieve a populated `Weather` bean (representing the forecast)

5. `index.jsp` returns the information contained in the `Weather` bean returned from `getWeather()` as an HTML table

JSPs backed by Java classes that access data is a common method for implementing dynamic web sites. Note how the most important aspect of your sequence was the call to `getWeather()`. That method does all of the work, retrieving the weather forecast based on the zip code. Exposing that method as a Web Service would allow programmatic access to your weather information. The next section details how to expose methods for Web Services using JAX-WS.

See Chapters 7 and 8 for more information on building web applications with Java.

Creating a Web Service from a Java Method

There are three major steps for exposing Java methods as a Web Service. These steps are the minimum necessary to expose and deploy a Web Service:

1. Apply annotations from `javax.jws` to annotate which classes are to be exposed as Web Services, and which methods in these classes are exposed as web methods. Also apply Java API for XML Binding (JAXB) annotations to web method parameters and return values to specify how they should be encoded in XML (annotations for JAXB are found in `javax.xml.bind.annotation`—see Chapter 5 for more information regarding JAXB).

2. Run the `wsgen` tool included in JDK 6 to generate additional JAXB classes needed for specifying the Web Service request and response container elements.

3. Deploy the Web Service.

The most difficult step is still deployment. Different containers will have different mechanisms for deployment. Because JDK 6 includes a web server, you will look at deploying services using only the JDK, and then in standard servlet containers, using Apache Tomcat as an example.

Using JAX-WS Annotations

The first step to creating a Web Service using JAX-WS is to annotate the Java class representing the service. Each Java class can represent one Web Service, and can have one or more of its methods exposed as web methods. The key annotations from JAX-WS are summarized in the following table.

Annotations (from `javax.jws`)	Function
WebMethod	Exposes a Java method as a Web Service method. This annotation is applied to methods, and can provide the WSDL operation name for the method. The WebMethod annotation must be used in conjunction with the WebService annotation applied to its class.
WebParam	Allows parameters in Web Services methods (methods marked with WebMethod) to specify their XML element name and namespace. Also allows providing additional WSDL information such as parameter type (IN, OUT, INOUT) and where in the SOAP message the parameter can be decoded.
WebResult	WebResult is similar to WebParam — it marks the return value of a Web Service method (methods marked with WebMethod). It allows for the customization of the XML element name and namespace for the return value.
WebService	Marks a Java class as a Web Service. This annotation must be present for methods on the class to be marked with WebMethod. The name of the service can be customized, as well as providing the location of a custom WSDL file.

The first step to exposing `WeatherGetter` as a Web Service is to annotate the class. The following code shows simple usage of the `WebService` and `WebMethod` annotations. The parameter `zipcode` is annotated to give it an element name that matches its usage (rather than the JAX-WS default XML element name for the first argument, `arg0`). With the following annotations, JAX-WS will generate WSDL for you that conforms to the WS-I Basic Profile 1.1 and can be parsed by any 1.1-compliant Web Services toolkit. An advantage to allowing JAX-WS to generate the WSDL for you (instead manually specifying a custom WSDL file) is that you can be confident it will comply with the 1.1 Basic Profile, and allow for easy interoperability. Most 1.1 Basic Profile Web Service toolkits support automatic binding stub generation for services. By having your WSDL 1.1 Basic Profile–compliant, it is easy for toolkits to automatically generate bindings. The default SOAP binding for JAX-WS is SOAP document/literal binding. Document/literal binding merely means the payload of the SOAP messages is XML that can be described by XML Schema (and encoded as raw XML, not SOAP RPC–encoded XML).

```
...
import javax.jws.WebMethod;
import javax.jws.WebParam;
import javax.jws.WebResult;
import javax.jws.WebService;
...
@WebService(name="WeatherService")
public class WeatherGetter {
...
  @WebMethod
  public @WebResult(name="weather") Weather getWeather
             (@WebParam(name="zipcode") int zipCode) {
...
```

JAX-WS annotations will not let you specify the XML format for the Java type of the return value of `getWeather()`, the `Weather` bean. They will let you specify the element name, but JAXB annotations are used for control over how it serializes.

Note that this is possible for both method parameter types and return value types, but in the weather example, you only have a primitive type for your one parameter — so no JAXB bindings are possible for `zipcode` *other than changing the element name via the JAX-WS* `WebParam` *annotation.*

The `Weather` bean is annotated in the following code segment to customize its XML representation (which is what is returned in your Web Services' response SOAP message):

```
...
import javax.xml.bind.annotation.XmlElement;
...
public class Weather {
...
@XmlElement(name="barometer")
  public float getBarometer() {
...
  @XmlElement(name="barometer-description")
  public String getBarometerDescription() {
...
  @XmlElement(name="general-description")
  public String getDescription() {
...
```

```
@XmlElement(name="high-temperature")
public int getHighTemp() {
...
  @XmlElement(name="low-temperature")
  public int getLowTemp() {
...
```

Because JAX-WS works in conjunction with JAXB, all method parameters and return values in web methods must be serializable by JAXB. The main requirements for JAXB-serializable classes are: they must have a default no-arg constructor, and all fields or properties to be serialized within the class must also be types that are JAXB serializable. See Chapter 5 for more information on those requirements.

Running wsgen

Before JAX-WS annotated classes can be deployed as Web Services, the `wsgen` tool must be run. The `wsgen` tool generates the SOAP envelope messaging elements, the elements that represent the request for a particular method in a service, and the element representing the response. The only time you will not have to run `wsgen` is if your service methods only have Java primitive types for both parameter and return values. The `wsgen` tool is located in your JDK 6 `bin` directory. To run it, specify your classpath and the fully qualified class name of your class having the `WebService` annotation. For this example, run the `wsgen` tool on the compiled `WeatherGetter` class file by issuing the following command:

```
wsgen -cp . book.WeatherGetter
```

Running `wsgen` on `WeatherGetter` produces the following files:

```
./book/jaxws/GetWeather.class
./book/jaxws/GetWeatherResponse.class
./book/jaxws/GetWeather.java
./book/jaxws/GetWeatherResponse.java
```

The two classes generated, `GetWeather` and `GetWeatherResponse`, are JAXB annotated Java Beans, representing a `getWeather()` request message and its corresponding response message. If you tried to deploy this Web Service without running `wsgen`, you would receive a `ClassNotFoundException`, because the runtime will be looking for the generated classes.

Deploying Your Web Service with JDK 6

New to JDK 6 is an internal web server. This web server can be used to deploy Web Services using only the Java 6 runtime. Deploying Web Services developed with JAX-WS is quick and easy when only using the JDK. In practice, if you are developing server-side applications, it could help you quickly test some of your services (though most likely your services will rely on some other Java EE container's services forcing you to test on your application server). One of the potential uses for the internal web server is on the client side. Client-side apps that use Web Services can now have two-way conversations with their app servers — allowing app servers to call Web Services that reside back on the client. To deploy Web Services using the JDK's internal web server, you use the `java.xml.ws.Endpoint` class. Simple deployment is straightforward and illustrated in the following code:

```
public static void main(String[] args) throws Exception {
    WeatherGetter wg = new WeatherGetter();

    // create and start a new webservice end point on port 8080
```

```
       // using our WebService, WeatherGetter
       Endpoint endpoint =
                       Endpoint.publish("http://localhost:8080/services/weather", wg);

       // run our web server for 5 minutes by sleeping main thread,
       // then shutting down web server
       //
       // note: if you were to comment out these next two lines of code,
       // the web server would continue to run till you sent the process the TERM
       // signal (ctrl-c)
       Thread.sleep(1000 * 60 * 5); // sleep for 5 minutes

       // unpublish the web service (and stop the web server)
       endpoint.stop();
   }
```

Note how the static method `Endpoint.publish()` creates a new Web Service endpoint and publishes it to the URL specified (and in the preceding example, starting up the internal HTTP server running locally on port 8080). After you have published a Web Service, you can access its WSDL. This is useful for generating client stubs, which you can do with JAX-WS, but also with other Web Service toolkits in other languages. The WSDL for a service published with JAX-WS can be found by appending '?wsdl' to the URL of the endpoint. Your `WeatherGetter` service's WSDL would be published here:

```
http://localhost:8080/services/weather?wsdl
```

Deploying Your Web Service with Tomcat

The reference implementation of JAX-WS included in JDK 6 contains a servlet and support classes for deploying JAX-WS services into standard servlet containers. Apache Tomcat is the reference servlet container implementation and also widely used in production. You will deploy your `WeatherGetter` service on Tomcat to demonstrate how to deploy JAX-WS Web Services to a standards-compliant servlet container. From reading this section, you should also be able to deploy to the JBoss Application Server, and any other application server that uses Apache Tomcat for its servlet container. Once application servers implement Java EE 5, each will have a different custom mechanism for deploying JAX-WS Web Services. Follow the directions of your application server for Web Services deployment, and if your application server does not yet implement Java EE 5, follow the instructions here to deploy to your standards-compliant servlet container (ignoring the Tomcat-specific steps if not deploying on Tomcat).

The steps required to deploy Web Services on Apache Tomcat are as follows:

1. Download and install the latest version of Apache Tomcat (version 5.5.17 was the latest at the time of this writing). The latest 5.5.x version can be downloaded from http://tomcat.apache.org/download-55.cgi.

2. Deploy your web application normally (copy your web application directory to `TOMCAT_HOME/webapps`).

3. Create the `sun-jaxws.xml` configuration file specifying your Web Service endpoints, and add Sun's Web Service servlet and context listener to your `web.xml`. Make sure the `sun-jaxws.xml` file is deployed to your web application's `WEB-INF` directory. See the following two sections for details.

Configuring web.xml and sun-jaxws.xml

Configuring your web application within Tomcat to enable JAX-WS Web Services requires you to enable a special servlet context listener and servlet in your web application:

```
com.sun.xml.ws.transport.http.servlet.WSServletContextListener
com.sun.xml.ws.transport.http.servlet.WSServlet
```

The bold text in the following `web.xml` application shows how these components were added to your weather application. Note especially the `<servlet-mapping>`, as the `<url-pattern>`, because the URL pattern must match a URL endpoint in your `sun-jaxws.xml` file:

```
<?xml version="1.0" encoding="UTF-8"?>
<web-app>
    <listener>
        <listener-class>
            com.sun.xml.ws.transport.http.servlet.WSServletContextListener
        </listener-class>
    </listener>
    <servlet>
        <servlet-name>jaxservlet</servlet-name>
        <servlet-class>
            com.sun.xml.ws.transport.http.servlet.WSServlet
        </servlet-class>
        <load-on-startup>1</load-on-startup>
    </servlet>
    <servlet-mapping>
        <servlet-name>jaxservlet</servlet-name>
        <url-pattern>/weather</url-pattern>
    </servlet-mapping>
    <welcome-file-list>
        <welcome-file>
        index.html
        </welcome-file>
    </welcome-file-list>

</web-app>
```

Sun's `WSServlet` requires the `sun-jaxws.xml` configuration file. This file must reside in the `WEB-INF` directory of your web application. Your web application's Web Service endpoints are defined here. For each endpoint, three attributes are required:

❑ **name:** Name of your Web Service (any unique name will do).

❑ **implementation:** The fully qualified class name of your Web Service class (marked with the `WebService` annotation.

❑ **url-pattern:** The URL pattern relative to your web application's root URL. This URL pattern must match map back to Sun's `WSServlet`. Make sure the pattern here is the same as it in one of your `WSServlet` `<servlet-mapping>` elements in your `web.xml` file.

The `sun-jaxws.xml` configuration file for your weather application is shown here:

```xml
<?xml version="1.0" encoding="UTF-8"?>
<endpoints xmlns="http://java.sun.com/xml/ns/jax-ws/ri/runtime" version="2.0">
  <endpoint
      name="weather"
      implementation="book.WeatherGetter"
      url-pattern="/weather"/>
</endpoints>
```

Though this example only defined one endpoint in your `sun-jaxws.xml` file, you can define multiple endpoints. That's all there is to it—Tomcat is now configured to run the weather Web Service.

Don't forget to include the classes wsgen generates in your web application's classpath. Also, at the time of this writing, the JAX-WS implementation included in the JDK was not the completely updated with the latest JAX-WS RI from Sun. If you receive `ClassNotFoundExceptions` for the Sun servlet context listener or servlet, download the latest JAX-WS RI and put the jars in your `TOMCAT_HOME/shared/lib` directory. You can download the latest JAX-WS RI from `https://jax-ws.dev.java.net/`.

Writing a Web Service Client

Writing a Web Services client when you have the WSDL handy for the Web Service is quick and simple. Because WSDL defines the interface and data types in a particular Web Service (or multiple Web Services), classes to access the Web Service can be auto-generated (much like RMI stubs). JAX-WS provides a tool, `wsimport`, for this purpose, whenever you want to write a client for a Web Service you just generate stubs from its WSDL.

Running wsimport

The `wsimport` tool comes with JDK 6 and can be found in the `bin` directory. It generates Web Service client stub classes from WSDL. To write a client to connect to your weather Web Service, point `wsimport` at your WSDL:

```
wsimport http://localhost:8080/weather/weather?wsdl
```

The `wsimport` tool outputs JAXB-annotated classes that represent your message XML types as well as your actual stub classes. All of the classes generated correspond to some section of the WSDL file. The XML schema found in the `<types>` section of the WSDL document produces JAXB-annotated classes for the actual content of your XML messages. A class representing the `<service>` WSDL element is generated, and provides a way to access the entire set of web methods described in the WSDL file. In the weather example, the following classes were generated by `wsimport`:

```
./book/GetWeather.class
./book/GetWeatherResponse.class
./book/ObjectFactory.class
./book/package-info.class
./book/Weather.class
./book/WeatherGetter.class
./book/WeatherGetterService.class
```

Note how no Java source files were generated. The `wsimport` tool can generate these as well with the `-s` option. You should rarely need to modify the generated sources, but if you are curious how JAX-WS client classes are annotated, it is worth a look.

Looking back at two WSDL snippets from the weather example, you can see which elements `WeatherGetterService` and `WeatherGetter` were generated from:

```
...
  <service name="WeatherGetterService">
    <port name="WeatherGetterPort" binding="tns:WeatherGetterPortBinding">
      <soap:address
            location="http://localhost:8080/services/weather"></soap:address>
    </port>
  </service>
</definitions>
```

The rest of the generated classes are JAXB-annotated describing the XML schema found in the WSDL `<types>` section.

Generating Stubs Supporting Asynchronous Invocation

By default, `wsimport` does not generate stubs that support asynchronous Web Service invocation. This feature is considered a JAX-WS customization and as such to enable it you will have to create a JAX-WS bindings XML file. These binding files configure JAX-WS extensions and are XML based. To support asynchronous invocation of all of the Web Services described in a particular WSDL file, use a JAX-WS bindings file similar to this one:

```
<bindings
    wsdlLocation="http://localhost:8080/weather/weather?wsdl"
    xmlns="http://java.sun.com/xml/ns/jaxws">
        <enableAsyncMapping>true</enableAsyncMapping>
</bindings>
```

Note that the URL specified in `wsdlLocation` must point to the same WSDL URL passed to the `wsimport` tool. Running `wsimport` with your bindings file now looks like this:

```
wsimport -b bindings.xml http://localhost:8080/weather/weather?wsdl
```

You can customize many more aspects of JAX-WS to Web Service bindings. For more information about these customizations, see this guide at the following URL:

```
http://java.sun.com/webservices/docs/2.0/jaxws/customizations.html
```

I recommend always generating stubs that support asynchronous invocation. The only difference between these stubs and the stubs generated by default is a couple of new methods for each web method. You may end up needing them later, and it never hurts to have a couple of unused methods. Hopefully, `wsimport` will automatically generate stubs supporting asynchronous invocation in the future, without requiring a bindings file.

Calling a Web Service

Depending on how you ran `wsimport`, you can use its generated stubs to call Web Services either synchronously or asynchronously. Synchronous invocation blocks on the current thread until the Web Service call has completed. Synchronous invocation is often appropriate for most server-side applications, because you are already running in a multithreaded application server. On the client side, or any area with user interaction, asynchronous invocation becomes especially useful. Asynchronous Web Service calls are non-blocking, so when the Web Service completes, an event is triggered. For user interfaces, or other areas where you do not want a thread to hang until the Web Service completes (which like any network I/O can have outages, delays, and so on), asynchronous Web Service calls are appropriate.

Both synchronous and asynchronous Web Services calls require the same stub objects. First you must create the main service object. The main service object for generated stubs derives from `javax.xml.ws.Service` (and is annotated with `javax.xml.ws.WebServiceClient`). For every `<port>` element in the source WSDL, there will be a method in the main service object to retrieve that port representing that Web Service endpoint. Those port objects are where the actual Web Service calls happen. Creating your generated main Web Service object for the weather example, `book.WeatherGetterService`, and retrieving the port for the one Web Service method, `getWeather()`, looks like this:

```
import book.Weather;
import book.WeatherGetter;
import book.WeatherGetterService;


...


        WeatherGetterService wgs = new WeatherGetterService();
        WeatherGetter wg = wgs.getWeatherGetterPort();
```

Using `WeatherGetter`, you can either call `getWeather()` synchronously or asynchronously. Before getting into too much client coding, look at some of the key classes used for calling Web Services from JAX-WS clients.

Key Classes and Interfaces (from javax.xml.jws)	Function
AsyncHandler<T>	Callback interface for asynchronous Web Service invocation. Follows asynchronous coding patterns much like the java.util .concurrent package.
BindingProvider	Gives access to the request and response message contexts for client-side Web Services. You can set standard JAX-WS properties here, such as username and password for basic HTTP authentication.
Response<T>	Derives from Future interface from java.util.concurrent, and provides the mechanism to get the result of an asynchronous Web Service invocation.
Service	All generated service classes by wsimport derive from this class. This class requires the WSDL describing a Web Service to function, and is the starting point for retrieving ports to actually call Web Services.

Synchronous Invocation

As the following code shows, synchronous invocation is just a simple method call. Pass `WeatherGetter.getWeather()` an integer zip code, and receive a JAXB-annotated Weather bean that was generated by `wsimport` as the return value:

```
import book.Weather;
import book.WeatherGetter;
import book.WeatherGetterService;

public class WcMain {
  public static void main(String[] args) throws Exception {

    WeatherGetterService wgs = new WeatherGetterService();
    WeatherGetter wg = wgs.getWeatherGetterPort();

    Weather w = wg.getWeather(12345);

    System.out.println(w.getGeneralDescription());
    System.out.println(w.getBarometer() + " : " + w.getBarometerDescription());
    System.out.println(w.getLowTemperature() + " / " + w.getHighTemperature());
...
```

The output from using your weather Web Service is:

```
Sunny
30.761734 : Rising
55 / 70
```

Asynchronous Invocation

Because you generated stubs with asynchronous invocation support, there will be getWeatherAsync() style methods available. Note in the following code the call to getWeatherAsync() — you still pass the integer zip code parameter, but because getWeatherAsync() is non-blocking, you pass it an implementation of the javax.xml.ws.AsyncHandler<T> interface. This interface consists of one callback method. Because the getWeather() web method has a response body of the type book.GetWeather Reponse, this is the type T you use to parameterize AsyncHandler. The following code illustrates creating an anonymous implementation of AsyncHandler<GetWeatherResponse> to receive the callback:

```
import book.Weather;
import book.WeatherGetter;
import book.WeatherGetterService;
import book.GetWeatherResponse;

import java.util.concurrent.Future;
import javax.xml.ws.AsyncHandler;
import javax.xml.ws.Response;


public class WcMain {
  public static void main(String[] args) throws Exception {
    WeatherGetterService wgs = new WeatherGetterService();
    WeatherGetter wg = wgs.getWeatherGetterPort();

    Future f = wg.getWeatherAsync(12345, new
                                        AsyncHandler<GetWeatherResponse>()
        {

            public void handleResponse(Response<GetWeatherResponse> response) {
```

```java
          try  {
            if (!response.isCancelled() && response.isDone()) {
              System.out.println("Async call back");

              GetWeatherResponse msg = response.get();
              Weather w = msg.getWeather();

              System.out.println(w.getGeneralDescription());
              System.out.println(w.getBarometer() + " : " +
                                        w.getBarometerDescription());
              System.out.println(w.getLowTemperature() + " / " +
                                        w.getHighTemperature());
            }
          } catch (Exception ex) {
            ex.printStackTrace();
          }
        }
      });

    // to cancel the async invocation: f.cancel(true)

    // sleep for 10 seconds to give our asyc call time
    // to complete (the async call happens on a background
    // daemon thread, so if this main thread terminates, the
    // VM will terminate regardless of the background thread's
    // activity)
    Thread.sleep(10000);
  }
}
```

Note that the return type from `getWeatherAsync()` is of type `java.util.concurrent.Future`. Using this instance of `Future`, you could cancel your request before it completes using the `cancel()` method:

```java
f.cancel(true); // cancels the asynchronous request
```

Take a look into the callback mechanism provided via the `AsyncHandler<T>` interface. It is called when the Web Service has completed and returned its result or if an error occurred. It follows the same pattern as any generic asynchronous operation that is based on the `java.util.concurrent` package. The `javax.xml.ws.Response<T>` is actually an extension of the `Future` interface, and in addition to normal `Future` capabilities such as checking for completeness and the capability to get the result of the asynchronous call (in your case, the `GetWeatherResponse` object), it also exposes the Web Service response context.

In the following code, first check to make sure the request has completed. If so, you can retrieve the message payload. Note that if any error occurred during the Web Service call, an exception will be thrown on the call to `get()`:

```java
public void handleResponse(Response<GetWeatherResponse> response) {
    try
    {
          GetWeatherResponse msg = response.get();
```

WSDL Location

There is one important fact you need to know about the JAX-WS reference implementation included in JDK 6. The `javax.xml.ws.Service` class, the base class of all Web Service client classes, parses the WSDL from the Web Service during its initialization in its constructor. What this means is that in the following line of code that initializes the `WeatherGetterService`, the WSDL file is downloaded and parsed:

```
// wsdl file is retrieved and parsed within this constructor
WeatherGetterService wgs = new WeatherGetterService();
```

The WSDL is downloaded from the WSDL URL passed in to the `wsimport` *tool*. If the URL is not valid or the file cannot be parsed, an exception is thrown. Oftentimes during development you will probably have either a local test server or a development server, and stubs generated for this server will always by default try to download WSDL from your development server (or local machine). The URL endpoint locations found in the WSDL are then used for the Web Services. This means if you download WSDL from a development server, it will most likely point to the services on the development server, and not your production server. To change where the WSDL is initially parsed, you can do one of the following:

❏   Use the service constructor that specifies the WSDL URL.

❏   Save a copy of the WSDL and load it from either the file system or the classpath (as a resource), and pass the WSDL URL for the file.

❏   Regenerate the stubs, pointing `wsimport` to your production WSDL file.

Option one is most recommended, and how JAX-WS was intended to be used. The following code shows how to initialize a `WeatherGetterService` instance with a WSDL file in a different location from the one used with `wsimport`:

```
WeatherGetterService wgs = new WeatherGetterService
                (new URL("http://production:8080/weather/weather?wsdl"),
                    new QName("http://book/", "WeatherGetterService"));
```

Note how not only you specify the URL of the WSDL file, but which `<service>` element in the WSDL file specifies your service. Changing the URL of the WSDL file is also the intended mechanism for changing the actual URL endpoint for the Web Service as well. Nowhere can you programmatically specify the URL endpoint of the actual Web Service; rather, you must point the service to a different WSDL location has the new location of the URL endpoint.

Saving a copy of the WSDL file (and potentially modifying it to change the location of the Web Service URL endpoints is a valid option to pursue, especially if the WSDL on the server is either large or your network connection to the server is slow. One advantage of always parsing the WSDL from the server though is that you will immediately know if the server Web Service has been updated and your generated code is no longer valid (an exception will be thrown on WSDL parse).

Be aware that anytime you construct a service object, the WSDL is downloaded and parsed. If you constantly interact with large WSDL files, you may wish to break some of them up into smaller, faster parsing pieces.

Web Service Security with Basic HTTP Authentication

Access control is an evolving part of Web Services. Some Web Services incorporate a username and password as part of the actual message, and do custom user verification with every Web Service call. More complex implementations of access control use the WS-Security set of standards provided by the Organization for the Advancement of Structured Information Standards (OASIS). WS-Security is a powerful security mechanism that integrates username tokens, XML digital signatures, and message encryption into SOAP messages. WS-Security is not supported out of the box by JAX-WS or in JDK 6. WS-Security is beginning to be adopted, and both Sun and Microsoft implement it as extensions to their normal Web Service toolkits. WS-Security is promoted because it uses identification information in the SOAP header and can therefore be passed around multiple Web Services all the while keeping the identity of the sender — especially because with WS-Security you can digitally sign pieces of a message as originating from a given entity. As messages are then routed through a complex SOA, what information came from whom is always known.

Though WS-Security is definitely the way of the future, most production Web Services do not need its complex distributed levels of security. The main use case for WS-Security is for routing messages and keeping the security information intact. If you are implementing a single server and not routing messages, you may not need WS-Security. Once WS-Security is more mature and integrated out of the box with JAX-WS, it will make sense to use it all the time.

Enabling Basic HTTP Authentication on the Server

Basic HTTP authentication often more than suffices for determining the identity of the calling party. All servlet containers support basic HTTP authentication and Tomcat integrates it with its security realms. Following is the `web.xml` file from the weather web application example, with basic HTTP authentication enabled. Note how it only allows authenticated users in the `tomcat` role to use the weather Web Service in the `<auth-constraint>` element:

```
...
<security-constraint>
  <web-resource-collection>
    <web-resource-name>
      Weather web service
    </web-resource-name>
    <url-pattern>/weather/*</url-pattern>
  </web-resource-collection>
  <auth-constraint>
      <role-name>tomcat</role-name>
  </auth-constraint>
</security-constraint>

<login-config>
  <auth-method>BASIC</auth-method>
  <realm-name>UserDatabase</realm-name>
</login-config>

</web-app>
```

The particular realm used in this example is Tomcat's default realm, where users, passwords, and roles are specified in the `TOMCAT_HOME/conf/tomcat-users.xml` file. In a production environment, you would want to use a database-backed realm. See Tomcat documentation for how to use and configure different realm types. The following code lists the `tomcat-users.xml` file. Only users with the `tomcat` role will be able to use the Web Service based on the authentication constraint placed in the `web.xml` file:

```
<?xml version='1.0' encoding='utf-8'?>
<tomcat-users>
  <role rolename="tomcat"/>
  <role rolename="role1"/>
  <user username="tomcat" password="tomcat" roles="tomcat"/>
  <user username="both" password="tomcat" roles="tomcat,role1"/>
  <user username="mytestusername" password="itspassword" roles="tomcat"/>
  <user username="role1" password="tomcat" roles="role1"/>
</tomcat-users>
```

Those two files have now configured the Web Service for basic HTTP authentication. Any callers will have to specify a username and password that has the `tomcat` role for access. You don't even have to change the Web Service `book.WeatherGetter` code if all you want to do is limit access. Suppose that you have a different type of Web Service, one where different results would be returned depending on who the calling user is. The `javax.xml.ws.WebServiceContext` class does just that and provides your Web Services with the connected users' `java.security.Principal`. `WebServiceContexts` are provided to your Web Service classes through the Java EE resource injection feature. The following code is all that is necessary for your Web Service class to receive a `WebServiceContext` instance:

```
...
import javax.annotation.Resource;
import java.security.Principal;
import javax.xml.ws.WebServiceContext;
...
@WebService(name="WeatherGetter")
public class WeatherGetter {
  @Resource WebServiceContext wsContext;
...
```

Note, though, that the `WebServiceContext` object is only valid inside of `WebMethod` annotated methods — do not access it from elsewhere. The following code then allows you to get a user's identification through the `Principal` object, and check to see to which roles the user belongs:

```
@WebMethod
  public @WebResult(name="weather") Weather
            getWeather(@WebParam(name="zipcode") int zipCode) {

    Principal usrPrincipal = wsContext.getUserPrincipal();
    if (usrPrincipal != null) {
      logger.info("User '" + usrPrincipal.getName() +
                            "' has accessed getWeather() service.");
    }

    if (wsContext.isUserInRole("tomcat")) {
      // can perform special behaviors here based upon user roles
      // and login names
      //
      // this is especially useful when different users have
      // different accesses and permissions in a database or file system
      // etc.
          ...
  }
...
```

Note that if the `Principal` is `null`, it means no user has been authenticated (and is what would happen had you not enabled HTTP basic authentication). As you can see, enabling HTTP authentication is simple and built right in to the JAX-WS framework.

When using basic HTTP authentication, passwords are sent in the clear. You should always send HTTP passwords using a secure HTTPS connection. Do not allow users to access your Web Services under normal HTTP if you are using basic authentication.

Enabling Basic HTTP Authentication on the Client

Using basic HTTP authentication on the client side is even easier than implementing it on the server. There are two different ways to do it. The first uses the normal `java.net` JDK method of doing basic HTTP authentication. Because the JAX-WS implementation in the JDK utilizes `java.net` for its HTTP support, this works. The other way is to set a couple of properties in the request context of the `WeatherGetter` object generated by `wsimport`.

First look at using the JDK's native support for basic HTTP authentication. This has an advantage over using the JAX-WS request context. Remember that JAX-WS must parse the WSDL file upon the construction of your client service object. If that URL is also protected by HTTP authentication (which it most likely will be because most of the time the WSDL URL is the same as the Web Service endpoint URL, but with the addition of the query string '?wsdl'), then an exception will be thrown on service creation and you will be unable to call the service. The JDK basic authentication route avoids this, because the same authentication credentials will be automatically applied to the WSDL URL as well.

The `java.net.Authenticator` class handles requests for basic HTTP authentication. By default, it always returns a `null` `java.net.PasswordAuthentication` object, and you will be unable to use the `java.net.URL` class to access any URL that is protected by basic HTTP authentication. To override this standard behavior, you must extend the abstract `Authenticator` class and provide your own `getPasswordAuthentication()` implementation. The simple authentication class that follows only provides user credentials if you are using the HTTPS protocol, and connecting to the specified weather Web Service host:

```java
import java.net.Authenticator;
import java.net.PasswordAuthentication;

public class BasicHTTPAuthenticator extends Authenticator {

  @Override
  protected PasswordAuthentication getPasswordAuthentication() {
    // only return the password if we are using https
    // (we don't want our password sent in the clear)
    if ("https".equalsIgnoreCase(this.getRequestingProtocol()) &&
                    "localhost".equalsIgnoreCase(this.getRequestingHost())) {

      return new PasswordAuthentication("mytestusername",
          new char[] { 'i', 't', 's', 'p', 'a', 's',
                                              's', 'w', 'o', 'r', 'd' });

    }

    return null;
  }
}
```

Note that if you were writing a graphical client, or one with user interaction, you could write an implementation of `java.net.Authenticator` that prompts the user for their username and password. To use your implementation of `java.net.Authenticator`, set it as the JDK's default authenticator by using Authenticator's static `setDefault()` method as shown:

```
Authenticator.setDefault(new BasicHTTPAuthenticator());
```

Now transparently, if either the WSDL URL or your Web Service endpoint requires HTTP authentication, the JDK will automatically pass your username and password (they will only be passed if authentication is required, and in your implementation, if the transport is HTTPS).

The other mechanism for sending the username and password to your Web Service endpoint requires less code, but will fail if the WSDL URL also requires authentication. You can get around the WSDL URL problem by specifying your own URL, as demonstrated earlier in this chapter. The `javax.xml.ws.BindingProvider` interface allows access to the request and response contexts for the SOAP messages. From here, you can set a few standard properties, including the username and password for basic HTTP authentication. For classes generated with `wsimport`, any interface representing a WSDL `<port>` (in this case, `book.WeatherGetter`), will also implement `BindingProvider`. The following code illustrates setting the username and password using the JAX-WS standard username and password properties:

```
import javax.xml.ws.BindingProvider;
...
    WeatherGetterService wgs = new WeatherGetterService();
    WeatherGetter wg = wgs.getWeatherGetterPort();

    ((BindingProvider) wg).getRequestContext()
      .put(BindingProvider.USERNAME_PROPERTY, "mytestusername");
    ((BindingProvider) wg).getRequestContext()
      .put(BindingProvider.PASSWORD_PROPERTY, "itspassword");

    //call web service with zip code 12345, with basic http authentication
    Weather w = wg.getWeather(12345);
...
```

Again, it is important to note that you should always use HTTPS for security when sending basic HTTP authentication.

Putting It All Together: Weather System Tray App

One client-side possibility for a weather forecast Web Service is an application that runs in the system tray that allows the user to check the current weather forecast. Using the new system tray API in JDK 6, putting together an application to monitor the weather using your Web Service is straightforward. When using Web Services from a thick client, such as a Swing application or system tray app, asynchronous invocation is the way to go. Asynchronous calls do not block the GUI thread, and integrate with the `java.util.concurrent` API, making multithreaded programming in Java easier than before. With thick client apps, the only alternative to asynchronous invocation is creating and managing your own background threads, and invoking the Web Service synchronously on these threads. This is a perfectly valid approach (if JAX-WS did not support an asynchronous invocation model, it would be the only approach). For the system tray app, use the asynchronous invocation method.

One big advantage to the JAX-WS asynchronous model is the ability to cancel a request that has been sent cleanly and simply. You will need this ability almost always with asynchronous programming, and one of the difficulties of using your own background thread is that the main way to cancel is by either aborting threads (highly discouraged, because it can cause JVM deadlocks), or interrupting the thread. Interrupting the thread causes an `InterruptedException`, which you can then handle as a cancel request. If possible, use the JAX-WS asynchronous invocation model, and you can avoid this extra complexity.

Weather Watcher Application

The Weather Watcher application will be an application running in the system tray, and provide the user with the ability to get the latest weather forecast from a user-specified zip code. It will communicate using the JAX-WS asynchronous invocation model, and provide the user the ability to cancel a weather request that has already been sent. Figure 11-17 shows the context menu for the Weather Watcher system tray application. When a user selects Get Weather, the application will initiate an asynchronous call to your weather Web Service.

Figure 11-17

The Weather Watcher application is implemented in one Java class, `book.WeatherWatcher`. There are two main areas of interest in the code: the first is the configuration of the system tray icon, and the second is the asynchronous invocation of the weather Web Service. JDK 6 makes creating tray icons a breeze. In the constructor, set up the system tray icon, and hook up all of the events. The asynchronous invocation occurs in the `book.WeatherWatcher.actionPerformed()` method (`book.WeatherWatcher` implements `java.awt.event.ActionListener`), and is kicked off whenever the user clicks Get Weather.

The key imports for using asynchronous invocation are highlighted in the following code segment, as well as the field `future`, which allows you to cancel Web Services requests already kicked off:

```
...
import java.awt.AWTException;
import java.awt.Image;
import java.awt.MenuItem;
import java.awt.PopupMenu;
import java.awt.SystemTray;
import java.awt.Toolkit;
import java.awt.TrayIcon;
import java.awt.event.ActionEvent;
import java.awt.event.ActionListener;
import java.net.Authenticator;
import java.net.PasswordAuthentication;
import java.util.concurrent.Future;

import javax.swing.JOptionPane;
import javax.swing.SwingUtilities;
```

```
import javax.xml.ws.AsyncHandler;
import javax.xml.ws.Response;

public class WeatherWatcher implements ActionListener {

  private static class BasicHTTPAuthenticator extends Authenticator {
... (same basic http authentication as shown previously in this chapter)
  }

  private TrayIcon icon;

  private WeatherGetterService service;
  private WeatherGetter weatherGetter;

  private int zipcode = 12345;

  private MenuItem getWeatherMI;
  private MenuItem cancelMI;

  // used for cancelling requests
  private Future future;
...
```

In the `WeatherWatcher` constructor, you create the popup menu the tray icon displays as a context menu when the user right-clicks the icon in the system tray. Note the bolded code segment where the Cancel menu item's (`cancelMI`) click event is hooked up; this code segment cancels an active Web Service request. In this application, the Cancel menu is only enabled for user interaction when a Web Service is kicked off, and subsequently disabled when the Web Service is either cancelled or terminates:

```
public WeatherWatcher() throws AWTException {
  Authenticator.setDefault(new BasicHTTPAuthenticator());

  service = new WeatherGetterService();
  weatherGetter = service.getWeatherGetterPort();

  // if unsupported, throw exception first before
  // doing anything else
  SystemTray sysTray = SystemTray.getSystemTray();

  Image wImage = Toolkit.getDefaultToolkit().getImage(
      WeatherWatcher.class.getResource("book-weather-icon.png"));

  PopupMenu menu = new PopupMenu();

  getWeatherMI = menu.add(new MenuItem("Get Weather"));
  getWeatherMI.addActionListener(this);

  cancelMI = menu.add(new MenuItem("Cancel"));
  cancelMI.addActionListener(new ActionListener() {
    public void actionPerformed(ActionEvent evt) {
      if (future != null && !future.isDone()) {
        future.cancel(true);

        getWeatherMI.setEnabled(true);
```

```
            cancelMI.setEnabled(false);
        }
    }
});
// initially disable the cancel menu item, since there is no active request
cancelMI.setEnabled(false);

menu.add(new MenuItem("-"));

menu.add(new MenuItem("Configure Zipcode")).addActionListener(
    new ActionListener() {
... (retrieve user input for zipcode field)
    });

menu.add(new MenuItem("Exit")).addActionListener(new ActionListener() {

  public void actionPerformed(ActionEvent evt) {
    System.exit(0);
  }
});

this.icon = new TrayIcon(wImage, "Weather Watcher", menu);

sysTray.add(this.icon);
  }
...
```

The `actionPerformed()` method of the `WeatherWatcher` class is where weather Web Services requests are started. Because `WeatherGetter.getWeatherAsync()` is called, the request is non-blocking and starts up in a background thread. When the request terminates (either successfully or fails with an exception), the anonymous `AsyncHandler<GetWeatherResponse>`'s `handleResponse()` method is called:

```
// called when user clicks "Get Weather" context menu item
// initiates asynchronous web service call
public void actionPerformed(ActionEvent evt) {
  this.getWeatherMI.setEnabled(false);
  cancelMI.setEnabled(true);

  future = weatherGetter.getWeatherAsync(zipcode,
      new AsyncHandler<GetWeatherResponse>() {

        // note that this reponse method is on another thread,
        // so we have to get back on the GUI thread to do any
        // updates to our GUI components
        public void handleResponse(Response<GetWeatherResponse> resp) {
          try {
            final Weather w;

            if (!resp.isCancelled() && resp.isDone()) {
              // if there was an exception during the web service processing,
              // it will be thrown here
              GetWeatherResponse gwr = resp.get();
              w = gwr.getWeather();
            } else {
```

```
                // user cancelled the request, re-enable menus and return
                try {
                    SwingUtilities.invokeAndWait(new Runnable() {

                        public void run() {
                            cancelMI.setEnabled(false);
                            getWeatherMI.setEnabled(true);
                        }

                    });
                } catch (Exception ex) {
                    ex.printStackTrace();
                }

                return;
            }
    ...
```

All execution in `handleResponse()` occurs on a different thread. This is extremely important—it means whenever you want to update your GUI components you have to get back on the GUI thread. Remember that the `javax.swing.SwingUtilites` class facilitates doing just that. Use its `invokeAndWait()` method to execute code back on the GUI thread. Even if you did not utilize the JAX-WS asynchronous invocation model, you would still have to do this whenever you execute GUI code on a thread other than the GUI thread. If you did not use the asynchronous model for the client, whenever a request was active, the system tray icon would be unresponsive, and there would be no way to see what the previous forecast was, or cancel the current request—basically the application would be held hostage and user interaction denied until the web request completed. Using the asynchronous invocation model avoids this problem.

The following code either displays the result of the successful Web Service call to the user, or displays an error message if the Web Service request terminated with an exception:

```
        try {
            // display the weather forecast received to the user,
            // and set the tooltip so the user can view it later
            SwingUtilities.invokeAndWait(new Runnable() {

                public void run() {
                    cancelMI.setEnabled(false);
                    getWeatherMI.setEnabled(true);

                    StringBuffer msg = new StringBuffer();

                    msg.append("Zipcode: " + zipcode + "\n\n");
                    msg.append(w.getGeneralDescription() + "\n");
                    msg.append(w.getBarometer() + " : "
                        + w.getBarometerDescription() + "\n");
                    msg.append(w.getLowTemperature() + " / "
                        + w.getHighTemperature());

                    icon.displayMessage("Weather Report", msg.toString(),
                        TrayIcon.MessageType.INFO);

                    icon.setToolTip(msg.toString());
```

```
                          }
                    });
              } catch (Exception e) {
                 e.printStackTrace();
              }

        } catch (final Exception ex) {
           // there was an error during our web service request, display
           // the error to the user
           try {
              SwingUtilities.invokeAndWait(new Runnable() {

                 public void run() {
                    cancelMI.setEnabled(false);
                    getWeatherMI.setEnabled(true);

                    icon.displayMessage("Error Getting Weather", ex
                       .getMessage(), TrayIcon.MessageType.ERROR);
                 }

              });
           } catch (Exception ie) {
              ie.printStackTrace();
           }
        }
     }

     });
  }

...(main method)

}
```

The result of a successful Web Service request is shown in Figure 11-18. Web Services provide a powerful mechanism to expose data normally retrieved by a standard browser-based web application to a variety of clients, and the Web Service import tools provided with JAX-WS make it quick and easy to incorporate Web Services into your clients.

Figure 11-18

Using TCPMon to Simulate a Slow Connection

During the development of distributed systems, many developers will often run both the client and the server on their machine. This has the effect of making many network communications seem much faster than they actually will be in production, and never really gives them worst-case scenarios, such as server machines being unavailable (with potentially long waits for connection timeouts), or network congestion and server load, effectively slowing down communications. Just in the Weather Watcher example from the previous section, you ran both the client weather system tray app and the Tomcat server on the same machine. The side effect here was that the weather request happened so fast you were unable to test the Cancel functionality — which allows the user to cancel an outbound request. Apache TCPMon provides a method for simulating slow connections, which allows you to test your application more thoroughly. In the weather watcher case, it allows you to test the Cancel functionality because the request to the server will take enough time that you'd have an opportunity to test canceling before it successfully returned. It's also a good idea to do this type of testing because it will really highlight parts of your client app that maybe did not have a Web Service request threaded (and as such will freeze your app for a while), or show you different user interaction patterns that could only happen while a request was outbound.

Configuring TCPMon for simulating a slow connection is straightforward. As you can see in Figure 11-19, you can set the number of bytes to send before a connection pause. The settings shown in the figure make your Web Service request take about six to eight seconds, providing ample time to test the Cancel request functionality of your application.

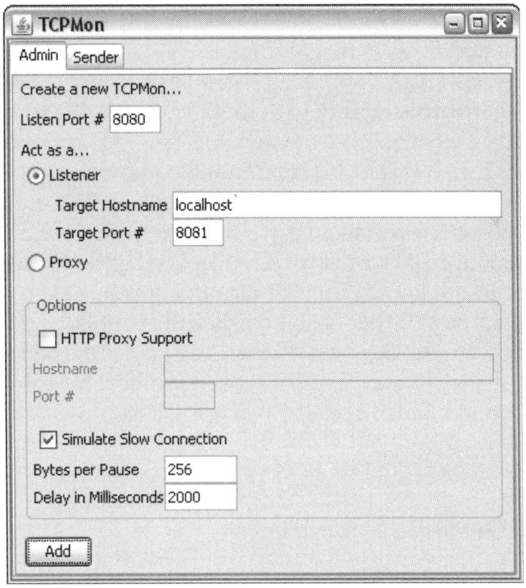

Figure 11-19

Note how in Figure 11-19 you start a listener on port 8080 and forward all requests to port 8081. Doing so means that if Tomcat is running on port 8081 instead of its default port of 8080, TCPMon will be entirely transparent to your client app — your weather application still connects to `http://local host:8080/weather/weather`. To configure Tomcat to run on port 8081, modify the `TOMCAT_HOME/conf/server.xml` file as shown here:

```
    ...
    <!-- Define a non-SSL HTTP/1.1 Connector on port 8080 -->
    <Connector port="8081" maxHttpHeaderSize="8192"
            maxThreads="150" minSpareThreads="25" maxSpareThreads="75"
```

595

```
                    enableLookups="false" redirectPort="8443" acceptCount="100"
                    connectionTimeout="20000" disableUploadTimeout="true" />
    ...
```

Other Client-Side Possibilities

Web Services give client applications language and platform freedom. They can be thick or thin clients, and can use the information in your services in a variety of ways. Information-centric applications could integrate a variety of Web Services. Applications could query for map information, for traffic information, and weather forecasts, and overlay it all on one view. Customized applications could be written to display information from your various online accounts, such as car insurance information, bills you need to pay, your various bank account and retirement plans, and tie the information all together in an automated way. Once more and more public web sites begin to offer Web Services, these possibilities will continue to balloon. If you are deploying a service for a particular customer, if you Web Service enable it, they can find uses for it and integrate with other services you do not even know about. Web Services enable the current generation of dynamic web sites to share their data with potentially any application, not simply web browsers and users manually retrieving their data.

Web Services Interoperability Technologies Project (WSIT)

The Web Services Interoperability Technologies Project (WSIT) is a Sun-sponsored project on java.net to implement many extensions for JAX-WS. Many standards from OASIS are in the process of being implemented and tested for interoperability with the Microsoft .NET platform. WS-Security and the many other WS-* standards are being implemented, focusing on security, messaging, metadata, and quality of service. The WSIT project is a large undertaking and one of its goals is transparency to the end user. It will integrate with the JAX-WS model for client Web Service connectivity, and wsimport will automatically generate classes that will handle WS-Security, reliable messaging, and so on. To the client Web Services programmer, the goal is transparency. Deploying Web Services is where you will have to be not only aware of these technologies, but pick the ones appropriate for your server, or for different service points in your SOA. The WS-* set of standards will eventually make Web Services into a reliable platform for mission-critical applications. It will then have all of the benefits of CORBA, but be more platform independent, and have its simpler XML-based protocol for communications. To follow the WSIT project (also called project Tango), see the following URL:

```
https://wsit.dev.java.net/
```

The set of standards from OASIS can be found here:

```
http://www.oasis-open.org/committees/tc_cat.php?cat=ws
```

These technologies are still maturing, and at the time of this writing, project Tango (which has only released its first milestone release), only interoperates with Microsoft technology preview of its extensions to its Web Service stack. Now that JAX-WS is a core part of the Java platform, it should not be too much longer for these technologies to mature. In the meantime though, by beginning to move your existing Web Services to JAX-WS (and creating new ones using JAX-WS), you will be in a good position to adopt these technologies when they mature. Interoperability should always be the number one goal when developing and deploying Web Services — because the whole point is cross-platform communication.

Summary

In this chapter, you have learned some possible ways to enable Java components in your application to communicate with external components in other applications or systems that could have been written in a variety of languages. Sockets provide the building blocks for all other technologies discussed in this chapter. With TCP/IP, they provide a reliable byte stream over a network that any language with a socket API can use. This is the lowest level of interprocess communication. Sockets are, however, not in themselves a guarantee of communication between two different components; a common protocol must also be spoken. In this chapter you implemented a small portion of the HTTP specification to gain an understanding of the immense undertaking implementing a protocol can be. RMI, CORBA, and Web Services are all built on top of sockets and TCP/IP. RMI and CORBA implement complex protocols allowing them to provide such features as reliability, sessions, and transactions, and event callbacks. They are cornerstone technologies for many existing enterprise systems. Java EE makes extensive use of RMI, because RMI combined with JNDI allows for the objects of a system to be transparently spread across multiple machines without any changes in the application's code. RMI and CORBA have become intertwined to some degree since support for CORBA's IIOP protocol was added to RMI. Now RMI and CORBA have basic interoperability, and this makes it easier for developers to integrate legacy CORBA systems into their modern Java EE equivalents.

None of the technologies used in this chapter is inherently better than any other. The right tool is needed for the right job. Sockets provide a low-level API that allows for the optimization and creation of new protocols. Some projects may require this — the remote control of external hardware, such as robotic devices, can usually be done best starting with sockets, and then building a more developer-friendly API layered on top. RMI and CORBA provide great foundations for distributed systems, and an understanding of them is necessary to utilize the full power of Java EE. The network latency implications of remote method calls must also be considered in any distributed system. Web Services complement existing web portals. They will be the simple mechanism by which information on the World Wide Web is shared for use by machines, not just by human eyes. Distributed applications and systems will probably make use of more than one component-to-component technology. As the integration of systems and information becomes easier with more platform-agnostic APIs and technologies, a whole new breed of information-centric applications can arise.

Web Services are the future of distributed computing, and enable the evolution of the current World Wide Web of unstructured information to one of structured information. Web Services are not as advanced technologically as RMI or CORBA, but there is power in their simplicity. Web Services require minimal development effort to implement and, because all of their underlying protocols are human readable, are easy to debug. With the OASIS WS-* standards, Web Services are on the path to support transactions, reliable messaging, and stronger security models. Once projects like WSIT and Microsoft's Indigo mature, these next-generation Web Service goals will be a reality.

12

Service Oriented Integration

The purpose of this chapter is to introduce you to a number of techniques and APIs for performing systems integration. Building a new system from scratch is quite an undertaking, but it is not the norm today — most companies have an extensive legacy IT investment. Their systems were developed over time to meet a specific need. Whether the need was customer service, order fulfillment, or finance, there was something that drove the tremendous cost and heartache associated with IT development.

Eventually the systems that represent the IT infrastructure of a corporation grow to the point where sharing data and collapsing stovepipes not only starts to make sense; it's the only option.

This chapter differs from a number of the other chapters in this book because it is focused on specific solutions for software integration. Throughout this book you have learned a number of APIs, tools, and techniques for building software. This chapter, on the other hand, examines some specialized issues related to integrating and managing distributed applications.

Service Oriented Architecture

One of the biggest design challenges is making systems that will be stable as they adapt to change over time. Service Oriented Architectures (SOA) are shown to be more stable because they reuse core business functions. Figure 12-1 shows a graphic depiction of a service oriented architecture.

In an SOA the IT investment a company has made is leveraged by creating Service Layers around their existing applications. These services provide a standard interface to application functions that span the enterprise. A number of enabling technologies facilitate this design. The next section discusses some of these technologies and where they are used in building an SOA.

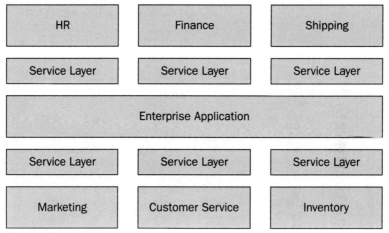

Figure 12-1

Enabling Technology

Three APIs stand out as important tools for building a service oriented architecture:

JAVA Technology	Relevance
Web Services and XML Technology	Web Services are the public face of a service oriented architecture. They define the information contract between two systems.
Java Management Extension (JMX)	JMX provides the service infrastructure to deploy and manage applications across a network.
Java Messaging Service (JMS)	JMS provides location-independent processing of information via message endpoints.

Web Services are covered in Chapter 11, so they will not be discussed here. Instead, this chapter focuses on the service fulfillment side of SOAs by looking at enabling technologies for integration, as well as Integration Patterns for designing distributed systems.

To understand the basis for this type of approach you first look at some underlying technologies of JMX. JMX is the Java standard for managing remote resources. Following that, you examine JMS for loosely integrating systems via Message-Oriented Middleware (MOM).

Java Management Extensions

Java Management Extension (JMX) is a technology for managing and monitoring applications systems and network devices. This technology allows you to deploy specialized Java classes called MBeans to a software agent and interact with them at runtime.

Why Is JMX Important?

As of JDK 1.5, JMX is a standard part of the Java Platform. It is also the foundation for many of the J2EE application servers including JBoss, Websphere, and Weblogic. By understanding JMX technology, it will be easier for you to work with these products as well as develop your own extensions with this technology.

The JMX Architecture

JMX is composed of a three-layer architecture. Each layer has its own responsibility in creating manageable resources. The layers are Instrumentation, Agent, and Remote Management. Figure 12-2 shows the high-level architecture.

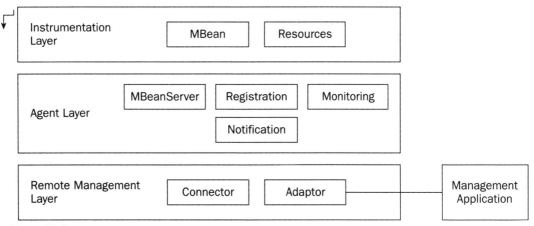

Figure 12-2

The following table describes the role of each layer within the architecture.

Layer	Description
Instrumentation	Defines the resources, called MBeans, to be managed in the JMX architecture. This can be anything from applications, services, to network devices.
Agent	The infrastructure that allows for management, deployment, event notification, and monitoring. All communication with the Instrumented resources happens through the Agent layer. The most significant component is the MBeanServer.
Remote Management	Defines the external communication with the agent by specifying protocol adaptors and connectors. An adaptor allows a client application to communicate with an MBeanServer. An MBeanServer must deploy at least one adaptor. There are numerous adaptors for different protocols. HTTP, RMI, and SMTP are a few basic adaptors for communicating with an MBeanServer.

Now that you understand the architecture at a high level, you can create a simple example to utilize a few of the capabilities of the technology.

Creating and Managing a Standard MBean

The simplest JMX example is actually quite powerful. The steps in the process of deploying a managed bean are as follows:

1. Create a managed bean, by specifying an interface that complies with the MBean specification. In this example, call it WorkerMBean.

2. Deploy the WorkerMBean to an MBeanServer.

3. Manipulate the MBean via the standard management console.

First, look at the code for the WorkerMBean. It consists of an interface and an implementing class. For standard MBeans, the interface name must end with the MBean suffix. The interface defines an attribute called Running by defining the setRunning() and isRunning() methods. This is consistent with standard JavaBean naming conventions. The interface also defines three operations, start(), stop(), and calcGreeting(). This interface defines services that will be exposed to the MBeanServer:

```
package wrox.ch12.jmx;

public interface WorkerMBean {

public boolean isRunning();
public void setRunning(boolean running);
public void start();
public void stop();
public String calcGreeting( );

}
```

The next step is to implement the interface. There are three rules that must apply to the implementing class:

❑ The implementing class must be in the same package as the MBean interface.

❑ The implementing class must be named the same as the interface minus the MBean suffix (in this case, Worker).

❑ The implementing class must have a public zero parameter constructor.

Here is the implementation of the example. The key is that you have an MBean with methods to monitor its state, in this case Running. You have a simple business method calcGreeting(), that represents the service you are providing:

```
package wrox.ch12.jmx;

import java.util.Calendar;

public class Worker implements WorkerMBean {

boolean running = false;

public boolean isRunning() {
```

```
        return running;
    }

    public void setRunning(boolean running) {
        this.running = running;
    }

    public void start() {
     running = true;
    }

    public void stop() {
     running = false;
    }

    public String calcGreeting() {

        if (!isRunning())
            return "not available";

        Calendar time = Calendar.getInstance();
        if (time.get(Calendar.AM_PM) == 0) {
            return "good morning";
        } else {
            return "good evening";
        }

    }
}
```

The next step is to deploy this MBean to an MBeanServer as part of a running Agent. First request the MBeanServer from the running JVM. Then create an ObjectName to reference the MBean. All MBeans are required to have a unique name called the ObjectName. Finally, register the WorkerMBean with the MBeanServer:

```
package wrox.ch12.jmx;

import java.lang.management.ManagementFactory;

import javax.management.MBeanServer;
import javax.management.ObjectName;

public class Agent {

 public static void main(String[] args) {
     Worker worker = new Worker();
     MBeanServer mbs = ManagementFactory.getPlatformMBeanServer();

     try {
        ObjectName name = new ObjectName("wrox.ch12.jmx:type=Worker");
        mbs.registerMBean(worker, name);
        System.out.println("Agent Started..");
        Thread.sleep(Long.MAX_VALUE);
     } catch (Exception e) {
```

```
                    e.printStackTrace();
        }
    }
}
```

Because all MBeans are uniquely referenced within an MBean server, their object name has a special format. An `ObjectName` is made up of two parts, a domain and a name value pair separated by a colon:

```
wrox.ch12.jmx:type=Worker
```

This is the name assigned to this MBean with the domain being `wrox.ch12.jmx` and the descriptive name being `type=worker`.

The next step is to run the agent and connect to the agent via the standard management console. Several consoles are available. You will be using JConsole included with JDK 1.6. Open two command prompts and type to start the agent:

```
C:\> Java -Dcom.sun.management.jmxremote wrox.ch12.jmx.Agent
```

And the console:

```
C:\>jconsole
```

You should see a login prompt that looks like Figure 12-3.

Figure 12-3

JConsole is the management application you are going to use to connect to and manipulate your managed resources. As you can see from Figure 12-3 there are two types of connections: Local and Remote.

An example of a remote connection will be provided later. For now, select Local and select the name of the Agent you started, `wrox.ch12.jmx.Agent`.

There is a lot of useful information in the JConsole application such as the health and memory usage of the agent JVM. Select the MBeans tab so you can interact with the MBean you have deployed, as shown in Figure 12-4.

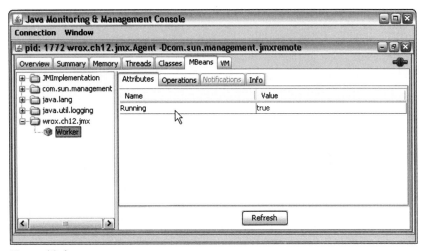

Figure 12-4

The MBeans tab shows all the manageable Java objects deployed to the JVM. Select the Operations sub-tab and click the calcGreetings button. You should see Figure 12-5.

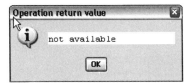

Figure 12-5

This is because you prevented the service from running until you explicitly started it. So click the Start button, and then click calcGreetings again. You should see Figure 12-6.

Figure 12-6

This demonstrates a stateful interaction with a Java object in a running JVM. This is possible by following the standard JavaBean naming convention and by deploying a bean to an MBean server. This is a simple example but the sky is the limit on services and devices you can manage via JMX.

The next example exercises more of the management services of the API via the `MBeanServer` interface. The following section explores Java Messaging Service and makes the JMX components message-driven.

JMX Management

Two JSRs define JMX technology:

❑ JSR 003: Java Management Extensions (JMXTM) Specification API 1.2

❑ JSR 160: Java Management Extensions (JMX) Remote API 1.0

The examples in this section illustrate the management features of the JMX API. You will do the following:

1. Create a `RemoteAgent` that is accessible via an RMI registry.

2. Connect to the agent via a remote client.

3. Query for MBeans deployed to an MBeanServer.

4. Deploy a Monitor MBean and receive notifications when the MBean changes.

RemoteAgent

You can tell by the package declaration that the `RemoteAgent` uses the `javax.management` and the `javax.management.remote` packages. The remote package defines the standard for creating a connector server so the agent can receive external process requests:

```
package wrox.ch12.jmx;

import javax.management.MBeanServer;
import javax.management.MBeanServerFactory;
import javax.management.remote.JMXConnectorServer;
import javax.management.remote.JMXConnectorServerFactory;
import javax.management.remote.JMXServiceURL;
```

The following code creates an `MBeanServer`, registers the `ConnectorServer`, and then starts the connector to listen for incoming requests:

```
public class RemoteAgent {

  public static void main(String[] args) throws Exception {
      MBeanServer mbs = MBeanServerFactory.createMBeanServer();
      JMXServiceURL url = new
JMXServiceURL("service:jmx:rmi:///jndi/rmi://localhost:9999/server");
JMXConnectorServer server = JMXConnectorServerFactory.newJMXConnectorServer(url,
null, mbs);
```

```
        System.out.println("starting rmi connector server");
        server.start();
    }
  }
```

To run the agent, first start the RMI Registry on port 9999:

```
C:\>rmiregistry 9999 &
```

Then start the agent. The agent will bind to the RMI Registry and register the application stubs required to communicate with the `MBeanServer`:

```
c:\>java wrox.ch12.jmx.RemoteAgent
```

With the agent started you will be able to connect to it via the JConsole application as you did in the previous example. This time select Remote connection and specify the following as the connection string:

```
service:jmx:rmi:///jndi/rmi://localhost:9999/server
```

The application should behave in the same way even though you are connecting through a different connector. The connector provides transparent access to the `MBeanServer`.

RemoteClient

Right now there are not any MBeans of interest deployed to the server. The next step is to use a remote client to deploy and manipulate them via the `MBeanServer`:

```
package wrox.ch12.jmx;

import java.util.Iterator;
import java.util.Set;

import javax.management.MBeanServerConnection;
import javax.management.ObjectName;
import javax.management.Query;
import javax.management.QueryExp;
import javax.management.remote.JMXConnector;
import javax.management.remote.JMXConnectorFactory;
import javax.management.remote.JMXServiceURL;

public class RemoteClient {

  MBeanServerConnection connection = null;
```

The client starts out by creating the same URL you used in creating the server. Then connect to the server remotely:

```
public RemoteClient() throws Exception {
  JMXServiceURL url = new JMXServiceURL(
            "service:jmx:rmi:///jndi/rmi://localhost:9999/server");
  JMXConnector connector = JMXConnectorFactory.connect(url);
  connection = connector.getMBeanServerConnection();

.}
```

With the connection interface you can manipulate the managed resources. The deploy method creates three workers. Notice that the same type of object can be deployed to the same server as long as the `ObjectName` is unique:

```
void deploy() throws Exception {
    connection.createMBean("wrox.ch12.jmx.Worker",
                new ObjectName("wrox.ch12.jmx:type=Worker,number=1"));
    connection.createMBean("wrox.ch12.jmx.Worker",
                new ObjectName("wrox.ch12.jmx:type=Worker,number=2"));
    connection.createMBean("wrox.ch12.jmx.Worker",
                    new ObjectName("wrox.ch12.jmx:type=Worker,number=3"));
.}
```

The next method, `lookup()`, is an example of using the `MBeanServer` query interface. This query will return all the MBean deployed to the `wrox.ch12.jmx` domain. The wildcard * will match any character name within the `wrox.ch12.jmx` domain:

```
void lookup() throws Exception {
  ObjectName on = new ObjectName("wrox.ch12.jmx:*");
  Set set = connection.queryNames(on, null);
  for (Iterator iter = set.iterator(); iter.hasNext();) {
      ObjectName bean = (ObjectName) iter.next();
      System.out.println("deployed..=" + bean.toString());
  }
}
```

To build on that the `checkRunning()` method also does a lookup of deployed MBeans. But it also requires that the attribute named `Running` is set to the value of `true` via the `QueryExp`. Also notice the getter and setter pair for the `Running` property is a capital R. This differs from the standard JavaBean naming convention for properties:

```
void checkRunning() throws Exception {
  ObjectName on = new ObjectName("wrox.ch12.jmx:*");
  QueryExp exp = Query.eq(Query.attr("Running"), Query.value(true));
  Set set = connection.queryNames(on, exp);
  for (Iterator iter = set.iterator(); iter.hasNext();) {
    ObjectName bean = (ObjectName) iter.next();
    System.out.println("running.. MBean =" + bean.toString());
  }
}
```

The method `remove()` does the opposite of deploy — it removes the MBeans that match certain criteria:

```
void remove() throws Exception {
  ObjectName on = new ObjectName("wrox.ch12.jmx:*");
  Set set = connection.queryNames(on, null);
    for (Iterator iter = set.iterator(); iter.hasNext();) {
      ObjectName bean = (ObjectName) iter.next();
      System.out.println("removing..=" + bean.toString());
      connection.unregisterMBean(bean);
    }
}
```

The client also creates a standard `StringMonitor` to track changes to an MBean's attributes:

```
public void addMonitor( ) throws Exception {
  connection.createMBean("javax.management.monitor.StringMonitor", new
ObjectName("wrox.ch12.jmx:name=WorkMonitor"));
  }

public static void main(String[] args) throws Exception {
  RemoteClient rc = new RemoteClient();
  rc.remove();
  rc.deploy();
  rc.lookup();
  rc.checkRunning();
  rc.addMonitor();
  }
}
```

Now the client deployment is complete. Next, you use the `WorkMonitor` to track changes to the `WorkerMBean`'s attributes.

WorkMonitor

Through the management console you can see and send properties on the `WorkMonitor` so it will report a notification to the console when an attribute changes. Figure 12-7 shows the attributes of the `WorkMonitorMBean`.

Figure 12-7

The steps to implement the monitor are as follows:

1. Add the `objectName` of the `WorkerMBean` you would like to monitor using the `addObservedObject()` method — in this case `wrox.ch12.jmx:type-Worker,number=2`.

2. Set the attribute you would like to monitor via `ObservedAttribute`. You are monitoring the `Status` attribute.

3. Next, set the `StringToCompare` attribute for the value you would like to monitor.

4. Choose `NotifyDiffer` or `NotifyMatch` from the attribute list.

5. Finally, invoke the `start()` operation to start monitoring.

You will now be able to tab over to the `wrox.ch12.jmx:type-Worker,number=2` MBean and change the `Status` attribute. You should see a notification was generated from your `WorkMonitorMBean`. Figure 12-8 shows the output from JConsole.

Attributes	Operations	Notifications[1]	Info			
TimeStamp	Type			Event	Source
15:49:07:765	jmx.monitor.string.differs		0	javax.management.monitor.MonitorNotificatio...	wrox.ch12.jmx:name=WorkMonitor

Figure 12-8

This section has only scratched the surface with regard to what you can accomplish with JMX technology. You have learned how to create remote management resources that you can communicate with via numerous standard adaptors and connectors. The examples have shown you how to discover services based on name and attributes, as well as monitor internal states and report notification messages. In the next section you look at another integration technology, Java Messaging Service, or JMS.

Java Messaging Service

In the previous section you looked at creating MBeans. In this section you look at developing JMS components to build loosely coupled systems. Then, using what you learned in the previous section, you will deploy and manage these components as MBeans.

Why Is JMS Important?

JMS is a standard Java API for interacting with Message-Oriented Middleware (MOM). Before JMS 1.0 each messaging vendor would develop their own API, locking a system integrator into a proprietary solution.

Messaging systems allow you to perform location-independent processing. This lends itself naturally to systems integration and distributed processing systems. In messaging systems, software components do not communicate directly with one another. They communicate via sending and receiving information between message destinations or endpoints. The next section discusses the two types of endpoints provided in the JMS API, queues and topics, and explains the difference between them.

Endpoints: Queues and Topics

Queues and topics differ only in how messages are consumed (that is, removed) from the endpoint. Using the queue model, each message is received only once. This differs from the topic model where every component registered with the topic is sent a copy of the message.

Two analogies can be used to keep track of the difference. Queue is analogous to waiting in line at the bank. At the bank you wait and as a teller is available your request is handled in turn. The more tellers available to handle customers, the more customers can be handled. This shows that as you add consumers to a queue you decrease the workload for each consumer.

A topic is just the opposite. The more consumers you have for a topic, the more messages you send. In that way a topic is like a newspaper boy's delivery route. The more houses he has, the more peddling he does. You choose one destination type over another based around these lines. If you want to keep multiple systems informed of the same thing, use a topic. If you are looking to divide and conquer a set of requests, use a queue.

Fortunately, with the release of JMS 1.1 the majority of classes in the JMS API work for both types of destinations, as described in the following table. Prior to that, there was a separate set of classes for each destination type. This not only simplifies your application design, but also allows you to send messages between a queue and a topic and vice versa using the same message transaction—something you could not do before JMS 1.1. Transaction support is discussed when you review the `Session` object in the next section.

Class	Description
Destination	The generic term for a queue or a topic—in other words, a message endpoint. A destination is typically created as part of an administrative process at design time, but there are ways to create and destroy them at runtime for a specific purpose.
Connection Factory	The administrative object for creating connections to a JMS server. The `ConnectionFactory` implementation is bound to a JNDI registry for the client to look up at runtime.
Connection	Allows for the creation of a messaging session with a JMS server.
Session	The heart of the message exchange because it defines the message transaction support and the acknowledgment. It is also the factory interface for creating the consumer, producer, and message types.
MessageConsumer	Allows a client to receive messages from a JMS server either synchronously or asynchronously.
MessageProducer	Used to send messages to a JMS destination.
Message	The base interface for sending information to and from a destination. There are several subclasses that describe the type of payload a message can contain, such as a serialized object, byte stream, or text.

Sending and Receiving Messages

There are three components to the example demonstrating sending and receiving messages via JMS:

Component	Purpose
MessageClient	Shows you how to connect to a JMS server and send messages via the JMS API.
JMSWorker	An asynchronous message client deployed as an MBean.
JMSAgent	Defines the `MBeanServer` to expose the `JMSWorker` MBean for management.

Before looking at the design of these components, you have to configure your JMS server. The next section describes this process using JBoss as the JMS server.

Configuring the JMS Server

This first example is to set up a messaging system exercising the core portions of the JMS API. For this example, you will be using a JMS 1.1-compliant server, JBoss 4.03. JBoss is an open source J2EE application server available free of charge. You can download JBoss from its web site at www.jboss.org. You will need to run the installer and start JBoss. The command is as follows:

```
C:\jboss-4.0.3\bin\run.bat
```

The next step is to create the Destinations you will be using for the example. Open the jbossmq-destinations-service.xml file located in the %jboss_home%\server\default\deploy\jms directory. Append the following code to the bottom of the file just before the ending server:

```
<mbean code="org.jboss.mq.server.jmx.Queue"
    name="jboss.mq.destination:service=Queue,name=work-start">
</mbean>
<mbean code="org.jboss.mq.server.jmx.Queue"
    name="jboss.mq.destination:service=Queue,name=work-complete">
</mbean>
```

You should recognize the elements described in this file. All of the resources in JBoss are deployed as MBeans. The code attribute of the mbean tags specifies the class, and the name attribute specifies the object name.

Now, set up the client application so you can communicate with the JMS server.

When you create a queue or topic in JBoss it is bound to the JNDI registry. Your client must look up the object in the registry to send and receive messages. To do that you have to configure your client to be able to locate the object registry so when you create your InitialContext() through JNDI you will point to the correct server information. This is done by putting a jndi.properties file in your class path. Your file will look like this for JBoss:

```
java.naming.factory.initial=org.jnp.interfaces.NamingContextFactory
java.naming.factory.url.pkgs=org.jboss.naming:org.jnp.interfaces
java.naming.provider.url=localhost:1099
```

The resources org.jnp.interfaces.NamingContextFactory and org.jboss.naming:org.jnp.interfaces must be in your application's classpath. They are available in the jbossall-client.jar file. Your provider.url property will be different if you are running your JMS server on a different computer than your client. If you get the following error it is because your JNDI service is not available at the host and port you specified:

```
javax.naming.CommunicationException: Could not obtain connection to any of these
urls: localhost:1099 and discovery failed with error:
javax.naming.CommunicationException: Receive timed out [Root exception is
java.net.SocketTimeoutException: Receive timed out] [Root exception is
javax.naming.CommunicationException: Failed to connect to server localhost:1099
[Root exception is javax.naming.ServiceUnavailableException: Failed to connect to
server localhost:1099 [Root exception is java.net.ConnectException: Connection
refused: connect]]]
```

There are three components in this example: a client, MessageClient, to demonstrate sending messages to a destination; an MBean, JMSWorkerMBean, to register and listen for messages asynchronously; and a JMSAgent for deploying the MBean and making it available for management.

MessageClient

The import section of the message client shows all the classes involved in sending a message. The two main packages are javax.jms.* and javax.naming.*:

```
import javax.jms.Connection;
import javax.jms.ConnectionFactory;
import javax.jms.Destination;
import javax.jms.JMSException;
import javax.jms.MessageProducer;
import javax.jms.Session;
import javax.jms.TextMessage;
import javax.naming.InitialContext;
import javax.naming.NamingException;

public class MessageClient {
  Destination destination = null;
  ConnectionFactory factory = null;
```

The constructor of the message client looks up the ConnectionFactory and the Destination from the JNDI registry. Each lookup returns the standard interface defined by the specification. The implementing class is JMS vendor-specific and hidden from the client code, making it portable to other JMS servers:

```
  public MessageClient(String destinationName) {

    InitialContext ic = null;

    try {
      ic = new InitialContext();
      destination = (Destination) ic.lookup(destinationName);
      factory = (ConnectionFactory) ic.lookup("ConnectionFactory");
    } catch (NamingException e) {
      e.printStackTrace();
    }

  }
```

The send() method performs the work of the client by creating a Connection, Session, Message Producer, and Message. The Session object is key to understanding the JMS API. The Session defines the transactional boundaries and message acknowledgment support for the message exchange:

```
  public void send(String text) throws JMSException {

    Connection con = factory.createConnection();
    Session session = con.createSession(false, Session.AUTO_ACKNOWLEDGE);
    MessageProducer producer = session.createProducer(destination);
    TextMessage message = session.createTextMessage(text);
    System.out.println("message ready to send: " + message);
```

```
      producer.send(message);
      producer.close();
      session.close();
      con.close();
    }
```

The `main()` method provides a test driver for the application. You passed in XML to send as the body of the `TextMessage`. This is not a requirement, but a good design decision to integrate with various systems that are not Java-based:

```
    public static void main(String[] args) {

      try {
        MessageClient ms = new MessageClient("queue/work-start");
        ms.send("<document>Welcome to JMS</document>");
      } catch (JMSException e) {
        e.printStackTrace();
      }
    }
  }
```

To run the client, execute the following command:

```
  C:\>java -cp jbossall-client.jar wrox.ch12.jms.MessageClient
```

JMSWorkerMBean

The `JMSWorkerMBean` describes the same methods from the previous `WorkerMBean` example. This will define the methods you can invoke through the JConsole application or any JMX remote client. This interface is defining the life cycle of the `JMSWorker`. You can connect and disconnect from the JMS server using the `start()` and `stop()` methods. You can also modify the destination the `Worker` uses to receive messages:

```
  package wrox.ch12.jms;


  public interface JMSWorkerMBean {
    public void start();
    public void stop();
    public boolean isRunning();
    public void setRunning(boolean running);
    public void setDestination(String name);
    public String getDestination();


  }
```

JMSWorker

The `JMSWorker` MBean is an example of an asynchronous message client. The class implements the `MessageListener` interface, allowing the `JMSWorker` to be registered with the JMS server and receive messages when they are sent to destination:

```
package wrox.ch12.jms;

import javax.jms.Connection;
import javax.jms.ConnectionFactory;
import javax.jms.Destination;
import javax.jms.JMSException;
import javax.jms.Message;
import javax.jms.MessageConsumer;
import javax.jms.MessageListener;
import javax.jms.MessageProducer;
import javax.jms.Session;
import javax.naming.InitialContext;
import javax.naming.NamingException;
```

The `JMSWorker` class must look up the `ConnectionFactory` and `Destination` just like the message client:

```
public class JMSWorker implements MessageListener, JMSWorkerMBean {

  private ConnectionFactory factory;
  private Connection connection;
  Session session;
  private Destination destination;
  private boolean running = true;
  private String destinationName = null;

  public JMSWorker(String destinationName) {
    this.destinationName = destinationName;
    try {
      InitialContext ic = new InitialContext();
      factory = (ConnectionFactory) ic.lookup("ConnectionFactory");
      destination = (Destination) ic.lookup(destinationName);
    } catch (NamingException e) {
      e.printStackTrace();
    }
  }
```

The message listener interface `javax.jms` package forces the `JMSWorker` class to implement the `onMessage()` method. Notice that this does not make the `onMessage()` manageable via JMX, because it is not part of the `JMSWorkerMBean` interface:

```
  /*
   * (non-Javadoc)
   *
   * @see javax.jms.MessageListener#onMessage(javax.jms.Message)
   */
  public void onMessage(Message message) {
    try {
      System.out.println("message received:" + message.toString());

      } catch (JMSException e) {
      e.printStackTrace();
    }
```

```
    }
    public boolean isRunning() {
     return running;
    }
    public void setRunning(boolean running) {
     this.running = running;
    }

    public String getDestination() {
     return destinationName;
    }
    public void setDestination(String name) {
     this.destinationName = name;
    }
```

To start receiving messages asynchronously, a MessageListener must be registered with the JMS server via the MessageConsumer interface. The start() method of the JMSWorker is a good place to control this because the start() method is manageable via JMX and the component can be started and stopped based on any number of operational criteria:

```
    public void start() {

     try {
       connection = factory.createConnection();
       session = connection.createSession(false, Session.CLIENT_ACKNOWLEDGE);
       MessageConsumer consumer = session.createConsumer(destination);
       consumer.setMessageListener(this);
       connection.start();
     } catch (JMSException e) {
       running = false;
       e.printStackTrace();
     }
     running = true;
    }
```

The stop() message will tell the JMS server to stop invoking the onMessage() method for this component:

```
    public void stop() {
     try {
       connection.stop();
     } catch (JMSException e) {
       e.printStackTrace();
     }
    }
   }
```

That concludes the asynchronous message listener. Next, the JMSAgent will deploy the JMSWorker from management via the MBeanServer.

JMSAgent

This is the same as the previous agent that used the JVM platform `MBeanServer` to deploy MBeans. The only difference is that once deployed you are calling the `start()` method via the `invoke()` method on the `MBeanServer`:

```
package wrox.ch12.jms;

import java.lang.management.ManagementFactory;

import javax.management.MBeanServer;
import javax.management.ObjectName;

public class JMSAgent {

 public static void main(String[] args) {
   JMSWorker worker = new JMSWorker("queue/work-start");
   MBeanServer mbs = ManagementFactory.getPlatformMBeanServer();

   try {
     ObjectName name = new ObjectName("wrox.ch12.jmx:type=Worker");
     mbs.registerMBean(worker, name);
     mbs.invoke(name, "start", null, null);
     System.out.println("JMS Agent Started..");
     Thread.sleep(Long.MAX_VALUE);
   } catch (Exception e) {
     e.printStackTrace();
   }
 }
}
```

Start the JMS agent by issuing the following command:

```
c:\>Java -Dcom.sun.management.jmxremote wrox.ch12.jms.JMSAgent
```

You should see "JMS Agent Started..." as the console output.

When the `JMSWorker` receives the message, it prints the message to the standard output. There are two parts to a JMS message, the `Header` and the `Body`. The `Header` contains properties associated with the message. Here is the message printed to the console:

```
message recievedSpyTextMessage {
Header {
   jmsDestination   : QUEUE.work-start
   jmsDeliveryMode  : 2
   jmsExpiration    : 0
   jmsPriority      : 4
   jmsMessageID     : ID:14-11437513428751
   jmsTimeStamp     : 1143751342875
   jmsCorrelationID: null
   jmsReplyTo       : null
   jmsType          : null
```

```
      jmsRedelivered   : false
      jmsProperties    : {}
      jmsPropReadWrite: false
      msgReadOnly      : true
      producerClientId: ID:14
   }
   Body {
      text             :<document>welcome to JMS</document>
   }
   }
```

The following table discusses some of the intended uses for these properties. In the section that follows, you will see examples where these Header properties will be relevant.

Property	Usage
jmsMessageID	Each message is assigned a unique identifier. The message ID is that identifier, and provides a unique tracking mechanism.
jmsCorrelationID	Used to associate messages to each other. This can be thought of as a parent-child relationship. You could have a situation where one message is broken into sub-messages where the CorrelationID can be used to identify the original message.
jmsTimeStamp	The time the message was created.
jmsReplyTo	The message's return address. You can use this property to specify a temporary destination available for a specific message exchange.
jmstype	Can be used in conjunction with a message filter, so you can register a MessageConsumer that will only receive messages matching the type specified.

In the previous example you deployed the MessageListener JMSWorker as an MBean. It is not required that you do this. The J2EE 1.2 EJB container defines a message-driven enterprise bean. The EJB solution is recommended if your messages are transactional in nature. Because the EJB container supports declarative transactions at the method level, you could create a transaction that includes receiving a message and updating a database. The JMX approach is limited in that sense, but offers some flexibility in monitoring. When you have to interact with legacy systems where transactions are not possible, monitoring is a real asset. Message-driven beans run in an instance pool as part of the EJB container. You might want to deploy each instance separately to manage individually. Also, the JMX solution allows you access to all of the methods that you expose through the MBean interface. For example, if you need to change any of the MBean properties, you could do it at runtime.

JMS allows you to interact with Message-Oriented Middleware via a standard interface. Now that you understand the fundamentals of JMX and JMS, you will be able to build components to support a number of integration scenarios. The next section describes common integration patterns and discusses where you might leverage them as a solution.

System Integration Patterns

Chapter 3 discusses a number of software design patterns used in application development. This section examines a few patterns for doing software integration. The concepts are still the same, but the pieces are bigger. The emphasis in integration design is *loose coupling*, which looks to limit the dependencies between software systems, thus fostering software reuse and reducing the potential of simple code changes rippling across your software architecture.

Processing Chain

Message components like the example demonstrated previously work well as part of a distributed processing chain. Figure 12-9 defines a processing chain.

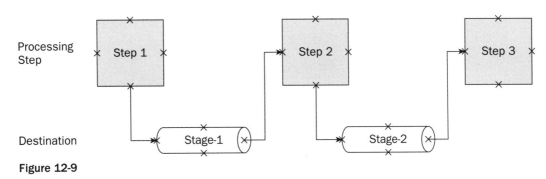

Figure 12-9

Using this approach you break each process into a series of steps. Each step reads from an input destination, performs some processing, and sends the results to an output destination. This has proven to be a very scalable solution.

Using the MBean approach you can create an interface to expose destinations as managed attributes:

```
public interface ProcessorMBean {
    public void setInputDestination(String queue );
    public void setOutputDestination(String queue );
}
```

Processing chains are common in back-end systems. They are useful in service fulfillment as well. By breaking a problem down into a series of discrete processes or events, the constrained events can be load balanced more efficiently when compared to scaling a process as a whole.

Request-Reply

Using JMS is also useful in request and reply scenarios common in web-based programming. With this architecture pattern you are using a temporary queue as a bucket to collect your results. There are only a few modifications to the `MessageClient` and `JMSWorker` classes to fulfill this scenario. Figure 12-10 illustrates the ideas expressed in this pattern.

619

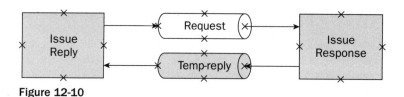

Figure 12-10

Modify the `MessageClient` to create a temporary queue, then set the queue as a `ReplyTo` property on the message you are about to send. This information will be used by the `JMSWorker` class to issue a response:

```
Session session = conn.createSession(false, Session.AUTO_ACKNOWLEDGE);
Destination temp = session.createTemporaryQueue();
TextMessage request = session.createTextMessage();
request.setText("<message>please respond</message>");
request.setJMSReplyTo(temp);
```

Once the message has been sent, the client waits on the temp queue until the request is processed or a timeout has been reached:

```
MessageProducer mp = session.createProducer(queue);
mp.send(request);
mp.close();
MessageConsumer mc = session.createConsumer(temp);
TextMessage reply = (TextMessage) mc.receive(WAIT_THRESHHOLD);
```

Finally, modify the `JMSWorker` class to handle the response. If the `ReplyTo` property has been set, send the message to the `ReplyTo` destination after it has been processed:

```
/*
 *
 * @see javax.jms.MessageListener#onMessage(javax.jms.Message)
 */
public void onMessage(Message message) {

  try {
  System.out.println("message received:" + message.toString());

  if (message.getJMSReplyTo() != null) {
    System.out.println("responding message");
    MessageProducer producer =session.createProducer(message.getJMSReplyTo());
    producer.send(message);
    producer.close();
  }
  } catch (JMSException e) {
    e.printStackTrace();
  }
}
```

This example used a queue to scale your request and response programming model. The next section examines divide and conquer based on a message pattern known as split and aggregate.

Split-Aggregate

Split and Aggregate are two components that work together to divide and conquer a large job. This is a great solution for increasing performance throughput for a system. Anytime you are processing a collection of tasks or items you could loop through the collection and process each individually. However, if each individual task is process intensive, large batch processing can cause a performance bottleneck.

Figure 12-11 shows a simple process looping through items in a purchase order and verifying that they are in stock.

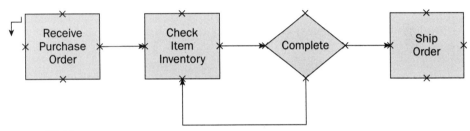

Figure 12-11

Instead of processing the request in batch, send each item to a queue while still referencing the original purchase order for each item. This would map to a series of message-based components described in Figure 12-12.

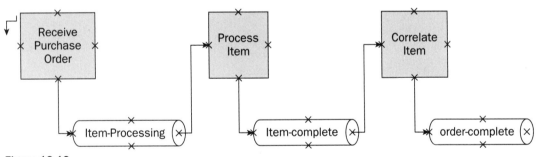

Figure 12-12

This process entails three basic steps: divide a request into a series of smaller requests while retaining enough information to reconstruct the original message, process the sub-message, and finally, determine when the request is complete. The following is a walkthrough of these concepts:

1. Receive Purchase Order divides the order into individual Item messages and sets the correlation identifier of the message to that of the purchase order. The following code shows you how to set the `Header` properties to be used by the correlation step:

```
session.createProducer(destination);
String parent = m.getJMSMessageID();
String[] children = getChildren(m);
for (int i = 1; i < children.length; i++) {
  Message child = session.createMessage();
  child.setJMSCorrelationID(parent);
  child.setIntProperty("count", children.length);
  child.setIntProperty("index", i);
  producer.send(child);
}
```

2. Process Item picks each item off the destination and checks the inventory. This process can be scaled by adding physical nodes to your processing architecture.

3. Finally, at the correlation step, each completed item is stored until all the items from the order are complete. This is called a *state-full filter*. Basically, for each parent PurchaseOrder the message aggregate has an object that stores the partial information and determines if it should forward to the next step:

```
public void aggregate(TextMessage m) throws JMSException {

PurchaseOrderAggregate poa = (PurchaseOrderAggregate)
map.get(m.getJMSCorrelationID());
  if (poa == null) {
    poa = new PurchaseOrderAggregate(m.getIntProperty("count"));
    map.put(m.getJMSCorrelationID(), poa);
  }
  poa.add(m.getText(), m.getIntProperty("index"), m.getIntProperty("count"));

  if (poa.isComplete()) {
    PurchaseOrder po = poa.getPurchaseOrder();
    send(po);
  }

}
```

❑ Here is a sample aggregate that counts the number of items received compared with the number of items sent:

```
package wrox.ch12.jms;

public class PurchaseOrderAggregate {

PurchaseOrder po = new PurchaseOrder();
int received;
int count;

public PurchaseOrderAggregate( int count ) {
  this.count = count;
}
```

❑   As each item is added, the `Aggregate` class increments a counter until all items are received. A state-full filter does not always have to store each message part. For example, in an auction scenario you would only be interested in retaining the highest bidder:

```
public void add( String item, int index, int count) {
received++;
po.addItem(item);
}
public boolean isComplete( ) {
  if (received == count ) return true;
    return false;
}
PurchaseOrder getPurchaseOrder( ) {
    return po;
  }
}
```

This concludes the section on integration design patterns. With these patterns you will be able to address a number of integration scenarios. For future reading, consult the book *Enterprise Integration Patterns* by Gregor Hohpe, which goes into further detail regarding these as well as several other patterns.

Summary

In this chapter you learned some core technologies involved in building integration solutions consistent with a Service Oriented Architecture. You looked at JMX as the foundation for manageable services and JMS for distributed processing. In addition to these technologies, you learned about patterns of integration that promote loose coupling as a core design principle.

13

Java Security

Security becomes ever more important as people flock to the Web and a large number of sites (such as Amazon and online banks) store personal information about their customers, not to mention a wide variety of uses in custom enterprise solutions with multiple users. Java provides security in two major ways. Java Cryptography provides user identification/authentication and signing of digital messages. Java Authentication and Authorization Services provides programmatic access control and user authorization, granting access to various program features based on permissions and security policies. This chapter gives you a solid foundation in these APIs and shows you how to utilize them effectively. Additionally, the new digital signing of XML documents, introduced in JDK 6, is discussed.

The Java implementation of security addresses many standard facets of security such as access control, public/private key generation and management, signing of digital content, and management of digital certificates. This chapter looks at what Java provides in its various security packages and delves into the concepts of security.

Java Cryptography Architecture and Java Cryptography Extension (JCA/JCE)

The *Java Cryptography Architecture* (JCA) was first introduced in JDK 1.1. Since its initial release, the JCA went from providing APIs for digital signatures and message digests to including certificate management and fine-grained configurable access control. The other important features of a security implementation are encryption of data for communication, key management and exchange, and Message Authentication Code (MAC) support. These features are all found in the *Java Cryptography Extension* (JCE), which was integrated into the standard Java API in version 1.4 of the Java 2 SDK release. Combining the functionality provided by JCA with JCE presents you with a rich set of security and cryptography-related routines for your security needs.

JCA Design and Architecture

The JCA forms the core of the security API. It was designed with two important principles in mind. First, the JCA is implementation-independent and interoperable. Implementation independence is achieved through the use of *cryptographic service providers* (or, more simply, *providers*). A provider implements a cryptographic service such as generating random numbers or creating digital signatures. Interoperability ensures that different providers will still work with each other. For example, different providers implementing routines using the same algorithm should work such that a message encrypted by one provider can be decrypted by another provider. The second principle is that of algorithm independence and extensibility. Algorithm independence is achieved through the specification of *engine classes* that provide a specific cryptographic service, such as a key generator or a message digest service. Algorithm extensibility ensures that these engine classes can be updated with new algorithms easily.

The JDK comes with a default implementation of the cryptographic service providers. This provider package is named SUN and has the following providers:

❑   Implementation of DSA (Digital Signature Algorithm)

❑   Implementation of MD5 and SHA-1 message digest algorithms

❑   Key pair generator to generate public and private key pairs for the DSA algorithm

❑   DSA algorithm parameter generator

❑   DSA algorithm parameter manager

❑   DSA key factory that supports converting public keys to and from private keys

❑   SHA1PRNG pseudo-random number generator

❑   X.509 Certificate path builder and validator for PKIX

❑   A certificate store using the PKIX LDAP V2 Schema

❑   Certificate factory for X.509 certificates and *Certificate Revocation Lists* (CRLs)

❑   A keystore

All of these providers are discussed in more detail in this chapter. All examples in this chapter use the default implementation of providers in the SUN package. Consult the third-party documentation if you are using another provider package.

Engine Classes

An engine class provides the interface to a specific cryptographic service. This interface dictates how programmers use a particular service. There can be a number of different implementations for a particular engine class, such as Signature implementations that use SHA-1 or MD5 algorithms. Each engine class has a corresponding *Service Provider Interface* (SPI), which is an abstract class that is encapsulated by the engine class. The SPI class must be subclassed in order to create a concrete implementation. Each engine class also has a factory class that is used to create a specific instance of the engine class (and its enclosed SPI class) using the `getInstance` factory method.

The Java SDK defines 12 engine classes, three of which (the certificate path classes and the certificate store) were introduced in the 1.4 version of the Java 2 SDK. These engine classes and their descriptions are shown in the following table.

Engine Class	Description
MessageDigest	Calculates the message digest (or hash) of data
Signature	Digitally signs data and verifies signatures
KeyPairGenerator	Generates a public and private key pair
KeyFactory	Converts opaque cryptographic keys into transparent representations of the underlying key material
CertificateFactory	Creates public key certificates and CRLs
KeyStore	Creates and manages a keystore, which stores and manages public/private keys and certificates
AlgorithmParameters	Manages parameters for a particular algorithm, including encoding/decoding of parameters
AlgorithmParameter Generator	Generates a set of parameters for a specified algorithm
SecureRandom	Generates random (or pseudo-random) numbers
CertPathBuilder	Builds certificate chains (or certification paths)
CertPathValidator	Validates certificate chains
CertStore	Retrieves certificates and CRLs from a repository

The naming convention of SPI classes is the text Spi appended to the engine class name. For example, the SPI for the SecureRandom engine class is SecureRandomSpi. Each engine class has a getInstance method that is used to request a particular algorithm and also a particular provider if needed.

Installing a different provider package is done by either placing the JAR file in your classpath or deploying the JAR file as an extension in your JRE. The provider must then be placed in the list of approved providers in the java.security file. This file is found in the lib/security directory of your JDK or JRE installation. The property in this file takes the following form:

```
security.provider.n=masterClassName
```

The n is replaced with a number, such as 1 or 2. Using numbers provides a way to rank providers, and this list of providers is searched top down when no specific provider is specified in a call to one of the engine classes' getInstance methods. The masterClassName is replaced with the fully qualified class name of the master class for the provider package. This file contains the following lines for specifying providers in the JRE that comes with the current Java 6.0 SDK:

```
security.provider.1=sun.security.provider.Sun
security.provider.2=sun.security.rsa.SunRsaSign
security.provider.3=com.sun.net.ssl.internal.ssl.Provider
security.provider.4=com.sun.crypto.provider.SunJCE
security.provider.5=sun.security.jgss.SunProvider
security.provider.6=com.sun.security.sasl.Provider
security.provider.7=org.jcp.xml.dsig.internal.dom.XMLDSigRI
security.provider.8=sun.security.smartcardio.SunPCSC
security.provider.9=sun.security.mscapi.SunMSCAPI
```

Next, take a closer look at using each of the engine classes. Examples utilize the default implementations provided by the SUN package.

Calculating and Verifying Message Digests

The `MessageDigest` engine class takes an arbitrary length byte array as input and calculates a fixed-length hash value, known as a message digest. This is a one-way operation. It is impossible to take a message digest and derive the original input. If this were possible, then the world would have the best compression algorithm in existence, which a guy I know actually tried to implement in high school. This is a vital aspect of a message digest because it keeps the original input out of the picture. Additionally, with the complexity of the message digest algorithms, it is computationally infeasible to find two sets of input that hash to the exact same value. Therefore, you can view a message digest as a fingerprint of data because each input set hashes to an (almost) unique value.

Take a look at using the factory creation method in action. This is the same across all engine classes, so it is described in detail here but glossed over for the other engine classes. Each engine class has three static methods that conform to the following signatures:

```
static [engine class name] getInstance(String algorithm)
static [engine class name] getInstance(String algorithm,
                                       String provider)
static [engine class name] getInstance(String algorithm,
                                       Provider provider)
```

The second two forms of the `getInstance` method allow you to specify a particular provider. The last form allows you to pass in an instance of a provider, and the second form lets you just use the name of a provider. All strings, including algorithm, are case-insensitive. The `[engine class name]` is replaced with the actual class name of the engine class.

The SUN package comes with two message digest algorithms: MD5 and SHA-1. The MD5 algorithm accepts input and generates a 128-bit message digest for the given input. For those familiar with MD4, the MD5 algorithm is slightly slower than MD4 but has greater assurance of security. One key benefit to the MD5 algorithm is that it can be coded in a fairly straightforward manner, not needing any complicated or large lookup tables. Although secure, it has actually been discovered that it is computationally feasible to find two sets of input that hash to the same value. This violates one of the principles of message digests. Due in part to this fact, SHA-1 is also available. SHA-1, short for Secure Hash Algorithm, was developed by the NSA and first published in 1995. It is based on some of the same principles as MD5, but produces a message digest that is 160 bits long. The maximum input size SHA-1 can take is in the neighborhood of 2 quintillion bytes (2^{64} bits).

After invoking the `getInstance` factory method, an initialized `MessageDigest` is available. The next step is to provide the `MessageDigest` object with the input and then ask it to calculate the message digest. Three methods are available to pass input data to the `MessageDigest`:

```
void update(byte input)
void update(byte[] input)
void update(byte[] input, int offset, int len)
```

The first form accepts a single byte of input. The second takes an array of bytes, and the length of the array is used as the length of the input. The last form takes an array of bytes, but it allows for the calculation of a message digest based on a subset of the array starting at position offset. The input size is described by `len`.

There are three methods that calculate the message digest, which is then returned as an array of bytes:

```
byte[] digest()
byte[] digest(byte[] input)
int digest(byte[] buf, int offset, int len)
```

The first `digest` method calculates the message digest based on the input already passed in via one of the update methods. The second form is a convenience method that returns a message digest based on input passed in to the method. The third form is not a convenience method. It calculates the message digest based on the input set via one of the update methods and then stores the message digest in the `buf` byte array that is passed in to the method. The `len` parameter dictates the maximum length available for the message digest, and offset dictates where in the array the message digest should start getting written. The return value is how many bytes were stored in `buf`.

You can use the `MessageDigest` engine class to ensure the integrity of data. Say you're writing the security and data integrity component of a system that is used globally. You want to ensure that data is not altered. One way to accomplish this is to store a collection of message digests that correspond to sensitive data that is communicated across the globe. These message digest values are stored in a base system and then the message digest can be recalculated when each piece of data arrives at its destination. A component can be developed to look up the message digests from the base system (because they are small and shouldn't be communicated with the data) and compare them to a newly calculated message digest. Here's an example implementation of a class that instantiates and computes the message digest and then compares it to an already looked up message digest value:

```java
import java.security.MessageDigest;
import java.security.NoSuchAlgorithmException;

public class MessageDigestExample {
    public static void main(String args[])
    {
        try {
            MessageDigest sha = MessageDigest.getInstance("SHA-1");
            byte[] data1 = {65,66,67,68,69};
            byte[] data2 = {70,71,72,73,74};

            sha.update(data1);
            sha.update(data2);
            byte[] msgDigest = sha.digest();

            // Can also combine the final update with digest like this:
            // byte[] msgDigest = sha.digest(data2);

            System.out.println("--- Message Digest ---");
            for(int i=0; i<msgDigest.length; i++) {
                System.out.print(msgDigest[i] + " ");
            }

            System.out.println("");
        } catch(NoSuchAlgorithmException nsae) {
            System.out.println("Exception: " + nsae);
            nsae.printStackTrace();
        }
    }
}
```

The SHA-1 algorithm is specified in the call to `getInstance`, returning an initialized `MessageDigest` object that computes the message digest according to the SHA-1 algorithm. The update method is invoked twice, simulating a multipart operation. The message digest that is calculated is a series of numbers shown in the following output:

```
--- Message Digest ---
-97 103 -17 -58 -81 -87 95 26 -17 -101 51 81 -42 -80 29 126 5 -111 -73 72
```

This array of numbers can be recomputed and compared on the recipient's side to ensure the data is the same that was originally communicated.

Digital Signing and Verification of Data

Digitally signing data is accomplished using a private key, and the verification of that signature is done with the public key. This ensures that the data originated from the specific person that signed it with their private key, much like signing a credit card receipt. The private key is used to sign a collection of bytes, and a short, fixed-length signature is generated (much like a message digest). This signature can then be verified using the public key. This process is illustrated in Figure 13-1. This is a primarily programmatic view of using the DSA algorithm. In actuality, the DSA algorithm is used with a message digest algorithm such as MD5 or SHA-1 (to which you already have access through the `MessageDigest` engine class). The actual message digest becomes input to the DSA algorithm along with the private key. On the other side, the data is then encoded into a message digest again and serves as input to DSA along with the public key in order to verify the integrity of the data.

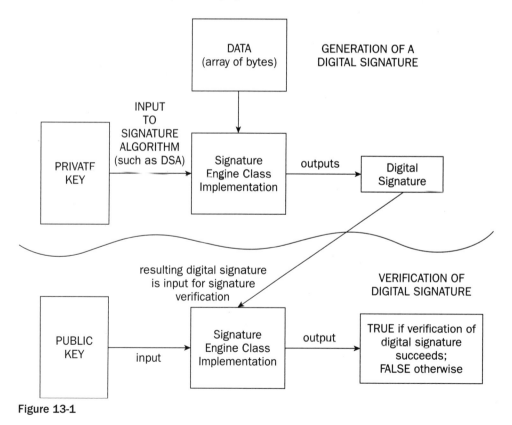

Figure 13-1

Much like message digests, there are two vital principles for a Digital Signature Algorithm. The first principle is that the public key that corresponds to the private key can be used to verify the integrity of the data. The second is that the digital signature and the public key do not reveal anything about the private key. The actual `Signature` object can be in one of three states. Consult the following table for the list of states that an object of the `Signature` class can assume.

Signature State	Description
UNINITIALIZED	The state assumed immediately after creation.
SIGN	Signifies the object is initialized for signing. Set after a call to `initSign`.
VERIFY	Signifies the object is initialized for verifying a signature. Set after a call to `initVerify`.

The SUN package comes with an implementation of the Digital Signature Algorithm (DSA). DSA is part of the Digital Signature Standard (DSS) that was developed by the NSA in 1991. Either SHA-1 or MD5 can be used with the DSA algorithm. Hopefully, the value of engine classes is making itself apparent. It becomes easy to combine a message digest function with a digital signature function. Just like the `MessageDigest` engine class, the `Signature` engine class has the same three `getInstance` methods. An instance of a `Signature` class must be initialized after creation using the following method in order to prepare it to digitally sign data:

```
final void initSign(PrivateKey privateKey)
```

After this method is called, the `Signature` class assumes the `SIGN` state. The next step is to send data to the `Signature` object and actually sign it. This is accomplished by the `update` and `sign` methods:

```
final void update(byte b)
final void update(byte[] data)
final void update(byte[] data, int offset, int len)
```

The first form accepts a single byte of data. The second takes an array of bytes, and the length of the array is used as the length of the data. The last form takes an array of bytes, but it allows for the calculation of a signature based on a subset of the array starting at position offset. The data size is described by `len`. The first form of the `sign` method returns the signature in an array of bytes. The second form places the signature in the `outbuf` array starting at offset and going for a maximum length of `len`:

```
final byte[] sign()
final int sign(byte[] outbuf, int offset, int len)
```

The value returned is how many bytes were stored in the `outbuf` array. After a `sign` method returns, the `Signature` object is left in the `SIGN` state and is still configured with the programmed private key. Call `initSign` again to utilize a different private key.

The other operation that the `Signature` engine class supports is verifying data. The `Signature` object must first be set to verify data by invoking an `initVerify` method:

```
final void initVerify(PublicKey publicKey)
final void initVerify(Certificate certificate)
```

Either a public key object or a certificate can be used to verify a digital signature. After initVerify is invoked, the Signature object assumes the VERIFY state. The update methods are used to send data into the Signature object to verify. Their usage does not differ from passing in data for signing. A verify method is then invoked to determine if the signature generated from the data and public key match the private key:

```
final boolean verify(byte[] signature)
final boolean verify(byte[] signature, int offset, int length)
```

The digital signature takes the form of a byte array. The second form of verify is used to specify the location (at offset) and the length (specified by length) of the signature in the byte array. If it all matches up, verify returns true. However, if the public key does not match the signature or the signature is invalid, false is returned. After verify returns, the Signature object is left in the VERIFY state still programmed with the public key that was passed in to initVerify. Call initVerify again to use a different public key.

One common use of public and private keys is signing and then verifying the source of communication. For example, assume you work for a government contractor and are tasked with constructing a secure communication system that is essentially secure email. The secure email client must have the capability to digitally sign messages going out and also verify messages that are delivered. The details of generating and managing keys are saved for subsequent discussion. Assume the keys are available. You might develop a utility class listed in the following example to assist with the signing and verifying of secure communication:

```java
import java.security.Signature;
import java.security.KeyPair;
import java.security.PublicKey;
import java.security.PrivateKey;
import java.security.NoSuchAlgorithmException;
import java.security.InvalidKeyException;
import java.security.SignatureException;

public class SignatureExample {
    public byte[] signData(byte[] data, PrivateKey key)
    {
        try {
            Signature signer = Signature.getInstance("SHA1withDSA");

            signer.initSign(key);

            signer.update(data);

            return(signer.sign());
        } catch(NoSuchAlgorithmException nsae) {
            System.out.println("Exception: " + nsae);
            nsae.printStackTrace();
        } catch(InvalidKeyException ike) {
            System.out.println("Exception: " + ike);
            ike.printStackTrace();
        } catch(SignatureException se) {
```

```
                System.out.println("Exception: " + se);
                se.printStackTrace();
        }

        return(null);
}

public boolean verifySig(byte[] data, PublicKey key, byte[] sig)
{
        try {
                Signature signer = Signature.getInstance("SHA1withDSA");

                signer.initVerify(key);

                signer.update(data);

                return(signer.verify(sig));
        } catch(NoSuchAlgorithmException nsae) {
                System.out.println("Exception: " + nsae);
                nsae.printStackTrace();
        } catch(InvalidKeyException ike) {
                System.out.println("Exception: " + ike);
                ike.printStackTrace();
        } catch(SignatureException se) {
                System.out.println("Exception: " + se);
                se.printStackTrace();
        }

        return(false);
}

public static void main(String args[])
{
        SignatureExample sigEx = new SignatureExample();
        KeyPairGeneratorExample kpge = new KeyPairGeneratorExample();
        KeyPair keyPair = kpge.generateKeyPair(717);

        byte[] data = {65,66,67,68,69,70,71,72,73,74};
        byte[] digitalSignature = sigEx.signData(data,
                                        keyPair.getPrivate());
        boolean verified;

        // This verification will succeed
        verified = sigEx.verifySig(data, keyPair.getPublic(),
                                digitalSignature);
        if(verified) {
                System.out.println("** The digital signature " +
                                "has been verified");
        } else {
                System.out.println("** The digital signature is " +
                                "invalid, the wrong " +
                                "key was used, or the data has" +
```

```
                                            " been compromised");
        }

        System.out.println("");

        // Generate a new key pair. Guaranteed to be different
        // and incompatible with first set.
        keyPair = kpge.generateKeyPair(517);
        // This verification will fail
        verified = sigEx.verifySig(data, keyPair.getPublic(),
                                   digitalSignature);
        if(verified) {
            System.out.println("** The digital signature has" +
                               " been verified");
        } else {
            System.out.println("** The digital signature is " +
                               "invalid, the wrong " +
                               "key was used, or the data " +
                               "has been compromised");
        }
    }
  }
}
```

The `KeyPairGeneratorExample`, explained subsequently, is used to obtain a public and private key. The data is signed with the private key and verified with the public key.

Digital Key Creation and Management

Two representations of keys are made available by the security API. *Transparent representations* of keys allow you to retrieve specific information about the key, such as the algorithm parameter values used to calculate the key. *Opaque representations* of keys keep these values hidden and only allow you access to the algorithm used to create the key, the encoding used, and the encoded form of the key itself. Transparent representations of keys inherit from a tagging interface called KeySpec. Because this is a tagging interface, no methods are defined inside the interface. Key interfaces provided in the `java` `.security.spec` package are listed in the following table.

Key Interface	Description
DSAPrivateKeySpec	A DSA private key specification
DSAPublicKeySpec	A DSA public key specification
RSAPrivateKeySpec	An RSA private key specification
RSAPrivateCrtKeySpec	An RSA private key specification using Chinese remainder theorem
RSAMultiplePrime PrivateCrtKeySpec	An RSA multiple prime private key specification using the Chinese remainder theorem
RSAPublicKeySpec	An RSA public key specification
EncodedKeySpec	An encoded key specification. PKCS8EncodedKeySpec and X509EncodedKeySpec are two provided implementers.

As opposed to transparent representations of keys, opaque representations inherit from the Key interface. Unlike the KeySpec interface, the Key interface defines three methods that all concrete implementations must implement. These three methods are described next.

The `algorithm` method returns a string representation of the algorithm used to create the key:

```
String algorithm()
```

The `getEncoded` method returns the encoded version of the key (which can then be packaged and transmitted) according to a standard encoding format such as X.509 or PKCS #8:

```
byte[] getEncoded()
```

The `getFormat` method returns the name of the particular encoding format used to encode the key:

```
String getFormat()
```

The `java.security.interfaces` package contains 12 interfaces that inherit directly from the Key interface. These are the various types of keys that are standard in the Java API and are listed in the following table.

Key Interface	Description
DHPrivateKey	A Diffie-Hellman private key
DHPublicKey	A Diffie-Hellman public key
DSAPrivateKey	A DSA private key
DSAPublicKey	A DSA public key
PBEKey	A PBE (password-based encryption) key, supporting a SALT value
RSAMultiPrime PrivateCrtKey	An RSA multiprime private key using the Chinese remainder theorem. Consult PKCS#1 for more information.
RSAPrivateCrtKey	An RSA private key using the Chinese remainder theorem. Consult PKCS#1 for more information.
RSAPrivateKey	An RSA private key
RSAPublicKey	An RSA public key
PublicKey	Used as a tagging interface for all public key interfaces/classes
PrivateKey	Used as a tagging interface for all private key interfaces/classes
SecretKey	Used as a tagging interface for all secret key interfaces/classes

The `KeyFactory` engine class is used to convert transparent representations of keys to opaque representations and vice versa. The standard `getInstance` methods are available to create a `KeyFactory`. There are two methods to convert a transparent representation to an opaque representation: one for public keys and one for private keys. There is one method defined for the reverse operation. These methods are described subsequently.

The generatePublic and generatePrivate methods take a transparent representation of a key (a class that inherits from KeySpec — directly or indirectly) and return either the opaque representation of the public key or the opaque representation of the private key:

```
PublicKey generatePublic(KeySpec keySpec)
PrivateKey generatePrivate(KeySpec keySpec)
```

The getKeySpec method accepts the opaque representation of the key through the key parameter and a class that specifies which key specification class to convert the key to and return:

```
KeySpec getKeySpec(Key key, Class keySpec)
```

From more of a client perspective, the KeyPair class and KeyPairGenerator and KeyStore engine classes are used to create, store, and manage public/private keys and certificates. The KeyPair class defines the following two methods:

```
PrivateKey getPrivate()
PublicKey getPublic()
```

The first method returns the private key currently stored, and the second returns the public key. The KeyPairGenerator engine class is used to generate these pairs of private and public keys and uses the KeyPair class to store them.

The KeyPairGenerator engine class generates a pair of keys in either an algorithm-independent manner or an algorithm-specific manner. Which of these is used depends on how the KeyPairGenerator is initialized. The following two methods are for algorithm-independent initialization. Because all algorithms use the basic concepts of size and randomness, this initialization is available when initialization based on a specific algorithm isn't necessary:

```
void initialize(int keysize, SecureRandom random)
void initialize(int keysize)
```

The meaning of the keysize parameter varies for each algorithm. Other algorithm parameters are given preconfigured parameters. For example, a DSA algorithm might assign its parameters different values based on the specified keysize. If a random number generator is not passed in, randomness is generated via a default system generator.

These forms of initialize perform the initialization based on specific parameters that are passed through the params parameter. If a random number generator is not passed in, randomness is generated from the system:

```
void initialize(AlgorithmParameterSpec params, SecureRandom random)
void initialize(AlgorithmParameterSpec params)
```

This method creates and returns a KeyPair object. Each call to this method returns a separate and distinct pair of keys:

```
KeyPair generateKeyPair()
```

Here's an example implementation of a method that utilizes the KeyGenerator class to generate a private key and public key and store them in a KeyPair object (this is used in other examples in this chapter):

```java
import java.security.KeyPairGenerator;
import java.security.KeyPair;
import java.security.SecureRandom;
import java.security.NoSuchAlgorithmException;
import java.security.NoSuchProviderException;
import java.security.PublicKey;
import java.security.PrivateKey;

public class KeyPairGeneratorExample {
    public KeyPair generateKeyPair(long seed)
    {
        try {
            // Get a DSA key generator from first
            // provider that provides it

            KeyPairGenerator keyGenerator =
                        KeyPairGenerator.getInstance("DSA");

            // Get a random number generator using
            // algorithm SHA1PRNG from the SUN provider package.
            SecureRandom rng =
                    SecureRandom.getInstance("SHA1PRNG", "SUN");

            // Configure RNG and initialize key pair generator
            rng.setSeed(seed);
            keyGenerator.initialize(1024, rng);

            return(keyGenerator.generateKeyPair());
        } catch(NoSuchProviderException nspe) {
            System.out.println("Exception: " + nspe);
            nspe.printStackTrace();
        } catch(NoSuchAlgorithmException nsae) {
            System.out.println("Exception: " + nsae);
            nsae.printStackTrace();
        }

        return(null);
    }

    public static void main(String args[])
    {
        KeyPairGeneratorExample kpge = new KeyPairGeneratorExample();

        KeyPair kp = kpge.generateKeyPair(717);
        System.out.println("-- Public Key ----");
        PublicKey pubKey = kp.getPublic();
        System.out.println("   Algorithm=" + pubKey.getAlgorithm());
        System.out.println("   Encoded=" + pubKey.getEncoded());
        System.out.println("   Format=" + pubKey.getFormat());

        System.out.println("\n-- Private Key ----");
        PrivateKey priKey = kp.getPrivate();
        System.out.println("   Algorithm=" + priKey.getAlgorithm());
        System.out.println("   Encoded=" + priKey.getEncoded());
```

```
            System.out.println("   Format=" + priKey.getFormat());
        }
    }
```

This class utilizes a specific random number generator, SHA1PRNG, from the SUN provider package. It is then seeded with the value specified in the call to `generateKeyPair`. If you take a look at the output, you will see a difference between the private and public key:

```
-- Public Key ----
    Algorithm=DSA
    Encoded=[B@1a46e30
    Format=X.509

-- Private Key ----
    Algorithm=DSA
    Encoded=[B@3e25a5
    Format=PKCS#8
```

The public key is encoded in the X.509 format, and the private key is encoded in the PKCS#8 format. PKCS stands for Public Key Cryptography Standards, and the eighth standard defines the format for private keys. The usage of X.509 for the public key means that a public key certificate was generated. A certificate allows the connecting of a trusted source with a public key, ensuring the public key is coming from the person that it claims it is.

Storing and Managing Keys

A *keystore* is a database of public keys, private keys, and certificates. By default, this database is stored in a file named keystore in the user's home directory. The SUN provider package provides this behavior through a proprietary format named JKS. Each private key in this file is protected by a password, and the file itself is also protected by a password. The `KeyStore` engine class provides a robust interface for implementing a keystore provider. There are two types of entries that a `KeyStore` stores. The first, a *key entry*, contains sensitive key information such as private keys and the authenticating certificate chain, or a secret key. The second, a *trusted certificate entry*, contains a certificate authenticating the owner of a specific public key. The manner in which the keystore is persisted depends upon the implementation; thus, it is not specified by this engine class. The `KeyStore` engine class provides methods to load and save a keystore, access aliases of entries, determine entry types, manage the entries themselves, and retrieve information about the keystore. The standard `getInstance` methods are available to create a keystore.

The `load` method loads a keystore from the specified input stream. The optional password is used as a way to verify the integrity of the keystore. If no password is specified, this integrity check is not performed. Pass in null in place of an input to create an empty keystore:

```
final void load(InputStream stream, char[] password)
```

The `store` method saves the current keystore to the specified output stream. If a password is specified, it is used to calculate a checksum of the keystore data and is appended to the end of the output stream. This checksum is used by `load` to perform an integrity check:

```
final void store(OutputStream stream, char[] password)
```

Each keystore entry has an associated alias that takes the form of a string. The `aliases` method returns an enumeration of the entry aliases in the keystore:

```
final Enumeration aliases()
```

The `isKeyEntry` and `isCertificateEntry` methods provide a way to check the type of a keystore entry. The first, `isKeyEntry`, returns `true` if the entry specified by `alias` is a key entry, and returns `false` otherwise. The second, `isCertificateEntry`, returns `true` if the entry specified by `alias` is a certificate entry and returns `false` otherwise:

```
final boolean isKeyEntry(String alias)
final boolean isCertificateEntry(String alias)
```

The `setKeyEntry` method adds a new key entry to the keystore (if `alias` does not correspond to an existing entry) or changes the key at the preexisting alias in the keystore. If the key is passed in as an array of bytes, the key should be in protected format, such as an `EncryptedPrivateKeyInfo` in the PKCS #8 standard. The alternate form of `setKeyEntry` uses a password to protect the key. The `chain` parameter is used to pass in a certificate chain as a trust source for the key:

```
final void setKeyEntry(String alias, Key key,
                       char[] password, Certificate[] chain)
final void setKeyEntry(String alias, byte[] key,
                       Certificate[] chain)
```

The `setCertificateEntry` method adds a new certificate entry to the keystore (if `alias` does not correspond to an existing entry) or changes the certificate at the entry named by `alias` (if a certificate entry already exists):

```
final void setCertificateEntry(String alias, Certificate cert)
```

The `deleteEntry` method removes the entry associated with `alias` from the keystore:

```
final void deleteEntry(String alias)
```

The `getKey` method returns the key entry from the keystore that is associated with `alias`. The `password` is used to retrieve the key:

```
final Key getKey(String alias, char[] password)
```

The `getCertificate` and `getCertificateChain` methods return the certificate or certificate chain (array of Certificate) specified by `alias` in the keystore:

```
final Certificate getCertificate(String alias)
final Certificate[] getCertificateChain(String alias)
```

The `getCertificateAlias` method returns the alias associated with a specified certificate from the keystore:

```
final String getCertificateAlias(Certificate cert)
```

Along with key management, Java provides a way to specify parameters to cryptographic algorithms, such as changing the constants used by a particular algorithm.

Algorithm Management

Algorithms have parameters associated with them, such as values of constants for the DSA algorithm. The actual values of these parameters are revealed in transparent representations through classes that implement the AlgorithmParameterSpec interface. This interface defines no methods, which thus makes it a tagging interface. Opaque representations of algorithm parameters are addressed by the `Algorithm Parameters` engine class. No direct access to the values of the algorithm parameters is available. The following methods, along with the expected `getInstance` methods, are defined in the `Algorithm Parameters` engine class. After object creation using `getInstance`, one of the `init` methods must be invoked to initialize the object:

```
void init(AlgorithmParameterSpec paramSpec)
void init(byte[] params)
void init(byte[] params, String format)
```

The byte array `params` contains the parameters in an encoded format. The form of `init` that only takes a byte array uses the default decoding format ASN.1 to decode the parameters. The last form of `init` accepts the byte array of parameters and format, the string representation of a decoding scheme. The first form accepts a reference to a transparent representation of the algorithm parameters. Note that initialization can only occur once. You cannot reuse an `AlgorithmParameter` object like you can a `SecureSignature` object.

The following two methods return a byte array containing the encoded parameters. The default decoding used is ASN.1. You can specify a specific decoding format by passing its name in `format`. The default implementation of this engine class as provided in the SUN provider package disregards the `format` parameter:

```
byte[] getEncoded()
byte[] getEncoded(String format)
```

The following returns a reference to a transparent representation of the encoded parameters. The `paramSpec` parameter is used to specify a particular `AlgorithmParameterSpec` class, such as passing in `DSAParameterSpec.class` to get a `DSAParameterSpec` object returned:

```
AlgorithmParameterSpec getParameterSpec(Class paramSpec)
```

The `AlgorithmParameterGenerator` is an engine class to generate parameters for a particular algorithm. Creating an object of this class is the same as any other engine class. A particular algorithm and possibly a provider are passed to a `getInstance` method. After object creation, the object must be initialized using one of the `init` methods. After initialization, you can invoke `generateParameters` to actually generate the parameters for the specified algorithm:

```
void init(int size, SecureRandom random)
void init(int size)
void init(AlgorithmParameterSpec genParamSpec, SecureRandom random)
void init(AlgorithmParameterSpec genParamSpec)
```

Each algorithm uses two core pieces of information to generate parameters: a size and a way to create random numbers. This size could be a number of bits or a number of bytes, all depending on the specific algorithm. The use of `SecureRandom` shows the interoperability of the engine classes. Any provider's random number generator can be used with any other provider's `AlgorithmParameterGenerator` to generate parameters. If no random number generator is specified, a system-provided source of random numbers is used. The first two forms only allow the specification of a single size, so default values are used for other algorithm parameters. The last two forms provide for the specification of each algorithm's parameter. Because there are no requirements made based on the `AlgorithmParameterSpec`, each algorithm has its own `AlgorithmParameterGenerator` that works with the algorithm's `Algorithm ParameterSpec` to generate the parameters.

The following generates and returns a set of algorithm parameters encoded in an `AlgorithmParameters` object:

```
AlgorithmParameters generateParameters()
```

Java has support for random number generators, an integral part of cryptographic support that Java provides.

Random Number Generation

A *random number generator* (RNG) is a vital part of encryption algorithms. Because most random number generators start with a *seed value*, a value that causes a predictable string of numbers to get generated, random number generators are often termed *pseudo-random* because they are not truly random. The engine class for random number generators is `SecureRandom` and, as expected, has the standard set of `getInstance` methods.

The operations available on the random number generator are seeding the generator, obtaining a random number (or sequence of random numbers), and obtaining a random seed that can be used to seed a random number generator. These operations are accomplished via the following methods:

```
synchronized public void setSeed(byte[] seed)
public void setSeed(long seed)
```

Invoking a `setSeed` method isn't strictly necessary. When the `getInstance` method is invoked, the random number generator should set itself to a random state. However, it is possible to increase the randomness by which the generator works by passing in a long value or a sequence of bytes as a seed. Each subsequent call to `setSeed` increases the randomness. A seed passed in later does not replace an earlier seed; it extends it into a more random organization.

The byte array `bytes` is filled with a sequence of randomly generated bytes up to the array's allocated length:

```
synchronized public void nextBytes(byte[] bytes)
```

The following method returns a byte array of size `numBytes`. This byte array can then be used as a seed to the random number generator:

```
byte[] generateSeed(int numBytes)
```

Here's a brief example using the `SecureRandom` class to generate random numbers:

```java
import java.security.SecureRandom;
import java.security.NoSuchAlgorithmException;

public class SecureRandomExample {
    public static void main(String args[])
    {
        try {
            SecureRandom rng = SecureRandom.getInstance("SHA1PRNG");
            rng.setSeed(711);

            int numberToGenerate = new Integer(args[0]).intValue();
            byte randNumbers[] = new byte[numberToGenerate];

            rng.nextBytes(randNumbers);
            for(int j=0; j<numberToGenerate; j++) {
                System.out.print(randNumbers[j] + " ");
            }

            System.out.println("");
        } catch(NoSuchAlgorithmException nsae) {
            System.out.println("Exception: " + nsae);
            nsae.printStackTrace();
        }
    }
}
```

In this example, the user passes in how many numbers to generate on the command line as the first (and only) parameter. The same seed is used every time this program is executed, so the same sequence of numbers will always get generated. If you execute this program and ask for five numbers, you will get the same output as listed in the following example:

```
111 100 -92 -59 -49
```

Much of what you have seen has been in Java for a while. Java 6 introduces support for XML digital signatures, an important facet of a cryptographic package since Web Services have become popular.

XML Digital Signatures

New in Java 6 is an implementation of JSR 105, the Java XML Digital Signature API Specification. This specification implements the W3C's XML-Signature Syntax and Processing at `www.w3.org/TR/xmld sig-core`. The new package `javax.xml.crypto` and its sub-packages are provided to implement this specification. These packages are used to create and validate XML signatures in a variety of scenarios provided by canonicalization and transform algorithms. A natural result of adding this functionality is that SOAP messages can be signed without needing an external library. Therefore, this is of significant interest to any developers working on Web Services. The following table describes these packages at a high level.

Package	Description
`javax.xml.crypto`	Main interfaces such as AlgorithmMethod (parent interface of DigestMethod, SignatureMethod, Transform, and others), URI-Reference (parent interface for Reference, DOMURIReference, and others), and other key interfaces. Also provides `KeySelector` class for finding and returning a key from a `KeyInfo` object
`javax.xml.crypto.dom`	DOM-specific classes, such as `DOMStructure` and `DOMCrypto Context`. This package is used in conjunction with XMLSignature Factory and KeyInfoFactory.
`javax.xml.crypto.dsig`	The core functionality for XML signatures. Key interfaces are Reference, DigestMethod, SignedInfo, and others. Most significant is the XMLSignatureFactory, which knows how to create concrete instances of the interfaces.
`javax.xml.crypto` `.dsig.dom`	Provides DOMSignContext and DOMValidateContext, DOM versions of XMLSignContext and XMLValidateContext.
`javax.xml.crypto` `.dsig.keyinfo`	Provides classes for creating and using `KeyInfo` objects. Also provides a `KeyInfoFactory` class for generating `KeyInfo` objects.
`javax.xml.crypto` `.dsig.spec`	Provides interfaces and classes for representing input parameters to algorithms such as digest, signature, and canonicalization.

You can generate three main types of signature: a detached signature, an enveloping signature, and an enveloped signature. The detached signature is separate from the content it is signing. An enveloping signature signs content inside the signature element itself (thus, the `Signature` element envelopes the content). An enveloped signature ultimately is located in the document it signs, though it does not include itself in the signature calculation (think of the content as a sibling element to the `Signature` element). Included in the code for this book is a custom utility class named `XMLSignatureHelper` that simplifies some of the work needed for basic scenarios of signing and validating XML signatures. The important fragments of this code will be used for the examples in this section.

The terminology used in the Java classes is the same as that which is used in the W3C's document. The following are the most important classes introduced in these packages:

❑   `Reference`: A `Reference` encompasses a digest algorithm and a digest value, and possibly any of the following: an identifier of what was signed, the type of the data, and any transforms that were applied. This element is used to store how certain content was signed and the value of that signature. More than one `Reference` can appear in a document. A `Reference` URI that is null (equal to "") refers to the same document that the element appears in.

❑   `Signature`: This is the root element of an XML signature. At a minimum it contains a `SignedInfo` and a `SignatureValue`. Optionally, it may include zero or more `KeyInfo` elements and zero or more `Object` elements.

❑   `SignedInfo`: The `SignedInfo` element contains a `CanonicalizationMethod` (describing which Canonicalization algorithm was used), a `SignatureMethod` (describing the signature algorithm used) and one or more `Reference` elements.

❑ `Transform`: Instances of `Transform` perform some manner of manipulation on the XML document. Multiple `Transform` instances can be specified when creating a `Reference`. The `Transform` instances are applied to an initial document, the output from each `Transform` serving as input to the next `Transform` in the list. After all `Transform` instances have been applied the document is then signed. The following table lists default `Transform` instances included in JDK 6.

Transform	Description
`Transform.BASE64`	Requires an octet stream for input. An XPath node-set will be converted into an octet stream if given as input. The output is base64-encoded character data.
`Transform.ENVELOPED`	Removes the `Signature` element from the content that is being signed. This provides for the `Signature` element becoming part of the content (that is, being enveloped by the content).
`Transform.XPATH`	Uses the existing XPath language to assist in isolating a portion of a document to sign.
`Transform.XPATH2`	The XPath Filter 2 transform algorithm. This was established to provide a method that is computationally simpler than using just XPath. See www.w3.org/2002/06/xmldsig-filter2 for more information.
`Transform.XSLT`	Provides for the application of an XSL style sheet. Requires an octet stream as input and output is an octet stream. The W3C document recommends that an output method of `xml` is used for XML and HTML documents. Also, it recommends canonicalizing the output from this `Transform` in order to help interoperability.

❑ `Canonicalization`: A `Canonicalization` algorithm is a transform performed on an XML document to put it in a normalized form. For example, line breaks may all be normalized to #xA, white space outside elements are normalized, white space within elements does not change, attribute values are surrounded by double quotes, and so forth. This enables the validation of XML signatures against documents that change in insignificant ways (such as additional white space added during transport). See www.w3.org/TR/2001/REC-xml-c14n-20010315 and www.w3.org/TR/2002/REC-xml-exc-c14n-20020718/ for a specific description of canonicalization. JDK 6 comes with four standard `Canonicalization` algorithms described in the following table.

Canonicalization Algorithm	Description
`CanonicalizationMethod.EXCLUSIVE`	Possibly excludes ancestor content, essentially isolating a chunk of XML. This makes it easy to sign a piece of an XML document and then extract it from a document for signature validation if necessary. XML comments are discarded.
`CanonicalizationMethod.EXCLUSIVE_WITH_COMMENTS`	Same as `EXCLUSIVE` but preserves XML comments.

Canonicalization Algorithm	Description
CanonicalizationMethod .INCLUSIVE	The standard canonicalization algorithm provided. Referred to as INCLUSIVE to distinguish it from EXCLUSIVE. This algorithm discards XML comments.
CanonicalizationMethod .INCLUSIVE_WITH_COMMENTS	Same as INCLUSIVE but preserves XML comments.

❑ DigestMethod: Describes the digest algorithm that is applied to the signed object. The default digest methods included with JDK 6 are described in the following table.

Digest Method	Description
DigestMethod.RIPEMD160	The RIPEMD-160 digest algorithm.
DigestMethod.SHA1	The SHA1 digest algorithm.
DigestMethod.SHA256	The SHA256 digest algorithm.
DigestMethod.SHA512	The SHA512 digest algorithm.

❑ DigestValue: Contains the value of the digest, encoded in base64.

❑ KeyInfo: An optional element that can contain the key needed for signature validation. It may include keys, names, certificates, and other information relating to this data.

Signing Documents

As mentioned previously, there are three main ways to sign a document. A detached signature, one stored external to the data being signed, is most easily accomplished by specifying a URI in a Reference object and then saving the signature to an empty document. An enveloped signature is accomplished using a Transform specified when creating the Reference object. An enveloping signature is created by adding an Object element as a child of the Signature element containing the content that is signed. The following sections examine these scenarios in detail.

Signature Process

The basic process for signing a document is same for all signature types. The way the Reference object is configured and the way the signature method is invoked are the key differences. This process is as follows:

1. Obtain an instance of XMLSignatureFactory.

2. Obtain a Reference instance by invoking XMLSignatureFactory's createReference method.

3. Obtain a SignedInfo instance by invoking XMLSignatureFactory's newSignedInfo method.

4. Create a KeyInfo object containing the public key of a key pair.

5. Obtain an `XMLSignature` object by invoking `XMLSignatureFactory`'s `newXMLSignature` method.

6. Sign the document by invoking `XMLSignature`'s `sign` method.

Detached Signature

A detached signature exists outside (or along side) the content being signed. The detached signature can be stored in a separate document or as a sibling element to the signed content (in which case the signature can be viewed as both detached and enveloped). Using the `XMLSignatureHelper` class, creating a detached signature is accomplished using the following code:

```
try {
    XMLSignatureHelper sigHelper = new XMLSignatureHelper();

    sigHelper.createReference(args[0], "SHA1");
    sigHelper.createSignedInfo();
    sigHelper.generateKeys("DSA", 512);
    Document doc = sigHelper.getSignedDocument();

} catch(Exception e) {
    System.out.println("EXCEPTION: " + e);
    e.printStackTrace();
}
```

When instantiating the `XMLSignatureHelper`, an `XMLSignatureFactory` is automatically created by the following code:

```
String providerName = System.getProperty("xmlSignFactoryProvider",
                          "org.jcp.xml.dsig.internal.dom.XMLDSigRI");

signatureFactory = XMLSignatureFactory.getInstance("DOM",
        (Provider)Class.forName(providerName).newInstance());
```

This code allows for the specification of a different provider via the system property `xmlSignFactory Provider`. If this system property is not available, the default provider for XML signature classes is used which provides DOM-oriented signature creation/validation.

The `createReference` method creates a `Reference` to a specific URI with the digest method `SHA1`. The other three digest methods, `SHA256`, `SHA512`, and `RIPEMD160` can be specified as a literal string. This `Reference` is created using the following code:

```
reference = signatureFactory.newReference(this.uri, this.digestMethod);
```

The `uri` points to the document to sign and the `digestMethod` is one of the digest methods listed in the previous section.

Next, the `SignedInfo` object is created using default values. The `SignedInfo` used by this helper class is created using this code:

```
signedInfo = signatureFactory.newSignedInfo(
            signatureFactory.newCanonicalizationMethod
              (CanonicalizationMethod.INCLUSIVE_WITH_COMMENTS,
```

```
                          (C14NMethodParameterSpec) null),
          signatureFactory.newSignatureMethod(SignatureMethod.DSA_SHA1,
                                null),
              Collections.singletonList(reference));
```

The default `CanonicalizationMethod` used is `INCLUSIVE_WITH_COMMENTS`, and the default signature method used is `DSA_SHA1`.

Next, a public and private key are generated and packaged correctly for the signing:

```
KeyPairGenerator kpg = KeyPairGenerator.getInstance(keyMethod);
kpg.initialize(keySize);
keyPair = kpg.generateKeyPair();

KeyInfoFactory kif = signatureFactory.getKeyInfoFactory();
KeyValue kv = kif.newKeyValue(keyPair.getPublic());

keyInfo = kif.newKeyInfo(Collections.singletonList(kv));
```

The `KeyPairGenerator`, described earlier in this chapter, is utilized here to generate keys based on a specific algorithm. For this example `DSA` is used with a key size of 512. Once the key pair is generated, a `KeyInfoFactory` is created. This is a class introduced to create `KeyInfo` objects to store key information. This `keyInfo` stores a single `KeyValue` object, which in turn stores the public key of the generated key pair.

Finally, the document is signed by invoking `getSignedDocument`. This method creates an empty document and stores the signature to this document, accomplished by the following code:

```
DocumentBuilderFactory dbf = DocumentBuilderFactory.newInstance();
dbf.setNamespaceAware(true);
Document doc = dbf.newDocumentBuilder().newDocument();

DOMSignContext signContext = new DOMSignContext(keyPair.getPrivate(),
                                                doc);
signature = signatureFactory.newXMLSignature(signedInfo, keyInfo);
signature.sign(signContext);
```

The `DOMSignContext` is used to specify where the `XMLSignature` should be marshaled. In this case it is the empty document just created. The signature is created based on the `SignedInfo` object and `KeyInfo` object created in the previous two code snippets; however, the content is *not* signed yet. The actual signing of the content is accomplished by invoking `signature.sign` method with the `sign` context as a parameter. Now the `doc` contains the `Signature` element.

The following is a class that uses the `XMLSignatureHelper` to create a detached signature based on an URI specified on the command line. Here's the code, then an example execution:

```
public class DetachedExample {
 public static void main(String[] args)
 {
     try {
          XMLSignatureHelper sigHelper = new XMLSignatureHelper();

          sigHelper.createReference(args[0], "SHA1");
```

647

```
                sigHelper.createSignedInfo();
                sigHelper.generateKeys("DSA", 512);
                Document doc = sigHelper.getSignedDocument();

                TransformerFactory tf = TransformerFactory.newInstance();
                Transformer trans = tf.newTransformer();
                trans.transform(new DOMSource(doc),
                                 new StreamResult(System.out));
        } catch(Exception e) {
                System.out.println("EXCEPTION: " + e);
                e.printStackTrace();
        }
    }
}
```

The `Transformer` is used to print the document to `System.out`. Using `http://www.yahoo.com` as the URI provides the following output:

```
<?xml version="1.0" encoding="UTF-8"?>
<Signature xmlns="http://www.w3.org/2000/09/xmldsig#">
  <SignedInfo>
    <CanonicalizationMethod Algorithm="http://www.w3.org/TR/2001/REC-xml-c14n-
20010315#WithComments"/>
    <SignatureMethod Algorithm="http://www.w3.org/2000/09/xmldsig#dsa-sha1"/>
    <Reference URI="http://www.yahoo.com">
      <DigestMethod Algorithm="http://www.w3.org/2000/09/xmldsig#sha1"/>
      <DigestValue>cF1Fjd7BkEvUUPPI6uTMX7RzCOc=</DigestValue>
    </Reference>
  </SignedInfo>

<SignatureValue>VlEJx3OiLZ7Nto6RXrBe1ODKfMI5mEUAcVps0FcduvjhyAyygfvmwA==</Signature
Value>
  <KeyInfo>
    <KeyValue>
      <DSAKeyValue>

<P>/KaCzo4Syrom78z3EQ5SbbB4sF7ey80etKII864WF64B81uRpH5t9jQTxeFu0ImbzRMqzVDZkVG9xD7n
N1kuFw==</P>
        <Q>li7dzDacuo67Jg7mtqEm2TRuOMU=</Q>

<G>Z4Rxsnqc9E7pGknFFH2xqaryRPBaQ01khpMdLRQnG541Awtx/XPaF5Bpsy4pNWMOHCBiNU0NogpsQW5Q
vnlMpA==</G>

<Y>u89DetQcoLgKRJVvx5LZY6FrNUrxyoG5ZwvUIHCVFTdbWUOcPwbE01tfsSIoRntm355QTQCOF/BgeyRP
hB03wA==</Y>
      </DSAKeyValue>
    </KeyValue>
  </KeyInfo>
</Signature>
```

The `SignedInfo` element contains information about the canonicalization algorithm used, the signature algorithm used, and the `Reference` element that specifies the URI to the content and the digest information. The `SignatureValue` element contains the actual signature (using the DSA algorithm). The `KeyInfo` element is optional and here it specifies the P, Q, G, and Y parameters used by the DSA algorithm.

Enveloping Signature

An enveloping signature is where the `Signature` element contains the signed content in an `Object` element inside the `Signature`. The main difference between this and the detached example is that the `Reference` object is created with the URI #object (because the content will be in an `Object` element) and when the root element of the content to sign is specified when signing. This specifies which content will flow into the `Object` element.

Take a look at a simple XML file that will be used for both the enveloping and enveloped (discussed next) examples:

```
<?xml version="1.0" encoding="UTF-8"?>
<toyList>
    <toy name="action figure" description="GI Joe"/>
    <toy name="ball" description="Red Ball"/>
</toyList>
```

This time, the `Reference` is created using the following code:

```
reference = signatureFactory.newReference("#object", this.digestMethod);
```

This creates a reference to an `Object` element that will contain the data that what will be signed.

The creation of the `SignedInfo` and generation of keys is done in the same manner as the previous example. The code to load a document for signing is as follows:

```
DocumentBuilderFactory dbf = DocumentBuilderFactory.newInstance();
dbf.setNamespaceAware(true);

Document doc = dbf.newDocumentBuilder().parse(args[0]);
NodeList nl = doc.getElementsByTagName(args[1]);

if(nl.getLength() == 0) {
    System.out.println("Cannot find '" +
                        args[1] + "' element");
    System.exit(1);
}

Node n = nl.item(0);
XMLStructure content = new DOMStructure(n);
```

The `parse` method of the `DocumentBuilder` class can load a local file or content pointed to by a URI. After the `Document` is initialized, the root node that encompasses the content for signing is discovered by calling `getElementsByTagName` and then creating an `XMLStructure` object containing this `Node`. The assumption here is that the first node (or only node) by the given name is signed.

The code to sign the content is as follows:

```
XMLObject obj = signatureFactory.newXMLObject(Collections.singletonList(content),
                                  "object", null, null);

DOMSignContext dsc = new DOMSignContext(keyPair.getPrivate(), doc);

signature = signatureFactory.newXMLSignature(signedInfo, keyInfo,
                          Collections.singletonList(obj), null, null);

signature.sign(dsc);
```

An `XMLObject` is constructed to provide the `Object` element with the `toyList` XML file as content. The `SignContext` is again constructed with the private key and document. The signature is then constructed with the previously created `SignedInfo` and `KeyInfo`. The third parameter to `newXMLSignature` is a `List` of `XMLObjects` — in this case, the `Object` element that contains the content. The `sign` method is then invoked to actually sign the content. Because this is an enveloping signature, the `Signature` contains the `toyList` XML file. The signed document is as follows:

```
<?xml version="1.0" encoding="UTF-8"?>
<Signature xmlns="http://www.w3.org/2000/09/xmldsig#">
  <SignedInfo>
    <CanonicalizationMethod Algorithm="http://www.w3.org/TR/2001/REC-xml-c14n-
20010315#WithComments"/>
    <SignatureMethod Algorithm="http://www.w3.org/2000/09/xmldsig#dsa-sha1"/>
    <Reference URI="#object">
      <DigestMethod Algorithm="http://www.w3.org/2000/09/xmldsig#sha1"/>
      <DigestValue>IK6hYVxCaZRGE3bsw3fiiGBXQ0g=</DigestValue>
    </Reference>
  </SignedInfo>

<SignatureValue>IMW58kXbcAELpkm3cUsUnoM0V+lsa1gBypDEmqkqVeJoW9foFIDx+A==</Signature
Value>
  <KeyInfo>
    <KeyValue>
      <DSAKeyValue>
<P>/KaCzo4Syrom78z3EQ5SbbB4sF7ey80etKII864WF64B81uRpH5t9jQTxeEu0ImbzRMqzVDZkVG9xD7n
N1kuFw==</P>
<Q>li7dzDacuo67Jg7mtqEm2TRuOMU=</Q>
<G>Z4Rxsnqc9E7pGknFFH2xqaryRPBaQ01khpMdLRQnG541Awtx/XPaF5Bpsy4pNWMOHCBiNU0NogpsQW5Q
vnlMpA==</G>
<Y>RIM/yrVLk79mDFwpA7VT+rKfmPGMX5ehIMevdOlCG158U7Ggu8irLnF4Ix9jSOLnCXGnk+U1wJWhZ1UA
Z73Ogw==</Y>
      </DSAKeyValue>
    </KeyValue>
  </KeyInfo>

  <Object Id="object">
    <toyList xmlns="">
      <toy description="GI Joe" name="action figure"/>
        <toy description="Red Ball" name="ball"/>
    </toyList>
  </Object>
</Signature>
```

The `toyList` document is contained by the new `Object` element that the `Reference` points to. Notice that the `xmlns` attribute was added to the `toyList` element, which is added by the `Canonicalization` algorithm.

Enveloped Signature

An enveloped signature is where the signed content contains the `Signature` element. As mentioned previously, it is possible to have an enveloped and detached signature in the case where the actual `Signature` element is a sibling to the content (therefore, it is detached from the content it signs). When creating the `Reference`, the `ENVELOPED Transform` is specified in the List of Transforms in the call to `newReference`. This `Transform` causes the `Signature` element to become a child of the root element of the content being signed. Creating the `Reference` with this specific transform is performed by the following code:

```
reference = signatureFactory.newReference(this.uri, this.digestMethod,
            Collections.singletonList(
                signatureFactory.newTransform(Transform.ENVELOPED,
                                              (XMLStructure)null)),
            null,null);
```

This invocation is similar to the others with the only difference being a `Transform` is specified.

The document is loaded by invoking the `DocumentBuilder.parse` method, same as in the previous example. This document is passed directly to the signing routine and comes out modified, with the `Signature` element ultimately becoming part of the document. The signing is accomplished by the following code:

```
DOMSignContext dsc = new DOMSignContext(keyPair.getPrivate(),
                                        doc.getDocumentElement());

signature = signatureFactory.newXMLSignature(signedInfo, keyInfo);

signature.sign(dsc);
```

The `getDocumentElement` of the `Document` class is used to point the signing context to the root element of the document. This node is where the `Signature` element will be appended. The signed document is as follows:

```
<?xml version="1.0" encoding="UTF-8"?>
<toyList>
  <toy description="GI Joe" name="action figure"/>
  <toy description="Red Ball" name="ball"/>
  <Signature xmlns="http://www.w3.org/2000/09/xmldsig#">
    <SignedInfo>
    <CanonicalizationMethod Algorithm="http://www.w3.org/TR/2001/REC-xml-c14n-
20010315#WithComments"/>
    <SignatureMethod Algorithm="http://www.w3.org/2000/09/xmldsig#dsa-sha1"/>
    <Reference URI="">
      <Transforms>
        <Transform Algorithm="http://www.w3.org/2000/09/xmldsig#enveloped-
signature"/>
      </Transforms>
```

```
              <DigestMethod Algorithm="http://www.w3.org/2000/09/xmldsig#sha1"/>
              <DigestValue>yjRwVuUgEXOkadbGekceHYUXHfY=</DigestValue>
          </Reference>
        </SignedInfo>


    <SignatureValue>BiqzvYOaWHsqj0aL+FReC2TyGGtNVeXWa7wmwEuunNxo7/oUMz1zuA==</Signature
    Value>
        <KeyInfo>
          <KeyValue>
            <DSAKeyValue>
    <P>/KaCzo4Syrom78z3EQ5SbbB4sF7ey80etKII864WF64B81uRpH5t9jQTxeEu0ImbzRMqzVDZkVG9xD7n
    N1kuFw==</P>
    <Q>li7dzDacuo67Jg7mtqEm2TRuOMU=</Q>
    <G>Z4Rxsnqc9E7pGknFFH2xqaryRPBaQ01khpMdLRQnG541Awtx/XPaF5Bpsy4pNWMOHCBiNU0NogpsQW5Q
    vnlMpA==</G>
    <Y>2lz2sepCjKpyQe6f3O+kb1MJNYLy9yQs3isoiQNS7DYElPjO/mswxSHVjOfERGFzfUIr7E1B0+ngKYmY
    qs5xkQ==</Y>
            </DSAKeyValue>
          </KeyValue>
        </KeyInfo>
      </Signature>
    </toyList>
```

The `Signature` element is appended to the root element, `toyList`, thus enveloped by the content it signed. Notice that the `Reference` URI is empty, indicating it is signing the document itself that the `Reference` belongs to. Also notice that the `Reference` element now has a `Transforms` element with the enveloped signature listed as a `Transform`. Before the signature is validated in this document, the `Transform` is used to prevent the `Signature` element itself from becoming part of the data the signature is validated against.

Validating a Signature

Validating a signature involves creating a validation context, unmarshalling the signature using the `XML SignatureFactory`, and invoking the validate method of the `XMLSignature` object. The `DOMValidate Context` has two constructors: one accepts a key to use, and the other accepts a `KeySelector` object. A `KeySelector` is a selector that can extract a key from a `KeyInfo` object. In the following example a custom `KeySelector` will be shown to extract a key from the `KeyInfo` element in the document. This is suitable to validate the output generated by previous examples because the `KeyInfo` element is in the XML content:

```java
public class KeyValueSelector extends KeySelector {
    public KeySelectorResult select(KeyInfo keyInfo, KeySelector.Purpose purpose,
                        AlgorithmMethod algMethod, XMLCryptoContext xmlContext)
    throws KeySelectorException {

        if (keyInfo == null) {
            throw new KeySelectorException("keyInfo cannot be null");
        }

        SignatureMethod signatureMethod = (SignatureMethod)method;
        List list = keyInfo.getContent();
```

```
        for (int i=0; i<list.size(); i++) {
            XMLStructure xmlStructure = (XMLStructure)list.get(i);

            if (xmlStructure instanceof KeyValue) {
                PublicKey pubKey = null;

                try {
                    pubKey = ((KeyValue)xmlStructure).getPublicKey();
                } catch (KeyException ke) {
                    throw new KeySelectorException(ke);
                }

                return new SimpleKeySelectorResult(pubKey);
            }
        }

        throw new KeySelectorException("KeyValue element not found");
    }
}
```

The `SimpleKeySelectorResult`, not listed here, is a trivial implementation of the `KeySelector Result` interface. It holds the `PublicKey` and provides a `getKey` method to return the key. The parameters to the select method provide the necessary information to find and extract the key. Note that this is a basic implementation of a key selector and does not handle cases such as multiple keys (with potentially different algorithms) within the same `keyInfo` object.

The method from `XMLSignatureHelper` to validate a signature is shown next:

```
public boolean validateSignature(Document doc) throws MarshalException,
                                        XMLSignatureException, Exception
{
    NodeList nl = doc.getElementsByTagNameNS(XMLSignature.XMLNS, "Signature");

    if (nl.getLength() == 0) {
        throw new Exception("'Signature' element must be present");
    }

    DOMValidateContext validateContext =
            new DOMValidateContext(new KeyValueSelector(), nl.item(0));

    XMLSignature signature =
            signatureFactory.unmarshalXMLSignature(validateContext);

    return(signature.validate(validateContext));
}
```

First, the `Signature` element is found, and then the validation context is established based on the `KeyValueSelector` implemented and the `Signature` node. Next, the signature is unmarshaled using `unmarshalXMLSignature`. Finally, the validation is actually performed by invoking the `validate` method of the `Signature` object. This method returns true if validation is successful and false otherwise. Additionally, a method is provided in the `XMLSignatureHelper` named `validateReferences` that validates each `Reference` individually in order to show which succeed and which fail. Using the `validate` method of the `Signature` object performs overall validation of the signature.

Certificate Management

Certificates are a vital part of the security picture. Because public keys are, by definition, public, how can you verify that the public key truly belongs to the person that claims to own it? This is accomplished using a certificate. A trusted third party, such as Verisign or Entrust, issues a certificate to an entity (a person, an organization, and so forth) verifying that this entity is trusted. A public key associated with a certificate is then trusted to come from the owner of the associated certificate. A *certification path* is a sequence of trust from one authority to another. For example, one certificate authority (CA) can issue a certificate for one public key, and the subject of this certificate is then used as a CA for another public key. This establishes a path of trust, and each step must be validated for the entire trust relationship to stand up.

The Java Security Architecture provides classes in the `java.security.cert` package to manage and utilize certificates. The `CertificateFactory` creates certificates, certification paths, and certification revocation lists (CRLs) from their corresponding encodings. The `CertPathBuilder` builds certification paths (or chains). The `CertPathValidator` provides the functionality to validate the certification path stored in a `CertPath` object. The `CertStore` class provides a repository for storing both trusted and untrusted certifications and CRLs. All of these classes are engine classes and thus have the standard `getInstance` methods for creating an instance of one of these classes.

CertificateFactory

The `CertificateFactory` engine class is a factory class that can generate certificates, certificate paths, and CRLs. The standard `getInstance` methods are available for object creation.

To generate a certificate, one of the following methods is used:

```
final Certificate generateCertificate(InputStream inStream)
final Collection generateCertificates(InputStream inStream)
```

The first form creates a single certificate from a provided input stream, and the second creates a collection of zero or more certificates from a provided input stream.

Creating a CRL is similar to creating certificates:

```
final CRL generateCRL(InputStream inStream)
final Collection generateCRLs(InputStream inStream)
```

The first form creates a single CRL from a provided input stream, and the second creates a collection of zero or more CRLs from a provided input stream. The `CertificateFactory` can also create a certification path from a provided input stream:

```
final CertPath generateCertPath(InputStream inStream)
final CertPath generateCertPath(InputStream inStream, String encoding)
```

These methods provide a way to create a certification path from the input stream. The second form allows you to specify the encoding used for the certification path.

The following method creates a `CertPath` object and initializes it with the list of certificates passed in:

```
final CertPath generateCertPath(List certificates)
```

A list of certificate encodings supported by this factory is returned. The default encoding is listed first:

```
final Iterator getCertPathEncodings()
```

Following are engine classes used to support the building and validating of certificate paths.

CertPathBuilder

The `CertPathBuilder` engine class is used to create a `CertPath` from a set of `CertPathParameters`. The nature of these parameters is algorithm-specific. The standard `getInstance` methods are provided for object creation. A single method is provided to build the `CertPath`:

```
public final CertPathBuilderResult build(CertPathParameters params)
        throws CertPathBuilderException, InvalidAlgorithmParameterException
```

The `CertPathBuilderResult` contains a `getCertPath` method that returns the `CertPath` that is built using this method. Using this interface allows for ease of grouping and copying (via clone) of the path that is built.

CertPathValidator

The `CertPathValidator` is an engine class that validates a certificate path. The standard `getInstance` methods are provided. A single method is provided to validate the certificate path:

```
public final CertPathValidatorResult validate(CertPath certPath,
                                        CertPathParameters params)
        throws CertPathValidatorException,
            InvalidAlgorithmParameterException
```

If the validation succeeds, an instance of a class implementing the `CertPathValidatorResult` interface is returned. Otherwise, a `CertPathValidatorException` is thrown, signaling an invalid certificate path. The `CertPath` and `CertPathParameters` that are passed in must be compatible with the algorithm, or an `InvalidAlgorithmParameterException` is thrown.

Another important engine class is the `CertStore`. As its name implies, this class provides support for storing certificates and CRLs.

CertStore

The `CertStore` is an engine class designed to store certificates and CRLs. The `getInstance` methods are augmented with a `CertStoreParameters` parameter. The revised `getInstance` methods are listed next:

```
public static CertStore getInstance(String type,
                                    CertStoreParameters params)
public static CertStore getInstance(String type,
                                    CertStoreParameters params,
                                    String provider)
public static CertStore getInstance(String type,
                                    CertStoreParameters params,
                                    Provider provider)
```

The `type` parameter represents the name of a repository type, such as LDAP or Collection for Java collections. The specific `CertStoreParameters` are specific to each repository type.

The parameters used to initialize the `CertStore` can be retrieved using the following method:

```
public final CertStoreParameters getCertStoreParameters()
```

To retrieve certificates and CRLs from a `CertStore`, the concept of a *selector* is introduced. This selector defines the criteria used to select a set of certificates or CRLs to return. The following methods are provided to select and return a set of certificates or CRLs:

```
public final Collection getCertificates(CertSelector selector)
        throws CertStoreException
public final Collection getCRLs(CRLSelector selector)
                         throws CertStoreException
```

Each method returns a collection of their corresponding objects. The selector interfaces both define a single method named `match` that accepts a certificate or a CRL and returns `true` if the specified object matches some criteria, or `false` otherwise. Concrete implementations of these interfaces are available as part of the security library, such as X509CertSelector and X509CRLSelector, which verify whether a certificate or CRL matches the format of X509 certificates/CRLs.

Java Cryptography Extension

The Java Cryptography Extension (JCE) specifies other cryptographic services that are important for a more complete security package. The JCE is based on the same architecture as the JCA and is thus provider-based. The default provider package that comes with J2SDK 1.6 is named SunJCE. The services provided by the JCE are as follows:

❑ **Encryption/Decryption:** Converts a non-encrypted *plaintext* (or *cleartext*) message into an encrypted form using a key or performing the opposite operation.

❑ **Password-Based Encryption (PBE):** Derives an encryption key from a given password, sometimes based on a salt (a random number) to extend the time needed for a brute force attack, which thus makes a brute force attack more infeasible.

❑ **Cipher:** An object that carries out the encryption and decryption of information based on a particular algorithm.

❑ **Key Agreement:** A protocol that enables two or more parties to establish the same cryptographic keys without needing to share secret information.

❑ **Message Authentication Code (MAC):** A short code that is used to verify the integrity/origination of information, similar to using a digital signature to verify data integrity/origination.

The engine classes provided by the JCE are `Cipher`, `KeyGenerator`, `KeyAgreement`, and `Mac`. These engine classes and classes related to each are discussed in detail in this section.

The Cipher Engine Class

The `Cipher` engine class is the largest engine class in the JCE. It provides both encryption and decryption support. The JCE also introduces `CipherInputStream` and `CipherOutputStream`, which provide secure input and output streams when combined with a `Cipher` object. The `getInstance` methods available on the `Cipher` object differ from the `getInstance` methods of engine classes from the JCA.

The `transformation` parameter is used to specify a particular transformation and takes the form of algorithm/mode/padding or just algorithm. Specifying DES or DES/ECB/PKCS5Padding (the default algorithm/mode/padding provided by the SunJCE) are both valid. The `provider` parameter lets you specify which provider should be used. If no provider is specified, a provider is located that provides the requested transformation:

```
public static Cipher getInstance(String transformation);
public static Cipher getInstance(String transformation,
                                 String provider);
```

After object creation, the `Cipher` object must be initialized with an operating mode and other information. There are eight forms of the `init` method:

```
public void init(int opmode, Key key)
public void init(int opmode, Certificate certificate)
public void init(int opmode, Key key, SecureRandom random)
public void init(int opmode, Certificate certificate,
                 SecureRandom random)
public void init(int opmode, Key key,
                 AlgorithmParameterSpec params)
public void init(int opmode, Key key,
                 AlgorithmParameterSpec params, SecureRandom random)
public void init(int opmode, Key key,
                 AlgorithmParameters params)
public void init(int opmode, Key key,
                 AlgorithmParameters params, SecureRandom random)
```

The `opmode` parameter can take one of four integer values that are defined as final integers in the `Cipher` class. These operating modes are listed in the following table.

Operating Mode Constant's Name	Description
ENCRYPT_MODE	Configures `Cipher` to encrypt data
DECRYPT_MODE	Configures `Cipher` to decrypt data
WRAP_MODE	Configures `Cipher` in key wrapping mode to convert a key to bytes that can be securely transported
UNWRAP_MODE	Configures `Cipher` to unwrap a previously wrapped key

You can pass in a key through the `key` or `certificate` parameters (for a certificate that contains a key). The `params` parameter contains parameters for the particular algorithm requested, and `random` is used to utilize a different random number generator than the system source of randomness.

If the mode is `DECRYPT_MODE`, the `Cipher` requires a key and appropriate parameters. If these are not specified, an `InvalidKeyException` or `InvalidAlgorithmParameterException` is thrown. If the `Cipher` is configured for `ENCRYPT_MODE`, these parameters are configured with already defined values unless explicitly passed in to the `init` method.

Encrypting/Decrypting Data

Data can be passed to a `Cipher` object in parts or all at once. The `update` method is used to pass in a chunk of data at a time, and the `doFinal` method is used to either pass in all of the data at a single time or signal the end of a sequence of data that was passed in through the `update` method:

```
public byte[] update(byte[] input)
public byte[] update(byte[] input, int inputOffset,
                     int inputLen)
public int update(byte[] input, int inputOffset,
                  int inputLen, byte[] output)
public int update(byte[] input, int inputOffset,
                  int inputLen, byte[] output, int outputOffset)
```

These methods allow you to pass a piece of data to the `Cipher`. Using these methods lets you process more data than you have at a single time. The last two forms store the encrypted/decrypted data in a buffer passed in, as opposed to returning the data in the first two forms.

The following methods are used to either process all the input at once or signal the end of input after repeated calls to `update`:

```
public byte[] doFinal(byte[] input)
public byte[] doFinal(byte[] input, int inputOffset,
                      int inputLen)
public int doFinal(byte[] input, int inputOffset,
                   int inputLen, byte[] output)
public int doFinal(byte[] input, int inputOffset,
                   int inputLen, byte[] output,
                   int outputOffset)
public byte[] doFinal();
public int doFinal(byte[] output, int outputOffset)
```

The first four forms let you combine the operation of passing in the rest of the data and retrieving the result. The last two forms signal the end and then obtain the result. The last form returns the length of the output.

Wrapping and Unwrapping Keys

The following method is used to take a key and convert it to a sequence of bytes that can be safely and easily transported. The key is encrypted using the `Cipher` so secure transmission is possible. For the recipient to unwrap the key, you also need to transmit the name of the key algorithm and the type of the key (either `SECRET_KEY`, `PRIVATE_KEY`, or `PUBLIC_KEY`).

```
public final byte[] wrap(Key key)
```

This method takes a wrapped key and unwraps it using the specified algorithm and key type. The `wrappedKeyType` is either `SECRET_KEY`, `PRIVATE_KEY`, or `PUBLIC_KEY`:

```
public final Key unwrap(byte[] wrappedKey, String wrappedKeyAlgorithm,
                        int wrappedKeyType)
```

The following method is useful to determine the size of the output in order for the client code to allocate enough space in its buffer for the encrypted/decrypted data:

```
public int getOutputSize(int inputLen)
```

Two classes are provided for chaining a cipher in file input/output operations. The CipherInputStream inherits from the FilterInputStream class. The CipherOutputStream inherits from FilterOutput Stream. Data passing through the each of these is encrypted or decrypted using an associated Cipher object. Usage of CipherInputStream and CipherOutputStream are straightforward. Take a look at the example to see them in action.

Here is a class that provides an interface to using the Cipher class by itself and also utilizing the Cipher InputStream and CipherOutputStream classes. This example could be modified rather easily to work as a utility class using the Cipher engine class:

```java
import java.security.*;
import java.security.spec.*;
import javax.crypto.*;
import javax.crypto.spec.*;
import java.io.*;

public class CipherExample {
    private Cipher m_encrypter;
    private Cipher m_decrypter;

    public void init(SecretKey key)
    {
        // for CBC; must be 8 bytes
        byte[] initVector = new byte[]{0x10, 0x10, 0x01, 0x04,
                                       0x01, 0x01, 0x01, 0x02};

        AlgorithmParameterSpec algParamSpec =
                          new IvParameterSpec(initVector);

        try {
            m_encrypter = Cipher.getInstance("DES/CBC/PKCS5Padding");
            m_decrypter = Cipher.getInstance("DES/CBC/PKCS5Padding");

            m_encrypter.init(Cipher.ENCRYPT_MODE, key, algParamSpec);
            m_decrypter.init(Cipher.DECRYPT_MODE, key, algParamSpec);
        } catch (InvalidAlgorithmParameterException e) {
            System.out.println("Exception: " + e);
        } catch (NoSuchPaddingException e) {
            System.out.println("Exception: " + e);
        } catch (NoSuchAlgorithmException e) {
            System.out.println("Exception: " + e);
        } catch (InvalidKeyException e) {
            System.out.println("Exception: " + e);
        }
    }

    public void write(byte[] bytes, OutputStream out)
```

```
{
    try {
        CipherOutputStream cos =
                        new CipherOutputStream(out, m_encrypter);

        cos.write(bytes, 0, bytes.length);

        cos.close();
    } catch(IOException ioe) {
        System.out.println("Exception: " + ioe);
    }
}

public void read(byte[] bytes, InputStream in)
{
    try {
        CipherInputStream cis =
                        new CipherInputStream(in, m_decrypter);

        int pos=0, intValue;

        while( (intValue = cis.read()) != -1) {
            bytes[pos] = (byte)intValue;
            pos++;
        }
    } catch(IOException ioe) {
        System.out.println("Exception: " + ioe);
    }
}

public byte[] encrypt(byte[] input)
{
    try {
        return(m_encrypter.doFinal(input));
    } catch(IllegalBlockSizeException ibse) {
        System.out.println("Exception: " + ibse);
    } catch(BadPaddingException bpe) {
        System.out.println("Exception: " + bpe);
    }

    return(null);
}

public byte[] decrypt(byte[] input)
{
    try {
        return(m_decrypter.doFinal(input));
    } catch(IllegalBlockSizeException ibse) {
        System.out.println("Exception: " + ibse);
    } catch(BadPaddingException bpe) {
        System.out.println("Exception: " + bpe);
    }

    return(null);
```

```
        }

    public static void main(String args[])
    {
        try {
            CipherExample ce = new CipherExample();

            SecretKey key =
                        KeyGenerator.getInstance("DES").generateKey();

            ce.init(key);

            System.out.println("Testing encrypt/decrypt of bytes");
            byte[] clearText = new byte[]{65,73,82,68,65,78,67,69};
            byte[] encryptedText = ce.encrypt(clearText);
            byte[] decryptedText = ce.decrypt(encryptedText);

            String clearTextAsString = new String(clearText);
            String encTextAsString = new String(encryptedText);
            String decTextAsString = new String(decryptedText);

            System.out.println("  CLEARTEXT: " + clearTextAsString);
            System.out.println("  ENCRYPTED: " + encTextAsString);
            System.out.println("  DECRYPTED: " + decTextAsString);

            System.out.println("\nTesting encrypting of a file\n");

            FileInputStream fis = new FileInputStream("cipherTest.in");
            FileOutputStream fos =
                            new FileOutputStream("cipherTest.out");

            int dataInputSize = fis.available();

            byte[] inputBytes = new byte[dataInputSize];
            fis.read(inputBytes);
            ce.write(inputBytes, fos);
            fos.flush();
            fis.close();
            fos.close();

            String inputFileAsString = new String(inputBytes);
            System.out.println("INPUT FILE CONTENTS\n" +
                                    inputFileAsString + "\n");

            System.out.println("File encrypted and saved to disk\n");

            fis = new FileInputStream("cipherTest.out");

            byte[] decrypted = new byte[dataInputSize];
            ce.read(decrypted, fis);

            fis.close();
            String decryptedAsString = new String(decrypted);

            System.out.println("DECRYPTED FILE:\n" +
```

```
                                    decryptedAsString + "\n");
            } catch(IOException ioe) {
                System.out.println("Exception: " + ioe);
            } catch(NoSuchAlgorithmException e) {
                System.out.println("Exception: " + e);
            }
        }
    }
}
```

The `KeyGenerator` engine class is used to generate a `SecretKey`. This class accepts a `SecretKey` as an initialization parameter, which is then used by the various instances of the `Cipher` class.

KeyGenerator

The `KeyGenerator` engine class is used to generate secret keys for symmetric algorithms. The standard `getInstance` methods are available. After object creation, one of the following methods is used to initialize the `KeyGenerator`.

The following are the algorithm-independent initialization methods:

```
public void init(SecureRandom random)
public void init(int keysize)
public void init(int keysize, SecureRandom random)
```

The following are the algorithm-specific initialization methods:

```
public void init(AlgorithmParameterSpec params)
public void init(AlgorithmParameterSpec params, SecureRandom random)
```

The algorithm-independent initialization allows you to specify a RNG or a keysize — or both — as parameters used to initialize the key generator. The algorithm-specific initialization methods accept a set of parameters (and possibly a RNG also) that are used with the chosen algorithm. What these parameters are depend on the algorithm used.

After the `KeyGenerator` is created and initialized, the `generateKey` method is called to generate a secret key:

```
public SecretKey generateKey()
```

Consult the previous `Cipher` example for a use of the `KeyGenerator` in action.

SecretKeyFactory

`SecretKeyFactory` is very much like the `KeyFactory` in the `java.security` package; however, this engine class only works on secret (symmetric) keys. This class is used to convert keys back and forth between their transparent and opaque representations. The standard `getInstance` methods are used to create a `SecretKeyFactory` object. Three main methods are used to manipulate keys: `generateSecret`, `getKeySpec`, and `translateKey`.

The following converts a key specification into a `SecretKey` object. If the factory cannot convert the key using the current algorithm, an `InvalidKeySpecException` is thrown:

```
SecretKey generateSecret(KeySpec keySpec)
```

This converts a key into a key specification in the format specified by the `keySpec` parameter. If the factory cannot perform the conversion due to the algorithm or some other mismatch (such as incompatible formats), an `InvalidKeySpecException` is thrown:

```
KeySpec getKeySpec(SecretKey key, Class keySpec)
```

This translates a `key` object from an unknown or untrusted provider to a `key` object from this factory:

```
SecretKey translateKey(SecretKey key)
```

A useful class that JCE provides is `SealedObject`, a class that can encrypt and decrypt any object that is serializable.

Protecting Objects through Sealing

The `SealedObject` class is used to encrypt any class that is serializable. It is used with an instance of the `Cipher` class. The constructor of `SealedObject` is used to specify an object to seal an initialized `Cipher` object. One of three `getObject` methods is later used to decrypt the object. The name of the algorithm used to encrypt the object can be retrieved using the `getAlgorithm` method:

```
Object getObject(Cipher c)
Object getObject(Key key)
Object getObject(Key key, String provider)
```

The first form decrypts the object using a provided `Cipher`. The second decrypts the object using the algorithm that encrypted the object and requires a key for decryption. The final form allows you to specify a specific provider along with the key needed to decrypt the object.

Here's an example of creating a custom class, sealing it, and then unsealing it:

```java
import java.security.*;
import java.security.spec.*;
import javax.crypto.*;
import javax.crypto.spec.*;
import java.io.*;

class CustomerData implements Serializable {
    public String name;
    public String password;
}

public class SealedObjectExample {
    private SecretKey secretKey;
    private Cipher encrypter, decrypter;

    public SealedObjectExample()
    {
        try {
```

```java
                    secretKey = KeyGenerator.getInstance("DES").generateKey();

                    encrypter = Cipher.getInstance("DES");
                    encrypter.init(Cipher.ENCRYPT_MODE, secretKey);

                    decrypter = Cipher.getInstance("DES");
                    decrypter.init(Cipher.DECRYPT_MODE, secretKey);
            } catch(NoSuchAlgorithmException e) {
            } catch(InvalidKeyException e) {
            } catch(NoSuchPaddingException e) {
            }
    }

    public SealedObject seal(Serializable obj)
    {
            try {
                    return(new SealedObject(obj, encrypter));
            } catch(IOException e) {
            } catch(IllegalBlockSizeException e) {
            }

            return(null);
    }

    public Object unseal(SealedObject so)
    {
            try {
                    String algorithmName = so.getAlgorithm();

                    // can use algorithmName to construct a decrypter

                    return(so.getObject(decrypter));
            } catch(IOException e) {
            } catch(IllegalBlockSizeException e) {
            } catch(BadPaddingException e) {
            } catch(ClassNotFoundException e) {
            }

            return(null);
    }

    public static void main(String args[])
    {
            CustomerData cust, unsealed;
            SealedObject sealed;
            SealedObjectExample soe = new SealedObjectExample();

            // configure a CustomerData object
            cust = new CustomerData();
            cust.name = "Paul";
            cust.password = "password";

            // Seal it, storing it in a SealedObject
```

```
        sealed = soe.seal(cust);

        // Try unsealing it
        unsealed = (CustomerData)soe.unseal(sealed);
        System.out.println("NAME: " + unsealed.name);
        System.out.println("PASSWORD: " + unsealed.password);
    }
}
```

The only requirement on the class that will be sealed is that it inherits from `Serializable`. The `Sealed Object` class contains the sealed object, and to unseal the object, all that is necessary is the `SealedObject` object. It is possible to retrieve the name of the algorithm used to seal it using the `getAlgorithm` method on the `SealedObject` class. A `Cipher` object is also needed to perform the unsealing operation.

Computing Message Authentication Codes

The `Mac` engine class computes a hash, similar to a message digest, for input data given a secret key. The `Mac` class has the standard `getInstance` methods for object creation. After creation, the object must be initialized using one of the following methods:

```
public void init(Key key)
public void init(Key key, AlgorithmParameterSpec params)
```

The key must be a `key` class that inherits from the `javax.crypto.SecretKey` interface, such as `Key Generator.generateKey()` or `KeyAgreement.generateSecret()`. Certain algorithms require that the algorithm used to generate the key be compatible with the algorithm specified in the `getInstance` call. If this is the case and the two algorithms are not compatible, an `InvalidKeyException` is thrown.

The `Mac` class follows similar semantics for sending data to the computation engine. Data can be passed in all at once using the `doFinal` method or passed in piece by piece using the `update` method (and then invoking `doFinal` to signal the end of the input):

```
public byte[] doFinal(byte[] input)
public byte[] doFinal()
public void doFinal(byte[] output, int outOffset)
```

The first `doFinal` method accepts a byte array containing the input data, computes the message authentication code, and returns that in a byte array. The second form is used to signal the end of input after several invocations of the `update` method. The last form can be used after a sequence of `update` methods to both accept the last chunk of data and signal the end of input. The `outOffset` parameter specifies where in the output array to start reading data, and the data ends at the end of the array.

The following three methods are useful for sending data to the `Mac` class a piece at a time:

```
public void update(byte input)
public void update(byte[] input)
public void update(byte[] input, int inputOffset, int inputLen)
```

The first method accepts a single byte of input. The second method takes an array of bytes. The third allows you to pass in an array and specify where in the array (starting at `inputOffset`) to read the data, and the length of the data (`inputLen`). After you are done calling `update`, don't forget to call a version of `doFinal` to signal the end of input and calculate the message authentication code.

Here's an example of creating an instance of the `Mac` class and computing the message authentication code for data. This example leverages the previous `KeyGeneratorExample`:

```
import java.security.*;
import javax.crypto.*;
import java.io.*;

public class MacExample {
    public static void main(String args[])
    {
        try {
            String inputString = "Test input string";

            KeyGenerator keyGen = KeyGenerator.getInstance("HmacMD5");
            SecretKey secretKey = keyGen.generateKey();

            Mac mac = Mac.getInstance(secretKey.getAlgorithm());
            mac.init(secretKey);

            // the Mac class needs data in byte format
            byte[] byteData = inputString.getBytes("UTF8");

            // Compute the MAC for the data all in one operation
            byte[] macBytes = mac.doFinal(byteData);

            String macAsString =
                    new sun.misc.BASE64Encoder().encode(macBytes);

            System.out.println(
                "The computed message authentication code is: "
                + macAsString);
        } catch (InvalidKeyException e) {
        } catch (NoSuchAlgorithmException e) {
        } catch (UnsupportedEncodingException e) {
        }
    }
}
```

Computing the message authentication code is very similar to computing the message digest using the `MessageDigest` engine class. The main difference is that a key is required. Here, the key is generated via the `KeyGenerator`. Normally, this key would be saved or transmitted for verifying that the MAC matches the data. The `Mac` class is created with the same algorithm used for the key and then initialized with the key.

Program Security Using JAAS

JAAS stands for Java Authentication and Authorization Service. This package used to be an extension, but it was made part of the J2SDK in the 1.4 release of the JDK. Authentication is the process by which the user of the application (any type of Java program, including applets, servlets, and so forth) is verified. Authorization is the process by which an authenticated user is granted permission for executing actions, such as modifying specific files that are access-controlled. Authentication and authorization work together to provide access control for your program, but these are separate concepts.

User Identification

For access control to work, there must be a way of storing the user's identity. This is accomplished using a `Subject`, a grouping of information that identifies the source of all requests, such as a particular user that is logged in to the system. A `Subject` has associated principals, which are other identifying characteristics of a `Subject`, such as a user's Social Security number or name. A `Subject` also has public and private credentials, such as a public and private key, but it can be any object.

You won't usually need to instantiate a `Subject`; however, two constructors are provided:

```
public Subject();
public Subject(boolean readOnly, Set principals,
               Set pubCredentials, Set privCredentials);
```

The first constructor creates a `Subject` that isn't read-only and has empty (not null) sets of principals, and public and private credentials. The second constructor gives you an idea of the information the `Subject` possesses.

These two methods allow you to change and retrieve the read-only state of the subject. If the `Subject` is marked read-only and an attempt is made to change the principals or credentials, an `IllegalState Exception` is thrown:

```
public void setReadOnly();
public boolean isReadOnly();
```

These methods allow you to retrieve a handle to the set of principals, or public or private credentials. Once you have this handle, you can use the methods on the `Set` class to manipulate the contents of the set. Modifying this set modifies the set in the `Subject`:

```
public Set getPrincipals();
public Set getPrincipals(Class c);
public Set getPublicCredentials();
public Set getPublicCredentials(Class c);
public Set getPrivateCredentials();
public Set getPrivateCredentials(Class c);
```

Each version of this access method has a `Class` parameter that allows you to retrieve only those principals/ credentials that are of a specific type. However, these methods return a new set that does not correspond to the internal set of the `Subject`.

A `Subject` can be associated with an `AccessControlContext`. This is a snapshot of context from an `AccessController` that governs how security checks are performed. You can access this through the following method:

```
public static Subject getSubject(final AccessControlContext acc);
```

Note that this is a static method. This method returns the `Subject` currently associated with the specified `AccessControlContext` or null if there is no association.

Executing Code with Security Checks

The `Subject` class provides `doAs` and `doAsPrivileged` methods to execute code that contains security restrictions. The `java.security.PrivilegedAction` interface must be implemented by another class in order to package code for use with the `doAs` or `doAsPrivileged` methods. Only one method is defined in this interface:

```
public Object run();
```

Any code in the `run` method executes with the `Subject` passed to the `doAs` or `doAsPrivileged` method. If permission for all the operations in the code is not granted to the `Subject`/principals, then a `SecurityException` is thrown. The value returned can have any meaning you wish to associate with it or simply return null if you don't need to pass any information back.

The `doAs` method executes a specified block of code as a particular `Subject`:

```
public static Object doAs(final Subject subject,
                          final java.security.PrivilegedAction action);

public static Object doAs(final Subject subject,
                  final java.security.PrivilegedExceptionAction action)
        throws java.security.PrivilegedActionException;
```

These methods first associate the `Subject` with the current thread's `AccessControlContext` and then execute the action. The first form expects the method to return, and the second allows checked exceptions to be thrown from the executing code.

The `doAsPrivileged` method operates the same as the `doAs` method, but it allows you to specify which `AccessControlContext` to use instead of the one attached to the current thread:

```
public static Object doAsPrivileged(final Subject subject,
                          final java.security.PrivilegedAction action,
                          final java.security.AccessControlContext acc);

public static Object doAsPrivileged(final Subject subject,
                  final java.security.PrivilegedExceptionAction action,
                  final java.security.AccessControlContext acc)
            throws java.security.PrivilegedActionException;
```

These provide a third parameter to both methods for using a different `AccessControlContext`.

Principals

A principal can be of any class type as long as the class inherits from `java.security.Principal` and `java.io.Serializable`. The `Principal` interface defines the following methods:

```
boolean equals(Object another)
```

The `equals` method returns `true` if the principal passed in matches the current principal and returns `false` otherwise.

The `toString` method returns a string representation of this principal:

```
String toString()
```

The `hashCode` method returns a hash code for this principal:

```
int hashCode()
```

The `getName` method returns the name of this principal:

```
String getName()
```

When an entity submits itself to authentication, it must provide credentials (information that the security system can use to verify the entity). For example, a user logging in to a system must provide a username and password.

Credentials

Credentials can be of any type, and no requirements are placed on what interfaces a credential class must implement. However, JAAS provides two interfaces that bestow behavior on a credential class that might prove useful. These interfaces are `Refreshable` and `Destroyable`.

The `javax.security.auth.Refreshable` is useful for a credential that requires a refresh of its state (perhaps the credential is valid only for a specific length of time). Four methods are defined on this interface.

The `isCurrent` method should return `true` if the credential is current or return `false` if it has expired or needs a refresh of its state:

```
boolean isCurrent()
```

The `refresh` method refreshes the current state of the credential, making it valid again. The `javax.security.auth.Destroyable` interface gives a credential semantics for destroying its contents:

```
void refresh() throws RefreshFailedException
```

The `isDestroyed` method returns `true` if the credential's contents have been destroyed and returns `false` otherwise:

```
boolean isDestroyed()
```

The `destroy` method destroys the contents of the credential:

```
void destroy() throws DestroyFailedException
```

Methods that require contents to be valid should throw the `IllegalStateException` after `destroy` is called.

Authenticating a Subject

The basic manner in which a subject is authenticated is through a `LoginContext` object. A `LoginContext` then consults another class for the specific authentication services. The sequence of steps that occurs when a `LoginContext` is used for authentication is as follows:

1. A `LoginContext` object is instantiated.

2. The `LoginContext` consults a `Configuration` to load all `LoginModules` for the current application.

3. The `login` method of the `LoginContext` is called.

4. Each `LoginModule` then attempts to authenticate the subject. The `LoginModule` should associate principals/credentials with a successfully authenticated user.

5. The success or failure of the authentication is communicated back to the application.

Configuration

The configuration file contains a number of configurations per application for authentication. Each configuration has a name (usually the application name) and then a list of login modules to use for authentication. The configuration can have one set of login modules under the name `other` to specify an authentication scheme to use when no others match the name specified. Each set of login modules adheres to the following syntax:

```
NAME {
        LoginModuleClass  FLAG  ModuleOptions;
        LoginModuleClass  FLAG  ModuleOptions;
}
```

The `LoginModuleClass` is the fully qualified name of a `LoginModule`. The `FLAG` can be one of the values in the following table.

Flag Name	Description
Required	The `LoginModule` is required to succeed; however, if it fails, `LoginModules` specified after the current one still execute.
Requisite	The `LoginModule` is required to succeed. If it fails, control returns to the application. No further `LoginModules` are executed.
Sufficient	The `LoginModule` is not required to succeed. If the `LoginModule` succeeds, control is immediately returned to the application. Control passes down the list of `LoginModules` even if this one fails.
Optional	The `LoginModule` is not required to succeed, and control passes down the list if this one succeeds or fails.

The `ModuleOptions` is a space-separated list of login module-specific `name=value` pairs.

LoginContext

The `LoginContext` class provides a clean approach to authenticating subjects while leaving the authentication details to `LoginModules`. This makes it easy to change the configuration for an application by adding or removing a `LoginModule`. The `LoginContext` class provides the following constructors:

```
public LoginContext(String name) throws LoginException
public LoginContext(String name, Subject subject) throws LoginException
public LoginContext(String name, CallbackHandler callbackHandler)
       throws LoginException
public LoginContext(String name, Subject subject,
                    CallbackHandler callbackHandler)
       throws LoginException
```

The `name` parameter corresponds to an entry in the configuration used for the application. The first and third forms of the constructor create an empty subject because one isn't passed in. If a `LoginModule` has to communicate with the user, it can do so through a `CallbackHandler`. For example, if a username and password are required, a class can inherit from `javax.security.auth.callback.Callback Handler` and retrieve the information from the user. The `CallbackHandler` interface defines a single method:

```
void handle(Callback[] callbacks)
       throws java.io.IOException, UnsupportedCallbackException
```

One or more callbacks can be specified, allowing you to separate username and password entries into two separate callbacks all managed by a single `CallbackHandler`.

The `LoginContext` also provides `login` and `logout` methods.

This method causes all configured `LoginModules` to authenticate the subject. If authentication succeeds, you can retrieve the subject via `getSubject()`. The subject may have revised credentials and principals after all authentication is performed:

```
public void login() throws LoginException
```

The `logout` method removes credentials/principals from the authenticated subject:

```
public void logout() throws LoginException
```

Essentially, the code used for an application to log in, obtain an authenticated subject, and then log out looks like the following snippet:

```
LoginContext loginContext = new LoginContext("BasicConsoleLogin");

try {
    loginContext.login(); // utilizes callbacks
    Subject subject = loginContext.getSubject();

    // ... execute specific application code here ...

    loginContext.logout();
```

```
    } catch(LoginException le) {
        // authentication failed
    }
```

The `LoginContext` retrieves the set of `LoginModules` to execute from the configuration under the name `BasicConsoleLogin`.

Authorization

Authentication provides for more of a black-and-white approach to security. The user (or other entity) is either authenticated or not. JAAS provides authorization for granting degrees of access to an entity. Each application can use a policy file that contains a list of permissions for various targets. The policy file provides a way to grant permissions to both code and principals.

The `javax.security.auth.AuthPermission` class exists to guard access to the `Policy`, `Subject`, `LoginContext`, and `Configuration` objects, providing a layer of security on these classes as well. Consult the documentation for this class for a full list of permissions that it provides.

The policy file contains a list of grant sections that grant permissions to code or principals. The `grant` keyword is used to start a grant section, followed by zero or more optional elements: `signedBy`, `codeBase`, and `principal`. The basic format looks like the following:

```
grant signedBy "signer_names",
        codeBase "URL",
        principal principal_class_name "principal_name",
        principal principal_class_name "principal_name",
        ... {

permission permission_class_name "target_name", "action",
                    signedBy "signer_names";
permission permission_class_name "target_name", "action",
                    signedBy "signer_names";
    ...
};
```

You can only specify `signedBy` and `codeBase` a maximum of one time, but the `principal` element can be specified more than once. All of these are optional elements. By not specifying any at all, the permissions specified apply to all executing code, regardless of its source.

As one example of a policy file, the `java.policy` that is located in the `jre/lib/security` directory that comes with Java has a policy that opens permissions wide to Java extensions:

```
grant codeBase "file:${{java.ext.dirs}}/*" {
        permission java.security.AllPermission;
};
```

The `codeBase` element is used to specify all code located in the `java.ext.dirs` (a system property) directory, which hence grants `AllPermission` to all code in the Java extensions directory.

The `signedBy` element is used to grant permissions only when the code is signed by the specified entity.

There are many available permissions in the Java API, such as `java.io.FilePermission`, `java.net.NetPermission`, and `java.security.AllPermission`. Each permission has its own set of actions, such as `FilePermission`, needing to know which operations are valid on a particular file (read, write, and so forth). Consult the online documentation for specific details on each permission.

Summary

In this chapter, you learned about Java cryptography and security. Security is very important in online systems and systems that have multiple users. You now know some of the basics of security, such as generating and using keys, including digital signing and key management. Also introduced were the new XML digital signature packages. You have seen how Java supports a variety of security mechanisms from data encryption to access control, and you have an overview of how to go about securing your application.

14

Packaging and Deploying Your Java Applications

This chapter describes how to package and deploy your Java applications including client-side and server-side applications. It discusses Java Web Start, JAR packaging, JAR signing, building WAR files, and CLASSPATH manipulation. You'll walk through the different types of Java applications and get a brief introduction to each as well as information on a few useful utilities that you can use when creating, configuring, and deploying your own applications.

Examining Java Classpaths

One of the most potentially frustrating aspects of Java is the classpath. If you have coded in Java even for a short length of time, you're already familiar with the classpath. It is a system environment variable that directs the Java Virtual Machine (VM) to a set of classes and/or JAR files. This is how the VM knows where code used by the program resides.

At times, you wind up needing a class and have no idea which JAR file has this class. You might add a bunch of JAR files to your classpath, hoping you'll accidentally add the right one in, never truly knowing which JAR files are not needed. Many people complain about DLL Hell on Windows, but a similar mismanagement of the classpath and the many files it points to can create the same situation with Java. If you use a development environment such as Eclipse, you are somewhat insulated from this problem because it is easy to manage your classpath through the GUI. However, in a deployment scenario, you may not have the luxury of a graphical tool to help manage the classpath. A seemingly small problem (one JAR left off the classpath, for example) may take seconds to fix if you know where the class is or — if you don't know — much longer. Also, having multiple versions of the same class in your classpath can lead to particularly difficult bugs to track down.

Another problem with classpaths is length limits on the environment variable imposed by the operating system. I've seen more than one project with an insane number of JAR files (each with a long path) specified within the classpath. Sometimes there is no great solution to this problem. If the classpath works and nobody needs to tweak it after deployment, you should be fine. However, long classpaths are troublesome during development and might even grow too long for the environment space after deployment.

Here are a few suggestions to attempt to manage long classpaths. First, know where your application is executing from and utilize relative paths instead of absolute paths. Second, attempt to group your application and its libraries into as few JAR files as possible. A more complicated but useful solution is grouping the common utility JAR files (perhaps third-party JAR files used by your application) and placing these in the extensions directory within the installed JRE. By default, this extensions directory is lib/ext beneath the JRE directory. By installing a JAR file as an extension, it no longer needs to appear on the classpath. You must ensure that the JAR file is placed within the correct JRE though. This might entail you installing your own JRE with your application, but this too cannot be done lightly. This should be only done with JAR files that are shared across multiple applications running within the same JRE. Using the relative path strategy is wiser for JAR files used by only a single application.

In hoping to alleviate your burden a little, here are a couple of utility programs that may help you in managing your classpath. The first class is a straightforward utility that accepts a list of classes stored inside a file and verifies that each class is present somewhere within the classpath (or in one of the JAR files in the classpath). The file containing the class list is passed in on the command line. Each line in the file contains a single fully qualified class name:

```java
import java.io.*;

public class ClassPathVerifier {
    public static void main(String args[])
    {
        try {
            BufferedReader br = new BufferedReader(
                                new InputStreamReader(
                                new FileInputStream(args[0])));
            String clsName="";

            while( (clsName = br.readLine()) != null) {
                try {
                    Class.forName(clsName);
                    System.out.print(".");
                } catch(Exception e) {
                    System.out.println("\nNOT FOUND: " + clsName);
                }
            }

            br.close();
        } catch(IOException ioe) {
            System.out.println("IOException: " + ioe);
            ioe.printStackTrace();
        }
    }
}
```

This class uses the simple technique of passing a class name into the Class.forName method. If no exception is thrown, the class is found. To show progress, a single period is printed for each class that is successfully loaded. If you manage multiple classpaths, this utility can be used to ensure that a set of classes is always available.

A utility that packs more of a punch is listed next. The purpose of this next utility is to find which JAR file(s) a class is inside. You need not specify a fully qualified class name — any portion of the class name and package will do. This means that you can even search for a package instead of a particular class:

```java
import java.io.*;
import java.util.zip.*;
import java.util.StringTokenizer;

public class ClassSearch {
    private String m_baseDirectory;
    private String m_classToFind;
    private int m_resultsCount=0;
```

An interesting method that uses a bit more complex code is the `searchJarFile`. This method, shown in the following example, actually opens a JAR file and searches inside it for a given class name:

```java
public void searchJarFile(String filePath)
{
    try {
        FileInputStream fis = new FileInputStream(filePath);
        BufferedInputStream bis = new BufferedInputStream(fis);
        ZipInputStream zis = new ZipInputStream(bis);
        ZipEntry ze = null;

        while((ze=zis.getNextEntry()) != null) {
            if(ze.isDirectory()) {
                continue;
            }

            if(ze.getName().indexOf(m_classToFind) != -1) {
                System.out.println("  " + ze.getName() +
                                "\n    (inside " + filePath + ")");
                m_resultsCount++;
            }
        }
    } catch(Exception e) {
        System.out.println("Exception: " + e);
        e.printStackTrace();
    }
}
```

The `findHelper` method searches directories and subdirectories for JAR files:

```java
public void findHelper(File dir, int level)
{
    int i;
    File[] subFiles;

    subFiles = dir.listFiles();
```

```
            if(subFiles == null) {
                return;
            }

            for(i=0; i<subFiles.length; i++) {
                if(subFiles[i].isFile()) {
                    if(subFiles[i].getName().toLowerCase().indexOf(".jar") != -1) {
                        // found a jar file, process it
                        searchJarFile(subFiles[i].getAbsolutePath());
                    }
                } else if(subFiles[i].isDirectory()) {
                    // directory, so recur
                    findHelper(subFiles[i], level+1);
                }
            }
        }
    }
```

The method `searchClassPath` is used to find a class in the JAR files specified in the given classpath:

```
    public void searchClassPath(String classToFind)
    {
        String classPath = System.getProperty("java.class.path");
        System.out.println("Searching classpath: " + classPath);
        StringTokenizer st = new StringTokenizer(classPath, ";");

        m_classToFind = classToFind;

        while(st.hasMoreTokens()) {
            String jarFileName = st.nextToken();
            if(jarFileName != null &&
                jarFileName.toLowerCase().indexOf(".jar") != -1) {
                searchJarFile(jarFileName);
            }
        }
    }
```

The `findClass` method is kicked off from the main method and takes two parameters. One parameter is the base directory that will be used as a starting point to begin the class search. The second parameter is the class name that you are looking for. If the class name is found in any JAR files that exist in the base directory or its subdirectories, the JAR filename and location are printed out to the console:

```
    public void findClass(String baseDir, String classToFind)
    {
        System.out.println("SEARCHING IN: " + baseDir);
        m_baseDirectory = baseDir;
        m_classToFind = classToFind;
        m_classToFind = m_classToFind.replaceAll("\\.", "/");

        File start = new File(m_baseDirectory);

        System.out.println("SEARCHING FOR: " + m_classToFind);
        System.out.println("\nSEARCH RESULTS:");

        findHelper(start, 1);
```

```
        if(m_resultsCount == 0) {
            System.out.println("No results.");
        }
    }
}
```

The `main` method shown in the following example is the driver method of the utility class and takes a base directory and class name for which to search:

```
public static void main(String args[])
{
    if(args.length < 1 || args.length > 2) {
        System.out.println("Incorrect program usage");
        System.out.println("  java ClassSearch <base directory>" +
                            " <class to find>\n");
        System.out.println("    searches all jar files beneath base" +
                            " directory for class\n");
        System.out.println("");
        System.out.println("  java ClassSearch <class to find>\n");
        System.out.println("    searches all jar files in classpath" +
                            " for class\n");
        System.exit(1);
    }

    ClassSearch cs = new ClassSearch();

    if(args.length == 1) {
        cs.searchClassPath(args[0]);
    } else if(args.length == 2) {
        cs.findClass(args[0], args[1]);
    }
}
}
```

This class uses the zip library in Java along with the directory search facilities of the `File` class to search for a class/package specified on the command line. An alternate usage allows you to search for a class within the JAR files listed in the classpath. This allows you to find every JAR file that has a class, which thus resolves a mess in the classpath. Here's an example usage of the program. This assumes that the JDK is installed in `C:\Program Files\java\jdk1.6.0`:

```
c:\>java ClassSearch "c:\program files\java\jdk1.6.0" RSAPrivateKey
SEARCHING IN: c:\program files\java\jdk1.6.0
SEARCHING FOR: RSAPrivateKey

SEARCH RESULTS:
  com/sun/deploy/security/MozillaJSSRSAPrivateKey.class
    (inside c:\program files\java\jdk1.6.0\jre\lib\deploy.jar)
  com/sun/deploy/security/MSCryptoRSAPrivateKey.class
    (inside c:\program files\java\jdk1.6.0\jre\lib\deploy.jar)
  sun/security/mscapi/RSAPrivateKey.class
    (inside c:\program files\java\jdk1.6.0\jre\lib\ext\sunmscapi.jar)
  sun/security/pkcs11/P11Key$P11RSAPrivateKey.class
    (inside c:\program files\java\jdk1.6.0\jre\lib\ext\sunpkcs11.jar)
  java/security/interfaces/RSAPrivateKey.class
```

```
        (inside c:\program files\java\jdk1.6.0\jre\lib\rt.jar)
    java/security/spec/RSAPrivateKeySpec.class
        (inside c:\program files\java\jdk1.6.0\jre\lib\rt.jar)
    sun/security/rsa/RSAPrivateKeyImpl.class
        (inside c:\program files\java\jdk1.6.0\jre\lib\rt.jar)
```

This execution of the utility shows the various JAR files that contain either RSAPrivateKey or a related class (because a substring search is performed with the specified class name). If you search for a more obscure class, such as ByteToCharDBCS_EBCDIC, you'll find the charsets.jar file in your search results. This utility can be used to find which JAR file a class is in but also every JAR file that contains this class. You can find a class you need or resolve classpath confusion if the same class is in a number of JAR files and an older version of a class you developed is being used although you've specified the newer version on the command line.

Investigating the Endorsed Directory

In an installation of a Java Runtime Environment, there are packages that are not part of the standard Java API. These packages are common third-party libraries and are considered *endorsed*, which means they are distributed as an extension to the Java API. One example of an endorsed package is the org.omg .CORBA package providing CORBA functionality. Because these packages are available to Java programs, it is possible that there is a conflict when you distribute third-party libraries that already exist in the endorsed directory. Java provides a mechanism called the *Endorsed Standard Override Mechanism*, which gives you a way to install newer versions of libraries in the endorsed directory.

To override the endorsed standards, place JAR files in the endorsed directory within the JRE. This directory is named endorsed and is located in the JRE installation beneath the lib directory, both on Windows and on Unix. If you have multiple JREs or JDKs installed, make sure you place the JAR files in the correct endorsed directory such that the VM that executes will recognize these JAR files. If you want to use a different directory for overriding the endorsed standards, specify it in the java.endorsed.dirs system property. In this property, you can list one or more directories that have JAR files you wish to use. These directories are delimited by the value of the File.pathSeparatorChar, which is system-specific.

There is a fixed list of standard APIs that you can override, shown in the following table. Note that you cannot arbitrarily override a package in the standard Java API.

Packages that Can Be Overridden	Packages that Can Be Overridden
javax.rmi.CORBA	org.omg.DynamicAny
org.omg.CORBA	org.omg.DynamicAny.DynAnyFactoryPackage
org.omg.CORBA.DynAnyPackage	org.omg.DynamicAny.DynAnyPackage
org.omg.CORBA.ORBPackage	org.omg.IOP
org.omg.CORBA.portable	org.omg.IOP.CodecFactoryPackage
org.omg.CORBA.TypeCodePackage	org.omg.IOP.CodecPackage
org.omg.CORBA_2_3	org.omg.Messaging
org.omg.CORBA_2_3.portable	org.omg.PortableInterceptor
org.omg.CosNaming	org.omg.PortableInterceptor.ORBInitInfoPackage

Packages that Can Be Overridden	Packages that Can Be Overridden
org.omg.CosNaming.Naming ContextExtPackage org.omg.CosNaming.Naming ContextPackage org.omg.Dynamic	org.omg.PortableServer org.omg.PortableServer.CurrentPackage

Exploring Java Archives

Java wouldn't be where it is today without the creation of its archive file format. The JAVA ARchive, which programmers generally refer to as a JAR file, is a way to bundle multiple files, including other JARs, into a single file that is suffixed with the .jar extension. JAR files use the same format to compress their files as those of the zip format. So, you can open a JAR file in a program that understands the normal zip compression and edit away. This makes the format of JAR files portable across different operating systems because most operating systems understand the zip format or have utilities that were created for them to manipulate zip files. JAR files can greatly reduce the download time of classes, images, audio, and other large files by compressing them. Applets and their resources can be compressed into a JAR file, significantly reducing the amount of time it takes to download the applet.

JAR files can also be digitally signed for architectures that require a substantial amount of security requirements to be imposed on the applications being constructed. By digitally signing a JAR file, you can always tell who the author of the JAR file was and if the file has been tampered with. There are two new enhancements to JAR support originally introduced in Java 5:

❑   Faster access to the contents of JAR files has been accomplished with a new parameter addition, -i, to the command-line JAR tool that allows you to create a JAR file index.

❑   A new API has been added for the *delete-on-close* mode that is used when opening JAR files.

The major feature that separates the JAR file from a normal zip file is that of its *manifest* file that is contained in the JAR file's META-INF directory. The manifest file allows you to invoke special features like package sealing and the ability to specify the JAR as an executable JAR file. The manifest file is similar to the format of a properties file in that it accepts NAME-VALUE pair entries that are used for changing specific settings about the JAR file. Along with the manifest file, there are also other files that can be created in the META-INF directory of a JAR file. More about this subject is discussed subsequently. The indexing support allows you to include an INDEX.LIST in the META-INF directory, which is automatically generated when you invoke the JAR tool and specify the -i option, allowing for quicker class loading times.

Manipulating JAR Files

The JDK contains a command-line tool called the *jar tool* that is used to create JAR files via the command line. You execute the jar tool by simply typing **jar** at a console window. If you can't get the tool to run, it's most likely that you don't have Java set up correctly for your environment. Reread the install instructions for your environment that comes with your JDK. You can always run the tool from the JDK/BIN directory, but it is highly recommended that you adjust your environment so that you can run the tool from anywhere. The correct syntax for executing the jar tool is shown in the following example:

```
jar {ctxu}[vfm0Mi] [jar-file] [manifest-file] [-C dir] files ...
```

Before you create your first JAR file, it is important to understand the options that can be used to create a JAR file. Otherwise, it will seem like a big mystery as to why certain options were chosen to create the JAR file. The following table lists the options and a description of the options for the jar tool.

Option	Description
c	Used to create a new archive.
t	Lists the table of contents for the archive file. This is a great way to inspect the contents of the JAR file right after you have created it to make sure it was created successfully and the way you anticipated.
	Note: The f option is usually combined with the t option to reduce the amount of typing you have to do.
x	Used to extract the specified files or all the files from the JAR file.
u	Allows you to update a JAR file with specified new or changed files. More likely you will use a tool that knows how to update a zip file format or an IDE that can update JAR files for you because this task can be quite cumbersome if you have a lot of files to update.
v	The verbose option allows you to get more feedback from the jar tool as it creates the JAR. It is helpful when debugging issues.
f	Specifies that the JAR file to update is on the command line.
m	Signifies that you are supplying the JAR tool with a manifest file that is to be included in the JAR.
0	The zero option tells the jar tool to not compress the files and just package them into the archive.
M	Prevents the default manifest file from being created. Manifest files are optional in JAR files.
i	Introduced in Java 5, this option is used to generate index information for the JAR file into its META-INF directory under the file named INDEX.LIST.
C [DIR]	Instructs the jar tool to change the directory to the one specified and to JAR the files that are being referenced.

Now it is time to show you just how easy it is to create a JAR file. This example will contain two Java files and an images directory. Normally, the Java files would be compiled into classes, and the source code would be removed, but this example simply demonstrates how almost any type of file can be contained in a JAR file. The chess directory contains two source files and a directory, images, that contains the bitmap of the board.

Once you know the files and directories you want to archive, you can issue a jar tool command with the options cvf from the root directory and literally compress the entire chess directory (see Figure 14-1) as well as any subdirectories under it. The c option is used to create the archive, the v option specifies verbose, and the f option signifies that you will be supplying the name of the JAR file to create on the command line.

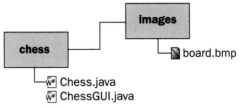

Figure 14-1

Here is an example of the jar tool in action:

```
C:\>jar -cvf chess.jar chess
added manifest
adding: chess/(in = 0) (out= 0)(stored 0%)
adding: chess/Chess.java(in = 0) (out= 0)(stored 0%)
adding: chess/ChessGUI.java(in = 0) (out= 0)(stored 0%)
adding: chess/images/(in = 0) (out= 0)(stored 0%)
adding: chess/images/board.bmp(in = 0) (out= 0)(stored 0%)
```

The chess.jar file is now created and contains all the files under the C:\chess directory. A default manifest file was automatically generated by the jar tool in the META-INF directory of the JAR file. It contains nothing more than a version string. Figure 14-2 shows the new JAR structure.

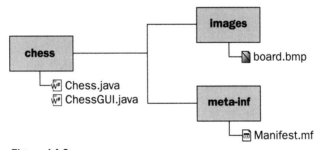

Figure 14-2

You can also use the jar tool to see the contents of the chess.jar file by specifying the t option on the file. Here is an example of how to view the table of contents of a JAR file:

```
C:\>jar -tf chess.jar
META-INF/
META-INF/MANIFEST.MF
chess/
chess/Chess.java
chess/ChessGUI.java
chess/images/
chess/images/board.bmp
```

Notice that the JAR utility added a META-INF directory and the file MANIFEST.MF. Besides viewing the contents of a JAR file, you can also extract the contents of the JAR file. This may be necessary if you ever get into a situation when you need to unpack the JAR to patch or edit files in the JAR file. To extract a JAR file, you will need to specify the x option. In this example, the xvf options are used. Refer to the option table in this section for more information on options and their uses:

```
C:\>jar -xvf chess.jar
   created: META-INF/
  inflated: META-INF/MANIFEST.MF
   created: chess/
 extracted: chess/Chess.java
 extracted: chess/ChessGUI.java
   created: chess/images/
 extracted: chess/images/board.bmp
```

The command simply extracts the JAR file to the current working directory. Now you can edit the files and repackage them if need be.

Examining the Basic Manifest File

The manifest file can be thought of as a file that contains metadata information about the JAR file it belongs to. By using the manifest file, you can version control, digitally sign, and seal the JAR files, packages, and extensions. When you first create your JAR file, if you didn't specify the -M option, a default manifest will be created for you. The M option prevents the default manifest file from being created. The default manifest file looks something like this, depending on the version of Java you are using:

```
Manifest-Version: 1.0
Created-By: 1.6.0-rc (Sun Microsystems Inc.)
```

The manifest file is broken up into two general parts: a main section and an individuals section where information about different files or packages can be listed. You don't have to list every file you have in the JAR file in the manifest file. In fact, you don't have to list any unless you plan to sign particular files in the JAR file. If you do, then those files must be listed.

Information in the manifest is broken up by name-value pair entries. The colon (:) character is used to separate the name from the value. This is similar to property files except in property files, the delimiter is an equals (=) sign. Any attributes that Java can't understand are ignored, but the attributes can still be used by the application. Therefore, these attributes are sometimes referred to as application-specific attributes. The following table describes several of the most common main attributes you will run across and gives a brief description of each.

Attribute	Description
Manifest-Version	The value of this attribute is the manifest file version.
Created-By	Generated by the jar tool, this is the version of Java that was used to create the JAR. It also includes the name of the vendor who created the Java implementation.
Signature-Version	The value of this attribute contains the signature version of the JAR file and must contain a valid version number string with this specific format: digit+{.digit+}*

Attribute	Description
Class-Path	The class loader uses this value to create an internal search path that will look for extensions or libraries that this application needs. URLs are separated by spaces.
Main-Class	This attribute is needed if you are creating a self-executing JAR file. You need to specify the name of the class file that contains the main method. When you specify the name, do not include the `.class` extension, or your JAR will not execute.
Sealed	This attribute has only two possible values: true or false. If true, all the packages in the JAR file are sealed unless they are defined individually to be different. If sealed, the class loader will only load classes from the JAR file that are in the same package as the first class loaded from the JAR.

Though the manifest is not an exciting file to read about, it definitely is worth exploring so you have a general understanding of the power and flexibility it provides JAR files.

Examining Applets and JARs

One of the most common uses for JAR files is to bundle applet code inside of JAR files and make them accessible, like any other applet via a web browser. Because of this feature, a special attribute called an extension in the manifest can be used to incorporate other packages in your applets. For more information on applets, see the "Analyzing Applets" section within this chapter.

Here is a list of the extension attributes that can be used to optimize your applets.

Attribute	Description
Extension-List	This attribute is where you list the optional packages that you would like to include in your applets. The package names should be separated by a single space.
(extension)-Extension-Name	The unique name of the package that the Java plug-in will use to determine if the package is installed is stored in this attribute.
(extension)-Specification-Version	This attribute lets the Java plug-in know which is the minimum version required of the package to use.
(extension)-Implementation-Version	This attribute lets the Java plug-in know which is the minimal version of the package that is required. If the version is too old, the plug-in will attempt to download a newer version of the package.
(extension)-Implementation-Vendor-Id	This attribute is used to assign a vendor ID to the optional package. Again, the Java plug-in will compare the vendor IDs to make sure it is getting the correct optional package.
(extension)-Implementation-URL	In order for the Java plug-in to know where to get the latest version of the package, this attribute would have to be set with the URL that tells the Java plug-in where to download the latest optional package.

Signing JAR Files

Signing JAR files is important for security-aware applications. It ensures that the JAR file has not been tampered with and the file is from the original author. JAR files are signed using a special utility tool called jarsigner, which can be found in your JAVA_HOME/BIN directory. JAR files can also be signed by using the java.security API via code. The jarsigner tool signs the JAR files by accessing a keystore that has been created by the keytool utility that is used to create public and private keys, issue certificate requests, import certificate replies, and determine if public keys belonging to third parties are trusted. The private key is used to sign the JAR file by the jarsigner tool, and only people who know the private key's password can sign the JAR file with it.

When a JAR file is signed by the jarsigner tool, all of the entries in the META-INF directory are signed. Even non-signature-related files will be signed. Generally speaking, signature-related files end in the following extensions: *.RSA, *.SF, *.DSA, and SIG-*.

You can sign the JAR file using the java.security API; however, compared to using the jarsigner tool, there will be a lot more work for you to do. When a JAR file is successfully signed, it must contain an updated manifest file, signature file, and signature block file. Entries for each file signed are created in the manifest file and look like the following example:

```
Name: com/wrox/SampleSigned.class
SHA1-Digest: fcavHwerE23Ff4355fdsMdS=
```

Now that you know the high-level view of JAR signing, it is time to show you a concrete example of how to sign a JAR and use all the wonderful tools that the Java SDK provides you with. Note that all these tests will not be with valid certificates or keystores; rather, you will create example keystores for testing purposes. This is great when you need to develop applications that require you to sign JAR files but don't have access to a certificate or keystore. The following example shows you how to use the keytool to generate a keystore and create a self-signed test certificate that you can use with the jar tool to sign the chess.jar file that you created earlier in this chapter.

The first thing you want to do is create a keystore that you can use for creating a self-signed certificate. The following are the steps involved in generating the key:

1. Execute the keytool as shown. This will create a myKeystore file that will contain your key:

```
C:\>keytool -genkey -keystore myKeystore -alias myself
```

2. It will prompt you to enter a password for the keystore. Simply enter **password**:

```
Enter keystore password:  password
```

3. Next, you will be asked to fill in several lines of data about yourself. Here is what you enter to generate the key:

```
What is your first and last name?
  [Unknown]:  John Doe
What is the name of your organizational unit?
  [Unknown]:  IT
What is the name of your organization?
```

```
   [Unknown]:  Wrox
What is the name of your City or Locality?
   [Unknown]:  Springfield
What is the name of your State or Province?
   [Unknown]:  Ohio
What is the two-letter country code for this unit?
   [Unknown]:  US
Is CN=John Doe, OU=IT, O=Wrox, L=Springfield, ST=Ohio, C=US correct?
   [no]:  Yes
```

4.   The last step is to enter a password for the private key. Here, you'll see the word **password** entered again:

```
Enter key password for <myself>
        (RETURN if same as keystore password):  password
```

Your new `myKeystore` file should be generated. You can open it up and view it in a text editor if you want, but the majority of the contents are encrypted. Even though you have a keystore, you still cannot sign a JAR file until you have a certificate that you can use for signing. Fortunately, the keytool is able to generate a self-signed certificate for you. This is simply done by issuing the following command:

```
C:\>keytool -selfcert -alias myself -keystore myKeystore
```

This command will prompt you for your keystore password. When you created the keystore, you made it using the word *password* as your password so that is what you should enter. This command can some-times take a minute or two to complete, depending on your system:

```
Enter keystore password:  password
```

You now have a certificate and are ready to sign the JAR file. However, how do you know for sure that the certificate and the keystore are okay? The easiest way is to issue a keytool command with the option `-list` on the command line. This will display the contents of the keystore. Here is the output of the command:

```
C:\>keytool -list -keystore myKeystore
Enter keystore password:  password
```

Again, you have to enter your password to access the information in the keystore. The output after entering your password is shown in the following example:

```
Keystore type: jks
Keystore provider: SUN

Your keystore contains 1 entry

myself, Jul 21, 2004, keyEntry,
Certificate fingerprint (MD5): 96:0B:2C:20:EA:DB:87:7A:64:DA:9F:68:21:85:B6:9A
```

The output shows the type of keystore you are using, the provider, and the certificate fingerprint. If you get the preceding printout, you are ready to sign the JAR file. In order to sign the JAR file, you must now use the jarsigner tool. Taking the keystore you generated earlier, issue the following command at a command prompt:

```
C:\>jarsigner -keystore myKeystore chess.jar myself
Enter Passphrase for keystore: password

Warning: The signer certificate will expire within six months.
```

You have now successfully signed your first JAR file! To verify that the jarsigner tool successfully signed the JAR file that you specified, extract the JAR file and review its contents. You should now see two new files in the JAR file: one called `Myself.dsa` and the other called `Myself.sf`. The `.dsa` (digital signature) file is unreadable, but the `.sf` file can be read. The contents of it are shown in the following example:

```
Signature-Version: 1.0
Created-By: 1.6.0 (Sun Microsystems Inc.)
SHA1-Digest-Manifest-Main-Attributes: XpKykodQ7e3bKKW8wqLFO8VocOU=
SHA1-Digest-Manifest: eL4xJ2eU5oyO7h4VVYW0hs1pEj0=

Name: chess/images/board.bmp
SHA1-Digest: wvxwx9Dqd+jbKoe8e7raVxSfNzI=

Name: chess/ChessGUI.java
SHA1-Digest: J1WKkQ915/82bHxMdf4nzrmphH0=

Name: chess/Chess.java
SHA1-Digest: Y4jU1kFH64RojRERTRBEIZRC+uc=
```

These three new entries show the signature for each of the files that were signed by the jarsigner. These entries are now also shown in the `manifest.mf` file:

```
Manifest-Version: 1.0
Created-By: 1.6.0(Sun Microsystems Inc.)

Name: chess/images/board.bmp
SHA1-Digest: 2jmj715rSw0yVb/vlWAYkK/YBwk=

Name: chess/ChessGUI.java
SHA1-Digest: 2jmj715rSw0yVb/vlWAYkK/YBwk=

Name: chess/Chess.java
SHA1-Digest: 2jmj715rSw0yVb/vlWAYkK/YBwk=
```

Another way to verify that the jarsigner signed the JAR file correctly is to run the jarsigner tool with the `-verify` option on the JAR file you want to verify. So, go ahead and issue the following command on the JAR file you just signed:

```
C:\>jarsigner -verbose -verify chess.jar
```

You should see the following output if it was successful:

```
 289 Wed July 21 21:28:58 EDT 2004 META-INF/MANIFEST.MF
 410 Wed July 21 21:28:58 EDT 2004 META-INF/MYSELF.SF
1008 Wed July 21 21:28:58 EDT 2004 META-INF/MYSELF.DSA
```

```
          0 Wed July 21 13:36:18 EDT 2004 META-INF/
          0 Wed July 21  13:27:02 EDT 2004 chess/
sm        0 Wed July 21  13:26:32 EDT 2004 chess/Chess.java
sm        0 Wed July 21  13:26:42 EDT 2004 chess/ChessGUI.java
          0 Wed July 21 13:27:14 EDT 2004 chess/images/
sm        0 Wed July 21 13:27:08 EDT 2004 chess/images/board.bmp


  s = signature was verified
  m = entry is listed in manifest
  k = at least one certificate was found in keystore
  i = at least one certificate was found in identity scope

jar verified.
```

If the validation failed, the jarsigner tool would either throw a security exception, or, if the JAR file was not signed at all, it would send a message back stating that the JAR file is unsigned (signature missing or not parsable).

If you have made it through all of these steps, congratulations! You now know how to sign your own JAR files. This is critical when you need to ensure security on a JAR file. JAR files are generally signed when using Java Web Start applications and especially applets, but signing can definitely be done for all the JAR files you create.

JAR files can also be signed by multiple people. What will happen is the signatures for each of the people who ran the jarsigner tool will be stored in the META-INF directory just as is the case when one person signs it. You can even sign the JAR file with different versions of the JDK so that there are a lot of security options you can do using the tools that have been mentioned for signing JAR files and creating keystores. Before moving on, take a closer look at the options that can be used with the jarsigner tool.

Option	Description
keystore <url>	Required when signing a JAR file and will default to the .keystore file in your user.home directory if you do not specify the keystore file to use. You can specify a full path and filename of the keystore file for the URL parameter.
storepass <password>	Used to supply the password that is required to access the keystore you plan to use when signing your JAR file.
storetype <storetype>	Used to specify the keystore type to be used. The security.properties file has an entry called keystore.type, and the jarsigner tool will default to that value if no storetype is provided.
keypass <password>	Your password for your private key if it is different from the store password. If you don't supply this option, you will be prompted for the password, if necessary.
sigfile <filename>	Specifies the base of the filename to use for generating the .sf and .dsa files. This option allows you to override the default values generated by the jarsigner tool.

Table continued on following page

Option	Description
signedjar <filename>	You can specify another name for the JAR file that will be signed. If you don't specify a name, the JAR file you are issuing the command on is overwritten. For example, you could use `chess_secure.jar` for the name if you want to have signed and unsigned copies of `chess.jar`.
verify <jarfile>	An option for verifying that the JAR file is signed properly.
verbose	Tells the jarsigner tool to output more information during the signing process to help with debugging issues.
certs	Should be used with verbose and verify together. It will display certificate information for each signer of the JAR file.
tsa <url>	Allows you to specify the location of the Time-Stamping Authority.

Examining the JAR Index Option

Downloading JAR files that are required by applets can be slow and painful, and searching them for the appropriate classes they contain used to be linear. Linear searching of a JAR file for a class can result in slow performance, wasted bandwidth, and waiting too long to initiate a download of a JAR file the applet may be missing. With the JARIndex algorithm, all the JAR files in an applet can be stored into an index file, which makes class loading times much faster — especially in determining what needs to be downloaded.

The jar tool has a new option, -i, which means index. This option will generate index information about the classes, packages, and resources that exist inside the JAR file. This makes access times much quicker. The information is stored in a small text file under the META-INF directory called INDEX.LIST. When the JAR is accessed by the class loader, it reads the INDEX.LIST file into a hash map that will contain all the files and package names in the hash map. Instead of searching linearly in the JAR file for the class file or resource that the class loader needs, it can now query the hash map, resulting in quicker access times. The INDEX.LIST file is always trusted by the class loader, so manipulating it manually is not wise. If you make a mistake and the class loader can't locate a resource or file, it will throw an InvalidJarIndexException so that you can capture the error and correct it. You can generate an index of the JAR file chess.jar that you created in previous examples by issuing the following command:

```
C:\>jar -iv chess.jar
```

The contents of the JAR file now contain an INDEX.LIST file in the META-INF directory:

```
C:\>jar -tf chess.jar
META-INF/INDEX.LIST
META-INF/
META-INF/MANIFEST.MF
chess/
chess/Chess.java
chess/ChessGUI.java
chess/images/
chess/images/board.bmp
```

The INDEX.LIST file contains the following information:

```
JarIndex-Version: 1.0

chess.jar
chess
chess/images
```

The INDEX.LIST file is simply text and is compressed inside the JAR file, so the memory footprint of the INDEX.LIST file is light, to say the least.

Creating an Executable JAR

Java supports the capability to make JAR files executable. If a JAR file is executable, it can be run from a console or command prompt by typing the following:

```
java -jar jar-file-name
```

Also, if you are in Windows and your application is GUI-driven, simply double-click an executable JAR, and it will automatically run.

Making your JAR file executable is extremely simple. Just follow these procedures when creating your JAR file, and you will instantly be able to make it executable:

1. Compile all of your Java source code.

2. Create a manifest file, and enter in (at a bare minimum) the Manifest-Version and Main-Class properties. The Main-Class should point to the name of the class that contains the main method in the JAR file:

```
Manifest-Version: 1.0
Main-Class: Test
```

3. Create the JAR file using the following syntax:

```
jar -cmf myManifest.mf test.jar *
```

4. Execute the JAR using the -jar option:

```
java -jar test.jar
```

The test.jar that was created should now execute without any problem if you specified the appropriate class in the manifest file that contains the main method for the application. It is extremely useful to make JAR files self-executing when the JAR files are GUI-driven applications and not based upon initial user input that would normally be supplied to the program via its ARG list in the main method of the application.

Analyzing Applets

Java applets are one of the notable features of the Java programming language. Applets are programs that are designed to run within web browsers that are compatible with and support Java. Applets can be

691

embedded directly in HTML and can be used on web pages to process user input or display information such as the current weather forecast. Applets can also exist outside of the web browser and can have a much more robust feature set built into them like a standalone application would. The downside of making an applet that contains the same amount of features as, say, a standalone Swing application is that, the larger the applet, the more time it would take to download the applet for the user to use. The reason for this is that applets are downloaded every time a user accesses the web page containing the applet. However, this is becoming less of an issue as the caching abilities of the Java plug-in improve with each new release of Java.

Basic Anatomy of an Applet

The basic anatomy of an applet is shown in the following class. You'll notice that there is no main method as is required by a standard Java application. Applets do not require such a method and only require you to extend the class that will be run from the `Applet` class. Instead of having a starting point method, applets have methods that are event-driven. There are five basic event-driven methods that are useful when developing a basic applet: `init`, `start`, `stop`, `destroy`, and `paint`. These methods are demonstrated in the following code:

```java
import javax.swing.*;
import java.awt.*;

public class Welcome extends JApplet {

    public void init() {
        System.out.prinln("Initializing Applet");
        repaint();
    }

    public void start() {
        System.out.println("Starting Applet");
        repaint();
    }

    public void paint(Graphics g) {
        g.drawString("Welcome to Java Applets!", 100, 50);
    }

    public void stop() {
        System.out.println("Stopping Applet");
        repaint();

    }

    public void destroy() {
        System.out.println("Destroying Applet");
        repaint();
    }

}
```

The five methods shown in the preceding code are described in the following table.

Method	Description
init	Used to initialize the applet when it is either loaded for the first time or reloaded thereafter.
start	After the applet has been initialized, the start method will be called. Here, you can fire off threads or begin execution of code.
stop	If the user leaves the web page that the applet is on or exits the web browser, this method is called. This allows you a chance to clean up code such as threads or code that is in the middle of being executed.
destroy	Your last chance to perform any final cleanup that is necessary before the applet is unloaded.
paint	Called any time the GUI needs to be updated based on users' interaction with the applet.

You do not have to override all of these events to get a basic applet to work. For example, you could just override the paint method that displays a string containing the words, "Hello World!" and the applet would function just fine. There are also many other event methods that you can override that will allow you to react to user actions. For example, if you need to capture the mouse-down event, you could do this by overriding the method mouseDown. These are standard AWT events. In more advanced applet implementations, you would most likely use Swing to build your applet.

Packaging an Applet for Execution

Applets are not executed the same way as normal Java applications. They are generally embedded in an HTML page and executed by a Java-compatible browser such as Internet Explorer. Internet Explorer uses the Java plug-in to execute applet code. For development purposes, you can also execute applets that are embedded in HTML files by using the appletviewer command. For example:

```
appletviewer com/wrox/Welcome.html
```

The preceding example executes the applet that is embedded in the Welcome.html file. The HTML code is shown in the following example:

```
<HTML>
  <HEAD>
     <TITLE> Welcome to Java Applet </TITLE>
  </HEAD>
  <BODY>
     <APPLET CODE="Welcome.class" CODEBASE="com/wrox/" WIDTH=200 HEIGHT=50>
        <PARAM NAME="exampleParam" VALUE="whatever">
     </APPLET>
  </BODY>
</HTML>
```

The <APPLET> and </APPLET> tags designate the specific tags belonging to the applet that will be executing. The CODE attribute is used to reference the class name that contains the compiled applet class.

693

The CODEBASE attribute is optional and specifies the base directory of where the applet's class is stored. If you do not use this attribute, the directory where the HTML file resides is used as the base directory.

The <PARAM> and </PARAM> tags allow you to specify specific parameters that you may want to pass to the applet when it is loaded. These tags have two attributes: a NAME and a VALUE. The VALUE can then be retrieved in code via the init method of the applet as depicted in the following example:

```
public void init() {
    String sValue = getParameter("exampleParam");

    if (sValue != null) {
        // This will print out the value "whatever"
        System.out.println(sValue);
    }
}
```

The getParameter method is used to retrieve the value of a specified parameter. In this case, you are retrieving the exampleParam value and displaying it to the user.

Examining Applet Security

When creating an applet and deploying it, certain security restrictions are enforced upon applets by the Java Environment. Applets usually cannot make network connections to any other machines except to that of the host they were downloaded from. Applets are generally restricted from writing or reading files from the client's machine. Also, applets cannot start applications that reside on the client's machine. These are not all the restrictions enforced on applets, but rather the most obvious. You can relax security restrictions by using Security Objects and Access Control Lists.

Applets cannot read or write files if they are considered untrusted. All applets that are downloaded are considered untrusted unless specified otherwise. To make an applet trusted, applets must be signed by an identity marked as trusted in your database of identities. Generally, your web browser can also ask you if you trust the server that the applet is coming from. This aids in giving the applets more rights to your computer. When developing applets on your machine, they are generally trusted because they are being accessed from your local machine. So, you may not see the security restrictions that a remote user would see when downloading your applet. It is important that you understand what your applet users can and cannot do before deploying your applet. Refer to your Java documentation for more information on Applet Security specifics.

Exploring Web Applications

Web applications are applications that can be deployed on application servers as Web ARchive files or, as the Java community calls them, WAR files. WAR files are the same format as JAR files, and, in fact, developers use the jar tool to create WAR files. The difference is the directory structure and files that comprise the WAR file are different than a standard JAR. WAR files generally contain JSPs, servlets, HTML, images, audio files, XML files, and numerous other files that you may find while surfing a normal web site.

So, static and dynamic content make up WAR files, but WAR files themselves are used for two basic reasons. One is to be front-end presentation oriented, concentrating heavily on user experience. The second is a service-oriented approach, which means that the WAR file is used to provide a service to other applications that are calling it. The most common term used for this type of web application is *Web Service*. You can have an enormous architecture that is comprised of Web Services that may use the *Simple Object Access Protocol* (otherwise known as SOAP) to communicate. If you add security on top of the SOAP layer, you will have a complicated system to package and deploy because you will need to manage certificates, keystores, signed JARs, SSL, and other security-related components and protocols. Therefore, WAR files can become much more difficult to deploy in enterprise-level usages.

However, in its simplest form, WAR files are easy to use and are a dream for packaging and compressing web site resources that are comprised of static and dynamic data like form processing or shopping carts. The WAR file format allows the whole web site to be portable and makes it easy to deploy on other vendor application servers that are J2EE compliant.

Examining the WAR Directory Structure

As stated previously, there are differences between a JAR file and a WAR file. WAR files have additional file and directory structures that are used for deploying the WAR file on to the application server of choice. Figure 14-3 is an example of a web application that is deployed on Tomcat.

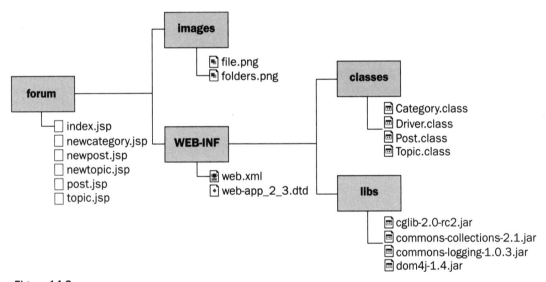

Figure 14-3

This is the forum example web application directory structure that was used in Chapter 6. This file is named forum.war, and, at the root level, it contains all the JSPs needed for the user interface components. The images directory simply stores images that are used by the JSPs. The WEB-INF is the important directory and is the directory that distinguishes a WAR file from a JAR file. The web.xml in the directory is a required file and is officially called the web application deployment descriptor. The classes directory is where you would store your compiled classes that can be used by JSPs or servlets. The libs directory contains all the necessary JAR files to make your web application work.

Understanding the WAR Deployment Descriptor

The web application deployment descriptor is used to configure your web application. In this example, this deployment descriptor is called web.xml. The deployment descriptor contains the following basic XML elements that are configurable and must appear in this order.

Element	Description
icon	Has two child elements that represent the small icon and the large icon for a GUI tool.
display-name	Contains a short name this is intended for tools to use. It doesn't have to be unique.
description	Used to describe information to the parent element and is used in a number of different elements.
distributable	By having the distributable element present, you are signifying that the web application is programmed to be distributed in a servlet container.
context-param	Used to initialize a web application's servlet context.
filter	Specifically used to map servlets or URL patterns for web applications.
filter-mapping	Used by the container to decide which filters to map a request to.
listener	This element and its sub-elements are used to declare web application listener beans. You simply specify the class that is the listener bean.
servlet	The servlet element and its sub-elements are used to designate a specific class or JSP as a servlet and to provide specific configurations for that servlet.
servlet-mapping	Simply defines a mapping between a servlet and a specific URL pattern.
session-config	Useful for configuring the session information for a web application.
mime-mapping	Allows you to map between a file extension and a mime type.
welcome-file-list	Used to determine the first page to be displayed when users hit your web application.
error-page	When errors occur, the mapping in this element allows you to map an error code to an error page.
taglib	Use this element to describe the JSP tag library.
resource-ref	Allows you to specify external resources to use in your web application.
security-constraint	Allows you to associate security restraints with a particular resource.
login-config	Used to specify the authentication method to be used for the web application as well as any authentication constraints.
security-role	Allows you to define security roles for your web application.
env-entry	Used to specify environment entries that can be picked up by classes, JSPs, and so forth that exist in your web application.

Although the table explains the different elements and attributes used when creating a deployment descriptor, it can be confusing to try and understand how to use them. The following is a sample `web.xml` file for Tomcat that will hopefully shed some light on how to appropriately use some of the elements discussed in the previous table:

```xml
<?xml version="1.0" encoding="ISO-8859-1"?>

<!DOCTYPE web-app
    PUBLIC "-//Sun Microsystems, Inc.//DTD Web Application 2.3//EN"
    " http://java.sun.com/dtd/web-app_2_3.dtd">
<web-app>
```

Deployment descriptors are XML files; therefore, they require a standard prolog that is displayed in the previous example:

```xml
    <display-name>HelloWAR</display-name>
    <description> HelloWAR </description>


<servlet>
    <servlet-name>HelloServlet</servlet-name>
    <servlet-class>HelloServlet</servlet-class>
    <load-on-startup>1</load-on-startup>
</servlet>
```

The `<servlet>` element allows you to specify information about a servlet that exists in the web application — in this case HelloServlet. The `<load-on-startup>` attribute signifies that the application server should load the servlet upon startup:

```xml
<!-Creating mime type mappings -->
<mime-mapping>
    <extension>txt</extension>
    <mime-type>text/plain</mime-type>
</mime-mapping>
<mime-mapping>
    <extension>html</extension>
    <mime-type>text/html</mime-type>
</mime-mapping>
<mime-mapping>
    <extension>htm</extension>
    <mime-type>text/html</mime-type>
</mime-mapping>
<mime-mapping>
    <extension>gif</extension>
    <mime-type>image/gif</mime-type>
</mime-mapping>
<mime-mapping>
    <extension>jpg</extension>
    <mime-type>image/jpeg</mime-type>
</mime-mapping>
```

The `<mime-mapping>` element contains two attributes called `<mime-type>` and `<extension>`. These are used specifically for mapping mime types to file extensions:

```
<welcome-file-list>
  <welcome-file>index.html</welcome-file>
</welcome-file-list>
```

One of the most common elements, `<welcome-file-list>`, is shown in the preceding example. This element has an attribute called `<welcome-file>` that lets you specify the file to be loaded when a user first accesses your web application:

```
<security-constraint>
    <web-resource-collection>
        <web-resource-name>Hello View</web-resource-name>
        <url-pattern>/hello.jsp</url-pattern>
    </web-resource-collection>
    <auth-constraint>
        <role-name>tomcat</role-name>
    </auth-constraint>
</security-constraint>

  <login-config>
      <auth-method>BASIC</auth-method>
      <realm-name>Hello View</realm-name>
  </login-config>

  <security-role>
      <description>
        An example role defined in "conf/tomcat-users.xml"
      </description>
      <role-name>tomcat</role-name>
  </security-role>

</web-app>
```

The `<security-constraint>` element contains attributes that allow you to assign roles to specific web resources. In this example, the role of Tomcat is being assigned to `hello.jsp`. This means that only users with the specified role of Tomcat can view the JSP. The `<security-role>` element shows you how to define a role in the web application deployment descriptor.

Packaging Enterprise JavaBeans

Chapter 10 discusses the various classes that are needed to develop different types of EJBs and also has a good loan calculator example that will help you get your feet wet with EJBs. The inherent problem with deploying EJBs is that the EJB specification isn't specific enough about the deployment process and allows the vendors of application servers to interpret the art of deploying EJBs the way they see fit. Now, the vendors have an opportunity to interject their own proprietary deployment requirements. This makes it a painful experience if you want to move your EJBs from one vendor to another. So, the best advice is to simply read the specific documentation on the vendor of choice that you want to house your EJBs.

All is not lost though in terms of deployment standardization. One common file must exist in all EJBs — the `ejb-jar.xml` that resides in the `META-INF` directory of your EJBs' JAR file. The `ejb-jar.xml` file is the basic EJB deployment descriptor that must be used by the EJB container to locate the necessary classes, interfaces, security restrictions, and transaction management support. The `ejb-jar.xml` file will usually coexist with the vendor's application server deployment descriptor. For example, if you were to use JBoss as your application server, you would have to also configure a `jboss.xml` file with your EJBs. Chapter 10 has a good demonstration and explanation of what type of information is contained in the `ejb-jar.xml` file. It is recommended that you review the examples that are in Chapter 10 for specific information on how to deploy and package an EJB application.

Inspecting Enterprise Archives

Once you have developed your EJBs and WARs, you should have all the components of a full application — from the business logic (and maybe database logic) to the user interface for the Web. You may have just a couple files or perhaps a large number of files. Either way, you might be looking at your application and wondering if there is a way to tidy up that directory. If you have multiple applications that use distinct EJBs and WARs, then you're almost definitely thinking, "There must be some way to easily group and distinguish these two applications." Your thinking would be correct, and this is where Enterprise Archives (EARs) come into the picture. Even though mistakenly called Enterprise Applications at times, this name might be more meaningful, because inside an EAR file resides all your EJBs and WARs.

An EAR file has its own descriptor file, much like EJBs and WARs. Other than that the directory structure of an EAR is arbitrary, you can develop any scheme that best suits your application. An EAR file may look like Figure 14-4. Note that there is one WAR file but multiple EJB JAR files packaged inside the EAR. This grouping is useful to make your application a single, logical unit.

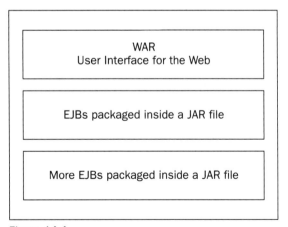

WAR
User Interface for the Web

EJBs packaged inside a JAR file

More EJBs packaged inside a JAR file

Figure 14-4

The EAR Descriptor File

The descriptor file is named `application.xml` and is located in the `META-INF` directory in the EAR file. The main component of this file is the `module` element. The following is an example of this file:

```xml
<?xml version="1.0" encoding="UTF-8"?>

<application xmlns="http://java.sun.com/xml/ns/j2ee"
             xmlns:xsi="http://www.w3.org/2001/XMLSchema-instance"
             xsi:schemaLocation="http://java.sun.com/xml/ns/j2ee
             http://java.sun.com/xml/ns/j2ee/application_1_4.xsd"
             version="1.4">

  <display-name>Example EAR file</display-name>
  <description>Simple example</description>

  <module>
    <ejb>ejb1.jar</ejb>
  </module>

  <module>
    <ejb>ejb2.jar</ejb>
  </module>

  <module>
    <web>
      <web-uri>mainUI.war</web-uri>
      <context-root>web</context-root>
    </web>
  </module>
</application>
```

Each instance of the `module` element specifies a particular module to load. This module can be an EJB (using the `ejb` element), a web application (using the `web` element), a connector (using the `connector` element), or a Java client module (using the `Java` element). The `context-root` element for web applications specifies the root directory to use for the execution of the web application.

Deployment Scenario

The previous section described a straightforward approach to packaging and using EAR files. What happens, though, if you have multiple applications that all depend upon some central component? Take a look at Figure 14-5. In this scenario, a second EAR file depends upon a component packaged in the first.

Although this scenario may seem like it solves the problem, it just ends up creating new deployment problems. First, Application A has no dependency on Application B, but the opposite is not true. If Application A were to fail or be brought down for maintenance, then Application B would also be down. Second, you have to create some way of adding the stub code to Application B that is necessary to utilize the EJBs in Application A. This is not addressed by the J2EE specification.

Another option is to package all these components into the same EAR file, effectively combining multiple applications into a single file. Of course, this approach has problems, too. In the real world, two different applications will have different deployment and uptime requirements. One application might have to always be available to its users, but the other one might have different memory requirements or only need to be up during the night. This makes packaging both applications within the same EAR file a poor choice due to the disparate requirements.

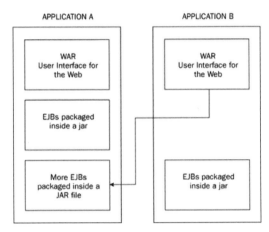

Figure 14-5

Another significant problem whenever there is a shared component between two or more applications is version incompatibility. Because the shared component usually has a single owning entity, classes inside the shared component might change method signatures, and this may break other applications that weren't expecting the method to change.

So, any route you choose seems to have its own set of problems. There is one other deployment scenario. You can take the shared component and place it inside each application's EAR file. This makes one EAR file totally separate from another. This still presents a deployment problem though. What happens when the API changes but the component used by all EARs is only updated in one EAR? This scenario makes it easy for different EAR files to all have different versions of this common component.

The basic approach you should take when deciding how to package your various enterprise applications and shared components is to consider each deployment scenario and pick the one that will (hopefully) cause the fewest nightmares for you in the future. Consult the following table for a summary of these deployment scenarios and rough guidelines as to when to use each one.

Scenario	When to Use
Shared component external to EARs	❑ Applications have different runtime requirements. ❑ API of shared component is not expected to change, or it is easy to update all applications that use the shared API.
Shared component packaged in a single EAR	❑ Applications have compatible uptime requirements and system requirements. ❑ API of shared component is not expected to change, or it is easy to update all applications that use the shared API.

Scenario	When to Use
Placing shared component in each EAR	❑ Each EAR is on a different system, and the systems cannot communicate with each other. ❑ The shared component is expected to stay relatively the same over time, or updating each EAR with a new version is easy.

Jumping into Java Web Start

Web-based solutions have become the standard for delivering client/server applications even though web browsers were never intended to be used to deliver anything other than static content. Developers continue to stretch the bounds of web technologies in search of the best solution. Applets appeared to be the answer because they delivered such a strong feature set and were able to be embedded in a Java-supporting web browser. Applets still require a significant amount of download time and are still not as rich as a thick client is. *Java Web Start* is based on the Java Network Launch Protocol (JNLP) and the Java 2 platform. Java Web Start was introduced as a standard component in Java 1.4. Because of Java Web Start's unique architecture, it only takes one click to download the application you wish to launch from a web browser. The link that you click is the JNLP file that tells Java to launch Web Start and download the application.

This section teaches you how to package and deploy a Java Web Start application through an example of an all-time favorite game, tic-tac-toe.

Examining the TicTacToe Example

This example goes into detail on how to create, package, deploy, and launch a Java Web Start application. The game is not exceptionally smart and could be enhanced by adding an artificial intelligence (AI) capability. An AI would have been overkill for the purpose of this demonstration. The following table is a list of files that make up the TicTacToe example.

File	Description
tictactoe.jnlp	The Java Network Launch Protocol file that contains all the specific attributes to tell Java Web Start how to launch the application. It is also the file that the user clicks on to execute the application.
ttt.htm	Contains a link to the `tictactoe.jnlp` file used to launch the application.
TTTMain.java	The source file with the main method in it that drives the application.
TTTGui.java	Contains all the Swing code necessary to handle the user interaction with the game.
TTTLogic.java	Contains all the game logic and is used to determine who wins, whose move it is, and what positions are open on the board. This is the perfect spot to add an artificial intelligence capability.
tictactoe.jar	The signed JAR file that contains the compiled code and will be launched by Java Web Start.

The `tictactoe.jar` file, the `ttt.htm` file, and the `tictactoe.jnlp` must all be deployed to a web server so the user can download the application. When the user clicks the link that is in the `ttt.htm` file, the following window is displayed to the user (see Figure 14-6).

Figure 14-6

This window is displayed until the application is downloaded. Once it is downloaded, the application is launched, and the user can begin using it. If there is no specific code to tie the application to network use, the user can also use the application offline! Try that with an applet! The TicTacToe application shown in Figure 14-7 appears as any normal thick client would.

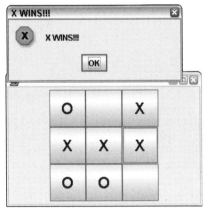

Figure 14-7

This is what makes Java Web Start so powerful and the technology of the future. It is just now starting to catch on in the world of distributed computing and is proving to have all the security features required to be a strong enterprise solution to complicated applications that require heavy client-side processing. Also, by moving the processing to the client, you eliminate the load on the server.

TicTacToe.JNLP

Before you actually create and deploy the JNLP file, you do have to make sure that whatever web server you are using is configured to properly handle the JNLP mime type. To do this, simply add an entry in your deployment descriptor for the JNLP extension. In Tomcat, you can do this in the `WEB-INF/web.xml` file with the following XML entry:

```
<mime-mapping>
    <extension>jnlp</extension>
```

```
    <mime-type>application/x-java-jnlp-file</mime-type>
  </mime-mapping>
```

Now that you are sure the web server can handle the JNLP extension, you can create the JNLP file:

```
  <?xml version="1.0" encoding="utf-8"?>
  <jnlp
    spec="1.0+"
    codebase="http://localhost/ttt"
    href="tictactoe.jnlp">
```

The `<spec>` attribute is used to denote the JNLP specification version. The next attribute, `<codebase>`, is used as a base directory to locate resources on the web server. The final attribute, `href`, is used to point to the JNLP file:

```
    <information>
        <title>TIC TAC TOE</title>
        <vendor>TTT Team</vendor>
        <homepage href="http://localhost/ttt/ttt.htm"/>

        <description>TICTACTOE GAME</description>

        <description kind="short">
            A demo of the capabilities of JAVA WebStart.
        </description>

        <offline-allowed/>
    </information>
```

The `<information>` element supplies Java Web Start with general information about the application. It has a `<title>` attribute to signify the title of the application. It also has a `<vendor>` attribute to denote the company, organization, or supplier of the application. There is also a `<homepage>` attribute that is used to tell the person where to go to get more information on the application. The `<description>` attribute is used to give the application a description. There is also a short `<description>` attribute if you need to supply one; finally, the `<offline-allowed>` attribute signifies the application can be used offline. If this attribute is not supplied, the application cannot be launched without being first connected to the network:

```
    <security>
        <all-permissions/>
    </security>
    <resources>
      <j2se version="1.6"/>
      <jar href="tictactoe.jar"/>
    </resources>
    <application-desc main-class="com.wrox.TTTMain"/>
  </jnlp>
```

The security of a Java Web Start application is the same as that of an applet — it is restrictive unless instructed otherwise. You are specifying an `<all-permissions/>` attribute that gives the application full access to the client's machine. The `<resources>` element defines attributes that are needed in order to run properly. The `<j2se>` attribute signifies which Java platform to run the application on. The `<jar>` attribute tells Java Web Start which classes are required to run the application. Keep in mind that there can be multiple <jar> tags depending on your needs. The final element is the <application-desc> element that is instructing Java Web Start to run the com.wrox.TTTMain class. The importance of the <application-desc> tag is to let Java Web Start know that it is to run an application, not an applet:

```
<html>
<head>
<meta http-equiv="Content-Language" content="en-us">
<meta http-equiv="Content-Type" content="text/html; charset=windows-1252">

<title>TIC TAC TOE GAME!</title>
</head>

<body topmargin="0" leftmargin="0" link="#000080" vlink="#000080">

<center><A HREF="tictactoe.jnlp">Click Here to Launch TICTACTOE Game</A></center>

</body>
</html>
```

The ttt.htm file is shown in the previous example and is illustrated to teach you how to set up an HTML file to launch a Java Web Start application. As you can see, all that is required is to have the HREF tag point to the JNLP file.

TTTMain.java

The TTTMain class is the simple driver class for the application. Java Web Start calls this class to launch the application:

```
public class TTTMain {
  public static void main(String[] args) {
    TTTLogic tLogic = new TTTLogic();
    TTTGui tg = new TTTGui(tLogic);

    // Set the GUI visible
    tg.setVisible(true);
  }
}
```

This class creates the TTTLogic object that is to be used by the GUI. So, when users interact with the application, the GUI can track their interactions using this object.

TTTLogic.java

This class contains the most complicated code for the example. It keeps track of player moves, player turns, player positions, and whether or not there is a winner. There is a member variable called m_nBoard, which is a two-dimensional array that always keeps track of which squares are occupied on the board:

```
public class TTTLogic {
  int [][]m_nBoard;
  int m_nX, m_nO;

  boolean m_bXTurn;
```

The `TTTLogic` constructor sets the values for X and O in the `m_nX` and `m_nO` variables and sets the default to turn to X. Finally, it clears the board array by setting it with all zeros:

```java
public TTTLogic() {

    m_nX = 1;
    m_nO = 2;

    m_bXTurn = true;

    // Initialize array
    m_nBoard = new int[3][3];

    // Clear the board
    for (int x = 0; x < 3; x++){
        for (int y = 0; y < 3; y++) {
            m_nBoard[x][y] = 0;
        }
    }
}
```

The `getMarker` method takes an `x` and a `y` parameter. The `x` parameter represents a row, and the `y` parameter represents a column. The method will return the value for the particular square on the board that is requested. For example, an `x` value of 0 and a `y` value of 2 would result in the value of the upper-right corner square being returned:

```java
public int getMarker(int x, int y) {
    return m_nBoard[x][y];
}
```

The `setMarker` is the opposite of `getMarker` and actually sets the marker value of a specified square. It knows which mark to put in by determining whose turn it is using the `this.getXTurn` method. Once the marker has been set, the method advances the turn to the next player:

```java
public boolean setMarker(int x, int y) {
    int nIsFree = 0;

    nIsFree = getMarker(x, y);

    if (nIsFree == 0) {
        if (this.getXTurn() == true) {
            m_nBoard[x][y] = m_nX;
            this.setXTurn(false);
        } else {
            m_nBoard[x][y] = m_nO;
            this.setXTurn(true);
        }
        return true;
    }
    return false;
}
```

The `getWinner` method is a large method that determines who the winner is by executing different checks on the board. The checking for the O winner was purposely removed to save space in the chapter:

```java
public int getWinner() {
    // 1 = X
    // 2 = O
    int nWinner = 0;
    int nCount = 0;

    // -------- CHECK FOR an X winner
    // check the across boxes first for X
    for (int x = 0; x < 3; x++){
        nCount = 0;
        for (int y = 0; y < 3; y++) {
            if (m_nBoard[x][y] == m_nX) {
                nCount++;
            } else {
                break;
            }
        }
        if (nCount == 3) {
            nWinner = m_nX; // X Wins!
            return nWinner;
        }
    }
```

So far, you have checked the across squares to see if there is a winner. If the winner is X, the value of `m_nX` is returned. Next, you will check the down squares and see if X has won:

```java
    // check the down boxes first for X
    for (int y = 0; y < 3; y++){
        nCount = 0;
        for (int x = 0; x < 3; x++) {
            if (m_nBoard[x][y] == m_nX) {
                nCount++;
            } else {
                break;
            }
        }
        if (nCount == 3) {
            nWinner = m_nX; // X Wins!
            return nWinner;
        }
    }
```

Finally, you need to check diagonally to see if X has won. If not, then you will need to search to see if O has won:

```java
    // Check Diagonals
    if (m_nBoard[0][0] == m_nX && m_nBoard[1][1] == m_nX &&
        m_nBoard[2][2] == m_nX) {

        nWinner = m_nX; // X Wins!
```

```
            return nWinner;
        } else if (m_nBoard[2][0] == m_nX && m_nBoard[1][1] == m_nX &&
                m_nBoard[0][2] == m_nX) {
            nWinner = m_nX; // X Wins!
            return nWinner;
        }

        return nWinner;
    }
```

The method `getXTurn` is used to determine if it is player X's turn or not. The `setXTurn` allows you to set whether it is player X's turn:

```
public boolean getXTurn() {
    return m_bXTurn;
}
public void setXTurn(boolean bTurn) {
    m_bXTurn = bTurn;
}

}
```

TTTGui.java

The `TTTGui` is too big to display here, so what you are seeing is an example of what occurs when the button representing square 0,0 is pressed by the user. The same code exists for almost all other buttons with a few coordinate changes:

```
private javax.swing.JButton getJbtOne() {
    if (jbtOne == null) {
        jbtOne = new javax.swing.JButton();
        jbtOne.setName("jbtOne");
        jbtOne.setPreferredSize(new java.awt.Dimension(55,55));
        jbtOne.setText("");
        jbtOne.setFont(new java.awt.Font("Dialog", java.awt.Font.BOLD, 24));

        jbtOne.addActionListener(new java.awt.event.ActionListener() {
                public void actionPerformed(java.awt.event.ActionEvent e) {
                    boolean bXTurn = m_TLogic.getXTurn();
                    if (m_TLogic.setMarker(0,0)) {
                        if (bXTurn) {
                            jbtOne.setText("X");
                        } else {
                            jbtOne.setText("O");
                        }
                    }
                }
```

When the button is pressed, the first thing that happens is the code saves the player's turn in the `bXTurn` variable and then tries to set the marker on the space. If `setMarker` is successful, the appropriate symbol is used to mark the square the user chose:

```
                int nWinner = m_TLogic.getWinner();

                if (nWinner != 0) {
                    if (nWinner == 1) {
                        JOptionPane.showMessageDialog(null, "X WINS!!!",
                                    "X WINS!!!", JOptionPane.OK_OPTION);
                    } else {
                        JOptionPane.showMessageDialog(null, "O WINS!!!",
                                    "O WINS!!!", JOptionPane.OK_OPTION);
                    }
                }
            }
        }
    });
}
    return jbtOne;
}
```

Before the method is complete, it checks to see if it has a winner. If the user who clicked the square has won, the method will pop up a message box declaring the winner! The application must now be reset in order to play another game.

Summarizing Java Web Start

From the examples of code that you have seen, there is one step that wasn't mentioned — signing the JAR file. The necessary steps to sign JAR files are discussed under the JAR section of this chapter. To summarize, you should configure your web server to understand requests for JNLP files. You'll then need to create the JNLP file that describes the application to be launched with Java Web Start. You should package your application in a JAR file and sign the JAR file using the jarsigner tool. Finally, you should create the HTML page that will be used to access your JNLP file. That's all that is needed to turn your application into a Java Web Start application!

Using Ant with Web Archives

Ant is an open source application used for scripting many tasks and is commonly used for building Java applications. It has a vast array of built-in configuration management functions that are configured through XML tags. Ant essentially is a tool to do away with the dreaded makefiles of the past that required programmers to write an enormous amount of fragile, shell-based commands that had to be flexible enough for the user's environment and demands. Ant uses Java to do its necessary work, and, instead of shell-based commands, Ant has a concept called *Ant tasks* that performs almost every configuration/build task a programmer could want. You can download the latest binary distribution of Ant from `http://ant.apache.org`.

Installing Ant

Once you have downloaded your Ant distribution of choice, you simply extract the file to a directory of choice. You can extract Ant to a root directory and it creates starts by creating its own directory, such as `C:\apache-ant-1.6.5`.

The main directory of interest beneath Ant's root is the `bin` directory because this directory contains the scripts that execute Ant. You will need to configure your environment to be able to execute the Ant scripts from a console or command prompt. To do so, simply follow these three steps:

1. Set `JAVA_HOME` to point to the directory where your JDK is installed.

2. Create an environment variable called `ANT_HOME`, and set it to the directory where Ant is installed — for example, `ANT_HOME= C:\apache-ant-1.6.5`.

3. Finally, add the `ANT_HOME\bin` directory to your `PATH` environment variable so Ant can be accessible from any directory in any console window.

If you did not download a binary distribution of Ant, you will have to consult the instructions that come with Ant on how to build the source code for the particular platform you are on.

Building Projects with Ant

Ant is extremely easy to build with once you understand the basics of what is involved with creating Ant build files. Ant requires you to create an XML file called a build file that contains a project element and at least one target element. Each target can have multiple task elements that can perform a variety of operations from deleting files to compiling source code. With Ant, you can incorporate property files that you can read in, and you can also access system properties at any time during the execution of the build file.

A basic Ant system for building a project generally consists of a simple `build.xml` file and sometimes a properties file for loading in specific settings like a location of a third-party JAR. The `build.xml` file will need to contain a project and a target element. Here is a quick example of the syntax of a basic `build.xml` file that just displays a "Hello World!" message:

```xml
<project name="antTest" default="Hello" basedir=".">
  <description>A very simple build.xml file</description>

  <target name="Hello">
    <echo message="Hello World!"/>
  </target>
</project>
```

To run this example, you would change directory to the directory that contains the `build.xml` file from a console window and simply type **ant**. Ant will automatically look for the file named `build.xml` as a default. Once Ant finds the file, it executes it based on the default target supplied in the project element of the build file. In this case, the default target and only target is Hello. The output is shown in the following example:

```
C:\btest>ant
Buildfile: build.xml

Hello:
     [echo] Hello World!

BUILD SUCCESSFUL
Total time: 0 seconds
```

The Ant manual does a terrific job of explaining the different XML elements such as `project`, `target`, `classpath`, `filesets`, and so forth, so there isn't a need to explain them in-depth here. What is needed is to show you how to glue them all together. This next example shows you how to create a complete

Web ARchive (WAR) file using Ant. This example contains two files: a `mybuild.properties` file to contain the properties you will read in for Ant to use, and the staple `build.xml` file that is the main build file that Ant will execute. The following is the content of the `mybuild.properties` file:

```
# Xerces home directory
xerces.home  = C:\\xerces-2_6_2

# The name of the .jar file to create
jar.name     = myantwebapp.jar

# The name of the .war file to create
war.name     = myantwebapp.war
```

The first property shows a third-party tool location that you will need for compiling and packaging the source code. The next two properties list the name that you want the JAR and the final WAR file to be called. It's time now to dissect the complex `build.xml` file. This file is made up of four targets, three of which are dependent upon another target. When a dependency occurs in an Ant target, Ant must execute the dependency first. So, if target D is dependent on target C, and target C is dependent on target B, and target B is dependent on target A, Ant would execute the targets in the following order: A, B, C, then D. The `<project>` tag defines a name for the project and requires you to supply a default target to execute. In this case, you want Ant to run the `createWAR` target first:

```
<project name="MYANTWEBAPP" default="createWAR" basedir=".">
    <description>This a real world example of using ANT.</description>
```

The `createWAR` target has a dependency chain, as explained in the A, B, C, and D target example. The `basedir` attribute is asking which directory it should use as a base for execution. The period (`.`) signifies the current directory.

Now, you are telling Ant to read in the properties from `mybuild.properties` and to also create four additional properties: `src`, `jsps`, `build`, and `dist`:

```
<property file="mybuild.properties"/>

<!-- set global properties for this build -->
<property name="src"       location="src"/>
<property name="jsps"      location="jsp"/>
<property name="build"     location="build"/>
<property name="dist"      location="dist"/>
```

These can now all be accessed by their property name with the following syntax — `${propertyname}` — in the Ant build file:

The `<path>` tag will be used by the build file to incorporate the files in the path into a classpath that will be used to compile source code. Here, two Xerces JAR files are being built into a path element named `everything`:

```
<path id="everything">
    <fileset dir="${xerces.home}">
        <include name="xercesImpl.jar"/>
        <include name="xml-apis.jar"/>
    </fileset>
```

711

```
            <pathelement location="${build}"/>
    </path>
```

The first target, `clean`, gets executed first and simply deletes the build and distribution directories:

```
<target name="clean" description="Deletes the build and dist directories" >
    <delete dir="${build}"/>
    <delete dir="${dist}"/>
</target>
```

The `<delete>` tag is an Ant task. Ant has a multitude of tasks that can perform many operations. Refer to the Ant manual for more information. The second target, `init`, depends on `clean`:

```
<target name="init" depends="clean">
    <mkdir dir="${build}"/>
    <mkdir dir="${dist}"/>
</target>
```

Once `clean` deletes the `build` and `dist` directories, the `init` target re-creates them. These two targets ensure that the `build` and `dist` directories will be empty before you start compiling your source code. The third target, `createJAR`, depends on `init` and uses the Ant task `<javac>` to compile any source code that is in the `src` directory:

```
<target name="createJAR" depends="init"
        description="Compiles source and creates new JAR" >

    <javac classpathref="everything" classpath="${src}" srcdir="${src}"
                            destdir="${build}"/>

    <mkdir dir="${dist}/lib"/>

    <echo message="Creating jar: ${dist}\lib\${jar.name}"/>
    <jar destfile="${dist}/lib/${jar.name}" includes="**/*.class"
          basedir="${build}" compress="true" index="true" update="true"/>
</target>
```

You should also take note that the `classpathref` references the path that was built earlier called `everything`. The `<javac>` task will use the `everything` path in its `classpath` for compiling the source files. After the files are compiled, a handy Ant task called `<jar>` is used to create a JAR file into the `lib` directory that was created. The final target, `createWAR`, depends on `createJAR` and is used to create a WAR file:

```
<target name="createWAR" depends="createJAR">

    <copy preservelastmodified="true" overwrite="true"
                                    todir="${jsps}/WEB-INF/lib">
        <fileset dir="${dist}/lib">
            <include name="${jar.name}"/>
        </fileset>
    </copy>
```

```
        <mkdir dir="${dist}/war"/>

        <war destfile="${dist}/war/${war.name}" webxml="${jsps}/WEB-INF/web.xml"
                        update="true">

            <fileset dir="${jsps}" includes="*.html,*.jsp,*.doc"
                        excludes="*.jar,*.war"/>

            <webinf dir="${jsps}/WEB-INF" includes="*.wsdd,*.lst"/>
            <lib dir="${jsps}/WEB-INF/lib" includes="*.jar,*.war,*.zip"/>
            <zipfileset dir="${jsps}/images" prefix="images" excludes="*.psd"/>

        </war>
    </target>

</project>
```

The JAR file was created and moved to the WAR file's `WEB-INF/lib` directory because it has utilities that the WAR file needs. The other files, which you can see in the `fileset`, are then moved into position to create the WAR file. The WAR file is created using another handy Ant task called `<war>`.

This Ant build file example can now be run over and over every time you need to recompile and package your program. This example shows just how useful and easy it is to use Ant. If you need to replace Xerces with a new version, all that is required is a property change to `mybuild.properties`. However, this example barely touches on all the different Ant tasks that are available to you. The Ant manual that comes with the Ant distribution should explain all the tasks in great detail.

Summary

Packaging and deploying Java applications vary depending on the program you are currently working on. This chapter touched on the most popular types of Java applications that you will come across. It took you through the intricacies of the different Java archive files — JAR, WAR, and EAR — and kept going right into applet land. It also supplied you with a few helpful tools for managing your classpath and an explanation of already existing Java tools that can aid you in your packaging efforts such as the jarsigner and keytool tools.

This chapter discussed the great innovations of Java Web Start and how it can be the technology of the future for deploying thick, rich clients to users over browser-based technologies. Finally, this chapter examined the usefulness of Ant and how it can make a developer's building and configuration management woes a thing of the past.

Index

SYMBOLS AND NUMERICS

2-byte Unicode strings, 433
200 (HTTP response code), 532
403 (HTTP response code), 532
404 (HTTP response code), 532
500 (HTTP response code), 532
@AroundInvoke annotation, 481, 484
@AttributeOverride annotation, 490
@Column annotation, 479
@deprecated annotation, 27
@Discriminator annotation, 488
@EJB annotation, 490
@Entity annotation, 487
@Id annotation, 478
@Interceptors annotation, 481
@MappedSuperclass annotation, 489
@OneToMany annotation, 478
@overrides annotation, 27
@PersistenceContext annotation, 487
@PersistenceContexts annotation, 487
@PersistenceUnit annotation, 487
@PersistenceUnits annotation, 487
@Remote annotation, 483
@Resource annotation, 380–381
@Stateless annotation, 497
@TransactionAtrribute marking, 508
@TransactionManagement annotation, 508
@Transient annotation, 512

A

abstraction, 126
access
   to databases, 311
   to fields, 442–445
   in JNI, 442–445
access control, 585–586
accessor methods, 104
Action classes. See also specific types, e.g.: XWork
      Action
   IoC and, 401
   in WebWork, 399
   of XWork, 399, 412–415
ActionListener interface, 163, 205, 217–218
actionPerformed method, 163, 205, 213
Adapter pattern
   using, 126
   Adaptee interface in, 133
   Adapter interface in, 133
   Client interface in, 132
   discussed, 131–132
   Target interface in, 132
addActionListener method, 205
addFolder method, 466
adding data
   in EJB database, 476, 477
   in EntityManager API, 477–478
   in Hibernate, 412
   to Model 2 system, 417–419
   web application visualization for, 416
   XWork Action for, 413–414

addMouseListener method, 183
addTableData method, 185
addTree method, 185
AdjustmentListener, 234
advanced programming, 455–460
Agent layer, 601
Aggregate, 621
agility, 81–82
AJAX (Asynchronous JavaScript and XML), 381–384
AJAXTags library, 382–384
algorithm(s)
  in JCA, 640–641
  management of, 640–641
algorithm method, 635
AlgorithmParameter object, 640
AlgorithmParameterGenerator engine class,
    627, 640, 641
AlgorithmParameterSpec interface, 640
ALL logging level, 38
Ambler, Scott, 81
AnnotatedElement interface, 31–32
annotation(s)
  @deprecated, 27
  @overrides, 27
  custom, 27
  defined, 26
  discussed, 292
  doclet API for, 28–29
  functions of, 292–293
  for Java classes, 290–292
  in JDBC 4.0, 333–334
  in metadata, 26–27
  in Query interface, 333
  for resource injection in EJB, 487
  at runtime, 31
  source-level, 27
  usage of, 293–295
  XML schema and, 301–302
  XmlAccessorType, 296–297
  XmlAttribute, 297
  XmlElement, 297
  XmlElementWrapper, 297–298
  XmlJavaTypeAdapter, 298–300
  XmlRootElement, 295
  XmlTransient, 300–301
  XmlType, 295–296
AnnotationDesc.ElementValuePair method, 29
AnnotationTypeDoc method, 29
AnnotationTypeElementDoc method, 29

AnnotationValue method, 29, 30
Ant (Apache)
  development scenarios with, 94–101
  discussed, 93–94, 125
  Hibernate build file for, 408–409
  installing, 709–710
  in JMeter, 118
  Maven 2 and, 106
  project building with, 710–713
  TestNG and, 108, 109
  Web ARchive use with, 709–713
Apache Ant. See Ant
Apache Axis, 538
Apache Derby. See Derby
Apache TCPMon. See TCPMon
API (Application Program Interface). See also specific
    types, e.g.: Java API for XML Binding
  for Hibernate, 340–341
  in Java programming, 124
  for Service Oriented Architecture, 600
applet(s)
  discussed, 691–692
  in JAR, 685
  packaging, for execution, 693–694
  security analysis for, 694
  structure of, 692–693
APPLET tags, 693
appletviewer command, 693
Application Component, 401
application data
  for configuration, 239–241
  discussed, 237–239
  saving, 239
application development (Model 2), 396
Application Program Interface (API). See also specific
    types, e.g.: Java API for XML Binding
  for Hibernate, 340–341
  in Java programming, 124
  for Service Oriented Architecture, 600
applicationScope implicit object, 366
@AroundInvoke annotation, 481, 484
array(s)
  functions of, 437–442
  of generic types, 14
  in JNI, 436–442
  length property of, 18
  native code for, 438, 440
  of objects, 436, 437

of primitive types, 436, 437–442
usage of, 436–437
ArrayList class, 7, 8
assertions, in JMeter, 119
assignment conversion, 21
asterisk, 60, 61
ASyncHandler, 583
asynchronous invocation, 581, 583–584
Asynchronous JavaScript and XML (AJAX), 381–384
@AttributeOverride annotation, 490
authentication
checks for, 668
on client, 588–589
codes for, 665
configuration for, 670
credentials for, 669
defined, 666
execution of, 668
HTTP, 586–588, 588–589
in JCE, 665–673, 667–672
LoginContext for, 671–672
of messages, 665–666
principals in, 668–669
with security checks, 668
on server, 586–588
of subject, 670
of user identity, 667
authorization
defined, 666
in JCE, 672–673
autocommitting, 5
Axis (Apache), 538

B

back-end
passing data to, 494–495
queries in, 505
bank applications
communication for, 520
EJBs for, 520
Java EE for, 520
Basic Profile (WS-I), 567–568
batch updates
using PreparedStatement, 327–328
using Statement object, 326–327
using statements, 326–328
BatchUpdateException, 326–327
bean classes, 482
Beck, Kent, 91

binding, 568
body (SOAP), 570
BorderFactory class, 186
BorderLayout manager, 158–164
BorderLayoutPanel, 159–160
bound type parameters, 12–13, 299
boundary meta-characters, 62–63
bounded type variables, 12–14
bounds, 12–13
boxing conversions
context for, 21
defined, 7, 19
discussed, 19–20
with generics, 21
BoxLayout manager, 164–172
browsing data
in Hibernate, 412
in Model 2 system, 416, 419–422
web application visualization for, 416
XWork Action for, 412–413
Buest, Cedric, 106
buf byte array, 629
buffers, direct byte, 456
bugs (defect), 80, 87–88
building, with design patterns, 127–131
building process, 84
bundling, resource, 44
business tier (J2EE), 93
ButtonGroup component, 161
buttonPanel, 226–227
ButtonText variable, 160
bytecode, 7, 8
bytes array, 641

C

C (programming language)
data types, 432
Java objects in, 442–449
strings in, 432
variable arguments in, 18
Call Level Interface, X/Open SQL (CLI), 312
Call method, 448
callable statements (JDBC 4.0), 318, 324–326
CallMethod functions, 445–447
CallNonVirtual functions, 447, 448
CallNonVirtual method, 448
CallNonVirtualVoid function, 449
CallVoidMethod, 448, 449, 470
canImport method, 221–222

Canonicalization class, 644–645
CardLayout manager, 202–207
Cartesian join, 353
cascade property, 350
case implementation, 412–415
CDO (Collaborative Data Objects), 460
CenterPanel, 138
certificate(s)
  for digital signature verification, 632
  in JCA, 654–656
  management of, 654–656
  trusted, 638
  type parameters for, 656
certificate path, 654
Certificate Revocation List (CRL), 626, 654, 656
CertificateFactory engine class, 627, 654–655
CertPathBuilder engine class, 627, 655
CertPathValidator engine class, 627, 654, 655
CertStore engine class
  defined, 627
  discussed, 654–656
Chain of Responsibility pattern, 173–175, 177
ChainingInterceptor, 400
ChangeListener, 135
character classes
  in meta-characters, 63
  in regular expressions, 63
checkall function, 386, 389
checks, authentication, 668
ChildLogger, 58, 60
cipher, 656
Cipher engine class
  data encryption/decryption with, 658
  in JCE, 656–665
  key wrapping/unwrapping in, 658–662
  sealing objects in, 663–665
CipherInputStream class, 659–662
CipherOutputStream class, 659–662
CLASS policy, 26
ClassCircularityError, 459
classes
  defining, 407–408
  in generics, 14
  in Hibernate, 407–408
  in Java Serialization API, 242–243
  JAXB, 280–281
  for XML Digital Signatures, 643–645
ClassFormatError, 459
Class.forName method, 676–677

classpaths, 675–680
clazz, 457
clean target, 111–112
clearFolderList method, 466
cleartext (plaintext), 656
CLI (X/Open SQL Call Level Interface), 312
client
  HTTP authentication on, 588–589
  for JMS, 613–614
  for MBeans, 607–609
  remote, 607–609
  for Web Services, 580–589
  writing, 580–589
client layer
  in three-tier model, 314
  in two-tier model, 313
client programming, 524–525
client tier (J2EE), 93
closing, result sets, 332
CloudScape, 3
CMP (Container-Managed Persistence), 496–497
CMT. See under Contact Management Tool
code(s)
  for authentication, 665
  executing, 431–432
  Java, 428–429
  for JNI, 428–429, 431–432
code phase (Waterfall methodology), 88
code reuse
  in JSP 2.0, 361–362
  with .tag files, 361–362
  with .tagx files, 361–362
CodeTag annotation, 27
coding
  in Extreme Programming, 91
  during software development, 83
cohesion, high, 126
Collaborative Data Objects (CDO), 460
collection classes, 7
collection mapping, 348–350
CollectTask, 96
color definition, 274, 300
Colors enum, 24
@Column annotation, 479
Command interface, 142–143, 162, 164, 211–213
Command pattern, 142–146, 190, 203
CommandManager interface, 142, 143
Common Object Request Broker Architecture (CORBA)
  using, 553–554
  classes in, 558

for communication, 547–563
COS Naming for, 550–551
discussed, 547–548
for distributed file system notifications (example),
554–563
IDL of, 548–550
Internet InterORB Protocol for, 551
in JDK, 547
Object Request Broker in, 550
RMI compatibility with, 551
RMI-IIOP for, 551–553
**Common Object Service (COS) Naming, 550–551,
559–560**
communication
during software development, 81
**communication, component-to-component. *See*
component-to-component communication**
compatibility issues, of Model 2, 403–405
compile target, 112
complex types, 274
complexity, 396
component(s)
defined, 519
discussed, 519
mapping, in Hibernate, 347–348
component class, 151
Component injecting, 401
componentPanel, 226
component-to-component communication
for bank applications, 520
CORBA for, 547–563
discussed, 519, 520
interprocess, 521–522
network architecture supporting, 521–522
RPC/RMI for, 542–547
scenarios for, 520–521
sockets usage for, 522–541
for web browsing, 520
for web portals, 521
for Web Services, 563–596
composite class, 152–154
Composite pattern
component class in, 151
composite class in, 152–154
discussed, 150–151
leaf class in, 151–152
concurrency, 329
Concurrent Versioning System (CVS), 85
CONFIG logging level, 38

config target, 116
configuration
application data for, 239–241
for authentication, 670
in Hibernate, 339–340, 409–410
of Hibernate, 409–410
internal data changes in, 266–268
in JMeter, 119
loading, 248–249
management of, 84–85
in Model 2 architecture, 422–424
reading, from disk, 246
saving, 248
verification and validation for, 258–259
writing, to disk, 245–246
configuration object
deserialization of, 258
in Enterprise JavaBeans, 240
ConfigurationType, 277, 282
Connection class, 611
Connection interface, 315–316
connection management, 316–318
ConnectionFactory class, 611
ConsoleCorbaServer, 562–563
ConsoleHandler, 48–49
constants, in enumerations, 24
construction phase (UP), 91
constructors, 25
contact management system, 406
Contact Management Tool (CMT), 366–375, 370–375
ContactMgmtTool, 390–391
ContactMgmtTool POJO, 390–391
ContactMgmtToolDAO JavaBean, 388, 390–391
Container-Managed Persistence (CMP), 496–497
Context class, 229
context-root element, 700
continuous integration, 85
control
of access to Web Services, 585–586
IoC, 397–399
control gates (Waterfall methodology), 88
controller (MVC), 394
controller component (MVC), 140–142
cookie implicit object, 366
**CORBA. *See* Common Object Request Broker
Architecture**
**COS (Common Object Service) Naming, 550–551,
559–560**
coupling, low, 126

C++ programming
data types, 432
Java objects in, 442–449
javah for, 429–430
strings in, 432
variable arguments in, 18
crashing, in Java virtual machine, 432
`createMenuBar` **method, 218–219**
`createReference` **method, 646**
credentials, 669
`Criteria` **interface, 340, 350–352**
CRL (Certificate Revocation List), 626, 654, 656
cryptographic service providers, 626
`CustomHolder` **class, 11–12**
CVS (Concurrent Versioning System), 85

D

data
adding, 417–419
browsing, 419–422
in C/C++, 432
changing, 424–426
decryption, 658
for digital signing, 632–634
encryption, 658
insertion of, 477–478
integrity of, 629
in JNI, 432
in Model 2, 417–422, 424–426
removing, 412
types of, 432
verification of, 631–632, 632–634
data model, 238
`DatabaseMetaData`, **325**
databases
access to, 311
in Derby, 4–5
discussed, 311–312
with Hibernate, 335–353
`ij` creation of, 4
with JDBC API, 312–335
databases, persisting applications with
discussed, 311–312
with Hibernate, 335–353
with JDBC API, 312–335
`DatagramSocket` **class, 523**
`DataSource` **interface, 317–318**
`DBPanel` **constructor method, 184**
`Decorator` **class, 170**

Decorator pattern, 165–166
decryption
with `Cipher` engine class, 658
defined, 656
`DECRYPT_MODE`, **657**
`defaultReadObject` **method, 254**
`DefaultWorkflowInterceptor`, **401**
`deleteEntry` **method, 639**
`DeleteGlobalRef` **function, 454**
`DeleteLocalRef`, **442, 451**
`DeleteWeakGlobalRef` **function, 454**
deleting data. See removing data
Dependency Injection (DI), 474, 487. See Inversion of Control
dependency mediation, 102
dependency scope, 103
deployment, of Web Services (WS), 575–580
deployment descriptor
for Interceptors, 482
for WAR files, 696–698
for WebWork framework, 422–423
`@deprecated` **annotation, 27**
Derby (Apache)
using, 4–7
benefits of, 3
defined, 3
development of, 3
discussed, 4, 7
for Hibernate configuration files, 339
`ij` use in, 4–5
location of, 317, 341
in network mode, 6
descriptors, method, 445–446
deserialization
of `Configuration`, 258
defined, 241
discussed, 252
inside Swing actions, 246–247
by value, 304
design, 126–127
design patterns
Adapter pattern, 131–134
building with, 127–131
Command pattern, 142–146
Composite pattern, 150–154
defined, 124
discussed, 123–124
importance of, 124–127
for inheritance loops, 129–131

for interfaces, 129
MVC pattern, 134–142
single class design, 127
Strategy pattern, 146–150
TeacherResponsibilities and, 128
design phase (Waterfall methodology), 88
Destination class, 611
destroy method, 669, 692, 693
detached signature
defined, 643
discussed, 646–649
in XML Digital Signatures, 646–649
DHPrivateKey interface, 635
DHPublicKey interface, 635
DI (Dependency Injection), 474, 487
Dialect class, 339
Dialog class, 215–216
digest method, 629
DigestMethod class, 645
DigestValue class, 645
digital keys
creation of, 634–638
JCA for, 634–640
management of, 634–640
storing, 638–640
digital signature
as byte array, 632
detached, 646–649
enveloped, 649–652
on JAR files, 681
types of, 643
validating, 652–653
XML Digital Signatures, 649–653
Digital Signature Algorithm (DSA), 626, 630
Digital Signature Standard (DSS), 630
digital signing
data verification for, 632–634
with detached signatures, 646–649
of documents, 645
with enveloped signatures, 649–652
in JAR, 686–690
JCA for, 630–634, 642–654
process for, 645–646
validating signatures in, 652–653
with XML Digital Signatures, 645–646
direct byte buffers, 456
Direct Web Remoting (DWR), 384–391
directories, endorsed, 680–681
discipline, 82

@Discriminator annotation, 488
displayMessage method, 192, 193
distributed file system notifications (example), 554–563
distributed objects, 545–547
DLL files, 430–431
doAs method, 668
doclet API (Javadoc API), 28–29, 30–31
Document class, 651
Document Object Model (DOM), 238
document signing. See digital signing
document type definition (DTD), 338
doGet method, 253
DOM (Document Object Model), 238
domain model
for contact management system, 406
defined, 336
in Model 2 architecture, 405–412
DOMSignContext, 647
doTag method, 364
dragEnter method, 168–169
dragExit method, 168–169
driver(s)
in JDBC 4.0, 312–313, 327
in JDBC API, 327
DriverManager, 316–317
DropMode, 221
DropTargetListener interface, 167
DSA (Digital Signature Algorithm), 626, 630
DSAPrivateKey interface, 635
DSAPrivateKeySpec, 634
DSAPublicKey interface, 635
DSAPublicKeySpec, 634
DSS (Digital Signature Standard), 630
DTD (document type definition), 338
DWR (Direct Web Remoting), 384–391
dwReplacement method, 359–361
dwr.xml file, 390
dynamic registration, 456–459

E

EAR (Enterprise ARchives). See also specific types, e.g.: Web ARchive
deployment of, 700–701
descriptor file for, 699–700
inspecting, 699
EAR descriptor file, 699–700
eastPanel component, 161
echo server, 526–530

education, for software development, 84

EIS (Enterprise Information System), 93

EJB. *See* Enterprise JavaBeans

EJB 3 (Enterprise JavaBeans 3), 474

@EJB annotation, 490

EJBContext interface, 487

ejb-jar.xml file, 699

EL. *See* Expression Language

elaboration phase (UP), 91

elements
  initial setting for, 437
  in native arrays, 439

ElementType, 26

Ellipse2D class, 180

ellipses, in variable arguments, 18, 19

email client
  development of, 460–471
  JNI for, 460–471
  system design for, 460–461
  user interface of, 461–471

EncodedKeySpec, 634

encryption
  with Cipher engine class, 658
  defined, 656

ENCRYPT_MODE, 657

ENCTYPE FORM attribute, 379–380

enctype tag, 379–380

endorsed directories, 680–681

Endorsed Standard Override Mechanism, 680

endpoints, 579

engine classes, 626–628

engine.js script, 385

enhanced for loop. *See* for loop

EnsureLocalCapacity function, 453

Enterprise ARchives (EAR). *See also specific types, e.g.:*
    Web ARchive
  deployment of, 700–701
  descriptor file for, 699–700
  inspecting, 699

Enterprise Information System (EIS), 93

Enterprise JavaBeans (EJBs)
  for bank applications, 520
  configuration object in, 240
  discussed, 473–474
  EL features in, 359
  entities in, 475
  features of, 474
  inspecting, 699
  interceptor classes in, 481–485
  JPA of. *See* Java Persistence API

  for many-to-many relationships, 506–517
  Object-Relational Mapping vs., 473
  for one-to-many relationships, 496–506
  packaging, 698–699
  persistence capabilities of, 485–496
  problems with, 473, 480
  serialization, 262–263
  session beans and, 480–481
  usage of, 240
  XMLEncoder/Decoder API for, 262–263

Enterprise JavaBeans 3 (EJB 3), 474

entities
  in EJBs, 475, 478
  in JPA, 475
  of Plain Old Java Object, 475

@Entity annotation, 487

entity beans, 480

EntityManager API
  acquisition of, 476
  adding data in, 477–478
  defined, 475
  discussed, 476–480
  persistence in, 476
  Query method for, 478

enumerations
  constants in, 24
  defined, 24
  discussed, 24–26
  with fields and methods, 25–26
  in JDK 5, 24
  with methods, 25–26

EnumMap, 25

enums, 25

EnumSet, 25

envelope (SOAP), 570

enveloped signature
  defined, 643
  discussed, 649–652
  in XML Digital Signatures, 649–652

equals method, 668

eraseItems method, 390

ErrorManager, 56

EventPanel method, 196–197

exception(s), 15–16

exception handling, 449–451

ExceptionCheck function, 449

ExceptionClear function, 450

ExceptionDescribed function, 450

ExceptionOncurred function, 449

execMethods, 448
executable JAR, 691
execute method, 200, 205, 211–213, 227–228
Executer interface, 15–16
executeTests method, 34
execution (code)
  of authentication, 668
  using JNI, 431–432, 445–449
  of JSP page, 376
  of methods, 445–449
existing protocols, 541
ExitAction, 140–141
Expression Language (EL)
  in JSP 2.0, 359–361, 365–366
  in JSTL 1.1, 374–375
  in Model 1 Architecture, 357
eXtensible Markup Language. *See under* XML
Externalizable classes, 243
Externalizable interface, 243, 259–260
Extreme Programming (XP), 87, 91–92

F

FatalError function, 450, 452
field(s)
  access to, 442
  enumerations with, 25–26
field access, 442–445
field descriptors, 446
file manipulation (JAR), 681–684
file naming, 50
file system
  for Maven 2, 102
  notification events, 554, 556, 558–561
  POM files on, 102
FileHandler, 49–50
FileItem class, 379–380
FileManager bean, 378, 380–381
fill method, 181
fillTable function, 386–387
Filter interface, 55–56
findClass method, 678–679
findHelper method, 677–678
finding data (EJB), 476
FINE logging level, 38
FINER logging level, 38
FINEST logging level, 38
FinishButton class, 228
fireTableDataChanged method, 187
FLAG, 670

flexibility, 395, 426
FlowLayout manager, 173–177, 226–227
folders, storing and retrieving, 464–465
for loop, enhanced
  defined, 7
  improvements on, over JDK5, 17–18
  syntax for, 16–17
foreach, 16
formal type parameters, 8, 9
Formatter class, 52–55
formPanel method, 197–198, 200
FROM clause, 475
FromReflectedMethod function, 459–460
front-end
  with AJAX, 382
  DWR library for, 391
  Java EE for, 520
function signatures (prototypes), 430
Function Tag Library, 366–368

G

Gang of Four (GoF) design patterns, 158
generatePanel method, 233
generateParameters, 640
generatePrivate method, 636
generatePublic method, 636
generate-web target, 112
generation (sequence) pattern, 49
generics (parameterized types)
  using, 14
  arrays of, 14
  bounded type variables, 12–14
  boxing with, 21
  class instances in, 14
  defined, 7
  discussed, 7–8
  exceptions and, 15–16
  in JDK 5, 7
  methods for, 15
  type erasure, 8–11
  wildcards, 11–12
Getahead, 384
GetArrayElements, 438
GetArrayLength, 437, 442
GetArrayRegion, 439
getCertificateAlias method, 639
getCertificateChain method, 639
getColor method, 226–227, 229
getConnection method, 388

`getContactData` method, 388–389
`getContactMgmtTool` method, 389
`getDate` method, 201–202
`getDeclaredAnnotations`, 32
`getElementById` method, 389
`getEncoded` method, 635
`GetFieldID`, 443–444, 446
`getFolderList` function, 467
`getFormat` method, 635
`getInstance` method
  for `Cipher` objects, 657
  for engine classes, 627, 628
  for `KeyFactory`, 635
`getKeySpec` method, 636, 639
`getLocalAddr` method, 358
`getLocalName` method, 358
`getLocalPort` method, 358
`getMarker` method, 706
`GetMethodID`, 446
`getName` method, 669
`GetObjectArrayElement`, 437, 442
`GetObjectClass` function, 447, 459
`getPanel` method, 229
`getParameter` method, 694
`getProcedures` method, 326
`getRandomNumbers`, 105
`getRecentFiles`, 267
`getRemotePort` method, 358
`getSplashScreen` method, 216–217
`GetStaticField`, 444
`GetStaticMethodID` function, 447
`GetStringChars`, 434, 436
`GetStringLength`, 434
`GetSuperClass`, 459
`getValues` method, 231–232
`getWinner` method, 707–708
`getXturn` method, 708
global references
  using, 453
  creating and destroying, 454
  defined, 451
  local references with, 455
  weak, 453
GoF (Gang of Four) design patterns, 158
`Graphics2d` method, 180
greedy operators, 64–65
`GridBagConstraints` class, 189, 192–193
`GridBagLayout` manager, 189–194
`GridLayout` class, 161

`GridLayout` manager, 169–171, 177–189
GROUP clause, 475
`GroupLayout` manager, 207–214

H

`handleNext` method, 230–233
`handlePrevious` method, 230–233
Handler class
  methods for, 46–48
  stock handlers for, 48–51
  use of, 46
`hashCode` method, 9, 669
`hashtableQuestions` collection class, 162
HAVING clause, 475
header files, javah for, 429–430
header implicit object, 366
headers (SOAP), 570
`headerValues` implicit object, 366
Hibernate
  API, 340–341
  components of, 336–337
  configuration of, 409–410
  `Criteria` interface in, 350–352
  discussed, 335–336
  many-to-one relationship in, 345–346
  mapping files in, 338–339, 347–350, 424
  Model 2 architecture support for, 402–403
  persistent objects in, 337–338, 342–344, 407
  persisting applications with, 335–353
  Plain Old Java Object vs., 337
  `Query` interface in, 352–353
  setup for, 341, 409–410
  usage example for, 341–353
  utility classes in, 341–342
  WebWork support for, 402–403
  in XDoclet, 113, 115–116, 115–117
Hibernate API
  many-to-many relationships in, 345–346
  role of, 337
Hibernate configuration file
  discussed, 339–340
  role of, 337
Hibernate mapping file
  defined, 338
  discussed, 338–339
  role of, 337
Hibernate Query Language (HQL), 340, 352–353
`HibernateAction` class, 404–405
`HibernateFactory` object, 402

HibernateInterceptor, 403–404
holdability, of result sets, 329–330
Holtz, Lou, 82
horizontal components, 397
HQL (Hibernate Query Language), 340, 352–353
HTML files, 530
HTMLTableFormatter, 58
HTTP 1.0, 533
HTTP authentication
  on client, 588–589
  on server, 586–588
HTTP GET
  background on, 532–533
  implementation with, 533–538
  for protocols, 532–538
HTTP Input tag, 379–380
HTTP protocol
  elements of, 531–532
  in JDK, 541, 588
  response codes in, 532
  in web applications, 521, 522
  for Web Services, 571

I

IBM, 3
@Id annotation, 478
id property
  in Hibernate database, 339, 407
  for mapping, 339
IDE (integrated development environment), 84
identification, user, 667
IDL (Interface Definition Language), 548–550
ignoreflag, 387–388
IIOB. See Internet InterORB Protocol
ij (interactive JDBC scripting tool), 4–5
impl package classes, 277
implementation
  with HTTP GET, 533–538
  in Web Services, 579
implicit objects, 366
importData method, 221–222
IN parameters
  pitfalls of, 322–323
  in prepared statements, 320–323
  setting, 320–322
inception phase (UP), 91
index option (JAR), 690–691
indirect measurement, 87
InetSocketAddress class, 523, 524

INFO logging level, 38
ignoreflag attribute, 385–386
inheritance, 126
inheritance loops, 129–131
init method, 692, 693
initComponents () method, 160
initialElement, 437
initialize, 636
initParam implicit object, 366
Injector interface, 398
INOUT parameter, 324
InputScreen, 249
insensitive result sets, 329
insideCircle method, 182
inspecting
  Enterprise ARchives, 699
  Enterprise JavaBeans, 699
  WAR files, 699
installation wizards (Swing), 225–234
installing
  Ant (Apache), 709–710
  JDBC API, 313
Instrumentation layer, 601
integrated development environment (IDE), 84
integration
  service-oriented, 599
  during software development, 85
  systems, 599
interactive JDBC scripting tool (ij), 4–5
interceptor classes
  deployment descriptor for, 482
  in EJBs, 481–485
  InvocationContext for, 481–482, 484–485
  life cycle of, 485
  StatelessSession interface for, 482–484
  styles of, 482
  in WebWork, 400–401
@Interceptors annotation, 481
Interface Definition Language (IDL), 548–550
interface design, 129
International Organization for Standards (ISO), 312
internationalization, of strings, 433
Internet InterORB Protocol (IIOB)
  for CORBA, 547
  discussed, 551
  for objects passed by value, 551
  for RMI, 545
interprocess communication, 521–522
InterruptedException, 588

`InvalidJarIndexException`, **690**
inverse attribute, **350**
Inversion of Control (IoC, dependency injection)
  defined, 396
  discussed, 146
  in Model 2 architecture, 397–399, 426
  Plain Old Java Object for, 398
invocation protocol
  asynchronous, 581, 583–584
  in JSP 2.0, 363–365
  method, 21
  synchronous, 582–583
  of Web Services, 581–584
`InvocationContext`, **481–482, 484–485**
`InvocationContext` **reference, 481, 484**
`Invoker` **interface, 142, 144–145**
IoC. *See* **Inversion of Control**
`IOException`, **15–16**
`IsAssignableFrom` **function, 459**
`isCertificateEntry` **method, 639**
`isCurrent` **method, 669**
`isDesktopSupported` **method, 222–223**
`isDestroyed` **method, 669**
`isKeyEntry` **method, 639**
ISO (International Organization for Standards), 312
`IsSameObject` **function, 455**
`Iterable` **interface, 17**
iterator(s), **16**
`iterator` tags, **421**

J

J2EE web application
  architecture of, 93
  defined, 125
  design patterns in, 125
  WebWork as, 422
JAAS (Java Authentication and Authorization Service),
  625, 666
`JAddEventButton` **class, 200**
Jakarta Commons Net Package, 541
Jakarta Commons Upload, 378
JAR. *See* **JAVA ARchive; Java ARchive**
jar tool, 681–684
jarsigner, 686
Java 5 Tiger release, 106
Java API for XML Binding (JAXB)
  advantages to using, 307
  disadvantages to using, 307
  discussed, 270–271

  in JDK, 308
  object graphs, 277–280, 283
  pitfalls of, 302–307
  runtime compatibility for, 277
  serialization in, 290
  usage of, 307–308
  value serialization in, 302–305
  version compatibility for, 277
  WSDL for, 308
  XML Schema Definition in, 271
Java API for XML Binding classes, 280–281
  annotations, 292–301
  usage of, 283–290
  from XML schema, 276–277
Java ARchive (JAR)
  applets in, 685
  creation of executable JAR, 691
  discussed, 681
  and endorsed directories, 680–681
  exploring, 681
  file manipulation in, 681–684
  index option for, 690–691
  and Java classpaths, 675–680
  for license files, 253, 254
  manifest files for, 684–685
  signing, 686–690
Java Authentication and Authorization Service (JAAS),
  625, 666
Java class annotations, 290–292
Java code
  discussed, 428–429
  native methods for, 427
  strings in, 432
  variable arguments in, 18
Java Cryptography Architecture (JCA)
  algorithms in, 640–641
  architecture of, 626
  certificate management in, 654–656
  design of, 626
  for digital keys, 634–640
  for digital signing, 630–634, 642–654
  discussed, 625
  engine classes for, 626–628
  `MessageDigest` class in, 628–630
  RNG in, 641–642
  security and, 625–626
  XML Digital Signatures in, 642–654
Java Cryptography Extension (JCE)
  authentication in, 665–673, 667–672
  authorization in, 672–673

`Cipher` class in, 656–657, 656–665
discussed, 625
`KeyGenerator` engine class in, 662
for license files, 254
message authentication code in, 665–666
sealing objects with, 663–665
`SecretKeyFactory` in, 662–663
security and, 625, 656
services of, 656
Java DataBase Connectivity. *See under* **JDBC**
Java Development Kit. *See under* **JDK**
Java drivers, 312
Java EE. *See* **Java Enterprise Edition**
Java Enterprise Edition (Java EE)
for bank applications, 520
discussed, 519
for RMI, 547
Java Foundation Classes (JFC)
discussed, 157–158
layout managers, 158–214
Mustang release, 214–225
Java logging
defined, 34
discussed, 35–36
`ErrorManager`, 56
examples of, 56–60
`Filter` interface, 55–56
`Formatter` class, 52–55
`Handler` class, 46–51
`Level` class, 45–46
`Logger` class, 38–42
`LogManager` class, 36–42
`LogRecord` class, 42–45
Java Management Extensions (JMX)
architecture for, 601
discussed, 600
importance of, 601
MBeans in, 602–610
relevance of, 600
for SOA, 600–610
Java Messaging Service (JMS)
client for, 613–614
discussed, 610
importance of, 610
`JMSAgent` in, 617–618
`JMSWorker` MBean in, 614–616
message functions in, 611–612
queues in, 610–611
receiving messages with, 611–612
relevance of, 600

sending messages with, 611–612
server configuration for, 612–613
for SOA, 610–618
topics in, 611
Java meta-characters, 63, 64
**Java Naming and Directory Interface (JNDI), 317–318,
380, 474**
Java Native Interface (JNI)
using, 428
advanced programming with, 455–460
arrays in, 436–442
code for, 428–429
creating, 429–431
data types in, 432
discussed, 427, 432
dynamic registration with, 456–459
for email client development, 460–471
exception handling using, 449–451
executing code using, 431–432
field access using, 442–445
local reference in, 452
method execution using, 445–449
NIO support in, 456
object references in, 451–455
program writing with, 427
reflection functions in, 459–460
strings in, 432–436
threading using, 455–456
Java Network Launch Protocol (JNLP), 702–704
Java objects. *See* **object(s)**
Java Persistence API (JPA)
discussed, 474–475
entities in, 475
entity manager of, 476–480
features of, 474, 475
for Plain Old Java Object, 474
query language of, 475–476
select statements in, 475–476
Java persistence query language, 475–476
Java preferences. *See* `Preferences` **class**
Java Remote Method Protocol (JRMP), 545
Java Runtime Environment, 680
Java SDK, 626–627
Java Serialization API
classes in, 242–243
discussed, 241–242
extending and customizing, 257–261
format customization, 258–260
implementation, into applications, 253–257
steps for, 243

Java Serialization API (continued)
strengths and weaknesses in, 261
time-based licensing using, 249–253
`transient` keyword for, 257
usage of, 261–262
versioning in, 260–261
XMLEncoder/Decoder API vs., 269

Java Server Page (JSP)
for EJB 3 components, 513
EL features in, 359

Java Socket API, 523

Java Standard Template Library. *See* JSTL 1.1

Java strings, UTF-8 format for, 433

Java virtual machine
crashing, 432
string usage in, 432

Java Web Start applications
discussed, 702, 709
TicTacToe example for, 702–709

Java2DPanel class, 179–180, 182–183

Java2DPanelMouseclickPrint class, 188–189

JavaBeans (Enterprise). *See* Enterprise JavaBeans

Javadoc API (doclet API), 28–29, 30–31

javah, 429–430

javap utility, 446

JavaScript
AJAXTags libraries as alternative to, 382
and DWR, 384

javascript function, 385

JAXB. *See* Java API for XML Binding

JAXB 1.0, 271, 277

JAXB 2.0, 271, 277, 280

JAXB classes (JDK 6), 276

JAXBContext, 281

JAXBElement, 280–281

JAXBException, 287, 289

JAX-WS, 575–577, 579

JBoss, 612–613

JButton component, 160, 174, 205

JButton setText() method, 162

JButtonCoins method, 176

JButtonSave component, 200–201

JButtonStrategy1 class, 203–204, 205–206

JButtonStrategy2 button, 204

JButtonStrategy2 class, 206

jbyte, 434

JCA. *See* Java Cryptography Architecture

JCE. *See* Java Cryptography Extension

jchar, 432, 434

JConsole, 604–605

JDBC 3.0, 335

JDBC 4.0
using, 315–316
annotations in, 333–334
connection management in, 316–318
`DataSource` interface in, 317–318
discussed, 311
`DriverManager` in, 316–317
drivers in, 312–313, 327
result sets in, 328–333
statements in, 318–328
transaction management in, 334–335

JDBC API (Java DataBase Connectivity API)
classes in, 243
in Derby, 5–6
discussed, 312–313
drivers in, 327
establishing data source for Contact Management Tool, 373
installing, 313
parameters in, 353
persisting applications with, 312–335
`setObject` method for, 323–324
three-tier model of, 314–315
two-tier model of, 313–314

JDBC-net pure Java driver, 312

JDBC-ODBC bridge driver, 312

JDK (Java Development Kit)
CORBA support in, 547
dependencies in, 103
HTTP support in, 541, 588
JAXB in, 308
manipulating JAR files, 681–682
versioning in, 260
XMLEncoder/Decoder API in, 269

JDK 5
enumerations in, 24
features of, 3
for loop enhanced from, 17–18
generics in, 7

JDK 6
changes in, 3
Derby in, 3
JAXB classes in, 276
WS deployment with, 577–578

JFC (Java Foundation Classes)
discussed, 157–158
layout managers, 158–214
Mustang release, 214–225

JFormattedTextField class, 174

JFrame (BorderLayout) container, 158

JKS, 638

JMeter, 117–120

JMeter 2.1, 119

JMS. *See* Java Messaging Service

JMSAgent component, 611, 617–618

JMSWoker component, 611, 614–616

JMX. *See* Java Management Extensions

JNDI (Java Naming and Directory Interface), 317–318, 380, 474

JNextButton component, 228

JNI. *See* Java Native Interface

JNIMailBridge, 460, 465

JNINativeMethod structure, 457, 459

JNLP (Java Network Launch Protocol), 702–704

JPA. *See* Java Persistence API

JPanel, 138

JPanel (FlowLayout) container, 158

JPreviousButton component, 227–228

JQuestionButton, 162

JRadioButtonAnswer class, 162

JResetButton button, 164

JRMP (Java Remote Method Protocol), 545

JSP (Java Server Page)
  for EJB 3 components, 513
  EL features in, 359

JSP 2.0
  code reuse in, 361–362
  discussed, 357–358
  Expression Language in, 359–361, 365–366
  invocation protocol in, 363–365
  .jspx page extensions in, 362–363
  for Model 1 architecture, 357–365, 376–380
  Servlet 2.4 support in, 358
  web application visualization with, 376–380

JSP custom tags (WebWork), 417

.jspx page extensions, 362–363

JSR 105, 642

JSTL 1.1
  discussed, 366
  Function Tag Library in, 366–368
  for Model 1 architecture, 366–375
  SQL transactions in, 368–370
  web application visualization with, 370–375

jstring data type (C/C++), 432, 433

JTextArea component, 233

JTextField, 221, 231–232

JTree object, 208

JUnit, 85

K

key agreement, 656

key entry, 638

key interface, 634–635

key unwrapping, 658–662

key wrapping, 658–662

KeyFactory engine class
  defined, 627
  for representation conversion, 635

KeyGenerator engine class, 662

KeyInfo class, 645

KeyPair class, 636

KeyPairGenerator engine class
  defined, 627
  for key management, 636

KeySelectorResult interface, 653

keysize parameter, 636

KeySpec interface, 634

keystore, 638–639

KeyStore engine class
  defined, 627
  discussed, 638
  for key management, 636

King, Gavin, 402

L

language features
  boxing conversions, 19–21
  discussed, 7
  enumerations, 24–26
  for loop, enhanced, 16–18
  generics, 7–16
  metadata, 26–34
  static data importing, 21–23
  unboxing conversions, 20–21
  variable arguments, 18–19

Larman, Craig, 90

layout managers
  BorderLayout manager, 158–164
  BoxLayout manager, 164–172
  CardLayout manager, 202–207
  discussed, 158
  FlowLayout manager, 173–177
  GridBagLayout manager, 189–194
  GridLayout manager, 177–189
  GroupLayout manager, 207–214
  SpringLayout manager, 194–202

lazy attribute, 350

lazy (reluctant) operators, 65

leaf class, 151–152
learning curve (Model 2), 395
len parameter, 628, 629
Level class, 45–46
license files
    JAR for, 253, 254
    JCE for, 254
life cycle
    of interceptor classes, 485
    of JMSWorker, 614
    with Maven, 101, 106
listeners, in JMeter, 119
listkey, 419
listvalue, 419
load method, 638
loading, 248–249, 287–290
load-on-startup attribute, 697
local references
    creating and deleting, 451
    defined, 451
    global references with, 455
    management of, 452–453
    memory Issues of, 452
localized strings, 433
Logger class
    levels of, 38
    methods for, 38–42
    usage of, 38
Logger objects, 34–35, 39–42
logging. See Java logging
LoggingInterceptor, 400
logic controllers, in JMeter, 119
login method, 223
LoginAction, 140
LoginContext, 670, 671–672
LogManager class
    configuration of, 37
    control methods in, 37–38
    properties of, 36
logout parameter, 671
LogRecord class, 42–45
    defined, 42
    methods for, 43
    for origination, 43–44
    for resource bundling, 44
    for setting information, 44–45
loops
    for checking, 506
    inheritance, 129–131
loose-coupling, 128, 619

M

MAC (message authentication code)
    defined, 656
    in JCE, 665–666
mail messages, 464–466
MailClient, 460
MailFolder class, 463
MailMessage class, 463
main method, 679
manifest files (JAR), 681, 684–685
manipulating result sets, 331–332
many-to-many relationships
    EJBs for, 506–517
    in Hibernate API, 345–346
    one-to-many relationships vs., 507
    web components for, 506–517
many-to-one relationship, 345–346
MAPI routines, 465–466
@MappedSuperclass annotation, 489
mapping
    of collections, 348–350
    components of, 347–348
    files for, 424
    in Hibernate, 338–340, 347–350
    properties for, 350
    property-to-column, 339
    XDoclet for, 110–111
marshaller
    in RMI, 544
    XML, 281–282
Maven 1, 101
Maven 2
    Ant and, 106
    archetypes in, 102
    discussed, 101–102
    transitive dependencies in, 102–106
MBeans
    creation of, 602–606
    in JConsole, 605
    JMSWorker, 614–616
    in JMX, 602–610
    in JMX architecture, 601
    management of, 602–606, 606
    remote client for, 607–609
    RemoteAgent for, 606–607
    WorkMonitor for, 609–610
MBeanServer, 603, 607
MD4 algorithm, 628
MD5 algorithm, 628

MD5 algorithms, 626
MDI (multiple document interface), 239
member variables, 442
memory, 452
MemoryHandler, 50–51
message authentication code (MAC)
   defined, 656
   in JCE, 665–666
Message class, 611
MessageClient component, 611
MessageConsumer class, 611
MessageDigest engine class
   calculating, 628–629
   defined, 627
   in JCA, 628–630
   verifying, 629–630
Message-Oriented Middleware (MOM), 600, 610, 618
MessageProducer class, 611
messages
   in JMS, 611–612
   receiving, 611–612
   sending, 611–612
meta-characters
   boundary, 62–63
   character classes in, 63
   discussed, 60
   Java, 63, 64
   POSIX, 63–64
   predefined types, 61–63
   in regular expressions, 61–63
   types of, 60
metadata
   AnnotationDesc, 29
   AnnotationDesc.ElementValuePair, 29
   annotations in, 26–27
   AnnotationTypeDoc, 29
   AnnotationValue, 30
   AnnotionTypeElementDoc, 29–30
   defined, 7
META-INF directory, 681, 683–684, 686, 689, 690
method descriptors, 445–446
method execution, 445–449
method invocations, 21
methodology
   discussed, 88
   Extreme Programming, 91–92
   observations on, 92–93
   Unified Process, 90–91
   Waterfall methodology, 88–89
methods, 25–26

methods parameter, 457
mgrBody object, 386–387
Microsoft .NET framework, 554, 596
middle layer, in three-tier model, 314
middleware
   message-oriented, 600, 610, 618
   for RMI, 546
mime-mapping element, 698
Mine, Philip, 269
model(s), 406
model (MVC), 394
model component (MVC), 136–137
Model 1 architecture
   discussed, 355–357
   EL for, 359–361, 365–366
   JSP 2.0 specification for, 357–365, 376–380
   JSTL 1.1 for, 366–375
   Model 2 architecture vs., 396
Model 2 architecture
   adding data to, 417–419
   advantages of, 395
   application development with, 396
   browsing data in, 419–422
   case implementation in, with actions, 412–415
   changing data in, 424–426
   compatibility issues of, 403–405
   configuring, 422–424
   disadvantages of, 395–396
   discussed, 393–395, 426
   domain model definition in, 405–412
   Hibernate support in, 402–403
   Inversion of Control in, 397–399
   Model 1 architecture vs., 396
   MVC in, 393–394
   need for, 393
   Plain Old Java Object in, 426
   problems with, 403–405
   process of, 394–395
   scope in, 395
   security in, 395
   use of, 395–396
   web application visualization in, 415–422
   with WebWork, 396, 399–402
ModelDrivenInterceptor, 400
mode-less, 215
modeling, 81
Model-View-Controller (MVC) pattern
   application initialization with, 136
   changes to, 135
   components of, 394

Model-View-Controller (MVC) pattern (continued)
controller component of, 140–142
discussed, 134–142, 393
in Model 2 architecture, 393–394
model component of, 136–137
purpose of, 134
view component of, 137–139
modularity
in Model 2 architecture, 426
of WebWork, 426
module element, 699–700
MOM (Message-Oriented Middleware), 600, 610, 618
MonitorEnter function, 456
mousePressed method, 181
MS Outlook, 460
multiple document interface (MDI), 239
Mustang release, 214–225
MVC pattern. See Model-View-Controller pattern
MyAdjustmentListener method, 234
MyTableModel class, 186–187

N

name parameter, 579, 671
named queries, 475
NamedQuery annotation, 506
naming (COS), 550–551, 559–560
naming files, 50
native API/part Java driver, 312
native arrays, 439
native code
for arrays, 438, 440
Java objects in, 437
sort routine in, 4389
native keyword, 428
native libraries, 431
native methods
using, 428–429
for Java code, 427
registering, 456–459
unregistering, 457
native-protocol pure Java driver, 312
navigating result sets, 330–331
.NET framework (Microsoft), 554, 596
NetBeans, 207
network architecture, 521–522
NewArray, 438
NewGlobalRef function, 453, 454
NewLocalRef function, 451
NIO direct buffers, 456

NIO support, 456
NoClassDefFoundError exception, 450
nodes, in Preferences class, 70, 72, 73
nonscrollable result sets, 329
non-static fields, 442
non-static methods, 445
NULL character, 433
NumberFormat class, 174
numBytes array, 641

O

OASIS, 596
object(s)
in ArrayList, 7
arrays of, 436, 437
in C/C++, 442–449
distributed, 545–547
point, 275
in RMI, 545–547
sealing, 663–665
object graph, 239
Object Graph Navigation Language (OGNL), 401
object graphs (JAXB), 277–280
object graphs serialization, 290
Object Management Group (OMG), 547
Object method, 30
object references
comparing, 455
global, 453–455
global references, 453–455
in JNI, 451–455
local, 451–453
local references, 451–453
Object Request Broker (ORB), 550
ObjectFactory class, 280
ObjectInputStream, 249, 265
object-oriented (OO) design, 126, 127, 234, 311
ObjectOutputStream, 249, 265
Object-Relational Mapping (O/RM)
in @Column annotation, 479
compatibility issues of, 403
EJBs vs., 473
solutions of, 344
tools for, 403
object-to-object communication, 548
OFF logging level, 38
OFX (Open Financial Exchange), 271
OGNL (Object Graph Navigation Language), 401
OMG (Object Management Group), 547

`omitCheckedItems` function, 385–386
`@OneToMany` annotation, 478
one-to-many relationships
  EJBs for, 478–479, 496–506
  many-to-many relationships vs., 507
  web components for, 496–506
OO design. *See* object-oriented design
opaque representations, 634, 635
Open Financial Exchange (OFX), 271
Open Systems Interconnection (OSI), 521
`OperatingSystems` enum, 24
operations, in `Preferences` class, 70–71, 74
`opMode` parameter, 657
`Optional FLAG`, 670
O/R mappings, standardized, 475
ORB (Object Request Broker), 550
`ORDER BY` clause, 475
O/RM. *See* Object-Relational Mapping
OSCAR, 540
OSI (Open Systems Interconnection), 521
`OutOfMemoryError`, 459
`@overrides` annotation, 27
`OwnerSession` interface, 507–508

P

package target, 112
packaging
  for applet execution, 693–694
  of EJBs, 698–699
`pageContext` implicit object, 366
`pageScope` implicit object, 366
`paint` method, 692, 693
`paintComponent(Graphics g)` method,
  166, 180, 183
`panelTable` method, 185, 197
`param` implicit object, 366
`PARAM` tag, 694
parameterized types, 8. *See also* generics
`params` parameter, 657
`paramSpec` object, 640
`paramValues` implicit object, 366
parentheses, inside regular expressions, 65
`ParentLogger`, 58
`parse` method, 649
parsing, file formats, 530
Password-Based Encryption (PBE), 656
password-based encryption (PBEKey), 635
Pattern-Matcher model, 61, 68
patterns. *See* design patterns

PBE (password-based encryption), 656
`PBEKey` interface, 635
persistence query language, 475–476
`@PersistenceContext` annotation, 487
`@PersistenceContexts` annotation, 487
`PersistenceDelegates`, 269
`@PersistenceUnit` annotation, 487
`@PersistenceUnits` annotation, 487
persistent objects
  in Hibernate, 337–338, 342–344, 407
  libraries for, 497
  properties of, 496
  role of, 337
`pigLatin` method, 359–361
PKCS (Public Key Cryptography Standard), 638
Plain Old Java Object (POJO)
  `ContactMgmtTool`, 390–391
  entities of, 475
  Hibernate vs., 337
  for IoC, 398
  JPA for, 474
  in Model 2 architecture, 426
  session beans as, 474
plaintext (cleartext), 656
platform-independent RPCs, 566–567
POA (Portable Object Adapter), 559
point objects, 275
POJO. *See* Plain Old Java Object
polymorphism, 126, 130, 149
POM (project object model), 103, 106
Popescu, Alexandru, 106
`PopLocalFrame` function, 452, 453
`populateTable` method, 184, 185, 187
`PopupMenu` class, 217–218
port types, 568
Portable Object Adapter (POA), 559
portlet, 361–362
POSIX meta-characters, 63–64
`PostPersist`, 501
post-processor tests, in JMeter, 119
`PostRemove`, 501
`Preferences` class
  using, 75–77
  discussed, 70
  events in, 73
  exporting, to XML, 74
  nodes in, 70, 72, 73
  operations in, 70–71, 74
  retrieving values for, 72–73
  setting values for, 73

prepared statements (JDBC 4.0)
 batch updates using, 327–328
 discussed, 318
 IN parameters in, 320–323
 setObject method for, 323–324
PreparedStatement, 327–328
pre-processor tests, in JMeter, 119
primary key, 500, 511
primitive types
 array type counterpart for, 436
 arrays of, 436, 437–442
 conversion of, to reference type, 19
 references to, 20–21
 types of, 438
principals, in authentication, 668–669
printf (), 432
PrintWriter class, 524
private key, 632
PrivateKey interface, 635
processing chain pattern, 619
programming
 client, 524–525
 scripting vs., 396
 sockets for, 524–525, 525–526
project building, with Apache Ant, 710–713
project object model (POM), 103, 106
PropertyChangeListener interface, 139, 174–175
property-to-column mapping, 339
propOrder value, 295–296
proprietary protocols, 540–541
protocol(s)
 defined, 521
 discussed, 530
 existing, 541
 HTTP GET for, 532–538
 HTTP specification for, 531–532
 implementation with, 530–541
 proprietary, 540–541
 reverse engineering with, 540–541
 for RPCs, 544–545
 with sockets, 530–541
 sockets and, 530–541
 specification for, 531–540
 TCPMon testing for, 538–540
 utilizing, 541
prototypes (function signatures), 430
provided scope, 103
providers (cryptographic service providers), 626
pseudo-random random number, 640

Public Key Cryptography Standard (PKCS), 638
public key object, 632
PublicKey interface, 635
PushLocalFrame, 453

Q

quality measures, 80
Query interface
 annotations in, 333
 for EntityManager API, 478
 in Hibernate, 352–353
 in Hibernate API, 340
 of JPA, 475–476
queues (JMS), 610–611

R

random number generation, 641–642
random number generator (RNG), 641
RDBMS (Remote Database Management System), 324
readObject method, 254
read-only result sets, 329
refactoring, 83
reference, 543
reference(s)
 conversion of, from primitive types, 19
 object. See object references
 to primitive types, 20–21
Reference class, 643
reflection API, 32–33
reflection functions, 459–460
refresh method, 669
RegisterNatives function, 457, 459
registerOutParameter, 324
registration
 dynamic, 456–459
 with JNI, 456–459
 for native methods, 456–459
registry (RMI), 545
regular expressions
 character classes in, 63
 defined, 34, 60
 Matcher class, 66–68
 MatchResult interface, 68
 meta-characters in, 61–63
 parentheses inside, 65
 Pattern class, 65–66
 repetition operators in, 64
 usage examples for, 68–70

relational database, 315–316
ReleaseStringChars, 434, 436
reluctant (lazy) operators, 65
@Remote annotation, 483
remote client (MBeans), 607–609
Remote Database Management System (RDBMS), 324
Remote Management layer, 601
Remote Method Invocation (RMI)
  CORBA compatibility with, 551
  defined, 542
  defining, 543
  distributed objects in, 545–547
  IIOB for, 545
  in Java EE, 547
  marshalling/unmarshalling in, 544
  middleware for, 546
  objects in, 544
  principles of, 542–543
  registry for, 545
  RMI-IIOP objects from, 551–553
  serialization in, 249
remote procedure calls (RPC)
  defined, 542
  platform-independent, 566–567
  principles of, 542–543
  protocols for, 544–545
  in Web Services, 566–567
remote reference, 542
RemoteAgent (MBeans), 606–607
removeAll method, 200, 227–228
removing data
  in EJB database, 476
  in Hibernate, 412
renewItems method, 390
renewResults function, 385–388
repetition operators, 64
replaceString, 435–436
Request Component, 401
request-reply pattern
  discussed, 619–621
  for SOA, 619–621
request-response flow, 399–400
requestScope implicit object, 366
Required FLAG, 670
Requisite FLAG, 670
@Resource annotation, 380–381
resource bundling, 44
Resource Injection, 486
restoreLogPanel method, 201–202

result sets
  using, 330
  closing, 332
  concurrency of, 329
  discussed, 328
  holdability of, 329–330
  in JDBC 4.0, 328–333
  manipulating, 331–332
  navigating, 330–331
  row insertion/deletion in, 332
  types of, 329
ResultSet interface, 315–316
retention, 26, 27
RetentionPolicy enumeration, 26
reuse
  code, 361–362
  at code-level, 124
  at design-level, 124
  in Model 2 architecture, 395
reverse containment, 130
reverse engineering, 540–541
RMI. See Remote Method Invocation
RMI-IIOP, 551–553
RNG (random number generator), 641
rootElement object, 280
RPC. See remote procedure calls
RSAMultiPrimePrivateCrtKey interface, 634, 635
RSAPrivateCRTKey interface, 634, 635
RSAPrivateKey interface, 634, 635
RSAPublicKey interface, 634, 635
RulesButton class, 164
runtime
  annotations at, 31
  JAXB version compatibility for, 277
RUNTIME policy, 26

S

sampler plans, in JMeter, 119
savepoint, 335
saving
  action implementation for, 284–287
  of application data, 239
  configuration, 248
scalability, 395
SchemaExport (Hibernate), 408, 409, 425
scope, 395
scripting, programming vs., 396
scrollable result sets, 329, 330

sealing objects, 663–665

searchClassPath method, 678

searchJarFile method, 677

SecretKey interface, 635

SecretKeyFactory, 662–663

Secure Hash Algorithm (SHA-1), 626, 628, 630

SecureRandom engine class
  defined, 627
  use of, 642

security
  of Applets, 694
  discussed, 625
  using JAAS, 666
  with JCA, 625–626
  with JCE, 625, 656
  in Model 2 architecture, 395
  user identification and, 667

security checks, 668

security-constraint element, 698

security-role element, 698

Select statements, 475

select tag (WebWork), 419

sendMail method, 464

sensitive result sets, 329

sequence (generation) pattern, 49

Serializable interface, 243, 249

serialization. See also Java Serialization API
  classes for, 243
  defined, 241
  inside Swing actions, 246–247
  in Java API, for XML Binding, 302–305
  JAXB, 290
  for object graphs, 290
  in RMI, 249
  strengths of, 261
  as temporary solution, 262
  by value, 302–305
  weaknesses of, 261
  XmlJavaTypeAdapter as root of, 306

serialVersionUID, 260

server
  HTTP authentication on, 586–588
  JMS configuration of, 612–613
  programming, 525–526
  sockets for programming of, 525–526

server layer
  in three-tier model, 314
  in two-tier model, 313

ServerSocket class, 523

Service Oriented Architecture (SOA)
  APIs for, 600
  discussed, 599–600
  for JMS, 610–618
  JMX for, 600–610
  processing chain pattern for, 619
  request-reply pattern for, 619–621
  Split-Aggregate pattern for, 621–623
  system integration patterns for, 619–623
  for Web Services, 563

Service Provider Interface (SPI), 626, 627

service-oriented integration, 599

servlet, for timeserver, 252

Servlet 2.4 support, in JSP 2.0, 358

servlet element, 697

session bean, 474, 480–481

Session class, 611

Session Component, 401

Session object
  in Hibernate API, 340, 402, 403
  transaction support in, 611

SessionFactory, 340–342

sessionScope implicit object, 366

sessionStatelessLocal, 494–495

SetArrayRegion, 439

setBackground method, 226–227

setCertificateEntry, 639

setEnabled method, 226–227

SetField, 443–444

setKeyEntry method, 639

SetLayout() method, 158

setListData method, 222

setMarker method, 706, 708

setMinimumFractionDigits method, 174

setObject method
  for JDBC API, 323–324
  for prepared statements, 323–324

setPreferredSize method, 179–180

setRecentFiles, 267

setSuccessor method, 175–176

setTabComponent method, 220–221

setText method, 231–232

setValueAt method, 186–187

setValues method, 230–232

setVerticalGroup method, 211

SEVERE logging level, 38

SHA-1 (Secure Hash Algorithm), 626, 628, 630

short iterations, 86

Show Tables command, 412

SIGN signature state, 630
Signature engine class
  defined, 627, 643
  states of, 630
  for verification of data, 631–632
signatures. *See* digital signature
SignedInfo class, 643
signing. *See* digital signing
Simple Object Access Protocol (SOAP)
  and WAR files, 695
  in WS, 567, 570–571, 642
  in WSDL, 567–568
SimpleFormatter, 52, 58
SimpleKeySelectorResult, 653
SimpleTagSupport class, 364
single class design, 127
SOA. *See* Service Oriented Architecture
SOAP. *See* Simple Object Access Protocol
socket(s)
  classes of, 523
  for client programming, 524–525
  for communication, 522–541
  communication with, 522–541
  defined, 521, 522
  in echo server, 526–530
  Java Socket API, 523
  protocol implementation with, 530–541
  protocols and, 530–541
  for server programming, 525–526
  types of, 523
Socket class, 523, 524
SocketEcho class, 526–529
SocketHandler, 49
software development principles, 80–88
software estimation, 87
source code, 83
source control, 85
SOURCE policy, 26, 27
source-level annotations, 27
specification, for protocols, 531–540
SPI (Service Provider Interface), 626, 627
spiral methodology, 89
SplashScreen class, 216–217
Split, 621
Split-Aggregate pattern, 621–623
SpringLayout manager, 194–202
SQL transactions, in JSTL 1.1, 368–370
stack trace, 450
standard transactions, 335

standardized O/R mappings, 475
start method, 692, 693
State class, 225, 229–234
State pattern, 203, 225
stateful session bean, 480
state-full filter, 622
@Stateless annotation, 497
stateless session bean, 480
StatelessSession interface, 482–484
statement(s) (JDBC 4.0)
  batch updates using, 326–328
  callable, 324–326
  interface for, 318–319
  prepared, 320–324
Statement interface, 315–316
Statement object
  batch updates using, 326–327
  execution methods for, 319
static data importing, 21–23
static fields, 442
static importing
  defined, 7
  discussed, 21–23
  syntax for, 22
static methods, 445
StaticParametersInterceptor, 400
stock formatters
  creating, 54–55
  discussed, 52
  SimpleFormatter, 52
  XMLFormatter, 52–54
stock handlers
  ConsoleHandler, 48–49
  FileHandler, 49–50
  for Handler class, 48–51
  MemoryHandler, 50–51
  SocketHandler, 49
  StreamHandler, 48
stop method, 692, 693
storage, of digital keys, 638–640
store method, 638
Strategy pattern, 126, 146–150, 203–204
StreamHandler, 48
string(s)
  in C/C++, 432
  functions of, 433–434
  internationalization of, 433
  in Java code, 432
  in Java virtual machine, 432
  in JNI, 432–436

string(s) (continued)
localized, 433
in native code, 435
replacing, 435
storage of, 432
types of, 432
`String` **method, 30**
Struts, 396
stubs
defined, 543
for Web Services, 581
sub-elements
in JAXB, 277
in WAR file attributes, 696
subject authentication, 670
`Subject` **class, 667, 668**
subtyping, 147
`Sufficient` `FLAG`**, 670**
SUN package, 626, 628, 630, 638
`sun-jaxws.xml`**, in Tomcat, 579–580**
superclass constructors, 25, 459
`supportsStoredProcedures`**, 326**
Swing API, 262
Swing applications
in `GroupLayout` manager, 208–210
layout managers in, 158, 190, 191
and Mustang release, 223
navigation flows in, 225–234
in `SpringLayout` manager, 196–197, 199
`switch` **statements, 24–25**
synchronizing objects, 455
synchronous invocation, 582–583
system design, 460–461
system integration patterns
processing chain pattern, 619
request-reply pattern, 619–621
for SOA, 619–623
Split-Aggregate pattern, 621–623
`System.load`**, 455**
systems integration, 599

T

`tabTest`**, 219–220**
`.tag` **files**
code reuse with, 361–362
conversion into Java code, 364
tag library (WebWork), 401, 417
`.tagx` **files, code reuse with, 361–362**
target, 26
TCP (Transmission Control Protocol), 523

TCPMon (Apache)
using, 539–540
acquiring, 539
discussed, 538–539
protocol testing with, 538–540
`TeacherResponsibilities`**, 128**
teamwork, 84
testing methods, 32–33, 85
TestNG, 85, 106–110, 125
`TestParameters` **annotation, 34**
`TestStrategy` **interface, 207**
`testStrategy` **method, 205**
`THEAD` **tag, 386–387**
thread synchronization, 455
ThreadGroups, 117, 119
threading, using JNI, 455–456
three-tier model, 314–315
`Throw` **function, 450**
`ThrowNew` **function, 450**
`throws`**, 15**
TicTacToe Java Web Start application example, 702–709
time-based licensing
discussed, 249–250
implementing, 250–252
using Java Serialization API, 249–253
timeserver in, 252–253
`TimerInterceptor`**, 400**
timers, in JMeter, 119
timeservers, 252–253
Tomcat
`sun-jaxws.xml` in, 579–580
Web service deployment on, 578
`web.xml` configuration in, 579
WS deployment using, 578–580
`ToReflectedField` **function, 460**
`ToReflectedMethod` **function, 460**
`toString` **method, 669**
traceability, 82–83
tracking bugs, 87–88
transaction(s)
in Hibernate API, 340
in JDBC 4.0, 334–335
management of, 334–335
SQL, in JSTL 1.1, 368–370
standard, 335
`@TransactionAtrribute` **marking, 508**
`@TransactionManagement` **annotation, 508**
`TransferHandler` **class, 221–222**
`Transform` **class, 644**
`@Transient` **annotation, 512**

transient keyword, 257
transition phase (UP), 91
translation, of JSP page, 376
Transmission Control Protocol (TCP), 523
transparent representations, 634, 635
transport protocols, 571
TrayDemo constructor, 216–217, 221
trayIcon object, 217–218
treePanel method, 186
trusted certificate entry, 638
Twain, Mark, 87
two-tier model, 313–314
type erasure, 8–11
type parameters. *See also* generics
    bound, 12–13, 299
    for certificates, 656
    formal, 8, 9
types section, 570
type-safe, 7, 8, 24

U

UDP (User Datagram Protocol), 523
UDT (User Defined Types), 323
UML (Unified Modeling Language) training, 81
unboxing conversions
    context for, 21
    defined, 7
    discussed, 20–21
uncheckall function, 386, 389
Unicode strings, 2-byte, 433
Unified Modeling Language (UML) training, 81
Unified Process (UP), 90–92
UNINITIALIZED signature state, 630
unmarshaller
    creation of, 281–282
    in RMI, 544
    XML, 281–282
unregistering native methods, 457
UnregisterNatives function, 457
UNWRAP_MODE, 657
unwrapped keys, 658–662
UP (Unified Process), 90–92
updatable result sets, 329, 331
update clause, 16
URL class, 533, 534, 579
User Datagram Protocol (UDP), 523
User Defined Types (UDT), 323
user identity authentication, 667
user interface, of email client, 461–471

UTF-8 format, for Java strings, 433
utility classes (Hibernate), 341–342
utility libraries
    discussed, 34–35
    Java logging, 35–60
    Preferences class, 70–77
    regular expressions, 60–70
util.js script, 385

V

validate method, 201–202
validation
    of configuration, 258–259
    of signatures, 652–653
    of XWork, 415
value deserialization, 304
value serialization, 302–305
ValueStack, 401
variable arguments
    in C/C++, 18
    defined, 7
    ellipses in, 18, 19
    in Java code, 18
velocity, 87
verification
    of configuration, 258–259
    of data, 632–634
    for digital signing, 632–634
    of MessageDigest, 629–630
VERIFY signature state, 630, 632
versioning, 260–261
vertical components, 397
view (MVC), 394
view component (MVC), 137–139
Visitor pattern, 190, 193–194
Visual Studio 2005, 430
volatility, in application, 126

W

WAR files. *See* Web ARchive
WARNING logging level, 38
Waterfall methodology, 88–89, 92–93
weak global references, 451, 453, 454
weather application example (WS), 564–566, 572–575,
    589–596
Web application(s), 694–695
web application deployment descriptor (web.xml),
    422–423

web application visualization
for adding data, 416
for browsing data, 416
with JSP 2.0, 376–380
with JSTL 1.1, 370–375
in Model 2 architecture, 415–422
Web ARchive (WAR files)
with Ant (Apache), 709–713
deployment descriptor for, 696–698
directory structure, 695
discussed, 694–695
inspecting, 699
`package` target in, 112
SOAP and, 695
structure of, 695
web browsers, 238
web browsing, 520
web component (EJB 3)
construction of, with tables, 496–506
deployment of, 506–517
for form usage, 485–496
for many-to-many relationships, 506–517
for one-to-many relationships, 496–506
web portals, 521
Web Services (WS)
access control in, 585–586
asynchronous invocation of, 581, 583–584
calling, 581–582
communication for, 563–596
deployment of, 575–580
discussed, 563–564
enabling example for, 564–566, 572–575, 589–596
endpoints attributes for, 579
invocation of, 581–584
of JAX-WS, 575–577, 579
JDK 6 for deployment of, 577–578
platform-independent RPCs in, 566–567
relevance of, 600
SOAP in, 570–571
stubs for, 581
synchronous invocation of, 582–583
Tomcat for deployment of, 578–580
transport protocols for, 571
weather application example for, 564–566, 572–575, 589–596
writing client for, 580–589
`wsgen` and, 577
`wsimport` tool for, 580–581
Web Services Description Language (WSDL)
discussed, 568–570

for JAXB, 308
location of, 585
SOAP in, 567–568
Web Services Interoperability Organization (WS-I)
Basic Profile of, 567–568
defined, 564
Web Services Interoperability Technologies Project (WSIT), 596
web sites
automated browsing on, 520
server-side applications for, 525
Web Services on, 563
Web tier (J2EE), 93
WebMethod annotation, 575
WebParam annotation, 575
WebResult annotation, 575
WebService annotation, 575
WebServiceContext, 587
WebWork
`Actions` in, 399
architecture of, 399–400
components in, 401
defined, 396
deployment descriptor for, 422–423
Hibernate support by, 402–403
interceptors in, 400–401
as J2EE web application, 422
Model 2 architecture with, 396, 399–402
modularity of, 426
OGNL in, 401
request-response flow in, 399–400
tag library, 401, 417
`ValueStack` in, 401
XWork as component in, 399
XWork in, 144
XWork wrapped to, 423
WebWork JSP custom tags, 417
WebWork2, 396
web.xml, 422–423, 579
welcome-file-list element, 698
WHERE clause, 475
wildcards, 11–12
WorkMonitor, 609–610
WorkPanel, 138, 139
World Wide Web Consortium, 270
WRAP_MODE, 657
wrapped keys, 658–662
wrapper, 423
writeObject method, 254
writing, configuration, 245–246

WS. *See* Web Services
WSDL. *See* Web Services Description Language
wsgen, 577
WS-I (Web Services Interoperability Organization)
Basic Profile of, 567–568
defined, 564
wsimport tool, 580–581, 585, 596
WSIT (Web Services Interoperability Technologies Project), 596

X

XDoclet, 110–117
clean target in, 111–112
as code generation engine, 113–114
compile target in, 112
config target in, 116
discussed, 125
generate-web target in, 112
Hibernate in, 113, 115–117
for mapping, 110–111
package target in, 112
usage of, 110
xjc command, 276–277
XML
annotations generating, 301–302
content creation, 283
for content creation, 283
data types in, 568
format for, 273–280
format of, 273–280
JAXB classes from, 276–277
marshaller, 281–282
marshalling/unmarshalling, 281–282
relevance of, 600
unmarshaller, 281–282
XML Digital Signature API Specification
classes for, 643–645
detached signatures in, 646–649
discussed, 642–643
document signing with, 645
enveloped signatures in, 649–652
in JCA, 642–654
signing process in, 645–646
validating signatures in, 652–653

XML document
for configuration objects, 271–272
in JSP20-compliant web containers, 362–363
XML schema
annotations generating, 301–302
JAXB classes from, 276–277
XML Schema Definition (XSD)
for configuration data model, 275–276
development of, 270
in JAXB, 271
for XML format definitions, 273–280
XmlAccessorType, 296–297
XmlAttribute, 292, 297
XmlElement, 292, 297
XmlElementWrapper, 292, 297–298
XMLEncoder/Decoder API
classes in, 265
customization of, 268–269
discussed, 262
EJB serialization using, 262–263, 265–269, 265–270
file format of, 264
Java Serialization API vs., 262–263, 269
in JDK, 269
usage of, 269–270
XML serialization format in, 263–264
XMLFormatter, 52–54, 58
XmlID, 292, 305
XmlIDREF, 292, 305
XmlJavaTypeAdapter, 293, 298–300
XmlRootElement, 280–281, 291, 293, 295
XmlTransient, 293, 300–301
XmlType, 295–296, 293296
XmlValue, 293
X/Open SQL Call Level Interface (CLI), 312
XP (Extreme Programming), 87, 91–92
XSD. *See* XML Schema Definition
XWork
validating, 415
as WebWork component, 144, 399
WebWork wrapped to, 423
XWork Action
for adding data, 413–414
for browsing data, 412–413
discussed, 399, 412–415